BICENTENNIAL
1807
WILEY
2007
BICENTENNIAL

THE WILEY BICENTENNIAL—KNOWLEDGE FOR GENERATIONS

*E*ach generation has its unique needs and aspirations. When Charles Wiley first opened his small printing shop in lower Manhattan in 1807, it was a generation of boundless potential searching for an identity. And we were there, helping to define a new American literary tradition. Over half a century later, in the midst of the Second Industrial Revolution, it was a generation focused on building the future. Once again, we were there, supplying the critical scientific, technical, and engineering knowledge that helped frame the world. Throughout the 20th Century, and into the new millennium, nations began to reach out beyond their own borders and a new international community was born. Wiley was there, expanding its operations around the world to enable a global exchange of ideas, opinions, and know-how.

For 200 years, Wiley has been an integral part of each generation's journey, enabling the flow of information and understanding necessary to meet their needs and fulfill their aspirations. Today, bold new technologies are changing the way we live and learn. Wiley will be there, providing you the must-have knowledge you need to imagine new worlds, new possibilities, and new opportunities.

Generations come and go, but you can always count on Wiley to provide you the knowledge you need, when and where you need it!

WILLIAM J. PESCE
PRESIDENT AND CHIEF EXECUTIVE OFFICER

PETER BOOTH WILEY
CHAIRMAN OF THE BOARD

PC Hardware Essentials

David Groth and Ron Gilster
with Megan Miller

BICENTENNIAL
BICENTENNIAL
1807
WILEY
2007
BICENTENNIAL
BICENTENNIAL

PUBLISHER
Anne Smith

PROJECT EDITOR
Brian B. Baker

MARKETING
Jennifer Slomack

SENIOR EDITORIAL ASSISTANT
Tiara Kelly

PRODUCTION MANAGER
Kelly Tavares

PRODUCTION EDITOR
Kerry Weinstein

CREATIVE DIRECTOR
Harry Nolan

COVER DESIGNER
Hope Miller

COVER PHOTO
© Comstock/Jupiter Images

Wiley 200th Anniversary Logo designed by: Richard J. Pacifico

This book was set in Berkeley Oldstyle Book by Aptara, Inc., printed and bound by R. R. Donnelley. The cover was printed by R. R. Donnelley.

Microsoft product screen shot(s) reprinted with permission from Microsoft Corporation.

Photo Credits: Figures 1-3, 1-5, 1-10, 2-2, 2-8, 2-9, 2-15, 2-18, 3-1, 3-7, 3-16, 4-2, 4-9, 4-10, 4-11, 5-3, 5-6, 7-6, 7-7, 7-8, 7-10, 7-11, 8-1, 8-2, 8-4, 8-5, 8-6, 8-11, 8-12, 8-13, 8-14, 9-13, 9-14, 9-23, 11-5, 11-13 © Azimuth Interactive, Inc. 2007.

To order books or for customer service please call 1-800-CALL WILEY (225-5945).

ISBN 978-0-470-07400-8

Printed in the United States of America

10 9 8 7 6 5 4 3 2

ABOUT THE AUTHOR

David Groth is a full-time author and consultant. He is the author of Sybex's best-selling *A+ Complete Study Guide, PC Chop Shop: Tricked Out Guide to PC Modding,* and is co-author of *Cabling: The Complete Guide to Network Wiring, Network+ Study Guide: Exam N10-003, i-Net+ Study Guide: Exam IK0-002, CompTIA Network+ Certification Kit (Exam N10-003),* and co-editor of *A+ Fast Pass.*

Ron Gilster has more than 35 years of experience in virtually every aspect of computing technology. He has extensive experience training, teaching, and consulting in computer-related areas, including working on mainframes, minicomputers, and virtually every type of personal computer and operating system that exists. He is the author of many books, including *PC Repair Bench Book, PC Hardware: A Beginner's Guide, PC Technician: Black Book, A+ Certification for Dummies, CCNA for Dummies, DSL Bible,* and is co-author of *CCDA for Dummies and Server+ Certification for Dummies.* He has held consulting and management positions with several high profile companies.

Megan Miller is an editor and writer with 20 years experience in publishing, technical project management, and interactive communications.

PREFACE

College classrooms bring together learners from many backgrounds, with a variety of aspirations. Although the students are in the same course, they are not necessarily on the same path. This diversity, coupled with the reality that these learners often have jobs, families, and other commitments, requires a flexibility that our nation's higher education system is addressing. Distance learning, shorter course terms, new disciplines, evening courses, and certification programs are some of the approaches that colleges employ to reach as many students as possible and help them clarify and achieve their goals.

Wiley Pathways books, a new line of texts from John Wiley & Sons, Inc., are designed to help you address this diversity and the need for flexibility. These books focus on the fundamentals, identify core competencies and skills, and promote independent learning. Their focus on the fundamentals helps students grasp the subject, bringing them all to the same basic understanding. These books use clear, everyday language and are presented in an uncluttered format, making the reading experience more pleasurable. The core competencies and skills help students succeed in the classroom and beyond, whether in another course or in a professional setting. A variety of built-in learning resources promote independent learning and help instructors and students gauge students' understanding of the content. These resources enable students to think critically about their new knowledge and apply their skills in any situation.

Our goal with *Wiley Pathways* books—with their brief, inviting format, clear language, and core competencies and skills focus—is to celebrate the many students in your courses, respect their needs, and help you guide them on their way.

CASE Learning System

To meet the needs of working college students, *PC Hardware Essentials* uses a four-part process called the CASE Learning System:

▲ **C:** Content
▲ **A:** Analysis
▲ **S:** Synthesis
▲ **E:** Evaluation

Based on Bloom's taxonomy of learning, CASE presents key topics in PC hardware in easy-to-follow chapters. The text then prompts analysis, synthesis, and evaluation with a variety of learning aids and assessment tools. Students move efficiently from reviewing what they have learned, to acquiring new information and skills, to applying their new knowledge and skills to real-life scenarios.

Using the CASE Learning System, students not only achieve academic mastery of PC hardware *topics*, but they master real-world *skills* related to that content. The CASE Learning System also helps students become independent learners, giving them a distinct advantage in the field, whether they are just starting out or seeking to advance in their careers.

Organization, Depth, and Breadth of the Text

▲ **Modular Format.** Research on college students shows that they access information from textbooks in a non-linear way. Instructors also often wish to reorder textbook content to suit the needs of a particular class. Therefore, although *PC Hardware Essentials* proceeds logically from the basics to increasingly more challenging material, chapters are further organized into sections that are self-contained for maximum teaching and learning flexibility.

▲ **Numeric System of Headings.** *PC Hardware Essentials* uses a numeric system for headings (e.g., 2.3.4 identifies the fourth subsection of Section 3 of Chapter 2). With this system, students and teachers can quickly and easily pinpoint topics in the table of contents and the text, keeping class time and study sessions focused.

▲ **Core Content.** The topics in *PC Hardware Essentials* are organized into 12 chapters.

Chapter 1, Understanding and Working with Personal Computers, introduces students to key computing concepts and terminology. It begins with an overview of the functions of computing and identifies the main PC components. Next it discusses how computers work by using circuits, binary calculations, and software to perform processing functions. The chapter outlines the main types of PCs students will encounter and concludes with an overview of some essential skills in understanding and working with PCs: troubleshooting steps, the required tools, working with clients, preventive maintenance, and safety concerns.

Chapter 2, Electricity and Power, looks at the important role that electricity plays in computing. It begins with a review of common electrical terminology and concepts. Next it looks at the multimeter and its use in measuring electrical circuits, as well as tools for safeguarding against electrostatic discharge. Then it moves on to discuss the various types of power problems that can affect a PC, and the devices that can be implemented to prevent or minimize power-related problems. The chapter concludes with an examination of the PC's power supply unit and the steps and techniques students can take in maintaining, troubleshooting, and replacing a power supply.

Chapter 3, Motherboards, focuses on the role of the motherboard and its components as the core of the PC. The chapter first identifies the main components of the motherboard and discusses the types and form factors of today's mother-boards. The chapter then takes a more in-depth look at the various motherboard components and their functions. Next, the chapter examines the BIOS chip, its role in the PC's boot process, and how the student can use errors generated during the boot process to troubleshoot a PC. The chapter concludes with a review of the techniques the student can use in installing and troubleshooting a motherboard, as well as a discussion of the main considerations important to selecting a new motherboard for a PC.

Chapter 4, Central Processing Units, takes an in-depth look at the PC's CPU. It begins with a review of the main types of CPU packages, sockets, and slots and discusses how CPUs are powered and cooled. Next the chapter examines how CPUs work and identifies the main properties and features used to evaluate and compare CPUs, and continues with a review of contemporary CPU tech-nologies. The chapter moves on to a historical overview of the CPU and discusses popular CPUs manufactured by Intel and AMD. The chapter concludes with a discussion of the techniques and important considerations in installing, cooling, upgrading, and troubleshooting CPUs.

Chapter 5, Memory, focuses on the types of memory used in a PC. It begins with a review of the role of memory in a PC and takes a look at the different types of RAM and ROM used by a PC. It moves on to a closer look at dynamic RAM: common form factors, technologies, features, and characteristics. The chapter concludes with a review of the techniques and considerations important in upgrading, installing, and troubleshooting a PC's memory.

Chapter 6, Bus Structures, reviews PC buses and their functions and exam-ines how expansion buses and cards are used to expand the capabilities of a PC. It begins with an overview of the types of internal buses found in a PC and looks at the system bus as a defining characteristic of the PC's overall speed. The chapter then discusses expansion buses and examines the various types of archi-tectures used for expanding the functionality of a PC. Next the chapter looks at the various types of system resources that come into play in managing PC devices, from I/O addresses to DMA channels. The chapter concludes with a discussion of the types of expansion cards used to upgrade a PC, along with the key steps a student will need to know when installing, upgrading, or troubleshooting an expansion card.

Chapter 7, Hard Drives, examines hard drives as the most popular form of secondary storage for PCs. It begins by examining the components and charac-teristics of hard drives and looks at how they read, write, and store data. Next, the chapter reviews industry standards for hard drives, including parallel ATA/IDE, SATA, and SCSI standards, and examines the methods used to install these hard drives. The chapter concludes with an examination of the essential concepts involved in managing hard drives, from formatting and partitioning a hard drive to defragmenting and troubleshooting steps.

Chapter 8, Removable Storage, reviews the wide variety of removable storage devices used with PCs, from tape drives to USB flash drives. It begins with an overview of the most popular types of removable storage. Then, it discusses floppy drive technologies and installation methods. The chapter next examines optical drives, including their technologies, characteristics, and standards, and looks at the steps needed to install and troubleshoot a CD or DVD drive. The chapter concludes with a review of flash memory storage and looks at the technologies and types of flash memory devices available today.

Chapter 9, Input and Output Devices, focuses on the various external devices used by PCs. It begins with an examination of the types of interfaces used by I/O devices, their ports and connectors, and reviews the role of the device driver in managing I/O devices. The chapter next discusses the techniques and considerations common to installing and troubleshooting any I/O device. The chapter moves on to a closer look at and comparison of the most popular I/O interfaces, from legacy interfaces to wireless interfaces. The chapter then examines individual I/O devices, discussing the key characteristic technologies of each, from input and pointing devices to scanners and digital cameras. Next the chapter looks at working with PC audio, discussing basic audio concepts and reviewing important audio components, such as sound cards. The chapter concludes with a review of display technologies and discusses important concepts in working with and troubleshooting monitor displays.

Chapter 10, Printers, examines printer technologies. It begins with an overview of the main types of printing technologies and looks at the key components and printing processes of a laser printer. It examines the various hardware and software interfaces commonly used for connecting a printer to a PC and reviews the steps needed to install a new printer. The chapter also reviews ways to upgrade a printer, common printer supplies, and printer maintenance techniques, and concludes with a look at common printer problems and troubleshooting steps.

Chapter 11, Portable Systems, focuses on technologies unique to portable systems and laptops. First it reviews the key differences between laptops and PCs and identifies common laptop components. It examines laptop power sources, displays, keyboards, and discusses technologies for internal laptop components such as motherboards, expansion buses, memory, and storage. Next, the chapter looks at PC card technologies, and their form factors and interfaces. The chapter concludes with a review of important concepts and techniques in maintaining and troubleshooting laptops and upgrading and installing laptop hard drives, memory, and batteries.

In today's world, most PCs are connected to some form of network. Chapter 12, Network Fundamentals, introduces basic network concepts and terminology. It begins with an overview of primary network components, types of networks, and network topologies. Next, it discusses network models, standards, protocols, major architectures, and examines network and TCP/IP addressing. The chapter moves on to a review of network transmission media and connectivity hardware, from NICs to routers and wireless access points. The chapter examines how to establish and configure wired and wireless network connections and reviews the various methods for connecting a PC to the Internet. The chapter concludes with an examination of key concepts important to troubleshooting network connections.

Pre-reading Learning Aids

Each chapter of *PC Hardware Essentials* features the following learning and study aids to activate students' prior knowledge of the topics and orient them to the material.

- ▲ **Pre-test.** This pre-reading assessment tool in multiple-choice format not only introduces chapter material, but it also helps students anticipate the chapter's learning outcomes. By focusing students' attention on what they do not know, the self-test provides students with a benchmark against which they can measure their own progress. The pre-test is available online at www.wiley.com/college/groth.
- ▲ **What You'll Learn in This Chapter.** This bulleted list focuses on subject matter that will be taught. It tells students what they will be learning in this chapter and why it is significant for their careers. It will also help students understand why the chapter is important and how it relates to other chapters in the text.
- ▲ **After Studying This Chapter, You'll Be Able To.** This list emphasizes capabilities and skills students will learn as a result of reading the chapter. It sets students up to synthesize and evaluate the chapter material, and relate it to the real world.

Within-text Learning Aids

The following learning aids are designed to encourage analysis and synthesis of the material, support the learning process, and ensure success during the evaluation phase:

- ▲ **Introduction.** This section orients the student by introducing the chapter and explaining its practical value and relevance to the book as a whole. Short summaries of chapter sections preview the topics to follow.
- ▲ **"For Example" Boxes.** Found within each section, these boxes tie section content to real-world examples, scenarios, and applications.
- ▲ **Figures and tables.** Line art and photos have been carefully chosen to be truly instructional rather than filler. Tables distill and present information

in a way that is easy to identify, access, and understand, enhancing the focus of the text on essential ideas.

▲ **Self-Check.** Related to the "What You'll Learn" bullets and found at the end of each section, this battery of short answer questions emphasizes student understanding of concepts and mastery of section content. Though the questions may either be discussed in class or studied by students outside of class, students should not go on before they can answer all questions correctly.

▲ **Key Terms and Glossary.** To help students develop a professional vocabulary, key terms are bolded in the introduction, summary, and when they first appear in the chapter. A complete list of key terms appears at the end of each chapter and again in a glossary at the end of the book. Knowledge of key terms is assessed by all assessment tools (see below).

▲ **Summary.** Each chapter concludes with a summary paragraph that reviews the major concepts in the chapter and links back to the "What You'll Learn" list.

Evaluation and Assessment Tools

The evaluation phase of the CASE Learning System consists of a variety of within-chapter and end-of-chapter assessment tools that test how well students have learned the material. These tools also encourage students to extend their learning into different scenarios and higher levels of understanding and thinking. The following assessment tools appear in every chapter of *PC Hardware Essentials*.

▲ **Summary Questions** help students summarize the chapter's main points by asking a series of multiple choice and true/false questions that emphasize student understanding of concepts and mastery of chapter content. Students should be able to answer all of the Summary Questions correctly before moving on.

▲ **Applying This Chapter Questions** drive home key ideas by asking students to synthesize and apply chapter concepts to new, real-life situations and scenarios.

▲ **You Try It Questions** are designed to extend students' thinking, and so are ideal for discussion or writing assignments. Using an open-ended format and sometimes based on web sources, they encourage students to draw conclusions using chapter material applied to real-world situations, which fosters both mastery and independent learning.

▲ **Post-test** should be taken after students have completed the chapter. It includes all of the questions in the pre-test, so that students can see how their learning has progressed and improved.

Instructor Package

PC Hardware Essentials is available with the following teaching and learning supplements. All supplements are available online at the text's Book Companion Website, located at www.wiley.com/college/groth.

▲ **Instructor's Resource Guide.** Provides the following aids and supplements for teaching an introduction to databases course:

  ▲ *Teaching suggestions.* For each chapter, these include a chapter summary, learning objectives, definitions of key terms, lecture notes, answers to select text question sets, and at least 3 suggestions for classroom activities, such as ideas for speakers to invite, videos to show, and other projects.

  ▲ **PowerPoint Slides.** Key information is summarized in 10 to 15 PowerPoint slides per chapter. Instructors may use these in class or choose to share them with students for class presentations or to provide additional study support.

  ▲ **Test Bank.** One test per chapter, as well as a mid-term, and two finals: one cumulative, one non-cumulative. Each includes true/false, multiple choice, and open-ended questions. Answers and page references are provided for the true/false and multiple choice questions, and page references for the open-ended questions. Questions are available in Microsoft Word and computerized test bank formats.

Student Project Manual

The inexpensive *PC Hardware Essentials Project Manual* contains activities (an average of five projects per textbook chapter) designed to help students apply textbook concepts in a practical way. Easier exercises at the beginning graduate to more challenging projects that build critical-thinking skills.

ACKNOWLEDGMENTS

Taken together, the content, pedagogy, and assessment elements of *PC Hardware Essentials* offer the career-oriented student the most important aspects of the information technology field as well as ways to develop the skills and capabilities that current and future employers seek in the individuals they hire and promote. Instructors will appreciate its practical focus, conciseness, and real-world emphasis.

We would like to thank the following reviewers for their feedback and suggestions during the text's development. Their advice on how to shape *PC Hardware Essentials* into a solid learning tool that meets both their needs and those of their busy students is deeply appreciated.

Neal Christensen, Mount Saint Mary College
Kathy Smith, Texarkan College
M. Allen Kent, Jr., Montana State University Billings
Brian Morgan, Marshall University
John Trifiletti, Florida Community College
Chris Brandt, Brown College
Mike Sahabi, Baker College
Harold Lamson, ITT Technical Institute
Diane Byrd, Katharine Gibbs
Kenny Lou, Cerritos College

We would also like to thank Carol Traver for all her hard work in formatting and preparing the manuscript for production.

BRIEF CONTENTS

CONTENTS

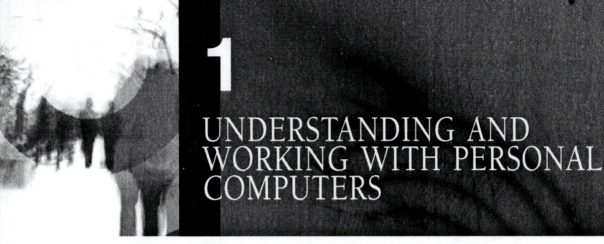

1

UNDERSTANDING AND WORKING WITH PERSONAL COMPUTERS

Starting Point

Go to www.wiley.com/college/groth to assess your knowledge of basic PC components and operations

Determine where you need to concentrate your effort.

What You'll Learn in This Chapter

▲ Types of computers and key PC components
▲ How PCs store data in bits and bytes and use binary and hexadecimal number systems
▲ PC case styles and form factors
▲ PC maintenance issues
▲ PC troubleshooting steps, issues, and resources

After Studying This Chapter, You'll Be Able To

▲ Identify the main components of a PC
▲ Convert a binary number to a decimal number
▲ Distinguish between bits and bytes
▲ Differentiate hexadecimal from decimal numbers
▲ Evaluate and select appropriate PC case styles
▲ Create a PC workspace and select appropriate tools
▲ Identify environmental and safety concerns involved in working with PCs
▲ Formulate a troubleshooting plan

INTRODUCTION

A **computer** is an electronic device that can process data automatically. When most people think of a computer, they think of a laptop or desktop computer; however, a computer is actually any type of electronic device that processes data. Types of computers include:

▲ **Supercomputers:** These are very expensive and fast computers used for intensive processing, such as in weather forecasting.

▲ **Mainframes:** Also called enterprise servers, mainframe computers are powerful, shared computers that many users can work on through different terminals.

▲ **Servers:** These are network computers from which workstation or client computers access and share files, printers, communications, and other services. Servers may also be dedicated to one specific task, such as storing shared files (file server) or controlling networked printers (print server).

▲ **Workstations:** These are high-end microcomputers typically used for tasks that involve intensive processing, such as engineering or high-end graphics.

▲ **Personal computers (PCs):** Also called microcomputers, these computers are used by individuals in home or business settings.

▲ **Handheld computers:** These are smaller computing devices designed primarily for portable personal information management.

▲ **Embedded computers:** Embedded computers are tiny computing devices embedded in consumer appliances, such as cell phones and microwave ovens.

All of these computer types consist of both **hardware**, or physical equipment, and **software**, programmed instructions that control the hardware.

PCs are the computers most of us use in daily life to connect to the Internet and perform tasks at work. Types of PCs, or microcomputers, include desktops (which are not portable) and laptops (which are). Laptops and desktop PCs use the same types of components, such as hard drives and central processing units (CPUs), although laptops and other portable computing systems use components designed to be smaller and to produce less heat than a desktop PC. However, the basic technologies and software used to run laptops and PCs are the same.

To understand how the various hardware components of a PC work, it is important to understand the basic processes used in a PC, and how its various hardware components interact with software. In addition, we'll also cover some basic information you should be familiar with before attempting to work with PC hardware, or build or disassemble a PC, including the types of tools you use to work on PC components and steps to follow when troubleshooting a PC.

1.1 Understanding How PCs Work

PCs are electronic devices; and use electrical signaling and charges to represent and manipulate data. Before discussing how PCs use electrical signaling, however, let's first review the basic functions and components that make up a PC.

1.1.1 The Four Main Functions of Computing

PCs are designed to process data. Most simply, data is information, such as a string of numbers or characters. For instance, the text of an email is data, as is a list of prices on a cash register receipt. When we work with data, we need ways to both create it and make changes to it. There are many different ways to manipulate or perform functions on data. Examples include:

▲ Creating documents, such as email and word-processing reports
▲ Creating a graphic display or chart
▲ Calculating numbers in a spreadsheet

Processing data with a computer involves four main functions (Figure 1-1):

1. **Input:** The PC must receive data from somewhere. Typing with a keyboard or transferring digital images from a camera are examples of input.
2. **Processing:** After the PC has the input data, it can perform tasks on it, or process it. If you are typing an email, the processing the PC does involves

Figure 1-1

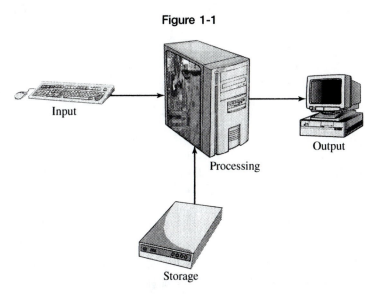

The four main functions of computing.

running the email application and inserting your typed words into the email file. Another example of processing would be adding two numbers together.

3. **Output:** Output is data that has been processed. An email you are writing, displayed on the monitor, is an example of output. Printed pages are another type of output.

4. **Storage:** The data that is input, processed, and output must be stored somewhere in the PC. There are two main types of storage:

   - **Primary storage:** Primary storage refers to the system memory that is used to store data temporarily for the CPU to process. This type of storage is designed to transfer small amounts of data very quickly to keep up with the speed of the CPU.

   - **Secondary storage:** Secondary storage refers to storage areas used to permanently hold larger amounts of data. For example, hard drives are used to store the data files that a user creates, such as an email archive.

All computers—from handhelds to supercomputers—perform these basic functions.

1.1.2 PC Hardware Components

A PC is made up of many distinct hardware components that contribute to the four main functions of a computer (Figure 1-2).

The main components in most computer systems include:

▲ **The case:** A PC case is the enclosure that encases all the components of a computer. The case is fitted with power buttons and indicators and a fan to circulate air.

▲ **The power supply:** The device in the computer that provides the power is the power supply.

▲ **The motherboard:** The motherboard, or system board, is the olive green or brown circuit board that lines the bottom of the computer. The motherboard is used to hold most of the essential electrical components of the PC, such as circuits and transistors, including the CPU. The motherboard typically also holds system memory, ports used to attach external devices through cables, and sockets for adding additional circuitry on expansion cards.

▲ **The CPU:** The "brain" of any computer is the central processing unit (CPU), also called a processor. This is a component made of highly complex electrical circuitry that does all the calculations and performs 90 percent of all the functions of a computer. There are many different types of processors for computers.

▲ **Memory:** The PC's system memory is special circuitry designed to temporarily hold the specific data that the CPU is working on at any given

Figure 1-2

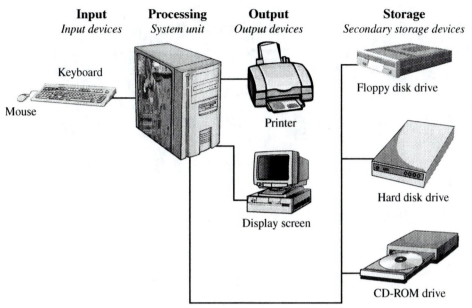

Input	**Processing**	**Output**	**Storage**
Input devices	*System unit*	*Output devices*	*Secondary storage devices*

Keyboard

Mouse

Printer

Display screen

Floppy disk drive

Hard disk drive

CD-ROM drive

Each of the four basic functions of a computer system
(input, processing, output, and storage) is performed by
specific hardware components.

The hardware components of a typical PC.

time. System memory is typically housed on small boards attached to the motherboard.

▲ **Buses:** Buses are the copper traces or wires on a motherboard that are used to transport data within the PC.

▲ **Expansion cards:** Expansion or adapter cards are used to add new circuits—and functionality—to a PC. For example, video adapter cards are used to give more processing power to display images. Other common types of expansion cards are sound cards and networking cards.

▲ **Storage devices:** Storage devices hold the data being accessed, as well as the files the system needs to operate and data that needs to be saved. The many different types of storage differ in terms of their capacity (how much they can store), access time (how fast the computer can access the information), and the physical type of media used. The most important storage device in a PC is its hard drive. This is a magnetic disk housed in its own case that is mounted in the PC. Other common storage devices include floppy drives and CD/DVD drives.

Figure 1-3

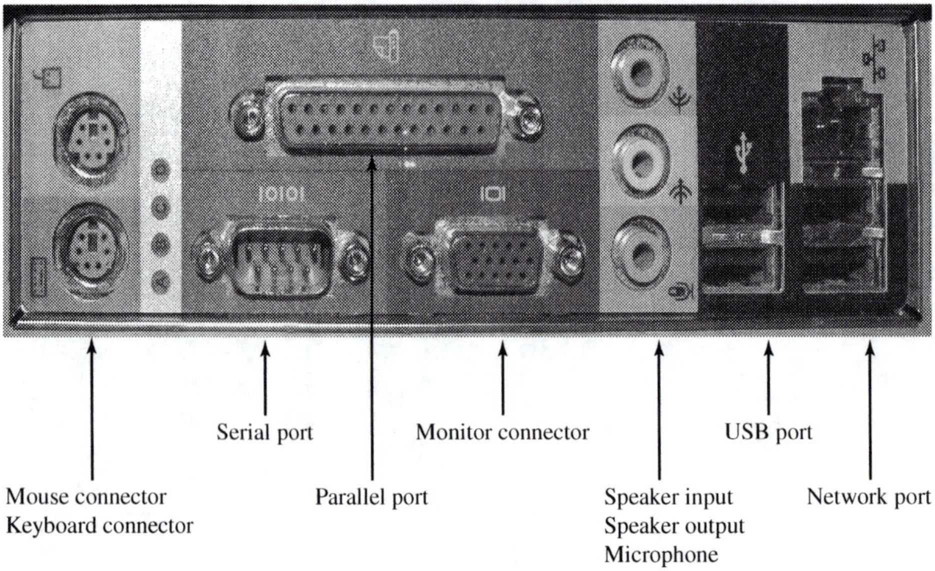

Serial port   Monitor connector   USB port

Mouse connector   Parallel port   Speaker input   Network port
Keyboard connector   Speaker output
                                                Microphone

Common ports on the back of a PC.

▲ **Input devices:** Input devices are used to send data to the computer. Common input devices are the keyboard and mouse.

▲ **Display devices:** The most common display device for a PC is a monitor, although other devices, such as TVs, can be used. There are two main types of monitor, flat-panel LCD (liquid crystal display) monitors and the older CRT (cathode ray tube) monitors, which use a similar type of display tube as a TV.

▲ **Ports and cables:** Ports and cables are used to attach external devices to the PC. There are many different types of ports for adding devices such as keyboards, mice, printers, and monitors (Figure 1-3). Each type of port requires using a cable designed to work with that port. External devices are designed to use specific ports and cables.

1.1.3 How PCs Work

PCs work by converting electrical signals and charges into binary information that the CPU can perform calculations on.

For example, when you type on a keyboard, you are pressing a mechanical key that sends off a series of electrical signals to the PC. The PC's processing circuits or chips are designed to be able to sense and react to specific types of electrical signals. Although there are many ways electrical signals can be sent and managed, essentially, what the PC does is convert the electrical signaling into a string of on and off values. It can do this because electrical components called transistors are designed to be able to hold one of two possible values: on or off. The transistors used in PC components are extremely tiny, and millions of transistors are wired together to hold large amounts of data as on and off values.

Binary and Decimal Numbering

The value of interpreting electrical signals or holding electrical charges as on or off values is that each charge can now be designated as one of two numbers: 1 or 0. Groups of these 1s and 0s can be then used to form larger numbers using the **binary number system.** In the binary number system, only two digits are used—1 and 0—and the number's value is the result of the number 2 being raised to various powers. This is true for all number systems. The decimal number system is based on values of the number 10 raised to increasing powers (Table 1-1). For example, the decimal number 459 represents 4×10^2 (400) + 5 × 10^1 (50) + 9 × 10^0 (9). In the binary number system, 459 would be represented as 111001011: 1×2^8 (256) + 1×2^7 (128) + 1×2^6 (64) + 0×2^5 (0) + 0×2^4 (0) + 1×2^3 (8) + 0×2^2 (0) + 1×2^1 (2) + 1×2^0 (1).

To convert a binary number to a decimal number, you add the decimal values for each position. The key is to remember that each position represents a power of 2, starting with 0 on the right end up through 7 (or higher) at the left end. For example, the binary number 00001010 contains

$0 * 2^0 = 0$ (any number to the zero power is worth 1)
$1 * 2^1 = 2$ (any number to the one power is the number)
$0 * 2^2 = 0$ (two times two)
$1 * 2^3 = 8$ (two times two times two)
Totaling 10 (the remaining positions are all zero)

So, 00001010 in binary is the same as 10 in decimal. Just count the positions, starting from the right with zero, and then calculate the powers of two for each position with a one. You add up the decimal values of each position to get the resulting decimal number, which in this case was 2 + 8 to get 10.

For the PC to use 1s and 0s as numbers, the single values held in transistors, called **bits,** are grouped into specific sizes or lengths to be seen as larger values.

Table 1-1: Comparing Decimal and Binary Numbers

Number System	Sample Number	3rd Position Value	2nd Position Value	1st Position Value	Decimal Value
Decimal	123	1×10^2 (100)	2×10^1 (20)	3×10^0 (3)	100 + 20 + 3 = 123
Binary	111	1×2^2 (4)	1×2^1 (2)	1×2^0 (1)	4 + 2 + 1 = 7

The engineering of PC processing, storage, and transferring components—the CPU, the memory, and buses—determines how big a binary value can be transferred or processed at a single time. Early computers were based on 8-bit transfers; today, many components work with 32-bit or 64-bit values.

To change input binary data into new values, or process the data, special, tiny circuits are used. At their most basic, these circuits can add, subtract, and compare values. Combinations of these circuits are used to perform ever more complex calculations, from multiplication and division through processing visual display data or performing very complex mathematical equations.

The Role of Software

A circuit can only behave in the defined ways it has been engineered. For performing more complicated interactions with data, PC hardware is designed to be managed by software. PC software is essentially lines of instructions, or code, written in a programming language and stored as data in the computer system. Some software is written in low-level machine programming languages, and is designed to interact with hardware directly as well as be manipulated by higher levels of software. The software on a PC with which users interact includes operating system software and application software:

▲ **Operating system software:** A PC's **operating system** is software designed to interact with the PC's hardware and with application software. For example, you type an email in application software, such as Microsoft Outlook or Mozilla Thunderbird. The email application software interacts with the operating system software (for example, Windows XP) to deliver input and receive output from the PC. In addition to the Windows family of operating systems, the Apple Macintosh PCs use Apple's operating systems, such as OS X. Another popular operating system is Linux. The function of the operating system is to provide a consistent environment for other software to execute commands and to give users an interface with the computer so they can send commands (input) and receive feedback or results back (output). To do this, the operating system communicates with the computer hardware to perform the following tasks:

- Data storage on hard drives and file management
- Device (hardware) access
- Memory management
- Output format

After the operating system has organized these basic resources, users can give the computer instructions through input devices such as a keyboard or a mouse. Some of these commands are built into the operating system; others are issued through the use of applications. The operating system is the center through which the system hardware, other software, and the user communicate. The operating system itself communicates with hardware using drivers. A **driver** is an extremely specific piece of software written for the purpose of instructing a particular operating system on how to access a piece of hardware. For example, each modem or printer has unique features and configuration settings, and the driver allows the operating system to properly understand how the hardware works and what it is able to do. Drivers are usually shipped with a hardware component on a floppy disk or CD-ROM that you use to install the hardware. In addition, the Windows operating system incorporates many generic and popular drivers for various common types of drivers.

▲ **Application software:** An **application** is software that is written to perform specific tasks and to supplement the commands available to a particular operating system. Each application is specifically compiled (configured) for the operating system on which it will run. For this reason, the application relies on the operating system to do many of its basic tasks. Examples of applications include Microsoft Word and Adobe Acrobat. When accessing devices and memory, the applications or programs can simply request that the operating system do it for them. This arrangement saves substantially on programming overhead because much of the executable code is shared—it is written into the operating system and can therefore be used by multiple applications running on that operating system.

1.1.4 Bytes, Words, and the Hexadecimal Numbering System

Although bits—1s and 0s—are at the foundation of PC computing, the PC operates on groups of bits at a time. The smallest grouping of bits that a PC today typically processes is a **byte**: a group of 8 bits. (Some computing systems may group more or less bits as a byte, but in modern PC architecture, a byte typically refers to 8 bits). A byte is sometimes called an octet because it is formed of 8 binary digits, such as "11001100." A byte can store up to 256 values, from the binary number 0000000 (0) to 11111111 (255). Bits are commonly expressed by a "b" and bytes expressed with a "B." Prefixes, such as kilo (meaning thousand), mega (meaning million), and giga (meaning a thousand million), are used with the terms bit and byte to express larger amounts of data. These terms mean slightly different things in a binary number system than in a decimal system. In a decimal number system, kilo means 1000, whereas in binary, kilo refers to 2^{10} or 1024 (Table 1-2).

When data is discussed in terms of how fast data is moving along a bus or how much data can be stored on a hard drive, you will hear the data expressed

Table 1-2: Decimal and Binary Unit Prefixes

Prefix	Decimal Value	Binary Value
Kilo	1000	1024
Mega	1000^2	1024^2
Giga	1000^3	1024^3
Tera	1000^4	1024^4
Peta	1000^5	1024^5
Exa	1000^6	1024^6

in terms of bits and bytes. For example, data may move at 56 KBps (56 kilobits per second) or at 40 MBps (40 megabytes per second). Storage amounts are usually discussed in terms of megabytes (MB), gigabytes (GB), or terabytes (TB).

For internal processing, bits are worked on in groups called words. A **word** can be any number of bits but is typically made of one or more bytes. PC architecture and applications are engineered and programmed to work with specific sizes of words. Early PCs worked with 8-bit words, and successive generations of PCs worked with 16-bit and 32-bit words. You will hear this referred to as 16-bit processing, 32-bit applications, etc. Today, PC architectures are moving from 32-bit processing to 64-bit processing.

Instead of using the decimal system or binary system for programming software, programmers often use a **hexadecimal number system**. The hexadecimal numbering system uses a base of 16, instead of 10 or 2. This means that for every position in a number, there are 16 possible values: 0 through 15, and the symbols used are the numbers 0-9 and the letters A (10), B (11), C (12), D (13), E (14), and F (15). Using a hexadecimal numbering system works well with bits and bytes because a single hexadecimal digit (1 through F) can express all the values that could be contained in 2 bytes, or 16 bits. Many values in operating system software and used to interact with PC hardware are expressed in hexadecimal values. To differentiate hexadecimal numbers from decimal numbers, the number is often followed by a small letter h, as in F00Ah, or has a prefix of 0x, as in 0xF00.

1.1.5 Types of PCs

PCs are generally categorized by the type of case they use. The type of case a PC has can determine the way its internal components are arranged, what types and numbers of components can be in the PC, and how the PC airflow is managed to help cool the components.

All the computer's components mount to the inside of the case—the case is essentially the mounting platform for all the electronic devices that make up the computer. Typically, cases are square or rectangular boxes, usually beige in color (although the current trend is for all-black cases and matching peripherals), and made of steel, aluminum, or plastic.

Cases are distinguished in two ways: by their case style, and by their form factor. In general, a **form factor** describes a components physical dimensions and specifications. The form factor that a PC case has describes the type of motherboard for which they are designed. You could have two cases with the same physical dimensions and look, but with completely different internal layouts suitable for their motherboards.

Case Styles

Case styles vary in the way they normally sit (vertically or horizontally) as well as the number of device bays they support. A device bay (or bay for short) is a large slot into which an expansion device fits (usually a disk drive of some sort). There are two bay sizes: 5 1/4-inch (typically used for CD-ROM and similar drives) and 3 1/2-inch (used for floppy, Zip, and hard disk drives).

Several common PC case styles are in use today (Figure 1-4):

▲ **Full Tower:** A full tower case is a computer case that stands approximately 20–25 inches tall, has at least five 5 1/4-inch drive bays, and is designed to stand vertically on the floor next to a desk (refer to Figure 1-3). This type of case may have wheels so you can move it easily when you need to unplug a cable or do other work on the computer. Often, it will have stabilizing feet to prevent it from tipping over. Full tower cases are often used for server computers because of the number of disk drives a server needs to hold. Full tower cases also have a lot of room inside. This space allows components to be separated and provides good airflow around them. Drawbacks to a full size tower include its size and expense.

Figure 1-4

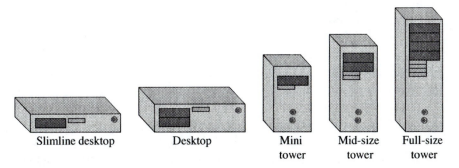

Slimline desktop   Desktop   Mini tower   Mid-size tower   Full-size tower

Common PC case styles.

Figure 1-5

Power supply

5.25" drive bays

3.5" drive bays

Expansion bays

Mid-size tower.

▲ **Mid-size Tower:** A mid-size tower (Figure 1-5) case stands between 16 and 19 inches tall, has at least three 5 1/4-inch drive bays, and is designed to stand vertically either on the floor or on a computer user's desk next to the monitor. This type of case doesn't have quite as much room inside as a full tower case, but it still has significant room for airflow and component layout and is less expensive than a full tower case.

▲ **Mini Tower:** A mini tower case is a computer case that stands about 12 to 15 inches tall, has one or two 5 1/4-inch drive bays, and is designed to stand next to a computer monitor (refer to Figure 1-4). It was designed to keep the small form factor of a desktop case but also keep the look of a tower. Mini towers are often used in low-end or entry-level computer systems to keep the price down. They are the cheapest possible tower-style case you can buy. The main drawback to mini tower cases is their relatively small size. Most components are packed inside these cases with relatively little room for airflow, so the cases tend to be used for computer configurations that don't have many components (housing all-in-one motherboards, for example).

▲ **Desktop:** Although the term "desktop" in general refers to a nonportable PC, a desktop *case* is designed to lie horizontally, with at least three 5 1/4-inch bays oriented horizontally and the 3 1/2-inch bays oriented vertically (Figure 1-6). Currently, the dimensions for a typical full size desktop case are about 15 to 17 inches wide and 5 to 7 inches high. This case design usually saves floor and desktop space, but costs about

Figure 1-6

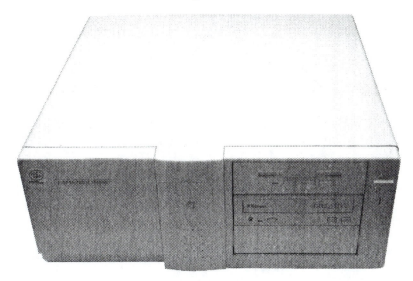

Desktop case.

the same as a similarly configured mini tower case and has less internal space. Desktop cases also don't necessarily cool as well as their vertically oriented cousins. For these reasons, sales of desktop systems today are much slower compared to similarly configured mini tower versions.

▲ **Slimline:** A slimline computer case is a thinner desktop case that usually has only one 5 1/4-inch drive bay, mounted horizontally (or possibly two, side by side). It's designed to take up the least amount of desktop space, and is the smallest standardized form factor. The only advantage of the slimline case is its small size. The small size, however, leads to one major disadvantage: heat. Heat shortens the life of computer components, and due to the small size of slimline cases, they require specialized cooling design (and they still do a poor job of cooling).

▲ **Proprietary cases:** Many PC manufacturers (such as Dell and Gateway) don't use standardized cases, but rather manufacture their motherboards and cases together to keep costs down. This results in what are known as proprietary case designs. A proprietary case is a computer case that is designed to work with only one particular motherboard and set of components and is typically designed for a specific purpose. Dell's computers are a perfect example of PCs that use proprietary cases. Although Dell's cases could be classified as mid tower or mini tower, they work only with Dell motherboards designed for the particular case and are therefore usually classified as proprietary.

Form Factors

Essentially, a form factor describes the motherboard's size, shape, and how it is mounted to the case. Form factors specifications now include:

▲ The size, shape, and function of the system case

▲ The type, placement, and size of the power supply

▲ The system's power requirements

▲ The location and type of external connectors

▲ The case's airflow and cooling systems

There are standard form factors used for cases, motherboards, and power supplies, and in general, when a PC is built, you choose a case, motherboard, and power supply that have the same form factor. Some of the most commonly used form factors are:

▲ **AT:** Uses a motherboard patterned after the original IBM PC AT motherboard.

▲ **Baby AT:** Uses a motherboard that is a smaller version of the AT form factor motherboard.

▲ **ATX:** Similar in size to the Baby AT, the ATX adds features. This is the most often used form in today's PCs. The ATX motherboard allows for easier installation of full-length expansion cards and cables and is easier to cool. There are several smaller version of the ATX form factor, including the mini ATX and micro ATX.

FOR EXAMPLE

You Get What You Pay For

As with any other product, there are varying degrees of quality and design among full tower cases. You could find two cases that look exactly the same outwardly, but are built completely differently. They might differ in metal type and thickness, fastener type, and whether the motherboard mounting plate can be removed to make motherboard mounting easier. As you look at the various types of available cases, remember that generally speaking, you get what you pay for. Cheaper cases are made of thinner gauge metal, use inferior fastening mechanisms, and generally don't have the fit and finish of the more expensive cases. The quality of the case is especially important when you are building the computer yourself.

Table 1-3: Case Design Comparison

Case Design	Number of 5 1/4" Bays	Footprint Size	Cooling	Cost
Full tower	5 or more	Largest	Excellent	$$$$
Mid tower	3 or more	Large	Good to excellent	$$$
Mini tower	1 or 2	Medium	Good	$$
Desktop	3 or more	Medium	Poor to good	$$
Slimline	1	Smallest	Poor	$
Proprietary	Varies	Varies	Varies	Varies

▲ **LPX:** LPX motherboards (and the smaller mini LPX) are lower-end motherboards that have only one expansion slot, but can use a riser card to add additional slots.

▲ **NLX:** An acronym for New, Low profile eXtended, this form factor is used in low-profile case types. It incorporates expansion slots that are placed on a riser board to accommodate the reduction in case size. However, this design adds another component to troubleshoot.

▲ **BTX:** The Balanced Technology Extended (BTX) motherboard was designed by Intel to deal with issues surrounding ATX (heat, power consumption, and so on). The BTX motherboard is larger than ATX, so there is more room for integrated components; there is also an optimized airflow path and a low-profile option.

Table 1-3 compares the case designs discussed in this chapter.

SELF-CHECK

1. What are the four main functions in computing?
2. Describe how PCs work with data.
3. What is meant by 32-bit computing?
4. Identify six types of PC case styles.

1.2 Troubleshooting PCs

For the most part, PCs are extremely reliable devices, composed of precisely manufactured and tested electronic circuits. Electronic components occasionally fail, however, and require diagnosing and repair or replacement. Mechanical parts, such as switches or fans, can also fail. Skilled technicians play an essential role in helping businesses and users maintain and repair computers, and technicians must develop both an understanding of how a PC's components functions as well as a method for troubleshooting a failing system.

Troubleshooting is the process of identifying a computer problem so that it can be fixed. Until you've had the opportunity to troubleshoot several computers with several different types of customers, the only way to gain the troubleshooting skills you will rely on as a certified technician is to learn from other people's experiences. This section summarizes basic guidelines and general tips for approaching the task of troubleshooting.

1.2.1 General Troubleshooting Steps

There are three main stages of troubleshooting:

1. **Identifying the problem:** Identifying or defining the problem means more than just determining that a component is not working. For example, a printer that won't turn on is experiencing a different problem from a printer that is printing garbage text.

2. **Isolating the cause of the problem:** After you have clearly defined a problem, you must work to determine what the cause is. For example, is the problem hardware or software-related? Is there a problem with an internal component of the PC or with a peripheral?

3. **Resolving the problem:** After you have determined the cause of the problem—for example, too little system hard drive space in the PC—you must then determine the best way to fix the problem. There are often several ways to resolve a problem. For example, you could add storage space in a PC by removing or compressing existing files, replacing a hard drive, or adding another hard drive or different type of storage. The best resolution should be appropriate to the user's needs, although it may be affected by the resources and time at your disposal or company policy.

The most common troubleshooting tips are condensed here into a seven-step process. When you troubleshoot a problem with a PC, try each step in order. If one step doesn't narrow the problem down, move on to the next step.

1. **Define the problem:** If you can't define the problem, you can't begin to solve it. You can define the problem by determining the steps that cause the problem. Find out exactly where and when the problem occurs, and see if the problem can be repeated using the following steps.

    • **How often does this happen?** Establishes whether a problem is a one-time occurrence (usually indicating a software-related memory error or the like) that can be solved with a reboot, or whether a specific sequence of events causes the problem to happen (usually indicating a more serious problem that may require software installation or hardware replacement).

- **Has any new software been installed recently?** New software can mean incompatibility problems with existing programs. For example, installing an application could overwrite a required utility file with a newer version of the same name, which an older program may not be able to work with.

- **Have any other changes been made to the computer recently?** If a change was made shortly before a problem started, there's a good chance the problem is related to the change. If the change involved a new hardware component, check to see that the hardware component was installed correctly.

2. **Check the simple stuff first:** Often, computer problems are the result of something simple. Some examples of simple problems are shown here:

- **Is it plugged in?** Cables must be plugged in on both ends to function correctly. Cables can be easily tripped over and inadvertently pulled from their sockets. Make sure cables are properly and firmly connected.

- **Is it turned on?** Computers and their peripherals must be turned on to function. Most have power switches that have LEDs that glow when the power is turned on.

- **Is the system ready?** Computers must be ready before they can be used. Ready means the system is ready to accept commands from the user. An indication that a computer is ready is when the operating system screens come up and the computer presents you with a menu or a command prompt. If that computer uses a graphical interface, the computer is ready when the mouse pointer appears. Printers are ready when the On Line or Ready light on the front panel is lit.

- **Is there an operator error?** Operator errors (missteps by yourself or a user) include improperly installed hardware or software, a mistake in typing a command, or error performing a procedure. If a problem occurs while you are performing a procedure, double-check the steps of the procedure to make sure you have followed all the steps in the correct order. You can also double-check that the procedure you are using is the right one, and that the documentation you are using isn't misleading or faulty.

- **Are there external signs of problems?** External signs of problems include sounds and visual signals that you are not expecting or should not be there. Can you hear any strange beeps or sounds coming from the PC? Is the monitor displaying correctly? Are any power indicator lights off?

3. **Reboot the computer:** Rebooting the computer clears the memory and starts the computer with a clean slate. If rebooting doesn't work, try powering down the system completely, and then powering it up again. Very often this will solve the problem.

4. **Determine if the problem is hardware related or software related:** This step is important because it determines what part of the computer you should focus your troubleshooting skills on. Each part requires different skills and different tools. To determine if a problem is hardware or software related, you can do a few things to narrow down the issue. For instance, does the problem manifest itself when you use a particular piece of hardware (a modem, for example)? If it does, the problem is more than likely hardware related. This step relies on personal experience more than any of the other steps do. You will without a doubt run into strange software problems. Each one has a particular solution. Some may even require reinstallation of the software or the entire operating system.

5. **For hardware problems, determine which component is failing:** Some hardware problems are easy to figure out. If the modem doesn't work and you know it isn't a software problem, the modem is probably the piece of hardware that needs to be replaced. With some computers, several components are integrated onto the motherboard. If you troubleshoot the computer and find a hardware component to be bad, there's a good chance that the bad component is integrated into the motherboard (for example, the parallel port circuitry) and the whole motherboard must be replaced—an expensive proposition, to be sure. To isolate hardware component problems, a common tactic is to swap out the potentially problematic component with a known good component. If the problem is resolved by using a known good component, you know the replaced component is at fault.

6. **Check documentation and run diagnostic tests:** The service manuals are your instructions for troubleshooting and service information. Almost every computer and peripheral made today has a set of service documentation in the form of books, service CD-ROMs, and websites. Depending on the type of problem, you can use Windows or third-party diagnostic tools or utility software to help pinpoint the problem.

7. **Check the internal hardware configuration:** Your last resort in troubleshooting is to open the PC and inspect the internal hardware. Make sure that cables are plugged in, components are receiving power, and any expansion cards or memory modules are properly inserted. If you suspect a problem lies with one of your expansion cards, you can remove and reinstall it to make sure the connection is secure.

When troubleshooting a PC hardware component, it is important to work methodically and change only a single hardware configuration at a time. For example, if you need to determine whether a problem with a mouse is related to the port it is plugged into on the PC or the mouse itself is failing, you will need to test each possibility separately: For example, trying a new mouse plugged into a different port would not tell you anything about the original mouse problem. In this circumstance, to isolate the problem, you could try to use the non-working mouse in a different port or try plugging a different mouse that you know is working, into the original port.

When you make any kind of configuration change during troubleshooting, you must change the computer back to its original state before making a different change. It is also very important to document the problem and the steps you take to identify it and resolve it. This will not only help you in working methodically, but also serve as a source of information for future troubleshooting problems.

1.2.2 Working with Clients

In most work situations, you will be troubleshooting a PC that belongs to someone else—a coworker or client—and you will need to be able to work effectively with non-technicians to identify problems and isolate their causes.

FOR EXAMPLE

FRUs

When a component has been deemed to be bad, it needs to be replaced. A replaceable component is called a **field replaceable unit (FRUs)** or **field replaceable module (FRM)**. FRUs can be individual parts (such as a lever or chip) or whole assemblies (like monitors, power supplies, and keyboards). In most cases you don't (or can't) replace individual parts. Most companies have gone to the strategy of using whole assemblies for FRUs. For example, you can't order a #2415 capacitor for a Compaq power supply from Compaq anymore. Instead, you order a #A5123G power supply assembly. The individual assembly costs more, but there is less labor involved in replacing a whole power supply than a single capacitor, so it's actually cheaper for the customer as well as the service centers.

When you determine that a particular component needs to be replaced, you look in a catalog (usually produced by the manufacturer) for the part number of the FRU you need. The catalog may also indicate the FRU's cost and shipping information. Some FRUs require an exchange of the old, broken component (called a core or exchange FRU). In this case, the catalog will indicate two prices: one for the FRU alone, and another for the FRU with an exchange. The price of the single FRU is usually double (sometimes triple) the price of a core FRU.

When going into a technical support or service situation, you should understand that the two primary reasons for a service call are as follows:

▲ Operator error, which is typically a user training or nontraining issue
▲ Recent changes made to a PC that are causing configuration conflicts or problems

A distant third reason for a service call is that one or more of the PC's components have stopped working.

There are several important considerations when working with users.

▲ **User level of technical knowledge:** Different users have different levels of understanding PC hardware and software. It is important to be able to identify the level of technical expertise the user has so that you can communicate effectively with them. A user that feels you are oversimplifying or talking down to them and using jargon will be less motivated to help with diagnosing a problem and managing its solution.

▲ **User role in defining the problem:** A user is, appropriately, most often concerned with the task or tasks they have been hired by their company to do. They may need to print a report properly and on time, and be far more worried or frustrated about completing their task and much less concerned with the internal workings of the printer or its maintenance. It is important to remember that users or clients you are working with were not hired because of their ability to manage or troubleshoot PC hardware, but rather their ability to perform work that is supported by the hardware. As such, regardless of the problem as you define it, the problem is never resolved until the problem as the user sees it is resolved. You may remove a paper jam from a printer, but until the user is able to print their document, the problem is not resolved.

▲ **User role in creating the problem:** It is not uncommon for a problem to be the result of human error, or for users to be embarrassed in admitting their role or lack of expertise as a contributing factor. To elicit the most accurate information from a user, use questioning techniques that are neutral in nature. Instead of "What were you doing when it broke?" be more compassionate and say, "What was going on when the computer decided not to work?" It sounds silly, but these types of changes can make your job a lot easier.

When you work with a user, the first task is to have the customer give you his or her version of what happened. Hopefully, the customer's description can include a re-creation of what happened on the PC and why he or she thinks that may be a problem. Even if the customer/user is unable to re-create the problem, you should ask about any hardware or software changes that were recently made to the PC. As you know, many PC problems are the result of changes that were made to the hardware or software. If the user's explanation of the problem matches the conditions with which you are familiar, you can start the process of identification, isolation, and resolution.

What may be the most valuable tools for troubleshooting a PC hardware problem are paper and a pen. You have a lot to write down as you begin troubleshooting the PC, including the user's comments and the PC's configuration. Additionally, observe the customer's environment as carefully as you can, especially the electrical setup that's used for the PC in question. Is the PC attached to a wall socket or a power strip? How many devices are sharing the electrical supply? Is the environment dust-free and otherwise clean? Is it humid or overly dry? All of these conditions tell you about the stresses and strains to which the PC is subjected.

However, do not assume any conclusions based on what you see. Ask the user how long the PC has been in its current location and electrical situation. Also, don't jump to conclusions about what the apparent problem may be without first speaking with the user. And when dealing with a user directly, always use the five Cs (courtesy, concern, consideration, conscientiousness, and cooperation) and the three Ls (listen, listen, and listen) of customer care.

1.2.3 Troubleshooting Resources

Although your personal experience and the experience of technicians you know may form the most valuable resource for your troubleshooting, there are a wide variety of resources you can use to troubleshoot difficult problems. Two important categories of resources include knowledge base resources and diagnostic tools and utilities.

Knowledge Base Resources

Knowledge base resources include:

▲ **Service documentation:** This includes items such as the owner's manual, the buyer's guide, and the service and replacement parts manuals. These books can be a valuable source of troubleshooting information. They can also contain replacement-parts information, such as which part(s) should be replaced when a particular component is found to be bad. In addition, they usually contain exploded diagrams of the model being repaired.

▲ **The Internet:** The Internet is an extremely valuable resource for troubleshooting guidance. There are several types of places to find troubleshooting resources and tips:

   • **Manufacturer websites:** One feature of most companies' websites is the knowledge base, an area that contains several pieces of information that can be very valuable to technicians working with its products. The knowledge base usually contains one or more **FAQ** (Frequently Asked Questions) files. These are summaries of the common questions that support technicians are asked and their answers. A knowledge base may also include reports of bugs that have been discovered or suspected in the company's products. If you are unable to find an answer in a company's knowledge base, you can usually go to the website's support page to ask your question directly.

- **Search Engines:** If you can't find an answer at the manufacturer's website, you can try entering your problem into one of the many search engines, such as Google.

- **Community resources:** Some websites are run by communities of technical individuals that can be a great source of information. Chances are, if you're having a computer or technical problem, someone else, somewhere in the world, has the solution. You can post your problem to any number of website bulletin boards and newsgroups and often receive a quick response, possibly within minutes.

▲ **Training materials:** Books and other training materials (such as the one you are reading right now) are excellent sources of information.

Diagnostic Utilities

Diagnostic utilities are software designed to help troubleshoot a computer problem. You can purchase some diagnostic tools from software vendors or download them from websites offering freeware and shareware. Windows offers a number of built-in utilities and software tools to help you determine the source of an problem. Some of the general hardware troubleshooting utilities or tools included in Windows are available through the Start>All Programs>Accessories>System Tools menu. Others you can access through the Control Panels Administrative Tools panel. You can also purchase additional diagnostic tools from third-party software vendors. Some may be available for free or at minimal cost, as freeware or shareware that can be downloaded from the Internet.

Common built-in Windows tools include:

▲ **Device Manager:** The Device Manager is a tool you can use to analyze hardware-related problems. The Device Manager displays all of the devices installed in a computer (Figure 1-7). If a device is malfunctioning, a yellow circle with an exclamation point inside it is displayed. With this utility, you can view the devices installed in a system and any of those devices that are failing, and also double-click on a device and view and set its properties. On the General tab, you will see the status of the device (whether it's working). The other tabs are used to configure the individual devices, add or update drivers, and verify the version of drivers installed.

Figure 1-7

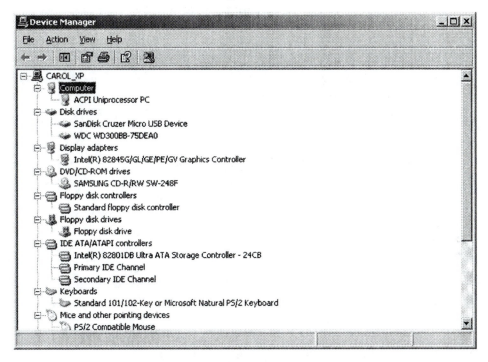

Windows XP Device Manager.

▲ **Computer Management Console:** The Computer Management Console can manage more than just the installed hardware devices. In addition to a Device Manager that functions almost identically to the one in Windows 9x, the Computer Management Console can also manage all the operating system services running on that computer. It contains an Event Viewer to show any system errors and events, as well as methods to configure the all of software components of computer's hardware.

▲ **Event Viewer:** The Event Viewer is a utility application included in the Windows NT/2000/XP/2003 operating systems that logs significant errors and events (such as an application failing to load or a user logging on to the system) during the operation of the computer. These log files can give a general indication of a Windows computer's health, and you can use it to help track down hardware- and software-related issues.

▲ **MSCONFIG.EXE:** MSCONFIG.EXE (a.k.a. the System Configuration Utility) allows a user to manage their computer system's configuration. For example, if you suspect a certain driver is causing problems during boot, you can use MSCONFIG.EXE to prevent that driver from loading.

▲ **Safe Modes:** If you don't press any keys at startup, Windows starts normally, loads all its drivers, and does not prompt for any interaction. However, occasionally Windows may not load properly, or a device may not function correctly. When Windows won't start properly, it is probably due to a driver or other piece of software not loading correctly. To fix problems of this nature, you should boot Windows in Safe mode. In Safe mode, Windows loads a minimal set of drivers so that you can disable the offending driver.

In addition to these utilities, Windows includes a number of command-line utilities you can use to configure and maintain your system. A **command line utility** is executed through the command line interface (CLI), which is a DOS-like text base interface. To open the CLI, or command prompt, open the Start menu, select Run, enter cmd in the Open field, and click OK. In the CLI, you type in a command and press Enter to execute the command.

To issue a command from the command prompt, you need to know the structure the command uses, generally referred to as its syntax. Typically, you type in the name of the command and then one or more words to indicate the component (such as a file or disk that the command operates on.) In addition, a command can be modified or configured by typing in a switch. Switches enable you to further configure the command's actions. A switch is a short phrase or letter, such as –r, that tells the command to perform some specific task.

Table 1-4: Sample Windows Text Commands

Command	Purpose
CHKDSK	Examines the machine's hard drives.
DEFRAG	Defragments (reorders and cleans up) a hard drive's files
DISKPART	Manages hard disk partitions
DRIVERQUERY	Displays information about drivers in use
FORMAT	Prepares a drive for use.
PRNCFG	Displays printer configuration information
RECOVER	Attempts to retrieve data from a damaged hard drive
SFC	System file checker; replaces damaged system files
SHUTDOWN	Allows you to shut down a PC
SYSTEMINFO	Displays system configuration info
VER	Checks the current version of the operating system.

In general, older versions of Windows, such as Windows 98, use more text-based commands than newer versions, such as Windows XP. Table 1-4 lists a few of the commands available in Windows XP.

For example, to use the CLI to check a hard drive for errors with the CHKDSK command:

1. Click Start and then click Run to open the Run dialog box.
2. In the Open text box, type cmd and press Enter to open the command-line interface.
3. In the command line window, type chkdsk and press Enter to run the chkdsk utility. To specify that chkdsk fixes any errors it finds, you use the switch /f, so instead of typing chkdsk, you would type chkdsk /f.

SELF-CHECK

1. What are the three main stages of troubleshooting?
2. At what point in the troubleshooting process should you open the PC to check internal hardware configuration?
3. List five types of intellectual resources for troubleshooting.
4. Define and give examples of a command-line utility.

1.3 Working with PCs

PCs need regular maintenance to keep them in good working order. Before working on a PC, however, it is important to plan an appropriate workspace and have the right tools. In addition, you must understand the hazards associated with PC components and be able to handle them safely.

1.3.1 PC Workspaces and Tools

For any work you do on a computer, you must have an adequate workspace. A good workspace is a level, flat surface about 4 feet wide by 4 feet deep and standing about waist height. The work area must be flat. If it's not, small parts could roll around and possibly get lost or damaged. Also, the area must be sturdy. A typical computer weighs about 25 pounds. In addition, the area must be well lit, clean, and large enough to hold all pieces (assembled and disassembled) and all necessary tools.

Before you begin, make sure all necessary tools are available and in working order. You should also lay out the parts you will be using (ideally, on a separate table or work surface). Make sure the documentation for the system you are working on is available (including owner's manuals, service manuals, and Internet resources). Three tools in particular that will be very handy are generally not considered traditional tools, but rather timesavers: an egg carton, a pen, and a notepad. An egg carton is perfect for organizing screws and small parts that might otherwise end up in the "extra parts" pile. You should use a pen and notepad to record anything that may easily be forgotten, such as cable positions, DIP-switch settings, and the locations from which you remove the components.

Some common hardware tools you use to work on PCs include:

▲ **Nonmagnetic screwdrivers:** Most of the larger components in today's computers are mounted in the case with screws. If these components need to be removed, you must have the correct type of screwdriver available. There are three major types:

- **Flat-Blade Screwdriver:** Also called a flathead or standard screwdriver. The type of screw that this screwdriver removes is not used much anymore (primarily because the screw head is easily damaged).
- **Phillips Screwdriver:** The most commonly used type of screwdriver for computers today is the Phillips screwdriver. Phillips-head screws are used because they have more surfaces to turn against, reducing the risk of damaging the head of the screw. More than 90 percent of the screws in most computers today are Phillips-head screws.
- **Torx Screwdriver:** The Torx type of screw has the most surfaces to turn against and therefore has the greatest resistance to screw-head damage. (Figure 1-8). The sizes of Torx drivers are given with the designation T-xx, where the xx is replaced with a number from 1 through 20. The most common sizes are T-10 and T-15, but for some notebook computers, you will need to have much smaller Torx drivers on hand.

Figure 1-8

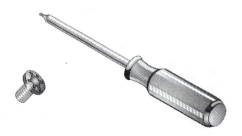

Torx screwdriver and screw.

- • **Tweaker:** One tool that is invaluable when working on a computer can be bought from different tool vendors and is often given away at trade shows. That tool is commonly known as a tweaker. It is a screwdriver that is shaped like a pen and is about the same size. It has a Phillips screwdriver on one end, a flat-blade screwdriver on the other, and clips easily into a shirt pocket.

Several screwdrivers are available with changeable tips, similar to bits for a drill. The advantage is that you can easily change these screwdrivers from a flat blade to a Phillips to a Torx just by changing the bits in the driver. The bits are usually stored in the handle of this type of screwdriver.

Although it may seem convenient, don't use a multiple-bit driver that is magnetized. Magnetism and computers don't make good friends. The magnetism can induce currents in conductors and burn out components without your knowledge. It could also erase magnetic disk storage media.

- ▲ **Needle-Nose Pliers:** These are great for grasping connectors or small screws when your hands are too big. If a needle-nose is still too large for the job, a standard pair of tweezers will work as well (Figure 1-9).

- ▲ **Flashlight:** Small flashlights will help you see components in a dark computer case. Maglite makes a powerful small flashlight that runs on two AA batteries. It also fits well into a toolkit.

- ▲ **Compressed Air:** Useful for removing dust from the inside of the PC case.

- ▲ **Antistatic wrist strap:** Antistatic wrist straps are essential devices that technicians use to prevent small electrical charges from damaging delicate PC components (Figure 1-10).

- ▲ **Multimeters:** A multimeter is a combination of several different kinds of testing meters, including an ohmmeter, ammeter, and voltmeter. In trained hands, it can help detect the correct operation or failure of several different types of components. You will learn how to use a multimeter in Chapter 2.

Figure 1-9

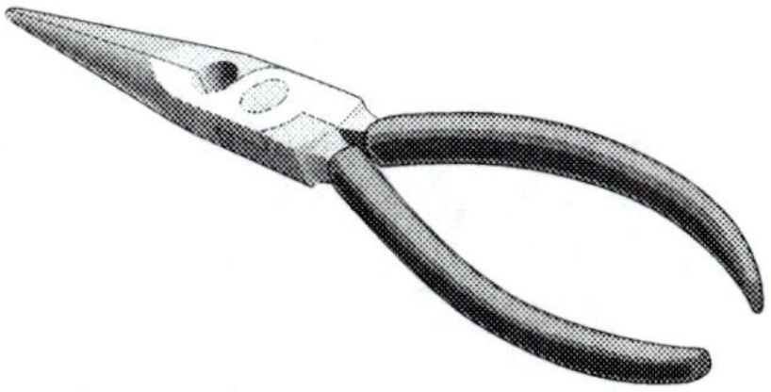

Needle-nose pliers.

Figure 1-10

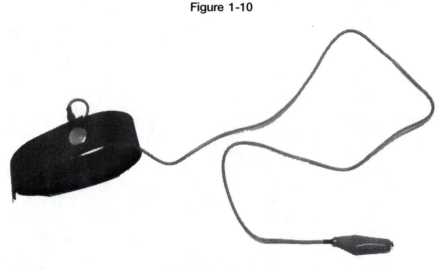

Antistatic wrist strap.

1.3.2 Preventive Maintenance

To keep a PC in good running order you must perform regularly scheduled maintenance inspections. Without regular care and maintenance, your PC won't perform as it should—it may even stop working, just like a car would without some form of regular attention. Therefore, the purposes of any preventive maintenance (PM) program are to reduce the need for repair and to extend the life of the computer. You can accomplish these goals only if you perform PM on a regular basis following a well-defined procedure. Virtually all PC owner's manuals include a chart or table that details the maintenance, adjustments, inspections, and cleaning that should be performed at specific, periodic intervals.

Items to regularly remove dust from and clean include:

▲ Keyboard

▲ Mouse

▲ Monitor

▲ Case

▲ Floppy drive

In addition, special tools are used to manage and maintain the files on a PC's hard drive. Hard drive management includes:

▲ Maintaining the files and file system to keep the raw data organized

▲ Running anti-virus programs

▲ Performing regular backups of data

FOR EXAMPLE

Maintaining the PC Case

Look over the case thoroughly for dust, corrosion, leaking battery acid. Normally, the inside and outside vents have dust accumulated on them, but if dust is gathering in a place that it shouldn't, the case may have a crack in it, a part may be missing, or some other problem may have developed. A common problem is that one or more of the slot covers that should be filling empty expansion ports on the case are missing. If the case is only lightly dusty, use compressed air to blow it out; be careful not to blow the dust into your eyes. If you must remove particles or debris, pick them out with tweezers, or if big enough, with your fingers. Because you are working inside the case, you must use electrostatic discharge (ESD) protection such as an antistatic wrist strap. Also check cables and wires for loose connections.

Using compressed air, blow out the outside vents of the power supply first and then clean the case's inside vents, drive bays, adapter cards, and outside vents. You can also use a small vacuum cleaner to clean the inside of the case. In fact, for some systems, a vacuum cleaner may be better than compressed air. Blowing the dust around can merely move it from one place to another inside the case. Sucking out the dirt and grime is sometimes better than blowing the dust under the edge of a loose component or connector. Several small vacuum cleaners designed specifically for PCs are available in both AC and battery-powered models. Most have either a small brush head or a relatively short hose on which brush attachments are mounted.

Anytime you open a PC, perform a little preventive maintenance. If nothing else, vacuum the system case to remove all the dust bunnies that have accumulated inside since the last time it was cleaned (if ever).

1.3.3 Environmental and Safety Concerns

There are several environmental and safety concerns that working with PCs present. These include:

▲ **Cleaning supplies:** The liquid cleaning compounds that are used to clean or condition the computer's components, case, and glass surfaces present safety and environmental problems to the user, the technician, and other people. Many of the chemical solvents and cleaners—and their containers—may require special handling because they're poisonous (or harmful in other ways). The best tool for finding out whether a chemical solution poses a threat to you, the user, or the world in general is a Material Safety Data Sheet (MSDS). An MSDS, which is used in the

United States, Europe, and most of Asia, is available for every potentially hazardous chemical product. (In Canada, the product safety information is referred to as Workplace Hazardous Materials Information System, or WHMIS.) An MSDS lists the proper handling and storage procedures for chemical cleaning solutions. Website resources you can use to look up any product that you're not sure of include:

- MSDS Search National Repository: www.msdssearch.com
- Vermont Safety Information on the Internet (SIRI): http://siri.org/msds/index.php

However, the label is the first place to look for safety information on a product. Usually, if a problem may exist for either you or the PC in using the product, the label cautions you.

▲ **Electrical hazards:** PC components, such as the power supply and monitor, can contain lethal amounts of voltage. For this reason, power supplies and CRT monitors should never be opened and worked on directly by technicians not certified or trained to do so. In addition tiny amounts of static electricity can damage the PC's sensitive electrical components, and technicians use equipment such as antistatic wrist straps to prevent this type of damage.

▲ **Fire Safety:** Repairing a computer isn't often the cause of an electrical fire. However, you should know how to extinguish such a fire properly. Four major classes of fire extinguishers are available, one for each type of flammable substance: A (water-based extinguishing material) for wood and paper fires, B (carbon dioxide) for flammable liquids, C for electrical fires, and D (metal powder or NaCl [salt]) for flammable metals like phosphorus and sodium. The most popular type of fire extinguisher today is the multipurpose, or ABC-rated, extinguisher. It contains a dry chemical powder that smothers the fire and cools it at the same time. For electrical fires (which may be related to a shorted-out wire in a power supply), make sure the fire extinguisher will work for class C fires. If you don't have an extinguisher that is specifically rated for electrical fires (type C), you can use an ABC-rated extinguisher.

▲ **Disposing of hazardous components:** Several components in a PC require special handling when you dispose of them. The list includes batteries, circuits and switches that contain mercury, a CRT monitor, and more.

- **PC batteries:** PC batteries, such as the lithium battery that provides power to the CMOS memory, shouldn't be disposed of in either fire or water. Batteries should be disposed of according to local restrictions and regulations covering the disposal or recycling of all batteries. Leaking batteries should be handled carefully. Make sure that you don't get the electrolyte—the chemicals inside the battery—in your eyes.

- **Monitors:** A CRT monitor contains the following contaminants: solvents and solvent vapors, metals (including a very high level of lead), photoresist materials, deionized water, acids, oxidizers, phosphor, ammonia, aluminum, carbon slurry, and a long list of other chemicals and caustic materials. For this reason, a monitor shouldn't just be thrown in the dumpster. In fact, federal regulations require monitors (actually CRTs in general) to be encased in concrete before being disposed of in water or a landfill. The best way to discard a monitor is through a disposal service that handles computer equipment.
- **Other problem components:** Other items that are related to the PC must be disposed of carefully. Most are common-sense items, but you may see a question on the exam that groups them as hazardous PC waste. Included in this bunch of items are laser-printer toner cartridges, refill kits, and the used or empty containers of chemical solvents and cleaners.

▲ **Security concerns:** In addition to the hazardous components contained in PCs, it is important to make sure that when you are disposing of data storage devices these devices no longer contain any sensitive information that could be accessed or misused by others. There are various techniques for doing this, but it is important to remember that simply deleting files via an operating system does not usually erase any raw data that is stored on the device.

SELF-CHECK

1. Describe an appropriate workspace for working on PCs.
2. Identify seven tools for working on PCs.
3. Which six PC components require regular maintenance and care?
4. What PC components contain environmental hazards?

SUMMARY

Personal computers (PCs) or microcomputers are made of distinct electrical components, such as the case, power supply, motherboard, CPU, memory, buses, expansion cards, storage devices, input devices, display devices, and ports and cables. There are four main functions in computing: input, processing, output, and storage. PCs work by converting electrical signals into groups of on/off values that are given the binary values of 1s and 0s. These are grouped to form larger values, typically in multiples of bytes, that are processed using specially designed electronic circuits. The number of bits that a PC can work on at a single time is called a word. PCs implement the binary and hexadecimal number systems in computing and programming. Whereas the decimal number system uses 10 as its base, the binary number system uses 2 and the hexadecimal number system uses 16.

To control the PC hardware, the PC uses software. Types of software include the operating system, which acts as an interface between hardware and other software, and application software.

PCs are generally categorized by the style of case they use (such as full tower, mid tower, etc) or their form factor. Their form factor primarily describes the type of motherboard the case is designed to hold, but also describes other physical specifications such as the type of power supply and cooling.

The three main stages in troubleshooting a PC include identifying the problem, isolating its cause, and resolving the problem. It is important to check simple causes first, such as making sure the PC has power. It is also to be able to work successfully with users and clients at all stages and use troubleshooting resources to aid your work.

When working on PCs, you should be aware of the types of tools used, appropriate workspaces, and the PC components that need regular maintenance, such as monitors, keyboards, mice, cases, floppy drives, and hard drives. In addition, you need to take special precautions for electrical hazards, fire, chemical hazards, and appropriately dispose of hazardous components.

KEY TERMS

Application

Binary number system

Bit

Byte

Command line utility

Computer

Diagnostic utility

Driver

Embedded computer

Field Replaceable Module (FRM)

Field Replacement Unit (FRU)

Form factor

Frequently Asked Questions (FAQ)

Handheld computer

Hardware

Hexadecimal number system

Mainframe

Operating system

Personal computer (PC)

Server

Software

Supercomputer

Word

Workstation

ASSESS YOUR UNDERSTANDING

Go to www.wiley.com/college/groth to evaluate your knowledge of personal computers.

Measure your learning by comparing pre-test and post-test results.

Summary Questions

1. What type of computer is used to manage networks?
   (a) supercomputer
   (b) mainframe
   (c) server
   (d) personal computer

2. Which of the following is an input device?
   (a) expansion card
   (b) bus
   (c) monitor
   (d) mouse

3. Which PC component is largely responsible for the processing function of the PC?
   (a) motherboard
   (b) storage device
   (c) CPU
   (d) memory

4. Which PC component stores data temporarily for the CPU?
   (a) hard drive
   (b) system memory
   (c) secondary storage
   (d) motherboard

5. What type of number is 0x1001?
   (a) binary
   (b) decimal
   (c) hexadecimal
   (d) octet

6. Which of the following is the number 28 in hexadecimal?
   (a) 11100
   (b) 1C
   (c) 0x1A
   (d) 28

7. What does the expression 3 GBps mean?

   (a) 3 gigabits per second

   (b) 3 gigabytes per second

   (c) 3 gigabits per sector

   (d) 3 gigabytes of storage

8. The PC case's form factor defines the type of motherboard the PC case can hold. True or false?

9. A large slot in the PC case that an expansion device fits into is called a(n):

   (a) expansion card

   (b) expansion slot

   (c) hard disk drive

   (d) drive bay

10. A Phillips screwdriver has the most surfaces to turn against and the greatest resistance to screw-head damage. True or false?

11. Which of the following is not an appropriate tool to use with a PC?

    (a) magnetized multiple-bit screwdriver

    (b) tweaker

    (c) pliers

    (d) Torx screwdriver

12. You can use a small vacuum cleaner to clean out the inside of a PC case. True or false?

13. What type of fire extinguisher is used for electrical fires?

    (a) Type A extinguisher

    (b) Type B extinguisher

    (c) Type C extinguisher

    (d) Type D extinguisher

14. Which of the following is not an external sign of problems that you check in troubleshooting?

    (a) unplugged cable

    (b) flickering LED

    (c) unusual sounds

    (d) none of the above

15. If you are troubleshooting a PC and can find nothing simple wrong, such as a lack of power or operator error, what should your next step be?

    (a) Open the PC case to see if any internal cables are unplugged.

    (b) Reboot the PC.

    (c) Run a hardware component diagnostic test.

    (d) Check documentation and other resources.

16. What does FRU stand for?

    (a) floppy replacement unit

    (b) field replaceable unit

    (c) floppy replaceable unit

    (d) frequently replaced unit

17. Which of the following software utilities tools are used to review the status of a hardware device?

    (a) Device Manager

    (b) Event Viewer

    (c) MSCONFIG.EXE

    (d) Safe mode

18. CLI is a command that allows you to copy line items within a file. True or false?

19. Which of the following is a type of operator error?

    (a) CPU calculation error

    (b) mistyped sentence

    (c) reversed cable

    (d) insufficient memory

20. There is typically only one way to resolve most common PC problems. True or false?

Applying This Chapter

1. Express the decimal number 35 in binary and hexadecimal.

2. Convert the binary number 1101101 into decimal.

3. How many bytes are in 20 KB?

4. A friend has purchased her first PC. Explain to her what she should do to care for the PC.

5. Your company has assigned an intern to help you in your work troubleshooting employee PC problems. What tasks could the intern assist with?

YOU TRY IT

PC Cases

You are building a PC. What type of case will you use? Find one or more online case manufacturers and select a case. What are the main features of this case?

Working with Clients

A client is having problems with his PC and has said that the PC isn't working. What are the first questions you will ask him?

Troubleshooting Resources

Determine the brand and model of the PC you use. What online resources are there that discuss common problems with your PC?

Disposing of a Monitor

Determine the type of monitor you have. If this monitor were broken, where would you dispose it? Find out where in your community or locale you can dispose of your monitor.

2
ELECTRICITY AND POWER

Starting Point

Go to www.wiley.com/college/groth to assess your knowledge of electricity and power.
Determine where you need to concentrate your effort.

What You'll Learn in This Chapter

▲ Basic electrical concepts and safety issues as they apply to the PC
▲ Power supply components, form factors, and connectors
▲ Power supply installation and troubleshooting

After Studying This Chapter, You'll Be Able To

▲ Choose an appropriate power supply for your system and motherboard
▲ Install or replace a power supply
▲ Troubleshoot power supply problems and determine whether the problem lies with the power supply, its connections to the system, or whether the problem is external
▲ Test resistance and voltage using a multimeter
▲ Identify the form factor of a power supply
▲ Identify the different devices available for protecting a power supply from over-or undervoltage
▲ Calculate the amount of power needed for a system

INTRODUCTION

The power supply unit, or PSU, is an integral part of the computer, providing the system with power to run everything from the motherboard and CPU to cooling fans. Although a simple power supply problem may just prevent power from reaching the PC, other power supply and electrical problems—from power brownouts to static electricity—can cause circuitry to slowly degrade. They can even cause outright failure of the system.

It is also important to understand the type of power supply that a system requires—different motherboards, CPUs, or expansion buses can require more or less power. Power supplies are categorized by their form factor—their physical dimensions and technology standards—and you need to match these correctly to the form factor of the motherboard and the case.

Although power supplies are fairly inexpensive and disposable components (it is far too dangerous to open them up and work on their circuitry), it is still important to be able to diagnose power issues. You should be able to determine if a power problem lies with the power supply itself, with its connections to the system, or is external, such as a problem with an electricity outlet. If the power supply itself is faulty, or if you determine that a PC requires more power than its current power supply is providing, you will need to be able to choose an appropriate power supply and install it.

2.1 Working with Electricity

Everything inside or attached to the PC system unit runs on electricity: motors, fans, switches, circuit boards, monitors, and connectors. Electricity has certain properties that can be measured, and a technician can test a component, such as a cable, for these properties to see if they are working properly.

Electricity is essential to the PC's functioning, but never forget that it is also a dangerous force. Fluctuating current from a power source or electrostatic discharge can degrade or ruin PC components. Electrical shocks can, of course, be fatal for humans. In this chapter, you will learn about various techniques and technologies available to help protect both you and the PC from electrical damage and to keep the power supply functioning properly and providing adequate power.

2.1.1 Electricity and the PC

Electricity is based on electrons, which are particles within atoms that have negative charges. In some materials, the atoms have free electrons that are able to move from atom to atom. These negatively charged electrons are attracted to move towards positive charges. When this movement is organized to flow in one direction, such as through a wire, electricity is created. The electrical charge of flowing electricity can be used as power to do "work:" to heat or to spin motors, for example.

Common Terms

Some common terms used to describe electricity and electrical components are:

▲ **Current:** The flow of electricity.

▲ **Circuit:** A specific path or loop that electricity is made to flow along. A closed circuit is complete, allowing current to flow. In an open circuit, current is stopped, for example, by an on/off switch.

▲ **Power:** The amount of work the electrical current is capable of producing.

▲ **Resistance:** The quality of impeding the flow of electricity. Some materials are more resistant to the flow of electricity.

▲ **Insulator:** A device or material that offers resistance to the flow of electricity.

▲ **Conductor:** A device or material that allows the flow of electricity. Some materials, like copper, are more conductive than others.

▲ **Continuity:** Describes the existence of a complete, working circuit.

▲ **Capacitor:** A device for storing electrical charge.

▲ **Resistor:** A device used to impede the flow of electricity.

Electricity flowing through a circuit is similar to water running through a hose. When you open a water faucet, the pressure in the water line forces the water to flow at some gallons-per-minute rate into the hose. The friction of the rubber hose reduces the force and rate of the water before it exits the hose. In a similar manner, an electrical power source, such as a battery, also has pressure, called voltage (Figure 2-1). When electricity flows into a wire from a source such as a battery, some of its pressure (or voltage) is lost due to resistance in the wire. Current, the flow of electricity, isn't needed for voltage to exist. (When a water faucet is off, water pressure still exists.) There is just no current.

It is important to remember that when an electrical circuit is open, voltage is still in the line although no current is flowing. If you touch the wire and close the circuit, the current begins to flow, and you can feel all of its pressure as a *shock*.

Common Electrical Measurements

Common electrical measurements include:

▲ **Amps:** Measures a current's strength or rate of flow. The amount of current needed to operate a device; for example, a hard disk drive needs 2.0 amps to start up, but only 0.35 amps for typical operation.

▲ **Ohms:** Measures a conductor's resistance to electricity. Resistance of less than 20 ohms means that current can flow through a computer system.

Figure 2-1

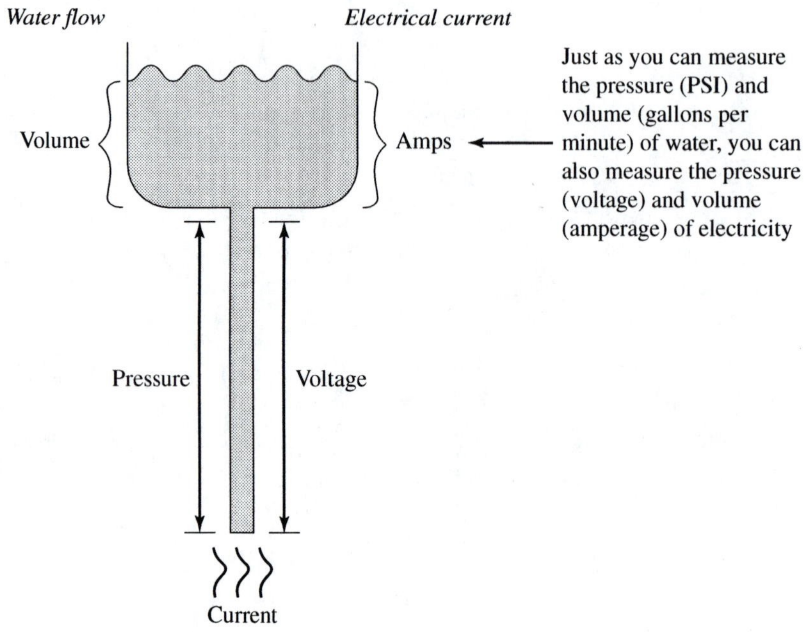

Water flow   Electrical current

Volume

Amps

Just as you can measure
the pressure (PSI) and
volume (gallons per
minute) of water, you can
also measure the pressure
(voltage) and volume
(amperage) of electricity

Pressure   Voltage

Current

Comparing electrical current to water flow.

▲ **Volts:** Measures the electrical pressure (often referred to as potential) in a
circuit.

▲ **Watts:** Measures the electrical power in a circuit range. A PC power supply is rated in a range of 200 to 600 watts.

Voltage, current, and resistance are interrelated measurements. Within a circuit,
lowering the resistance or increasing the current will produce higher voltage.
Described by Ohm's law, the relationship of voltage to current and resistance is:

$$Voltage = Current * Resistance$$

This formula can also be converted to define current or resistance:

$$Current = Voltage / Resistance$$

$$Resistance = Voltage / Current$$

So if you have two of any of the measurements, you can calculate the third.
The calculation for determining power is:

$$Power = Voltage \times Current$$

Types of Current

Electricity has two current types:

▲ **AC (alternating current)**: In alternating current, the current changes directions about 60 times per second, or 60 Hz. The voltage changing rapidly from a positive charge to a negative charge causes the current to also switch the direction of its flow in the wire. AC is the type of current supplied by power companies to the outlets in your house or office.

▲ **DC (direct current)**: Direct current maintains a constant level and flows in only one direction—always, predictably, and measurably, from a negative (or hot) charge to a positive (or ground) charge. DC is the type of current used inside the computer.

A PC's power supply converts power from the AC wall outlet into DC power for the computer's components to use. Peripheral devices, such as printers, external modems, and storage drives (including CD-ROM and Zip drives), use an AC power converter to convert AC power into DC power. Portable PCs, such as notebooks, palmtops, and PDAs (Personal Digital Assistants), are powered by batteries that supply DC voltage directly to the PC, or AC power converters.

FOR EXAMPLE

Current vs. Voltage—Which Is More Dangerous?

The number of volts in a power source represents its potential to do work. However, volts don't do anything by themselves. Current (amperage, or amps) is the force behind the work done by electricity. Here is an analogy: You have two boulders. One weighs 10 pounds, the other 100 pounds, and each is 100 feet off the ground. If you drop them, which one will do more work? The obvious answer is the 100 pound boulder. They both have the same potential to do work (100 feet of travel), but the 100 pound boulder has more mass, and thus more force. Voltage is analogous to the distance the boulder is from the ground, and amperage is analogous to the mass of the boulder. This is why you can produce static electricity on the order of 50,000 volts and not electrocute yourself. Even though this electricity has a great potential for work, it does very little work because the amperage is so low. This also explains why you can weld metal with 110 volts. Welders use only 110 (sometimes 220) volts, but they also use anywhere from 50 to 200 amps!

2.1.2 Multimeters

A **multimeter** measures the properties of AC and DC electrical circuits. A multimeter's main components (Figure 2-2) are:

▲ **A digital or analog display:** Shows the reading or measurement of the circuit being tested.

▲ **Two probes:** A red (positive) probe and a black (negative) probe. When you test a device, you place the red probe on the hot point, or high point, of the current and place the black probe on the ground, or low point. The voltage of the circuit is calculated as the difference in the readings of these two points.

Figure 2-2

A common digital multimeter.

▲ **A function selector switch.** A rotary or other type of switch is used to:

- Select the function being tested (such as AC voltage, DC voltage, or ohms)
- Select the range to which the meter is set. If you're measuring a battery using an older meter, you may have to set the range selector manually (to a range close to, but greater than, 1.5 volts). Newer meters, especially digital ones, automatically set their ranges appropriately and are called **auto-ranging multimeters.**

Using a Multimeter

You can make four measurements on a PC using a multimeter:

▲ **Amps:** Measure the strength of an electrical current

▲ **Farads:** Measure the capacitance of an electrical device (capacitance is a measure of the amount of electric charge stored for a given electric potential)

▲ **Ohms:** Measure the resistance in an electrical medium

▲ **Voltage:** Measure the electrical potential of a circuit

When preparing a multimeter for use, you must set three things:

▲ **The type of current you're measuring:** AC or DC (also known as VDC—voltage direct current).

▲ **What you're measuring:** Set the appropriate indicator or dial to voltage (volts), current (amps), or resistance or continuity (ohms).

▲ **The range of values expected:** If you're measuring voltage from the power supply, the voltage range is 3V to 12V, and for the AC wall plug's output, the range is around 105V to 125V. There are also **auto-ranging multimeters** that sense the incoming power and set the range automatically. Remember to put on your electrostatic discharge (ESD) wrist strap (described in Section 2.1.3) and connect it to either a static ground mat or the PC case.

Warning: *Never* connect a non–auto-ranging meter to an AC power outlet to measure voltage. This action will almost surely result in permanent damage to the meter mechanism, the meter itself, or both.

When you're measuring circuits, it is very important to have the meter hooked up correctly so that the readings are accurate. Each type of measurement may require that the meter be connected in a different way. Common measurements that you will make with the multimeter are:

▲ **Measuring voltage:** When measuring voltage, you must be sure you connect the probes to the power source correctly: With DC voltage, the red

Figure 2-3

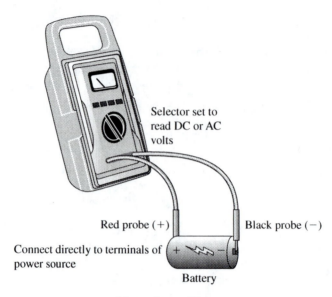

Selector set to
read DC or AC
volts

Red probe (+)   Black probe (−)

Connect directly to terminals of
power source

Battery

Measuring voltage.

probe (+) must connect to the positive (hot) side and the black probe
(−) to the negative (ground). (The position doesn't matter with AC voltage.) You also must change the selector to VDC (Volts DC) or VAC (Volts
AC), whichever is appropriate, to tell the meter what you are measuring
(Figure 2-3). Note that these settings protect the meter from overload.
If you plug a meter into a power supply while it's still set to measure
resistance, you may blow the meter. Follow these general steps to measure voltage:

1. Set the function selector to measure DC (or AC) voltage.

2. Choose the voltage range. This will usually be 20V or lower, based
   on what you are measuring.

3. Hold the black (negative) probe to a ground point on the circuit.

4. Touch the red (positive) probe to a hot point on the circuit.

▲ **Measuring resistance:** Resistance is the electrical property most commonly
   measured in troubleshooting components. A measurement of infinite resistance indicates that electricity cannot flow from one probe to the other:
   there is no continuity. If you use a multimeter to measure the resistance in
   a segment of wire and the result is an infinite reading, there is a very good
   chance that the wire has a break in it somewhere between the probes.
   Warning: *Do not* test resistance on components while they are mounted on
   a circuit board! The multimeter applies a current to the component being

Figure 2-4

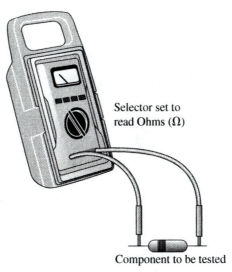

Selector set to
read Ohms (Ω)

Component to be tested

Measuring resistance.

tested. That current may also flow to other components on the board, thus damaging them. Follow these general steps to measure resistance:

1. Be sure the circuit (power connector, trace, or cable) has no power running through it. If the circuit to be tested is inside the PC, turn off the PC's power supply. You could damage your multimeter if you test a circuit that has power running through it.

2. Set the function selector to test ohms and set an appropriate range (Figure 2-4).

3. Touch the multimeter's probes to two metal points on the circuit. If you get a zero value, set the range higher or lower.

4. The multimeter should give a reading, buzz, or beep to indicate continuity in the cable. If you do not get buzzed or beeped, then either no continuity exists in the cable, or you have not made a good connection. Try a few more times—if you still get no reading, probably there is no continuity and you have discovered a bad cable.

▲ **Measuring current:** Although you will most often use the multimeter to measure resistance, you should also know how current (amps) is measured. The procedure is similar to those used for the other measurements. A major difference is that when you connect the multimeter to measure the current a circuit is drawing, you must connect the multimeter in series with the circuit being measured. Figure 2-5 illustrates the proper connection of a multimeter to measure current.

Figure 2-5

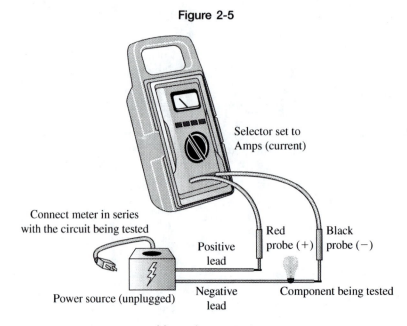

Selector set to
Amps (current)

Connect meter in series
with the circuit being tested

Red
probe (+)

Black
probe (−)

Positive
lead

Power source (unplugged)

Negative
lead

Component being tested

Measuring current.

Table 2-1 lists the type of problems that can be identified in some systems by using a multimeter and the property that is measured.

2.1.3 Electrostatic Discharge

When you shuffle your feet across a carpet and feel a shock when you touch a metal doorknob, you are discharging static electricity into the doorknob. This

Table 2-1: Troubleshooting with a Multimeter

Component/System	Property	Potential Faults
Power supply connectors	Volts	Defective power supply, cables, or connectors
Cable connections	Ohms	Broken or defective cable
Cable shielding	Ohms	Broken or defective cable sheath or insulation
Electrical devices	Volts or Ohms	Improper electrical operation to specifications

shock is **electrostatic discharge (ESD).** Essentially, electrostatic discharge (ESD) happens when two objects of dissimilar charge come in contact with one another. The two objects exchange electrons in order to standardize the electrostatic charge between them. This charge can, and often does, damage electronic components. ESD charges can cause problems such as making a computer hang or reboot.

Most PCs are designed for some ESD protection as long as their cases are intact and closed properly. Cases are chemically treated or have copper fittings designed to channel electrostatic discharge away from the sensitive components inside.

The danger from ESD damage begins when the case is opened and the fragile components on the motherboard are exposed. When a human with a static electrical charge touches anything inside the case, the charge can travel along the wires interconnecting the various electronic components. One of the wires may lead inside a component, and when the charge gets close enough to a metal part with an opposing charge, the internal wires and elements of components can explode or weld together. CPU chips and memory chips are particularly sensitive to ESD. Be extremely cautious when handling these chips.

Take a look at some ESD facts:

▲ Most of the computer's electronic components use three to five volts of electricity.
▲ An ESD shock of 30 volts can destroy a computer circuit.
▲ An ESD shock you can *feel,* such as on a doorknob, has around 3,000 volts.
▲ An ESD shock you can *see* carries about 20,000 volts.

The real problem with ESD damage is that not all of it is obvious. If an entire component is destroyed, you know it and you replace the piece. When a component has been damaged but continues to work, days, weeks, or even months may pass before the component fails completely. More frustrating is intermittent partial failures that can't be isolated.

There are several tools and precautions you can use to eliminate static electricity

▲ **Antistatic wrist strap:** The first and easiest method to use is the antistatic wrist strap, also referred to as an **ESD** strap. To use an antistatic wrist strap, attach one end to an earth ground (the positive, or ground, pin on an extension cord, an antistatic mat, or the chassis of the PC) and wrap the other end around your wrist (Figure 2-6). (The ground pin is usually indicated by a round hole below the long and short slots in an outlet.) The antistatic strap grounds your body and keeps it at a zero charge and offers more ESD protection than other solutions. Note

Figure 2-6

Pin connects to ground pin
(small round hole) or
earth ground

ESD strap

Outlet

Connecting an antistatic wrist strap.

that an antistatic wrist strap is a specially designed device to bleed electrical charges away *safely*. It uses a 1-megaohm resistor to bleed the charge away slowly. A simple wire wrapped around your wrist will not work correctly and could electrocute you. **Warning:** When working on the monitor, *never* wear an antistatic wrist strap. The monitor has a very large capacitor in it and a grounding strap invites all of its stored charge to run through your body—not a pleasant experience.

▲ **ESD mats:** It is possible to damage a device by simply laying it on a bench top. For this reason, you should have an **ESD mat**, also called an **antistatic mat**, in addition to an antistatic wrist strap. This mat drains excess charge away from any item coming in contact with it (Figure 2-7). ESD mats are also sold as mouse/keyboard pads to prevent ESD charges from interfering with the operation of the computer. Many wrist straps can be connected to the mat, thus causing the technician and any equipment in contact with the mat to be at the same electrical potential and eliminating ESD. There are even ESD bootstraps and ESD floor mats, which are used to keep the technician's entire body at the same potential.

▲ **Antistatic bags for parts: Antistatic bags** are important tools to have at your disposal when servicing electronic components because they protect the sensitive electronic devices from stray static charges. These silver or pink bags are designed so that the static charges collect on the outside of the bags rather than on the electronic components. However, keep in mind that unlike antistatic mats, antistatic bags do not "drain" the charges away, and they should never be used in place of an antistatic mat. Store all electrical components in antistatic bags when not in use.

▲ **Humidity control:** Dry air can cause static electricity, so another preventive measure you can take is to maintain the relative humidity at around 50 percent. Be careful not to increase the humidity too far—to the point where moisture begins to condense on the equipment.

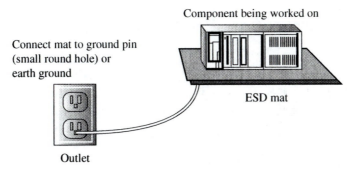

Using an ESD mat.

▲ **Antistatic spray:** You can use antistatic spray, which is available commercially, to reduce static buildup on clothing and carpets. In a pinch, a solution of dilute fabric softener sprayed on these items will have the same effect.

If an antistatic wrist strap or mat is not available, you can discharge excess static voltage by touching the metal case of the power supply. However, the power supply *must be plugged into a properly grounded outlet* for this technique to work as intended. Because the power supply is plugged in, you should be extra cautious so you don't get electrocuted. Also, maintain continuous contact to continuously drain excess charge away. As you can see, it is much easier and safer to have an antistatic wrist strap.

2.1.4 Power Problems

Unfortunately, it's rare for the power that comes out of the wall (what we normally call **line power**) to be consistently 110V, 60Hz. It may be of a slightly higher or lower voltage, it may cycle faster or slower, there may occasionally be no power, or (the worst) a 5000V spike may come down the power line from a lightning strike and destroy the expensive electronic components of your computer and its peripherals.

Most power problems go unnoticed because they are usually small enough that the computer's power supply can deal with them (all except a blackout, of course). But these power problems can lead to reliability problems in your computer.

Two types of damage can be done to the PC by electrical forces:

▲ **Catastrophic damage:** The device is destroyed in a single event.
▲ **Degradation:** The device is damaged over repeated instances and begins to fail or has intermittent problems.

There are three main classes of power problems:

▲ **Power quality problems:** Power quality problems occur when the power coming out of the wall has a different frequency than it normally does (60 Hz is standard in the United States). This type of problem manifests itself when stray electromagnetic signals are introduced into the line. This **electromagnetic interference (EMI)** is usually caused by the electromagnetic waves emitted by the electric motors in appliances. Additionally, televisions and other electronic devices (including computers) can produce a different type of interference, called **radio frequency interference (RFI)**, which is really just a higher-frequency version of EMI. If your power lines run near a powerful radio broadcast antenna or factory, it can also introduce noise into your power. Line noise can eventually burn out the power-regulating circuits in a PC's power supply. After this happens, any line noise on the power line could pass through the power supply to the motherboard, disk drives, and other internal PC components.

▲ **Power overage problems:** Power overage problems, which occur when too much power is coming out of the wall, are the most common type of power problem that causes computer damage. There are two main types of overage problems:

• **Spikes:** A **spike** is a power overage condition that exists for an extremely short period of time (a few milliseconds at most). High voltage spikes can degrade a PC's power supply.

• **Surges:** A surge lasts much longer than spikes (up to several seconds). Spikes are usually the result of faulty power transformer equipment at power substations. Surges can come from both power equipment and lightning strikes. Multiple surges over time can destroy equipment, and a lightning strike can send a powerful surge that damages any electrical equipment plugged in to the power lines.

▲ **Undervoltage power problems:** Undervoltage problems usually don't damage hardware. More often, they cause the computer to shut down completely (or at the very least, to reboot), thus losing any unsaved data in memory. There are three major types of undervoltage problems:

• **Sags:** A **sag** is a momentary drop in voltage, lasting only a few milliseconds. Usually, you can't even tell one has occurred. Your house lights won't dim or flicker (actually, they will, but it's too fast for you to notice), but your computer will react strangely to this sudden drop in power. A computer's normal response to this kind of disorientation is to reboot itself.

- **Brownouts:** A **brownout** occurs when voltage drops below 110V for a second or more. Brownouts are typically caused by an immediate increase in power consumption in your area and the lag time it takes for your power provider to respond by increasing production. You might notice when brownouts occur because the lights in your home will dim, but not go out, and then go back to full brightness a second or two later. You might also notice because your computer will reboot or the screen will flicker.

- **Blackouts:** A **blackout** occurs when the power fails completely and is typically caused by a power failure somewhere in your area. The problems caused by a blackout are usually more frustrating than damaging, but the fluctuation of power surrounding a blackout can harm your system. If you're in the middle of a long document (that you have not yet saved), or are defragmenting or fixing other hard disk problems (and the allocation tables aren't completely rebuilt) when the power goes out, you probably will have problems. More often, the damage occurs when the power returns suddenly (usually as a huge spike).

2.1.5 Solutions for Power Problems

There are a variety of devices sold to combat power problems (Table 2-2):

▲ **Line conditioners:** These devices are used to eliminate noise and produce "perfect" power of 110V/60Hz. Line conditioners remove most of the stray EMI and RFI signals from the incoming power. They also reduce any power overages to 110V.

▲ **Surge protectors:** The primary component of a surge protector, or suppressor, is a Metal Oxide Varistor (MOV). The MOV protects the computer by taking the hit from voltage spikes. One problem with the MOV is that one big spike or an accumulation of small surges over time can knock it out. MOVs are rated in terms of clamping speed (how long it

Table 2-2: Power Problems and Solutions

Protection Method	Protects Against
Line conditioner	Surges, low voltages
Surge suppressor	Some protection for surges and low voltages
SPS	Outage
UPS	Surges, low voltages, and outage

takes to go from the overvoltage to zero volts) and clamping voltage (at what voltage the MOV shorts out). Surge suppressors have three levels of clamping voltage that indicate the maximum number of watts the suppressor allows to pass through to anything plugged into it. The standard ratings are 330 (best), 400 (better), and 500 (good). The problem is that by the time the clamping voltage is reached, some of the overvoltage has gotten through to the power supply and damaged it. After a time, the power supply will be damaged permanently. Realistically, having a surge protector is better than not having one, but not much. It's better to use a line conditioner that can absorb the overvoltage than to use a circuit breaker. A few other characteristics you should look for when comparing surge suppressors are:

- **Energy Absorption:** Surge suppressors are rated in Joules, which measures their capability to absorb energy. The higher the rating, the better the protection: 200 Joules is basic protection, 400 is good protection, and 600 is superior protection.

- **Line Conditioning:** The line conditioning capability of a surge suppressor is measured in decibels. The more decibels of noise reduction, the better the line conditioning.

- **Protection Indicators:** Some surge suppressors have LED indicators to show that you are protected. How reliable these indicators are depends on how much you paid. Less-expensive surge protectors will absorb enough power over time to degrade the indicators. This is certain—if the LED is out, get a new protector. You can't know whether you're protected if a suppressor has no indicator.

A common misconception is that a power strip can protect your computer from power overage problems. Most power strips (the ones that cost less than $15) are nothing more than multiple outlets with a circuit breaker.

▲ **Backup Power Supplies:** There are two different battery-based power solutions to undervoltage conditions: the SPS and the UPS. Each takes a different approach to keeping the power at 110V. In both cases, you plug the units into the wall and then plug your computer equipment into the SPS or UPS.

- **Standby Power Supplies (SPS):** In an SPS, a battery is waiting to take over power production in case of a loss of line voltage. An SPS contains sensors that constantly monitor the line voltage and a battery. While conditions are normal, the line voltage charges the internal battery. When the line voltage drops below a preset threshold (also called the **cutover threshold**—for example, 105V), the sensors detect it and switch the power from the wall to the internal battery. When the power comes back above the threshold, the sensors detect the restoration of power and switch the power source back to the line voltage. The main problem with SPSs is that they take a few milliseconds (called switching time) to switch to the battery. During those few milliseconds, there is no voltage to the computer. This lack of voltage can cause reboots or crashes (rather like a brownout). An SPS is effective for preventing blackouts, but it does little for brownouts and sags.

- **Uninterruptible Power Supply (UPS):** The better choice for undervoltage problems is a UPS (Figure 2-8). A UPS works similarly to an SPS, but with one important difference: Power runs constantly runs from the line current to the internal battery and then from the battery to the PC. This means that there is no switching time during a power

Figure 2-8

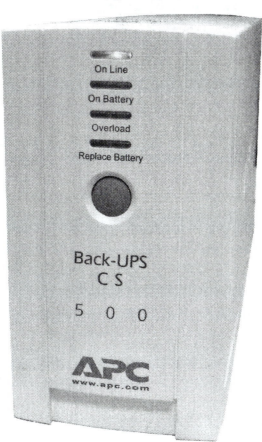

An uninterruptible power supply (UPS).

loss. Because the equipment is constantly operating off the battery, the UPS also acts as a kind of surge suppressor. **Warning:** Never plug a laser printer or copier into a UPS! The large surge of power they draw when they are first turned on (close to 15 amps) can burn out the inverter and battery.

Table 2-2 summarizes the various protection methods and the problems they address.

SELF-CHECK

1. Define current, power, and resistance.
2. What do amps, ohms, volts, and watts measure?
3. What are the three main classes of power problems?
4. What is ESD?
5. Describe the types of devices you can use to combat power problems.

2.2 Examining Power Supplies

The power supply is a black or silver box with a fan inside and cables coming out of it (Figure 2-9). It's located either at the back of the desktop case or at the top of the tower or mini-tower case. The power supply is distinctive because of its big yellow warning label. Power supplies contain transformers and capacitors that carry *lethal* amounts of current. They are not meant to be serviced. *Do not* attempt to open them or do any work on them.

2.2.1 Power Supplies and Their Components

The computer power supply is a type of switching power supply. It reduces the 110V incoming voltage to the various charges used by PC components and circuits by switching the power charge off and on. The power supply provides the following standard voltages to the motherboard and drives:

▲ **+5V:** The standard voltage of motherboards with all processors below 100 MHz (such as early Pentium, 486, and 386) and many peripheral boards.

▲ **+12V:** Used primarily for disk drive motors and similar devices. Modern motherboards also pass this voltage to ISA bus expansion slots.

Figure 2-9

A power supply.

▲ **−5V and −12V:** Included in most power supplies for compatibility with older systems. Most modern motherboards don't use either of these voltages. Power supplies that produce these values do so at very low (less than 1 amp) amperage. Check the label on your power supply.

▲ **+3.3V:** This is the standard voltage level for motherboards compatible with 100 MHz processors and faster. Upgraded motherboards must convert the 5V signal from the power supply into 3.3V for the processor, requiring a voltage regulator on the motherboard. Newer power supplies provide the 3.3V power for the CPU directly.

The PC power supply functions only when it has demand. A power supply without some demand will not function properly and may even damage itself. Never "test" a power supply without connecting it to at least one 12V line—for example, a disk drive.

Inside the power supply is a 1000-microfarad capacitor. Capacitors store electricity, even when the power is off. This capacitor performs line conditioning by absorbing any power coming in above the normal level and using it to replace

---

FOR EXAMPLE

Fan Speed Monitor Connectors

Some power supplies have a fan monitoring feature that allows your PC or monitoring software to regulate the speed of the PSU fan depending on the internal temperature of the PC. On these power supplies, you will find an additional 3-pin connector that attaches to a motherboard connector that is typically labeled "FAN." If you don't attach this connector, however, the fan will still work; its speed will just not be monitored.

---

power below normal levels. If you were to touch the capacitor, it would shock you—potentially with bodily harm or worse.

The primary power supply components (Figure 2-10) are:

▲ **Power cord:** Connects the power supply to the AC wall outlet.

▲ **Pass-through connectors:** Located on the back of the power supply. In the past, these connectors were used primarily to plug a monitor into the power supply, which enables you to turn the monitor on and off with

Figure 2-10

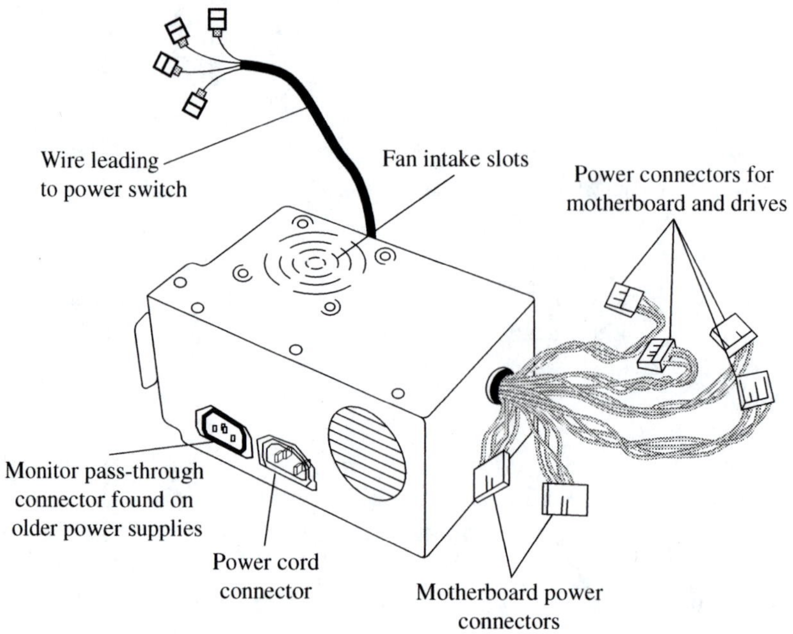

Power supply components.

the computer's power switch. This feature has all but disappeared from PCs because it's no longer necessary to plug the monitor into the power supply. When a monitor is plugged into the power supply's pass-through connector, the monitor is not being powered by the PC's internal power supply. It's called a pass-through plug because it passes the AC power through. You have only gained the convenience of turning the monitor on and off with the PC.

▲ **Power switch:** Where the main power switch is located on a PC depends on its form factor and its age:

• On older PCs, this switch extended through the case wall from the power supply on a back corner of the PC.

• In the newer ATX power supply, the switch is electronic, not physical. You don't so much turn the computer on or off as you request the motherboard to do it.

▲ **110V/220V selector switch:** Allows you to select between the two voltages. If a power supply has one, be sure it's set correctly (refer to Figure 2-9).

▲ **Power supply fan:** The power supply also contains the main cooling fan that controls airflow through the PC case. The power supply fan is the most important part of a PC's cooling system. Air is forced to flow through the computer case and over the motherboard and electronic components, which generate heat as they work. Any interruption to the airflow can cause sensitive components to degrade or fail. The power supply fan should be kept clean and clear. Only with the case closed and intact does the PC cooling system function at its optimum level. If a power supply's wattage rating is sufficient to supply the computer's electrical requirements, the fan should be adequate to handle the computer's cooling needs, although Pentium-class processors require additional cooling or heatsinks of their own.

2.2.2 Power Supply Form Factors

Power supplies are available in different **form factors.** The form factor of a power supply defines its size and the types of motherboard connectors it has. The power supply must match both the form factor of the case and the motherboard's power requirements. The form factor of a power supply is seldom an issue (except for upgrades and build-your-owns) because the power supply is usually purchased already installed in the case. In general, the form factors of the motherboard are the same for the case and the power supply. Power supply form factors (Figure 2-11) include:

▲ **AT:** This obsolete, older power supply has two connectors, the P8 and P9 connectors, which plug in side by side on the motherboard. You can identify this PSU by a cut-out corner that allows it to overhang part of

Figure 2-11

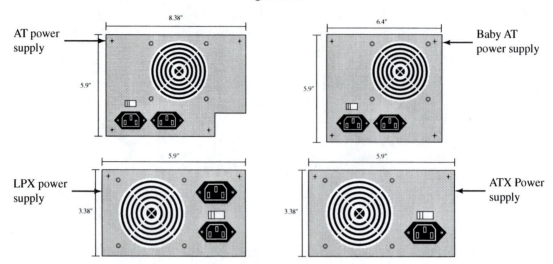

Power supply form factors.

the motherboard. There are desktop and tower versions of the AT PSU; the tower version has a power switch for the front of the PC case.

▲ **Baby AT/LPX:** The Baby AT power supply is about 2 inches narrower than the AT. It does use the same P8/P9 motherboard connectors but does not have the corner cutout. There are several versions of the Baby AT power supply for tower and desktop PCs. One version for low-profile desktops, the LPX, is much shorter than other Baby ATs and has a monitor pass-through and power cord outlet located at the side of the fan vent. The Baby AT and LPX form factors have been superseded by newer PSUs.

▲ **ATX/NLX:** The ATX power supply is virtually identical to the LPX but has a different internal construction and has no monitor pass-through power connector. It uses a single, 20-pin P1 motherboard connector. A major difference between ATX power supplies and earlier PSUs is in the ATX's "soft-power" feature. The ATX power supply turns on and off with electronic signaling and not a physical power switch. Additionally, some power is constantly supplied to the motherboard, even when the power is turned off. This allows the PC to be switched off by software, such as a Windows shutdown or to be booted automatically. NLX form factor motherboards use ATX PSUs, and for this reason you may see an ATX power supply referred to as an NLX power supply.

▲ **SFX form factor:** The SFX power supply (also called the Mini ATX or Micro ATX) is a smaller form factor designed for smaller Intel motherboards. It uses a P1 connector but doesn't include the −5-volt signal used by some older expansion bus cards.

▲ **ATX12V form factor:** The ATX12V is an update version of the ATX form factor. It adds an extra 4-pin +12V power connector, called the P4 connector, that enables the delivery of more current needed by the higher-end processors. Early ATX12V form factors also used a six-pin AUX (auxiliary) connector to provide additional power. Newer ATX12V PSUs use a 24-pin connector that combines the old standard 20-pin ATX connector and the auxiliary connector. ATX12V power supplies are backwardly compatible, and their 24-pin connectors can be fitted with adapters to connect to 20-pin motherboard connections. ATX12V power supplies are also used with a new motherboard form factor, the BTX (Balanced Technology Extended), which is designed for improved cooling.

The two main form factors today, Baby AT and ATX have different types of cooling fans:

▲ Baby AT cools the system by using the fan to blow air out of the case. However, this means that room air, including smoke and dust, is pulled in through the rest of the case to accumulate on internal components such as grills, wires, circuit boards, memory modules, and so on. This buildup can affect the cooling system's capability of cooling the motherboard and drives by restricting the airflow. Buildup also can possibly short out the motherboard or other components.

▲ The ATX power supply fan sucks air into the case, rather than blowing it out. This method helps keep the case clean by pressurizing the inside of the case. The power supply is situated on the board so that air blows straight over the processor and RAM. This design was originally intended to eliminate the need for a CPU fan, but as mentioned earlier, nearly all Pentium-class processors include their own fans and heatsinks.

2.2.3 Power Supply Connectors

Power supplies use different types of connectors to power the various devices within the computer. Each has a different appearance and way of connecting to the device:

▲ **Floppy drive power connectors:** Floppy drive power connectors (Figure 2-12), also called **Berg connectors**, are most commonly used to power floppy disk drives and other small form factor devices. This type of connector is smaller and flatter than any of the other types of power connectors. Notice that there are four wires going to this connector. These wires carry the two voltages used by the motors and logic circuits: 5VDC (carried on the red wire) and 12VDC (carried on the yellow wire) plus two

Figure 2-12

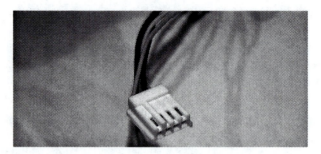

Floppy drive connector.

black ground wires. These connectors are keyed so they can't be installed backwards. (A keyed connector has a prong, lip, or other structural element to guide its placement.)

▲ **Standard peripheral power connector:** The standard peripheral power connector (Figure 2-13), also called a **Molex connector**, is generally used to power different types of internal disk drives such as hard drives and CD-ROM and DVD drives. This power connector, though larger than the floppy drive power connector, uses the same wiring color code scheme as the floppy drive or Berg connector, and you can use adapters to convert between the two.

▲ **Motherboard connectors:** In building a PC, its case, motherboard, and power supply must all work together and use the same or compatible

Figure 2-13

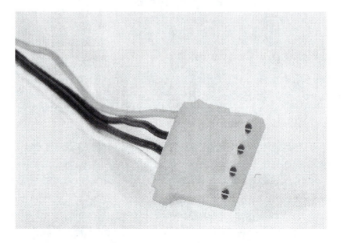

Standard peripheral power connector.

Figure 2-14

P8 and P9 connectors.

form factors. In using the proper form factor for a PSU, you can ensure that the motherboard receives the correct supply of voltages and that the power supply has the proper connectors for the motherboards sockets.

- **AT system connectors:** The AT system connectors are two 6-wire connectors, labeled P8 and P9 (Figure 2-14). They connect to an AT-only motherboard and deliver the power that feeds the electronic components on it. These connectors have small tabs on them that interlock with tabs on the power connector on the motherboard. If there are two connectors, you must install them in the correct fashion. To do this (on most systems), place the connectors side by side with their black wires together and then push the connectors onto the socket on the motherboard.

- **ATX system connectors:** The ATX system connector, also called a P1 connector (Figure 2-15), provides the six voltages required through one connector: a single, keyed, 20-pin connector (or 24 pin for newer ATX12V form factors). In addition to the main ATX 20- or 24-pin power connector, some ATX power supplies may have one or two additional power connectors, such as an **auxiliary power connector** (a 6-pin Molex connector) or a P4 connector/**ATX12V connector** (a 4-pin connector that delivers the extra power to the CPU). Newer power supplies may also have a **PCI express connector**, a 6-pin connector used to power newer PCI express graphics cards.

- **SATA drive connectors:** Newer power supplies may feature 15-pin connectors for powering newer SATA drives (Figure 2-16).

Figure 2-15

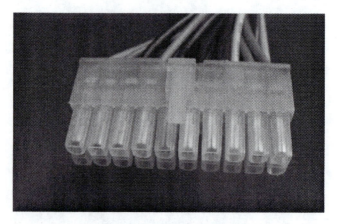

ATX 20-pin P1 connector.

▲ **Fan connectors:** Some power supplies include a 3-pin fan connector that attaches to the motherboard and is used to monitor and control the power supply fan.

Table 2-3 summarizes the different form factors and their associated connectors.

Figure 2-16

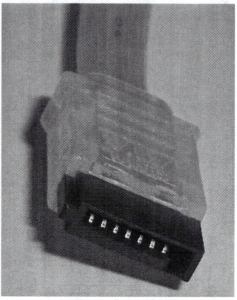

SATA drive connector.

Table 2-3: Form Factors and Connectors

Form Factor	Motherboard Connector
PC/XT/AT	AT
Baby AT/LPX	AT
ATX/NLX	ATX 20-pin
SFX	ATX
ATX12V	ATX 20-pin + Auxiliary or ATX 24-pin

SELF-CHECK

1. What type of current does the power supply provide?
2. What are the five voltages provided by the power supply?
3. What are the principle differences between a Baby AT and an ATX power supply?
4. What types of connectors would you expect to find on an ATX12V power supply?

2.3 Working with Power Supplies

Do not take the issue of safety and electricity lightly. Removing the power supply from its case presents a great risk. The current flowing through the power supply normally follows a complete circuit; when your body breaks that circuit, your body becomes part of the circuit.

The two biggest dangers with power supplies are burns and electrocution. These risks usually go hand in hand. If you touch a bare wire that is carrying current, you may get electrocuted. A large enough current passing through the wire (and you) can cause severe burns. (It can also cause your heart to stop, your muscles to seize, and your brain to stop functioning. In short, it can kill you.) Electricity always finds the best path to ground, and it will use you as a conductor if you are grounded.

Although it is possible to work on a power supply, doing so is *not* recommended. Power supplies contain several capacitors that can hold *lethal* charges *long after they have been unplugged!* It is extremely dangerous to open the case of a power supply. Besides, power supplies are inexpensive, so it will cost less to replace one than to try to fix it, and this approach is much safer.

2.3.1 Installing and Replacing Power Supplies

Remember that an ATX power supply is always on. Power is supplied to the motherboard even when the system power is off. Always disconnect the power cord from the back of the case before working on one.

To replace a power supply:

1. Turn off the computer and unplug the power cord from the wall outlet. Always be sure that the power supply is unplugged by removing its power cord from its back before you attach its connectors inside the PC.
2. Open the case and then disconnect all power supply connectors from the motherboard and any peripheral devices.
3. Remove the four screws that secure the power supply to the case, and lift or slide the power supply out. (You may need to remove expansion cards or drives to remove the power supply.)
4. If the new power supply has an input voltage selector switch, make sure the power supply is set to the correct input voltage (110V in the United States).
5. Insert the new power supply into the case and attach it to the case with its mounting screws (Figure 2-17).
6. Connect the power supply to the motherboard; either with P8/P9 connectors for an AT system, or a P1 (20- or 24-pin) ATX connector (Figure 2-18).

Figure 2-17

Installing a power supply.

Figure 2-18

Installing the ATX system connector.

7. Plug in any other motherboard connectors, such as P4, ATX auxiliary connector, PCI express connector, or fan connector.

8. Attach any Molex, Berg, or SATA connectors to the PC's hard drives, optical drives, floppy drives, and so on, and replace any expansion drives you may have removed.

9. Replace the PC case and plug the power cord back into the power supply. If the power supply has its own power switch, make sure it is in the On position.

10. Plug the computer back in and power it up. Verify that you hear the fan spinning and the computer and hard drives are working properly.

Be aware that different cases have different types of on/off switches. The process of replacing a power supply is a lot easier if you purchase a replacement with the same mechanism. Even so, remember to document exactly how the power supply was connected to the on/off switch. In addition, newer ATX power supplies have two switches: a main power switch on the back of the computer, and

---

FOR EXAMPLE

Installing Motherboard Connectors

P8/P9 connectors plug into the motherboard with the black wires adjacent in the center. Although it's easy to remove the P8/P9 AT system connector from the motherboard, the tabs on the connector can make it difficult to reinstall them. Here's a tip: Place the connector at a right angle to the motherboard's connector, interlocking the tabs in their correct positions, and then tilt the connector to the vertical position. The connector will slide into place easily. The single ATX system connector fits in only one direction. To install it, push the power connector onto the connector on the mother-board until it latches. This power connector cannot be installed the wrong way. If the connectors aren't mating properly, turn the connector around and try again.

---

the internal on/off switch activated by the motherboard. The switch at the back of the power supply must be turned on and the front case power switch properly connected to the motherboard. If neither is done, the computer won't turn on no matter how many times you hit the power switch.

2.3.2 Maintaining and Upgrading Power Supplies

The only moving parts on a power supply are the switch and the fan, so other than protecting against power quality issues, you will not need to perform regular maintenance on a power supply. However, because of the heat that a power supply generates that could damage internal electrical components, you should be alert to any signs that this heat is not being properly dissipated by the power supply fan or any case fans. If you notice that your PC is suddenly quiet, you may need to shut the PC down immediately. Some fans are controlled by PC software, and may power up, higher, lower, or off depending on the PC's internal temperature, so be sure to understand how any case fans and power supply fans operate by reading the documentation on your PSU, motherboard, and case.

Form factors of PCs are specifically designed to maximize air flow and cooling; using vents and fans coordinated around the placement of the PSU, motherboard, and CPU. For this reason, keep the case of your PC closed any time it is running and you are not working on it. Not doing this may result in unneeded heat stress on PC components. You can also make sure that case and PSU fans are clean (you can use cans of compressed air to blow dust off of them) and vents are not blocked.

If you are upgrading a computer with new components, you may also need to upgrade the PSU. Devices that may require more power (and special connectors) than your current PSU provides include PCI Express expansion cards, Serial ATA (SATA) drives, and powerful new CPUs.

In general, whenever you add a newer device to an older system, remember the power requirements of the newer device and the output level of your power supply. Power supplies are rated in watts. The higher the wattage, the more power the power supply (and thus your computer) will use. Most computers use power supplies in the 250- to 400-watt range.

If your current system is already drawing the maximum power output from the power supply and you try to add a component that draws more power than the component it replaces, you could have major problems. At the very least, the new component won't function. But, more possibly, you could blow a fuse on the power supply or cause damage to the other components in the computer.

Always calculate the power requirements of your system before you add a new component (especially components that draw more power, such as video cards and disk drives). You can do this by adding the power requirements (in watts) of each component (they either are printed on the devices or can be obtained from the manufacturer). Make sure the power supply is able to put out at least 10 percent more than your existing system requires. Typically, power supplies greater than 300 watts are sufficient for most home PCs.

To reduce the amount of electricity consumed by computers, the U.S. Environmental Protection Agency (EPA) established guidelines for energy efficiency under a program called *U.S. Green Star,* also known as *Energy Star.* On Green Star systems, the power supply works with the computer's components and some peripherals to reduce the power they use when idle. Green Star devices have a standby program that puts them into sleep mode after the device has been idle for a certain period. In sleep mode, the device reduces 99 percent of its power consumption and uses no more than 30 watts of power. In Windows XP, you configure the options for power saving through the Control Panel's Power Options dialog box.

2.3.3 Troubleshooting Power Supplies

Most power supply problems are usually easy to troubleshoot—nothing happens when you flip the switch. When that happens, first try disconnecting the power plug from the wall for a few minutes. Doing so will cause the power supply's internal relay to reset.

Common power problems include:

▲ **No power when you push the power button:** Often the power cord isn't pushed in all the way, you forgot to connect the front panel power switch connector to the motherboard (or it fell off), or the power supply has its own power switch that might be turned off.

▲ **Computer powers up for a moment, and then powers down and won't turn back on until you unplug it:** This is usually caused by a

CPU fan that won't turn on, isn't turning at the right speed, or is the kind that can't send speed information to the motherboard (that is, it isn't a three-wire fan).

▲ **A loud bang, smoke, or both at the back of the case:** More than likely, the power supply was set to the wrong input voltage. If you have this problem, you may have to replace the power supply.

If you're not getting any power to the PC, do the following:

▲ Check that power is getting to the power supply. If the fan isn't turning on, power is not reaching the power supply.

▲ Make sure that the power cord is firmly connected to the power supply.

▲ Make sure that any power strips are powered on and that the wall outlet is providing electricity.

▲ If the power supply has a 110/220 voltage switch, make sure that it's set correctly (110 is standard in the U.S.). Additionally, an ATX power supply's power switch should be turned on before the PC's power button is switched on.

▲ Check the power supply's connections to the motherboard.

If these steps don't work, open the case, remove the power supply, and replace it with a new one.

Although power line and wiring problem are not frequent, keep in mind that if you experience random symptoms, such as mysterious crashes, memory errors, lost data, or damaged chips, you may have a problem with your household electricity. Things that you can do to troubleshoot household line problems include making sure that your outlets are wired properly. To guard against these problems, you can make sure that no high-wattage devices are using the same outlet and use power protection such as surge suppressors, line conditioners, and UPSs.

SELF-CHECK

1. Under what circumstances would you upgrade a power supply?

2. What is the main reason you should replace a faulty power supply rather than fix it?

3. Describe how the P8 and P9 connectors are attached to the motherboard.

4. What are the troubleshooting steps you would take if the power supply is not switching on?

SUMMARY

The power supply converts alternating current provided through wall outlets to direct current that the PC requires. We measure electricity in terms of the rate of current (amps), the pressure in a circuit (volts), the resistance in a circuit (ohms), and its power or capability to do work (watts). You use a multimeter to measure the properties of electrical circuits. Multimeters consist of an analog or digital display, two probes, and a function selector switch. Auto-ranging multimeters automatically set the range.

The circuits in a PC are very vulnerable to shocks from electrostatic discharge. Technicians use antistatic wrist straps and ESD mats to protect the computer, and themselves, when working on a PC. Other tools and techniques for preventing ESD include antistatic bags, humidity control, and antistatic spray.

There are three main types of power problems: power quality problems, such as EMI and RFI; power overage problems (spikes and surges); and power under-voltage problems (sags, brownouts, and blackouts). Line conditioners are used to prevent power quality problems. Surge protectors provide some safety against surges and low voltages. They are rated in terms of clamping speed and clamping voltage. There are two types of backup power supplies, standby power supplies (SPSs) and uninterruptible power supplies (UPSs). An SPS provides backup power from its batteries only when line voltage drops. A UPS provides power continuously from its batteries.

Power supplies are rated in watts and provide the standard voltages of 3.3V, +5V, −5V, +12V, and −12V to the motherboard and drives. They contain transformers and capacitors with lethal amounts of current and are considered disposable and replaceable PC components. There are several power supply form factors. In use today are the older Baby AT, and several variations of the ATX form factor. All power supplies have a variety of connectors for providing power to the motherboard and devices such as floppy and disk drives. Common connectors are the floppy drive (Berg) connector, the standard peripheral (Molex) connector, and the motherboard connectors. Older Baby AT power supplies use a P8 and P9 connector. ATX power supplies may have a 20- or 24-pin motherboard connector. ATX12V form factors include a 4-pin P4 connector for supplying power needed by Pentium 4 and higher processors. Newer power supply units have connectors for PCI express buses and SATA drives. A power supply unit works in conjunction with the motherboard, and should be selected to match the motherboard and provide the correct power. When choosing a power supply, you should make sure that the power supply provides at least 10 percent more power than the combined power needs of all system components.

When installing a power supply unit, it is important to make sure it is set to use the correct input voltage (110V in the United States). You can tell that the installed power supply is working because you will hear the fan spin up. If

a power supply is not providing power to the PC, you can check the wall outlet, power cord, power switch, any power strips in use, the voltage switch, and
the motherboard connections.

KEY TERMS

Alternating current (AC)	Insulator
Amps	Line conditioner
Antistatic bag	Line power
Antistatic wrist strap	Molex connector
Auto-ranging multimeter	Multimeter
Berg connector	Ohms
Blackout	Power
Brownout	Radio frequency interference (RFI)
Capacitor	Resistance
Circuit	Resistor
Conductor	Sag
Continuity	Spike
Current	Standard peripheral power connector
Cutover threshold	Standby power supply (SPS)
Direct current (DC)	Surge
Electromagnetic interference (EMI)	Surge protector
Electrostatic discharge (ESD)	Uninterruptible power supply (UPS)
ESD mat	Voltage
ESD strap	Volts
Floppy drive power connector (Berg connector)	Watts

ASSESS YOUR UNDERSTANDING

Go to www.wiley.com/college/groth to evaluate your knowledge of electricity and power.

Measure your learning by comparing pre-test and post-test results.

Summary Questions

1. Electrical current is measured in _Amps____.
   (a) amps
   (b) ohms
   (c) volts
   (d) watts
2. Electrical resistance is measured in ohms. True or false?
3. What types of electrical measurements do multimeters make?
   (a) amps and ohms
   (b) amps and volts
   (c) amps, ohms, and volts
   (d) amps, ohms, volts, and farads
4. When the electrical power system fails completely, it's called a(n) _____.
   (a) brownout
   (b) blackout
   (c) overvoltage
   (d) undervoltage
5. What is the voltage of line voltage?
   (a) 110V
   (b) 12V
   (c) 5V
   (d) 3.3V
6. The PC operates on what type of electricity?
   (a) alternating current
   (b) direct current
   (c) switching current
   (d) directional current
7. Power supplies require little maintenance. True or false?
8. A PC conforming to the Green Star standard reduces its power consumption in Sleep mode to 99 percent. True or false?

9. Computer components can be damaged by an ESD charge of as little as
_____ volts.
(a) 2000
(b) 30
(c) 30,000
(d) 3 to 5

10. When connecting an ESD strap to an extension cord, you must connect
it to the ground pin. True or false?

11. A device that can supply backup power to a PC when the electricity fails
and provides for line conditioning as well is called a(n) _____.
(a) SPS
(b) UPS
(c) surge suppressor
(d) line conditioner

12. While you repair a PC with an ATX motherboard, it should be powered
up. True or false?

13. An _____ provides for ESD protection while a component is in transit between producer and consumer.
(a) antistatic wrist strap
(b) antistatic spray
(c) antistatic mat
(d) antistatic bag

14. ESD is the most common threat to PC hardware when being serviced by
a technician. True or false?

15. Which power problem is an undervoltage condition that results in the
complete loss of power?
(a) spike
(b) surge
(c) sag
(d) blackout

16. What electronic component in the PC power supply absorbs most power
spikes?
(a) resistors
(b) varistors
(c) coils
(d) capacitors

17. The device used to protect a PC against overvoltage is called a surge protector. True or false?

18. Which PC component should you NOT work on with an antistatic wrist strap?

   (a) laser printer

   (b) monitor

   (c) power supply

   (d) motherboard

19. Which of the following formulas is called Ohm's law?

   (a) Current = Voltage * Resistance

   (b) Resistance = Voltage * Current

   (c) Voltage = Current * Resistance

   (d) Power = Voltage * Resistance

20. To calculate power, you use the formula:

   (a) Power = voltage × current

   (b) Power = voltage / current

   (c) Power = voltage × resistance

   (d) Power = voltage / resistance

Applying This Chapter

1. If a circuit produces 600 watts and produces a 5 amp current, what is its resistance?

2. A client complains that his hard disk is making a lot of noise. After examining the computer and hearing the high-pitched noise for yourself, you notice that the noise seems to be coming from the fan in the power supply. Which component(s) should be replaced?

3. A client wants to purchase a surge protector for her PC. What will you advise her?

4. You are on the phone with a client and you need to determine what type of power supply she has. What questions will you ask her to identify the power supply? How will you tell if the power supply is a Baby AT, an ATX, or an ATX12V?

5. List the main steps in replacing a power supply.

YOU TRY IT

Protecting a PC

A client lives in a remote location that often experiences blackouts. On top of that, the wiring in her house is old—light bulbs tend to flicker. Explain the type of protection she should have for her computer. What will you recommend?

Troubleshooting Power

When you try to turn on the computer, you notice that it will not activate. The monitor is blank, and the fan on the power supply is not active. Turning the switch off and then back on makes no difference. What is the most likely cause of this problem? What steps will you take to troubleshoot the problem?

Upgrading a Power Supply

You have been asked to upgrade a PC's power supply. What considerations will you take into account before making a selection?

Using a Multimeter

You suspect that the floppy drive connector on a power supply is not working and you are going to test its voltage with a multimeter. How will you connect the probes?

3
MOTHERBOARDS

Starting Point

Go to www.wiley.com/college/groth to assess your knowledge
of motherboards and the BIOS.
Determine where you need to concentrate your effort.

What You'll Learn in This Chapter

▲ Motherboard types and form factors
▲ Motherboard components and what they do
▲ The BIOS chip and its functions
▲ Motherboard installation

After Studying This Chapter, You'll Be Able To

▲ Choose an appropriate motherboard for an upgrade
▲ Identify, remove and install a motherboard for inspection and/or
   replacement for maximum computer performance
▲ Upgrade a PC's BIOS to support a new device
▲ Interpret BIOS error signals and messages

INTRODUCTION

Every essential component directly or indirectly involved with making the PC function is either connected to or embedded on the motherboard. For all intents and purposes, the motherboard is the computer. How well a PC performs (or if it doesn't perform at all) depends upon the components housed on the motherboard. Even the data stored on separate hard drives communicates with and through motherboard components, as do the PC's input and output devices, from keyboards to digital cameras. For these reasons, it is important to be able to identify the components on the motherboard and understand how they work together.

There are different types of motherboards designed for different form factors, and different motherboards support specific types of processors and memory modules. Some motherboard types and their components are easier to upgrade than others. When you are upgrading an existing system or building a new system, you need to be able to choose a motherboard that will support the type of hardware you want to include with the PC. Because the motherboard's circuits are sensitive to ESD, you need to understand the proper safety precautions and steps for installing a motherboard.

One important motherboard component is the BIOS (Basic Input/Output System). This is a tiny startup program hardwired to the motherboard that allows the PC to start up, check the attached hardware, and find the operating system. The BIOS provides some key hardware troubleshooting tools and also allows you to configure the system hardware, such as specifying which hard drive the operating system is located on. You need to know how to interpret error messages from the BIOS and use it to configure hardware.

3.1 Identifying Motherboards

The motherboard is sometimes referred to as a system board, planar board, or logic board. It is a large printed circuit board (Figure 3-1) that's home to many of the essential parts of the computer: The motherboard binds the PC's operational components together. Even devices (such as printers, hard drives, and CD-ROMs) are either connected to or controlled by the devices or controllers on the motherboard.

3.1.1 Motherboard Components

Some of the key components of a motherboard include:

▲ **CPU:** The Central Processing Unit (CPU), or microprocessor, is the "brain" of the computer. This component does all the calculations and performs a majority of the functions of a computer.

Figure 3-1

Typical motherboard.

▲ **Chipset:** A group of chips that together help the processor and other peripheral devices plugged into the motherboard communicate with each other.

▲ **Buses:** A network of fine wires that interconnect the CPU with all the other components on the motherboard.

▲ **Memory slots and chips:** Memory or random access memory (RAM) slots contain the memory chips. The CPU uses memory chips as temporary holding places for the large amounts of data that it processes. The number and type of memory slots varies from motherboard to motherboard, but the appearance of the different slots is similar. Metal pins in the bottom make contact with the soldered tabs on each memory module. Small metal or plastic tabs on each side of the slot keep the memory module securely in its slot.

▲ **Expansion slots and cards:** The most visible parts of any motherboard are the expansion slots. These look like small plastic slots, usually from 3 to 11 inches long and approximately one-half inch wide. These slots are used to install various devices in the computer to expand its capabilities. Some devices installed in these slots may include video, network, and sound cards.

▲ **Ports and connectors:** Motherboards include a variety of ports and other connectors used for attaching peripheral devices such as printers, hard drives, or input/output devices such as keyboards.

3.1.2 Types of Motherboards

There are two major types of motherboards: integrated and nonintegrated:

▲ **Nonintegrated:** In a nonintegrated—or standard—motherboard, major assemblies, such as disk controllers and video circuitry, are installed separately through expansion cards. You can identify nonintegrated boards because each expansion slot is usually occupied by one of these components.

▲ **Integrated:** In an integrated system board, components that would otherwise be installed as expansion cards, such as video and/or audio circuitry, are constructed as part of the motherboard circuitry. Integrated system boards were designed for simplicity. However, when one component breaks you must usually replace the whole motherboard. On some integrated system boards you may be able to disable the malfunctioning component (e.g., the sound circuitry) and add an expansion card to replace its functions.

The line between integrated and nonintegrated system boards can be blurry. Many "nonintegrated" system boards today incorporate some commonly used circuitry such as disk controllers and sound cards onto the motherboard itself.

Occasionally, to save space, components of the video circuitry (and possibly other circuits as well) are placed on a thin circuit board called a **daughterboard** that connects directly to the motherboard.

In some computers, mostly high-end servers, you will find a different approach to the system board: the backplane. In a **backplane** design, *all* of the circuitry components, even the CPU and memory, are installed as separate daughterboards onto a board called the backplane. A **passive backplane** helps coordinate the components, but is basically just a holder for the daughterboards. An **active backplane**, or intelligent backplane, has some circuitry built into it to help speed up the system.

3.1.3 Motherboard Form Factors

The shape, packaging, and to a certain extent, the function of a motherboard are defined by its form factor. In a single PC, the motherboard, power supply, and system case usually have the same form factor; although some power supplies and cases can handle several motherboard form factors. The most common motherboard form factors are:

▲ **AT: AT motherboards**, also called full AT motherboards, are patterned after the motherboards found in the original IBM AT (Advanced Technol-

> ## FOR EXAMPLE
>
> ### Deluxe Integrated Motherboards
>
> Today, most motherboards include some embedded components. Inexpensive motherboards usually integrate generic video and audio sound adapters that are less full-featured than what you would find on expansion card versions designed for slots; for example, a typical embedded video chip would have less video RAM for graphics rendering. However, vendors such as Abit, Asus, and, Intel also produce deluxe, high-end motherboards that integrate embed high quality video and sound adapters from popular manufacturers. If you visit these manufacturers' websites, you will see all three types of motherboards for sale: integrated, standard, and deluxe.

ogy) PC. They are nearly square at 12 inches by 11 to 13 inches. AT motherboards are rarely found for sale today.

▲ **Baby AT:** The **Baby AT motherboard** uses the same number of components as the full AT, compressed into a smaller area, 8.5 inches by 10 to 13 inches. The baby AT (Figure 3-2) can be distinguished by:

- P8/P9 power connector for connecting
- Ribbon cables to connect ports to the board
- Expansion slots oriented parallel to the wide edge of the board

The baby AT design has some fundamental problems:

- Because the processor and memory are in line with the expansion slots, only one or two full-length expansion cards can be used.
- The processor is far from the power supply's cooling fan and tends to overheat unless a heatsink or processor fan is directly attached to it.

▲ **ATX:** Although similar in size (12 inches by 9.6 inches) the **ATX motherboard** adds features and addresses the Baby AT's design flaws. In general, the ATX motherboard allows for easier installation of full-length expansion cards and cables and is easier to cool. The ATX (Figure 3-3) is the most common motherboard today. ATX features and characteristics include:

- Expansion slots oriented parallel to the narrow edge of the board
- One-piece power connector
- Built-in IO ports on one side
- CPU oriented so that the power supply fan helps cool it
- CPU and RAM placed at right angles to the expansion slots, which allows you to install full-length expansion cards
- Supports an additional case fan, recommended for PCs with 3-D video accelerators, multiple hard drives, and other high-heat producing adapter cards.

Figure 3-2

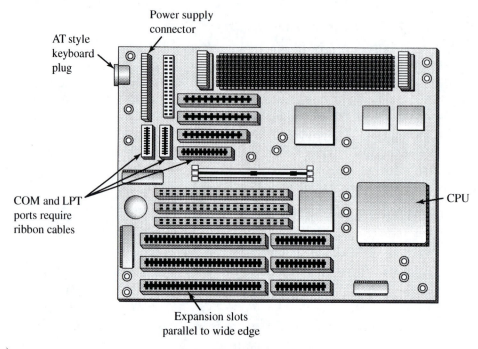

Baby AT motherboard.

Figure 3-3

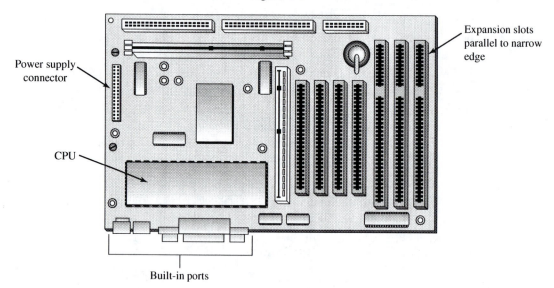

ATX motherboard.

- Soft power switching: The ATX motherboard can control the power on and off functions of the power supply.
- Provides split voltage (a range of voltages, usually 12v, 5v, and 3.3v) to the motherboard, eliminating the need for a voltage regulator included on earlier motherboards.

▲ **Micro ATX:** The Micro ATX is designed for smaller PC cases. It is a square 9.6 inches by 9.6 inches and has a reduced number of I/O ports and expansion slots (Figure 3-4).

Figure 3-4

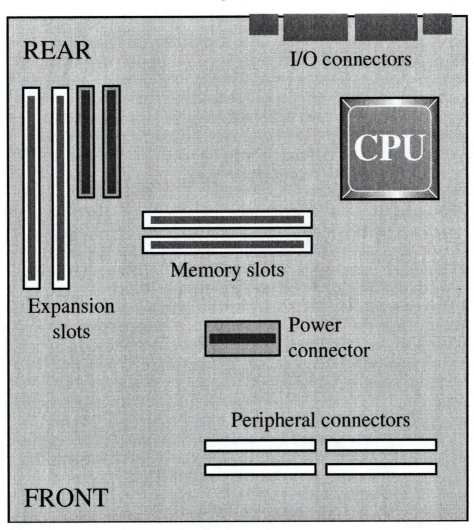

Micro ATX motherboard.

Figure 3-5

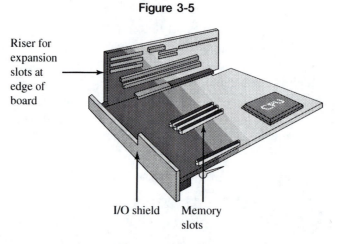

Riser for
expansion
slots at
edge of
board

I/O shield   Memory
slots

NLX motherboard.

▲ **NLX:** The NLX form factor is used in low-profile case types. **NLX motherboards** are unique because the expansion slots are placed sideways on a special riser card (Figure 3-5) to use the space optimally. These motherboard form factors are usually found in what are known as clone computers (those not manufactured by a Fortune 500 PC company).

▲ **BTX:** The newest **BTX motherboards** (Figure 3-6) are designed for better airflow in the PC case and are not backwardly compatible with the ATX form factor, except for the ATX power supply. Features include:

• Repositioning of the expansion slots, memory slots, CPU, and IO ports. The memory slots are parallel to and at opposite ends from the expansion cards, and at right angles to the I/O ports.

• Support for recent expansion bus technologies such as PCI and PCI express.

• Use of a thermal module (heat sink, fan, and duct) to vent out of the case.

• There are three BTX form factors sizes, the full size (326 × 266 mm) and two smaller sizes: microBTX (264 × 266 mm) and picoBTX (203 × 266 mm).

Some manufacturers (such as Compaq and IBM) design and manufacture their own motherboards, which don't conform to either the AT or ATX standard. This style of motherboard is known as a **proprietary design** motherboard.

Figure 3-6

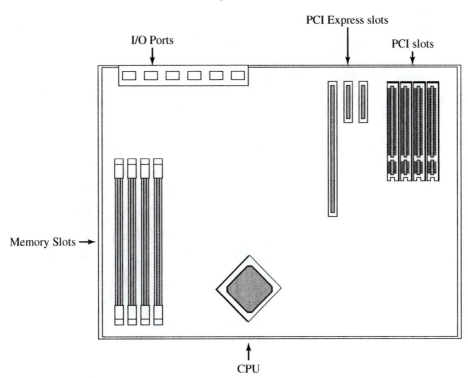

BTX motherboard.

SELF-CHECK

1. What is the main function of a motherboard?
2. What are the main differences between an ATX motherboard and a Baby AT motherboard?
3. What is a passive backplane?
4. What is the difference between an integrated and a non-integrated motherboard?

3.2 Examining Motherboard Components

The most important circuitry of the PC is located on the motherboard, and it is essential to understand what the main motherboard components are, and what their functions are (Figure 3-7). Some components are upgradeable or

Figure 3-7

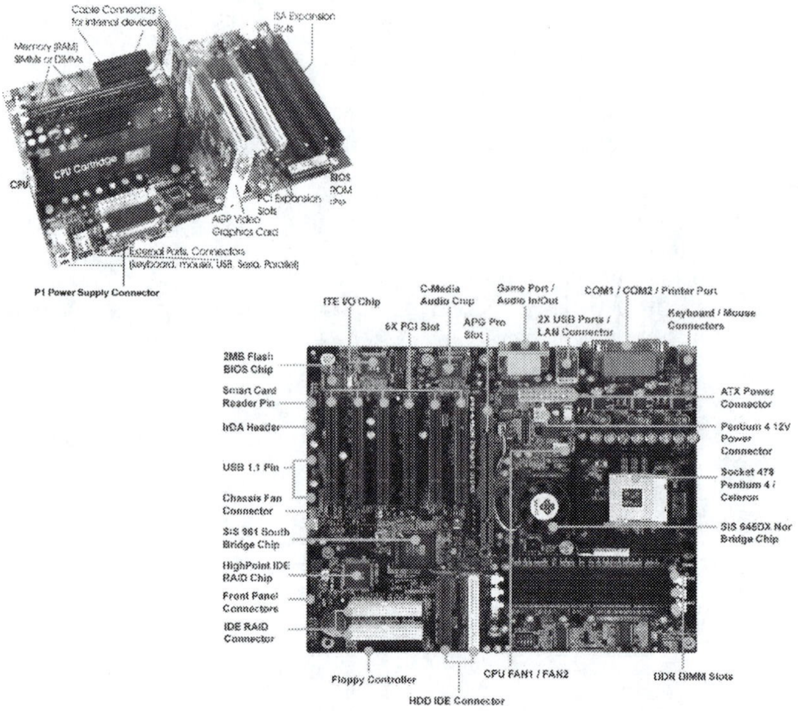

Motherboard components.

replaceable, such as the CPU and CMOS battery, while others are integral to the motherboard itself.

3.2.1 Central Processing Unit (CPU) and Processor Socket or Slot

The processor is usually the component that has either a fan or a heatsink (sometimes both) attached to it (Figure 3-8). These devices are used to draw away the heat a processor generates.

CPUs are attached to the motherboard via sockets or slots. Sockets are basically flat and have several rows of holes arranged in a square (Figure 3-9). Some processors are attached by special slots (Figure 3-10).

3.2.2 Motherboard buses

The CPU moves data values and signals around the computer on a network of fine wires that interconnect it to all the other components on the motherboard. This network is called the bus.

▲ The **internal bus** is comprised of the lines that move data within the motherboard.

Figure 3-8

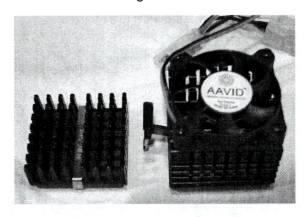

CPU with fan, and CPU with heatsink.

Figure 3-9

CPU socket.

Figure 3-10

CPU slot.

▲ The **external bus**, or **expansion bus**, is composed of the lines that communicate with peripherals and other devices attached to computer through the motherboard.

3.2.3 Chipsets

The chipset is a group of chips or circuits that together help the processor and other peripheral devices plugged into the motherboard communicate with each other.

The chipset controls the bits (data, instructions, and control signals) that flow between the CPU and system memory over the motherboard's buses. The chipset also manages data transfers between the CPU, memory, and peripheral devices. It supports the expansion bus and any power management features of the system. However, the chipset contains only enough instructions to issue control commands to device drivers, which are utility software programs that actually control the peripheral device.

Chipsets are matched to and integrated into the motherboard and usually cannot be upgraded without changing the entire motherboard. Usually, a particular chipset is matched to a single processor type; however, some chipsets support more than one processor.

The functions of chipsets can be divided into two major functional groups:

▲ **Northbridge:** The Northbridge subset of circuits provides support and control for:
- Communications between the CPU and memory
- High-speed peripheral communications using the PCI and AGP buses
- Communication between the Southbridge and the rest of the computer
- Any onboard video circuitry

Much of the true performance of a PC relies on the performance of the Northbridge chipset and its communication with the peripherals it controls.

▲ **Southbridge:** The Southbridge subset of circuits provides support for:
- Peripheral devices
- Controllers that are not essential to the PC's basic functions, such as the serial port controller
- Communications with the secondary expansion buses, such as USB, and legacy buses

The chipsets are not the only controller chipsets on the motherboard. The most prominent controller sets are the keyboard controller and a superset of input/output device controllers called the Super I/O controller. The Super I/O chip combines controllers that are common to all systems. Controller chips are also found on many high-end devices and adapter cards.

3.2.4 Expansion Slots

Expansion slots on the motherboard are used for adding additional circuitry on special cards called expansion cards. Expansion cards, which are also called adapter or sometimes controller cards, are designed to control specific hardware. Expansion cards exist for adding network interfaces, video and graphics capabilities, sound capabilities, and hard drive interfaces. If you look at the motherboard in your computer, you will more than likely find several types of expansion slots, such as:

▲ **ISA Expansion Slots:** An older type of expansion slot, Industry Standard Architecture (ISA) expansion slots are usually black and have two parts: one shorter and one longer. Some motherboards today, but not all, include an ISA slot for backward compatibility with old expansion cards.

▲ **PCI Expansion Slots:** Peripheral Component Interconnect (PCI) slots (Figure 3-11) are short (around 3 inches long) and usually white. The updated version of PCI, PCI-X, has longer white expansion slots (Figure 3-11).

Figure 3-11

PCI expansion slots.

▲ **PCI Express Expansion Slots:** PCI-Express slots come in a variety of lengths, and a motherboard may have several of different lengths (Figure 3-12).

▲ **AGP Expansion Slots:** Accelerated Graphics Port (AGP) slots were designed to be a direct connection between the video circuitry and the PC's memory. They are usually brown, located next to the PCI slots on the motherboard, and shorter than the PCI slots (Figure 3-12). Today, however, the newest video adapters use PCI-Express technology.

3.2.5 Memory Slots

For the most part, PCs today use Random Access Memory (RAM) memory chips arranged on a small circuit board. Although there are a variety of types, or form factors, of memory modules, the most popular today are DIMMs (Dual Inline Memory Modules) and RIMMs (Rambus Inline Memory Modules). Rambus is a trademarked name and RIMMs use a proprietary technology and are housed in a protective shield. You will learn more about the various types of RAM form factors in Chapter 5.

Today's DIMMs and RIMMs differ in the number of conductors, or pins, that the particular physical specification uses. Some common examples include 168-,

Figure 3-12

An AGP slot compared to a PCI slot.

184-, and 240-pin configurations. In addition, laptop memory comes in smaller form factors known as Small Outline DIMMs (SoDIMMs) and MicroDIMMs.

The RAM modules fit into memory slots on the motherboard. The number of memory slots varies from motherboard to motherboard. SIMMS memory slots are usually white; DIMMS are usually black and placed very close together. Metal pins in the bottom make contact with the soldered tabs on each memory module. Small metal or plastic tabs on each side of the slot keep the memory module securely in its slot.

3.2.6 Connectors

You will find the following types of connectors on a motherboard:

▲ **Power connectors:** The power connector (Figure 3-13) allows the motherboard to be connected to the power supply to receive power. Some modern motherboards will have additional power connectors, for PCI-express expansion cards, for example.

▲ **On-board floppy disk and hard drive connectors:** The disk drives used for storing data need a connection to the motherboard so the computer can "talk" to the disk drive. These connections are known as drive interfaces, and there are two main types: floppy disk interfaces and hard disk interfaces. The interfaces consist of circuitry and a port. Most motherboards produced today include both the floppy disk and hard disk interfaces on the motherboard.

▲ **Keyboard connectors:** The most important input device for a PC is the keyboard. All PC motherboards contain a connector that allows a

Figure 3-13

An ATX power connector on a motherboard.

keyboard to be connected directly to the motherboard through the case. There are two main types of keyboard connectors:

- **AT connector:** The older AT, or DIN-5, keyboard connector is round, about one-half inch in diameter, and has five sockets (Figure 3-14).

Figure 3-14

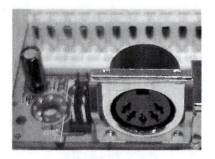

An AT keyboard connector.

Figure 3-15

A PS/2 keyboard connector on a motherboard.

- **PS/2 connector:** The PS/2, or DIN-6, keyboard connector (Figure 3-15) is smaller and more common than the AT connector.

Most new PCs contain a PS/2 keyboard connector as well as a PS/2 mouse connector right above it on the motherboard. The newest motherboards have color-coded the PS/2 mouse (green) and keyboard connectors (purple) to make connection of keyboards and mice easier.

▲ **Front Panel Connectors:** A series of connectors (Figure 3-16) to connect leads from the front panel to the motherboard. These connectors are

Figure 3-16

Front panel connectors.

used to control any power or status lights, reset and power switches, or simple onboard PC speakers used for warning beeps.

▲ **Peripheral Ports and Connectors:** Many different ports and connectors are used for attaching peripheral devices, such as printers and scanners. Some of the most common types of ports are:

- Serial (Male 9-pin and 25-pin)
- Parallel
- Universal Serial Bus (USB)
- FireWire (IEEE 1394)
- Video
- Ethernet
- Sound in/out
- Game ports

FOR EXAMPLE

Controllers, Ports, Connectors, Adapters, Interfaces

For any computing device to communicate and pass information to another device, there must be some way to manage and interpret the electronic signals. The engineering architecture—the wiring, signals, plug design, etc.—that allows two devices to communicate is called an interface. Besides the cabling, the hardware components of an interface that you use to connect the peripherals are ports, adapters, and connectors. *Ports* are the receptacles that *connectors* on cables plug into; and *adapters* are devices used to convert connectors or ports into a different type of port or connector. However, you may often see these three terms interchanged, along with the term *controller.* Strictly speaking, however, a controller is circuitry that is designed to manage the signals passed between devices; this circuitry may be embedded in the device, in a motherboard, or on an expansion card. Common controllers are floppy drive controllers, hard drive controllers, and keyboard controllers. Controllers match the data transfer speeds between peripherals and the CPU, and convert data from the type the CPU uses to the type of data the particular peripheral uses. Interface components, including controllers, ports, adapters, and connectors, are specifically designed to industry interface standards that describe the specific engineering for each component. Using standards for interfaces means, for example, that two different digital cameras can use (at separate times of course) the same USB port.

3.2.7 BIOS Chip

Aside from the processor, the most important chip on the motherboard is the **basic input/output system (BIOS)** chip. This special memory chip contains the BIOS software that tells the CPU how to interact with the rest of the hardware in the computer. The BIOS chip is easily identified: If you have a non-clone computer (Compaq, IBM, HP, and so on), this chip has on it the name of the manufacturer and usually the word BIOS. On clones, the chip usually has a sticker or printing on it from one of the three major BIOS manufacturers (AMI, Phoenix, or Award).

3.2.8 CMOS Battery

Your PC has to keep certain settings when it's turned off and its power cord is unplugged, such as the date, time, hard drive and memory configuration. Your PC keeps these settings, configured in a BIOS setup program, in a special memory chip called the **Complimentary Metal-Oxide Semiconductor (CMOS) chip.**

To keep its settings, the memory must have power constantly. When you shut off a computer, anything that is left in main memory is lost forever. To prevent the CMOS chip from losing its information, motherboard manufacturers include a small battery called the CMOS battery to power the CMOS. CMOS batteries come in different styles and sizes, but most look like either large watch batteries or small, cylindrical batteries.

3.2.9 Jumpers and DIP Switches

Jumpers and DIP switches are used to configure various hardware options on the motherboard. For example, some processors use different voltages (either 3.3 volts or 5 volts). You may need to configure the motherboard to provide the correct voltage for the processor it is using. You do so by changing a setting on the motherboard with either a **jumper** or a **DIP switch** (Figure 3-17). Motherboards often have either several jumpers or one bank of DIP switches. However, many motherboard settings today are either automatically detected or set manually in the CMOS setup program.

Figure 3-17

Jumper

Rocker-type DIP switch

Slide-type DIP switch

Jumpers and DIP switches.

3.2.10 Firmware

Firmware is the name given to any software that is encoded into a read-only memory (ROM) chip and can be run without extra instructions from the operating system. Most computers use firmware in some limited sense. The best example of firmware is the computer's BIOS setup program, used to set the options for the computer's BIOS (time/date and boot options, for example). Also, some expansion cards use their own firmware utilities for setting up peripherals.

3.2.11 Cache Memory

Cache memory is an extremely fast memory type that acts as a buffer, resolving the speed differences between RAM and the CPU. It holds frequently requested data and instructions so that they are immediately available to the CPU when needed.

Cache memory is categorized by its location:

▲ **Internal cache:** Also known as primary cache, internal cache is located inside the CPU chip, also called on the die, or on-chip.
▲ **External cache:** Also called secondary or off-chip cache, external cache is located on the motherboard outside the CPU.

Because it's faster than main memory and contains the most frequently used information, cache memory increases the performance of any system.

Cache is also identified by its level or proximity to the CPU:

▲ **Level 1 cache:** Level 1 (L1) cache is often used interchangeably with internal cache. L1 cache is placed internally on the processor chip and is the cache memory closest to the CPU.
▲ **Level 2 cache:** Level 2 (L2) cache was traditionally placed on the motherboard close to the CPU; and because it was not inside the CPU, it was designated as the second level of cache. Today, many CPU manufacturers include L2 cache in the CPU.
▲ **Level 3 cache:** L2 cache placed on the motherboard is often referred to today as Level 3 (L3) cache.

L1 cache cannot be increased without changing the CPU. On the other hand, L2 (or L3) cache can be upgraded on most motherboards. External cache modules plug into special cache module mounts or cache memory expansion sockets on the motherboard.

3.3 Understanding BIOS

The system **BIOS** is software that contains all the code required to control the keyboard, display screen, disk drives, serial ports, and various other PC components.

The BIOS is stored permanently on a read-only memory (ROM) chip on the motherboard. This ensures that it will always be available and will not be damaged by disk failure. The problem is that ROM is usually much slower than RAM, so many systems copy the BIOS to RAM each time the computer boots (this is known as **shadowing**).

3.3.1 The Functions of BIOS

The BIOS is responsible for checking that the PC's hardware is working properly and then getting the operating system running. Although many operating systems now contain their own device-oriented programs to improve performance, the BIOS contains a program for almost every activity associated with accessing hardware, including programs for starting the system, testing the hardware, reading and writing to and from storage devices, and moving data between devices.

The BIOS performs three vital functions for the computer:

1. **Booting the PC:** The instructions that start up the PC and load the operating system into memory and keep it running are part of the group of instructions that are collectively referred to as the **system BIOS**. The process of starting up the computer and loading the operating system is commonly called booting the computer, or simply the **boot sequence**. The BIOS is in charge of the boot sequence. When the PC is powered on, the BIOS supplies the PC with its first set of instructions. The instructions supplied by the BIOS are what the PC executes during its power on or boot sequence until it is able to fetch and execute instructions on its own.

2. **Verifying the hardware:** The hardware configuration of a PC is stored in the CMOS chip. When the system starts the boot sequence, the BIOS

starts a **Power-On Self-Test (POST)** program that verifies the data in the CMOS to the physical devices it can detect on the system.

3. **Providing the interface between hardware and software:** The BIOS provides the interface between the hardware and the software (such as the operating system, device drivers, and application software). In older PCs, the BIOS was completely responsible for hardware management. Modern operating systems, such as Windows XP, take over most hardware management after the boot process is complete.

3.3.2 The Boot Process

When you power up your PC, the processor is ready to work, but its memory is empty and it has no instructions. The BIOS is the mechanism on the system that provides the first instructions to be executed.

Each time the PC starts up, the CPU looks for the initial instructions to start the ball rolling. Because the processor can't execute any instructions to find these instructions, they must be available in the same place every time. The location of the instructions is hard-wired to a fixed, standard location, called the **jump address**. The CPU uses the jump address to find its initial instructions on the BIOS ROM chip and load the BIOS into memory.

The BIOS is loaded to a designated area of RAM called the high memory area. The CPU gets its instructions from this location and begins executing the BIOS program, which starts the boot sequence.

Several BIOS programs exist in a PC. Besides the main BIOS program, there are also device BIOS programs to control many of the peripheral devices. For example, most video cards have their own BIOS programs that provide additional instructions used for controlling the video display. Hard drives and many SCSI adapters also have their own BIOS programs.

Although what the BIOS actually does during its boot sequence varies slightly from manufacturer to manufacturer, the following basic steps are performed during the boot sequence (Figure 3-18):

1. **Power supply initializes:** When the PC is powered on, the internal power supply initializes. The power supply doesn't immediately provide power to the rest of the computer. It determines whether it can supply the proper voltages and then sends out a POWER GOOD signal. When the chipset receives this signal, it issues a SYSTEM RESET signal to the processor.

2. **Primary part of BIOS loads to RAM:** When the processor receives the SYSTEM RESET signal, it accesses the jump address for the start of the BIOS boot program and loads the BIOS program into RAM. The jump address contains the actual address of the BIOS boot program on the ROM BIOS chip. The jump address is usually located in a predefined area in system memory.

Figure 3-18

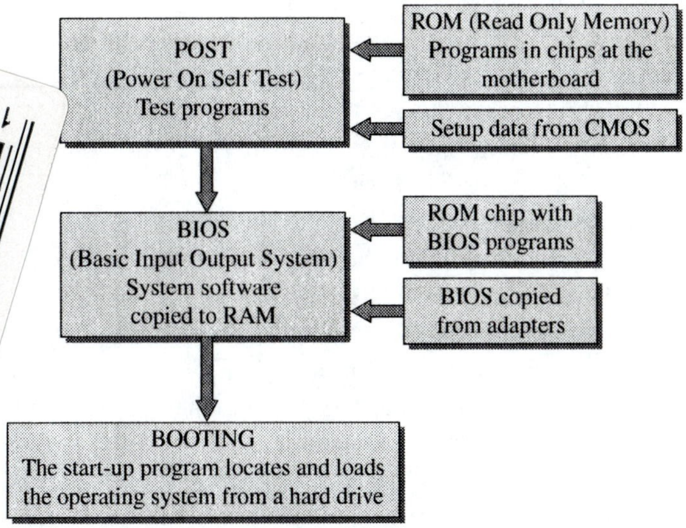

Summary of PC boot sequence.

3. **Type of boot confirmed**: There are two types of boots:
   - **A cold boot** occurs when the PC's power is switched on.
   - **A warm boot** is performed whenever the PC is restarted or reset with the power already on. A warm boot does not run the POST routine, but reestablishes the operating system and drivers on the PC.

4. **Power On Self Test (POST) begins**: If any fatal errors happen during the POST process (problems that prevent the PC from operating normally), the appropriate error beep codes sound or perhaps an error message displays, and the boot process stops. At this point in the boot process, only the system speaker can notify the user of errors.

5. **Video adapter software loads**: If all is well, the boot sequence continues, and the system BIOS loads the device BIOS of the video adapter (if there is one) and loads it to memory. The video adapter's information displays on the monitor.

6. **Other device BIOS loads**: Any other device-specific BIOS, such as those for the hard drives or SCSI devices, are loaded. At this time:
   a. **The BIOS startup screen loads**: Immediately after the BIOS loads the video and other device-specific BIOS, it displays the BIOS startup

screen. Although this display varies by manufacturer, it generally includes the following information:

- **Version:** The BIOS manufacturer and the BIOS program's version number and version date.
- **Startup program keys:** The keyboard key or keys used to access the BIOS setup program. These are often the Delete (Del) key or a Function (F1 or F2) keys.
- **Energy Star:** If the BIOS supports the Energy Star standard (also known as the Green standard), an Energy Star logo is displayed.
- **Serial number:** The BIOS program's serial number is specific to the combination of the motherboard, chipset, and program version.

   b. The BIOS begins a series of tests on the system, including a count of the amount of memory detected on the system. Because the display is now available, any errors found now are displayed as messages on the monitor instead of a beep from the system speaker.

7. **CMOS configuration tested:** The system determines whether the devices listed in the CMOS configuration data are present and functioning, including tests for device speeds and access modes.

8. **Ports assigned and devices configured:** The serial and parallel ports are assigned their identities, and a message is displayed for each device found, configured, and tested. If the BIOS program supports Plug and Play (PnP), any PnP devices detected are configured. Although it usually goes by much too fast to read, the BIOS displays a message for each device it finds and configures.

9. **The hardware configuration is confirmed:** At this time the BIOS displays a summary screen that details the computer as the BIOS sees it. This summary screen signals that the system is verified and ready for use. What's displayed depends on the manufacturer and version of the BIOS. It usually includes information about the PC's various devices and components, such as:

- Processor
- Coprocessor: If a math coprocessor or floating point unit (FPU) is installed on the system, it is indicated as "Installed." Virtually every modern processor has an integrated FPU and is indicated as "Integrated."
- Clock speed (Refers to the speed of the CPU)
- Floppy disk drives
- Hard drive, CD-ROM, and DVD drives
- Memory

- Video type: (Refers to the type of graphics processing used by the monitor)
- Serial ports
- Parallel ports

10. **The operating system is located and loaded:** The CMOS data contains the sequence in which storage devices are to be checked by the BIOS to locate the operating system. Typically, the first hard drive is listed first, but the BIOS can be set to have the BIOS check the floppy disk, a CD-ROM, or another hard drive first. If the boot program is not found on the first device listed, the next device indicated is searched, and then the third, and so on until the boot program is found. If no boot device is found, the boot sequences stop and an error message ("No boot device available") is displayed. Otherwise, the operating system is started and takes over control of the PC.

A **boot failure** occurs when the computer is unable to complete the boot process and load the operating system. Boot failure is typically caused by a loose or missing component, including, but not limited to, the CPU, BIOS chip, chipset, RAM, expansion card, or cable. If you are unable to pinpoint the component that is causing the boot to fail, you can remove expansion cards one at a time until the system boots. In practice, many boot and operational problems on a PC are fixed by merely rebooting the PC. Rebooting should always be a standard first step in your troubleshooting procedure. A successful POST sequence is usually signaled by the BIOS sounding of a single beep before displaying the BIOS summary screen.

Other devices can also cause boot time errors:

▲ An improperly installed motherboard may indicate other device problems.
▲ Newly installed RAM can cause fatal memory errors to appear at POST time if the RAM either is the wrong speed or uses a different data width.
▲ An improperly connected keyboard can cause a "Keyboard not found" error message.

3.3.3 CMOS Settings

The **BIOS setup** program, also referred to as the CMOS setup or BIOS screen, manages the hardware configuration, or **CMOS settings**, stored in CMOS memory. On some occasions, you will use the BIOS setup to configure or troubleshoot your PC. For example, you may need to configure a new hard drive added to the PC, tell the PC which hard drive contains the operating system, or disable a port.

The BIOS setup is available for only a very short time during the boot sequence. You access it during startup by pressing a specific key, such as F2 or the DEL key, or combination of keys. These startup keys are displayed during the initial boot process.

The initial screen of the BIOS setup program typically displays a menu of configuration categories each of which leads to one or more additional menu screens and options. You navigate through the menus and options typically by using the up, down, left, and right arrows. To select a menu or option, you may need to press [Enter] or a combination of keys specified for that option. (There is often a "hint" box that displays more information about any selected option or menu.)

The CMOS settings included in the BIOS setup, although somewhat standardized, vary with the BIOS. However, on most PCs, the configuration data is managed and maintained on two levels:

1. **Standard:** The standard configurations menu typically allows you to configure:
   - The system date and time
   - Hard drives
   - Floppy drives
   - Video display

   Some BIOS setup programs enable you to set which errors you want the BIOS to stop (halt) during the POST and boot sequence via a "Halt on" option. The choices range from all errors (a good choice), to no errors (a bad choice).

2. **Advanced** configuration: The advanced configuration options typically allow you to configure options specific to:
   - The motherboard
   - The CPU
   - The chipset

In addition to the standard and advanced setup options, you will often find configuration menus for:

▲ **Plug and Play options:** Some older operating systems (such as Windows NT) don't directly support PnP, which means that the BIOS must deal with any PnP device configurations.

▲ **Power management:** Options used to control the system when it is automatically powered down through power conservation settings.

▲ **Integrated peripherals:** Defines the configuration of the devices that are integrated into the motherboard, such as serial and parallel ports, audio, and USB ports.

▲ **Security and passwords:** The capability to set the user and supervisor password for the BIOS and the CMOS settings is included on a separate menu or in the advanced features menu on older systems. If the user password is set, the computer isn't allowed to boot until the proper password is entered. The supervisor password protects the BIOS setup program's settings and the system configuration. Without the supervisor password, a user can't access the CMOS settings, but the system will boot. If you choose to set either of these passwords, you put yourself in the situation of really needing to remember them, but there are second chances. If you forget the user password and remember the supervisor password, you can access the BIOS setup and clear or change the user password. If you forget both passwords, your only recourse is to open the computer and use the password-clear jumper (Figure 3-19) located on the motherboard near the CMOS chip and its battery. You can also clear the CMOS settings, including all advanced settings that you may have changed and the passwords, by removing the CMOS battery.

Both for troubleshooting purposes and security, keep a written, secure, record of the CMOS settings each time the BIOS configuration changes or for every new PC added to a network.

Figure 3-19

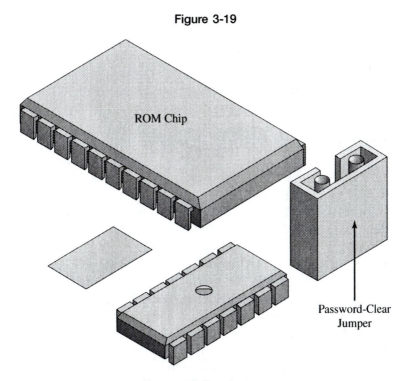

Password-clear jumper.

3.3.4 Updating the BIOS

Because the BIOS determines what devices a computer can utilize before the operating system loads, there might be times when you need to update the BIOS to support a new component. The most common reason to upgrade the BIOS is to support hard drives that are larger than the limit imposed by BIOS code.

However, if a PC has an apparent compatibility problem with a field replaceable module (FRM), a BIOS upgrade is not automatically needed. Essentially, the BIOS should not be upgraded except to solve an isolated specific (and documented) compatibility or performance issue. Use only the BIOS or motherboard manufacturer's software, and apply only the BIOS versions (obtained only from the manufacturer) that are listed as compatible with the PCs motherboard, processor, and chipset.

Older motherboards require the BIOS ROM to be physically replaced to upgrade it (usually by the motherboard manufacturer) but these are rare. Virtually all new systems use flash BIOS. **Flash BIOS** is stored on a flash memory chip. **Flash memory** is a type of reprogrammable ROM called EEPROM (Electrically Erasable Programmable Read Only Memory). It is updated, or flashed, using **flashing** software. Note that because the flashing software overwrites the information on the chip, if you make a mistake in updating the BIOS, your computer can become unbootable.

Flashing the BIOS has a few risks:

▲ When you begin flashing a BIOS ROM, you absolutely must complete the process. If the flashing process is interrupted—for example, a power failure occurs or the flashing software has a bug—depending on where you are in the flashing process, the probability of having a corrupted BIOS chip is high.

▲ Flashing the wrong BIOS version is another way to corrupt the BIOS ROM. Some flashing software will load whatever BIOS version you give it without question. The flashing utilities from the larger BIOS companies (such as Award, Phoenix, and AMI) include features that check the version of the flash file against the model of motherboard and let you know of any mismatch.

A corrupt BIOS leaves you in a real Catch-22 situation. To flash your BIOS ROM, you must boot the PC, and you can't boot the PC with a corrupted BIOS. However, most modern BIOS has a "**boot block.**" This is a tiny area of the BIOS that is not updatable and which contains a utility program that will run a floppy drive from which you can run a flashing program. If your BIOS is corrupt, but has a boot block, it will boot your PC to the floppy. Some new motherboards, called **Dual BIOS motherboards**, include a second, backup BIOS that is used when the primary BIOS is corrupt.

FOR EXAMPLE

Back Up the BIOS

Most flashing software includes the ability to back up the current BIOS before flashing the chip. Always take advantage of this step before performing the flash process, even if you have used the software before. Also, do not assume that because two computers are the same make and model and were purchased at the same time, you can use the same backup as protection against errors for both machines. Manufacturers are constantly revising BIOS software. Perform the backup for every computer you update.

To flash your BIOS:

1. Using the serial number and model number of the motherboard, locate on the manufacturer's website the web page that allows you to download the latest revisions to your PC's BIOS.
2. Following the instructions on the manufacturer's website, download the flashing software and update file to your PC.
3. If you don't already have one, either create a bootable disk (or CD), or visit www.bootdisk.com for a boot disk for your operating system.
4. Copy the .bin file (something like bios.bin) from the BIOS update and the flashing utility (something like AWDFLASH.EXE) to the boot disk.
5. Reboot the PC to the boot disk and at the A:\ prompt, enter the name of the flashing utility and enter the name of the BIOS update file when requested. Be sure not to interrupt this process at all.
6. Remove the floppy disk and reboot your PC. Check the BIOS settings against the written backup you created to ensure that any advanced settings are carried forward.

To safeguard the flashing process:

▲ Avoid flashing your BIOS in an electrical storm.
▲ Be sure your computer is protected against power surges or brownouts by an uninterruptible power supply (UPS).
▲ Check twice that you are flashing your BIOS with the current version.

After you flash your BIOS, you still may have the flashing software on your PC and that means there is a chance of accidental flashing. If this happens and you replace the BIOS with the same complete version, there should be no harm. However, if the accidental flashing is interrupted, or your current BIOS is replaced by an older or incompatible version either inadvertently or maliciously, the effect is the same as no BIOS at all—a PC that won't boot.

Most motherboards that support flash BIOS include a jumper block that can be set to disallow flash updates. To flash the BIOS ROM, the flashing security jumper has to be in the correct position. If you plan to flash your BIOS, open the system case and check the position of this jumper. After you flash the BIOS, reset this jumper and you're prevented from accidentally flashing it again. Another good reason to use the flashing security jumper is to prevent access from computer viruses that attempt to change the flash BIOS code.

If you have updated your BIOS but the system will not boot because it can't see the hard drive (and perhaps other devices as well), one or more CMOS settings may need to be adjusted. Using the written record of the CMOS settings that you made before you flashed the BIOS, enter the Setup program and verify that all the BIOS configuration settings are correct. The BIOS CMOS has default settings, and any settings that were changed in the past must be changed again.

3.3.5 POST Errors

If the PC has the most current and compatible BIOS version, any problems that are generated by the BIOS will most likely occur during the POST and boot processes. If the POST process detects errors, it generates a signal to indicate where in the process the error occurred and which device had the error.

The POST process generally continues past nonfatal problems. However, if a fatal error is detected, such as "no memory is found," the POST process signals its error code and halts the boot process immediately.

The BIOS uses the following two means of notifying you of a problem during the boot sequence:

▲ **Beep codes:** The system speaker emits a series of short and long tones to indicate a problem in an essential system component during the hardware phase of the boot sequence. Each BIOS manufacturer has a unique set of beep codes that it uses to signal boot errors. However, every BIOS does have a single beep sound at the end of the POST routine.

▲ **Error messages:** The BIOS displays error messages on the monitor that indicate a problem has occurred in the final stages of the boot cycle.

The onscreen POST error messages all typically indicate a serious system problem. Examples of boot sequence error messages are:

▲ **BIOS ROM checksum error—System halted:** The BIOS is corrupt, and you need to contact the motherboard or BIOS manufacturer for recovery procedures, if any exist.

▲ **CMOS battery failed:** The CMOS battery needs to be replaced.

▲ **CMOS checksum error—Defaults loaded:** The CMOS has become corrupt, likely because of a weak battery that needs to be replaced.

▲ **Display switch is set incorrectly:** Some motherboards have a jumper that sets the type of video display that is being supported. This error indicates that the jumper and the video configuration in the CMOS are different.

▲ **Floppy disk fail:** The BIOS cannot find the floppy disk controller (FDC). If the PC does not have a floppy disk drive, set the CMOS Floppy Disk Drive value to None (or Auto). If the FDC is included in the chipset, make sure that the drive's cables are all seated properly.

▲ **Hard disk install failure:** This is a similar error to the Floppy disk fail error message. The POST cannot find or initialize the hard drive controller (HDC). Make sure that the adapter card—if there is one—is seated snuggly and that the drive cables are connected properly.

▲ **I/O card failure:** This error indicates that an expansion card has failed or has a parity error at a certain address.

▲ **Keyboard error or no keyboard present:** Make sure that the keyboard is attached correctly and that no keys are pressed during the POST. Make sure that nothing is lying on the keyboard, such as a book.

▲ **Memory test fail:** This message indicates that an error was detected during memory testing. The message should also include information about the type and location of the memory error, such as a memory parity error at xxxx, where xxxx is the location of the memory error.

▲ **Primary/Secondary master/slave hard disk fail:** The POST process has detected an error in either the primary or secondary master or slave PATA hard drive. Check the cabling and the master/slave jumpers.

Most system BIOSs display a 3- or 4-digit error code along with the error message to help you pinpoint the apparent source of the problem. The documentation for the BIOS system or the motherboard should list the codes that are used on a particular PC.

POST error codes are grouped by device or service types in hundreds (Table 3-1). For example, a 600-series error indicates a problem with the floppy disk drive or the floppy disk drive controller. The error code that's displayed is a number between 600 and 699, with each number identifying a specific problem.

Other boot errors can look like POST errors when they are more often caused by a new or recent addition to the system. For example, after a new hard drive is installed, the system may boot to a blank screen if the new drive is not properly configured in the CMOS settings. A new hard drive that has not been partitioned or formatted will likely cause a No operating system error.

Table 3-1: POST Error Codes

Error Series	Error Category
1XX	Motherboard errors
2XX	RAM errors
3XX	Keyboard errors
5XX	Color graphics adapter errors
6XX	Floppy disk drive errors
14XX	Printer error
17XX	Hard drive errors
30XX	Network interface card (NIC) errors
86XX	Mouse error

 SELF-CHECK

1. What are the primary functions of the BIOS?
2. What is the POST?
3. How do you enter the BIOS setup program?
4. How do you update the BIOS?
5. What types of error messages does the BIOS give during startup?

3.4 Working with Motherboards

Because motherboards contain delicate circuitry that is easily damaged by ESD, you should take precautions to minimize any damage to the motherboard. Handle the motherboard as little as possible, and keep it in an antistatic bag whenever it is removed from the PC case. Make sure to keep liquids well away from it, and always wear an antistatic wrist strap when you are working with a motherboard.

3.4.1 Installing a motherboard

To install a motherboard:

1. **Remove the motherboard from its box:** Remove the motherboard from the box and set it on your work surface inside its antistatic bag. Ground yourself using an antistatic wrist strap. Then, carefully remove

Figure 3-20

Motherboard mounting plate.

the motherboard from its antistatic bag (be careful not to touch any exposed conductors) and set it on top of the bag.

2. **If necessary, install the CPU, CPU heatsink and fan, and RAM memory chips** (see Chapters 4 and 5). This must be done on a flat surface, and must be done before the motherboard is installed in order to avoid bending or flexing the motherboard.

3. **Open the case:** Remove the side (or top, if you are installing into a desktop case) cover of the case so you can access the mounting holes inside the computer case. To do this, you may need to remove some screws, slide a latch, or release some other fastening mechanism that is holding the case cover in place.

4. **Locate the motherboard mounting plate:** Position the case so that the mounting plate is at the bottom of the case (Figure 3-20).

5. **Install the mounting standoffs:** Connection pins and soldered joints often stick out the back of the motherboard. If you were to just lay the motherboard in the computer and power it up, the metal case would cause electrical shorts between these components and damage the motherboard. For this reason, you must mount the motherboard on small metal or plastic spacers, known as **standoffs**. These small items hold the motherboard away from the motherboard mounting plate in the case and prevent the components of the motherboard from touching the mounting plate and shorting out. There are two types of standoffs (Figure 3-21):

Figure 3-21

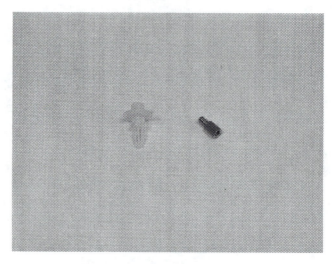

Push-in and screw-in standoffs.

- **Push-in standoffs** are typically made of nylon plastic and have a small one-way barb that fits into any of the mounting holes in the motherboard. To install them, you push the barb into the motherboard and slide the small tab on the bottom into a precut hole in the mounting plate.
- **Screw-in standoffs** are usually made of brass. They simply screw into the mounting plate into a predrilled, pretapped hole.

These standoffs must be installed before you can install the motherboard. You will notice several threaded holes and cutouts in the mounting plate. These holes are where you place the standoffs and mount the motherboard. There are also several mounting holes in the motherboard, each with a silver-colored ring around it (Figure 3-22). These holes are used to connect the motherboard to the standoffs. The mounting plate is configured to accept multiple motherboard configurations. Not all holes in the motherboard will necessarily line up with holes/slots in the mounting plate. However, the motherboard must be supported at least on its four corners and at one spot near the middle of the board, to minimize flexing of the motherboard during device installation (which may cause cracks).

After you have determined which locations will work for your motherboard, mark them with a marker. Then, install the standoffs in those marked locations, using the appropriate type for the kind of hole or slot (small brass screw-in standoffs for the tapped holes, plastic push-ins for the slots).

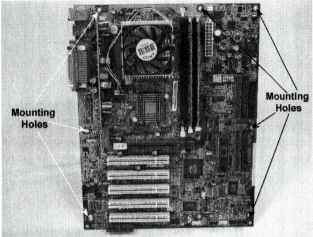

Motherboard mounting holes.

6. **Remove the back-panel cutouts:** Most cases come with a back panel that has standard cutouts (also known as punchouts) for the standard on-board ports (keyboard, mouse, serial, and parallel). There are also cutouts that have metal covers on them for the other onboard ports your mother-board might have (LAN, video, sound, and so on). For your motherboard to fit properly and the ports to be exposed, you must remove these metal covers from the cutouts. Note that because the AT and ATX have different board layouts for their components and expansion slots, they will have different case layouts for the cutouts where expansion ports and slots go at the back of the case. Therefore, an ATX motherboard will not fit into a case designed for an AT motherboard (and vice versa).

7. **Connect the front-panel leads:** Front-panel switches, lights, and periph-eral ports all have cables or leads that must be run to pins on the moth-erboard. Refer to your motherboard's manual to locate the motherboard pin(s) on which each lead's connector should be installed. Typically, the pins are in groups on the motherboard and labeled as to their function. After you have located the proper pins, slip the connector over the pins, making sure to orient the connectors properly as per the motherboard's documentation (+ to +, − to −, and so on).

8. **Install and secure the motherboard:** Finally, just slip the motherboard into the case. You may have to push the motherboard against the back-panel cutouts to make it line up with its mounting standoffs. Then, put one screw in to secure the motherboard. The screws are included with the

---

FOR EXAMPLE

Installing Front-Panel Connectors

When you're installing the front-panel connectors to a motherboard, often you will have to act as a kind of translator between the motherboard manufacturer and the case manufacturer. For example, a case manufacturer may label its front-panel USB ports as USB port #0 and port #1, while the motherboard will label its USB connectors as #1 and #2. In this case, you would need to install the front-panel #0 USB connector to the motherboard's #1 USB connector and the front-panel #1 connector to the motherboard's #2 connector. You often need to interpret what each company is trying to accomplish when you use parts from two different companies.

---

standoffs (both usually come in the box of hardware that comes with the case). You can use two hands to push the motherboard down onto any plastic push-in standoffs. Finally, put screws through the motherboard holes into any remaining standoffs. Some new case designs allow the motherboard to be attached to a hinged plate with only the spacers locking it into place.

9. **Reconnect all cables:** The final step is to connect all appropriate cables (including the power connector) to the motherboard and peripherals. It is very important to reattach the power cable. Not doing so can result in a damaged motherboard or an exploded power supply.

3.4.2 Upgrading Motherboards

There are four major considerations when looking to upgrade a motherboard:

▲ **CPU:** A new or existing CPU will need to be compatible with the motherboard and the motherboards chipset. In fact, you will more often base a system upgrade on a new CPU, rather than a new motherboard.

▲ **Form factor:** The motherboard, the power supply, and the case need to be compatible. If you aren't changing the PC's case, you are limited to the form factor of the case or those that will fit into it.

▲ **Fan and heatsink:** Different CPUs require different cooling devices.

▲ **Documentation:** Motherboards with good documentation are essential.

Other considerations to take into account when upgrading a motherboard include.

▲ **Bus speed:** The bus speeds supported by a motherboard and chipset must be matched to the processor.

▲ **Type of memory used:** Most motherboards today will only accept certain form factors and speeds of memory. If you upgrade a motherboard and do not want to upgrade RAM at the same time, make sure the new motherboard supports the RAM you have.

▲ **Cache memory:** Many motherboards have upward of 512K of L2 or L3 cache memory. Additional cache can be added to the motherboard, but it must be matched to the motherboard's bus speed,

▲ **Expansion bus:** Unless the new motherboard will replace some of the cards with built-in connectors, the current expansion cards will need compatible slots on the new motherboard.

▲ **BIOS:** The BIOS of a new motherboard should support the hardware standards and drive interfaces your system will use. BIOS from different manufacturers will have different security features, reporting, and user interfaces, so you will want to explore the BIOS feature set of a motherboard before you make a purchase.

▲ **Chipset:** The chipset is matched to the processor and the motherboard. Usually, this is a part of the motherboard and cannot be replaced.

▲ **Power supply:** The power supply shares the form factor with the case and motherboard. You will need to make sure that any new or existing power supply will connect to the motherboard and supply the right voltages for the motherboard, the CPU, any SATA drives or PCI express slots.

▲ **Built-in controllers and interfaces:** You may want more or fewer built-in controllers and plugs on the motherboard. Consider the connections and adapter cards on the current motherboard in making this choice.

To replace an existing motherboard:

1. Power down the system, unplug it, and remove any components or cables attached to it (be sure you document cable locations, expansion-card positions, and so on before removing them so you can put them back in the same location).

2. Remove any expansion cards from the system, cables connected to other peripherals, and the front panel button and light connectors. You can remove the CPU, heatsink, and memory if you want, but it will probably be easiest to remove them after the motherboard is removed from the computer case. Make sure anything that connects the motherboard to any other part of the computer has been disconnected.

3. To remove the motherboard, remove the screws holding the motherboard to the mounting brackets; then, slide the motherboard to the side to release the spacers from their mounting holes in the case (Figure 3-23).

Figure 3-23

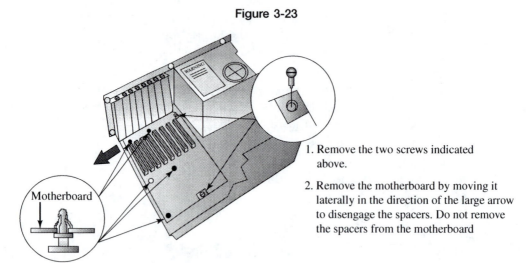

1. Remove the two screws indicated above.

2. Remove the motherboard by moving it laterally in the direction of the large arrow to disengage the spacers. Do not remove the spacers from the motherboard

There are five spacers holding the motherboard off the case. A spacer is shown above, viewed from its side.

Removing a motherboard.

4. Remove the new motherboard from its packaging and transfer the memory, CPU, and CPU heatsink from the old motherboard to the new motherboard (again, assuming they are compatible—if they aren't, you must purchase a compatible CPU and memory and install them).

5. Follow the steps from Section 3.4.2 for inserting a new motherboard.

3.4.3 Troubleshooting Motherboards

Most motherboard (and CPU) problems manifest themselves by the system appearing completely dead. However, "completely dead" can be a symptom of a variety of problems, not only with the motherboard or CPU but also with the RAM or the power supply.

The motherboard's functions are tested, for the most part, by the POST routines. 100 series errors and beep codes during startup indicate the biggest problems. There are very few problems that don't show up in the POST.

You can use a POST card to help narrow down the problem. A POST card is a circuit board that fits into an expansion slot in the motherboard and reports numeric codes as the boot process progresses. If the POST card stops at a certain number, you can look up the number in the manual that came with the card to determine the problem.

When the motherboard fails, it is usually because it has been damaged. Most technicians cannot repair motherboard damage; the motherboard must be replaced. Motherboards can become damaged due to physical trauma, exposure to ESD, or short-circuiting.

One common problem becomes visible when the system constantly loses its clock—the time resets to 12:00 on 12/01/83, for example. At the same time, you may begin seeing "1780—Hard Disk Failure" problems. When you try to reset the time, it sets correctly. But as soon as you turn off the computer and turn it back on, the time is lost.

These symptoms indicate that the system's CMOS is losing the time, date, and hard-disk settings (as well as other system settings). The solution is to replace the battery. When you do this, you will also have to reset the system settings.

SELF-CHECK

1. What is a standoff?
2. To what component of the PC's case is the motherboard attached?
3. What are the three major factors to consider when upgrading a motherboard?
4. What is a POST card?
5. What types of problems would you expect to see when the CMOS battery is failing?

SUMMARY

The motherboard is a circuit board that binds the PC's operational components and circuits. Nonintegrated motherboards place circuitry on expansion cards; integrated motherboards have circuitry embedded in the motherboard itself. In a backplane design, all of the circuitry is installed on daughterboards attached to a backplane. Motherboard form factors include the AT, Baby AT, ATX, MicroATX, NLX, and BTX, although some manufacturers have their own proprietary designs.

Key motherboard components include the CPU, internal and external buses, expansion slots, memory slots, connectors for floppy and hard drives, keyboard and mouse connectors, peripheral connectors, jumpers and DIP switches, various firmware, and external (L2 or L3) cache memory. Some of the most important circuitry on the motherboard is its BIOS chip and its chipset.

The chipset controls the data that flows between the CPU and RAM over the motherboard's buses and helps the CPU communicate with peripheral devices. The Northbridge subset of the chipset supports CPU/memory operations and high-speed peripherals, and the Southbridge subset supports secondary peripherals.

The BIOS chip stores the BIOS program that starts up the PC, checks its hardware with the POST routine, and locates and loads the operating system. Any errors during POST are reported through beep codes or through numbered POST error messages. The PC's hardware configuration settings are stored in its CMOS settings. The BIOS setup program, accessed during startup through BIOS-specific startup keys, allows you to access and configure these settings.

The BIOS chip is typically a Flash memory chip which you upgrade with flashing software. A faulty flashing procedure will make a computer unbootable. Most major motherboard manufacturers provide security features, such as a backup BIOS, boot block, or security jumpers, to safeguard against accidental or faulty flashing.

A motherboard is mounted on the case's mounting plate using standoffs, which prevent the connection pins and soldered joints on the back of the motherboard from touching the metal case. Although a case's mounting plate will have a variety of mounting holes for mounting different sizes of motherboards, some cases and cutouts will require specific motherboard form factors.

Beside the form factor, other considerations when choosing a new motherboard include the CPU, quality of documentation, RAM supported, cache memory, expansion slots, BIOS, chipset, power supply, fan and heatsink, and built-in controllers and interfaces.

Although the POST routines essentially test the functioning of the motherboard, a motherboard fails when its circuitry has been damaged. Unless the damaged circuitry is limited to a replaceable part such as the CPU, the motherboard will typically have to be replaced.

KEY TERMS

Active backplane

AT motherboard

ATX motherboard

Baby AT motherboard

Backplane

Basic input/output system (BIOS)

Boot block

Boot failure

Boot sequence

BTX motherboard

Bus

Cache memory

Chipset

CMOS battery

CMOS settings

CMOS setup program

Cold boot

Complimentary Metal-Oxide Semiconductor (CMOS) chip

Controller

Daughterboard

DIP switch

Direct-solder method

Dongle

Dual BIOS motherboards

Expansion bus

Expansion cards

Expansion slot

External bus

External cache

Firmware

Flash BIOS

Flash memory

Flashing

Integrated motherboard

Internal bus

Internal cache

Jump address

Jumper

Level 1 cache

Level 2 cache

Memory slot

NLX motherboard

Nonintegrated motherboard

Northbridge

Passive backplane

POST card

Power On Self Test (POST)

Proprietary design

Riser card

Shadowing

Southbridge

Standoffs

System BIOS

Warm boot

ASSESS YOUR UNDERSTANDING

Go to www.wiley.com/college/groth to evaluate your knowledge of motherboards and the BIOS.
Measure your learning by comparing pre-test and post-test results.

Summary Questions

1. Which statement best describes the purpose of the motherboard?
   (a) supplies DC power to the peripheral devices
   (b) interconnects the primary components of the PC
   (c) executes all instructions of the PC
   (d) stores and processes the data of the PC

2. All of the PC's circuitry components, even the CPU and memory, are installed as separate boards in a _____ design.
   (a) daughterboard
   (b) riser card
   (c) nonintegrated
   (b) backplane

3. The most common motherboard form factor today is the ATX. True or false?

4. CPUs are attached to the motherboard via sockets or _____.
   (a) adapters
   (b) slots
   (c) riser cards
   (d) heatsinks

5. The data lines on the motherboard that communicate with peripherals and other attached devices are called the _____.
   (a) expansion bus
   (b) chipset
   (c) controllers
   (d) Southbridge

6. Which type of expansion slot was designed to be a direct connection between video circuitry and the PC's memory?
   (a) PCI
   (b) PCI Express
   (c) AGP
   (d) ISA

7. A parallel connector is used to attach a keyboard to the motherboard. True or false?

8. A cable that is used to connect some ports to the motherboard is called a dongle. True or false?

9. Some hardware options are configured on the motherboard itself by using DIP switches and _____.

    (a) jumpers

    (b) standoffs

    (c) back-panel connectors

    (d) front-panel connectors

10. Any software that is encoded into ROM and can be run without extra instructions from the operating system is called _____.

    (a) firmware

    (b) CMOS

    (c) BIOS

    (d) cached software

11. Cache located on the motherboard, as opposed to in the CPU, is called external cache. True or false?

12. The practice of copying the BIOS to RAM each time the computer boots is called caching. True or false?

13. The location of the CPU's first instructions in the boot process is hard-wired to the _____.

    (a) BIOS

    (b) CMOS

    (c) jump address

    (d) high memory area

14. A startup that occurs when the PC is reset while it's the power is already on is called a partial boot. True or false?

15. In which of the BIOS setup screens would you expect to find options for configuring a CPU?

    (a) Standard Configuration

    (b) Advanced Configuration

    (c) Integrated Peripherals

    (d) Plug and Play options

16. What is the main risk associated with upgrading the BIOS?

    (a) The BIOS will become corrupt.

    (b) The chipset will become corrupt.

(c) The CMOS settings will be lost.

(d) The jump address will be lost.

17. A POST error code in the 300s will indicate a problem with the memory. True or false?

18. To accommodate a motherboard's onboard ports, what element of the case must you remove?

(a) standoffs

(b) cutouts

(c) back panel

(d) front-panel

19. What is the purpose of the boot block?

(a) Prevent the system from rebooting during flashing.

(b) Reboot the system when the power supply is dead.

(c) Restore the BIOS if it becomes corrupted.

(d) Restore the supervisor and user passwords.

20. Which motherboard component is used to resolve the speed differences of the CPU and RAM?

(a) chipset

(b) BIOS

(c) cache memory

(d) expansion bus

21. Which motherboard form factor places expansion slots on a special riser card and is used in low-profile PCs?

(a) AT

(b) Baby AT

(c) ATX

(d) NLX

Applying This Chapter

1. A client wants to build a series of simple PCs to be used solely for web and catalog access from their library. Would a nonintegrated or integrated motherboard be appropriate in building this system? Why?

2. There is an unlabeled motherboard in your company's storeroom. You notice that it has three very long, black expansion slots. Is this likely to be a newer or an older motherboard?

3. A client wants to improve his computer's speed. What components on the motherboard should he consider upgrading?

4. During the boot sequence of a new PC, you hear two short beeps followed by a long beep, but the operating system still loads. Is the PC fine? What should you assume or do about this?

5. A friend is going to install a new motherboard. What precautions will you advise her to take?

Troubleshooting a Motherboard Installation

A client has just installed a new motherboard, and the system will no longer boot to the operating system. What questions will you ask to help determine the cause of the problem?

Upgrading the BIOS Safely

You have installed a hard drive on your PC that requires you to upgrade the BIOS. What safety measures are there or can you take to prevent corrupting the BIOS?

Identifying a Motherboard

A friend who is upgrading her own computer has given you the motherboard of their old computer. How will you go about determining what type of motherboard it

is, and what, if any, parts of the motherboard could be used on another board?

Comparing Motherboards

You are building a new PC and need to choose a motherboard. Explore the product pages at the websites of motherboard manufacturer ASUS (ASUS.com) and Biostar (Biostar.com). Choose a recent motherboard from each company and compare the following features: CPUs supported, chipset, memory supported, expansion slots, ports and interfaces. Of the two, which would you choose, and why? (There will probably be some terms or features you don't recognize at the websites; such as some CPU or hard drive technologies, you can explore these features or just concentrate on the ones covered in this chapter.)

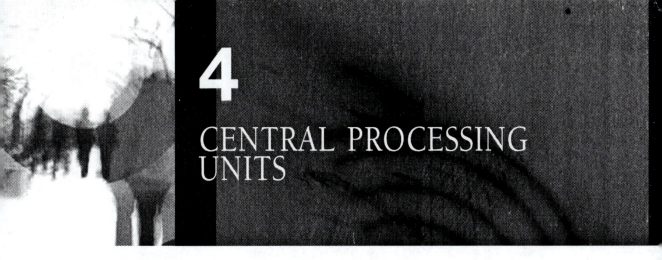

4

CENTRAL PROCESSING UNITS

Starting Point

Go to www.wiley.com/college/groth to assess your knowledge of central processing units (CPUs).
Determine where you need to concentrate your effort

What You'll Learn in This Chapter

▲ CPU packages, slots, and sockets, voltages, and cooling mechanisms
▲ CPU features and technologies
▲ Popular CPU manufacturers and CPU families
▲ CPU installation and troubleshooting steps

After Studying This Chapter, You'll Be Able To

▲ Identify a failing CPU
▲ Determine and analyze CPU specifications so that you will know when a CPU should be upgraded
▲ Use your understanding of CPUs and their specifications to select an appropriate CPU for a PC
▲ Safely remove and install a CPU that is compatible with a computer's motherboard
▲ Install a cooling mechanism for a CPU

INTRODUCTION

Everything that a computer can do for you is performed by its central processing unit, or CPU. The CPU performs all the arithmetic, logic, and computing actions of a PC. You may see your PC as a word processor, a computer game, a World Wide Web browser, an email tool, or any of the other tasks that you perform on your PC. In fact, each of these tasks is software that is made up of thousands of instructions that the CPU executes one at a time to create the actions that you see and use. The CPU, which is also called a microprocessor or processor, is a discrete piece of electronic circuitry that uses digital logic to perform the instructions of your software.

CPUs are housed on the motherboard and exchange data with the motherboard circuitry and memory through buses. Manufacturers use a number of ways to both package the CPU and attach the CPU package to the motherboard. When you upgrade a CPU or select a CPU for a new system, you need to be able to ensure that the CPU is compatible with the motherboard. Many motherboards can accommodate several models of CPUs, and you need to compare CPUs for performance and suitability. Manufacturers often build CPUs suited for certain types of systems: Some CPUs are built for professional servers and workstation PCs; others are built for gaming PCs or home user desktop PCs. Although in most cases, you will choose to upgrade or purchase a motherboard and CPU together, you may occasionally need to replace a failing CPU. Because the CPU itself generates a lot of heat, you need to make sure that it is installed with an appropriate cooling mechanism.

4.1 Examining the CPU

You can easily identify which component inside the computer is the CPU because it is a large square lying flat on the motherboard with a very large heatsink and fan. Or, if the CPU is installed in a slot, it is a large one-half inch thick expansion card with a large heatsink and fan integrated into the package. It is located away from the expansion cards (Figure 4-1).

4.1.1 CPU Packages

When you look at a CPU (Figure 4-2), you see its packaging, not the processor itself. Typically, the CPU's **package** is ceramic or plastic. This outer covering protects it's the processor's **core** (also called the die), which contains the microchip and the wiring that connects the chip to the CPU's mounting pins. The mounting pins, in turn, are attached to the motherboard through a **socket** or **slot**.

Figure 4-1

The location of a CPU in a typical PC.

Prior to 1981, CPUs were found in a rectangle with two rows of 20 pins known as a Dual Inline Package (DIP) (Figure 4-3). There are still integrated circuits that use the DIP form factor. However, the DIP form factor is no longer used for PC CPUs. (A processor form factor is the way the package of the processor is laid out, including how many pins it has, and the

Figure 4-2

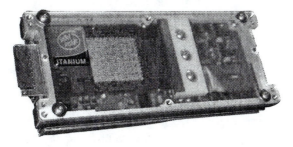

A Pentium Itaniam CPU.

Figure 4-3

 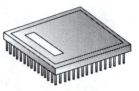

DIP (Dual In-line Package)   PGA (Pin Grid Array)

DIP and PGA packages.

composition and size of the processor itself.) There are a variety of CPU package types, including:

▲ **Pin Grid Array (PGA):** In a **PGA package**, the mounting pins are located on the bottom of the chip in concentric squares. These pins interface with the small wafer of silicon inside the processor package and are inserted into a motherboard socket. PGA packages typically incorporate a metal heat slug or plate on top to help with thermal conductivity. The pins on the bottom of the processor are laid out such that the processor can be inserted only one way (to prevent accidental damage by incorrect installation). The earliest CPUs were packaged in the Ceramic PGA (CPGA). The early Pentium CPUs used a variation that staggered the pin pattern (to cram more pins onto the package) and was called the Staggered PGA (SPGA). Other types of PGA packages include:

• **Plastic PGA (PPGA):** The PPGA package is similar to the PGA package type; however, the pins are staggered a bit differently. The pins are arranged so that the processor can be inserted only one way into its socket.

• **Flip Chip PGA:** In the **Flip Chip-PGA (FC-PGA)** package, the internal processor die in the package is put in with the die toward the top, so an attached heat sink is closer to the part that puts out the heat. This arrangement makes for much more efficient cooling of the processor. As with other PGA types, the pins are arranged so that the processor can go into its socket only one way.

• **Flip-Chip PGA2:** The FC-PGA2 package type is almost identical to the FC-PGA package type, with one important difference: The FC-PGA2 package includes what is known as an Integrated Heat Spreader (IHS). This is a copper or metal plate attached directly to the processor during manufacturing.

• **Organic PGA:** Similar to a CPGA, except that the ceramic is replaced by organic plastic material such as fiberglass.

- **Micro Pin Grid Array (μPGA or microPGA):** Developed by AMD for its newest processors, the **micro-PGA** packages pack more pins into a smaller area. Types of AMD micro PGA include the ceramic micro-PGA.

▲ **Ball Grid Array (BGA):** In a Ball Grid Array, there are no mounting pins projecting from the bottom of the chip; this eliminates the threat of bent pins on the bottom of the processor. Instead of pins, there are solder balls that connect to grips on the motherboard socket. Otherwise, these package styles look similar. Types of BGA include the Plastic Ball Grid Array (PBGA) and the micro BGA.

▲ **Ceramic Column Grid Array (CCGA):** This is similar to a Ball Grid Array, except that round columns, or posts, are used in place of balls.

▲ **Land Grid Array (LGA):** Similar to the PBGA, the Land Grid Array (LGA) uses mounting connections on the motherboard socket as opposed to the CPU's packaging. The Land Grid Array uses gold pads called lands instead of pins. Types of LGA include:

- **Flip-Chip Land Grid Array (FC-LGA):** This is used with some Pentium 4 775-pin CPUs.

- **OLGA on Interposer (OOI):** The OLGA on Interposer (OOI) package type is the type most often found on Pentium 4 processors with 423 pins. OLGA stands for Organic Land Grid Array, which is the way the pins are laid out on this type of package. The OOI package has an Integrated Heat Spreader, similar to FC-PGA2.

▲ **Single Edge Contact Cartridge (SECC):** The **SECC package** is a style of processor package in which the CPU is soldered directly to a small circuit board that has many gold finger contacts. These fingers make a connection with the contacts in a motherboard slot connector. The SECC is covered with a plastic shell to protect the processor and has a metal plate to provide heat dissipation. This cartridge may also have an integrated L2 cache (Figure 4-4).

▲ **SECC2:** The **SECC2 package type** is similar to the SECC package type, but the SECC2 plugs into the Slot 1 connector and does not use the thermal plate. SECC2 was used with later model Pentium II and early model Pentium III processors.

▲ **Single Edge Processor Package (SEPP):** The **SEPP package** is similar to an SECC package, but it does not have the plastic housing covering the circuit board. The early Intel Celeron processors used the SEP package, which has 242 contacts.

▲ **Pin Array Cartridge:** Developed by Intel and used with its Itanium CPUs, the PAC is a cartridge that does not use a slot, but fits into a special socket on the motherboard.

Figure 4-4

SEPP

SECC

A SEPP and a SECC.

4.1.2 CPU Sockets and Slots

The CPU must make physical and electrical contact with the motherboard in order to be used. It does so by using a processor socket or slot. The processor socket serves two purposes: It physically holds the processor in place through the use of clips and/or friction, and it allows the motherboard to electrically connect to the processor.

Processor sockets and slots are primarily differentiated by the number of pins on the processor they connect to (or the number of contacts they make), the physical layout of the socket or slot, and the type of processor they support.

Popular socket types include:

▲ **Socket 7:** A socket type that mounts the 321-pin SPGA of some processors in a Zero Insertion Force (ZIF) socket. A Zero Insertion Force socket is just that—it takes no effort to insert the processor into the socket. The processor drops into place and is held there by the friction of two sliding plates. Super Socket 7 is an extension of the Socket 7 design that is used for the AMD K6 processors and is backwards compatible with Socket 7.

▲ **Socket 8:** A 387-pin SPGA zero-insertion-force (ZIF) socket for the Pentium Pro processor. The pins are arranged in a 24 × 26 matrix that is

Figure 4-5

A Socket 370 mounting.

more rectangular than the Socket 7. Voltages used with the Socket 8 fall in the range of 3.1 to 3.3V.

▲ **Socket 370:** A 370-pin socket designed for the Celeron processor in Plastic Pin Grid Array (PPGA) packaging, but used for several later processors. Its name comes from the number of pins that it supports. (Figure 4-5). For PCs with Slot 1 motherboards to use the (at the time) new Socket 370 processors, a device called a slocket was developed. This is basically a circuit board that plugs into a Slot 1, but it has a socket (typically a Socket 370) on it. This device allows Socket 370-based chips to be plugged into Slot 1 motherboards. During the time the Socket 370 was released, many motherboard manufacturers released motherboards with both a Slot 1 and Socket 370 to satisfy demand for both socket types with a single motherboard. The Socket 370 has been revised several times with slightly different electrical specifications to support newer CPUs.

▲ **Socket 423:** Along with the Socket 478 mounting, this is one of two sockets used for the Pentium 4 processor. According to Intel, the Socket 423 mounting is optimized for Windows XP.

▲ **Socket 478:** Along with the Socket 423, the Socket 478 mounting (Figure 4-6) is one of the two types of sockets used for Pentium 4 processors. The Socket 478 is similar in appearance to the Socket 423, but it supports more pins for extra capabilities.

Figure 4-6

A Socket 478 Pentium 4 mounting.

▲ **Socket A:** Also called Socket 462, this is an American Micro Devices (AMD) 462-pin socket developed for its Athlon and Duron processors.

▲ **Sockets 745, 939, and 940:** Sockets, named for their pin count, developed by AMD for its CPUs.

More recent socket types include:

▲ **Socket T (LGA775):** A 775-pin LGA socket developed for the recent Intel CPUs. The Socket T allows the CPU's heatsink/fan to connect directly to the motherboard.

▲ **Socket AM2:** A 940-pin socket type for the latest AMD CPUs, not compatible with Socket 940 CPUs.

Slot type connections use a single slot mounting on the motherboard that mounts the processor in the same manner that is used for memory modules or expansion cards. The packaging technologies that mount in slot connectors include SEPP and SECC packages.

Types of slots include:

▲ **Slot 1:** Technically called the SC-242 (Slot Connector—242 pins) connector, this is a proprietary Intel connector that is used for Celeron, Pentium II, and Pentium III processors. Until the development of this processor slot, all processors were either directly soldered to the motherboard or used a socket with holes for the pins on the processor. Intel went to this Slot 1 design initially because it allowed for higher bus rates than its predecessor, the Socket 7. However, the large form factor tended to limit airflow and make overheating more of an issue (Figure 4-7). The Slot 1 connector supports SEPP and SECC processors.

▲ **Slot 2:** Technically the SC-330 connector, the Slot 2 connector is an Intel mounting for its Pentium II Xeon and Pentium III Xeon chips. This slot style enhances the capability of multiple processors that are installed in the same PC to work together. The Slot 2 functions similarly to the Slot 1 setup, but has more leads on the connector between the card and the motherboard slot; it also allows the CPU to communicate with the L2 cache at the CPU's full clock speed, thus enhancing performance. Slot 2 is primarily designed for use in high-end workstations and servers.

▲ **Slot A:** AMD Athlon processors use this slot style, which is physically the same as a Slot 1 connector. The Slot A looks the same as a Slot 1, and they are physically the same size, so the two are compatible

Figure 4-7

Slot 1

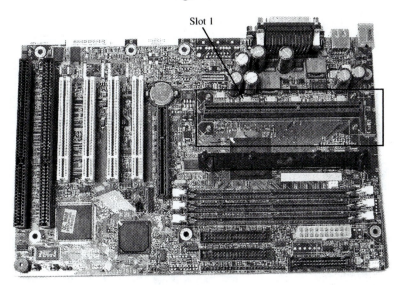

A Slot 1 connector.

Table 4-1: Socket and Slot Supported Package and CPU Types

Socket/Slot Type	Pins	Supported Package Types	Intel/AMD CPU types
Socket 7	321	CPGA	Intel Pentium and Pentium MMX, AMD K5/K6
Socket 8	387	Dual pattern SPGA	Intel Pentium Pro
Socket 370	370 & 418	PPGA, FC-PGA, FC-PGA2	Intel Pentium III and Celeron
Socket 423	423	OLGA/OOI	Intel Pentium 4, Celeron
Socket 478	478	micro-FC-PGA, micro FC-PGA2	Intel Celeron and Pentium 4
Socket A	462	CPGA, OPGA	AMD Duron, Athlon, and Sempron
Socket T	775	FC-LGA	Intel Pentium 4, Celeron D, Pentium D, and Core Duo
Socket 754	754	micro-PGA/BGA	Athlon 64 and Sempron
Socket 939	939	micro-PGA	AMD Athlon 64, 64FX, and Opteron
Socket 940	940	micro-PGA (ceramic)	AMD Athlon 64 FX, and Opteron
Socket AM2	940	CPGA, OPGA	AMD Athlon 64, 64FX, 64 Dual-core, and Sempron
Slot 1	242	SECC/SECC2/SEPP	Pentium II, Pentium III, and Celeron
Slot 2	330	SECC	Pentium II and Pentium III Xeon
Slot A	242	SECC	Athlon

mechanically (the processor from one can fit into the other). However, electronically they are completely different, so they are ultimately incompatible. The Slot A allows for a higher bus rate than a Socket 7 or Super 7 and is used primarily with the AMD K7 processor family.

Table 4-1 summarizes the above information.

4.1.3 Powering the CPU

The first CPUs operated on a single voltage level (originally 5V). Today's CPUs are dual-voltage; they use two levels of power:

▲ **I/O voltage:** The I/O, or external voltage the CPU uses when it communicates with motherboard components. This is typically 3.3V today.

▲ **Core voltage:** The core, or internal voltage level used by the micro-components of the processor. The internal voltage number is important; because the higher the voltage, the more heat the processor generates.

A **voltage regulator module (VRM)** is a small device on the motherboard that provides the CPU with its core voltage. For example, if a processor requires 1.5V, the VRM steps down the voltage so the processor has the correct voltage. On some motherboards the VRM is a replaceable module and on others the VRM is built in to the motherboard itself. Typically, the VRM is located very near the processor mounting slot or socket.

The VRM has two main functions:

▲ To protect the processor from spikes or other electrical events coming from the power supply
▲ To ensure that a steady flow of power is fed to the processor

Some VRMs are voltage ID (VID) programmable. This means that on power up, the CPU tells the VRM what voltage it needs, and the VRM supplies that voltage.

4.1.4 Cooling the CPU

At temperatures above its normal operating temperature, a processor begins to perform poorly, shuts down, or becomes permanently damaged. The form factor for the case, motherboard, and power supply that supports a particular processor is designed to provide cooling to keep the processor at or near its optimal operating temperature. Case fans and power supply fans contribute to cooling, but processors operate at high temperatures and need additional cooling. For example, the Pentium III processor operates at 100 degrees Celsius (about 212 degrees Fahrenheit, the boiling point of water).

Early microprocessors were cooled primarily by the airflow inside the case that was created by a system fan in the power supply. This process was called radiant cooling. Any heat that was radiated by the processor was cooled by air being sucked by the fan into the system case.

There are two main CPU cooling methods today:

▲ **Air cooling:** The most popular type of CPU cooling is the air-cooled method. Air-cooled processors use a large block of copper or aluminum, called a **heatsink**, that is shaped into fins or fingers (it looks a little like a bed of nails). A small fan is usually mounted on top of the heatsink to provide the moving air to cool them (Figure 4-8).
▲ **Liquid cooling:** Liquid cooling involves the use of a smaller block of aluminum (called a **water block**) mounted to the processor. Instead

Figure 4-8

Processor heatsink and fan.

of fins, the block has two small connectors for a water inlet and outlet. These are connected to a small pump and a radiator. Cool water is
pumped into the water block. It flows through a series of back-and-forth
channels where it absorbs heat from the processor. The heated water
travels to a radiator where it is cooled by air blown over the fins of the
radiator. The cooled water then returns to the pump and is ready to do
it again. Most liquid cooling systems use ordinary water; some use other
liquids such as nitrogen.

FOR EXAMPLE

Checking the Temperature

Some motherboards have thermal sensors that report on the temperatures
inside the case or near components like the CPU. Motherboards with built-
in thermal sensors report current temperatures in the CMOS settings. However, the CMOS settings are accessed during startup, so the temperatures at
this point may not reflect how hot your CPU gets. There are software utilities that you can download or purchase that you can use to monitor temperatures while the PC is running. You can also purchase circuit boards that
monitor internal temperature and will shut the computer off if it reaches
high temperatures. For critical network servers, heat sensors can potentially
save a lot of money in repair costs.

The newest PC form factor, BTX, was designed by Intel to improve airflow and cooling. A BTX motherboard is designed for the CPU to be housed in a thermal module that includes a large heatsink and fan. Some new CPUs are designed with a **throttling** feature that slows the CPU when it reaches a certain temperature and turn the PC off if the CPU's heat gets high enough to cause damage.

SELF-CHECK

1. How is the CPU connected to the motherboard?
2. What is the difference between an SEPP and an SECC?
3. What voltage levels do CPUs use?
4. What is a heatsink?

4.2 CPU Features and Technologies

Technically speaking, a CPU is an integrated circuit that contains millions of transistors interconnected by small aluminum wires. The CPU's processing capabilities control and direct the activities of the PC by interacting with the other electronic components on the motherboard, such as the main memory, bus structures, cache memory, and device interfaces. Although CPUs today share some of the same basic technical operations with the earliest CPUs, CPU technologies have vastly improved over the last decade. When comparing and selecting CPUs, you need to understand some of the modern technologies used with today's processors.

4.2.1 CPU Basic Operations

The role of the CPU is to control and direct all the activities of the computer using both external and internal buses. The CPU is a processor chip consisting of an array of millions of **transistors**, semi-conductor devices that at their most basic level act as switches for electronic signals. Essentially, through vast combinations of switches turning on and off, and sending intricate routines of 1s and 0s, the CPU is able to perform complex calculations and operations on data.

The CPU's function is to take and process instructions. An example of a simple instruction is adding two numbers in a calculator program. Instructions, whether originating from software or an input/output device, are loaded into RAM and then sent over the system bus to the CPU.

Components of a CPU include:

▲ **The control unit:** The CPU circuitry that coordinates the rest of the CPU's actions and interactions

▲ **The arithmetic logic unit (ALU):** The CPU circuitry that performs generic logical and mathematical operations

▲ **The registers:** Temporary storage areas for data with which the CPU is working

There are four basic steps that the CPU performs for each instruction. The steps are kind of an assembly line that is called the **pipeline**.

1. **Fetch:** The control unit fetches an instruction stored in memory, either from RAM or memory located within the CPU
2. **Decode:** The control unit determines what type of instruction it is
3. **Execute:** The ALU performs operations (such as adding and subtracting numbers, or comparing two values) as per the instructions
4. **Writeback:** The ALU writes the results of the executed step to memory

4.2.2 CPU Features

The speed and efficiency the CPU performs its operations depends on several factors. Properties and features used to rate and compare CPUs include:

▲ **CPU speed:** The CPU's speed is the frequency at which it executes instructions. This frequency is measured in millions of cycles per second, or megahertz (MHz); or billions of cycles per second, or gigahertz (GHz).The CPU has an internal and an external speed. The external speed corresponds with the motherboard's speed, based on its system crystal. The system crystal pulses, and these pulses are used to time and coordinate operations on the motherboard. Each pulse is called a **clock tick**. A CPU's speed as described in its specifications is its internal speed. The CPU has traditionally communicated with the motherboard and the rest of the PC through the chipset's Northbridge over the **frontside bus (FSB)**. This bus is also called the system or external bus. This bus runs at the speed of the external clock and influences how fast the PC runs as a whole. The CPU runs internally at a faster speed than the frontside bus (and the external clock). The **clock multiplier** is the number used to define the working speed of the processor relative to the speed of the frontside bus. For example, if the frontside bus was 166 MHz and the clock multiplier was set to 12.5, the CPU would be running at 2075 MHz internally. Today, some CPU designs are moving away from using the frontside bus as the CPU's main communication line and developing faster buses that link components directly to each other so they can take advantage of increasing CPU speeds.

▲ **Word size:** Data is operated on in groups of bits called words. The **word size** (or number of bits of data) that a single CPU register can store determines the amount of bits the CPU can operate on at one time. A 32-bit register can store a 32-bit word. The larger the word size, the faster the CPU can operate on complex data. A CPU with a 32-bit word size is said to have a 32-bit architecture. Older CPUs worked with a 16-bit word-size, and most CPUs today have either a 32-bit word size or 64-bit word size.

▲ **Data path:** Data is transferred to the CPU at a specified rate that is determined by its data path: The **data path** refers to how much data can be transferred during a single operation to the CPU. The width of the CPU's data path is defined by the bus that feeds the CPU. A 64-bit frontside bus will transfer 64 bits at a time to the CPU. The data path does not need to be the same size as the word size. A CPU with a 32-bit word size and a 64-bit frontside bus will be able to fill two registers at a time with each 64 bits of data input.

▲ **Maximum addressable memory:** In addition to the data buses that feed the CPU, the CPU also works with address buses. The **address buses** carry information from the main memory that tells the CPU where the data is stored. For the most part, the width of the address bus defines how many memory addresses the CPU can work with. As an analogy, you can compare the address bus to the address of a house. If the house numbers for a street were limited to two digits, the street could have only 100 addresses (00 to 99). For an address bus that communicates in binary language, a limit of two digits would give four addresses (00, 01, 10, and 11). Thus, the larger the address bus, the more combinations of 0 and 1 are permitted to pass through at one time. A CPU with a 24-bit address bus can access as much as 16MB of RAM, and a CPU with a 32-bit address bus allows access to up to 4GB of RAM. CPUs are designed to work with maximum amounts of system memory.

▲ **Cache memory:** The CPU stores frequently used data and instructions in cache memory. Cache memory is a small amount of RAM separate from system memory that is fast enough to keep up with the processor. The processor contains an internal cache controller that integrates the cache with the CPU. The controller stores frequently accessed RAM locations to provide faster execution of data and instructions. Levels of CPU cache memory include:

• **L1 cache:** This cache is built directly into the CPU.

• **L2 cache:** Originally built into the motherboard, L2 cache is now frequently found built into the CPU or its packaging (Figure 4-9). It is connected to the CPU via a bus called the **backside bus.**

• **L3 cache:** L3 cache is usually located external to the CPU on the motherboard although it may be built into the CPU packaging.

Figure 4-9

In 80486 and older Pentium I PCs, the Level 2 cache was often a set of socketed (removable) chips mounted on the motherboard

The AMD Duron (950 MHz, socket A form factor) has its L2 cache mounted directly on the CPU die

L2 cache.

L1 cache is the fastest, smallest, most frequently accessed, and most expensive type of cache memory. The CPU looks for stored data first in the L1 cache, and then in the L2 cache (and then in any L3 cache).

▲ **Instruction set:** CPUs include a hardwired set of low-level instructions called **instruction sets** that define the complex executions the CPU can perform. Software programmers use the instruction sets in programming software. Types of instruction sets, or Instruction Set Architectures (ISAs) include:

- **CISC (Complex Instruction Set Computing):** A traditional instruction set that had a large number of instructions. The more instructions an instruction set has for a programmer to use, the fewer complex instructions are needed in the software. However, more complicated instruction sets tend to slow the CPU.
- **RISC (Reduced Instruction Set Computing):** RISC decreased the number of instructions to include only the most common instructions to speed up the CPUs operations.
- **VLIW (Very Long Instruction Word):** A superscalar instruction set designed for parallel execution of instructions at the software level. This is in contrast to superscalar CPUs that use hardware such as two or more ALUs to execute multiple instructions at the same time.

Modern processors work with instruction sets and extensions that are a combination of the CISC and RISC types, including:

- **x86:** A 16-bit CISC-based ISA used with (and named for) the earliest Intel CPUs
- **IA-32:** Also called i386 or x86-32, this is basically a 32-bit version of the x86 ISA
- **IA-64:** A 64-bit ISA based on VLIW principles
- **AMD64:** Also called x86-64 or x64, this is a 64-bit version of the x86 ISA designed by AMD
- **EM64T (Extended Memory 64 Technology):** Intel's version of AMD64
- **MMX (MultiMedia Extension):** Designed by Intel to handle complex multimedia functions
- **SIMD (Single Instruction Multiple Data):** Designed by AMD to improve on the complex calculations needed for three-dimensional graphics
- **SSE (Streaming SIMD Extension):** An improvement upon SIMD and 3D graphics processing. SSE2, SSE3, and SSE4 are further improvements

▲ **Microcode efficiency:** CPUs contain **microcode**, or microprograms, that are designed to operate on the instruction sets. Two CPUs that use the same instruction set may have different microcode that operates more or less efficiently than the other. Extensions of instruction sets, such as the MMX instruction set, will have accompanying microcode to manipulate the instructions. Microcode may be stored in RAM or ROM chips within the CPU.

▲ **Transistors and process:** CPUs can be compared by the number of transistors they are made with. The number of transistors used has dramatically increased (from 3.3 million in the first Pentium in 1993 to over 300 million in recent Pentium D CPUs) by using ever smaller transistors

---

FOR EXAMPLE

CPU Speed and the Frontside Bus

Compare two hypothetical CPUs: The Brainium and the Fanthalon. The Brainium is offered at 1600, 1800 and 2000 MHz speeds, all with a frontside bus speed of 133 MHz; the Fantathlon is offered at 1400, 1600 and 2200 MHz speeds with a 166 MHz frontside bus. Which is faster? With all other things being equal (your system and any other CPU technologies) you don't have to do any complicated speed-benching or calculations. All of the Brainium CPUs will communicate to your PC at 133 MHz, and all of the Fantathlon CPUs will communicate at 166 MHz. For most ordinary computing needs, the differences between these CPU speeds will matter little: the frontside bus speed is key in passing information back and forth from the CPU, and the slowest of these Fanthalons will be faster than the speediest Brainium.

---

and circuits. CPUs today are often compared by the size of the transistors, measured in nanometers. A nanometer is one billionth of a meter. A CPU with transistors 90 nm wide may be described as built with a 90-nm **process**. A CPU's process may also be described in terms of microns, thousandths of meters.

4.2.3 CPU Technologies

Because the CPU ultimately defines everything you can do with a computer, and because its speed is a major factor in the speed of a PC, manufacturers are continuously working on new technologies to help improve speed and performance. Some of these techniques include:

▲ **Pipeline management:** In a simple, traditional four-step pipeline, each step is completed within one clock tick, meaning that the entire process needs four ticks to complete and start again on another instruction. To speed up this process, CPU manufacturers employ a number of techniques. For example, CPUs today incorporate a Floating Point Unit to handle calculations on very long numbers that would slow down the ALU. Other techniques to help increase the pipeline speed and efficiency include:

• **Superscalar architecture:** In **superscalar** architecture, the CPU has hardware features that allow it to process more than one instruction at a time. For example, a CPU might have two or more ALUs. A CPU with two ALUs can execute two mathematical operations at the same time.

- **Pipelining:** In a process called **pipelining**, the CPU operates with two or more pipelines. As one fetched instruction is sent to the next decoding step, another instruction can be fetched and worked on. The four steps of the pipeline are often further broken down into smaller steps, allowing more instructions to be staggered and worked on at the same time.

▲ **Multithreading:** A standard processor can operate on one set of software instructions (called a thread), at a time. Even though a user may have several programs open at the same time and be working on several different documents, the processor simply multitasks, switching between threads too quickly to notice. In multithreading, the CPU is designed to work on two or more sets of software instructions at the same time. CPU manufacturers have developed several multithreading technologies, including superthreading and hyperthreading, which use different techniques for handling the threads. From a users' perspective, a CPU that can work with two threads allows a single CPU to perform as if it were two CPUs.

▲ **Multicore Processors: Multicore** processors have two or more CPUs housed in a single die. A dual-core processor has two CPUs, and a quad-core processor has four CPUs. A dual-core processor is theoretically twice as fast as a single-core processor. However, to harness this speed, application software must be programmed to work with multiple processors.

▲ **64-bit processing:** The latest high-performance CPUs are built with a 64-bit architecture or word-size. This means that these CPUs are able to operate at twice the speed of a 32-bit CPU. However, software applications (including operating systems) are programmed for specific word-sizes: for instance, 32-bit software will not run on a PC with a 16-bit architecture. Although most 64-bit processors are designed to run older software by using special compatibility modes, the full benefits of having a 64-bit CPU aren't realized without using 64-bit software. There is some 64-bit software available, and Microsoft has released a 64-bit version of Windows XP, but there is still relatively little consumer software designed for 64-bit systems. Nevertheless, the latest 64-bit CPUs are also designed with new technologies that improve the speed of older software.

▲ **Bus technologies:** Because the frontside bus determines how much data the CPU can receive at a time, the speed of this bus essentially determines the overall speed of the system. As CPU speeds increase, especially with the use of multithreading and multi-core CPUs, manufacturers are moving away from using the frontside bus and incorporating point-to-point buses that link the CPU directly to separate components.

SELF-CHECK

1. What are the four basic steps that a CPU performs?
2. What is an instruction set?
3. What is multithreading?
4. Explain the difference among L1, L2, and L3 cache.

4.3 CPU Manufacturers

Many different manufacturers make CPUs for PCs. The market leaders in the manufacture of chips are Intel Corporation and Advanced Micro Devices (AMD). Other chip manufacturers whose CPUs you may come across when working on PCs are: Via, Transmeta, NexGen (later purchased by AMD), and Cyrix (later bought by Via). However, Intel processors still make up over half of the IBM-compatible personal computer processor market.

4.3.1 Early Intel Processors

When the first PC was introduced, IBM decided to go to the chip manufacturer Intel for a CPU. Since then, Intel has been the CPU supplier for almost all IBM-compatible computers. Early Intel CPUs manufactured before the mid-90s include:

▲ **808x series:** The Intel family of PC processors started in the late 1970s with the 8088. The 8088 was rectangular, using a DIP array of its 40 pins (Figure 4-10). It originally ran at 4.77MHz with 29,000 transistors. It was used primarily in the IBM PC. Next to be released was the 8086 (it was actually developed before the 8088), which had a 16-bit external data bus; however, the processor used an 8-bit bus for compatibility with older systems.

▲ **80x86 series:** After the 808x series, in the 1980s came the 80x86 series, otherwise known simply as Intel's x86 series. It included the following CPUs:

• **80286:** The 80286 was the first to implement the Pin Grid Array (PGA).

• **80386/80386DX:** This was the first Intel x86 processor to use both a 32-bit data bus and a 32-bit address bus. Overall, the 386 ranged in speed from 16MHz to 33MHz, supported multitasking, and was significantly faster than the 286. 80386SX was a version of the 80386DX with a 24-bit data path.

• **80486:** With the 486 chip family, Intel introduced a technology known as **clock doubling**. It worked by allowing a chip to run at the

Figure 4-10

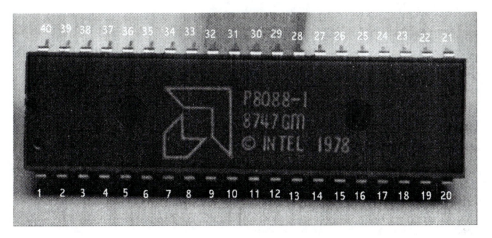

Intel 8088 CPU.

bus's rated speed externally, but running the processor's internal clock at twice the speed of the bus. For example, Intel designed a chip that ran at 33MHz externally and 66MHz internally. This chip was known as the 486DX2. Not long after, clock tripling was used, and so on. Today, the term clock multiplier is used to specify the difference between the speeds of internal and external speeds.

▲ **The Pentium Family:** Also called the P5 line of chips, the Pentium, introduced in the 1990s and was offered in speeds from 60 to 166 MHz. A newer version, the MMX, had speeds up to 266 MHz. The Pentium chip was basically a combination of two 486DX chips in one larger chip. The benefit to the two-chips-in-one architecture was that each chip could execute instructions independently of the other. This was a form of parallel processing that Intel called superscalar. Pentiums required special motherboards, because they run significantly hotter than previous processors. They also required the use of a heatsink on top of the processor to absorb and ventilate the heat. (The designers said the processor typically generates heat to the tune of 185° Fahrenheit!) The Pentium features included:

- 64-bit data path and 32-bit address path
- 32-bit multitasking using RISC (Reduced Instruction Set Computer) design techniques
- A superscalar architecture that executes two instructions in the same clock cycle
- Expanded the data bus to 64 bits and included high-speed internal cache

4.3.2 Modern Intel Processors

The Intel CPUs you are most likely to see in computers today are:

▲ **The Pentium Pro Family:** Beginning with the Pentium Pro in 1995, the Pentium Pro (or P6) family of CPUs were a series of fairly large processors with greater memory than previous familes. Characteristics of the P6 line include:

- Superpipelining: using up to 14 stages in the pipeline
- Built-in L2 cache
- Dynamic execution: Instead of processing instructions in a strictly sequential, first-come, first-served method, dynamic execution analyzes and predicts what instructions will follow current instructions and performs instructions out of sequence. This allows for more efficient management of the pipeline.

P6 chips include:

- **The Pentium Pro:** The Pentium Pro was developed as a network server processor. It is specially designed to support 32-bit network operating systems, such as Windows NT, and to be used in configurations of one, two, or four processors, with 1 megabyte of advanced Level 2 (L2) cache.

- **Pentium II:** The Pentium II is the Pentium Pro processor with MMX technology added. The P-II, as it is commonly referred to, is excellent for multimedia work that requires support for full-motion video and 3D images. The most unique thing about the Pentium II, compared to earlier Intel processors, is that it uses an SECC package type to attach to the motherboard instead of the standard PGA package used with the earlier processor types. The processor is a card that can easily be replaced—you simply shut off the computer, pull out the old processor card, and insert a new one. The Pentium II is designed to be used by itself in a computer. For multiprocessor servers and workstations, Intel also released a separate processor, the Pentium II Xeon, based on the same Pentium II circuitry. Generally speaking, multiprocessor Pentium II servers with between four and eight processors use the Pentium II Xeon.

- **Celeron:** Developed for use in desktop and portable computers, the first Celerons were a low-cost version of the Pentium II processor.

- **Pentium III:** The Pentium III was released in 1999 and uses the same SECC connector as its predecessor, the Pentium II. At the time, the Pentium III was the highest-powered processor in the Intel arsenal. It features 9.5 million transistors, a 32K L1 cache, 512K of L2 cache, and clock speeds of 450 MHz to 1 GHz. It included 70 new instructions and was optimized for voice recognition and multimedia. Aside from faster speeds, one of the more significant features of the Pentium III is the processor serial number (PSN), a unique number electronically encoded into the processor. This number can be used to uniquely identify a system during Internet transactions. Some Pentium IIIs and all Pentium 4s have gone back to the PGA package. Similar to the Pentium II, the Pentium III has a multiprocessor Xeon version.

- **Xeon:** The Xeon processors, both Pentium II and Pentium III, are successors to the Pentium Pro processors. The Xeon is a network server processor that is capable of addressing and caching up to 64GB of memory with its 36-bit memory address bus. Xeon processors can be configured with four to eight CPUs in one server. More recent versions of this workstation/server CPU include the 32-bit and 64-bit Xeon MPs (for multiple processing) and Dual Core Xeons.

▲ **Pentium 4 and NetBurst Based CPUs:** Using the first totally new processor design since the Pentium Pro, the Pentium 4 (P4) processor has clock speeds that exceed 2 GHz, about twice the speed of the Pentium III. It uses an Intel technology called NetBurst microarchitecture, which features:

- Hyperpipelining: In Hyperpipelining, the pipeline was increased to up to 31 stages.
- Rapid Execution Engine: In this technology, the CPU's ALUS operate at twice the speed of the CPU.

Other Intel NetBurst CPUs include Pentium D, and newer versions of the Celeron and Xeon CPUs. Newer versions of the Celeron are also based on Pentium designs but have (depending on the version) more limited performance power than their Pentium equivalents and are marketed as lower-end or budget CPUs.

▲ **Itanium and Itanium 2:** The Itanium was Intel's first 64-bit processor. The Itanium is designed to work with 64-bit software and multiple operating system platforms, and on higher performing workstations and servers. The Itanium was designed for scalability: It can scale to 512 processors. The Itanium 2 has a similar design but has higher CPU speeds, bus speeds, and more cache memory.

▲ **Intel Core:** Intel's latest CPU architecture is called Intel Core Microarchitecture. Key design concepts include multi-core processors and lower power consumption. The next iteration is called Core 2 and features 64-bit processing support.

Table 4-2 provides a summary of the history of the Pentium and higher Intel processors. Table 4-3 shows the physical characteristics of Pentium processors.

Table 4-2: History of Intel Processors

Chip	Year Added	Data Bus	Address Bus	Speed	Transistors	Other Specifications
Pentium	1993	64	32	60–200	3.3 million	Superscalar
Pentium Pro	1995	64	32	150–200	5.5 million	Dynamic execution
Pentium II	1997	64	36	233–450	7.5 million	32KB of L1 cache, dynamic execution, and MMX technology
Pentium II Xeon	1998	64	36	400–600	7.5 million	Multiprocessor version of Pentium II
Celeron	1999	64	36	400–600	7.5 million	Value version of Pentium II
Pentium III	1999	64	36	350–1000	9.5–28 million	SECC2 package
Pentium III Xeon	1999	64	36	350–1000	9.5–28 million	Multiprocessor version of Pentium III
Pentium 4	2002	64	36	1200–3100	42 million	20KB L1, 256–512KB L2 on chip
Itanium	2001	64	64	1000–1600	25 million	64-bit instruction set
Itanium 2	2002	128	64	1200–2330	220 million	Upgraded version of the Itanium
Pentium D	2005	64	36	2666–3733	230–376 million	First Intel multicore desktop CPU
Intel Core Solo	2006	64	36	800–1200	151 million	First CPU with Intel's Core micro-architecture
Intel Core Duo	2006	64	36		151 million	Low-power dual core CPU

Table 4-3: Physical Characteristics of Pentium-Class Processors

Processor	Speed (in MHz)	Socket	Pins	Voltage	L1 Cache
Pentium-P5	60–66	4	273	5V	16KB
Pentium-P54C	75–200	5 or 7	320 or 321	3.3V	16KB
Pentium-P55C	166–333	7	321	3.3V	32KB
Pentium Pro	150–200	8	387	2.5V	32KB
Pentium II	233–450	SECC	N/A	3.3V	32KB
Pentium III	450–1130	SECCII or 370	N/A	3.3V	32KB
Pentium 4	1300–3400+	423, 478	423 or 478	1.3–1.7	20KB
Pentium D	2666–3733	FC-LGA	775 lands	1.25–1.4	2×16K

4.3.3 AMD Processors

Advanced Micro Devices (AMD) has made a very profitable business out of being Intel's main competitor in the PC CPU market. Generally speaking, AMD's CPUs are roughly comparable in speed to Intel's chips. However, they end up being about 10 percent cheaper on average. Many individuals who build their own systems love AMD's chips because they seem to have a better "bang for the buck" factor. Table 2-7 lists some of the processors made by AMD.

Earlier, popular AMD CPUs include:

▲ **K5/K6:** The K5 and K6 CPUs were AMD's 64-bit competitor to Intel's Pentium (P5) CPU competitor. They offered twice as many instruction pipelines as the P5.

▲ **Athlon (K7):** The Athlon was similar to the Pentium II and Pentium III in Intel's P6 line, but used a newly designed core and a 200 MHz frontside bus.

▲ **Athlon XP:** AMD designed the Athlon XP (Figure 4-11) to work with Windows XP using a "QuantiSpeed" architecture, allowing the CPU to process more work per clock cycle.

▲ **Duron:** AMD's Duron processor was designed to compete with Intel's Celeron CPU and give better performance. This made the Duron a popular budget CPU.

AMD's current CPUs include:

▲ **Sempron:** The Sempron is a newer, budget-minded chip from AMD designed to compete with Intel's Celeron "D" processors and has speeds ranging from 1.5–2.0GHz.

Figure 4-11

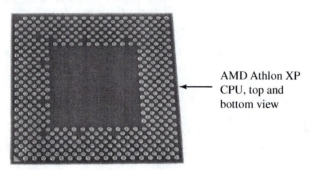

AMD Athlon XP CPU, top and bottom view

Athlon XP CPU.

▲ **Opteron:** The Opteron is a 64-bit CPU designed for use with servers and to compete with Intel's Itanium.

▲ **Athlon 64:** Athlon's latest 64-bit CPU architecture features support for a new bus technology called HyperTransport used to connect the motherboard circuits. In addition to the Athlon 64, AMD offers an Athlon 64

FOR EXAMPLE

Advertised Speed and Real Speed

Two CPUs from different manufacturers that have the same speed and frontside bus speed (say, 2 GHz and 200 MHz frontside bus) may have very different performance levels, depending on the technologies they incorporate in the chip. For this reason, CPU manufacturers often market their CPUs with a performance rating (PR) speed that's intended to reflect actual performance. AMD started this practice in the 1990s because many of their CPUs outperformed Intel's CPUs of the same speed. The original AMD PR system would give a CPU a PR speed of the Intel CPU that it matched in terms of overall performance. Benchmarking tests essentially backed up AMD's PR system. However, Intel has recently introduced its own PR system. The lack of any hard and fast standards and the diversity of CPU technologies have made the PR systems used today somewhat murkier. In general, they tell you what CPU "speed class" the CPU manufacturer thinks their CPU belongs to. And in reality, you may come across a customer who wants to know why their 3 GHz CPU is shown in their CMOS settings as being a 1.8 GHz chip. Assuming that the CPU settings in the CMOS are correct, the PR system is a likely culprit.

Table 4-4: AMD Processors and Their Intel Equivalents

Chip	Socket	Speed (in MHz)	Transistors	Intel Equivalent
K6	7	166–300	8.8 million	Pentium MMX–Pentium II
K6-II	7/Super 7	266–550	9.3 million	Pentium II
K6-III	Super 7	400–600	21.3 million	Pentium II
Athlon Classic	Slot A	500–1000	22 million	Pentium III
Athlon Thunderbird	Socket A	650–1400	37 million	Pentium III
Athlon XP Palomino	Socket A	1333–1733	37.5 million	Pentium III–4
Athlon XP Thoroughbred	Socket A	1467–2250	37.2–37.6 million	Pentium 4
Duron	Socket A	600–1300	25 million	Celeron
Sempron	754, AM2	1500–2000	37–69 million	Celeron
Opteron	939, 940	1600–2800	106	Xeon MP
Athlon 64	754, 939, AM2	1800–2400	68.5–154 million	Pentium D
Athlon 64 FX	939,940, AM2	2200–2800	105–233 million	Pentium 4 (Extreme Edition)
Athlon 64 X2	AM2, 939	2000–2600	150–233 million	Pentium D

FX designed for high-performance multimedia and gaming and the Athlon 64 Dual Core X2, a dual-core version of the Athlon 64.

Table 4-4 provides a summary of the history of AMD Processors and their Intel equivalents.

SELF-CHECK

1. What are three features of the Pentium P5 family of chips?
2. What are three Intel CPUs that use the NetBurst architecture?
3. What is clock-doubling?
4. What types of Athlon CPUs does AMD make?

4.4 Working with CPUs

Because the CPU is a major component of a PC's performance and speed, selecting one will often be your main consideration when building, customizing, or upgrading a PC. You will also need to be able to replace a faulty CPU, make sure it is cooled properly, and recognize what symptoms a faulty or overheating CPU shows.

4.4.1 Upgrading the CPU

Occasionally, there may come a time when you need to upgrade your computer's CPU. You may want top performance, or you may need to upgrade an entire system. Generally speaking, you can't just remove your old processor and replace it with a different one. As processor architectures change, so do motherboard architectures, and the new CPU will need to have the proper amount and type of supporting circuitry. You must use a processor that matches the socket type and chipset speed. If it is slower, it may overheat and fail; if it is faster, it will only be able to run at the rate of the external clock (multiplied by its clock multiplier.)

So, if you want to upgrade from a 1.8GHz Pentium 4 to a 1.9GHz Pentium 4, chances are good that it will work with no problems. However, if you want to upgrade from an AMD Athlon Thunderbird to a Pentium 4, you will have to replace the motherboard (and possibly the RAM as well) in order to make the upgrade successful—the Thunderbird and the Pentium 4 use completely different architectures and require different motherboards and supporting circuitry.

The CPU is arguably the most important component of the PC, and selecting a new CPU should be done with care. Whether you are selecting a CPU for a new or existing computer, you will want to take into account:

▲ **The general purpose of the computer:** The same features you might want in a CPU for a gaming system, such as the latest 3D graphics support, will be different from the features you need for a database server.

▲ **Motherboard compatibility:** The CPU that can be used to upgrade the PC depends on the motherboard, its form factor, and its chipset. One CPU may work with an existing motherboard and socket, another CPU may need to be installed with a new compatible motherboard and RAM. The manufacturer of your motherboard should have documentation on their website that lists what CPUs each motherboard is compatible with. When you are building a new PC, you will need to make sure these components are all compatible.

When you have determined the features you need from the CPU and any form factor restrictions you may have, you can compare appropriate CPUs by their speed and cache memory. You will also want to investigate the technologies the CPU uses, such as multithreading, multicore, and thermal throttling. It is a good idea to research peer, interest group, and industry reviews of the CPU.

A main factor to consider of course is your budget. In general desktop CPUs fall into three categories, based on price and performance:

▲ Low-end processors (such as the Celeron and entry-level AMD Athlons) provide decent performance at a minimal price and can be used for basic computing.

▲ Mid-level processors (such as the slower Pentium 4 and AMD Athlon XP) provide a good balance of speed without costing a lot. Most processors for home computers come from this range.

▲ The high-end processors (such as the newest Pentium 4 and AMD Athlon XP) are the highest performance processors, but you must be prepared to pay a premium for their speed. Most gamers and graphics professionals use these processors in their computers.

To upgrade a processor, you simply need to remove the old CPU and heatsink and replace them with the new processor and heatsink. A new heatsink isn't absolutely necessary, but your new, faster processor will put out more heat than the one being replaced, so it's a good idea to upgrade them both at the same time.

4.4.2 Installing a CPU

Before installing a CPU, make sure that the processor and the motherboard are compatible. Review the CPU documentation to see what type of packaging it

FOR EXAMPLE

Identifying Your CPU

The surest way to determine which CPU your computer is using is to open the case and view the numbers stamped on the CPU. However, you may be able to get an idea without opening the case because many manufacturers indicate the type of processor by using a model number that contains some combination of numbers for the processor type and speed. For example, a Whizbang 466 could be a 486 DX 66MHz computer. Similarly, a 75MHz Pentium computer might be labeled Whizbang 575.

Another way to determine a computer's CPU is to save your work, exit any open programs, and restart the computer. Watch closely as the computer returns to its normal state. You should see a notation that tells you what chip the computer is using.

has. The pins on the back of the processor packaging are locked into place by the locking mechanism on the socket. The two most common types of locking mechanisms used on sockets are the zero-insertion-force (ZIF) and the low-insertion-force (LIF) mechanisms. In these two mechanisms, there is little difference between the force that's required to insert the processor in the socket; the LIF just requires slightly more force to seat the processor than the ZIF.

To prepare for a CPU installation, make sure the computer is powered off and you are working with an antistatic wrist strap.

Most processors will come with instructions for installing the CPU on the motherboard. To install a socket-mounted CPU:

1. **Locate the processor socket.** The socket is a large plastic square with a square hole in the middle, it's usually white or light brown, and it's surrounded by lots of small pinholes.

2. **Release the locking arm.** The locking arm on the left side of the socket is tucked up under a locking lip. When the arm is pushed down slightly, it releases and can be raised into an unlocked position. Or, you may have to push the lever gently to one side to release it from its locking tabs (Figure 4-12).

3. **Remove the CPU from its packaging and determine which way it should be inserted.** After you have opened the socket, remove the processor from its packaging. Be very careful not to bend any pins on the processor. In fact, don't even touch the pins because you may damage them. They are almost impossible to straighten properly, and if they're bent or damaged, the processor may not fit properly into the socket.

Figure 4-12

The locking arm on a CPU socket.

Figure 4-13

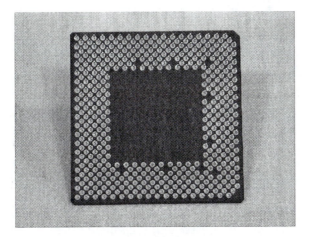

CPU pin alignment.

4. **Determine how the CPU aligns with the socket.** The processor has two sides: the side with many small pins and the top side. On the top side, notice that there is a small dot. Also notice that on the pin side, the pins are arranged in a square with two corners cut off. These cut-off corners match up with a similar pattern in the socket (Figure 4-13). There may be other locating features that help you align the processor with the socket.

5. **Insert the CPU.** At this point, the processor can be inserted into the socket. Above all, do not force the insertion of the processor. You will break something.

6. **Lower the locking arm.** After the processor is in place, lower the locking arm and tuck it back under its locking lip. The processor should be locked into place and ready to process!

Note that after a CPU is installed, you will need to install a cooling mechanism. Never operate the computer without a heatsink or other cooling mechanism installed. You can permanently damage the processor in a manner of seconds.

The heatsink and fan are typically one unit and are installed together. Heatsinks, fans, and water blocks are attached to the CPU by:

▲ Mounting points on the processor

▲ **Thermal interface material (TIM):** A special compound that comes in two styles:

• **Thermal grease**, a dielectric gel that comes in tubes. This is the most popular method.

- **Thermal contact patch,** which looks like double-sided tape stuck to the heatsink. Some processors may come with a thermal contact patch already on the heatsink.

Installing a heatsink and fan can be a complex process. Improper attachment of the heatsink can damage the processor. The general steps for installing a heatsink/fan follow: (If you have a water block, instead of a heatsink and fan, the procedures are similar—you just won't have a fan. Instead, you'll have a water reservoir, a pump, hoses, and a radiator that must be installed.)

1. **Apply thermal grease or a thermal contact patch to the processor.**
   The thermal compound works by eliminating the very small air gaps that occur between the processor and heatsink due to the uneven metal surface of the heatsink, thus creating the largest possible surface area for the greatest heat transfer efficiency. You apply the thermal compound on the processor die (the small chip in the center of the big CPU chip package) or use the thermal contact patch that comes with the heatsink, if it has one. (Don't use both—if the heatsink has a thermal contact patch, just use that and no thermal grease.) When you apply thermal grease, you need to be careful about the amount you spread: It should be an amount equal to about one-half grain to one full grain of rice onto the processor die. The amount of compound is critical. Too much, or too little, and you won't get good heat transfer. There should be just enough to cover the die with a very thin layer of material.

2. **Position the heatsink over the processor socket.** If necessary, reorient the heatsink until its flat smooth bottom fully covers the CPU's surface and the clips on the metal bank running through the heat sink are in position over the corresponding tabs in the socket.

3. **Permanently fasten the heatsink to the processor socket with a spring-loaded clamp.** This step requires very accurate positioning of the heatsink and careful handling of the clamp to ensure no damage is done to the CPU or its housing.

4. **Connect the heatsink's fan wires to the motherboard:** Most motherboards today have a special connector known as the CPU_FAN connector (Figure 4-14). This connector powers the fan for the CPU and also monitors its speed. The connector is usually what is known as a three-pin fan connector. PC fans can use either two or three wires. The first two wires are for power and ground, and the third wire (usually a yellow wire) is for speed sensing. That way, the fan can report its speed to the motherboard or other sensing device. This is very important for CPU fans because if the CPU fan isn't spinning at the proper speed, the CPU won't get adequate cooling. By using a three-wire fan, the

Figure 4-14

The CPU-FAN connector.

motherboard can constantly tell if the fan is spinning properly and can shut down the computer (or not let it boot up) if the fan doesn't spin up properly. There are usually at least two fan connectors on a typical motherboard today: one for the CPU's fan and the others for other case fans, chipset fans, and so on. Some motherboards will refuse to boot unless they can detect that a CPU fan is attached and spinning at the proper speed.

After a CPU and its cooling mechanism are installed, you should start up the PC and determine that the system recognizes the CPU. You can go into the BIOS Setup to make sure the new CPU is recognized and to locate the CPU configuration in the CMOS settings.

When you install a CPU, most of the newer computers automatically detect the speed of the CPU that is installed and adjust three main parameters for its proper function:

▲ CPU clock speed
▲ Clock multiplier
▲ Core voltage

Most motherboards today will detect which processor you've installed and set these parameters accordingly. However, it is possible to modify them yourself for better performance. For example, most motherboards today will let you adjust the clock rate. Dialing a higher clock rate than the CPU is rated for is called overclocking. Overclocking is not recommended, because of the significant potential to ruin your CPU or cause other problems. Overclocking will also invalidate the CPU's warranty.

4.4.3 Upgrading the Cooling System

Processors are designed to run within a certain temperature range. The operating temperature range varies among processors and their packaging types. On average, processors operate in the range of 40 degrees Celsius (about 100 degrees Fahrenheit) to 90 degrees Celsius (about 200 degrees Fahrenheit). For example, a Pentium III CPU in an SECC (Single Edge Connector Container or Slot 1) package should run at 75 degrees Celsius (167 Fahrenheit), but in its FC-PGA (Flip Chip–Plastic Grid Array) package, the CPU runs at 85 degrees Celsius (185 degrees Fahrenheit). These are die temperatures that indicate the temperature at the core of the processor packaging, not the temperature at which the processor dies.

In some cases, you may decide that you want to upgrade the CPU's cooling system. You can do this in several ways:

▲ **Add additional case fans or replacing existing fans.** By adding more fans, you can bring more cool air to the heatsinks that need it. Fans are rated by the amount of air they can move in a minute (cubic feet per minute [CFM]). If you want to increase the cooling performance of your system, either add more fans to bring air in and out of the case, or replace the existing fans with fans rated at a higher CFM. However, fans with higher CFM rates tend to be noisier.

▲ **Replace the heatsink.** You can get a bigger heatsink, or one with more surface area (more fins or larger fins). You can also install a heatsink made of a better heat-conducting material, such as a copper-aluminum combination.

▲ **Improve the efficiency of the heat sink.** One way of increasing the efficiency (even if only slightly) of a heatsink is to use a different thermal compound. A thermal compound increases the efficiency of heat transfer by increasing the contact area between the CPU and the heatsink. By using a different thermal compound, you can decrease the temperature by as much as 5°C. You can also improve the contact between the heatsink and the processor. You can eliminate some of the small air gaps between the processor and heatsink through lapping. Lapping is a process by which the heatsink or water block surface is sanded using a very flat surface (like a sheet of glass) and progressively finer grits of sandpaper until the surface is as flat as it can get. However, lapping has risks: If done improperly, it can cause an even larger air gap between processor and heatsink. So, if you're going to do it, be forewarned that it can be costly if done wrong.

▲ **Use a different type of cooling mechanism.** Because heat is a serious issue in PC performance, manufacturers are coming up with new cooling techniques, including.

- **Liquid cooling** is a relatively new technology whereby a water block is used to conduct heat away from the processor (as well as chipsets). Water is circulated through this block to a radiator, where it is cooled. The theory is that you can achieve better cooling performance through the use of this technology. For the most part, this is true. With air cooling, the lowest temperature you can achieve is room temperature. However, with liquid cooling, the pump is submerged in the coolant (generally speaking), so as it works it produces heat—which adds to the overall system temperature. The main benefit of liquid cooling is silence. Only one fan is needed: the fan on the radiator to cool the water. So, a liquid-cooled system can run extremely quietly. Liquid cooling, although more efficient than air cooling and much quieter, is generally more expensive than air cooling methods. In addition to the price, the other drawback is the possibility of a leak. Water and electronic components don't mix. Thankfully, most water cooling systems use quality hose and clamps and leaks are extremely rare. If you install a liquid cooling system, it is a good idea to double- and triple-check your connections and run the system for a day or two without a motherboard to see if leaks develop.

- **Phase change cooling:** A new type of PC cooling is phase change cooling. The cooling effect of a liquid that is changing to a gas is used to cool the inside of a PC. This cooling method is very expensive, but it works. Most often, external air conditioner, such as pumps, coils, and evaporators, cools the coolant, which is sent ice cold to the heatsinks on the processor and chipset. Think of it as a water cooling system that chills the water below room temperature. Using this technology, it is possible to get CPU temperatures in the range of −20°C (normal CPU temps hover between 40°C and 50°C).

4.4.4 Troubleshooting CPU Problems

If a CPU is broken, it must be replaced. However, problems relating to the CPU are usually not a problem with the CPU itself. A problem with the CPU is more likely to be the result of cooling (or the lack of it), power (or the lack of it), or compatibility issues with the motherboard and chipset.

The symptoms of a CPU that is beginning to fail are as follows:

▲ The PC will not boot.

▲ The PC boots but does not start the operating system.

▲ The PC crashes during startup and when running applications.

▲ The PC has sudden POST parity error problems in many devices.

▲ The PC locks up after a few minutes of operation.

If a PC boots without problems, but consistently halts or freezes after a few minutes, the CPU is probably overheating. One way to verify this is to shut down the PC, wait a few minutes to let the CPU cool, and then boot the PC. If the same problem happens after the PC operates for a while, the CPU probably has a cooling problem.

Some troubleshooting steps that you can use to check out the CPU, heatsink, and fan are as follows:

▲ Examine the heatsink and fan to determine whether they are in place or are cracked or broken. (If the CPU is not fitted with a heatsink or a cooling fan and it is a Pentium class or higher processor, you have found the problem.)

▲ Carefully grasp the heatsink (lightly touch it first—it can be very hot!), and try to move it slightly back and forth. If it is loose, you may not have a proper seal between the heatsink and fan.

▲ Remove the heatsink and fan, and verify that the CPU is properly secured in its socket or slot. If the CPU is inserted in a ZIF (zero insertion force) socket, make sure that the ZIF socket arm is locked and anchored. Reattach the heatsink and fan, making sure that they are attached securely.

If the PC displays the same symptoms as an overheating problem but the system is not overheating, the problem may be that the system clock jumpers on the motherboard or the BIOS settings for the system timers are incorrectly set. If the CPU and the motherboard are using different clock timings, it may take a while for them to get so far out of sync that the system halts. Refer to the documentation for the motherboard and CPU to get the proper clock setting, and adjust the clock accordingly.

If the PC is sounding a POST beep code that indicates a CPU fault, the CPU is probably not getting power. Using a multimeter, check the power outputs to the motherboard. If any of the leads are low or dead, replace the power supply. If the power is as it should be, you may have a dead CPU and it should be replaced. If the new CPU fails to solve the problem, you have isolated the problem to the motherboard itself.

If the system boots okay but freezes consistently when running a certain application or group of applications, the situation is too unique for normal diagnostics. Try running repetitive tests on the CPU using a third-party diagnostics package, such as Pc-Check from Eurosoft or AMIDiag from AMI. If the diagnostics indicate a CPU problem, replace the CPU and test again. If the same problem appears, expand the testing to the motherboard and chipset. You may end up testing the system completely, only to find that the problem is a corrupted file in the application software. Remember to shut down and unplug the PC before removing the CPU and to observe all standard antistatic procedures when handling the CPU. Be careful not to bend any of the pins because you may want to reinstall the CPU later. Use care when installing the new CPU because bent pins almost always ruin the PC. If a new CPU fails to correct the problem, you will need to replace the motherboard.

SELF-CHECK

1. What three price and performance categories do CPUs fall into?
2. What are the basic steps for installing a CPU?
3. List three types of CPU cooling methods.
4. What are three symptoms of a CPU that is beginning to fail?

SUMMARY

CPUs are discrete pieces of circuitry that perform all of a PC's essential, logical and computing tasks. CPUs chips are encased in packages that connect to the motherboard via sockets or slots. Types of packages include those that attach to sockets, such as PGA, BGA, CCGA, and LGA, and those that attach to slots, such as SECC, SECC2, and SEPP. A particular CPU package is designed for a corresponding socket or slot.

CPUs operate at two voltages: an external voltage used to communicate with motherboard components (typically 3.3V today) and an internal, or core voltage. A VRM is used to step down the external voltage for the CPU. Because CPUs generate a lot of heat, special cooling mechanisms, such as a heatsink/fan combination, are used to cool them.

CPU components include a control unit, ALU, and registers. The operations a CPU performs are designed around a four-step process: fetch, decode, execute, and writeback. CPUs are rated and compared by their speed, clock multiplier, word size, data path, addressable memory, cache memory, instruction set architecture, microcode efficiency, and number of transistors or process. One of the main factors that limits the performance of a CPU is the frontside bus speed.

Manufacturers employ a variety of technologies to enhance CPU performance and speed, including superscalar architecture, pipelining, multithreading, using multiple cores, new bus technologies, and 64-bit architectures.

Early Intel processors included the 808x series, the 80x86 series, and the first Pentiums. Popular Intel desktop processors you are likely to see today are the Pentium Pro, Pentium II, Celeron, Pentium II, Xeon, Pentium 4, and Pentium D. Intel's latest CPUs include the Itanium and Intel Core CPUs. Early AMD processors include the K5/K6 and Athlon. Popular AMD desktop processors you are likely to see today include the Athlon XP, Duron, and its latest CPUs, the Sempron, Opteron, and Athlon 64 family.

When you select a CPU for a system, ensure that it is compatible with the motherboard and chipset. When you install a socketed CPU, release and engage a locking mechanism on the socket and make sure that the CPU's pins are aligned with the socket before inserting it. You will also need to install a cooling mechanism such as a heatsink/fan. If the CPU fails, you can only replace it. However, one CPU-related problem that you can address is an overheating CPU. A PC that boots properly but consistently halts or freezes after a few minutes is an indication of an overheating CPU. You can monitor the temperature of the CPU to determine if it is overheating and make changes to or upgrade the cooling mechanism to fix this problem.

KEY TERMS

Address bus	Die
Arithmetic Logic Unit (ALU)	FC-PGA package
Backside bus	Frontside bus
BGA package	Heatsink
Cache memory	Instruction set
CCGA package	I/O voltage
Clock doubling	Land Grid Array (LGA) package
Clock multiplier	Lapping
Clock rate	Liquid cooling
Clock speed	Microcode
Clock tick	Micro-PGA package
Control Unit	Multicore
Core	Multitasking
Core voltage	Multithreading
CPU clock	Overclocking
CPU clock speed	PGA package
Data path	Phase-change cooling

Pipeline

Pipelining

Process

Registers

Semiconductor

SECC package

SECC2 package

Single Edge Processor Package (SEPP)

Slocket

Slot

Socket

Superscalar

Thermal contact patch

Thermal grease

Thermal interface material (TIM)

Throttling

Transistor

VRM

Water block

Water cooling

Word size

ASSESS YOUR UNDERSTANDING

Go to www.wiley.com/college/groth to evaluate your knowledge of CPUs. *Measure your learning by comparing pre-test and post-test results.*

Summary Questions

1. The _____ is a processor packaging that mounts into a single slot on the motherboard.
   (a) FC-PGA
   (b) SEPP
   (c) SECC
   (d) PPGA

2. Socket 370 is used to mount Celeron chips with 370 pins. True or false?

3. What motherboard component regulates the voltage to the CPU?
   (a) power supply connectors
   (b) VRM
   (c) heatsink
   (d) system bus

4. Water-cooling systems use a _____ on the CPU instead of a heatsink.
   (a) cooling tube
   (b) block of ice
   (c) fan
   (d) water block

5. Which CPU component acts as a temporary storage area for the data the CPU is working on?
   (a) control unit
   (b) ALU
   (c) registers
   (d) FPU

6. The CPU specification that defines the working speed of the CPU relative to the speed of the frontside bus is the _____.
   (a) data path width
   (b) word size
   (c) clock multiplier
   (d) cache memory size

7. A CPU that can use two or more ALUs is called superscalar. True or false?

8. Which CPU was the first to use clock doubling?
   (a) 8088
   (b) 80286
   (c) 80386
   (d) 80486

9. Which of the Pentium families introduced Dynamic Execution?
   (a) Pentium
   (b) Pentium Pro
   (c) Pentium 4
   (d) Intel Core

10. Which Athlon chips were designed to compete with Intel's Celeron?
    (a) K5 and K6
    (b) Athlon Classic and Thunderbird
    (c) Duron and Sempron
    (d) Opteron and Athlon 64

12. A CPU that is faster than the motherboard:
    (a) will run at the speed of the motherboard times the clock multiplier
    (b) will run at the speed of the motherboard
    (c) will run at the speed of the frontside bus
    (d) will fail and overheat

13. The ZIF locking mechanism requires slightly more force to seat the processor than the LIF. True or false?

14. You can improve the efficiency of an existing heat sink by using a different thermal compound. True or false?

15. If a PC boots without problems but consistently halts or freezes after a few minutes, the most likely cause is:
    (a) the CPU is failing
    (b) the BIOS system timers are incorrectly set
    (c) the CPU is not getting power
    (d) the CPU is overheating

16. What socket or slot did AMD develop for its Athlon and Duron processors?
    (a) Socket 478
    (b) Socket T
    (c) Socket A
    (d) Socket AM2

17. The L2 cache communicates to the CPU through the frontside bus. True or false?

18. A processor with two CPUs is called a multicore CPU. True or false?

19. Which processor package type is the same as the SECC, but without the plastic covering?

    (a) Socket A

    (b) Slot A

    (c) SEP

    (d) SECC2

20. The first released version of the Pentium 4 used which type of processor socket?

    (a) Socket A

    (b) Slot 1

    (c) Socket 370

    (d) Socket 423

Applying This Chapter

1. You are upgrading a PC and choosing a new CPU. What factors will come into play in your selection?

2. You are building a new, custom PC. What types of cooling systems are available for the CPU?

3. You have selected a compatible CPU for a motherboard you are upgrading. What steps will be involved in installing the CPU in a socket on the motherboard?

4. A friend is installing a new heatsink on her CPU and has never used thermal grease before. What advice do you have for her?

5. A CPU for sale on e-Bay is described as: Intel Xeon MP, 603-pin FC-BGA/mPGA, 2.70 GHz, 400 MHz bus, L1/L2/L3: 12K/512K/2048K, 13nm, 1.475V. Explain what these terms mean.

CPUs and Motherboards

You have come into possession of an Asus K8V-MX motherboard and you are considering using it for a new system. What socket does this motherboard have? Go to Asus.com to research which CPUs this motherboard supports.

Selecting a CPU

A client wants you to build a custom gaming PC, and the first thing you will do is select the CPU. Go to AMD.ccm and find which CPUs they recommend for gaming. What are comparable Intel CPUs? Select a model from each manufacturer and compare the CPUs in terms of speed, instruction set support, packaging, cache memory, and other architectural technologies. Which of the two would you purchase, and why?

CPU Troubleshooting

A client recently installed a new CPU on her motherboard. Each time she has used the PC since, the system works fine for a few minutes, but then powers off. What could be causing this? What troubleshooting steps will you take?

64-bit Processing

A family member wants to build an inexpensive PC that he will use mostly for connecting to the web and managing his electronic documents, such as tax records and photos, but he is also quite keen on having a speedy system and the latest 64-bit processor. What will you advise him regarding the choice of CPU?

5
MEMORY

Starting Point

Go to www.wiley.com/college/groth to assess your knowledge of memory.
Determine where you need to concentrate your effort.

What You'll Learn in This Chapter

▲ Memory types and categories
▲ System memory form factors and motherboard compatibility
▲ Installation steps for memory modules
▲ Symptoms and causes of memory problems

After Studying This Chapter, You'll Be Able To

▲ Discuss how memory works in a PC
▲ Identify different memory form factors
▲ Discuss and compare DRAM technologies
▲ Select appropriate DRAM modules for upgrading a PC
▲ Install a DIMM
▲ Identify a failing memory module and troubleshoot memory problems

INTRODUCTION

Although the CPU is the most important component of a PC, system memory is arguably the second most important. System memory acts as a temporary storage area for the data with which the CPU works. Data, such as operating system files and application files, is stored permanently on secondary storage devices, but these devices operate far more slowly than the CPU. To speed up the interaction between the CPU and data storage, memory chips are used to house frequently used or anticipated data.

There are various technologies and locations for PC memory, but the memory most people are familiar with is the system memory, which you will often hear referred to as RAM (random access memory). As a PC technician, you need to know about the various types, locations, and components used for PC memory, and how the memory interacts with the CPU and the operating system. Today, memory is one of the most popular, easy, and inexpensive ways to upgrade a computer, and you need to know how to match memory to the PC and install RAM properly.

5.1 Examining Memory

For the CPU to perform its functions, it must receive data and instructions. Data and software instructions can be stored permanently in PCs on hard drives, but for the CPU to work quickly, they are loaded into storage areas called **memory**. Memory is composed of electronic components, such as transistors and semiconductors, which hold signals as binary 1s and 0s.

5.1.1 Memory and the PC

There are two categories of memory: volatile and nonvolatile. **Volatile memory** only holds data or signals while it receives power. When power is switched off, the data it holds is lost. **Nonvolatile memory** retains its signals, or data, even when the power is switched off.

You will find two basic types of memory in a PC:

▲ **Read-only memory (ROM):** ROM is nonvolatile memory, typically used to store essential, small programs such as the BIOS.

▲ **Random-access memory (RAM):** RAM is memory used to hold the instructions and data in use by the operating system and software applications before and after the data is passed to the CPU. It is called "random" because the data stored in it is accessed nonsequentially: The CPU doesn't need to read each successive bit to find a particular piece of data. (A tape drive, in contrast, is sequential; as the data on it is recorded in a sequential

Figure 5-1

Banks of RAM memory modules installed on a motherboard.

stream.) The RAM used for the main memory on a PC is volatile. RAM is by far the faster of the two types of memory. In fact, RAM is often used to shadow the BIOS ROM to improve its performance during the boot process.

Memory locations in the PC include:

▲ System memory, installed in banks of RAM memory modules on the motherboard (Figure 5-1)
▲ CPU cache memory, installed as part of the CPU (internal cache) or nearby on the motherboard (external cache)
▲ CPU registers
▲ BIOS chips on the motherboard or other expansion boards

In general, the transfer of data into memory in the PC follows this order:

1. When a computer starts up, the first instructions of the BIOS are loaded from the BIOS ROM chip into the CPU.

Figure 5-2

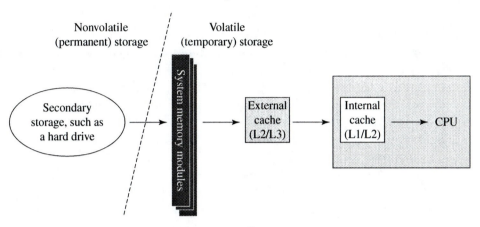

Movement of data to the CPU.

2. The BIOS loads the operating system, located on a hard drive, into system memory.

3. The operating system then loads additional software or data the PC user is working on (such as application software like Microsoft Word and data from a file being worked on) into system memory.

4. Smaller blocks of data that the CPU works with frequently are loaded from the system memory into its cache memory (Figure 5-2). Most CPUs have one or two levels of cache incorporated into the CPU (L1 or L2 cache) and use another level of cache located externally, either within the CPU packaging or on the motherboard (L2 or L3 cache).

5. The actual data the CPU is working on at any given moment is loaded from cache (or system memory, if the data is not in the CPU's cache) and stored in the CPU's registers.

6. When the CPU is finished working on a portion of data, the data is released ultimately back to RAM. When a user finishes working on a file and closes it, the file is written back to a hard drive and the space in system memory is freed for other data.

The CPU typically accesses memory through the motherboard's chipset. The chipset's Northbridge includes a memory controller chip that accesses system memory modules through the memory bus. The memory bus almost always operates at the same speed as the frontside bus and is often seen as part and parcel of the frontside bus. The memory bus has two main parts: a data bus and an address bus. The data bus is used for sending the raw data; the address bus is used to request data and communicate the specific address locations of data on

Interleaving

You may come across older systems with interleaved memory. Interleaving was a technology designed to shorten the time between accessing different portions of RAM. In interleaving, system memory was arranged in an even number of banks. When data is written to the banks, it is staggered between two banks. With this organization, while data is being read from one bank, the system can start preparing to read data from the next bank to speed the entire process up. If you are working on an older system, check to see whether it needs interleaved memory. If so, you will need to check the documentation to ensure you are placing memory modules in the correct bank slots.

the memory modules. The chipset communicates with the CPU over the frontside, or system bus. Today some newer CPU technologies incorporate the memory controller into the CPU or use specialized buses to communicate with memory.

5.1.2 Types of ROM

ROM stands for read-only memory. It is called read-only because it isn't designed to be written to. After information has been written to the ROM, it generally can't be changed. ROM is normally used to store the computer's BIOS because this information normally does not change. ROM chips are usually loaded with instructions called firmware during the manufacturing processes.

Other types of nonvolatile memory chips include:

▲ **Programmable Read Only Memory (PROM):** A PROM is essentially a blank ROM chip that can be programmed with data or instructions. A PROM burner or programmer is a special device used to write to the PROM, enabling you to store any data you want. The PROM burner induces high voltage (12 volts compared to the 5 volts used for normal PROM operations) to load the data to the chip. The higher voltage burns a memory location to turn its pre-existing binary 1 into a 0, if needed. This process is irreversible, so what you burn is what you get. For that reason, you may hear PROM memory referred to as One Time Programmable Memory.

▲ **Erasable Programmable Read Only Memory (EPROM):** An EPROM (pronounced "e-prom") is a type of PROM that allows data to be erased so that the chip can be reprogrammed. The EPROM has a small quartz crystal window on the top of the chip through which ultraviolet (UV)

Figure 5-3

A Flash BIOS chip.

rays access the circuitry. The UV light causes a chemical reaction that erases the EPROM by turning the 0's back into 1's again. To prevent accidental erasure of the EPROM chip, a label tape is normally placed over the quartz crystal window. EPROMs must be removed from a system to be reprogrammed, which is not always possible.

▲ **Electronically Erasable Programmable Read Only Memory (EEPROM):** An EEPROM (pronounced "e-e-prom") is the common BIOS chip on newer systems. An EEPROM chip can be reprogrammed like the EPROM; unlike the EPROM, it doesn't need to be removed from the motherboard.

▲ **Flash memory**: A type of EEPROM, commonly used for BIOS chips (Figure 5-3) and for removable data storage on small Flash memory cards, sticks or drives.

5.1.3 Types of RAM

RAM memory chips are packaged either singly as **Dual Inline Package (DIP) chips**, in groups of chips soldered onto a printed circuit board (PCB), or embedded into other chips, such as processors or controllers. When people refer to RAM, they are usually referring to the PC's main memory, or system memory, because a PC uses RAM for its main system memory. However, there are two types of RAM used in a PC.

▲ **Dynamic RAM (DRAM):** DRAM is what most people are talking about when they mention RAM. When you expand the memory in a computer, you are adding DRAM memory modules. DRAM chips are cheaper to manufacture than other types because they are less complex. They store signals as charges in tiny capacitors. *Dynamic* refers to the memory chips' need for dynamic refresh signals to keep the information that is written there. A special refresh logic circuit reads and then rewrites the contents of each DRAM address, regardless of whether it's in use.

▲ **Static RAM (SRAM):** *SRAM* is called static because the information doesn't need a constant update (refresh). It can retain its data using a very low voltage electrical charge. As long as it has a power stream, SRAM holds its charge and contents. SRAM stores information as patterns of transistor ons and offs to represent binary digits. This type of memory is physically bulky and more complex and expensive. The earliest PCs as well as some notebook computer systems, use SRAM chips for their main memory. However, today it is used most commonly for external cache memory. SRAM is available as either synchronous or asynchronous. Synchronous SRAM uses the system clock to coordinate its signals with the CPU, and asynchronous doesn't.

5.1.4 Memory and the Operating System

PC software is essentially long lists of instructions for performing different types of tasks. For the CPU to perform these tasks, the software must be loaded (by the operating system or in some instances by the BIOS) into easily accessed system memory.

Managing memory in early PCs and operating systems was a complex task. The first IBM PC's 8088 CPU was only able to address 1 MB of system memory and the early DOS operating system was designed to work with this constraint (in the early 80s, PCs commonly had 64K of system memory). The first 640K was called conventional memory; the rest (384K) was reserved for the BIOS and other system utilities. Essentially, the operating system and all applications had to run within the assigned 640K of conventional memory. Because of the constraints of conventional memory (and the introduction of CPUs that could address more RAM), later DOS versions added the capability to address extended, or expanded, memory: any memory above the first megabyte.

In addition to these memory constraints, early CPUs, such as the 8088, were designed to allow applications to directly communicate with RAM, in what is referred to as real mode. However, this design led to application and memory conflicts, and subsequent CPUs (and versions of Windows) were designed for what is called protected mode. In protected mode, the operating system acts as an interface between RAM and applications. Windows 9x versions supported 32-bit protected mode, and for compatibility with DOS applications, also had to support a 16-bit real mode and work with the following logical memory layout (Figure 5-4):

For the purposes of interacting with software, system memory is logically divided into the following sections:

▲ **Conventional memory:** The first 640KB of the first 1MB (1024K) of memory is called conventional memory and was used in older systems for running DOS applications and drivers.

Figure 5-4

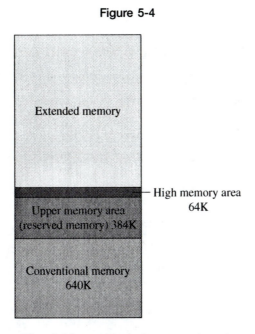

The divisions of logical memory layout.

▲ **Upper memory area:** The upper 384K of the first megabyte of memory, located directly above conventional memory. Reserved for the system BIOS and device drivers and special uses such as ROM shadowing.

▲ **High memory area:** The first 64K (less 16 bytes) of the second megabyte of memory. Although it's the first 64K of extended memory, it can be accessed in real, or 16-bit mode.

▲ **Extended memory:** Technically, this is all memory above 1MB, but in practice, it is any memory that's above the high memory area. Used by Windows for programs and data that are running in protected, or 32-bit mode.

The Windows NT family of operating systems (starting with Windows NT and including Windows XP and Server 2003) dispensed with support for real mode and the distinctions between different types of memory. Instead all memory is treated as the same block of memory and is managed by the operating system's memory manager.

One of the features of protected mode is the capability to use virtual memory. Windows is such a large OS and requires so much overhead that sometimes a PC doesn't have enough RAM to accommodate its needs. Rather than giving an out of memory error message to the user, Windows has a

Figure 5-5

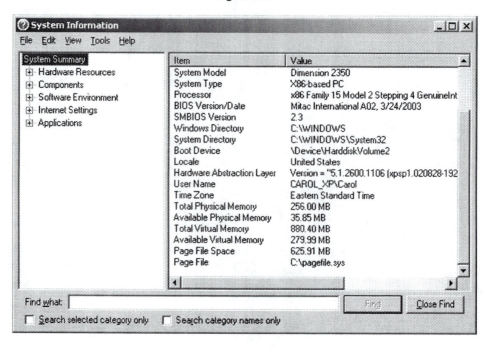

Accessing information about virtual memory.

workaround technique whereby it uses an unused part of the hard disk to simulate additional RAM, swapping data into and out of it from the real RAM. This is called **virtual memory**. The file on the hard disk used for the simulation is called a **page file** or **swap file**. Although this disk-based memory is slower than RAM, virtual memory considerably speeds up a PC system as a whole. Current Windows operating systems all use virtual memory. You can access information about a system's virtual memory via the System Information dialog box (Figure 5-5).

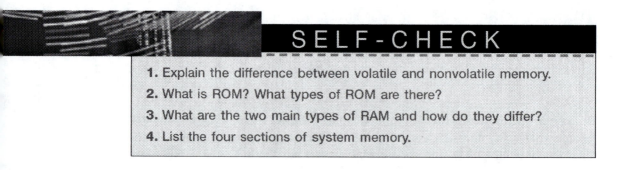

SELF-CHECK

1. Explain the difference between volatile and nonvolatile memory.
2. What is ROM? What types of ROM are there?
3. What are the two main types of RAM and how do they differ?
4. List the four sections of system memory.

5.2 Examining DRAM

5.2.1 DRAM Form Factors

Early PCs used DIP memory chips soldered on the motherboard. Because these took up so much space, DIP chips were then placed onto small, removable PCBs. These memory modules are inserted into slots on the motherboard. The modules are installed in banks. A **bank** may be a single or group of modules whose bit width adds up to the bit width the CPU works with. Individual memory slots on a motherboard are designed to hold particular chip form factors or styles. DRAM form factors include:

▲ **SIMM:** The first **Single Inline Memory Modules (SIMMs)** had nine small DIP chips on them. Four SIMMs could be installed in the same space as one row of DIP chips. To accomplish this, the SIMMs were installed very close to each other at approximately a 45-degree angle. Today you will find SIMMS on older PCs (486s and early Pentiums). The edge connector on a SIMM has either 30 pins or 72 pins. A SIMM's memory capacity ranges from 1MB to 16MB in either a one-sided or two-sided style, with chips soldered to one or two sides of the board. Because the Pentium processor uses a 64-bit bus, 32-bit SIMMs must be installed in pairs. Each SIMM bank has two sockets and both sockets must be filled before another bank receives a SIMM.

▲ **DIMM:** The **Dual Inline Memory Module (DIMM)** is the memory standard on most PCs today. "Dual" refers to the use of electrically separate contact pins on either side of the board. Because DIMMS are 64-bit, you usually need to install only one DIMM at a time. In comparison to the SIMM, a DIMM has 168, 184, or 240 contact pins as opposed to the 30 and 72 pins of the SIMM. A DIMM looks just like a SIMM, except that it's slightly larger. They may be single-sided, with chips on one side of the board, or double-sided, with chips on both sides. Some DIMMS designed for critical, high-end servers and workstations include buffers or registers that interact with the chipset's memory controller to provide extra stability and accuracy. Today, most PCs use DIMMS or RIMMS.

▲ **RIMM:** Where SIMM and DIMM are generic acronyms for a type of memory module, **RIMM** is a trademarked name for the Rambus memory module. A RIMM looks similar to a DIMM, but the RIMM has 184 pins on its edge connector. RIMMs transfer data in 16-bit chunks. A RIMM is packaged inside an aluminum sheath called a **heat spreader**. The heat spreader covers the entire assembly to protect against overheating.

▲ **SoDIMM:** Notebook computers and other computers that require much smaller components don't use standard RAM packages like the SIMM or

Figure 5-6

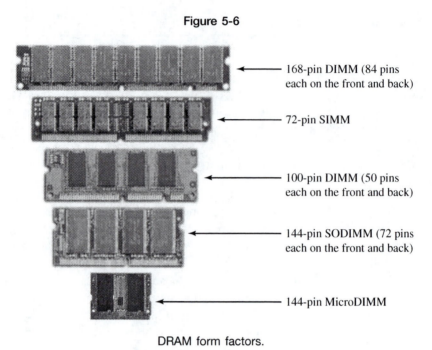

168-pin DIMM (84 pins each on the front and back)

72-pin SIMM

100-pin DIMM (50 pins each on the front and back)

144-pin SODIMM (72 pins each on the front and back)

144-pin MicroDIMM

DRAM form factors.

the DIMM. Instead, they use a much smaller memory form factor called a **Small Outline DIMM (SoDIMM)**. SoDIMMs are available in both 32-bit (72-pin) and 64-bit (144-pin) configurations. A smaller version of the RIMM, the SORIMM (Small Outline RIMM), is similar to the SODIMM except that is uses Rambus technology.

▲ **MicroDIMM:** The MicroDIMM is an extremely small RAM form factor, over 50 percent smaller than a SoDIMM. It was designed for the ultra-light and portable subnotebook style of computer. The MicroDIMM has 144 pins and is similar to a DIMM in that it uses 64-bit memory modules.

Figure 5-6 illustrates the various DRAM form factors.

5.2.2 DRAM Technologies

Over the past decade, manufacturers have developed different DRAM technologies in order to enhance the system memory speed. The following lists the characteristics of each of the DRAM technologies.

Early DRAM technologies were asynchronous. With asynchronous memory, the delivery of data from system memory wasn't timed with the system clock. The CPU had to wait a certain amount of time, called wait states, until

---

FOR EXAMPLE

Chip Creep

The angled design of DIPS in the early SIMM form factor was also meant to prevent **chip creep**, which happens when the chips that have been placed in sockets on the board begin to slowly move out of their sockets (due to the repeated heating and cooling of the system board). Here's an old technician's trick: If an older computer is having strange, irreproducible problems, open the case and reseat all socketed chips by pressing them down securely in their sockets. Most of the time, this technique will solve the problem. If it does, then the problem was caused by chip creep.

---

the system memory delivered data. Early asynchronous DRAM technologies included:

▲ **Fast Page Mode (FPM) DRAM: FPM DRAM**, at the time of the 486/Pentium transition, was the most common type of DRAM. It allowed data to be paged (swapped) into memory faster than earlier versions, thus providing better performance. It's generally compatible with motherboards with memory buses with speeds under 66 MHz.

▲ **Extended Data Out (EDO) DRAM: EDO DRAM**, introduced in 1995, increased performance over FPM DRAM by eliminating memory wait states. This means it eliminates a few steps to access memory, thus decreasing the time it takes to get information and thus increasing the overall performance of the computer. EDO memory had to be used in EDO-compatible motherboards. Burst Extended Data Out (BEDO) DRAM was a successor to EDO memory with pipelining technology added for faster access times. BEDO memory allowed much higher bus speeds than EDO memory.

EDO and FPM DRAM are no longer used today, although you may run across them in old PCs. You will more commonly find the following types of DRAM.

▲ **Synchronous DRAM (SDRAM): SDRAM**, also called **Single Data Rate (SDR) DRAM**, was the first generation of DRAM synchronized to the speed of the systems in which it will be used. Synchronizing the speed of the systems prevents the address bus from having to wait for the memory because of different clock speeds. SDR DRAM is rated by the bus speed it operates at. PC66 SDR DRAM runs at 66 MHz, PC100 runs at 100 MHz, PC133 runs at 133 MHz. SDR DRAM has been succeeded by the faster DDR and DDR2 SDRAMs.

▲ **Double Data Rate SDRAM (DDR SDRAM): DDR SDRAM** is clock-doubled, or **double-pumped**. The memory chip can perform reads and writes twice during a clock cycle (at the up or start of the cycle and the down or ending), thus doubling the effective memory executions per second. If you are using DDR SDRAM with a 100 MHz memory bus, the memory will execute reads and writes at 200 MHz and transfer the data to the processor at 100MHz. The advantage of DDR over regular SDRAM is increased throughput, and thus increased overall system speed. DDR SDRAM chips are identified by their peak data transfer rate in MBps, as opposed to a clock frequency rating in MHz. For example, a 100 MHz DDR SDRAM module isn't known as PC200; instead, it is called PC1600, for the peak bandwidth, or data transfer rate (64-bit $\times$ 2 $\times$ 100 MHz = 12,800 Mbps or 1600 MBps).

▲ **DDR2:** DDR2 is a successor to DDR memory. Still double-pumping, DDR2, like DDR, uses both sweeps of the clock signal for data transfer. Internally, DDR2 further splits each clock pulse in two, doubling the number of operations it can perform per FSB clock cycle. Through enhancements in the electrical interface and buffers, as well as through adding off-chip drivers, DDR2 nominally produces four times what SDR is capable of producing. DDR2 is not compatible with DDR, and cannot fit into the same slots. DDR2 has the same rating, or naming scheme as DDR, identifying modules by their perceived maximum throughput, in MBps. However, because some of these ratings are equivalent to DDR ratings, DDR2 memory is identified by the prefix PC2, as in PC2-3200. DDR3 SDRAM is the next incarnation of DDR DRAM in development, with proposed data rates up to 1600 MHz.

▲ **Rambus DRAM (RDRAM): RDRAM** is a proprietary DRAM technology developed by Rambus, Inc. that has memory speeds of up to 4.8 GBps and uses a proprietary Direct Rambus bus. RDRAM comes on a module that is similar to a DIMM, called a RIMM (Rambus In-line Memory Module). RDRAM, similar to DDR SDRAM, is double-pumped, and can transfer data on both the rising and falling edges of a clock cycle. 16-bit RDRAM RIMMs must be installed in pairs.

Other types of DRAM that you should be aware of are:

▲ **Synchronous Link DRAM (SLDRAM): SLDRAM** is an enhanced version of SDRAM memory that uses a multiplexed bus to transfer data to and from the chips rather than fixed pin settings. SLDRAM has transfer rates as high as 3 GBps. Unlike RDRAM, this is an open technology. It was developed by a consortium of memory manufacturers to compete with RDRAM but is no longer in use today.

▲ **Video RAM (VRAM): VRAM** is a specialized DRAM used on video cards and not for main memory. VRAM applies dual porting, which means that it can be written to and read from at the same time. This allows the processor and the refresh circuitry for the monitor to access VRAM at the same time. Another type of video RAM is Windows RAM (WRAM), also called Windows Accelerator RAM, which has essentially the same properties as VRAM.

Table 5-1 shows the progression of DRAM technology.

Table 5-1: Progression of DRAM Technologies

DRAM Model	First Used	Clock Rate	Form Factor	Peak Bandwidth	Voltage
Asynchronous DRAM					
FPM (60ns and 70ns)	1990	25MHz	30-pin SIMM (8-bit) 72-pin SIMM (32-bit)	200MBps	5v
EDO (50ns, 60ns, and 70ns)	1994	40MHz	72-pin SIMM 168-pin DIMM (64-bit)	320MBps	5v
Synchronous RAM					
SDRAM					
PC66	1996	66MHz	168-pin DIMM	528MBps	3.3v
PC100	1998	100MHz	168-pin DIMM	800MBps	3.3v
PC133	1999	133MHz	168-pin DIMM	1.1GBps	3.3v
RDRAM					
PC800	1999	400MHz (×2)	184-pin RIMM (16-bit)	1.6GBps	2.5v
PC1066	2002	533MHz (×2)	184-pin RIMM	2.1GBps	2.5v
RIMM 3200 (PC 800)	2002	400MHz (×2)	232-pin RIMM (32-bit)	3.2GBps	2.5v
RIMM 4200 (PC 1066)	2002	533MHz (×2)	232-pin RIMM	4.2GBps	2.5v

continued

Table 5-1 Progression of DRAM Technologies (continued)

RIMM 4800 (PC 1200)	2002	600MHz (×2)	232-pin RIMM	4.8GBps	2.5v
DDR SDRAM					
PC 1600 (200 MHz)	2001	100MHz (×2)	184-pin DIMM (64-bit)	1.6GBps	2.5v
PC 2100 (266 MHz)	2001	133MHz (×2)	184-pin DIMM	2.1GBps	2.5v
PC 2700 (333 MHz)	2002	166MHz (×2)	184-pin DIMM	2.7GBps	2.5v
PC 3200 (400 MHz)	2002	200MHz (×2)	184-pin DIMM	3.2GBps	2.5v
DDR2					
(PC2-3200) 400 MHz	2004	200MHz (×2)	240-pin DIMM (64-bit)	3.2GBps	1.8v
PC2-5300 (533 MHz)	2004	266MHz (×2)	240-pin DIMM	4.2GBps	1.8v
PC2-5300 (667 MHz)	2005	333MHz (×2)	240-pin DIMM	5.3GBps	1.8v
PC2-6400 (800 MHz)	2005	400MHz (×2)	240-pin DIMM	6.4GBps	1.8v
PC2-8000 (1000 MHz)	2006	500MHz (×2)	240-pin DIMM	8.0GBps	1.8V–2.2V

Data courtesy of CMP TechWeb and Kingston Technology 2000.

5.2.3 DRAM Features and Characteristics

The various types of memory can be described in terms of their operational characteristics, including the following:

▲ **Bit width:** Memory modules can be identified by the number of bits they can move at any one time. Today's modules are typically 32-bit or 64-bit. For example, most 168-pin SDRAM DIMMs are 64-bit. The CPU is designed to work with a certain bit-width of data, for example, and the data from system memory needs to be delivered in the same bit width. (For this reason, some modules must be installed in combination in banks to meet the requirements of the CPU's bit width.) Therefore, in systems that have a 64-bit bus, you can install SDRAM DIMMs singly to add memory to your system. However, if you have an older system that supports 72-pin DIMMs (which are 32-bit), and you have a system with a 64-bit bus, you would have to install them in pairs. Modules that include error correction capabilities will have wider bit widths to accommodate this extra data.

▲ **Capacity:** Individual memory modules are rated by their capacity—how many MB of data they can store. The capacity is determined by the number of memory chips installed on the module and the capacity of each chip. Each memory chip has a certain capacity, or density, calculated in Mb (megabits), as in a 64 Mb chip. A module with eight 16 Mb chips will hold 512 Mb. Translated to MB, this is 512 Mb/8 Mb per MB, or 64 MB. (Note that you may see the capacity of memory chips referred to as an expression of density: Mb x bit width. A 16 Mb chip may be 4 M (million bits) X 4 (bit width). Today, DIMM/RIMM memory modules are available in ranges from 32 MB to 2048 MB, but most systems use modules with 128 MB or more.

▲ **Speed/Bandwidth Rating:** This is the method used to rate a DRAM module in terms of speed differs depending on the type of technology used.

  • **Asynchronous DRAM** (FPM, EDO): This was rated for access time, the total time it took for a module to fulfill a data request from the CPU. A 60 ns access rate was faster than a 90 ns access rate.

  • **SDR DRAM:** This is rated by the speed of the bus it operates with, such as PC100 SDR RAM operates on a 100 MHz cycle.

  • **DDR DRAM:** DDR DRAM (and other DRAM that delivers data more than once per cycle) is rated by potential bandwidth, the amount of data that can be delivered per cycle. For example, a PC 2100 (266 MHz) DDR DRAM delivers 2100 MB/sec at a supported bus speed of 133 MHz.

▲ **Parity vs. non-parity: Parity** is a simple (and older) form of error checking used in computers and telecommunications. It works by adding an additional bit to a binary number and using it to indicate any changes in that number during transmission. There are two types of parity:

  • **Even parity** works by counting the number of 1s in a binary number and, if that number is odd, adding an additional 1 to guarantee that the total number of 1s is even. For example, the number 01101101 has five 1s; it will have a 1 in the parity bit position to make the total number of 1s even.

  • **Odd parity** works in a similar manner, but guarantees that the total number of 1s is an odd number.

When a character fails to have the appropriate number of bits, a parity error occurs and the system stops. A parity error can be the first signal of a host of problems, ranging from one-time anomalies to faulty memory. Faulty memory can be the cause of repeated memory parity errors. The limitation of the parity method for data integrity checking is that it can only detect an error. It has no mechanism to fix the error. When the parity method detects a parity error, it knows only that the count is wrong. It is easy to identify parity memory because instead of eight chips, it has nine (the extra chip is dedicated to the parity bit). Nonparity memory systems don't perform data integrity checks. You can't use nonparity memory in a parity system. Doing so generates a parity error as soon as the system boots up. You can turn off parity checking on some systems in the BIOS setup. Parity memory works fine in a nonparity system—the extra bit is ignored.

▲ **ECC vs. non-ECC: Error Correction Code (ECC)** is a data integrity method that is used in place of parity memory on many systems today. The difference between ECC memory and parity memory is that ECC can detect errors such as parity memory, but ECC can also correct errors to a point. ECC memory can detect up to 4-bit memory errors (which are rare) but it can correct only 1-bit errors. Like the parity method does with all errors, when ECC sees a multiple-bit error, it reports it as a parity error. ECC memory is more expensive than non-ECC memory, and the system must be able to support it properly. Most servers and high-end workstations can use ECC memory. However, it is not necessary for the average user.

▲ **CAS (Column Address Strobe) latency: CAS latency** specifies the time (in clock cycles) from when the request is made for information from memory to when the first bit of data is moved to the module's pins or connectors. The most common markings for CAS latency are CL2 (two clock cycles) and CL3. CL2 is a lower latency (meaning a faster access time) than CL3. There are also some memory chips labeled CL2.5.

▲ **Dual or Quad channel memory:** Some motherboard chipsets are designed with a **dual-channel** (or quad-channel) memory controller, allowing twice as much memory to be accessed in a cycle by having two 64-bit data channels to the RAM. Although this is a feature of the motherboard and not the RAM modules, you will hear a PC's memory referred to as dual-channel or single channel memory. Dual-channel memory requires DIMMS of equal capacity and speeds to be placed in designated pairs on the motherboard. Typically, a dual-memory capable motherboard will automatically use dual-channel memory when the memory modules are placed properly in the memory slots.

▲ **Gold vs. tin connectors:** The connectors on a DIMM or SIMM, and the contacts on the motherboard's memory slots, may be tin or gold. You need to use the same type of metal as the motherboard memory slots to prevent damage such as corrosion.

▲ **Single-ranked versus double-ranked:** In a double-ranked DIMM, the DRAM chips are split into two groups that are accessed separately by the memory controller. The chips of a single-ranked DIMM are not divided into separate groups. Some DIMMs designed for servers or workstations may have four ranks.

SELF-CHECK

1. What are the three main types of memory form factors for desktop PCs?
2. What is the difference between SDRAM and DDR SDRAM?
3. How are the different types of DRAM rated in terms of speed?
4. Explain bit width as it applies to memory modules.

5.3 Working with Memory

5.3.1 Upgrading Memory

There are two main reasons for upgrading memory:

▲ **To match the requirements of the operating system or other software.** You must ensure that you have enough memory to meet the requirements of any operating system upgrade (the requirements are usually listed on the operating system's packaging or promotional materials). You must also have enough memory to run the programs you are going to use as well as to keep the operating system in memory. This amount varies depending on the requirements of the programs installed. Every program has a list of how much memory you should have to run the program properly.

▲ **To improve the PC's performance.** You can improve performance by adding more memory to unoccupied memory slots or by replacing existing memory sticks with a faster variety. Adding more memory increases the performance of the computer because more of the operating system and other files being worked on can be loaded at once. Replacing the existing memory with faster memory accomplishes the same goal. However, you must replace *all* the existing memory with faster memory because one piece of slower memory will slow all the memory to the speed of the slowest chip.

Before a memory upgrade, you need to make sure you first check the type of memory your motherboard supports and then use only that memory. If your motherboard uses RIMMs, you must make sure you are buying and installing RIMMs. Also, if you have a non-DDR motherboard and install DDR memory, don't expect it to work properly. You will also need to match the memory to the motherboard speed. For example, if your system is capable of supporting PC3200 memory, make sure the memory installed in the system is PC3200 memory and not the slower PC2700 memory. If you are running memory that is operating at a slower speed than your system can handle, you are not taking full advantage of the performance features of that system.

Most often, stores that sell memory have a book or chart that can help you choose the right kind of memory to install. Or, you can go to the website of your motherboard's manufacturer, which should have a reference for the type of memory that goes in the system as well as how much memory can be installed into the system. Finally, you can look at the website of a major memory manufacturer, such as Crucial (Crucial.com) or Kingston (Kingston.com). Their websites tell which of their products work with which motherboards or systems.

5.3.2 Installing Memory Modules

When you are working with memory modules:

▲ Make sure you are electrically grounded. Just touching the case or power supply may not protect memory modules from ESD damage.
▲ Ensure that the PC power is off.
▲ Handle memory modules carefully. Don't bend or flex them, and always grasp them by the edges. Keep uninstalled modules in a safe place, preferably in an antistatic bag.

In a contemporary PC, a motherboard will typically have three DIMM or four RIMM closely spaced memory slots. These slots are about 4 inches long and have gray or white levers, called retaining clips, at either end. You may need to install memory in particular sockets for the system to work properly. For example, you may need to install the memory in pairs in sockets 1 and 3 on a particular motherboard, and singly on a different motherboard. Consult your motherboard's documentation to find out which sockets should be used.

The process for installing DIMMS and RIMMS is essentially the same:

1. Flip down the retaining clips on the sides of the socket in which you will be installing memory.

Figure 5-7

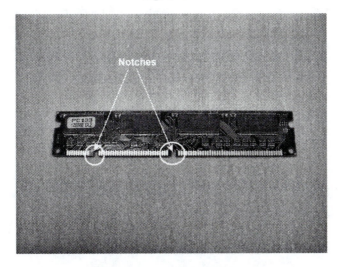

Notch in a memory stick.

2. Line up the memory so that it will fit into the socket. To do this, you must notice where the notches are on the bottom of the stick of memory (another term for a memory module). The stick should be oriented so that these notches (Figure 5-7) line up with the small bumps in the bottom of the memory slot (Figure 5-8) and so that the tin or gold fingers are down (toward the motherboard).

Figure 5-8

Bumps in a memory slot.

3. Slip the memory stick into the slot and push it down until it makes contact with the slot's retaining clips. After the memory makes contact with these clips, it will be increasingly difficult to push on the memory stick. However, you must continue to push until the memory seats into the bottom of the slot and the memory retainer clips fold over and latch into the sides of the memory stick, thus holding it in place.

There are some slight differences in the installation and removal process depending on the form factor of memory you are working with:

▲ **SIMMs:** To install a SIMM, align it with the socket at about a 45-degree angle. As the SIMM is lifted to a vertical position and seated in the socket, the clamping clips on the ends of the socket grab the module and hold it in place. To remove a SIMM, release the clamping clips very gently, push the module to a 45-degree angle, and then lift out the module (Figure 5-9).

▲ **DIMMs:** A DIMM is keyed to match the socket, so it only goes in one way. After the DIMM is aligned to the socket slot, firmly press down on the module until it seats in the socket slot and locks into place with a snap. Nearly all DIMM sockets have ejector tabs. To remove a

Figure 5-9

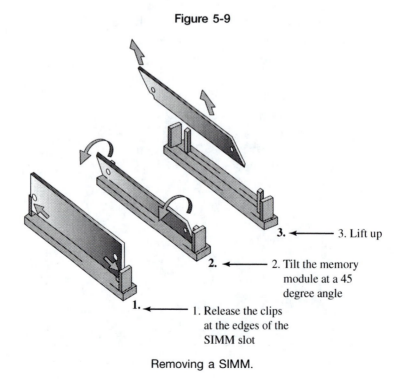

3. ◄——— 3. Lift up

2. ◄——— 2. Tilt the memory module at a 45 degree angle

1. ◄——— 1. Release the clips at the edges of the SIMM slot

Removing a SIMM.

DIMM, press down on the ejector tabs, and the module should pop up and out of the socket slot. Carefully lift the module out of the socket.

▲ **RIMMs:** If you are using 16-bit RIMM modules, both slots of the RIMM connector set must be occupied by two RIMMs or a single RIMM and what is called a C-RIMM (Continuity RIMM). A C-RIMM doesn't contain memory; it's only a pass-through module that completes the memory channel. You install a RIMM almost exactly as you would a DIMM—press down until the locking clips snap onto the module. To remove the module, press the ejector tabs outward; this pops the module out of the socket.

After you have installed the memory, and before replacing the system cover, boot the system to determine whether the new memory is being seen by the BIOS and operating system. If it isn't recognized, this may be due to either improper seating of the modules or using modules in a capacity or configuration that your PC doesn't support. Confirm that your memory is supported by your PC and installed properly.

5.3.3 Troubleshooting Memory

It is rare that you will encounter many problems with modern memory modules; in general, after you install and confirm that new memory is working, it will work for the life of the PC. However, memory problems are still encountered and typically fall in one of the following general areas:

▲ **Configuration:** The amount of memory that is installed is more than the PC or operating system supports, or the BIOS CMOS settings are incorrect.

▲ **Hardware:** At least one memory module is defective, or the memory modules that are installed are not compatible.

▲ **Installation:** The memory chips or modules are not properly seated in their sockets, or a socket is defective or needs cleaning.

One problem with diagnosing memory problems is that other PC components, such as software or the motherboard, can cause what may appear to be a memory problem. Knowing when a memory problem happened is often the best clue to the problem's source. Symptoms of hardware problems with memory include crashes, blue screens, and POST error messages. Memory problems typically occur in one of the following instances:

▲ **The first time that a new PC is started up:** The problem is most likely that the memory chips need to be reseated (in the best case) or are missing (in the worst case). If the problem does not appear to be memory-related, it may be a bad motherboard. Check with the manufacturer or the vendor.

▲ **Immediately after new memory is installed:** Check the part numbers and speed of the memory that was installed. Also, verify that the memory was properly installed or configured in memory banks, and ensure that if DIP (Dual In-line Packaging) or SIMM (Single In-line Memory Module) memory is in use, each bank was filled before memory was placed in another bank. You may also want to verify that the memory is appropriate for the motherboard, chipset, and processor. For example, the memory bus on a Pentium III PC is either PC100- or PC133- compliant, and so must be the memory modules. Different memory standards are available for a PC, but you must match the memory to the system. The part number of the memory holds a clue as to what it is. For the most part, if the memory's part number ends with a dash and a number, such as -60, it is industry-standard EDO (Extended Data Output) or FPM (Fast Page Mode) memory. If the part number ends with a slash and a number, such as /32, it is industry-standard SDRAM (Synchronous DRAM). SDRAM part numbers also indicate the standard to which they conform. For example, a Kingston Technology memory with the part number KTM66X64/128 is compliant with the Intel 66-MHz standard and is a 128MB Dual In-line Memory Module (DIMM).

▲ **Immediately after new software or operating system is installed:** More recent versions of software and operating systems typically require more memory than older versions. New software, especially beta versions, is notoriously buggy and can produce memory errors. The first step to correcting these errors, other than uninstalling the beta software, is to check for a BIOS upgrade or a service patch for the software. You should also check that you have enough memory installed for the operating system.

▲ **Immediately after hardware is installed or removed:** New hardware that is installed incorrectly or a connector or cable that is dislodged while removing a device can cause what appear to be memory errors accompanied by memory error messages. After checking the cables and connectors, check with the new hardware's manufacturer for newer device drivers or BIOS updates.

▲ **For no apparent reason:** If a PC has been running okay and suddenly begins having memory problems, check for corrosion on the contacts of the memory modules. Another possible cause is heat. The PC could have been running too hot and has finally damaged the motherboard, memory, or processor to the point of causing errors. Another suspect should be the power supply.

Typically, a PC will inform you of a problem in predictable ways. You should know the following problems and appropriate solutions:

▲ **The PC fails to boot and sounds a beep code:** Check the memory to ensure that it is properly installed and configured to the BIOS.

▲ **The PC boots, but the display is blank:** A dislodged card, a memory module that's not fully seated, or a memory module that the system doesn't support commonly cause a blank screen. Confirm that all expansion cards and memory modules are seated in their sockets, and verify that the installed memory is compatible with the system by checking memory part numbers. Installing nonparity RAM in a PC that has Error-Checking Code (ECC) memory, or placing SDRAM in a PC that supports only EDO (Extended Data Output) memory can cause the screen to be blank at boot up because the boot sequence cannot complete.

▲ **The PC boots, but the memory count is wrong:** The POST does a memory count that is displayed on the monitor. If the displayed number is not correct (it will always be less than it should be if it is wrong), the PC didn't recognize all of the installed memory. This could be caused by a wrong memory type being installed, such as dual-bank memory added to single-bank memory, in which case the POST sees only half of the memory added. Also, certain systems only accept specific memory modules and cannot see more than a certain amount of RAM.

▲ **The PC displays a memory error message, such as the following:**
   • Memory mismatch error
   • Memory parity interrupt at *nnnnn* (where *nnnnn* is the physical address of the faulty memory)
   • Memory address error at *nnnnn*
   • Memory failure at *nnnnn*, read *nnnnn*, expecting *nnnnn*
   • Memory verify error at *nnnnn*.

   These errors typically indicate problems between old memory and new memory or show a failing memory module. If removing a newly installed memory module eliminates the error, you should replace the old memory module with the new memory module. If the error shows up again, the new memory is either defective or is not compatible with the system. However, these error messages can also show up due to a motherboard problem.

▲ **Other memory problems:** Intermittent memory problems that show up sporadically as an error message, system crash, or spontaneous reboot, are notoriously difficult to diagnose. Hundreds of possible causes exist, including ESD (electrostatic discharge), overheating, corrosion, or a faulty power supply.

FOR EXAMPLE

Memory Testing Utilities

If you are trying to confirm that one of your various RAM modules is faulty, you can use a software memory diagnostic utility to pinpoint a specific defective module. Some PC manufacturers such as Dell and IBM have memory testing utilities designed for their PCs, or your PC's CMOS may have some diagnostic tests. You can also download memory testing utilities from the web such as Memtest-86.

▲ **Software-related memory problems:** The problems in this category include Registry errors, general-protection and page faults, and exception errors. Registry errors happen when the Windows operating system writes parts of the Registry to a defective portion of RAM. Software bugs cause faults and exception errors. For example, an application may not release its memory when completed or may try to occupy the same memory address as another application. Rebooting the PC usually solves these problems.

SELF-CHECK

1. What are the two main reasons for upgrading memory?
2. What factors determine the type of memory you use in a PC?
3. What is the basic procedure for installing memory?
4. What would cause the POST memory count to be different from the installed memory?

SUMMARY

The PC uses memory to speed up data transfers between data storage and the CPU. Data and software the PC is using is stored in system memory, and data that is frequently used is stored in cache memory. The CPU stores data it is working on in its registers. There are two categories of memory: volatile and nonvolatile. ROM is an example of nonvolatile memory; RAM is volatile. Types of ROM include PROM, EPROM, EEPROM, and Flash memory. Types of RAM include DRAM, used for system memory, and SRAM, commonly used for external cache.

For the operating system to work with memory, system memory is logically divided into four areas: conventional memory, the upper memory area, the high memory area, and the extended memory. Software and data that are currently in use are stored in extended memory.

Form factors for system memory include SIMMs, DIMMS, RIMMs, and for laptops, SODIMMs and MicroDIMMS. Types of DRAM technology include FPM DRAM, EDO DRAM, SDR DRAM, DDR DRAM, RDRAM, and DDR 2. In addition to their form factor and technology, DRAM modules are also identified and compared by their bit width, capacity, speed or bandwidth, type of error correction used (if any), such as ECC or parity, their CAS latency. DRAM modules may use single- or dual-channel memory, have gold or tin connectors. Some DIMMs are double-ranked, with the module's chips split into groups accessed separately by the memory controller.

You typically upgrade memory in order to support software or to improve overall performance. When you upgrade memory, it must be matched to the motherboard. The motherboard and the chipset will determine what type of memory can be used, its speed and its form factor.

The motherboard's documentation will specify how memory should be installed into the motherboard's slots. In general, to install a memory module, you must first release the retaining clips, line up the memory to the slot connectors, before inserting the module.

Memory problems on a PC are usually problems with configuration, hardware, or installation. Hardware memory problems have symptoms such as failure to boot and system crashes. A software memory problem may generate page fault and exception errors. However, problems with other hardware can exhibit similar symptoms and also generate memory errors. If you have a hardware problem with a memory problem, it will usually show up immediately after it is installed. Corrosion and power and heat problems may be the cause of a module failing later in its life.

KEY TERMS

Bank

Chip creep

Column Address Strobe
    (CAS) latency

Conventional memory

DDR2

Double Data Rate SDRAM
    (DDR SDRAM)

Double-pumped

Dual-channel memory

Dual Inline Memory Module
    (DIMM)

Dual Inline Package (DIP)
    chip

Dynamic RAM
    (DRAM)

Electronically Erasable
  Programmable Read Only
  Memory (EEPROM)

Erasable Programmable Read Only
  Memory (EPROM)

Error Correction Code (ECC)

Even parity

Extended Data Out (EDO) DRAM

Extended memory

Fast Page Mode (FPM) DRAM

Heat spreader

High memory area (HMA)

Memory

MicroDIMM

Nonvolatile memory

Odd parity

Page file

Parity

Programmable Read Only Memory
  (PROM)

Rambus DRAM (RDRAM)

Random access memory (RAM)

Read-only memory (ROM)

RIMM

Single Data Rate (SDR) DRAM
  (SDRAM)

Single Inline Memory Module
  (SIMM)

Small Outline DIMM (SoDIMM)

Static RAM (SRAM)

Swap file

Synchronous DRAM (SDRAM)

Synchronous Link DRAM
  (SLDRAM)

Upper memory area

Video RAM (VRAM)

Virtual memory

Volatile memory

ASSESS YOUR UNDERSTANDING

Go to www.wiley.com/college/groth to evaluate your knowledge of memory. *Measure your learning by comparing pre-test and post-test results.*

Summary Questions

1. What type of memory is used as general, temporary storage for the software and data a user is working on?
   (a) cache memory
   (b) registers
   (c) hard drives
   (d) system memory

2. Which type of ROM does not need to be removed from the system to be reprogrammed?
   (a) PROM
   (b) EPROM
   (c) EEPROM
   (d) All of the above

3. DRAM stores information as patterns of ons and offs in transistors. True or false?

4. The first 640K of memory is called upper memory. True or false?

5. Which memory form factor is most commonly used today?
   (a) DIP
   (b) DIMM
   (c) SIMM
   (d) RIMM

6. What technology characterized SDRAM?
   (a) SDRAM is clock-doubled.
   (b) SDRAM was synchronized to the clock.
   (c) SDRAM used static RAM.
   (d) SDRAM used a multiplexed bus rather than fixed pin settings.

7. Which of the following types of memory is able to correct 1-bit parity errors?
   (a) EDO
   (b) BEDO
   (c) Rambus
   (d) ECC

8. RIMMS must be installed in RIMM slots: True or false?

9. What is the difference between installing a SIMM and a DIMM?

    (a) The DIMM is installed at an angle.

    (b) The SIMM is installed at an angle.

    (c) SIMMs must be installed in pairs.

    (d) DIMMS must be installed in pairs.

10. Which type of errors indicates a software-related memory problem?

    (a) registry errors

    (b) crashes and blue screens

    (c) POST beep codes

    (d) startup failures

11. What is the most likely cause if the PC boots to a blank screen?

    (a) a memory module that is not fully seated

    (b) a parity error

    (c) a power-related memory problem

    (d) a software-related memory problem

12. Dual-channel memory is:

    (a) a DIMM in which DRAM chips are split into two groups

    (b) memory that can be accessed twice during a clock cycle

    (c) memory accessed by dual-channel memory controllers

    (d) memory whose chips are located on both sides of the module

13. An "8M × 16" memory chip will have a capacity of 128 MB. True or false?

14. What type of DRAM is used to support video cards?

    (a) VRAM

    (b) SLDRAM

    (c) RDRAM

    (d) SRAM

15. EDO is a type of asynchronous RAM designed to eliminate wait states. True or false?

16. If you are transmitting the 8-bit binary number 11010010 and are using even parity, what will the parity bit be?

    (a) 1

    (b) 0

    (c) Neither

    (d) Either

17. The memory type is most commonly used for L2 cache is SDRAM. True or false?

18. Which memory package is installed directly on the motherboard?
    (a) SRAM
    (b) RIMM
    (c) SIP
    (d) DIP
19. What Windows operating system feature uses hard disk space as extra memory storage?
    (a) BIOS
    (b) dynamic memory
    (c) virtual memory
    (d) extended memory
20. Why does system memory use DRAM as opposed to SRAM?
    (a) because DRAM can be dynamically updated
    (b) because DRAM is faster
    (c) because DRAM is less expensive
    (d) because DRAM can store more memory

Applying This Chapter

1. You are upgrading a PC and choosing a new CPU. What factors will come into play in your selection?
2. A RAM module is described on e-Bay.com as "DDR333 PC2700 DDR DRAM PC MEMORY 1 GB". What does this tell you about the module?
3. A friend wants to upgrade the memory on her PC to improve performance. What advice or recommendations do you have for her?
4. You are upgrading a PC to run Windows XP Professional. How will you determine whether you need to install new memory modules?
5. You are replacing RIMM memory modules on an older system. What are the special considerations involved when installing this type of memory?

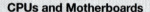

CPUs and Motherboards

You are building a PC with Intel Desktop Board D955XCS motherboard. Go to Intel.com and research what types of memory this motherboard supports.

Faster Memory

A client wants you to build a high-end PC for use with processor- and memory-intensive 3D-graphic applications, and asks that the PC has as much RAM as possible. What other memory considerations, other than the combined capacity of the memory modules, might help speed up the system?

Troubleshooting Memory

You have just installed new memory on a PC. When you start up the PC, it boots to a blank screen. What troubleshooting steps will you take?

What's Your Memory?

Find out the type and amount of system and cache memory on your system by checking the BIOS startup screen and the CMOS settings.

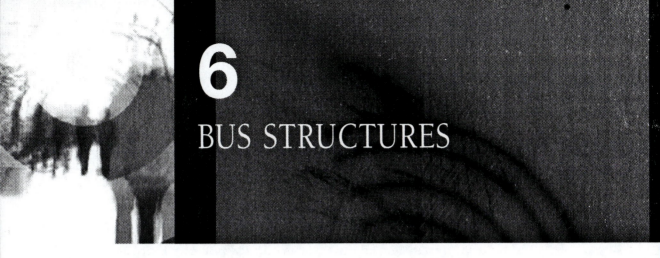

6
BUS STRUCTURES

Starting Point

Go to www.wiley.com/college/groth to assess your knowledge of bus structures.

Determine where you need to concentrate your effort.

What You'll Learn in This Chapter

▲ Bus types and characteristics
▲ Popular bus architectures
▲ The four types of system resources
▲ Installation steps for expansion cards

After Studying This Chapter, You'll Be Able To

▲ Identify and describe the two main bus structures found in the PC
▲ Discuss bus architectures in terms of their performance and use
▲ Identify the types of system resources and how they are used
▲ Evaluate and compare motherboards in terms of their supported bus structures and expansion slots
▲ Select an expansion card compatible with a motherboard's expansion buses and slots
▲ Install an expansion card
▲ Troubleshoot expansion card problems

INTRODUCTION

The bottom of any PC motherboard is an interconnecting maze of copper lines or pathways, called traces, that transport data, addresses, and instructions around the system. Each of these pathways is a bus, which is a group of tiny, very thin wires that carry signals. The PC uses different types of buses for communication inside the CPU, between motherboard components, and to peripherals.

Internal buses are used to connect separate components on the motherboard (the CPU, cache, and memory) and external buses are used to connect peripherals to the PC (including hard drives, monitors, and printers). Internal buses are usually referred to simply as buses, and external buses are more commonly discussed in terms of I/O ports, interfaces, and cables. This chapter examines the internal bus structures of the PC. You will learn more about the external buses used for hard drives in Chapter 7, and the common buses used for I/O devices in Chapter 9.

The PC's buses define how fast and how much data is transmitted between components. To be able to compare and evaluate PCs and motherboards in terms of their performance, you need to understand the different types of buses. Some of the most common upgrades to a PC are made by adding expansion cards, such as video cards, to the motherboard. The types of expansion cards you can use will depend on the types of buses used on the motherboard. Bus architectures or technologies have improved significantly over the past decade, and you need to be able to distinguish between older and newer technologies and understand how these technologies affect the ways you can upgrade a PC.

6.1 Understanding Buses

A **bus** is essentially a collection of wires, called **lines**, that transport data or power as electrical signals between two or more hardware devices or components. Buses are typically designed to be shared: more than two devices can communicate over the bus. A bus structure, or architecture, defines how the bus transmits data and what types of connectors or connections are used by devices to connect to the bus.

6.1.1 Introducing Buses

There are two main ways that buses transmit data:

▲ **Serial buses** transmit bytes one bit at a time over a single wire or line.
▲ **Parallel buses** are made up of groups of wires that transmit one or more bytes at a time. Each wire transmits one bit at a time.

Internal buses have traditionally been parallel, although new technologies have made serial buses faster. In a parallel bus, different wires or lines in a bus are often assigned different functions:

▲ **Data lines.** Each **data line** in a bus can transfer one bit at a time. A bus that can carry 32-bits of data at a time has 32 lines used for data, and is called a 32-bit bus.

▲ **Address lines.** Some lines are used to carry addresses, which refer to the location of stored data, as opposed to the data itself. Some buses transfer data and addresses on the same lines, and are called **multiplexed**.

▲ **Control signal lines.** Control signal lines are used to manage overall communications. For example, a control signal may be indicate whether data needs to be read or written.

▲ **Power lines.** Bus lines can also be used to carry small amounts of voltage for powering devices.

There are two main characteristics used to describe a bus's performance.

▲ **Width:** The size (its width, or capacity) of a bus determines the amount of data it can transmit. A 16-bit bus is capable of transmitting 16 bits of data at a time, and a 32-bit bus can transmit 32 bits of data. The wider a bus is in bits, the more data it can carry.

▲ **Speed:** The speed at which data moves on a bus is controlled by its clock speed, which is measured in megahertz (MHz). Higher bus speeds can transmit more data per second.

There are two main bus structures on every motherboard:

▲ **System, or frontside bus:** The **system bus**, or **frontside bus**, is an internal bus on the motherboard that interconnects main memory, the CPU, and all other components on the motherboard. This bus is sometimes referred to as the external bus because it is external to the CPU.

▲ **Expansion buses:** An **expansion bus** is an internal bus on the motherboard that is used to expand the motherboard's capabilities through the use of an expansion card. The expansion bus connects the chipset to expansion slots. Expansion cards, such as video or sound cards, are placed into the expansion slots. These cards typically have ports and connectors that jut out of the PC case that you use for attaching cables to external devices, such as monitors and speakers. A motherboard may have several types of expansion buses used for connecting various types of devices.

Synchronous buses are designed to operate synchronously with the system clock, and for this reason you may see them referred to as **"local" buses**. The system bus is a local bus. However, the term "local bus" is commonly used to differentiate between buses that communicate with components inside the PC and those that communicate with external devices.

The bus architectures used in a PC have an important effect on the PCs speed overall. For example, although a CPU may be capable of very fast data processing speeds, it is limited by the speeds of the buses supplying data to it, traditionally the frontside bus. And in fact, the data transferring speed between any two devices or components is dependent on the speed of the bus that connects them. A slow bus or data channel can act as a bottleneck, slowing processing speed.

6.1.2 The System Bus

The system bus, or frontside bus, connects the CPU to the chipset and other motherboard components (Figure 6-1). It provides the internal components of the computer with control signals, addresses, and data. It also supplies power.

Figure 6-1

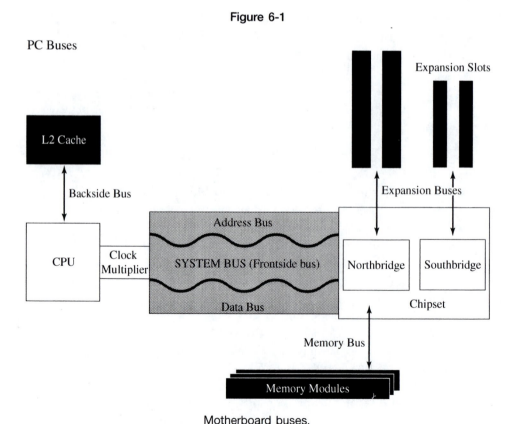

Motherboard buses.

Power comes to the motherboard straight from the power supply. The motherboard uses the system bus to distribute power to components mounted on or plugged into it.

The system bus runs at the same base speed as the system clock, but may be designed to transfer data twice during the clock cycle (double-pumped) or four times a cycle (quad pumped).

The address and data lines of the system bus are often discussed as distinct buses:

▲ **The data bus:** The **data bus** is used to send and receive data. The larger the bus width, the more data that can be transmitted (and, therefore, the faster the bus). Data in a computer is transferred digitally. A single wire carries 3.3V or 5V to indicate a 1 data bit; it carries 0 volts to indicate a 0 data bit. The greater number of wires allows more bits to be transmitted simultaneously.

▲ **The address bus:** Instead of data, the information the **address bus** sends is addressing information used to describe memory locations. These locations are used for data being sent or retrieved. The address bus carries a single bit of information, representing a digit in the address, along each wire. The size of the address bus corresponds to the number of address locations. The larger the address bus, the more

FOR EXAMPLE

Frontside or System Bus?

Because CPU, chipset, and motherboard architecture has changed significantly over the past decade and continues to change, you may hear the system bus referred to as the frontside bus, host bus, local bus, CPU or processor bus, main bus, or internal bus. What used to be a shared system bus in early PCs that connected all motherboard components was separated into two portions: the frontside bus, which connected the CPU to the chipset and main system memory, and the backside bus, which connects the CPU to L2 cache. The frontside bus is often described as the bus that connects the CPU to main memory. However, the frontside bus is being phased out in some motherboard and chipset architectures. One or more memory buses or channels may connect the Northbridge or the CPU directly to system memory, and new bus technologies may connect chips in a point-to-point (not shared) architecture. However, you can still assume that the term system bus or frontside bus refers to the main bus that supplies data, power, addresses, and control signals to and from the CPU.

memory address locations can be supported. The more memory address locations a processor can address, the more system memory (DRAM) a CPU can use.

The data bus and address bus are independent of each other, but for better performance, larger data buses require larger address buses.

6.1.3 Expansion Buses

Expansion buses, also called I/O buses, peripheral buses, or external buses, were created to let people easily expand the capabilities of their computer. Expansion buses on the motherboard are connected to **expansion slots,** into which you can fit circuit boards called expansion or adapter cards (Figure 6-2). The **expansion cards** themselves hold circuits and controllers for controlling specific types of

Figure 6-2

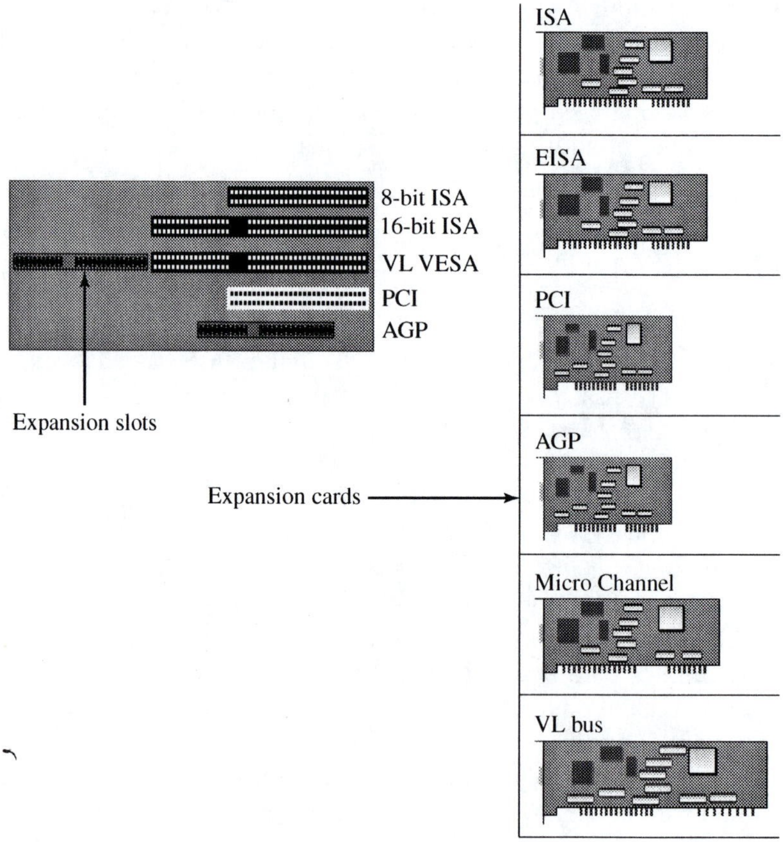

Expansion slots and cards.

peripherals and ports and adapters to attach the peripheral. For example, video cards allow PC users to upgrade the quality of their PCs graphic performance and will have an adapter for attaching a monitor.

Expansion buses and slots are designed to hold different types of expansion cards, so that you can use the same expansion slot for a video card, sound card, or other type of expansion card, as long as the card is designed for that type of expansion bus architecture. For example, you must use a PCI card to fit in a PCI expansion slot.

There are a number of different expansion bus structures, or architectures, that have been developed with ever increasing speeds and efficiencies. Some bus architectures were designed specifically for supporting video; others were developed as overall data transfer solutions.

The expansion buses communicate with the PC through the chipset: Some types communicate with the Northbridge, and others through the Southbridge. A motherboard may support several types of expansion buses, each with one or more corresponding expansion slots.

The expansion slots on a motherboard are the most visible part of the expansion buses. The expansion slot for any of the supported expansion bus architectures comprises a certain number of small metal spring edge connectors that line each side of the connector slot. The slot connectors match up with the tabs on the card's edge connectors (Figure 6-3).

Figure 6-3

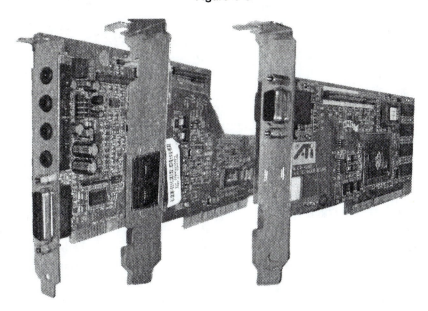

Expansion cards.

In order to coordinate with the CPU, the expansion card (and expansion bus), use different types of signals, including:

▲ **Clock signal:** This connection provides the card with the signal of the bus clock so that it can synchronize its communications with the buses of the motherboard.

▲ **Interrupt request (IRQ):** A request that tells the CPU to interrupt what it's doing to take care of the special needs of the device sending the IRQ. A device is given an IRQ number so that the CPU knows which device is making the request.

▲ **Direct memory access (DMA):** DMA channels allow certain devices to bypass the CPU and access system memory directly. DMA devices have the intelligence to handle their own data transfers to memory. Some bus architectures allow more DMA channels than others, but two devices can't share a DMA channel.

▲ **Input/Output (I/O) address:** Assigned to a device via its expansion slot. The I/O address, also called an I/O port or hardware port, allows the CPU to send commands directly to the device by writing them to an assigned area in memory that the device checks frequently. The I/O address is a one-way-only line that works like a reverse IRQ. The CPU uses the I/O address to send a command to the device. If the device responds, it uses the data bus or DMA channel to do so. Only one device can be assigned to an I/O address.

▲ **Bus mastering:** Allows one device to interact directly with another. Usually, the expansion card plugged into a slot has a bus master processor on the card that directs this activity. Most modern motherboards, especially those with the PCI bus, support bus mastering because it improves performance.

IRQs, I/O addresses, and DMA channels are a type of system resource. **System resources** are essentially communication channels or addresses that are used by the CPU to manage system devices like expansion cards.

Almost all PCs support multiple expansion bus interfaces. On these systems, provisions must be made to interconnect the different bus architectures and allow their devices to communicate with one another. This is accomplished using an **interface bridge**, which connects two dissimilar systems. A common bridge in Pentium systems was the PCI-ISA bridge supplied by the chipset. To see the interface bridges on your PC, you can use a Windows tool called the Device Manager that analyzes hardware-related problems. The Device Manager displays all of the devices installed (or recognized as installed) in a computer, organized by category. It allows you to view a device's status, properties, and resource assignments.

Figure 6-4

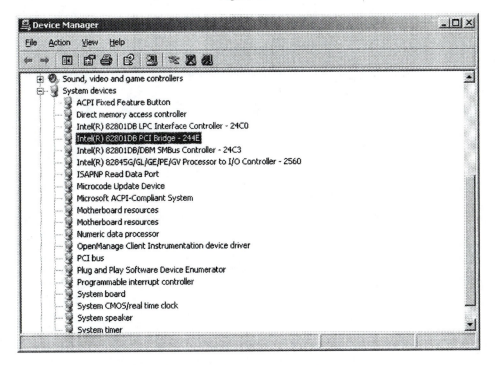

System devices node expanded.

To access the Windows XP Device Manager, open the Start Menu, right-click My Computer, and select Properties from the drop-down menu. In the System Properties dialog box, select the Hardware tab and click Device Manager. Expand the System devices node to view the interface bridges (Figure 6-4).

SELF-CHECK

1. Explain what a bus is.
2. What is the difference between the system bus and an expansion bus?
3. What are two characteristics used to describe a bus's performance?
4. What communication mechanisms do expansion buses and cards use to coordinate with the CPU and other components?

6.2 Examining Expansion Bus Architectures

Several expansion architectures have been used in PCs over the years, with successive generations of architectures supporting higher speeds and bandwidths. Expansion buses have typically been parallel buses, with higher bandwidths achieved through expanding the bus width. More recently, bus architectures have been using types of higher speed serial transmissions.

Because you may occasionally have to work with or support older PCs, you should be familiar with the popular architectures that have been used as well as with the types of architectures, slots, and cards used today.

6.2.1 Early Expansion Buses

Common expansion bus architectures that you will find on older PCs (and which are now obsolete), include the following:

▲ **8-bit Industry Standard Architecture (ISA) bus:** The 8-bit ISA bus, often called the PC bus or the 8-bit bus, was introduced with the first IBM PCs. It had 8 IRQ lines and 4 DMA channels. You will rarely encounter these.

▲ **16-bit ISA bus:** The ISA architecture was updated to a 16-bit bus, often called the AT bus, for use in early IBM AT (Advanced Technology) computers. It is commonly referred to simply as the ISA bus. For backward compatibility with 8-bit cards, the ISA bus added an additional short slot to the 8-bit bus slots to create a 16-bit connector (Figure 6-5). The 16-bit ISA added eight additional IRQs and doubled the number of DMA channels to 8. ISA expansion cards were designated to the appropriate IRQ or DMA numbers through jumpers and DIP switches. The 16-bit ISA architecture also separated the bus clock from the CPU clock to allow the slower data bus to operate at its own speeds.

ISA expansion cards use a connector similar to the 8-bit bus but with the additional connector for the 16-bit data and address lines. Most expansion cards made for the PC's 8-bit bus can be inserted into ISA slots, and they will function properly. Some 8-bit cards have a "skirt" extending below the bus slot. This skirt will not allow the 8-bit card to be inserted all the way into the ISA slot. For this reason, older motherboards included both 8-bit and 16-bit slots.

▲ **Micro-Channel Architecture (MCA):** Introduced with the IBM PS/2, MCA was the first 32-bit expansion bus. It featured bus mastering and a 10 MHz bus clock for expansion cards. The MCA expansion slot is about the same size as the ISA slot, but has about twice as many channels. MCA cards are also configured to their IRQ and DMA assignments

Figure 6-5

ISA expansion slots.

by software, a significant improvement over the jumpers and DIPs of the
ISA architecture.

▲ **Extended ISA (EISA):** EISA architecture was developed by a group of
companies to overcome the limitations of ISA and compete with MCA.
EISA has a 32-bit data bus, uses software setup, has more I/O addresses
available, and ignores IRQs and DMA channels. EISA uses only an
8 MHz bus clock to be backward compatible to ISA boards. In this case,
EISA supports ISA expansion cards along with its own.

▲ **VESA Local Bus (VLB or VL-bus):** VLB was used first on 486 systems
and grew from the need for the data bus to run at the same clock speed
as the CPU. VLB was developed by the Video Electronics Standards
Association (VESA) to support video capabilities and placed a port more
or less directly on the system bus with what was called a bus slot or a
processor direct slot.

See Table 6-1 for a comparison of the previously mentioned buses.

Table 6-1: Early Expansion Bus Architecture Characteristics

Bus	Bus Width (bits)	Bus Speed (MHz)	How Configured
8-bit ISA (PC bus)	8	8	Jumpers and DIP switches
16-bit ISA	16	8	Jumpers and DIP switches
MCA	32	10	Software
EISA	32	8	Software
VL-Bus	32	Processor speed (up to 40 MHz)	Jumpers and DIP switches

6.2.2 PCI Bus Architecture

With the introduction of Pentium-generation processors, all existing buses basically became obsolete. The Pentiums were 64-bit processors and using existing buses would have severely limited the performance of the new technology. Primarily for this reason, the **Peripheral Component Interconnect (PCI) bus** was developed.

PCI bus features and benefits include:

▲ **32-bit and 64-bit data path:** The PCI bus supports both 64-bit and 32-bit data paths, so it can be used in both 486 and Pentium-based systems.

▲ **Processor independent:** The PCI bus is processor-independent. The bus communicates with a special bridge circuit in the chipset's Southbridge that communicates with both the CPU and the bus. This has the benefit of making the bus almost universal. You can find PCI buses in PCs, Mac OS–based computers, and RISC computers. The same expansion card will work for all of them; you just need a different configuration program for each.

▲ **Higher clock speeds:** Another advantage of PCI over previous buses is its higher clock speed. PCI was originally designed to run at 33 MHz and in its current revision can run up to 66 MHz. The 64-bit data path using a 66 MHz bus gives PCI a maximum throughput of up to 512 Mbps.

▲ **Bus mastering:** PCI supports bus mastering expansion cards.

▲ **Backward compatibility:** The PCI bus uses a chipset that works with PCI, ISA, and Extended Industry Standard Architecture (EISA). It is possible to have a PC that contains all these buses on the same motherboard.

Figure 6-6

PCI expansion slots.

▲ **PnP support:** PCI cards are also **Plug and Play (PnP)**, which means they automatically configure themselves to the appropriate IRQ, DMA, and I/O port addresses.

Identification of PCI bus slots is simple. The finger slots in the bus (Figure 6-6) are packed together tightly. This connector is usually white. Older 32-bit PCI slots are shorter than 64-bit slots and contain two sections. 64-bit slots have three sections and are compatible with 32-bit cards.

In some systems that are a combination of PCI and ISA, each PCI slot is located next to an ISA slot. When you put a card in that PCI slot, you disable the ISA slot, and vice versa. Only one card will fit in a combination slot at a time.

Table 6-2: PCI Buses

Bus	Width	Clock/Bus Speed	Max Bandwidth
PCI	32-bit	33 MHz	133 MBps
	32-bit	66 MHz	266 MBps
	64-bit	33 MHz	266 MBps
	64-bit	66 MHz	533 MBps
PCI-X 64	64	66 MHz	533 MBps
PCI-X 133	64-bit	133 MHz	1066 MBps
PCI-X 266	64-bit	133 MHz/266 MHz double data rate	2132 MBps
PCI-X 533	64-bit	133 MHz /533 MHz quad data rate	4266 MBps

Variations of PCI were developed for low-profile desktops (low-profile PCI) and laptops (mini PCI). One variant, **PCI extended (PCI-X)**, was created for high-performance servers and workstations. It supports speeds from 133 to 533 MHz (higher bandwidth versions double or quadruple data transfers during a clock cycle) and supports 32-bit and 64-bit bus widths. See Table 6-2 for a comparison of PCI and PCI-X speeds and bandwidths.

6.2.3 Accelerated Graphics Port (AGP)

As Pentium systems became faster, PC game players wanted games that had better graphics, more realism, and more speed. The bus that was developed to meet this need was the **Accelerated Graphics Port (AGP)** bus. Based on PCI technol-

FOR EXAMPLE

3.3V and 5V PCI

Early PCI motherboards used 5.5VDC to power the expansion cards, and later boards use 3.3VDC. When you look at the connectors for these buses, the only difference you'll see is the placement of the blocker (called a key) in each connector—a 3.3VDC card can't be plugged into a 5.5VDC bus slot or vice versa. However, many boards have universal PCI connectors that will accept either type, and some PCI "universal" cards are designed to fit in either type of connector.

Figure 6-7

An AGP slot.

ogy, but designed specifically for supporting 3D graphics, AGP reduces the load on the PCI bus by providing a direct channel to the chipset's Northbridge; thus it gets much higher priority than the PCI bus. The original version of AGP uses a 32- bit width with a base speed of 66 MHz, twice the PCI bandwidth of 133 MBps at 266 MBps. Successive versions of AGP transferred data twice, four times, and eight times during the clock cycle to achieve higher throughputs.

Other, less common versions of the AGP interface include AGP Pro and 64-bit AGP, typically used in high-end graphics workstations. AGP is currently being phased out in favor of using newer PCI Express buses for video cards.

The AGP connector is similar in physical size and appearance to a PCI connector, but it's usually darker in color and offset from the other PCI slots to avoid confusion (Figure 6-7).

Table 6-3 describes the four types of AGP buses.

Table 6-3: AGP Buses

Bus	Width	Clock/Bus Speed	Max Bandwidth
AGP 1×	32-bit	66 MHz	266 MBps
AGP 2×	32-bit	66 MHz/133 MHz	533 MBps
AGP 4×	32-bit	66 MHz/266 MHz	1066 MBps
AGP 8×	32-bit	66 MHz/533 MHz	2133 MBps

6.2.4 PCI Express (PCIe)

PCI Express, or **PCIe**, is a high-speed serial local bus architecture. Most expansion buses are parallel buses: they transfer multiple bits at the same time (in parallel) by using additional wires for each bit. Serial data transfers essentially transfer data one bit at a time over a single connection, and older serial technologies were very slow compared with parallel. However, high-speed parallel buses have their own limits, including the increased costs and increased signal noise that come from using double- (or more) pumped data and from using large numbers of wires. Because of the desire for increased bus speeds that parallel buses cannot provide, new technologies have been developed using improved serial buses.

Benefits and features of the PCI Express technology include:

▲ **Point-to-point architecture:** The PCI Express serial architecture uses a point-to-point architecture. Each attached PCI device is essentially given its own bus, called a link. A link may be made of one or more lanes, with each lane able to transfer one byte at a time: a PCIe ×4 link has 4 lanes. Consumer desktop PCs use PCIe connectors with lane widths of ×1, ×4, ×8, and ×16.

▲ **Packet-based, routed data transfer:** Instead of separating addresses and read/write data, PCIe addresses and data are transferred together in single packets. Each packet has multiple bytes, which are broken down for high-speed transfer in one-byte segments over a link's lanes. Each PCIe lane connects to a single, shared PCIe switch, which routes the data to its correct destination.

▲ **High-bandwidth:** Each PCIe lane is bidirectional, and can transfer data at 250 MBps in one direction with a total bandwidth of 500 MBps for each lane. An ×4 PCIe lane has four times this bandwidth.

▲ **Support for multiple graphics cards:** Whereas AGP was designed for a single graphics card connection to the Northbridge, PCIe can support multiple graphics cards.

PCIe motherboard connectors come in different lengths that correspond to the number of lanes the connector supports. They may be short (×1) or quite long (×16), and a motherboard may have several different lengths of PCIe connectors on it. See Table 6-4 for a comparison of PCIe lane widths and bandwidths. Motherboards built with graphics performance in mind may have 2 ×16 PCIe slots. PCIe cards are created for working with a certain number of lanes, but the PCIe standard supports the use of connectors with either the same or higher lane width. For example, an ×8 PCIe card will work in an ×8 or ×16 connector (as long as the motherboard manufacturer has configured the slots for this use).

Table 6-4: PCIe Maximum Bandwidths

PCIe Width	Throughput	Bidirectional Throughput
×1	250 MBps	500 MBps
×2	500 MBps	1000 MBps
×4	1000 MBps	2000 MBps
×8	2000 MBps	4000 MBps
×16	4000 MBps	8000 MBps

Although PCIe is viewed as the successor to PCI, you will still find PCI/AGP motherboards, and PCIe motherboards with PCI connectors. PCIe is backwardly compatible with PCI on a software, or programming level. This means that operating systems and other software designed for working with PCI devices will be able to work with PCIe expansion cards without modification. However, PCI cards cannot be used in PCIe slots, and vice versa.

6.2.5 HyperTransport

HyperTransport is bus architecture developed by a consortium of manufacturers including AMD, Apple Computer, Sun Microsystems, NVIDIA, and Transmeta. Similar to PCIe, it is a next generation, point-to-point bus architecture using variable width data links and packet-based data transmissions, but is designed for more efficient data transfer than PCIe. In its current specification, Hyper-Transport has maximum bandwidths up to 41.6 GBps. The HyperTransport technology supports high-end expansion cards for servers and workstations that use HyperTransport eXpansion (HTX) connectors, similar to PCIe connectors. In consumer PCs, HyperTransport has primarily been used on motherboards as a replacement for the frontside bus.

SELF-CHECK

1. What two bus architectures were designed for supporting graphics cards?
2. List four benefits or features of the PCI bus architecture.
3. How would you identify ISA, AGP and PCI slots on a motherboard?
4. What is the difference between PCI and PCIe?

6.3 Understanding System Resources

The term **system resources** refers to the mechanisms, communications channels, or addresses used to interface, communicate, and control individual device adapters and controllers, along with the serial, parallel, and mouse ports. Usually, the CPU and the peripheral devices on a PC use the elements of the system resources as a set of communications channels.

The four system resources are:

▲ I/O (input/output) addresses (also known as I/O ports)
▲ Interrupt requests (IRQs)
▲ DMA (direct memory access) channels
▲ Memory addresses

A resource conflict occurs when two or more devices try to use the same resource at the same time. Today's Windows "Plug and Play" standards build in some flexibility to device resource needs. Plug and Play (PnP) is a configuration standard that allows the system BIOS and the operating system to configure expansion boards and other devices automatically so that you don't have to worry about setting DIP switches, jumpers and system resources (such as IRQ, I/O addresses, and DMA). In effect, you just plug in the device or adapter card and

---

FOR EXAMPLE

Understanding PnP

To use PnP on a system, four requirements must be met: The system BIOS must support PnP; the motherboard and its chipset must support PnP; the operating system running on the PC must support PnP; and the bus of the expansion slot used must be compatible with PnP. However, unless you are working with older PCs, you will rarely have to review a systems PnP capability. All versions of Windows since Windows 95 (including Windows 2000) fully support PnP (although Windows NT only partially supports it). PnP is compatible with ISA, EISA, MCA, PC Card (PCMCIA), and PCI devices and adapters. Almost all PCI and AGP cards, and all PCI Express cards, are PnP.

Older devices that are not Plug and Play are called legacy devices. A computer system that is described as "legacy-free" is a system that won't accept or recognize these older, legacy devices. You may also come across the term "Universal PnP." This is an evolving extension of Plug and Play that allows your PC to automatically recognize and configure network devices.

it works. If there is a conflict, Plug and Play works out compromises automatically in the background, so for the most part you will not encounter many resource conflicts. However, if you have multiple older devices that are not Plug and Play, you may encounter a resource conflict, and in these cases, you can use the Device Manager to change a resource assignment for one or more of the conflicting devices.

6.3.1 Input/Output (I/O) Addresses

Every device in the PC uses input/output addresses (which are also known as I/O addresses, I/O ports, or I/O port addresses). The address in the I/O address points to the location in memory that's assigned to a specific device to use for exchanging information between itself and the rest of the PC.

Virtually every device in the PC is assigned an I/O address and a segment of system memory to hold messages and data. The size of the memory segment varies with the amount of data a device must pass on to other devices; in general, the memory segment assigned to a device ranges from 1 to 32 bytes, with 4, 8, or 16 bytes being common. These areas of memory allow a device to work without worrying about what other devices or the processor may be doing.

For example, when a modem receives data, it wants to pass the data along to the PC for processing; where can the data be put? The modem writes the data to the I/O address of the port to which the modem is attached, and when the CPU is ready to process this data, it knows where to look. This process of using I/O addresses to complete input/output operations is called memory-mapped I/O.

I/O addresses are expressed in hexadecimal and written as 3F8h. Although the I/O addresses for a component are technically a range, such as 03E8–03EF for COM3, you more commonly refer to the first address in the range, called the base I/O address (03E8 in this case). The lowercase "h" indicates it's a hexadecimal address. Table 6-5 lists most of the common I/O address assignments used in PC systems.

You can use the Device Manager to review the I/O addresses being used. Click the View menu in the Device Manager and then select Resources by Type. Expand the Input/Output (IO) tree, if necessary (Figure 6-8). You can also find this information in the System Information utility, which can be accessed by selecting (All) Programs/Accessories/System Tools.

6.3.2 Interrupt Requests

An **interrupt** is a request from a device (other than the CPU) to the CPU for a service, action, or special action. When a device needs the CPU to perform a task (such as transferring data from memory or issuing an I/O), it sends a signal to the CPU using the IRQ line it is assigned. Each device is assigned a specific

Table 6-5: Common I/O Address Assignments

I/O Address Range	Device or Port Commonly Assigned
000-00Fh	DMA channels 0–3 controller
020-021h	IRQ 0–7 interrupt controller
060h, 061h	Keyboard
0F8-0FFh	Math coprocessor
130-14Fh	SCSI host adapter
170-177h	Secondary hard drive controller
1F0-1F7h	Primary hard drive controller
200-207h	Game port
220-22Fh	Sound cards
278-27Fh	LPT2 or LPT3
2E8-2EFh	COM4
2F8-2FFh	COM2
300-30Fh	Network cards
3B0-3BBh	VGA video adapter
3C0-3DFh	VGA video adapter
378-37Fh	LPT1 or LPT2
3E8-3EFh	COM3
3F0-3F7h	Floppy disk controller
3F8-3FFh	COM1

IRQ number (much like the food server) so that the processor knows the device to which it must respond.

Interrupt requests are sent to a special system component, called an interrupt controller, which is either a separate chip on the motherboard or incorporated into the chipset. The interrupt controller receives and verifies requests and passes them on to the processor. Two interrupt controllers have been on PCs since the 286, each managing eight IRQ lines with each IRQ tied directly to a particular device. The two interrupt controllers are linked, or cascaded, through IRQ 2, which is set aside for this purpose.

An IRQ is assigned to one specific device. Assigning two active devices to the same IRQ creates an IRQ conflict. An IRQ conflict can cause both devices

Figure 6-8

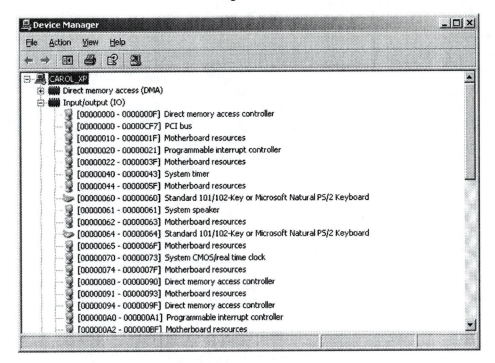

I/O assignments listed in Device Manager.

to perform sporadically (in the best case) or not at all (in the worst case). Similar devices can share IRQs, but they can't be used at the same time.

IRQs are assigned by the system BIOS during POST and the boot process, and there are default IRQ assignments for standard PC devices (Table 6-6). The way you reassign an IRQ or change the assigned IRQ of a device depends on the adapter card and the operating system. Some devices allow the IRQ to be changed and/or assigned in the BIOS setup. Older device adapters have jumpers to set the IRQ.

Windows 2000 and Windows XP systems handle IRQs a bit differently than earlier operating systems. Specifically, the IRQ Sharing feature, used on PCI devices on earlier systems, is expanded to include other ports and devices on motherboards that support the power management standard ACPI (Advanced Configuration and Power Interface). If you look in the Device Manager on a Windows XP system running on an ACPI motherboard, you should notice that several devices are sharing IRQ 9.

▲ On PCs running DOS and Windows 3.x, a device IRQ can be set through either a jumper on its adapter card or proprietary installation software.

Table 6-6: Default IRQ Assignments

IRQ #	Default Use	Description and Other Common Uses
0	System timer	Reserved interrupt for the internal system timer. Nothing else uses (or should use) interrupt 0.
1	Keyboard controller	Reserved interrupt for the keyboard controller. Nothing else uses (or should use) interrupt 1.
2*	Bridge to IRQs 8–15	In cascaded interrupt systems, IRQ 2 is used as a link to IRQs 8–15, which means it's not available for general use; if needed by an older system, it's replaced by IRQ 9. You may also see IRQ 2 assigned to programmable interrupt control, modems, COM3, or COM4
3	COM2	Many modems are preconfigured for COM2 on IRQ 3. It's also used as the default interrupt for COM4, if a system has four serial ports in use, and may be used for other devices such as expansion cards.
4	COM1	Normally used by the serial mouse. It's also the default interrupt for COM3 and may be used for other devices such as expansion cards
5	Sound card	Often the default IRQ for network interface cards. Used on some older systems for the hard disk drive and is the default interrupt for LPT2 (the second parallel port). Most sound cards are preset to IRQ 5.
6	Floppy disk controller	Reserved for the floppy disk controller (FDC). May also be used for tape controllers.
7	LPT1	This interrupt is normally used for the first parallel port, but may be used for other serial or parallel ports or other devices.
8	Real-time clock	Reserved for the real-time clock timer, which is used by software to track events to "real world" time. (IRQs 8–15 are not available on an 8-bit system.) Nothing else uses (or should use) interrupt 8.
9	None	A popular choice for network interface cards, but it's generally available for any use. It replaces IRQ 2 in cascading interrupt systems, so it should not be used if IRQ 2 is in use. Hardware MPEG 2 cards and SCSI host adapters can also use it.
10	None	This IRQ has no specific default settings; it is commonly used for video cards and modems.

Table 6-6: Default IRQ Assignments (continued)

IRQ #	Default Use	Description and Other Common Uses
11	None	No default assignment; it is used by some SCSI host adapters, PCI video cards, IDE sound cards, and USB controllers.
12	Motherboard mouse (PS/2) connector	On motherboards supporting a PS/2 mouse (mini-DIN connection on the motherboard), this IRQ is reserved for the PS/2 mouse. A PS/2 mouse on this interrupt frees up IRQ 4 (and COM1) for other uses. Some video cards may also use this IRQ.
13	Math coprocessor or floating point unit (FPU) unit	Reserved for the integrated floating point (386DX and later) or a math coprocessor (386SX and earlier).
14	Primary IDE adapter	Reserved for the primary IDE controller, which controls the first two IDE (ATA) disk drives. On PCs with no IDE devices, it can be reassigned in the BIOS setup for other uses, and is commonly used for SCSI controllers.
15	Secondary IDE adapter	Reserved for a secondary IDE controller, if present. Can be reassigned in BIOS, if needed, and is commonly used for SCSI controllers and network adapters.

*Interrupt 2 is a special case. Earlier (XT-based) PCs had only eight interrupts because those computers used an 8-bit bus. With the development of the AT, eight more interrupts were created (to match the 16-bit bus), but no mechanism was available to use them. Rather than redesign the entire interrupt process, AT designers decided to use interrupt 2 as a gateway, or cascade, to interrupts 9–15. In reality, interrupt 2 is the same as interrupt 9. You should never configure your system so that both interrupt 2 and 9 are used.

▲ On Windows 9x, Windows 2000, and Windows XP PCs, a device's IRQ assignment can be managed through the Device Manager. Using the Windows Device Manager, IRQ settings are changed or assigned in the properties of the individual device (Figure 6-9). The Device Manager will display a yellow or red exclamation point next to a problematic device to indicate that the device is either not working properly and may have a conflict or if it is disabled.

6.3.3 DMA Channels

A **direct memory access (DMA) channel** allows a device to bypass the processor to directly access memory. Those devices with a DMA channel assignment gain the advantage of faster data transfers that do not have to pass through the CPU. Not every device on the PC needs or uses DMA channels. DMA use is

Figure 6-9

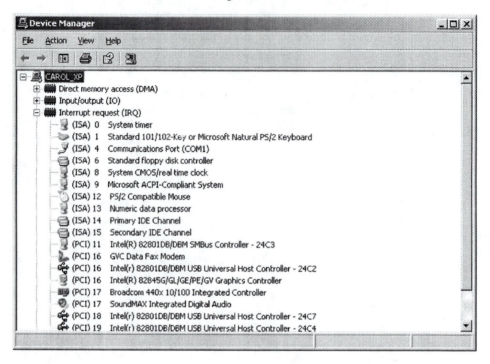

IRQ assignments listed in Device Manager.

common in some disk drives, tape drives, and sound cards. Most operating systems handle DMA assignments through PnP configuration, and newer buses (PCI, AGP, and PCIe) don't use DMA. One drawback to using DMA is that although the DMA device is working faster, the CPU may be put on hold, slowing everything else until the DMA data transfer is complete. Bus mastering allows devices to transfer data directly to each other, bypassing the CPU, and can be used instead of DMA channels for accessing memory.

A DMA channel can be assigned to only one hardware device. If two devices are assigned to the same DMA channel, both devices will have problems or the PC may crash. Table 6-7 lists common DMA channel usage. However, the assignments on your PC may assign the same devices to different channels, which is common.

DMA channel assignments can be set using one of these methods:

▲ Preset assignments of a device's adapter card, DIP switches, or jumpers on the device adapter card

▲ Assignments made during PnP configuration

▲ The BIOS setup utility

You can view DMA channel assignments in the Device Manager (Figure 6-10).

Table 6-7: DMA Channel Assignments

DMA Channel	Assignment
0	DRAM refresh
1	Sound card
2	Floppy disk drive
3	ECP or EPP parallel port
4	DMA controller
5	Sound card
6	Available
7	ISA IDE Hard Drive Controller

Figure 6-10

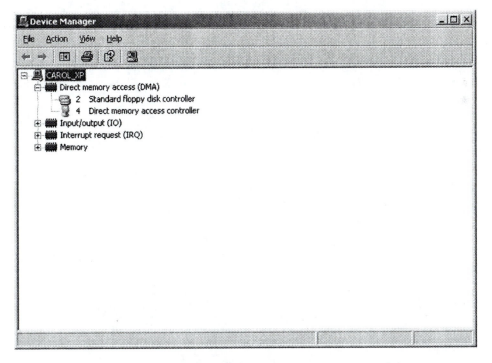

DMA assignments listed in Device Manager.

6.3.4 Memory Addresses

Memory addresses are areas of system memory (DRAM) that are assigned to be used exclusively by a specific device. Although not all devices require this, many devices use blocks of memory as part of their normal functioning. Network interface cards, for instance, often buffer incoming data in a block of memory until they can be processed. Doing so prevents the card from being overloaded if a burst of data is received from the network.

When the device driver loads, it lets the CPU know which block of memory should be set aside for the exclusive use of the component. This prevents other devices from overwriting the information stored there. (Of course, it also sets you up for hardware conflicts, because two components cannot be assigned the same address space.) Certain system components also need a memory address. Some of the more common default assignments are listed in Table 6-8, and you can view memory assignments in Device Manager (Figure 6-11).

S E L F - C H E C K

1. Explain how an I/O address is used.
2. What is an IRQ conflict?
3. What are DMA channels used for?
4. What does Plug and Play mean?

Table 6-8: Common Memory Address Assignments

Address	Assignment
F0000–FFFFF	System BIOS
E0000–EFFFF	In use on true IBM compatibles
CA000–DFFFF	Available on most PCs
C8000–C87FF	Hard-disk controller on an XT system
C0000–C7FFF	EGA/VGA display
B8000–BFFFF	CGA/EGA/VGA display
B0000–B7FFF	Monochrome display
A0000–AFFFF	EGA/VGA display
00000–9FFFF	System memory

Figure 6-11

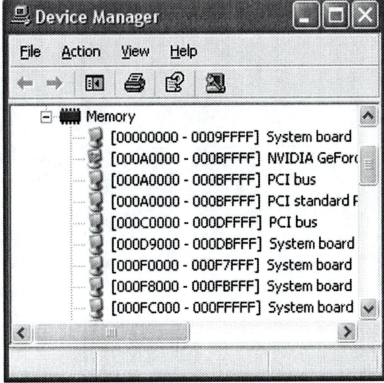

Memory assignments listed in Device Manager.

6.4 Working with Expansion Cards

6.4.1 Upgrading the PC with Expansion Cards

An **expansion card** is simply a circuit board you install into a computer to increase the capabilities of that computer. Most computers today use a separate video card because it can provide better performance than the on-board video circuitry. This is especially true of systems that are used for video games that require more advanced graphics.

Expansion cards include a connector for connecting to the motherboard, and a metal tab that holds ports or adapters. The metal tab allows the ports to be accessed from outside the PC's case. The type of ports on a card depends on the type of card it is and the peripherals it supports.

Expansion cards come in many different kinds, but the important thing to note is that no matter what function a card has, the card being installed must match the bus type of the motherboard you are installing it into (for example,

Figure 6-12

A video card.

you can only install a PCI network card into a PCI expansion slot). Four of the most common expansion cards that are installed today are:

▲ **Video cards:** Although motherboards include some built-in graphics support, **video or graphics cards** (Figure 6-12) are used to enhance a computer's graphic capabilities and work with the PC's monitor. A video card also is responsible for converting the data sent to it by the CPU into the pixels, addresses, and other items required for display. Some video cards can include dedicated chips to perform certain of these functions, thus accelerating the speed of display. With today's motherboards, most video cards are either PCIe or AGP expansion cards.

▲ **Sound Card:** Just as there are devices to convert computer signals into printouts and video information, there are devices to convert those signals into sound. These devices are known as **sound cards**. Many different manufacturers make sound cards, but the standard has been set by Creative Labs with its SoundBlaster series of cards. A sound card typically has small, round, 1/8-inch jacks on the back of it for connecting to microphones, headphones, and speakers as well as other sound equipment. Many sound cards also have a DB-15 game port which can be used for either joysticks or Musical Instrument Digital Interface (MIDI)

Figure 6-13

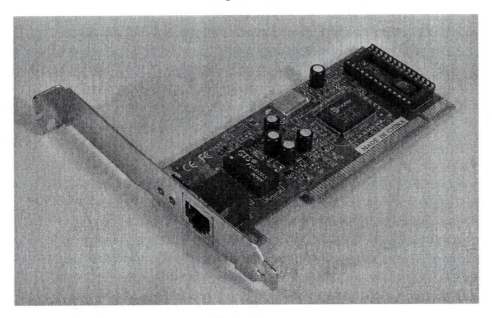

A NIC.

connections (allows a computer to talk to a digital musical instrument, such as a digital keyboard).

▲ **Network Interface Card (NIC):** A **NIC** (Figure 6-13) (also called a **network adapter**) is an expansion card that connects a computer to a network so that it can communicate with other computers on that network. It translates the data from the parallel data stream used inside the computer into the serial data stream of packets used on the network. NICs include connectors for the type of network (such as RJ-45 for UTP or BNC for coax). In addition to the NIC, you need to install software or drivers on the computer for the computer to use the network.

▲ **Modem:** Any computer that connects to the Internet via a dial-up connection needs a modem. A **modem** is a device that converts digital signals from a computer into analog signals that can be transmitted over phone lines and back again. Modem expansion cards have RJ-11 ports, or telephone jacks for connecting to telephone lines.

Although most cards use expansion slots to connect to the motherboard, some expansion cards use:

▲ **Audio Model Riser (AMR):** Some motherboards include AMR slots (Figure 6-14) into which AMR riser cards can be inserted to add support for

Figure 6-14

An AMR slot.

sound or modem functions. An AMR slot is typically located near a PCI slot that is disabled when an AMR card is in place.

▲ **Communications Network Riser (CNR):** CNR provides an on-mother-board slot (Figure 6-15) through which LAN or home networking, DSL, USB, wireless communications, audio, or modem system can be implemented on a PC. The CNR slot, available on many newer motherboards, connects through the USB bus to accept modems and networking devices configured from CNR slots.

Figure 6-15

A CNR slot.

6.4.2 Installing Expansion Cards

The process for upgrading a PC using expansion cards is basically the same for all types of slots (AGP, PCI, and so on). Just as with other types of components, it is critical to ensure that your motherboard will support the upgraded component. However, because expansion buses are designed to have some flexibility, this is less of a problem; their standards don't change nearly as fast as those for CPUs, chipsets, and memory.

If you are upgrading a card, you will need to remove the existing card (Figure 6-16). To do this, first remove anything plugged into the board, (such as a monitor attached through the case, or a PCIe power connector). Next, remove any mounting screws that are holding the boards in place, and put the screws somewhere where they won't be lost. Grasp the board by the top edge with both hands and gently rock it front to back (not side to side). After the board is out, place it in an antistatic bag to help prevent electrostatic discharge (ESD) damage while the board is out of the computer.

The general procedure for installing an expansion card is:

▲ **Prepare the case:** Locate the appropriate slot (on a recent PC, typically a PCI, AGP, PCIe slot) in the motherboard. You may need to remove the slot's corresponding I/O plate, or blank, (a piece of plastic or metal that covers the hole in the PC's case where the card's ports extend through). Figure 6-16 shows an example of a slot with the blank removed.

▲ **Insert the card:** Align the connector on the bottom of the card with the connector on the motherboard and insert the card into its connector. You should feel a slight amount of resistance. Push the card firmly into place with an even pressure on the front and back of the card. Stop pushing

Figure 6-16

A PC case with the I/O plate removed.

Figure 6-17

An installed expansion card.

when all of the card's connectors are making contact with the fingers in the expansion slot (Figure 6-17).

▲ **Secure the card:** Install the mounting screws through the tab in the expansion card to secure the card in place. In this case, you only have one screw to install, and it's located at the back of the computer. This screw holds the metal tab on the expansion card to the computer's case. If you are using a PCIe video card, you may also need to attach a PCIe power connector from the power supply.

PCI, AGP, and PCIe cards should automatically configure themselves in either an AGP or PCI slot. ISA cards may require manual configuration of the card's

FOR EXAMPLE

I/O Plates

You remove I/O plates by either taking out the screw holding it in place or using a pair of pliers to bend it back and forth until it breaks. Don't throw these plates away. If you ever want to remove a component, you will need to replace the blank so that dirt, dust, and other contaminants can be kept out. The most important function of a blank is to promote proper airflow over the internal components of your PC. PC manufacturers carefully design the placement of fans and air holes for their computers. Adding a new hole in the back of your computer will often result in less airflow rather than more. The end result is often a computer that overheats and burns out components.

resources. Although most cards use and are configured with software utilities called drivers that will load automatically when you boot up the system, you should check the manufacturer's website for any updated drivers. If there are any, you will need to download and install them.

For the most part, installing other expansion cards follows the same procedure. The only differences are what the cards look like and whether they need to be configured (and that depends on the bus). However, if you are installing multiple expansion cards on a new PC, it is best to install only the video card before the first power-up. After you have powered up the computer for the first time and configured any CMOS settings, shut down the computer, remove the power from the computer completely, wait 30 seconds for all power to discharge, and then install the next expansion card. Power up the computer so that the BIOS can configure the resources of the card; then, shut down the computer and repeat this procedure until all cards have been installed. This process will minimize the chances of resource conflicts because the BIOS has the opportunity to configure the cards one by one, and it's less likely to make a mistake configuring them all at once.

6.4.3 Troubleshooting Expansion Cards

An expansion card can malfunction because it either isn't installed properly, configured properly, or if over time, fails. If an expansion card isn't working, you will notice because the hardware device it is used to support stops working. If the device that the card supports doesn't work after you first install the card and attach the device, this is most likely an installation or configuration problem rather than a defect in the card itself.

To troubleshoot an expansion card installation:

▲ Check the manufacturer's installation and configuration instructions to make sure that you followed them, and make sure that you have the latest driver for the card

▲ Check the Device Manager to see if the card is recognized by the system and that there are no resource conflicts

▲ Make sure the card is seated properly in an appropriate slot

▲ Check the software included with the expansion card, it may include a diagnostic utility which you can use for troubleshooting. You can also use the Windows troubleshooting utility. To open the Windows Troubleshooting Wizard, open the Properties dialog box for the card by right-clicking the adapter in the Device Manager and selecting Properties. On the General tab of the Properties dialog box will be a button labeled "Troubleshoot."

However, if the expansion card has worked in the past, the problem may lie with the card or with the hardware device, or be a software issue. You may need to do some troubleshooting detective work to determine where the problem lies. For example:

▲ Check for basic hardware problems, such as functioning (and plugged in) power cords.

▲ Check software configuration issues, such as making sure that the card is configured properly and you have updated drivers.

▲ If you can, swap in a known good hardware device for the malfunctioning device to check that it is the card malfunctioning and not the hardware device. Conversely, you can swap in a known good card for the troublesome one to make sure that the card was the problem and not the slot.

If you can determine that software and configuration (or installation issues) aren't the cause of your problem, you most likely have a defective or failed circuit board. Circuit boards can stop working over time: components can overheat and connections or chips loosen. Scratches, oil, or dirt on circuit traces as well as EMI interference from other devices can cause a board to fail.

SELF-CHECK

1. Explain what an expansion card is and how it works with the motherboard.
2. List four types of common expansion cards.
3. Describe the steps for installing an expansion card.
4. What system tool do you use for managing system resources assignments?

SUMMARY

PC buses are groups of wires or lines used for transmitting data, control signals, power, and addresses between PC components. PC buses may be serial or parallel, external (connecting peripherals) or internal (used on the motherboard). A bus's performance is determined by its width and speed. The two main bus structures on the motherboard are the system or frontside bus and the expansion bus. The system bus connects the CPU with the chipset and system memory. It has two main parts: the data bus and the address bus. The expansion buses are used to attach peripherals through expansion cards inserted in expansion slots. To coordinate with the motherboard, expansion buses and cards use clock signals, IRQs, DMA, I/O addresses, and bus mastering. Interface bridges are used to interconnect different types of expansion buses on the motherboard.

Early expansion bus architecture includes the 8-bit (ISA), 16-bit ISA, MCA, EISA, VESA. Buses you will find on recent or new PCS include PCI, PCI-X, AGP, and PCIe. Expansion buses are migrating toward using advanced serial transmissions in place of parallel. Examples include PCIe and HyperTransport, which is most commonly used as a replacement for the frontside bus on AMD motherboards.

There are four types of system resources that devices, including expansion cards, may use to coordinate communications with the CPU: I/O addresses, IRQs, DMA channels, and memory addresses. If two devices use the same resource, a conflict will result, and prevent the devices from operating correctly. Some system resources are assigned by default to high-priority system devices, such as the keyboard or system timer, and cannot (or should not) be changed. Other resources can be reassigned through the Windows Device Manager. However, in current operating systems such as Windows 2000 and XP, a feature called IRQ sharing allows IRQs to be shared without conflict. DMA channels are also not often used, as bus mastering techniques allow devices to share the bus without conflicts or using DMA channels. Older expansion buses required expansion cards to have their system resources assigned manually through jumpers or DIP switches or software. Today, Plug and Play standards allow the BIOS to assign resources automatically during the boot sequence.

Expansion cards must be installed into a compatible expansion slot for their specific bus architecture. During an installation, you must be careful to avoid ESD or damaging the card's edge connectors. You may also need to remove a blank or I/O plate on the back of the PC case. If an expansion card is not working, the peripheral attached to it will not work properly. If you have just installed the card, this is most likely a configuration, systems resource, or seating problem. However, in troubleshooting, you may need to make sure that the problem lies with the expansion card as opposed to the peripheral.

KEY TERMS

Accelerated Graphics Port (AGP)

Address bus

Address line

AGP bus

Audio Modem Riser (AMR)

Bus

Bus mastering

Clock signal

CNR

Control signal line

Data bus

Data line

Direct Memory Access (DMA)

DMA channel

Expansion bus (I/O bus)

Expansion card

Expansion slot

Extended ISA (EISA)

HyperTransport

Industry Standard Architecture (ISA)

Input/Output (I/O) address

Interface bridge

Interrupt

Interrupt Request (IRQ)

Lines

Memory address

Micro-Channel Architecture (MCA)

Modem

Multiplexing

Network Interface Card (NIC)
   (network adapter)

Parallel bus

Peripheral Component
   Interconnect (PCI) bus

PCI-Express (PCIe)

PCI-Extended (PCI-X)

Plug and Play (PnP)

Power line

Serial bus

Sound card

Synchronous bus (local bus)

System bus (frontside bus)

System resources

VESA Local Bus (VLB or VL-bus)

Video (graphics) card

ASSESS YOUR UNDERSTANDING

Go to www.wiley.com/college/groth to evaluate your knowledge of bus structures. *Measure your learning by comparing pre-test and post-test results.*

Summary Questions

1. What are the two general types of bus structures on every motherboard?
   (a) the system bus and the expansion bus
   (b) the frontside bus and the system bus
   (c) the frontside bus and the backside bus
   (d) the local bus and the external bus

2. The system bus provides four different system necessities: data, addresses, control signals, and _____.
   (a) IRQ lines
   (b) DMA channels
   (c) power
   (d) system resources

3. Bus clock speed refers to:
   (a) the external speed of the CPU
   (b) the internal speed of the CPU
   (c) the speed of the hard drive
   (d) the speed at which data on the bus moves

4. What motherboard component do expansion buses typically communicate through?
   (a) CPU
   (b) I/O addresses
   (c) memory
   (d) chipset

5. Which bus architecture added 8 IRQs and 4 DMA channels?
   (a) 8-bit ISA
   (b) 16-bit ISA
   (c) MCA
   (d) EISA

6. What was the first 32-bit expansion bus architecture?
   (a) ISA
   (b) EISA
   (c) VESA Local Bus
   (d) MCA

7. What bus architecture was designed as a high-performance extension of PCI for servers and workstations?

   (a) PCI-X

   (b) PCI-Express

   (c) AGP

   (d) HyperTransport

8. What is the bit width of AGP 8×?

   (a) 16-bit

   (b) 32-bit

   (c) 64-bit

   (d) 128-bit

9. A PCle ×4 connector has:

   (a) four links

   (b) four lanes

   (c) four times the base bus speed

   (d) four PCI cards

10. Which of the following architectures is a point-to-point architecture often used as a replacement for the frontside bus?

    (a) PCI-X

    (b) PCI

    (c) AGP

    (d) HyperTransport

11. The CPU uses an IRQ to:

    (a) control devices attached to the system

    (b) generate a log file containing interrupt requests

    (c) identify a peripheral and find the software that controls it

    (d) protect the system from hardware device failures

12. What is the default I/O address for COM1?

    (a) 2F8-2FFh

    (b) 3F8-3FFh

    (c) 378-37Fh

    (d) 3F0-3F7H

13. What is the reserved IRQ for the keyboard?

    (a) IRQ 0

    (b) IRQ 1

    (c) IRQ 2

    (d) IRQ 3

14. What IRQ is often used for LPT1?

    (a) IRQ 5

    (b) IRQ 6

    (c) IRQ 7

    (d) IRQ 8

15. Newer buses, such as PCI, AGP, and PCIe, do not use DMA channels. True or false?

16. What are blocks of memory set aside for exclusive use of certain components called?

    (a) DMA channels

    (b) I/O addresses

    (c) IRQ lanes

    (d) memory addresses

17. What types of expansion cards typically use AMR slots?

    (a) video and audio

    (b) video and network

    (c) modem and network

    (d) audio and modem

18. To remove an expansion card, you should rock the board gently back and forth. True or false?

19. What are the most common resource problems?

    (a) IRQ conflicts

    (b) DMA conflicts

    (c) I/O address conflicts

    (d) memory address conflicts

20. What technique is used in modern bus architectures as a replacement for DMA channels?

    (a) point-to-point communication

    (b) bus mastering

    (c) parallel communications

    (d) serial communications

Applying This Chapter

1. What types of expansion slots would you expect to find in a newer PC?

2. What potential problems might you encounter when installing an expansion card?

3. A PC has a sound card that locks up whenever the parallel tape backup unit is used on the system. What is the most likely problem?

4. How can you determine if a problem you are having with a printer is the result of a systems resource conflict?

5. The Device Manager is showing that a scanner you have installed has an I/O address conflict at IRQ 4 with the communications port COM1. Which one can you change?

PCIe Compatibility

A friend wants to purchase a new PCIe graphics card for their system, which only has PCI and AGP slots. Explain what she will need to upgrade in her PC to accommodate the card.

Installing a PCI card

A friend recently purchased a PCI sound card from eBay, but it doesn't fit into the PCI slots on her motherboard. What might be the problem?

Identifying Motherboard Bus Technologies

You are building a new, custom PC and need to select a motherboard. Visit a motherboard manufacturer's website, such as ASUS.com, and determine which bus technologies and expansion slots are used in one of their new motherboards.

Troubleshooting

You have just installed a video expansion card. The system boots up and works well until you start up a new computer game, and then the system crashes. What type of problem could this be?

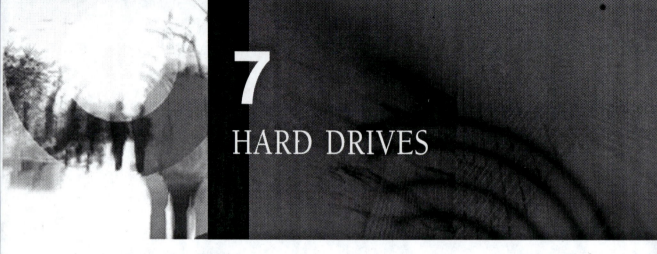

7
HARD DRIVES

Starting Point

What You'll Learn in This Chapter

▲ The components and characteristics of hard drives and how they work
▲ PATA and SATA standards for hard drives and how to install and configure an ATA hard drive
▲ SCSI standards for hard drives and how to install a SCSI hard drive
▲ Hard drive partitioning, formatting, and management

After Studying This Chapter, You'll Be Able To

▲ Compare hard drives in terms of industry standard ratings
▲ Identify recent hard drive standards
▲ Distinguish unique installation considerations for different hard drive technologies
▲ Choose an appropriate hard drive and interface for an existing PC Determine partitioning and formatting limits and options for a given operating system
▲ Install, partition, and format a hard drive
▲ Use system utilities to review the status of a hard drive
▲ Troubleshoot a faulty hard drive

INTRODUCTION

The system memory that is used by the PC to temporarily store data coming from and going to the CPU is often referred to as primary storage. In addition to system memory, PCs also need permanent, **nonvolatile storage** areas for larger amounts of data. Nonvolatile means that the data stored on a component is not lost when power to the component is turned off. These nonvolatile storage components are often referred to as **secondary storage**. Today, the most common secondary storage components are hard drives, and these typically store the bulk of the data that a PC uses. This data includes not just user documents and files, but also user and system software, such as Microsoft Word and Microsoft Office, and any files and data needed to support running these applications. Hard drives typically reside inside the computer (although there are external and removable hard drives) and can hold more information than other forms of storage.

7.1 Understanding How Hard Drives Work

One of the most common upgrades to a PC is adding or replacing a hard drive in order to gain more storage space. To choose a compatible drive for your system, it is important to understand a few of the basics of hard drives and how they work. Understanding the main characteristics of hard drives and how hard drives are rated will also help you compare equivalent hard drives from different manufacturers and select the one that is right for your needs.

7.1.1 Hard Drive Components

Hard drives, also called hard disk drives, hard disks, or fixed disks, consist of several small, identical disks called **platters** stacked together and placed in a sealed enclosure to protect them from dust or damage. The platters are made of aluminum or glass, and are coated with a thin layer of magnetic media that stores the actual data.

The platters are mounted through their centers on a small rod called a **spindle**. The disks are rotated about the spindle at a speed typically between 4,500 and 15,000 revolutions per minute (RPM). As they rotate, **read/write heads** float approximately 10 micro inches (about one-tenth the width of a human hair) above the disk surfaces and make, modify, or sense changes in the magnetic positions of the coatings on the disks. Read/write heads have sensors and magnets used for reading and writing magnetic charges on the platters' surfaces. The read/write heads are connected to an **actuator arm**, which is used to precisely position the heads over the correct area on the platters (Figure 7-1).

Hard drives also contain a **logic board** that contains the circuits and chips that control the drive's performance. The **disk controller** is the main circuit on

Figure 7-1

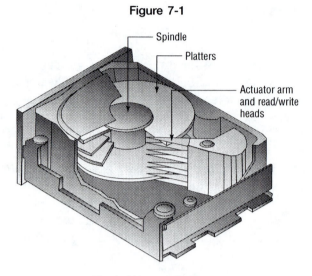

Hard drive components.

the logic board that controls everything from handling requests for data to managing the mechanics of the motor, actuator arm, and read/write heads.

Also essential to the functioning of a hard drive is the **host adapter**, or host bus adapter (HBA), logical circuitry that physically connects the hard drive to the "host"—the PC. The host adapter handles basic input/output processing, converting signals from the hard drive controller to signals the PC can understand. The host adapter may be an expansion card plugged into the motherboard or its circuitry may be built directly into the motherboard.

Hard drives come in several sizes. Older hard drives were designed to fit 5.25 inch drive bays but most modern desktop computer hard drives today are designed to fit in the standard 3.5 inch drive bays. Older hard drives were much taller than modern drives and are called "full-height." Modern drives are shorter, "half-height" or even slimmer. Inside the PC, internal hard drives are connected by cables to the power supply and to the host adapter.

7.1.2 Drive Geometry

To read and write data to the magnetic platters of a hard drive, the drive is electronically organized into sections recognized by systems software. This organization is called **drive geometry**. The components of a hard drive's physical geometry include:

▲ **Heads:** A hard drive usually has one read/write head for each surface of a platter; a drive with four platters has eight read/write heads.

▲ **Tracks:** Data is written to and read from the surfaces in concentric rings called tracks. The rings, or tracks, are numbered from the outside track in, with the outside track given the initial number 0. The total number of tracks that a surface can have depends on the drive's engineering; today's hard drives may have over 16,000 tracks on each surface.

▲ **Cylinders:** Because all heads are on a single actuator arm, the heads read the same track number on each surface at the same time. If the actuator arm moves to Track 12, all heads will be reading from Track 12 on the separate surfaces. The collection of tracks at a single actuator-arm position is known as a **cylinder** (Figure 7-2). The total number of tracks per surface is the same as the number of cylinders. In fact, the disks' tracks aren't treated as individual tracks on single disks; they're treated as cylinders, and manufacturers more commonly note the number of cylinders that a drive has. If you need to know the number of total tracks a hard drive has over all surfaces, you can multiply the number of heads by the number of cylinders.

▲ **Sectors:** To organize and locate separate chunks of data on a surface, the platter is divided into 60 or more wedges that divide short sections of tracks into smaller segments called sectors. Sectors are the smallest accessible portion of data on a track, and all sectors, regardless of their

Figure 7-2

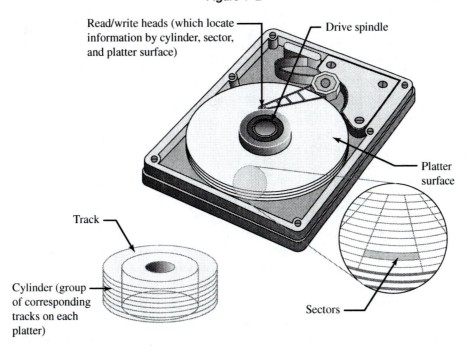

Read/write heads (which locate information by cylinder, sector, and platter surface)

Drive spindle

Platter surface

Track

Cylinder (group of corresponding tracks on each platter)

Sectors

Heads, tracks, sectors, and cylinders.

Figure 7-3

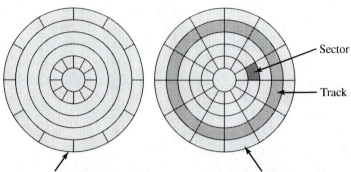

Zone-bit recording permits a variable number of sectors per track; tracks and cylinders at the edge of the drive can contain more sectors than those near the center

Traditional CHS drive geometry assigns a constant number of sectors to each track and cylinder across the entire disk platter

Sector

Track

Zone bit recording.

physical size, are defined as holding 512 bytes of data. When information is read from or written to a drive, the heads read or write a sector-sized division of a cylinder, from top surfaces to the bottom. In this physical geometry, with sectors defined by wedges, a certain amount of waste is built in: The sectors at the outer edges are physically quite a bit larger than inner sectors. To fit more sectors in to the outer tracks, zone bit recording (ZBR), or multiple zone recording was built in (Figure 7-3). ZBR divides the platters into different zones, nearer and further away from the spindle, and sectors within these zones are given a specified number of sectors per track. This allows outer tracks to have more sectors.

The PC's BIOS, however, is programmed to access each block of data through **CHS (cylinder, head, sector) addressing** and is unable to work with ZBR. To accommodate the needs of ZBR, drives were designed to have a logical geometry that was different from their physical geometry. The drive is given theoretical CHS values, which approximate the drive's total storage space. These values are its logical geometry and the hard drive controller uses these values to communicate with the BIOS. The drive itself is engineered to work with actual physical geometry (which can use ZBR) and can translate to and from the logical values needed by the BIOS using sector translation.

Sector translation uses a translation table that converts the actual physical geometry of a drive into the logical geometry used by the BIOS. An older method of sector translation, extended CHS (ECHS), uses logical values based on the traditional divisions of cylinders, sectors, and heads. Today, more drives use logical block addressing (LBA), which numbers all sectors on a drive sequentially, without reference to cylinders and heads.

7.1.3 Hard Drive Characteristics

There are a variety of characteristics and statistics that are used to rate and compare hard drives, including:

▲ **Capacity:** The capacity or size of a hard drive refers to how many bytes of data the drive can store. Capacity is determined by drive geometry. Each sector can contain 512 bytes, and a track can contain up to 63 sectors, so the total storage space of a hard drive can be determined by the following formula:

Capacity = 512 Bytes per sector × 63 Sectors per track × Cylinders × Heads

Typical PC hard drives today have capacities ranging from 40GB to 500GB and higher.

▲ **Spin speed:** The **spin speed** is how fast the platters are spinning, measured in revolutions per minute (RPM). Higher RPM values mean faster speeds and faster access to data. Depending on the model, disks today typically rotate between 4,500 RPM and 15,000 RPM.

▲ **Seek time:** Seek time is the time it takes for the read/write head to react to a request and position itself over a track. A seek from one track to the next (called a track-to-track seek) is usually quickest; a seek from the innermost to the outermost track (called a maximum, or full stroke seek) is longer. The average seek time is usually defined as the time it takes the head to move one-third of the way across the platter, which typically takes from 5 to 10 ms.

▲ **Rotational latency: Rotational latency** is the time it takes for a requested sector to travel to the head after the read/write head is in position, and is measured in milliseconds. Rotational latency is determined by the spin speed (RPM). Average rotational latency is the time it takes for a disk to turn 180°, and can be determined by the following formula:

Average Rotational Latency = (60)/(2 × RPM) × 1000.

The worst-case latency is the time for the disk to make a full revolution. Of the seek time and the latency period, the seek time is usually the longer wait.

▲ **Access time:** The **access time** measures the full amount of time that it takes to move the read/write head to the correct position and access the correct sector. The average seek time plus the average latency equals the drive's access time. The smaller the access time value, the faster the drive. The formula for access time is:

$$\text{Access time} = \text{Average seek time} + \text{Average Rotational Latency}$$

▲ **Interface:** The **interface** is the technology used to connect the hard drive to the rest of the system. The interface determines not only the type of physical connections and cables, but also the rate of data transfer to and from the hard drive. Interface technologies include the **Advanced Technology Attachment (ATA)** standards and the **Small Computer Systems Interface (SCSI)** standards, each of which is discussed in more detail later in this chapter.

▲ **Disk cache size:** To improve access times and data throughput, modern drives include a **disk cache** or buffer that may hold from 1 to 8 or more MB of data. The disk cache is used to store frequently used or recent data and helps to minimize the number of physical seeks to the hard drive.

▲ **Data transfer rate:** The **data transfer rate** measures the total amount of data that the drive can transfer over a specified time period, usually 1 second. The data transfer rate of a drive depends on its internal and external transfer rates. The external transfer rate measures the time taken to transfer data between the PC's RAM and the drive's disk cache. The internal data transfer rate measures how fast the drive can move data between its disk cache and the platter surface.

▲ **Data transfer mode:** The **data transfer mode** is the protocol used to transfer data to and from the hard drive. The data transfer mode is prescribed by the drive interface. SCSI hard drives use SCSI data transfer

FOR EXAMPLE

Real World Advice: Advertised Capacity

It is important to note that there is a difference between the actual capacity of a hard drive and its advertised capacity. Manufacturers use metric calculations for megabytes and gigabytes. Metric calculations assume that a kilobyte is 1000 bytes, a megabyte is a 1000 kilobytes, and so on. However, in the binary computations that PCs use, a true kilobyte is 2^{10} bytes, or 1024 bytes and a true megabyte is 1024 kilobytes. At very large drive capacities, this can mean there is a significant difference between what the manufacturer reports as the drive capacity and what your PC recognizes as the actual capacity. In addition, the final, usable capacity of a hard drive depends to a degree on the type of file system the drive is formatted with.

modes. Early parallel ATA drives used the PIO (Programmed Input/ Output) mode, which relied on the CPU to control the transfer of data from the hard drive. The DMA (Direct Memory Access) mode relieves the CPU of this duty, and transfers data directly to RAM. DMA modes can also be grouped into two categories: single word DMA modes and multiword DMA modes. Single word DMA transfers data one word (two bytes of data or 16 bits) at a time. Multiword DMA transfers several words at a time in a kind of burst. UltraDMA (UDMA) is the most recent version of DMA and has transfer rates up to 150MBps.

7.1.4 Reading and Writing Data

During writing, the head's magnet is energized to polarize a small portion of the magnetic material. During reading, the head recognizes any **flux transitions** (changes from nonpolarized segments to polarized segments and vice versa) and interprets combinations of these changes as binary 1s or 0s. The process of translating from binary to flux transition patterns is called **encoding**. The simplest encoding method is to interpret the presence of a flux transition as a 1 and the absence as a 0. More complex methods were devised to allow for better performance on more densely packed drives. Early encoding methods included Frequency Modulation (FM), Modified Frequency Modulation (MFM), and Run Length Limited (RLL). On today's drives, PRML (Partial Response, Maximum Likelihood) and EPRML (Extended PRML) encoding methods analyze much smaller fluctuations to determine the sequence of bits. These encoding methods allow for far greater density of tracks and sectors on hard disks than previous encoding methods.

To make it easier for the operating system to manage the storage space, the information encoded on the drive is written to groups of sectors known as **clusters**. A cluster is made up of up to 64 sectors grouped together (the actual number of sectors included in a cluster varies with the size of the hard drive).

Traditionally, encoding utilized longitudinal recording, writing, and reading parallel to the disk surface. New technologies of perpendicular, or vertical, recording (PR) allows writing to layers below the disk's surface plane, greatly increasing storage capacities.

None of these encoding methods are 100 percent perfect—all data transmission technologies will experience some very small rates of error. Data errors can also be caused by the magnetic fields fading over long periods of time. Hard drives are designed with error correction mechanisms to recognize errors and correct them during transmission. Essentially, error correction methods use the hard drive controller to write extra bits of data, called the error correction code (ECC) wherever it writes a segment of data to the disk. When that same data is read, the ECC is analyzed to see if any errors have crept into the data.

7.2 Understanding and Installing ATA Hard Drives

Early PCs needed separate controller cards attached to the motherboard to connect the drive to the computer and manage transfers. Later PCs improved on this technology with the development of integrated device electronics (IDE) drives that had embedded controller circuitry into the drives themselves. A succession of standards, known as the ATA (Advanced Technology Attachment) standards, specified how early IDE and later hard drives interfaced with the PC. The first ATA standards used a parallel bus, transferring 8 bits at a time, and are called **parallel ATA (PATA)**. Recent ATA standards specify the use of a faster, serial bus and are called **serial ATA (SATA)**.

7.2.1 Parallel ATA Standards

Parallel ATA (or PATA) standards that have been developed over the years include ATA-1 through ATA/ATAPI-7 standards, summarized in Table 7-1. ATA-7 is the last standard governing the parallel ATA interface; all recent and future standards govern the serial implementation of ATA, or SATA. Note that you will often hear ATA devices referred to as IDE, or Enhanced IDE (EIDE), devices. IDE and EIDE are marketing terms, however, and do not reflect real standards. The PATA standards were designed to be backwardly compatible; you can use a motherboard ATA hard drive connector to connect to any standard of ATA drive: however, the performance will be limited to the standard of the slowest component.

Some of the most significant advancements made during the period in which the ATA standards were developed include

▲ **LBA addressing:** Support for LBA was added by ATA-2.
▲ **Faster PIO, DMA, and UDMA modes:** Successive ATA standards improved on previous data transfer modes. See Table 7-2 for a summary of data transfer modes.

Table 7-1: ATA Standards*

Standard	Speed(s) (MBps)	PIO Modes	DMA Modes	UltraDMA Modes	ATAPI-Support?
ATA	3.3–8.3	0, 1, 2	Single Word 0, 1, 2 Multiword 0	N/A	No
ATA-2	11.1–16.7	3, 4	Multiword 1, 2	N/A	No
ATA-3	11.–16.7	All	All	N/A	No
ATA-4	16.7–33.3	All	All	0, 1, 2	Yes
ATA-5	44.4–66.7	All	All	3, 4	Yes
ATA-6	100	All	All	5	Yes
ATA-7	133	All	All	6	Yes

*Generally speaking, each ATA standard is backward compatible with the standard before it, so each row in Table 7-1 has the features of the rows above it.

▲ **SMART:** ATA-3 included the Self-Monitoring and Analysis Tool (SMART). SMART comprises several circuits within the disk controller that keep track of error conditions and general drive statistics. These circuits try to predict when a hard drive failure will occur and notifies the BIOS and the operating system of possible imminent failure.

▲ **ATAPI:** Early ATA standards included support only for hard drives. ATA-4 and later ATA standards include an additional set of standards for connecting

Table 7-2: Data Transfer Modes

PIO Mode	Maximum Transfer Rate (MBps)	DMA Mode	Maximum Transfer Rate (MBps)	UDMA Mode	Maximum Transfer Rate (MBps)
0	3.3	Single Word 0	2.1	0	16.7
1	5.2	Single Word 1	4.2	1	25
2	8.3	Single Word 2	8.3	2	33.3
3	11.1	Multiword 0	4.2	3	44.4
4	16.6	Multiword 1	13.3	4	66.7
5	22.2	Multiword 2	16.7	5	100

other devices such as CD-ROMs and tape drives, called the AT Attachment Packet Interface (ATAPI) standard.

▲ **80-conductor cable:** ATA-4 defined a new 80-conductor cable to avoid transmission problems. Use of this cable is mandatory with ATA-5 onward.

▲ **Cyclical Redundancy Checking (CRC):** CRC is an error-checking routine that works with the new higher speeds of UltraDMA.

▲ **SATA:** ATA-7 included the first standards for serial ATA (SATA), an implementation of the ATA interface that operates serially.

7.2.2 Serial ATA Standards

Serial ATA (SATA) came out as a standard recently and was first adopted in desktops and then laptops. Whereas ATA had always been an interface that sends 16 bits at a time, SATA sends only one bit at a time at faster rates. Additionally, SATA does not suffer the same cross-talk interference as a parallel interface, and so SATA cables can be longer, up to 1 m. Although the industry as a whole is moving towards using SATA drives, you will still find motherboards with both PATA and SATA interface connectors.

The first SATA standard developed was **SATA-1**, (also called SATA/150), which specified transfer speeds of 150 MBps. SATA-1 is backwardly compatible with ATA devices, which means that ATA-compatible operating systems, BIOS, and disk utilities will work fine with either parallel or serial ATA drives with no special modification. The latest SATA standard is **SATA-IO**, named after its oversight committee, the SATA International Organization. You will also hear SATA-IO referred to as SATA II or SATA 3G. SATA-IO specifications provide for transfer speeds up to 3.0GB, enhanced power management, and cable lengths up to eight meters. However, note that, unlike ATA standards, the SATA-IO standards are optional: A manufacturer does not have to include all SATA-IO features to label the drive as SATA-IO.

SATA-IO features include:

▲ **Port multipliers:** These devices allow up to 15 SATA devices to use the same bus.

▲ **Native command queuing.** Instead of having to execute hard drive requests in the order they are received, SATA drives can respond to sets of commands in the most efficient way.

▲ **eSATA:** External SATA (eSATA) allows external SATA drives to be connected to the host adapter.

▲ **Hot plug:** SATA drives are hot-pluggable, or hot-swappable. This means that the PC does not have to be powered down before attaching the hot-pluggable component.

7.2.3 Installing and Configuring ATA Hard Drives

Several concepts are essential for understanding how to install an ATA hard drive:

▲ **Master/Slave configuration:** PATA standards allow two separate PATA drives to share a single ribbon cable (and controller) using what is called a Master/Slave configuration. In this configuration, one drive is designated the Master. All signals from the host adapter are handled by the Master drive, which then forwards along any requests to the Slave drive. If you are using a Master/Slave configuration for two PATA drives using a single ribbon, you must configure one drive as Master and one as Slave. You do this typically through a jumper setting on the drive itself (Figure 7-4), but you should check the drive's documentation to see what the drive's Master/Slave settings are. You can choose the Cable Select drive setting when you are using a cable select ribbon, which designates one particular connector on the ribbon for the Master and the second for Slave (Figure 7-5). You use a Single setting when there is only one drive (a single Master) on the cable

▲ **IDE channel:** On most motherboards you will find two 40-pin PATA connectors, labeled **primary IDE channel** and **secondary IDE channel** (Figure 7-6). Each of these connectors can support a ribbon that

Figure 7-4

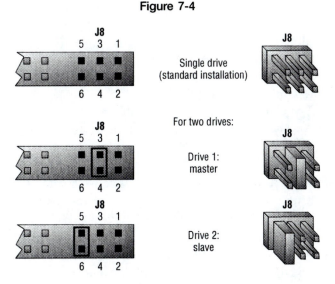

Master/Slave jumpers.

Figure 7-5

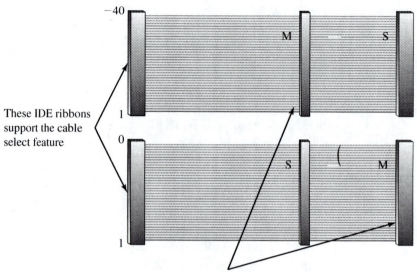

These IDE ribbons support the cable select feature

When the CS jumpers on both IDE devices are enabled, the device attached to the connector labeled M becomes the master drive; the drive attached to the connector labeled S becomes the slave drive

Cable select ribbons.

connects two drives. You will usually find a label or symbol pointing to one of the connector pins, Pin 1, to help in attaching a PATA ribbon.

▲ **Data cabling:** PATA data cables are ribbon cables (wide, flat cables) (Figure 7-7) and may have either 40 wires or 80 wires. They may have up to three connectors: for the motherboard and two PATA drives. The ribbon cable must be attached to the PATA connector on the motherboard correctly, with the Pin 1 edge on the ribbon cable connector matching up to Pin 1 on the motherboard connector. To help in making the proper connection, many ribbon cables have a colored stripe running on the edge of the cable that leads to Pin 1.

▲ **Power cable:** The PATA drive's power cable is attached to the power supply. It uses a Molex-type power connector that attaches directly to the drive in a matching connector port (Figure 7-8).

▲ **BIOS configuration:** Most new computers require little, if any, BIOS configuration to recognize a new drive. Most often, the only configuration necessary is the installation of the cable as well as changing the jumper settings. On older, pre PnP systems that don't' automatically recognize

Figure 7-6

Parallel ATA interface connectors.

Figure 7-7

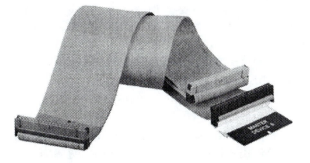

Ribbon cable.

Figure 7-8

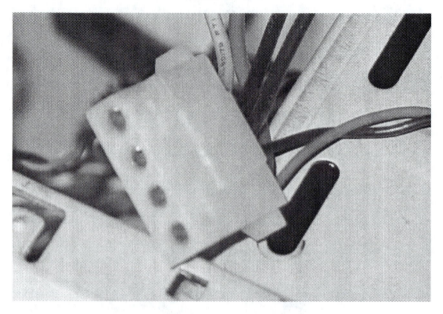

Molex power connector.

ATA drives, you may need to run a Detect IDE utility from the BIOS Setup program.

To install a PATA hard drive:

1. **Plan the installation:** Decide which drive bay and IDE controller and ribbon you will be using, and any Master/Slave configuration.
2. **Configure drive jumpers:** Set the drive jumpers to Master, Slave, Cable Select, or Single.
3. **Mount the drive:** To mount the drive, slide it into the drive bay, lining up the front end of the drive with the front of the bay. You may need to use screws to hold the drives in place. You can install a 3.5" drive into a 5.25" drive bay, by using a 5.25" to 3.5" rail mounting kit.
4. **Connect to the drive interface:** Connect the ribbon cable to the IDE interface and to the drive (Figure 7-9).
5. **Connect to the power supply:** Connect the power cable to the power supply.
6. **Power up the PC:** Reconnect any devices you may have disconnected in order to mount the drive and power on the PC. Confirm that the BIOS recognizes the drive.

FOR EXAMPLE

PATA Drive Placement

If you are installing two different PATA drives your best choice for drive placement is to use a separate IDE channel (and ribbon) for each. Using the same ribbon for the two drives will mean that, if one is built to a lower ATA standard, both drives will use the slower standard. If you need to choose a Master, choose the drive that is newer or faster. If you have three or more drives, designate drives that don't get a lot of use as the Slave drives.

7.2.4 Installing and Configuring SATA Hard Drives

Installing a SATA hard drive is virtually identical to installing an ATA Hard drive except for the following considerations:

▲ **Data cable:** The SATA data cable is much narrower than the PATA ribbon, and uses keyed connectors. Because SATA does not use Master/Slave configuration, a separate cable is needed for each SATA drive (Figure 7-10).

▲ **Power connector:** Serial ATA drives use a specific type power connector (Figure 7-11) that may not be on an older power supply. However, you can purchase adapters to convert SATA power connectors to Molex connectors.

▲ **SATA hard drives are hot pluggable:** They can be connected to the PC while it is running.

Figure 7-9

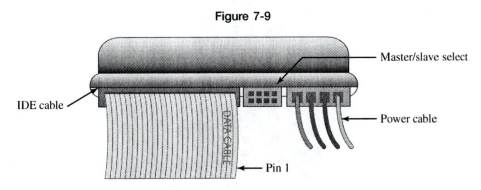

Installing a PATA hard drive.

Figure 7-10

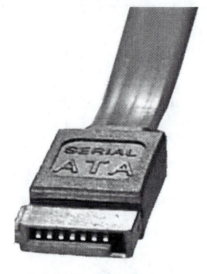

SATA data cable.

Figure 7-11

SATA power connector.

SELF-CHECK

1. List four features of SATA-IO.

2. What device sends requests to an ATA Slave drive?

3. How many wires does an ATA cable have?

4. How is installing a SATA drive different from installing a parallel ATA drive?

5. How many parallel ATA connectors and SATA connectors does a motherboard typically have?

7.3 Understanding and Installing SCSI Hard Drives

SCSI (pronounced *scuzzy*) is a technology developed in the '80s that specifies an interface for connecting a specified number of devices (including the host adapter) on a single, shared cable called the **SCSI bus**. SCSI is a very fast, flexible interface. You can buy a SCSI drive and install it in any Mac, PC, or Sun workstation with a SCSI host adapter. SCSI technology is not limited to hard drives; SCSI devices include printers, scanners, and tape drives. SCSI devices can be either internal or external to the computer. The SCSI host adapter is used to manage all the devices on the bus as well as to send and retrieve data from the devices. SCSI devices are smart devices; they contain a circuit board that can control the read/write movement. SCSI drives are typically utilized in server computers, rather than individual PCs.

7.3.1 SCSI Features

SCSI technology is characterized by some unique features:

▲ **Daisy-chaining:** SCSI devices are connected to each other and to the host adaptor by **daisy chaining:** Each device is connected in series with the next device on the bus (Figure 7-12). Internal SCSI devices attach in sequence to a single ribbon cable. External SCSI devices use separate cables to connect to the next device in the chain and usually have two ports: one for the incoming cable, another to connect to the next device in line.

▲ **Addressing:** Each device on the SCSI bus is assigned a unique number configured through either jumpers or DIP switches on the device. When the computer needs to send data to the device, it sends a signal addressed to that number.

Figure 7-12

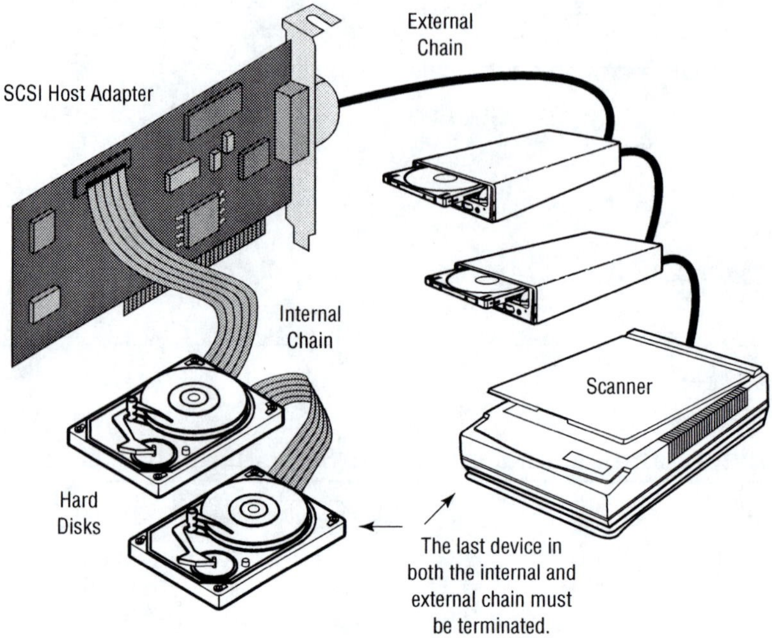

SCSI Host Adapter

External
Chain

Internal
Chain

Scanner

Hard
Disks

The last device in
both the internal and
external chain must
be terminated.

SCSI daisy chain.

▲ **Signaling:** Depending on the SCSI standard supported, SCSI devices use
different types of signaling:

- **Single-ended signaling: Single-ended (SE) signaling**, used in the
first SCSI standard, uses a positive voltage to represent binary 1, and
an absence of voltage to represent binary 0. The voltages are sent
over a single wire for each bit in the signal path (for example, eight
wires for an 8-bit SCSI bus). SE signaling limits the length of cabling
that can be used to around 6 meters.

- **High voltage differential signaling:** In **high-voltage differential
(HVD) signaling**, two wires are used, each carrying the electrical
opposite of the other. The receiving device takes the difference and
uses the resulting value. For example, if the wires are electrically
opposite (5V and –5V), the difference is zero, which represents a
binary 0. If one wire is 10V and the other is +1V, the difference is a
positive voltage, which represents a binary 1. Differential signaling is
much more tolerant of cable distances.

- **Low-voltage differential (LVD) signaling:** Low-voltage differential (LVD)
signaling works similarly to HVD signaling but uses lower voltages.

▲ **Bus mastering:** SCSI host adapters employ a technique called **bus mastering** that allows data to be transferred directly to system memory, bypassing the CPU. Bus mastering was designed to increase data transfer speeds and can also be used for transferring directly between peripherals.

▲ **Termination:** A device called a SCSI terminator (a terminating resistor pack) is configured at both ends of the bus to keep the signals from reflecting and causing interference. Termination may be external, in which a terminating block is plugged into a SCSI device's second port, or it may be internal, built into the device itself. SCSI buses use different types of termination, depending on the signaling used on the bus. LVD and HVD buses use LVD and HVD terminators respectively, although some LVD devices are equipped to switch between LVD termination and SE termination. There are three types of SE termination:

  • **Passive termination:** Passive terminators use resistors to absorb voltages; they are rarely used any more and work only with SCSI-1 devices.

  • **Active termination:** In active termination, the terminator contains (in addition to the terminating resistor) voltage regulators that actively take terminator power from the SCSI bus and use it for powering the termination of the bus.

  • **Forced Perfect Termination (FPT)** is a type of active terminator that resets voltages to the correct termination level, rather than absorbing or regulating voltages. This is the most reliable type of termination.

7.3.2 SCSI Standards

The three main SCSI standards are SCSI-1, SCSI-2, and SCSI-3. Each specifies a variety of speeds and secondary standards. Different SCSI standards have different requirements for cabling, maximum bus length, and maximum number of devices allowed on the SCSI bus. These requirements are summarized in Table 7-3:

▲ **SCSI-1:** The original SCSI standard supported eight devices on an 8-bit bus, using SE signaling. SCSI-1 was not universally accepted and devices from different manufacturers were not always compatible. The SCSI-1 standard is obsolete.

▲ **SCSI-2:** SCSI-2 defined two separate protocols:

  • **Fast SCSI:** Features data transfer speeds of up to 10MBps over the SCSI-1 8-bit cabling.

  • **Wide SCSI:** Provides for 16-bit and 32-bit SCSI bus structures.

  These two protocols can be used together to create a Fast-Wide SCSI bus to produce a transfer rate of 40MBps. SCSI-2 increased the number of devices that could be supported on the bus to 16 and added support

Table 7-3: SCSI Specifications

Name	Speed (MHz)	Width (Bits)	Transfer Rate (MBps)	Max Devices	Cable Type	Max Length (Meters)
SCSI-1:						
Asynchronous	5	8	4	7	A	6 (SE)/25 (HVD)
Fast-5 (Synchronous)	5	8	5	7	A	6 (SE)/25 (HVD)
SCSI-2:						
Fast-5 Wide	5	16	10	15	P	6 (SE)/25 (HVD)
Fast-10 (Fast SCSI)	10	8	10	7	A	3 (SE)/25 (HVD)
Fast-10 Wide (Fast Wide SCSI)	10	16	20	15	P	3 (SE)/25 (HVD)
SCSI-3:						
Fast-20 (Ultra SCSI)	20	8	20	7	A	1.5 or 3 (SE)/25 (HVD)
Fast-20 Wide (UltraWide SCSI)	20	16	40	7	P	1.5 or 3 (SE)/25 (HVD)
Fast-40 (Ultra2)	40	8	40	7	A	12 (LVD)
Fast-40 Wide (Ultra2 Wide)	40	16	80	15	P	12 (LVD)
Fast-80DT (Ultra160, Ultra3)	40	16	160	15	P	12 (LVD)
Fast-160DT (Utra320, Ultra4)	80	16	320	15	P	12 (LVD)
Fast-320DT (Ultra640, Ultra5)	160	16	640	15	P	2
Serial Attached SCSI (SAS)	n/a	1	300	128 (16,384 with expanders)	SAS	1

for HVD signaling. While SCSI-2 is backward compatible with SCSI-1 devices; the SCSI-1 devices can only operate at their original speeds.

▲ **SCSI-3:** SCSI-3 is a collection of standards, that includes the main SCSI Parallel Interface (SPI), also called **SCSI-3** or **Ultra SCSI,** and other SCSI-based interfaces such as iSCSI and Serial Attached SCSI (SAS). SCSI-3 introduced LVD signaling is the fastest implementation of SCSI.

▲ **Serial attached SCSI (SAS):** This is a version of SCSI that uses a serial cable and allows for more devices to be connected to the bus. It currently supports data transfer rates up to 300MBps

▲ **iSCSI:** Internet SCSI (iSCSI) combines Ethernet technologies with SCSI, and is used mainly for network attached storage. It can transfers data at rates up to 1GBps, over very long distances.

7.3.3 Installing SCSI Hard Drives

It is important to realize that the number of devices you can have on the SCSI bus is limited, as is the maximum length of the SCSI bus. Generally speaking, the faster the SCSI, the shorter the total length of the bus. Table 7-3 reviewed the device number and bus length limitations for the different types of SCSI.

Other issues central to installing SCSI devices are cabling, termination, addressing, and signaling.

▲ **Internal cabling:** Internal cabling is rated for the SCSI standard it supports. Terminated cables are available that come with a terminator block built into one end. There are two main types of SCSI internal cable:

- **A cable:** A 50-pin cable used with SCSI-1 and some types of 8-bit SCSI-2 and SCSI-3.
- **P cable:** A 68-pin cable used with most types of SCSI, including all 16-bit SCSI versions.

▲ **External cabling:** External cabling is also rated for the SCSI standard it supports. It uses thick, shielded cables that may have different connectors on either ends. The main connector types are:

- **Centronics:** A standard 50-pin Centronics.
- **Mini-Centronics:** This has the same basic shape as a Centronics connector but is smaller, with either 50 pin or 68 pin.
- **HD:** This connector has a D-shaped ring outside of a set of 50 or 68 pins, similar to a legacy parallel port connector.
- **VHD:** These are smaller versions of HD connectors and also have 50 or 68 pins.

▲ **Termination:** The first and last devices in the SCSI bus must be terminated. If you are using internal or external devices only, you terminate the

Figure 7-13

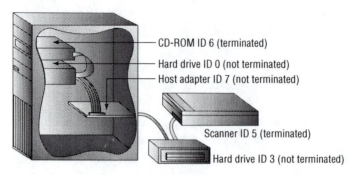

- CD-ROM ID 6 (terminated)
- Hard drive ID 0 (not terminated)
- Host adapter ID 7 (not terminated)

Scanner ID 5 (terminated)

Hard drive ID 3 (not terminated)

SCSI termination.

adapter and the last device in the chain only. However, if you are using a mix of internal and external devices, you must terminate the last device in the two chains, leaving the adapter unterminated (Figure 7-13). The type of terminator you use must be compatible with the type of SCSI signaling; SE (passive, active, or FTP), HVD, or LVD. If a device has built-in termination, you can, if you want, disable this (usually through a DIP switch or jumper, or through configuration software) and add a terminator.

▲ **Addressing:** All SCSI devices on a SCSI chain must be assigned a unique ID that identifies the device to other devices on the chain and to the SCSI host adapter. Depending on the SCSI version you are using, this ID is a number from 0 to 7 (Narrow SCSI) or 0 to 15 (Wide SCSI), and you assign the device its ID usually through jumpers or switches on the device itself. Some SCSI devices are assigned their IDs through their configuration software. SCSI host adapters must almost always be assigned the highest number allowed, either 7, or 15, and most host adapters expect that a bootable hard drive is located at address 0. You should check the documentation that comes with your SCSI host adapter to check the address assignments it expects. (Also, if you are configuring a SCSI chain with multiple devices, you will want to assign higher numbers to devices you use less frequently, as SCSI gives priority to the lowerSCSI IDs.). Some BIOS systems include a feature called SCSI Configured AutoMatically (SCAM) that sets SCSI device IDs through software. For this to work, the BIOS, the host adapter, and the peripheral device must support the SCAM adapter. However, SCAM was no longer continued with the SCSI-3 standard, so you will most likely find the SCAM feature on older systems.

▲ **Signaling:** Never put either SE or LVD devices on the same channel with HVD. Actual physical damage may result. Also, although SE and LVD

FOR EXAMPLE

Setting SCSI IDs

Different manufacturers of SCSI drives employ different ways of setting SCSI IDs on a device. You will usually find three or four sequential pairs of pins that represent a 3- or 4-digit binary number. The first pair represents 0001 (1), the second stands for 0010 (2), and so on. You set the ID by placing jumpers on ("shunting") the pairs, and it is the sum of the pins that have been shunted that determine the SCSI ID.

---

devices are electrically compatible, any SE devices on a chain with LVD devices will cause all devices to run at the SE device's slower rated speed. For best results, make sure all SCSI devices are the same type (SE, LVD, or HVD) on a single chain. Most SCSI devices are labeled with their signaling capability (Figure 7-14).

To install a SCSI drive, follow the same basic hardware installation steps mentioned for PATA drives. You don't have to modify the PC's BIOS settings. Because SCSI devices are intelligent, you tell the PC that no drive is installed, and let the adapter handle controlling the devices. However, if the drive is not recognized, you may need to do one of the following:

▲ If the device is bootable, you must set the host adapter to be BIOS enabled, meaning it has its own BIOS extension that allows the PC to recognize the device without a software driver.

▲ Load a driver for the adapter into the operating system. This method only works if you are booting from some other, non-SCSI device. If you have to boot from the SCSI drive, you must use the preceding method.

Figure 7-14

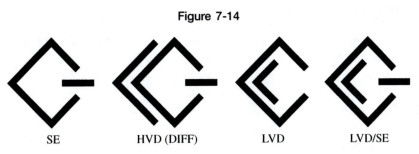

SE   HVD (DIFF)   LVD   LVD/SE

SCSI signaling labels.

7.4 Partitioning, Formatting, and Managing Hard Drives

Before a drive can be used, it must be formatted and partitioned. Low-level formatting creates the physical tracks and sectors (the CHS values) on the drive. Manufacturers always perform this low-level formatting on modern drives at the factory. Partitioning is the process of assigning part or all of the drive for use by the computer. A hard drive can have one or more partitions. High-level formatting is performed by the operating system on a logical drive to install a file system that can be used by the operating system. When you purchase a new PC, it is typically ready to use, with internal drives that are formatted and partitioned. However, if you purchase a separate, new drive that you will be installing on an existing PC, you will need to partition and format it.

A partitioned and formatted hard drive must still be managed on a regular basis. Managing your hard drive means protecting your data, checking the disks for disk and file errors, ensuring that you have an emergency boot disk to use if Windows won't start normally, and knowing what to do should a drive fail.

7.4.1 Partitioning

A partition is a continuous section of sectors that are next to each other. In DOS and Windows, a partition is referred to by a drive letter, such as C: or D:. Partitioning a drive into two or more parts gives it the appearance of being two or more physical hard drives.

A hard drive can have four partitions; these are called primary partitions. These primary partitions are seen as logical drives and can be assigned only one drive letter. Each hard drive must have one primary partition that is designated as the active partition. The active partition is used to start up the PC.

One primary partition on the hard drive can be converted to an **extended partition.** An extended partition can be logically subdivided into many logical drives.

The partition that contains the specific hardware files needed to start the drive and select an operating system is referred to as the **system partition.** On most systems, the active partition is the system partition. The partition that contains the operating system's executable and support files is called the **boot partition**. The boot partition can be (and often is) the same as the system partition but may also be on an extended partition. Some PCs are configured as multiboot computers, which have more than one operating system. On startup of a multiboot computer, you can choose which operating system to load. Therefore, on a multiboot system there will be just one system partition, but several boot partitions, one for each operating system installed.

Partitioning disks can improve drive efficiency. Under DOS and Windows, cluster sizes are automatically assigned in proportion to the drive size. The bigger the drive, the bigger the clusters, and large clusters can result in wasted disk space. Reducing the size of the drive through partitioning also reduces the cluster size.

At the beginning of each hard drive (in the very first sector) is a special file called the Master Boot Record (MBR). The MBR contains the partition information about the beginning and end of each partition, and there is only one MBR for each hard drive, even if the drive has many partitions and logical drives. However, if you have an extended partition, an additional Extended Master Boot Record (EMBR) is created to store information about the logical drives on that partition.

7.4.2 High-Level Formatting and File Systems

High-level formatting prepares a drive for writing and managing files. During formatting, the surface of the hard drive platter is briefly scanned to find any possible bad spots, and the areas surrounding a bad spot are marked as bad sectors that will not be used for storage. An operating system boot record is created along with the root directory, and a File Allocation Table (FAT) or Master File Table (MFT) is created. This table contains information about the location of files as they are placed onto the hard drive. Formatting also assigns a file system to the drive, and you must use a file system that your operating system supports: different operating systems support a number of file system formats (see Table 7-4).

The most common file systems for Windows operating systems are:

▲ **FAT16:** Used with DOS, Windows 3.x, and early versions of Windows 95. FAT16 (generally just called FAT) has a number of advantages. First, it's extremely fast on small (under 500MB) drives. Second, it's a file system that nearly all operating systems can agree on, making it excellent for dual-boot systems. However, FAT has a limit of 4GB per partition, making it unsuitable for today's large drives of 60GB and higher. The size of clusters that FAT uses to write files is also larger than later file systems, and on large drives, this wastes hard drive space.

FAT32: Introduced with Windows 95. FAT32 is similar to FAT but has a number of advantages. It supports larger drives and smaller allocation units. A disadvantage of FAT32 is that it isn't compatible with older DOS, Windows 3.x, and Windows 95 operating systems.

Table 7-4: Operating System Support for Different File Systems

Operating System	FAT16	FAT32	NTFS 4	NTFS 5
MS-DOS	Yes	No	No	No
Windows 95 (Original, A, B)	Yes	No	No	No
Windows 95C (OSR2)	Yes	Yes	No	No
Windows 98	Yes	Yes	No	No
Windows 98 Second Edition (SE)	Yes	Yes	No	No
Windows Me	Yes	Yes	No	No
Windows NT 4 Workstation	Yes	No	Yes	No
Windows 2000 Professional	Yes	Yes	No*	Yes
Windows XP Professional/Home Edition	Yes	Yes	No*	Yes
Windows Vista	Yes	Yes	No	Yes

*You convert NTFS 4 file systems to NTFS 5 as part of the Setup when upgrading from Windows NT 4 to Windows 2000, XP or Vista.

▲ **NTFS:** The NTFS file system was designed for the Windows NT operating system. NTFS includes enhanced attributes for compressing files, support for larger hard drives, improved security permissions, system logging, and disk spanning (using two or more hard disks as a single logical volume). NTFS4 is used only with Windows NT 4.0, and NTFS5 is used with Windows 2000, Windows XP and Windows Vista.

FOR EXAMPLE

FAT16 Cluster Sizes

A cluster is the basic unit used to store a file or a portion of a file. On hard disks, each cluster can contain 4, 8, 16, or more sectors, depending on the file system and the size of the partition. Under FAT16, a 2GB (2048MB) partition will have 64 sectors in a cluster. Because one sector always uses 512 bytes, each cluster on this 2GB partition will be able to hold 64 x 512 bytes or 32,768 bytes. When you write a file, the hard disk will use one or more entire clusters, even if the file doesn't fill a full cluster. On a 2GB FAT16 partition, a 4KB text file and a 30KB text file will both take up a full cluster; and a 34KB text file will occupy two full clusters. When you have hundreds or thousands of such files, a lot of disk space is wasted. The FAT32 file system allows smaller numbers of sectors per cluster, so is usually a better choice when you are using large hard drive volumes.

7.4.3 Partitioning and Formatting Utilities

Although you can use third-party software to partition and format a drive, Windows operating systems include partitioning and formatting utilities:

▲ **FDISK:** The FDISK utility is available with DOS or Windows 9x/ME. You can use FDISK to create, modify, or delete FAT16 or FAT32 partitions. To partition a boot drive, FDISK must be run from a command prompt on a startup floppy. To partition a secondary drive, you can run FDISK from the Window command prompt. FDISK can create only one primary partition and one extended partition (Figure 7-15).

▲ **FORMAT:** FORMAT is a command-line utility that allows you to prepare a disk to hold data. The FORMAT command can be used to format a disk. This utility is located in the C:\Windows\System32 folder but can be accessed from any command prompt. To use the FORMAT command, you type FORMAT X: (replacing X with the letter of the drive you are formatting). You can also further configure the formatting (such as specifying a files system) by adding a series of extra commands, called switches, to the command line. For a list of the switches available, use the command FORMAT /?.

▲ **My Computer:** You can access a Windows-based Format utility by right-clicking a drive icon in the My Computer window and selecting Format. This opens the Format Local Disk dialog box, which will guide you through the procedure.

▲ **Windows Setup:** When you are installing Windows NT, 2000, XP, or Vista Windows Setup will guide you through partitioning and formatting a drive, allowing you to choose sizes and file systems.

Figure 7-15

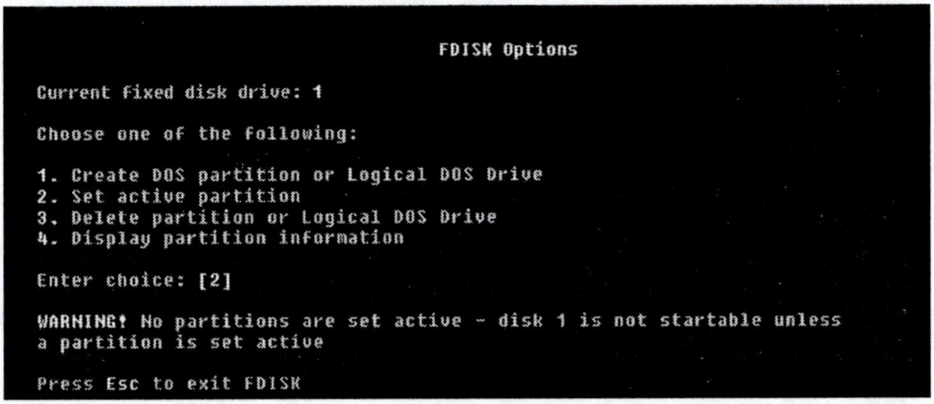

```
                              FDISK Options

Current fixed disk drive: 1

Choose one of the following:

1. Create DOS partition or Logical DOS Drive
2. Set active partition
3. Delete partition or Logical DOS Drive
4. Display partition information

Enter choice: [2]

WARNING! No partitions are set active - disk 1 is not startable unless
a partition is set active

Press Esc to exit FDISK
```

The FDISK Options menu.

Figure 7-16

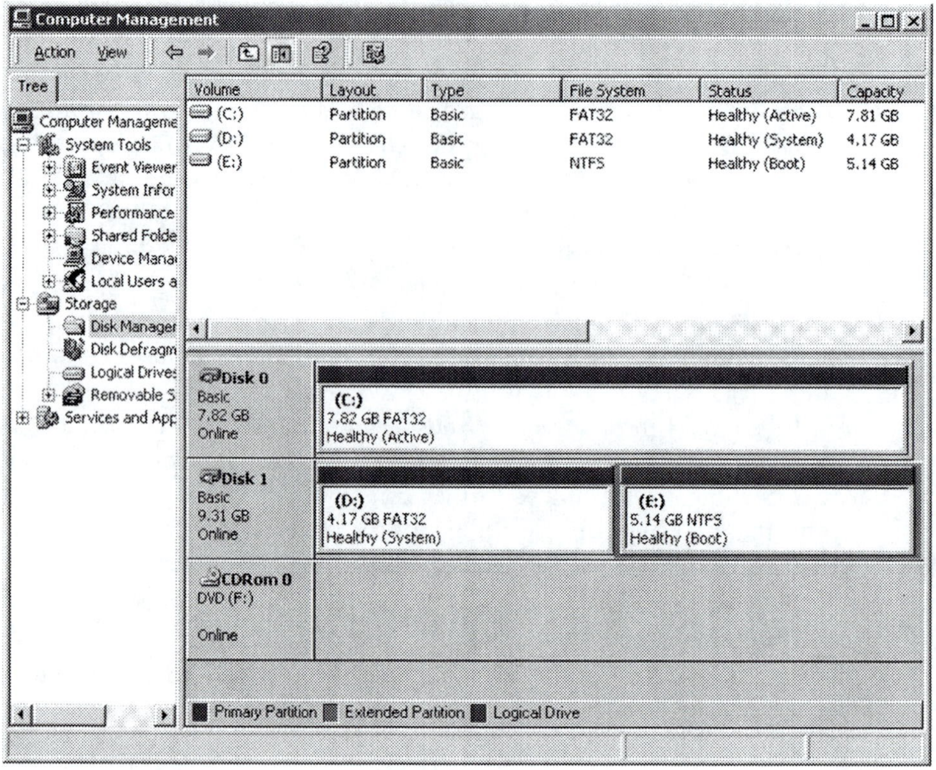

Disk Management utility.

▲ **Disk Management:** The Disk Management utility is available with Windows NT4, 2000, XP and Vista (Figure 7-16). (In Windows NT, this component is called Disk Administrator and looks somewhat different than in Windows 2000/XP/Vista.) You use Disk Management to partition and format drives. In Windows 2000/XP/Vista you can use Disk Management to create dynamic disks. Dynamic disks are a Microsoft technology that allows you to create logical "volumes" instead of partitions, and permits an unlimited number of these volumes.

▲ **Recovery Console:** The Recovery Console is a command-line utility available on Windows 2000 and XP Setup CDs that is designed for troubleshooting (In Windows Vista, the Recovery Console has been replaced by the Command Prompt). From the Recovery Console, you can format drives, stop and start services, and interact with files stored on FAT, FAT32, or NTFS. The Recovery Console isn't installed on a system by default, but you can add it as a menu choice at the bottom of the startup menu.

7.4.4 Managing a Hard Drive

To protect your hard drive from data loss and maximize its efficiency, there are several tasks you should perform regularly.

▲ **Backing up:** Data backups ensure that should a problem develop with your PC that jeopardizes your data, you have a copy of the data to restore when the problem is solved. It is important to not only backup user data, but also essential system files. Windows 2000, XP Professional and Vista include a Microsoft Backup utility that you can find on the Tools tab of a drive's Properties dialog box.

▲ **Protecting against viruses:** A computer virus is a malicious third-party program that can do considerable damage to your data and cause a hard drive to malfunction. Viruses are typically infected files or programs that are downloaded from the Internet or copied from infected disks. It is important to have a virus-protection program installed and to run the program regularly to scan your system.

▲ **Error-checking:** There are two types of errors a drive can develop in a hard drive. Physical errors are imperfections in the surface coat of the platters that prevent accurate data encoding. Logical errors are errors that occur in a drive's table of contents. For example, the location of a file may point to the wrong file. Logical errors are typically caused when an application, or the operating system freezes and crashes, losing data stored in system memory. You can use disk-checking utilities to detect and repair physical and logical errors. In Windows 9x (95, 98, and Me), you use ScanDisk. In Windows NT, 2000, XP, and Vista, you use Check Disk (Figure 7-17).

Figure 7-17

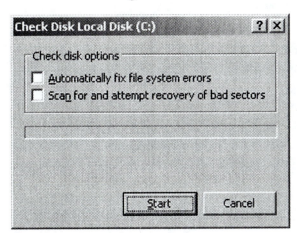

CheckDisk utility.

▲ **Defragmenting:** The operating system uses the first available cluster to write new files. If there is not enough contiguous (unbroken) space, the operating system will split a new file and write it to several locations. These split files are called fragmented, and they take longer to access by the read/write heads than nonfragmented files. To defragment your drive, you use the Windows Disk Defragmenter utility (Start > (All) Programs > Accessories > System Tools). Disk Defragmenter can tell you how much a drive is defragmented, whether defragmentation is recommended, and if you choose, defragment the drive (Figure 7-18).

For instances when a system's bootable hard drive crashes, you should make sure that you have an alternate way to start your computer. You do this through using a separate boot disk, either a floppy disk (for older systems) or a bootable CD. The disks you use depend on the operating system you are running.

▲ **Windows 9x:** In Windows 9x, you can create an emergency bootable floppy, from Add/Remove Programs in the Control Panel. When you boot

Figure 7-18

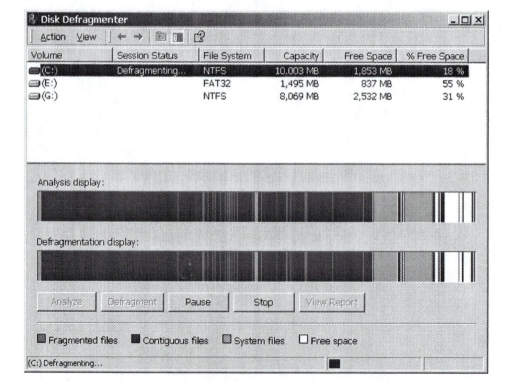

Disk Defragmenter utility.

from this floppy, you will be able to use troubleshooting utilities such as FDISK, FORMAT, and ScanDisk.

▲ **Windows NT/2000/XP/Vista:** These operating systems allow you to boot from their startup CDs. However, you should also create an Emergency Repair Disk (ERD). The ERD can check registry files, system files, the startup environment, and the boot sector. If it finds problems, it will tell you what files to use to fix the problems. In Window NT, you create an ERD by running RDISK.EXE located in \winnt\system32. In Windows 2000, you create an ERD by running the Emergency Repair Disk utility from the first screen of the Backup utility. In Windows XP, this emergency disk is called Automated System Recovery. You create the ASR disk using the Automated System Recovery Wizard button in the Backup utility. In Windows Vista, this functionality is called Windows Complete PC Restore.

7.4.5 Ensuring Drive Fault Tolerance

If the loss of data from a hard drive failure would be catastrophic to your organization, you need to use some method of **drive fault tolerance**. Drive fault tolerance means a hard drive is able to recover from an error condition and is implemented primarily with networked servers and data storage. Fault tolerance methods include:

▲ **Mirroring:** Mirroring uses two drives attached to a single host adaptor. When the OS writes data to the first drive, the same data is written to its duplicate, or mirror. If the first drive fails, the mirror drive is already online.

▲ **Duplexing:** Duplexing is the same as mirroring except it uses two separate host adaptors (one for each drive). Duplexing provides fault tolerance even if one of the controllers fails.

▲ **Disk striping with parity:** In striping, data files are subdivided and different portions written to separate disks. Striping data by itself improves only performance. To add fault tolerance, you need to use parity, or fault tolerance information computed for each block of data written to a drive. This parity information can be used to reconstruct missing data, should a drive fail.

▲ **Redundant Array of Independent Disks (RAID):** RAID is a storage technology that uses at least two hard drives in combination for high availability, fault tolerance, and performance. RAID drives are primarily used on servers. RAIDs can be created by using either hardware or software. A software RAID uses dynamic disks and is set up in the OS. Windows Server operating systems support RAID drives, as do Windows

2000, XP, and Vista. A hardware RAID is set up through drives that are physically connected to a RAID host adapter. Many RAID levels exist, each at a higher complexity than the next, including:

- **RAID 0:** Stripes data to multiple disks without parity or duplicating data. This RAID level only improves performance; it does not provide fault tolerance.
- **RAID 1:** Uses mirroring or duplexing with two drives
- **RAID 2:** Uses disk striping with parity with at least three drives; one of the drives is used only for parity information.
- **RAID 5:** The data and parity are striped across several drives in which the parity information for data on one drive is stored with the data on another drive.

7.4.6 Troubleshooting Inaccessible Hard Drives

Hard drive problems usually stem from one of three causes:

1. **The adapter is bad.** In this case, the BIOS will not recognize the drive. However, the drive will work properly when attached to a different host adapter. To fix this problem, replace the host adaptor.
2. **The adapter and disk are connected incorrectly.** To make sure that the hardware connection is working:
   - Check that the front panel drive LED lights up and stays on constantly. If not, the hard drive data cable is probably not properly connected.
   - Check both ends of the connecting cables to make sure they are plugged in: at the device and on the motherboard or adapter card, and check the power supply connectors. Make sure the drive's jumpers are properly configured. If another drive works with the same cable, the cable is working.
   - Install the drive on a different IDE channel. If this works, the original IDE channel may be at fault.
3. **The disk is bad.** If the BIOS recognizes the drive, but you are still having problems accessing the drive, the disk itself may be faulty. However, there are a number of different ways in which a drive may be faulty. To troubleshoot a disk, check for the following:
   - **Incorrect CMOS configuration:** Check the CMOS configuration for each hard drive. The information that you need should be in the documentation for each drive.
   - **Resource conflict:** Newly added hardware is conflicting with hard drive. Check the system resource settings to verify that a resource conflict has not been created by installing a new piece of hardware.

FOR EXAMPLE

Hard Drive Noise

During startup and while running, most hard drives produce certain characteristic noises. Pay attention to the normal sounds your hard drive makes—if you hear any unusual sounds (a high-pitched tone, a new clicking, rumbling, or grinding, or even any louder than normal noises continuing for over a month), this may be a signal that your hard drive is about to fail.

- **Corrupt or missing boot partition:** The boot partition on the hard drive may be corrupted. If the system files on the boot partition are corrupt, the system cannot boot properly. Copy your backed-up system files to the drive or use an ERD to repair the system files. You may have to format the partition and reinstall the operating system, should this fail to solve the problem. Also, verify that the boot partition has not been accidentally removed.

- **Virus infection:** The hard drive may be infected with a virus. Many viruses can corrupt the Master Boot Record on the hard drive and cause errors that show up as hard drive errors. If an antivirus program is not installed on the PC, install one and scan the hard drive.

- **Defective hard drive:** The hard drive may be defective. A louder-than-usual noise that the drive has been making for over a month may have been a sign that the bearings were seizing. Drives can experience mechanical problems; read/write problems; and circuitry problems.

Some of the common PC system error messages for hard drive problems are as follows:

- ▲ **Hard disk configuration error:** An incorrect CMOS configuration or a loose data cable causes this message.

- ▲ **Hard disk 0 failure:** Disk 0 is the Master drive on the primary IDE channel. This message is caused by an incorrect CMOS configuration or a bad connection to the power supply.

- ▲ **Hard disk controller failure:** Check the connection of the data cable on the drive and the power connectors.

When you are troubleshooting a SCSI hard drive, keep in mind the following:

- ▲ **CMOS setup:** The hard drive settings in the CMOS should be set to None or Auto-detect.

▲ **SCSI device drivers:** SCSI devices require device drivers. Make sure that the latest drivers are installed.

▲ **Host adapter and hard drive IDs:** The SCSI host adapter is almost always device 7 on the SCSI chain, and the first SCSI hard drive on the channel should be assigned as SCSI ID 0. If you have two or more SCSI hard drives, or any other SCSI devices, on the same SCSI cable, each device must have a unique SCSI ID number.

▲ **Termination:** If the SCSI hard drive is the only internal device or the last device on the internal SCSI channel, the hard drive must be terminated.

If nothing you do helps to resurrect a hard drive, you do have some options for trying to recover data on the drive. You can purchase a specialized data recovery utility program (one example is Ontrack's Easy-Recovery). These are designed to recover and reconstruct whatever file fragments are readable on the drive. A more expensive option is to send the drive to a data recovery service that specializes in retrieving data from failed drives.

SELF-CHECK

1. Describe low-level formatting, partitioning, and high-level formatting.
2. What is the difference between a primary partition and an extended partition?
3. What is a file allocation table?
4. List three partitioning utilities.
5. Describe the difference between a physical drive error and a logical drive error.
6. How does a file become fragmented?

SUMMARY

Key components of a hard drive system include platters coated with magnetic media, read/write heads, controller circuitry, and the host adaptor. Hard drive organization, called geometry, consists of heads, tracks, cylinders, and sectors. Characteristics used to rate and compare hard drives include capacity, spin speed, seek time, rotational latency, access time, interface, disk cache, data transfer rate, and data transfer mode. Hard drives connect to a host adaptor on the motherboard or a separate expansion card. They use a specific interface technology in order to communicate.

Popular interfaces include parallel Advanced Technology Attachment (ATA), Serial ATA (SATA), and Small Computer Systems Interface (SCSI). Each interface type has a succession of improved standards defining characteristics such as transfer rate and cabling.

Internal hard drives are mounted in a drive bay and use a data cable to connect to the motherboard and power cable to connect to the power supply. All drives need the appropriate cabling, connectors, and host adapters for connecting to the PC. Two ATA drives can be connected on a single cable to either a primary or a secondary IDE channel, but must be configured as either Master or Slave and the drives' positions will affect their performances. SATA drives do not share cables and do not require special configuration.

SCSI devices on a chain must be configured with a unique ID and devices at either end of the chain must carry a terminator resistor pack to prevent signals from reflecting. Depending on the SCSI standard, one of three signaling methods may be used: single-ended (SE), high-voltage differential (HVD), and low-voltage differential (LVD). SCSI chains are limited in total cable lengths and number of devices supported on a chain.

Hard drives must be partitioned and formatted before use. A drive manufacturer performs low-level formatting to define the drive's geometry. Partitioning divides a drive into separate areas defined by drive letters. A hard drive can have up to four primary partitions, or three partitions and one extended partition. The extended partition can contain numerous logical drives. High-level formatting prepares the logical drives by establishing a file system. Different operating systems support different files systems. Operating systems provide various utilities for partitioning and formatting. Windows 2000, XP and Vista support dynamic disks, which allow for unlimited numbers of volumes and combining disks as single volumes.

Managing a hard drive includes protecting data by making backups, guarding against viruses, checking drives for errors, defragmenting the file system, and ensuring that you have a means to boot the computer and troubleshoot a drive should it fail.

KEY TERMS

Access time

Active partition

Active termination

Actuator arm

Advanced Technology Attachment (ATA)

Boot partition

Bus mastering

Cylinder

Cylinder, Head, Sector (CHS) addressing

Daisy-chaining

Data transfer mode

Data transfer rate

Differential signaling

Disk cache

Disk controller

DMA (Direct Memory Access)

Drive fault tolerance

Drive geometry

Duplexing

Dynamic disks

Encoding

Error correction code (ECC)

Extended CHS (ECHS)

Extended partition

FAT16

FAT32

FDISK

File allocation table (FAT)

Flux transition

Forced perfect termination

Hard drive

High-level formatting

High-voltage differential (HVD) signaling

Host adaptor

Interface

Logic board

Logical Block Addressing (LBA)

Logical drive

Logical geometry

Low-level formatting

Low-voltage differential (LVD) signaling

Master Boot Record (MBR)

Mirroring

Multiword DMA

Nonvolatile storage

NTFS

Partitioning

Passive termination

PIO (Programmed Input/Output) mode

Platters

Primary partition

Read/write head

Redundant Array of Independent Disks (RAID)

Rotational latency

SCSI terminator

Secondary storage

Sector

Sector translation

Seek time

Serial Advanced Technology Attachment (Serial ATA)

Single-ended (SE) signaling

Single word DMA

Small Computer System Interface (SCSI)

Spanning

Spin speed

Spindle

Striping

System partition

Tracks

Virus

Volume

Zone bit recording (ZBR)

ASSESS YOUR UNDERSTANDING

Go to www.wiley.com/college/groth to evaluate your knowledge of hard drives. *Measure your learning by comparing pre-test and post-test results.*

Summary Questions

1. Which device converts signals from an ATA drive into signals the CPU can understand?

    (a) disk controller

    (b) host adapter

    (c) bus

    (d) connector

2. What is the name for the wedge-shaped areas into which a typical hard drive is divided?

    (a) tracks

    (b) sectors

    (c) clusters

    (d) spindles

3. Which of the following is not a drive performance characteristic?

    (a) data transfer rate

    (b) data transfer mode

    (c) signaling method

    (d) rotational latency

4. Which of the following does a hard drive controller use to detect and correct minor data loss?

    (a) EPRML

    (b) drive fault tolerance

    (c) duplexing

    (d) ECC

5. How many devices can be used by a single ATA channel?

    (a) 1

    (b) 2

    (c) 4

    (d) 7

6. How many devices can SCSI-1 support (including the controller)?

    (a) 8

    (b) 7

(c) 1

(d) 15

7. An ATA Slave drive only listens for data being sent to it from the Master drive. True or false?

8. Unlike SATA drives, parallel ATA drives can be removed or added while the computer is running. True or false?

9. Which of the following is *not* a form of SCSI signaling?

(a) single-ended

(b) differential

(c) VHD

(d) HVD

10. The SCSI-3 standard defined which of the following specifications?

(a) Fast-Wide SCSI, HVD, and bus mastering

(b) Wide SCSI, HVD, and SAS

(c) Ultra SCSI, LVD, and bus mastering

(d) Ultra SCSI, LVD, and SAS

11. A primary partition can hold up to four logical drives. True or false?

12. How do you low-level format an ATA drive?

(a) run FDISK

(b) execute FORMAT.COM

(c) you don't; it's done at the factory

(d) low-level formatting is done automatically during Windows Setup

13. Which of the following utilities will *not* allow you to partition a hard drive?

(a) FDISK utility

(b) FORMAT command

(c) Disk Management

(d) Recovery console

14. If you convert a basic disk to a dynamic one, it won't let you span or stripe volumes. True or false?

15. Which of the following is *not* a way to protect data?

(a) disk striping

(b) duplexing

(c) fault tolerance

(d) virus protection

16. Duplexing is the same as mirroring, except that it:

(a) uses parity to add fault tolerance

(b) uses disk striping to improve performance

(c) uses a separate host adapter for each drive

(d) uses dynamic disks

17. Which of the following is *not* a type of hard drive error?

(a) soft error

(b) high-level error

(c) surface error

(d) logical error

18. A fragmented file has data stored in non-contiguous _____.

(a) clusters

(b) cylinders

(c) tracks

(d) surfaces

19. Which of the following would you use to start your computer without the help of your hard drive?

(a) system disk

(b) ASR disk

(c) boot disk

(d) ERD disk

20. If a hard drive is not responding, what is one of the first troubleshooting steps you should take?

(a) Run an ERD.

(b) Check the BIOS.

(c) Reinstall the FAT.

(d) Repair the MBR.

Applying This Chapter

1. If a hard drive has 903 cylinders, 12 heads, 63 sectors per track, and 512 bytes per sector, what is its capacity?

2. If a drive is listed with a spin speed of 1200 RPM, what is its average rotational latency?

3. Explain to a novice technician how to properly connect an ATA data ribbon cable.

4. Compare and contrast the advantages of SATA and SCSI interfaces.

5. List the main steps used in installing any hard drive.

YOU TRY IT

Configuring and Positioning ATA Hard Drives

You are installing two ATA-7 hard drives using a parallel ATA interface to a computer. One of the new hard drives is significantly faster than the other. The computer system supports ATA-7 and already has an older ATA-6 internal hard drive and a CD-ROM drive. Describe how you will configure and position the drives.

Troubleshooting an ATA Installation

You need to explain to a technician over the phone how to take some simple troubleshooting steps with respect to a newly installed hard drive that isn't being recognized by the system. What steps will you ask the technician to perform?

Terminating SCSI Buses

You have installed an internal SCSI hard drive and two external SCSI devices: a scanner and a CD-ROM drive.

The scanner is the last device on the chain. Which device(s) should be terminated?

Purchasing the Right Drives

Your organization's multimedia developer needs 500GB of additional drive space with a fast response time, but your budget is limited to $300 or less. You have inspected the developer's system: it supports ATA-7 and has two internal ATA-drives with one drive bay open. The motherboard does have four SATA connectors and a free PCI slot for an additional expansion card. What interface will you recommend? Go online to research hard drives from Maxtor (Maxtor.com), Seagate (Seagate.com), and Western Digital (Westerndigital.com), and then determine the hard drive or drives you would recommend for the system. List the reasons why you think your proposed hard drive is a good choice over its competitors.

8
REMOVABLE STORAGE

Starting Point

Go to www.wiley.com/college/groth to assess your knowledge of removable storage.

Determine where you need to concentrate your effort.

What You'll Learn in This Chapter

▲ Popular removable storage technologies
▲ Optical drive technologies
▲ Flash memory technologies
▲ Installation steps for floppy and optical drives
▲ Symptoms and causes of problems with floppy, optical, and flash memory drives

After Studying This Chapter, You'll Be Able To

▲ Identify different types of optical drives
▲ Identify different types of flash memory devices
▲ Evaluate a removable storage device in terms of its technology, interface, and capacity
▲ Choose an appropriate technology and device for removable storage
▲ Install a floppy drive
▲ Install an optical drive
▲ Troubleshoot a failing storage device

INTRODUCTION

Although PCs are manufactured with internal hard drives for storing data, people also need ways to transfer data between computers or other devices such as digital cameras and portable audio players. Removable storage devices fulfill this purpose. Removable storage also allows you to keep data that you don't need quick access to (such as backups) off of your hard drive to save space or for security.

Some removable storage types such as floppy drives are based on magnetic disk technologies, such as hard drives. Other types of removable storage technologies include optical drives (Compact Disks (CDs) and Digital Video Disks/Digital Versatile Disks (DVDs)), flash memory devices, and tape drives.

Removable storage also provides a way for software manufacturers to distribute commercial software. Today, CDs and DVDs are the primary method used for retail software and most PCs have a CD or DVD drive. Before CDs and DVDs, floppies were the principal storage type used for software distribution. Floppies, other removable storage devices, such as Zip drives and Jaz drives, were once very popular, but they are being or have been phased out in favor of faster devices with higher capacities.

8.1 Examining Types of Storage

There are a variety of methods that have been used to store the data that a computer uses. Originally, computer information was contained in memory and printed to punch cards. When you wanted to retrieve the data, you ran the punch cards into a special reader; the information was read back into memory and could then be used. This proved to be a very limited storage medium in terms of capacity and ease of retrieval. A single page of data could take several pages of punch cards and the cards had to be put into the reader in the correct order or the program wouldn't run properly. New technologies in removable storage, as with hard drives, have been fueled by the need for media with greater storage capacities with higher data transfer speeds, and at reasonable costs.

8.1.1 Tape Drives

The discovery that computer signals could be recorded (and played back into the computer) with a tape recorder led to magnetic tape becoming the successor to punch cards. This was a much more efficient storage system than punch cards. Using a single, long tape reduced the possibility of getting the information out of sequence and made the data easier to access. Several early PC systems (such as the TRS-80 and the Apple II) came with cassette tape storage devices to load and store programs and data.

The major limitations of tape were its speed and precision. Tape was slow to store programs and data, and it was slow to access information because of its linear nature. **Tape drives** are sequential storage devices: If a piece of information is located at the end of a tape, you have to fast-forward through all the other information to get to the data you need. Although they are an older technology, tape drives are still used today because of their cost-effectiveness.

Tape drives can be external or internal, and today there are two basic types of tape cartridges: full-sized and mini. Mini cartridges are the more popular because their drive size fits into a normal PC drive bay. Tape cartridges use a long polyester ribbon coated with magnetic oxide wrapped around two spools. As the tape unwinds from one spool, it passes by a read/write head in the drive that retrieves or saves the information. It then proceeds to the other spool where it is kept until needed again. There are a great variety of tape drive and cartridge formats (Figure 8-1); with popular brands being Travan, quarter-inch cartridges (QIC), digital audio tape (DAT) and digital linear tape (DLT) and super DLT. Common cartridge storage sizes range from 4GB to 300GB and higher, although you can find expensive network tape drives with storage capacities in terabytes.

Figure 8-1

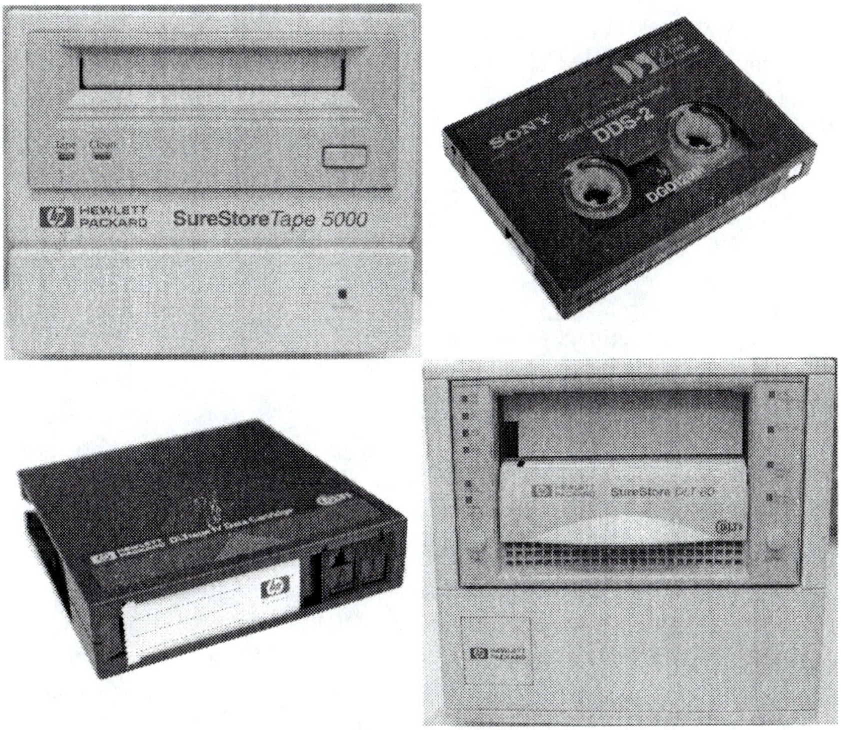

DAT and DT tape drives and cartridges.

FOR EXAMPLE

Selecting a Tape Drive

There are many competing standards for tape drives and cassettes. If you are purchasing a tape drive, make sure that the backup software you are using, the operating software for your system, and the tape drive are all compatible. As with any drive, you will also need to make sure that the tape drive also has a compatible interface (usually PATA or SCSI).

8.1.2 Removable Magnetic Disks

Magnetic disks, such as those used in hard drives, store data as patterns of transitions between positive and negative charges on a magnetized surface. Removable magnetic disks use the same types of technologies as hard drives, but are designed to be able to be easily inserted and removed, feature some type of protective casing, and typically have smaller capacities than hard drives. There is a wide variety of technologies that use the basic principles of magnetic disk storage, including:

▲ **Floppy disks:** The smallest member of this group is the **floppy disk** (1.44MB). It is called that because the thin magnetic disk used is flexible, and early floppies (5.25-inch floppies) had a thin protective casing that could actually be slightly flexed. Floppy disks are like fixed disks, but they have only one platter encased in a plastic shell. Later floppies (3.5-inch floppies) have a hard shell to protect the flexible disk inside. A floppy disk drive has either one or two read/write heads. Each head moves in a straight line on a track over the disk rather than on an angular path as with fixed disk systems. When the disk is placed into the drive, a motor engages the center of the disk and rotates it. This action moves the tracks past the read/write heads.

▲ **Zip and Jaz drives:** Iomega's Zip and Jaz drives (Figure 8-2) are detachable, external hard disks that are used to store a large volume (around 100MB for the Zip, 1GB and 2GB for the Jaz) of data on a single, floppy-sized disk. The drives connect to either a parallel port or a special interface card. The major use of Zip and Jaz drives is to transport large amounts of data from place to place. This used to be accomplished with several floppies. Jaz drives are no longer manufactured, and these two technologies have essentially been superseded by more popular CD and DVD disks.

▲ **Pocket hard drives:** A **pocket hard drive** is small, portable hard drives that are available in capacities from 2GB to 40GB and more, and

Figure 8-2

Zip and Jaz drives.

typically connect to the PC through a USB port. IBM's **Microdrive** is designed to fit into CompactFlash memory card slots (used with digital cameras and laptops) or a PC card Type II slot (used with laptops) and stores from 512MB to 8GB.

8.1.3 Optical Storage

Floppy drives were once the mainstay for PC removable storage, and almost all PCs came with at least one floppy drive. Today, optical storage has replaced the floppy, and almost all PCs come with at least one optical drive: Typically a CD (compact disk) drive (Figure 8-3), or a DVD (digital versatile, or video, disk)

Figure 8-3

An internal CD-ROM drive.

and CD combination drive that can read both CDs and DVDs. The primary difference between CDs and DVDs lies essentially in how much each data the disks can store; to look at, the disks themselves are virtually identical.

Whereas magnetic storage records data with magnetic charges, optical storage uses beams of light called lasers to record data in patterns of greater and lesser reflectivity on a shiny surface. Optical disks have become so popular because they can store far more data on a relatively similar physical size as floppy disk. While a 3.5-inch floppy can store, at best, 1.44MB of data, compact disks store 700MB or more and the smallest capacity DVDs store 4.7GB.

8.1.4 Flash Memory Devices

The same flash memory chips used for a PC's BIOS are also used for a variety of removable and portable storage devices. **Flash memory** (also called **flash RAM**) is nonvolatile memory and is a form of EEPROM (electrically erasable programmable read-only memory). Flash memory requires very little electricity and is solid state: It operates with no moving, mechanical parts such as the actuator arms of hard drives. Because of this, flash memory devices are very rugged and do not suffer the same types of physical wear and tear as magnetic hard drives. There are two popular types of flash memory devices that are used as portable data storage:

▲ **Memory cards:** A **memory card** is a small device, about the size of a large, thick postage stamp, that fits into a narrow slot on a digital camera or a card reader on a laptop or PC.

▲ **USB flash drives:** A **USB flash drive** is designed to function as a portable hard drive. They are typically narrow, pen-sized devices that can store up to 8GB and higher and connect to the PC through a USB port.

SELF-CHECK

1. Name three purposes of removable storage.
2. Identify four types of removable storage that use magnetic disk technology.
3. Besides magnetic disk, what other technologies are used for storing data?
4. Describe the difference in how magnetic disk and optical disk technologies store data.

8.2 Working with Floppy Drives

Today the floppy drive is almost unnecessary—most applications, hardware drivers, and utilities ship on CD-ROMs, and floppies are limited in their capacity. However, you will still find floppy drives on many PCs, and they are still used for storing or transferring small data files.

Two major sizes of floppy disk, or floppies, have been used, 3.5-inch (Figure 8-4) and 5.25-inch, although the 5.25-inch disks are now obsolete. Disk capacities range from 360KB to 1.44MB in various form factors (Table 8-1). Similar to hard drives, floppy disks are formatted with tracks and sectors. The density of a disk determines how closely the sectors and tracks can be packed. The lower density format is called double-density (DD), and the higher density is high density (HD).

Figure 8-4

A 3.5" HD floppy disk.

Table 8-1: Floppy Disk Types

Floppy Disk	Size	Capacity	Notes
5.25 inch Double-Density (DD)	5.25 inch	360KB	Obsolete. Cover notch in side with a sticker to write-protect.
5.25 inch High-Density (HD)	5.25 inch	1.2MB	Obsolete. Can often be distinguished from 5.25 inch DD by a reinforcement ring around the center hole. Same write-protect as DD.
3.5 inch DD	3.5 inch	720KB	Obsolete. Single square hole in corner with sliding tab for write-protection.
3.5 inch HD	3.5 inch	1.44MB	Current standard. Same write-protect tab as previously, plus extra square hole in adjacent corner to indicate HD capacity.

8.2.1 Floppy Drive Components

There are four major components to a **floppy disk drive** subsystem:

▲ **Storage medium, or disk:** The floppy disk itself is the removable medium on which information is stored in a floppy disk system. The two types, 5.25-inch disk and 3.5-inch diskette are not interchangeable. Most of these disks have a write-protect notch or tab that can be used to prevent accidental writing to the diskette.

▲ **Floppy drive:** Drives are built to accommodate one or the other sizes of floppy drive. There are three main types of form factors, or drive styles, available:

• **Full-height:** Large floppy drives used for 5.25-inch floppies and are about 1.63 inches high.

• **Half-height drives:** These drives (about 1 inch high) take up only about half the space (vertically) of full-height drives. This drive is the de facto standard in use today (Figure 8-5).

• **Combination:** The combination form factor contains both 1.2MB 5.25-inch and 1.44MB 3.5-inch drives in a half-height enclosure.

▲ **Floppy disk controller:** The **floppy disk controller** handles the communications between the floppy drive and the CPU. Three types of floppy disk controller interfaces are used in PCs:

Figure 8-5

Half-height 3.5-inch floppy drive.

- **Built-in controllers:** On most systems today, the motherboard includes a **floppy drive interface adapter.** This adapter is supported through the chipset, which integrates the floppy drive controller functionality.
- **Standalone cards:** Usually not a single purpose card, a **floppy controller card** installs into an expansion slot on the motherboard. For example, many floppy controller cards also include a game port, a serial port or two, a parallel port, and the disk interface.
- **Disk controller cards:** It was once common for a single card to provide the interface for the hard drive and the floppy disk. This reduced the number of expansion slots needed to install other system necessities.
▲ **Floppy Drive Cable:** The floppy drive çable is a 34-wire ribbon cable (similar to the EIDE ribbon cable used with PATA drives) with three connectors. One of these connectors attaches to the controller on the motherboard. The other two connect to the drives (one for drive A:, the other for drive B:). You can attach up to two floppy drives to a single controller.

8.2.2 Installing a Floppy Drive

Installing floppy drives is fairly straightforward. The steps are as follows:

1. Connect the cable to the drive (Figure 8-6).
2. Install the drive in the computer by physically mounting it in the computer case and connecting the power cable.
3. Connect the cable from the drive to the controller.
4. Connect the power supply to the drive. Find a floppy power connector (also known as a Berg connector) on one of the power cables coming from the power supply and connect it to the power pins on the floppy drive.

Figure 8-6

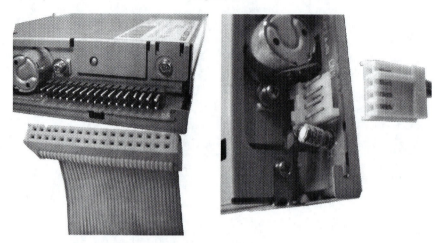

Floppy drive connectors.

There are two important considerations in connecting a floppy cable.

▲ You must align the cable so that Pin 1 of the cable (usually marked by a red stripe) is matched to Pin 1 of the controller and Pin 1 on the drive (usually either marked with a "1" or a white dot).

▲ You must make sure that you use the correct connector with the proper disk drive.

• The first set of connectors, in the middle of the cable, is for the B floppy disk drive (Figure 8-7).

• After the twist in the cable (that is, at the end of the cable) are the A floppy disk connectors. Some computer manufacturers may key the cable connectors so they can be connected in only one way.

The CMOS settings for the floppy should be discovered by the BIOS and configured at first boot-up. The CMOS settings indicate what types of floppy drives are connected (if any), their type (3.5-inch or 5.25-inch), and their capacity. You can configure all these settings within the CMOS setup program's floppy device settings, if necessary.

Floppy disks are formatted by the manufacturer, so you should be able to insert a floppy drive and use it immediately. If for some reason you have an unformatted disk, you can right-click the drive's icon in Windows Explorer and select Format from the sub-menu. Floppies are formatted with the FAT file system in Windows NT, 2000, and XP.

External floppy drives are also common today and are typically connected to the PC with a USB port (which also provides power) and do not require using a ribbon cable.

Figure 8-7

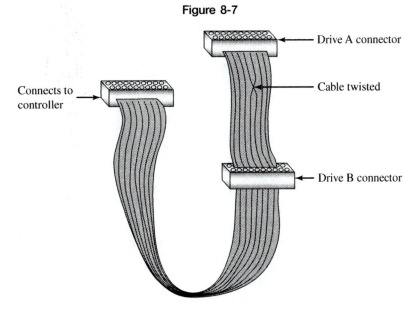

Floppy drive cable.

8.2.3 Troubleshooting Floppy Drives

Troubleshooting the floppy drive is also relatively simple. Common problems include:

▲ **Drive light that doesn't go out:** The most common problem after installation is a drive light that refuses to go out. This happens if the floppy drive cable is upside down on one side.

▲ **CMOS configuration problem:** In addition to needing the correct cable positions, the CMOS configuration also needs to be correct. They should reflect the right drive type and size of the floppy drive. If this information

---

FOR EXAMPLE

Emergency Floppies

Many people still believe that having a floppy drive on a PC is essential. The reason for this is that, on older PCs (running older Windows operating systems such as Windows 3x or 9x), if the hard drive crashed, the only way to boot up and repair the drive was to use emergency floppy disks. For a long time, creating a set of bootable floppies was an essential part of managing your PC. Today, however, all of the recent Windows operating systems (NT, 2000, XP, and Vista) come with bootable CDs that include repair utilities.

is wrong, most computers detect that the wrong drive type is selected, and an error occurs during boot-up.

▲ **Read/write problems:** If you receive error messages, such as "Data Error Reading Drive A," or have other problems when you try to read (open) or write from a floppy, you may have a read/write problem. A read/write problem can be caused by:

- **Dirty drives.** Read/write problems are often caused by a dirty drive. If this is the problem, you can fix it with a floppy-disk head-cleaning kit.

- **Misaligned read/write heads.** The mechanical arm in the floppy drive may become misaligned so that the format it creates is not properly positioned on the disk (thus preventing other floppy drives from reading it). Although commercial tools are available to realign floppy drive read/write heads it is usually cheaper to simply replace the floppy drive.

- **Bad media.** Most floppy drive problems result from bad media. Floppies are good for a finite number of uses, and they can go bad.

SELF-CHECK

1. What different types of floppy disks are there? Which type is used today?
2. What are the four main components of a floppy drive subsystem?
3. Describe how a floppy ribbon cable is connected.
4. List four possible causes of floppy drive problems.

8.3 Understanding Optical Drives

Optical drives are the most common method for removable storage today, and succeeded the floppy drive because they store more data. They are called optical because they use a narrow beam of light, called a laser, to read and write data. Compact disk (CD) drives have become standard equipment in PCs, and most software developers release their commercial software packages in CDs. Digital video disks (DVDs) are typically used for distributing and playing movies and some games, although they are becoming more popular in software distribution. Because DVD drives are designed to work with CDs, many PCs today are sold with DVD or DVD/CD combination drives.

8.3.1 Optical Drive Technologies

Optical disks store data in patterns of greater and lesser reflectivity. A manufactured CD has a layer (just below a protective acrylic surface) that is embedded with microscopic indentations called pits (Figure 8-8). The smooth, non-indented areas between pits are called lands. When the drive's laser beam is focused on this layer and the disk spins, light reflected from the optical disk surface is reflected back to a photosensor mechanism. The photosensor can detect when the reflected light is scattered as the laser moves over a less reflective pit and

Figure 8-8

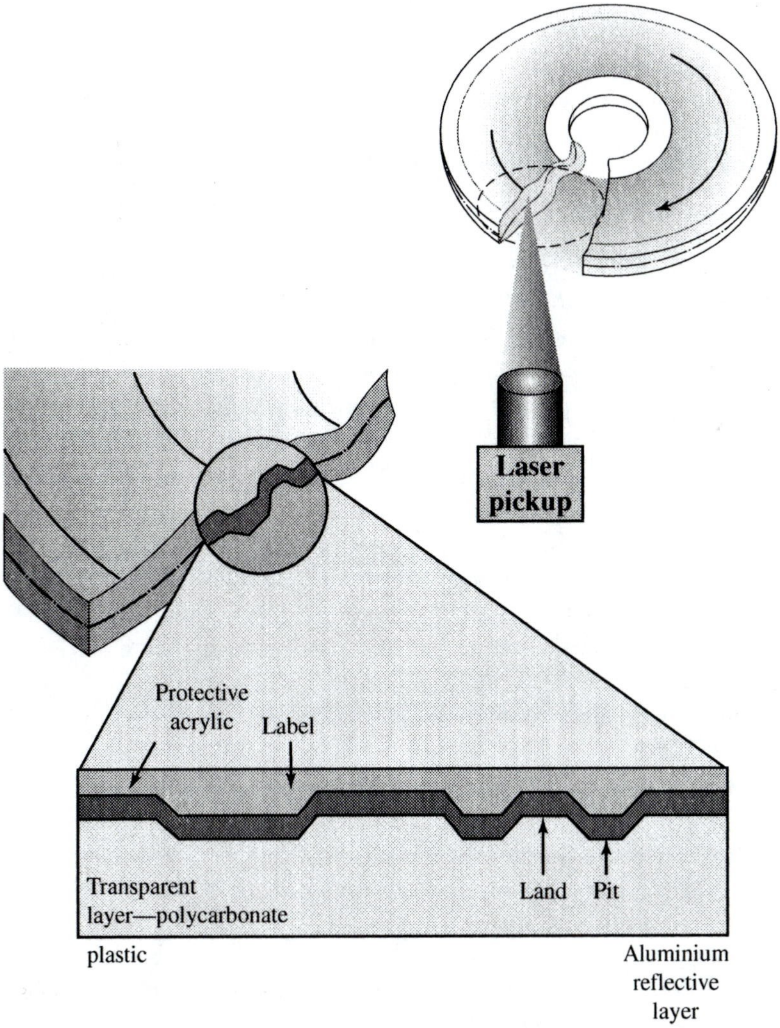

Laser
pickup

Protective
acrylic   Label

Transparent
layer—polycarbonate

plastic

Land   Pit

Aluminium
reflective
layer

Cross-section of a CD-ROM.

Figure 8-9

The binary stream is generated by reading the lengths of the pits and lands

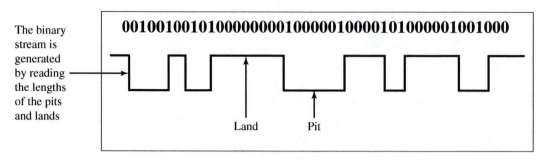

Land   Pit

Pits and lands.

when the reflected light becomes more focused, as the laser moves from a pit to a land. Whenever the photosensor detects a change (from a pit to land or vice versa), this is recorded as a binary one. If no change is detected within a certain time period, this is recorded as a binary zero. In this way, the sequence of pits and lands on an optical disk form a binary stream of data (Figure 8-9).

Pre-recorded CDs (CD-ROMS) are manufactured with embed physical indentations in a disk to create the pits; home CD burners use lasers that react with special dyes or chemicals in the disk surface to create less reflective areas or pits.

Some of the principles behind optical drive technology are similar to hard drive technologies. In both, a thin disk's surface is coated and then encoded with binary streams of data. As the disk spins, a sensor mechanism is positioned over the disk and detects the patterns of bits encoded in the surface. However, because of the difference in the type of encoding (optical versus magnetic), optical disk themselves are much hardier than magnetic disks (they do not easily lose their reflective encoding). They can therefore be handled (gently) by human hands without a high risk of losing data, and for this reason (in addition to their storage capacities), CDs and DVDs have become a very popular removable media.

Another difference is that while the magnetic disks use concentric tracks of data, optical disks have a single track that spirals from the center to the outer edge. In order for the optical drive to detect where separate files begin and end, optical drives use special file systems that divides the optical disk into sectors and creates the disks table of contents and directory structure. The two main file systems used on optical drives are:

▲ **ISO 9660:** The ISO (**International Standards Organization**) 9660 is an early optical file system developed for CD-ROMs. The first ISO-9660 specification had stringent limits on file name lengths and file structure,

> ⌐ FOR EXAMPLE ⌐
>
> ### ISO Images
>
> One type of file you may run into is an ISO image. An **ISO image** is a type of **disk image**: a single file that is an exact copy of all of the information on a disk, including its files and structural information, such as the file system and sectors. PCs can work with disk images as if they were actual drives, and disk images are useful for transferring entire hard drives (or optical disks) to new PCs or for backups of boot drives. ISO images are disk images made from optical disks (even those with file systems other than ISO 9660), typically by using third-party software.

so a variety of extensions to the ISO-9660 standard were developed to overcome these, such as the Joliet or Rock Ridge extensions. These extensions allowed for longer file names or other features such as multi-session recording. The ISO 9660 has for the most part been superseded by the UDF file system.

▲ **UDF:** The UDF (Universal Data Format) file system was developed essentially as a replacement for ISO 9660 and was designed to manage files on recordable CD or DVD drives. It supports large volume sizes and files and has fewer limitations than ISO 9660. It is also used on other media, such as flash drives.

One issue that optical drives posed in their design was how fast to spin the disks. Because of the uniform way in which pits and lands are encoded in the disk, there is much more data located at the outer edges of a disk than in the center. To enable a drive to read or write inner data at the same speed as reading outer data, early drives were designed to use CLV (constant linear velocity) (Figure 8-10). This means that the drive actually spins faster when reading or writing data closer to the center of the disk. However, with the advent of faster and faster drives, CLV reached some limitations due to the capability of the laser mechanism to be positioned quickly enough to accommodate the faster speeds. On faster drives, therefore, CAV (constant angular velocity) is used for reading data (CLV is always used for writing data). CAV means the disk spins at the same rate, such as hard drives, regardless of whether the laser is positioned. Today, many drives utilize zoned CLV (ZCLV) in which zones are specified on an optical disk and the drive uses a different CLV speed for each zone, reading more slowly at inner zones than at outer zones. Some drives may use one of the three velocity types (CLV, ZCLV, or CAV), depending on the format of optical disk that is placed in the drive.

Figure 8-10

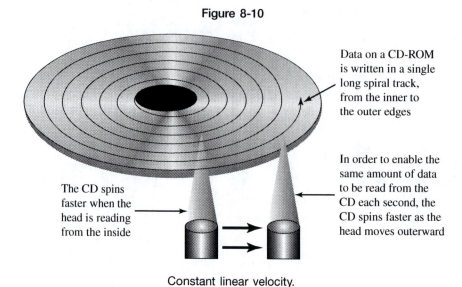

Data on a CD-ROM is written in a single long spiral track, from the inner to the outer edges

In order to enable the same amount of data to be read from the CD each second, the CD spins faster as the head moves outward

The CD spins faster when the head is reading from the inside

Constant linear velocity.

The two main types of optical drives, CDs and DVDs, CDs are the earlier technology, but they both operate similarly; using a laser beam of light to encode and read the pits and lands on a disk surface.

DVD improves on CD technologies in the following ways:

▲ **Storage capacities:** The first CD-ROMS could store 650MB; today the typical CD-R or RW capacity is 700MB, although you can find CD-R disks that can hold 800MB or 900MB. On a DVD, the pits and lands on the DVD disk's surface are spaced far more closely than on a CD, allowing for more data to be recorded on the disk. This means that a standard, single-sided DVD can hold 4.7GB, in comparison to a standard CD storage capacity of 700MB. See Table 8-2 for a list of the storage capacities of the various DVD disk standards.

▲ **Double-sided disks:** Some DVD disks are double-sided, allowing twice as much data storage.

▲ **Dual-layer disks:** More recent DVD drives have been developed that can read and write to two layers on a special, dual-layer DVD surface. A dual-layer DVD disk is manufactured with a second reflective layer below the first. The first layer is partially transparent, in order for the laser to penetrate to the second layer. Dual-layer disks are only available for recordable DVDs, not rewritable DVDs.

▲ **Compatibility with CDs:** DVD drives are able to read from CD-ROMs; and many combination drives can also write to CDs.

▲ **Improved Speeds:** DVDs are designed for faster reading and writing speeds.

Table 8-2: Common Optical Disk Capacities

Disk	Capacity
CD-ROM and CD-RW	650MB, 700MB
CD-R	650 to 900MB
DVD-5 (Single-sided, single-layered)	4.7GB
DVD-9 (Single-sided, dual-layered)	8.5GB
DVD-10 (Double-sided, single-layered)	9.4GB
DVD-18 (Double-sided, dual-layered)	17GB

8.3.2 CD and DVD Drive Standards

There are three main types of compact disk standards:

▲ **CD-ROM:** CD Read-Only Memory (CD-ROM) drives will only read from CDs; they will not write, or burn, CDs. CD-ROM disks are read-only, meaning that once information is written to a CD-ROM, it can't be erased or changed. Originally developed by the music recording industry as a replacement for vinyl records, CD-ROMs were soon adapted by the computer industry for recording and distributing digital data. Today, the bulk of commercial software applications today are distributed in CD-ROM format.

▲ **CD-R:** A Compact Disk Recordable (CD-R) drive can both read and write to disks. After a CD-R disk is written to, however, the CD-R drive cannot erase and write over existing data. Common CD-R disk capacities range from 650MB to 900MB, although the most common capacity is 700MB. To create the pits, or nonreflective areas, in a CD-R disk, the CD-R drive's laser heats up a portion of the chemically treated surface of the CD-R disk to make it less reflective. CD-R drives have for the most part been superseded by the more functional CD-RW drives.

▲ **CD-RW:** Similar to a CD-R, a Compact Disk Rewritable (CD-RW) can also read and write to compact disks, but it can also erase and write over data on CD-RW disks. The surfaces of a CD-RW disk are treated with a different chemical than that used in CD-R disks, one that allows the pits to be converted back to a reflective state and essentially "erased."

DVD formats, similar to CD formats, define whether the drive can read-only (DVD-ROM), write, or rewrite to a disk. However, there are a variety of competing formats for DVD writable and rewritable disks. The three main standards for DVD recording are:

▲ **DVD-R and DVD-RW:** DVD-R and DVD-RW disks were the first formats designed for commercial DVD players. The DVD-RW drives use a single sided DVD-5 (4.7GB) or double-sided DVD-10 (9.4GB) disk. DVD-R and DVD-RW standards are maintained by a consortium called the DVD Forum.

▲ **DVD+R and DVD+RW (also called DVD Plus):** DVD Plus standards have a few more features than DVD-RW, such as a better error management system. DVD+R and DVD+RW standards are maintained by a consortium called the DVD+RW Alliance.

▲ **DVD-RAM:** DVD Random Access Memory (RAM) drives use cartridges to place the disk in the drive (Figure 8-11), and unlike the other two standards (which are commonly referred to jointly as DVD±RW), encode data in concentric tracks instead of a single spiral track. DVD-RAM disks are not compatible with most DVD-ROM players or drives. DVD-RAM standards are maintained by the DVD Forum. In general, DVD-RAM supports higher read/write speeds and greater reliability than DVD±RW, but is more expensive.

Although today most DVD players support the first two standard categories, as well as other DVD formats, you should be sure to make sure that any DVD drives you purchase will be compatible with the type of disk you intend to use or play. DVD-Video disks are the disks that are used for DVD movie distribution.

Figure 8-11

DVD-RAM cartridge.

8.3.3 New Optical Storage Standards

There are two technologies on the market today that seek to become the next standard in optical storage; each one offers backward compatibility to the lesser CD and DVD technologies. One of these is known as High Density (or Definition) DVD (HD DVD). The other is known as Blu-ray Disc (BD). Both technologies employ similar blue-violet laser and encoding techniques, as well as disc size, with slightly differing results. The blue laser has a shorter wavelength than a standard CD or DVD laser, which allows more data to be stored in the same space because the laser can be focused more tightly to read data placed more closely. However, depending on the reception blue-laser technologies receive in the public sector, their times might come and go without much fanfare. Seemingly futuristic technologies, such as perpendicular and holographic recording, might be here before the market realizes it needs blue laser.

▲ **HD DVD:** HD DVD can hold high-definition video or large quantities of data. HD DVD has a single layer capacity of 15GB. Dual-layer and triple-layer formats exist that hold two and three times as much data, respectively. Publishers can include both standard DVD and HD DVD formats on a single disc. This coexistence means that consumers, manufacturers, and retailers have options during their transition to HD DVD because the newer HD DVD discs can play in a standard DVD player. The incentive to upgrade remains, however, due to the higher definition video awaiting owners on the same disc. If the HD DVD format is applied to standard DVDs that do not use the blue laser, it can result in capacities ranging from 5 to 18GB, offering a lower-cost alternative for those holding off on upgrading to HD DVD. HD DVD uses a single lens in its optical mechanism, unlike Blu-ray technology. Therefore, both red and blue LED lasers can be incorporated into HD DVD drives that are still more compact than those based on Blu-ray.

▲ **Blu-ray Disc:** Although Blu-ray Disc uses a similar technology to that of HD DVD, it gets the laser closer to the data and is able to store more data per layer, 25GB compared to HD DVD's 15GB. Manufacturers led by Sony make players backward compatible with DVDs and capable of the same high-definition video content. Initially, Blu-ray components were priced a bit higher than those based on HD DVD, but Blu-ray was the first to hit the market with a consumer-recordable version, including drives and media.

8.3.4 Optical Drive Characteristics

You can distinguish and compare CD and DVD drives by the following features:

▲ **Supported standards:** Although most CD drives you will find today are CD-RW, you may still encounter some CD-R only drives. For DVD drives, most drives are designed to support multiple formats, including DVD±RW; these are usually called multiformat or combination DVD drives. Drives with the DVD Forums' DVD Multi standard can read and write from **DVD±RW** as well as DVD-RAM, and some DVD burners are designed to read and/or write to dual layers (DL) disks. You may also see some drives labeled MultiRead. This is essentially a certification by The Optical Storage Technology Association (OSTA) that the drive can read a wide variety of disks. Specifically, MultiRead, or MultiRead 1 drives are CD drives that can read audio CDS, CD-ROM, CD-R, and CD-RW. MultiRead 2 drives are DVD drives that can read the CD disks listed in MultiRead1 as well as DVD-ROM, DVD-RAM, and DVD video and audio disks.

▲ **Internal or external:** Optical drives are available as internal drives to be inserted in a drive bay, or attached to a PC using an external cable, typically through a USB port.

▲ **Interface:** Common interfaces for optical drives are:

- **Parallel ATA/(ATAPI):** PATA/ATAPI (which you may more commonly see advertised as EIDE) drives will need to be connected to the motherboards IDE channels using an existing or second ribbon cable (also called an EIDE cable). You will need to follow the same rules for setting Master/Slave configurations as with a second hard drive (see Chapter 7). PATA optical drives are generally less expensive than drives with other interfaces.

- **SATA:** Serial ATA (SATA) is the new standard in drive interfaces, offering higher transfer speeds than PATA/EIDE.

- **SCSI:** Although less common than PATA/EIDE, you can find both internal and external optical drives that use the SCSI interface. You will need to follow the same rules for connecting a SCSI optical drive as you would for a SCSI hard drive; taking into account proper termination and SCSI addressing (see Chapter 7).

- **Universal Serial Bus (USB):** The USB interface is commonly used for external devices. USB it hot-swappable (you can attach devices while the PC is running). You will need to check which version of USB your PC uses and which the optical drive uses. USB 1.1 supports data transfer speeds up to 12Mbps; while USB 2.0 supports speeds up to 480Mbps. If you connect a USB 2.0 optical drive to an older USB 1.1 port on your motherboard, the drive's data transfer speeds will be limited to the USB 1.1 speeds.

- **IEEE 1394 (FireWire):** The IEEE 1394 interface (also called FireWire) is another relatively new high-speed serial bus (a competitor to USB, with similar transfer rates) that is used for external devices. You will often

Figure 8-12

Speed ratings on a CD-RW drive.

find newer external optical drives that allow for both USB and FireWire connections to the PC. Although most new laptops have FireWire ports, built-in FireWire ports are less common on PCs. However, you can install a FireWire expansion card to add this port to your PC.

▲ **Disk loading:** Although most optical drives use a sliding tray for inserting a disk, some models (such as DVD-RAM drives) may have protective caddies or cartridges that you put the disk into before inserting the caddy into the drive.

▲ **Read/Write/Rewrite Speeds:** The maximum data transfer rates of optical drives are commonly expressed as multiples of a base data transfer rate for writing, rewriting, and reading. Depending on the capabilities of the optical drive, it may have up to three speeds listed, as in 24X/20X/40X (Figure 8-12). The first rating is for writing (24X), the second for rewriting (20X), and the third for reading (40X). The base data transfer rate for CD drives is 150KBps; the base rate for DVD drives is 1.35MBps. To translate these rates to KBps or MBps, you would multiply the base rate times the designated "X" speed ratings. For example, a 24X write rating for a DVD-drive is, in MBps, equal to 24 X 1.35MBps, or 32.4MBps. Note that these X ratings refer to maximum data transfer rates; they don't take into account access times, for example, so these rates are for the most part theoretical maximums and approximations. DVD/CD combination drives may have up to six speed ratings—one set each for CD and DVD capabilities. In addition, in the technical specifications for an optical drive, manufacturers may give several speeds for a single function (writing, rewriting, or reading) depending on whether CAV, CLV, or ZCLV is used for a particular disk type.

▲ **Access time:** Similar to hard drives, optical drives are also rated by their access time, the amount of time it takes the read/write mechanism to locate data on the disk. Access times for optical drives are far slower than for hard drives, common access times for optical drives range between 100 and 200 ms.

▲ **Cache/Buffer:** Most optical drives will have disk cache, or buffer, of a few MB, to store often-used data, such as the disk file directory, to speed up the process of locating and reading files.

8.3.5 Installing a CD or DVD Drive

Adding a CD or DVD drive to a computer is a popular upgrade. As with any devices you are connecting to the PC, you need to choose a drive with an interface compatible with your motherboard. Internal CD-ROM and DVD drives usually use the PATA/EIDE interface as defined in the ATAPI (ATA Packet Interface) standard, but drives using a SCSI interface are also available. If the drive is a SCSI drive, most, but not all, come with its own host adapter card. Before installing a SCSI drive, verify that the PC already has a SCSI host adapter installed in an expansion slot or as part of the motherboard.

An external CD and DVD drive may also use the SCSI interface, but it's more common for an external CD or DVD drive to connect to the PC using a USB or IEEE 1394 (FireWire) interface. Remember that if you install a hard drive or other storage device (CD-ROM, DVD, tape drive, and so on) and it is faster than the interface it is connecting to, the new, faster device will only operate as fast as the slowest link in the chain (the onboard interface). For internal drives, you must also ensure that you have an available drive bay.

CD-ROM and DVD drives are installed using the same process as hard drives and usually occupy a half-height bay on the front panel of a PC so the user has access to the disk tray and drive controls. These drives are usually ATAPI devices and install on a PATA IDE data connection on the motherboard, or less commonly, an expansion card with an IDE connector.

When installing an IDE CD-ROM drive to a system that has an IDE hard drive installed, you must configure the CD-ROM as a Slave on the primary IDE ribbon cable or a Master or Slave on a second ribbon. However, some IDE CD drives can be configured only as Slaves, so you will need to check the optical drives manual to check for the correct configuration.

You install an internal optical drive using the same procedures as an internal hard drive. You must:

1. Prepare the drive bay.
2. Set any ATA or SCSI jumpers and IDs (Figure 8-13).
3. Install the drive in the bay.
4. Connect the data and power cables (and any other cables).

One unique installation step is the optional installation of an audio pass-through cable. This cable allows sound from DVDs and audio CDs to be passed directly to either the motherboard or the sound expansion card (Figure 8-14).

Figure 8-13

PATA CD-ROM drive jumpers connectors.

Figure 8-14

CD-ROM sound pass-through cable.

This cable is typically needed only on older systems, and you should check the documentation that comes with your drive and your sound card to determine what, if any, additional cables are needed, and whether it connects to the motherboard or sound card.

8.3.6 Troubleshooting Optical Drives

CD-ROM and DVD problems are normally media related. Although compact disc technology is much more reliable than that for floppy disks, it's not perfect. Another factor to consider is the cleanliness of the disc. On many occasions, if

FOR EXAMPLE

DVD Decoder Card Installation

If you are building a multimedia PC and want to work with or view high-quality video, you may also want to install a DVD decoder expansion card. A DVD decoder is used to convert video MPEG-2 files. MPEG-2 is a file format used for digital television and videos. Although DVD encoding can be done by software, some graphics cards and video capture cards incorporate higher-quality hardware-based DVD encoders, and there are also dedicated decoder cards that you can use. Many DVD drive kits will come with a cable, called a loopback cable, that you use to attach the DVD drive to a DVD encoder card. If you are using a decoder card, check the documentation to confirm how audio and loopback cables are installed. Typically, you will need two audio connections; one from the DVD drive to the decoder's Audio In port and the second from the Decoder's Audio Out port to the sound card. (If you are running an audio cable out from a CD drive in addition, this should now run to a second Audio-In port on the decoder). You will also need to connect the monitor to decoder's external monitor port, and the video loopback cable from the decoder to a video or graphics card.

a disc is unreadable, cleaning it with an approved cleaner and a lint-free cleaning towel will fix the problem.

If the operating system doesn't see the drive, start troubleshooting by determining whether the drive is receiving power. If the tray will eject, you can assume there is power to it. If you have a PATA/EIDE drive, check the BIOS Setup to make sure the drive has been detected. If not, check the Master/Slave jumper on the drive, and make sure the IDE adapter is set to Auto, CD-ROM, or ATAPI in BIOS Setup. When inside the case, ensure that the ribbon cable is properly aligned with Pin 1 and that both the drive and motherboard ends are securely connected.

To play movies, a DVD drive must have MPEG decoding capability. If DVD data discs will play but not movies, suspect a problem with the MPEG decoding.

If a CD-RW or DVD drive works normally as a regular CD-ROM drive but doesn't perform its special capability (doesn't read DVD discs or doesn't write to blank CDs), you may need to install third-party software to work with it. For example, with CD-RW drives, unless you're using a newer operating system such as Windows XP that supports CD writing, you must install CD-writing software in order to write to CDs.

If you are experiencing real slowdowns when using a PATA/EIDE optical drive, check to make sure that DMA (Direct Memory Access) is enabled for the drive. DMA allows data transfers to be made directly to RAM, bypassing the CPU, and without DMA enabled, an optical drive can severely slow down CPU operation. You will need to check the Properties box for the ATA/IDE controller that the drive is using (typically the primary or secondary IDE channel) and make sure that a DMA mode is selected. (You can access ATA/IDE controller properties through Device Manager; they are listed under IDE ATA/ATAPI Controllers.)

CD drives don't usually need to be cleaned during preventative maintenance. Clean one only if you're experiencing problems with it. Cleaning kits sold in computer stores provide the needed supplies.

SELF-CHECK

1. What are the three types of CDs?
2. What are the principle differences between CDs and DVDs?
3. List six features or characteristics used to differentiate between optical drives.
4. How is installing an optical drive different from installing a hard drive?

8.4 Understanding Flash Memory

Flash memory, the type of memory used on Flash BIOS chips has became popular technology for removable storage, and is most known for its use to store pictures taken by digital cameras. Today, flash memory devices have become very popular for a wide range of storage needs, because of their small size, easy portability, and solid-state ruggedness.

8.4.1 Flash Memory Basics

Flash memory stores data in cells that contain tiny transistors, and a flash memory chip is composed of grid of lines called columns and rows. The columns are called bitlines, and the rows are wordlines. At each intersection of the bitlines and wordlines is a cell with transistors, whose open or shut gates are used to define the value of the cell. If there is an electrical connection between the bitline and the wordline at the intersection, the cell's value is one (the default value); if there is no connection, the cell's value is 0. The connections the wordline makes between a series of bitlines are used to make up words, or bytes, of data. In a key difference from DRAM, flash memory transistors are engineered to retain their charges (and data) when power is switched off.

There are two types of flash memory—NAND and NOR—that differ in how the transistors are connected to each other.

The way NOR flash memory is constructed means that it functions similar to RAM (although it does not release its data in the absence of power), and is suitable for storing software programs. Cell phones typically use NOR flash memory. NAND is constructed to operate more like a storage drive, and is more suitable for storing data. Most flash memory storage devices use NAND flash memory. In general, NAND is faster at erasing and writing than NOR and can store data more densely. NOR flash memory is faster at reading data.

Although flash memory was originally designed to hold one bit per cell, newer (and more expensive) multicell flash memory technologies may hold two or more bits per cell.

The name "flash" came from the concept that its contents are erased in blocks when you apply a "flash" of voltage to blocks of data.

To increase the longevity of flash drives (which can generally be read and erased about a million times before some of the cells begin to degrade), a flash device may incorporate a technique called wear-leveling. Wear-leveling (which can also be implemented by some specialized file systems) distributes the data stored in flash memory to prevent some sections of cells wearing out faster than others. A flash memory device may use a flash-based file system or more typically (and especially with USB flash drives), a FAT16 or FAT32 file system.

Although flash memory was originally far more expensive, byte per byte, than magnetic storage, flash memory prices have dropped significantly, and today some hard drive manufacturers, such as Samsung, have developed solid-state hard drives using flash memory. Because they are solid-state and have no mechanical read/write heads that need positioning, flash hard drives have faster access times and can withstand bumps and jolts that could damage a regular hard drive. In addition, they store the same amount of data in a much smaller physical space than a hard disk drive. With fast PATA or SATA connections to the motherboard, flash hard drives can achieve the same high performance rates as magnetic disk drives.

8.4.2 Types of Flash Memory Devices

The types of devices that use flash memory include:

▲ **BIOS or firmware chips:** Most motherboards today use flash memory for their BIOS chips; firmware chips (memory chips used to hold essential software or data for a proprietary device, such as an expansion card, printer, or cell phone) also use flash memory.

▲ **Memory cards:** Memory cards are very tiny, often the size of a thick postal stamp, although there are many different formats and configurations. These cards are used in digital cameras to store photographs and for data storage in other mobile or handheld devices (Figure 8-15).

Figure 8-15

CompactFlash memory card.

Popular flash memory cards include CompactFlash, Memory Stick, Secure Digital, SmartMedia, and MultiMedia cards (MMC). Memory card types can be compared in terms of the following features:

- Physical format: The size of a memory card determines what slots it will physically fit into.
- Capacities available: Early memory cards had capacities of 16 or 32MB, but cards today may support up to 4GB and higher, depending upon the format.
- Encryption/security: Some card types include data encryption capability.

Memory cards connect to most hardware devices through a card slot. To connect to a PC, they typically use a card reader that connects to a PC's USB port. However, because they have become so popular and there are so many types of memory cards, several manufacturers sell multi-card readers designed to be inserted in a PC's drive bay. These readers have multiple slots and may read anywhere from 7 to over 50 types of memory cards. Windows XP should automatically recognize the card as a drive, which you can drag and drop files to and from, as with a regular drive. There is no common standard yet for rating the data transfer speeds of memory cards. Memory cards use different bus widths depending on their technology, some may use a 1-bit bus, others a 16-bit bus. Some memory cards are rated using the CD speed ratings, with a base rating of 1X being 150KBps. (A USB memory card reader is also limited to the speed of the USB port they use: USB 1.1 ports transfer a maximum of 12Mbps and USB 2.0 ports transfer a maximum of 480Mbps.) One of the most popular cards is the Secure Digital card, which was based on the MMC format but adds encryption features and a write-protect switch. Small versions of the Secure Digital card include the microSD and the miniSD, both of which can use the SD slot with adapters. A new, high-speed and

Figure 8-16

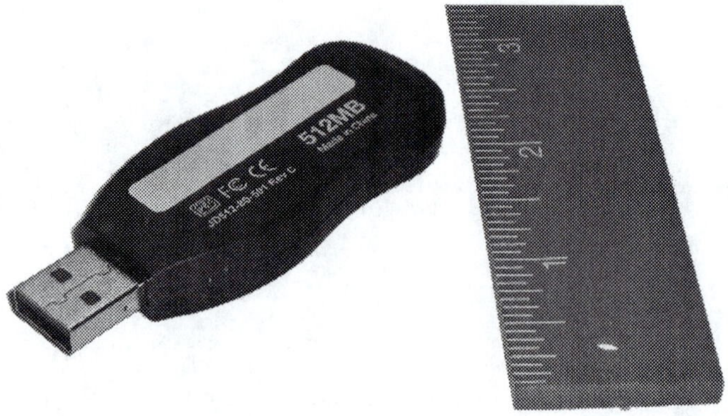

USB flash drive.

high-density version of SD called SDHC (Secure Digital High Capacity) is designed to support up to 32GB of memory.

▲ **USB flash drives:** Also known as thumb drives, pen drives, and pocket drives, USB flash drives are designed for removable storage for a PC. They are very small: Many such devices are mer ely extensions of the host's USB connector (and typically referred to as USB flash drives), extending out from the interface but adding very little to its width, making them very easy to transport, whether in a pocket or laptop bag (Figure 8-16). Most operating systems today (including Windows XP) will immediately recognize the flash drive and report it in Windows Explorer with a drive letter, ready for use. USB flash drives have emerged as the de facto replacement for other removable storage devices, such as floppies, edging out Zip and Jaz offerings from Iomega, as well as other proprietary solutions.

The components of a USB flash drive include:

- Flash memory chips
- USB connector
- Controllers to coordinate with the USB port and system clock
- LED to indicate if the drive is in use
- Write-protect switch

Some flash drives can be configured to be bootable or store and run desktop applications, and many have additional security features, such as an encrypted file system or fingerprint scanners. Flash drives are typically distinguished by the USB standard they support and their capacity. Typical capacities for USB flash drives range up to 8GB, although there are

---

FOR EXAMPLE

Flashy But Not Always Fast

Note that although new USB flash drives are designed to use the latest USB 2.0 interface specification, which supports transfer speeds up to 480MBps, most USB flash drives operate at speeds quite a bit slower than this, for example, as low as 8MBps. If you are comparing USB flash drives for a purchase, be sure to check the actual read/write speeds specified by the manufacturer.

---

some expensive USB flash drives with capacities up to 64GB. Wireless USB flash drives can connect wirelessly to the PC, using an enhanced wireless version of the USB interface.

▲ **Consumer electronics memory cards:** Memory cards are used in a variety of consumer electronics, from answering machines to cable TV set-top boxes.

▲ **Authentication devices:** Flash memory is also used in portable devices for carrying personal identification data. SanDisk's Personal Tag (P-Tag), is a very small removable card that the U.S. Army implemented to allow soldiers to carry their individual medical records. **Smart cards** are another flash-based authentication card. Smart cards are the size of a credit card, and contain a flash chip and sometimes a microprocessor. Smart cards, which have become popular in Europe, can be used for a variety of applications, from providing insurance information and personal identification to managing financial transactions. Some smart card designs require the card to be inserted into a smart card reader, while others have embedded antenna that can transmit information wirelessly.

8.4.3 Troubleshooting Flash Storage Devices

The most common problem that you might encounter with a USB flash drive, or other flash storage device, is that the drive isn't recognized by the operating system. If your operating system is pre Windows XP, or not Plug-and-Play compatible, you will need to make sure you download and install the latest drivers for your flash drive. Other reasons that the operating system doesn't recognize a flash drive include:

▲ **Physical installation issues:** The flash storage device, or more likely, the memory card, is inserted improperly into the PC or laptop card reader.

▲ **Corrupt formatting:** If the formatting on a flash memory device becomes corrupt, it may not be recognized by the operating system.

(Alternately, the OS may display some type of warning message; or the device may be recognized but not accessible.) Formatting can be corrupted when the following occurs:

- The flash drive or card is removed or disconnected while it is being read to.
- Power is lost while the drive or card is being written to. (This can happen if you switch off a digital camera while it is still writing to its memory card.)
- A camera's batteries run low or go dead.

Other things to check for if you are having problems with a flash drive include making sure the interface the card uses is working properly. For example, use a known working USB flash drive in the USB port to determine that the USB port is working properly. For a memory card, test the memory card reader by inserting a working memory card. Also check the compatibility of a memory card with your reader: If your memory card reader is old, it may have trouble recognizing a memory card with an updated interface.

SELF-CHECK

1. What are the benefits of using flash memory for storage?
2. How does flash memory store data?
3. List three types of flash memory devices.
4. What might cause a flash storage device not to be recognized by a PC?

SUMMARY

Removable storage is used for transferring data between computers and other devices, backups, storing data external to the computer, and commercial software distribution. Types of removable storage technologies include magnetic tape, magnetic disk (including floppy disks, LS-120, Zip disks, Jaz disks, and pocket hard drives), optical disks (CDs and DVDs), and flash memory (including memory cards and USB flash drives.)

Although several formats for floppy disks have been used, such as the 5.25" format, the currently used floppy disk is a 3.5-inch high density diskette that stores 1.44MB. Floppy drive subsystem components are the media (diskette), half-height drive, floppy drive controller (today integrated with the motherboard's chipset), and a 34-wire floppy drive cable, which typically has connectors for two floppy drives. Installation considerations for floppy drives include matching Pin 1 on the connectors to Pin 1 on the drives and motherboard connector, and using the second (furthest to the end) connector on the ribbon to the first "A" floppy drive. External floppy drives are typically connected through a USB port.

Optical drives include the CD and DVD. There are three types of CDs: CD-ROM, CD-R, and CD-RW. In addition to the read-only DVD-ROM (or DVD Video discs) there are several competing standards for DVD writeable or rewritable discs, DVD-R, DVD-RW, DVD-RAM, DVD+RW. New high-capacity DVD standards that utilize a different type of blue laser for writing more densely to the disk medium include Blu-ray and HD-DVD.

Optical drives may be connected through a variety of interfaces to a PC, including parallel ATA (EIDE), SATA, SCSI, USB, and FireWire. Performance characteristics for optical drive include data transfer rate (measured in multiples of a base speed of 1X (150KBps for CDs and 1.32MBps for DVDs), access times, cache or buffer size, CAV, CLV, or ZCLV spin speeds. Optical disks are usually written to in one or multiple sessions, although packet-writing through the use of third-party software allows optical disks to be treated like hard or floppy disks. Software utilities can also create a disk image (also called an ISO image for optical disks), which is a single file representing an exact digital copy of a drive and can be treated by the operating system as a drive.

Optical drives are installed in the same manner as hard drives, although they may require an audio cable to be connected to the sound card, or in the case of DVDs, a loopback cable connecting to an MPEG2 decoder.

Flash memory is solid-state storage and has no moving parts, such as a magnetic or optical disk. This allows flash memory storage devices to be extremely durable, although they are limited to about 1 million read/writes. Popular uses for flash removable storage include memory cards, typically used with digital cameras and laptops, and USB flash drives. Other flash memory uses include BIOS or firmware chips, consumer electronics, and authentication devices such as the Smart Card.

KEY TERMS

Blu-ray

Buffer

Cache

CD-Recordable (CD-R)

CD-Rewritable (CD-RW)

Combination drive

Compact Disk Read Only Memory (CD-ROM)

Constant angular velocity (CAV)

Constant linear velocity (CLV)

Digital Video Disk/Digital Versatile Disk (DVD)

Disk caching (disk buffering)

Disk image

DVD±R

DVD±RW

DVD-RAM

DVD-ROM

Flash memory

Floppy disk

Floppy disk controller

Floppy disk drive

Floppy drive cable

Floppy drive interface adapter

HD-DVD

ISO 9660

ISO image

Jaz disk

LS-120

Magnetic disk

Memory card

Microdrive

Optical disk

Optical drive

Pocket hard drive

Smart card

Tape cartridge

Tape drive

UDF

USB flash drive

Zip disk

Zoned CLV (ZCLV)

ASSESS YOUR UNDERSTANDING

Go to www.wiley.com/college/groth to evaluate your knowledge of removable storage.

Measure your learning by comparing pre-test and post-test results.

Summary Questions

1. What are the most common types of removable storage technology used today?
   (a) floppy drives and CD drives
   (b) optical drives and USB flash drives
   (c) CDs and DVDs
   (d) Zip drives and optical drives

2. Which is an older high-capacity storage technology used for backups?
   (a) CDs
   (b) CD-RW
   (c) tape drives
   (d) Zip drives

3. Which of the following does not use magnetic disk technology?
   (a) Jaz disk
   (b) Zip disk
   (c) CompactFlash memory card
   (d) IBM Microdrive

4. In optical media, binary digits are not indicated by pits and lands, but by the pattern of transitions between pits and lands. True or false?

5. Flash memory is categorized as a type of:
   (a) RAM
   (b) DRAM
   (b) ROM
   (c) EEPROM

6. How much data can a 3.5-inch HD floppy disk hold?
   (a) 360KB
   (b) 720KB
   (c) 1.2MB
   (d) 1.44MB

7. If you are installing just one floppy drive as drive A, which connector on the floppy drive cable should it be connected to?

   (a) The first drive connector (in the middle of the cable)

   (b) The second drive connector (at the end of the cable)

   (c) Either connector

   (d) Both connectors

8. Which of the following steps would tell you if a floppy drive's read/write heads are probably misaligned?

   (a) Format a disk using the drive and then see if the disk is readable in other drives.

   (b) Check to see if the drive light is not turning off.

   (c) Swap floppy components one at a time: the controller, cable, and drive.

   (d) Check for a POST error at boot up.

9. CD-R drives use special lasers to burn pits and lands into the disk. True or false?

10. A DVD data transfer speed of 24X is equivalent to which of the following?

    (a) 3.6MBps

    (b) 24MBps

    (c) 31.2MBps

    (d) 32.4MBps

11. How many GB can a double-sided, single layer DVD (DVD-10) hold?

    (a) 4.7GB

    (b) 8.5GB

    (c) 9.4GB

    (d) 17GB

12. What is the maximum capacity for a CD?

    (a) 700MB

    (b) 750MB

    (c) 1.4GB

    (d) 4.7GB

13. In three-part speed rating for an optical drive, such as "1X/2X/3X", what does the third rating (3X) describe?

    (a) the speed for reading

    (b) the speed for writing

    (c) the speed for rewriting

    (d) the speed for saving

14. A PATA internal optical drive cannot be configured as a master drive. True or false?

15. What are the two most popular file formats for optical discs?
    (a) FAT and UDF
    (b) FAT32 and NTFS
    (c) ISO 9660 and ISO 9661
    (d) ISO 9660 and UDF

16. An MPEG2 decoder is an expansion card that must be installed with a DVD drive. True or false?

17. If your optical drive is operating extremely slow, what would be the first thing you should check.
    (a) The BIOS configuration
    (b) The Master/Slave jumper settings
    (c) The DMA settings
    (d) The IRQ settings

18. Flash memory is erased and reprogrammed in large chunks called blocks. True or false?

19. The maximum number of erase/write cycles that flash memory is limited to is approximately:
    (a) 1000
    (b) 10,000
    (c) 100,000
    (d) 1,000,000

20. An authentication card that has been popular in Europe for purposes such as insurance, banking, pay-phone use, is called the:
    (a) P-tag
    (b) Smart card
    (c) Secure Digital card
    (d) SDHD card

Applying This Chapter

1. Your company is reviewing its backup strategies, and you need to describe the choices available. Which removable storage media have the highest capacities?

2. A friend wants to upgrade the internal CD-ROM drive in her older PC. What types of optical drives should she look at?

3. A coworker is replacing a floppy drive in an older PC, but only has experience in installing hard drives. What special considerations in installing a floppy drive can you advise them of?

4. A friend has just purchased and installed a CD drive, but the drive will not play their audio CDs. What could be the problem?

5. Your USB memory card is no longer recognized when you attach it to your PC's USB memory card reader. What could cause this?

Portability

Coworkers at your company often need to transport files between work and home, and have been using Zip and Jaz drives. Your company doesn't want to support this technology any more. What alternatives are there? Which would you recommend?

Optical Drive Speeds

A DVD drive on eBay is described as "16x8x16x DVD+RW. 16x6x16x DVD-RW / 8x DVD+R DL / 6x DVD-R DL / 48x32x48x CD-RW/." Explain what this means.

Selecting a DVD Drive

You are upgrading the CD-ROM drive on your PC. Go to the websites of several online DVD drive manufac-turers (such as Plextor.com, Toshiba.com), or search for optical drives using a search engine, and compare and review drives. Which will you select? Identify three reasons why you are selecting it, and list the drive's performance characteristics.

Selecting a USB Flash Drive

You work for a consulting firm whose executives need to transport highly sensitive data from their laptops to branch office PCs. Research the USB Flash drive tech-nologies from at least two flash drive manufacturers (such as Kingston.com and Lexar.com). Which USB flash drive might be most appropriate? Why?

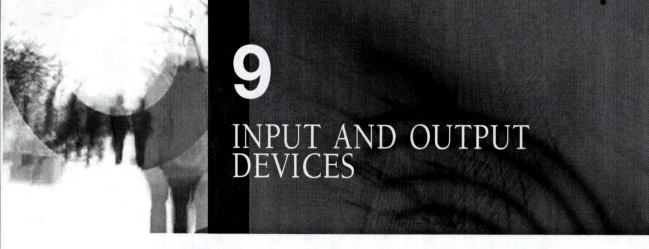

9

INPUT AND OUTPUT DEVICES

Starting Point

Go to www.wiley.com/college/groth to assess your knowledge of input and output devices.
Determine where you need to concentrate your effort.

What You'll Learn in This Chapter

▲ I/O interfaces, ports, connectors, and cables
▲ Common input and output devices
▲ Components of sound and display systems
▲ Installation steps for I/O devices
▲ Symptoms and causes of problems with I/O devices

After Studying This Chapter, You'll Be Able To

▲ Identify I/O ports and connectors
▲ Evaluate and compare current I/O interface technologies
▲ Identify different types of I/O devices
▲ Discuss and compare technologies used by popular devices, such as pointing devices, keyboards, scanners, digital cameras, sound systems, and monitors
▲ Select appropriate I/O devices for a PC
▲ Install and configure keyboards, mice, monitors, speakers, and other common I/O devices
▲ Troubleshoot problems with I/O devices

INTRODUCTION

A **peripheral** is a device that is not part of a PC, but is connected to the outside of the PC and increases its functionality. Peripherals connect with cables and special connectors to ports on the PC. Peripherals can be generally categorized by their function:

▲ **Storage peripherals,** such as removable storage drives and external hard drives

▲ **Networking peripherals,** including devices such as modems and NICs for connecting to networks

▲ **Input/output devices** used to input data to the computer, such as mice and keyboards,

▲ **Monitors and printers** used to display or otherwise translate data the PC has operated on

Some input/output devices have combined inputting/outputting functions, such as a Personal Digital Assistant (PDA).

9.1 Understanding Input/Output Peripherals

Input/output devices are often categorized by whether they input or output data, or perform both functions. Examples include:

▲ **Input peripherals:** Keyboards, mice, scanners, bar-code readers, Web-cams, digital cameras.

▲ **Output peripherals:** Monitors, printers, speakers, projectors (printers will be covered in Chapter 10).

▲ **Input/output peripherals:** Touch screens and PDAs.

9.1.1 Introduction to I/O Interfaces

The type of port to which a device connects depends on the interface with which the device is designed to work. An **interface** is a method of connecting two dissimilar items together. A **peripheral interface** is a method of connecting a peripheral or accessory to a computer, including the specification of cabling, connector type, speed, and method of communication used. Some types of interfaces can be used for a wide variety of devices, and other interfaces are used for specific types. For example, USB ports can be used for both removable storage devices and digital cameras, while special ports are used for monitors.

Common PC input/output (I/O) interfaces include:

▲ **Legacy serial:** Once a standard for I/O communications, the **serial interface** involves sending bits in a serial fashion, one bit a time. Serial means that the bits are sent in a series, a single-file stream.

▲ **Legacy parallel:** The **parallel interface** transfers data 8 bits at a time as opposed over multiple wires. The most common peripheral connected via a parallel connection is a printer, although Zip drives and scanners were also available for parallel connections. Parallel and serial ports are being phased out in favor of higher-speed serial interfaces.

▲ **USB:** A **Universal Serial Bus** (**USB**) is a high-speed serial bus that can connect multiple devices. USB supports connections to printers, scanners, and many other input devices (such as joysticks and mice).

▲ **IEEE 1394/FireWire:** The **IEEE 1394** standard is a high-speed serial bus standard that was developed by Apple and other manufacturers to meet the need for transferring the large amounts of data required by digital video. The standard is more commonly known as **FireWire**, the name given to it by Apple.

▲ **SCSI:** Small Computer System Interface (SCSI) is a high-speed parallel bus that is typically used to connect hard disk drives, printers, and scanners to a PC. Although it is most often found in server systems, SCSI can be added to desktop systems through the use of an expansion card. Serial Attached SCSI (SAS) is a recent SCSI interface standard that uses serial cables.

▲ **Wireless interfaces:** In addition to traditional interfaces that use cables and connectors for transmitting data, wireless interfaces specify communication through infrared (IR) pulses (light pulses) or radio frequency (RF).

You will learn more about these different types of I/O interfaces in Section 9.2.

9.1.2 Device Drivers

The interface describes how data is exchanged between the PC and an input/ output device, but the operating system communicates with hardware devices through utility software called **device drivers**. A peripheral may have one or more device drivers that it uses. When you purchase an input/output device, the package will typically contain a CD with the needed software and device drivers for that peripheral. A lot of standard I/O devices can work with generic drivers, drivers that are designed to manage the standard functions and signals from a basic category of devices, such as mice or keyboards. However, to get the full functionality of the device (such as special programmable mouse buttons), you need to make sure that you have the specific driver needed for that device. A manufacturer may have several versions of drivers for a device, each designed for a specific make or model and for a particular operating system.

9.1.3 Ports and Connectors

The ports that are available on a PC may be integrated with the motherboard or added through an expansion card. Some standard PC ports, often referred to as legacy ports, are being phased out in favor of higher-speed ports, such as USB and FireWire. **Legacy ports** include serial ports, parallel ports, and PS/2 keyboard and mouse ports; however, you will still need to be able to identify and work with these ports when you are working with older PCs.

Connectors are the hardware that allows a port to connect to a cable. Male connectors have pins, female connectors don't. The port connectors on a PC are usually female (and the connectors on cables male) because sockets are less prone to breaking than pins. It is easier and cheaper to replace a cable with broken pins.

The common ports and connectors types that are used with PCs include:

▲ **D-connectors: D-connectors** were once the most common style of connector found on computers, and are typically designated with DB-*n*, where the letter *n* is replaced by the number of pins (Table 9-1). D-connectors are shaped like a trapezoid (Figure 9-1) so that only one orientation between the plug and socket is possible. DB connectors are used for both serial and parallel communications.

▲ **RJ-Series: Registered jack (RJ) connectors** (Figure 9-2) are most often used in telecommunications. RJ connectors are typically square with multiple gold

Table 9-1: Common DB-Series Connectors

Connector	Gender	Use
DB-9	Male	Serial port
DB-9	Female	Connector on a serial cable
DB-25	Male	Serial port
DB-25	Female	Parallel port, or connector on a serial cable
DB-15	Female	Game port
DB-15	Male	Connector on a game peripheral cable
DB-15HD	Female	Video port (HD has three rows of 5 pins as opposed to two rows)
DB-15HD	Male	Connector on a monitor cable

Figure 9-1

A 25-pin female parallel (printer) port

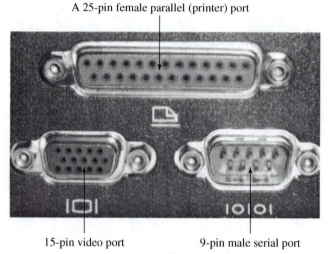

15-pin video port   9-pin male serial port

DB series ports and connectors.

contacts on the top (flat) side. A small locking tab on the bottom prevents the connector and cable from falling or being pulled out of the jack accidentally. The two most common RJ ports and connectors are:

- **RJ-11:** RJ-11 connectors are used most often in telephone hookups.
- **RJ-45:** RJ-45 connectors are larger than RJ-11 connectors and most commonly used for Ethernet network cables.

Figure 9-2

An RJ-11   An RJ-45
connector   connector

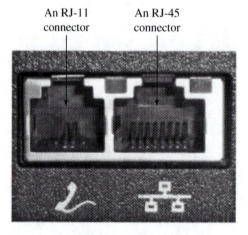

RJ ports and connectors.

Figure 9-3

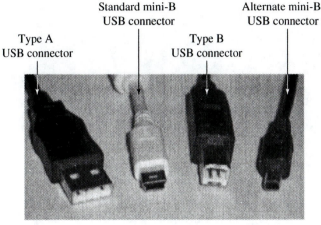

USB connectors.

▲ **Universal Serial Bus (USB):** USB uses a unique pair of connectors (Figure 9-3) and ports (Figure 9-4). USB Type A connectors are flat and thin and connect devices directly to a host: a PC or USB hub. USB Type B connectors are squarish and connect to the peripheral. A smaller version of the Type B connector, mini B, is also used for devices with a small form factor. Some manufacturers have developed

Figure 9-4

Type A USB ports.

Figure 9-5

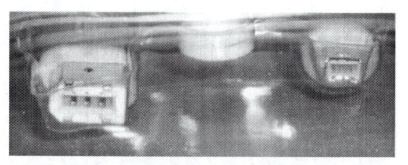

IEEE 1394/FireWire cable and connectors.

proprietary USB ports and connections for their devices. A USB cable will go into a USB port only one way and has a USB male connector on each end.

▲ **IEEE 1394/FireWire:** The FireWire connector looks a bit like a USB connector except that it's a bit larger and about halfway between rectangular and square (Figure 9-5). Most FireWire ports (Figure 9-6) and connectors are 6-pin; however, two of the wires in the cable are used for powering devices, and some FireWire devices may use external powering and have smaller 4-pin connectors. A new higher-speed version of FireWire uses a 9-pin connector and port.

▲ **PS/2:** A **PS/2 port** (also called a **mini-DIN connector**) is a mouse and keyboard interface port first used on the IBM PS/2 (hence the name). It is smaller than the older DIN-5 keyboard port and serial mouse connector (Figure 9-7). Most keyboards today still use the PS/2 interface, whereas most mouse devices are gravitating toward the USB interface. Mouse devices that have USB cables still may include a special USB-to-

Figure 9-6

IEEE 1394/FireWire port.

Figure 9-7

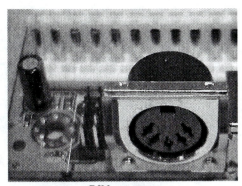

PS/2-style (mini-DIN) connnector   DIN connector

DIN and PS/2 (mini-DIN) connectors.

PS/2 adapter so they can be used with the PS/2 interface. PS/2 mouse and keyboard ports are not interchangeable.

▲ **Infrared:** An **infrared (IR) port** in a PC or notebook is a small, usually dark red, plastic window located usually on the front or side of the case (Figure 9-8). External IR ports can be attached to the PC through adapters to other ports. **Infrared** is a wireless communication method that uses electromagnetic radiation in the infrared band, and you use it to connect devices such as wireless keyboards and mice to the PC.

▲ **RCA: RCA jacks** (Figure 9-9) and **connectors** are used to transmit both audio and video information. Typically, when you see an RCA connector on a PC video card (next to a DB-15HD connector), it's for composite video output (output to a television or VCR). The RCA cables have two connectors, usually male, one on each end of the cable. The RCA male connectors on a connection cable are sometimes plated in gold to increase their corrosion resistance and to improve longevity.

Figure 9-8

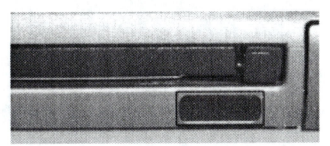

Infrared port.

Figure 9-9

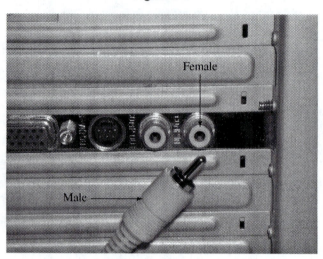

RCA jack (female) and connector (male).

▲ **HD/VHD connectors: High Density (HD) and VHD (Very High Density) connectors** have a shell similar to D-connectors and are used for SCSI devices, and may have 50 or 68 pins and latches or screws to hold the connection in place. SCSI ports are generally through SCSI interface extension cards.

▲ **Centronics:** The **Centronics connector** (Figure 9-10) consists of a central connection bar surrounded by an outer shielding ring. It has rows of flat contacts (36 for Centronics-36 or 50 for Centronics-50) instead

Figure 9-10

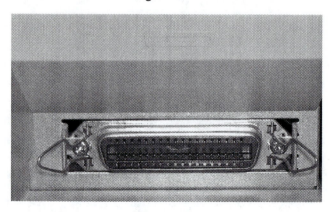

Centronics connector.

Figure 9-11

Male BNC connector

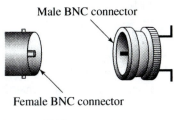

Female BNC connector

BNC connectors.

of pins, and latches at the sides to lock the connectors in place. The Centronics connector was used in parallel printer connections and SCSI interfaces. The smaller, high density mini Centronics connectors have 50 or 68 contacts packed more closely together.

▲ **BNC:** BNC (or **Bayonet Naur**) **connectors** are cylindrical connectors that twist together, similar to the coaxial cable connectors used with televisions. They are used in networking and sometimes in higher-end monitor connections. T-connectors are used to join two BNC connectors together (Figure 9-11).

9.1.4 Installing I/O Devices

Whenever possible, you should follow the manufacturer's exact instructions when installing any piece of hardware. Failure to do so may possibly damage the device and void the device's warranty.

Generally speaking, when you are connecting a new device to your computer, you should power down the computer, unplug it, and wait at least 30 seconds before attempting to install or remove any device. Follow the manufacturer's instructions for connecting the hardware (and insert the card, plug in the cable, or connect the device in whatever method it uses). Make sure it is firmly secured, and then power up the PC.

The device drivers may be loaded automatically through Windows Plug and Play (Windows has thousands of drivers built-in or available on its Setup CD) or Windows may prompt you to locate them on a CD or on your hard drive.

When you install or update a driver, Windows 2000 and higher will check to see if the driver is signed, and if it is not, will issue a warning sign. A **signed driver** is one that has been officially certified for security and stability for your operating system. Although you can use unsigned drivers, limiting your system to using only signed drivers will mean you will rarely have driver-based conflicts or problems.

If you are working with a non-Plug and Play device, you can install drivers by using the Setup program that comes with the hardware driver CD-ROM or the Windows Add Hardware Wizard. (After the driver is installed, you may be prompted to reboot the computer.)

After the device has been installed, you must configure its various options so that it functions the way you want it to. Often, this step is overlooked. Some people install the driver, and if the device works, stop there. However, you can often obtain the best performance with only a few more minutes of adjustment. Usually, to configure the device, you can use the Device Manager to view the properties of the device, or use a software utility that comes with the device. The latter method is more common with many peripherals and complex expansion cards.

9.1.5 Troubleshooting I/O Devices

Problems with input/output devices fall into several categories, and you can apply these general concepts for troubleshooting any device connected to the PC.

▲ **Hardware problems:** Cables, ports, and connections can be damaged. Check for bent pins in connections, or swap out potentially faulty components (a cable, or the device itself) with a known good component, to see where the problem lies. Make sure the cables for devices are within the maximum range allowed for the interface. Beyond the maximum range for a cabled interface, signal strength can lose strength or integrity.

▲ **Interface compatibility:** Devices must use the right port (with the correct interface and speed) for their connection, and using the wrong port, such as a PS/2 keyboard port in a PS/2 mouse port will cause errors or malfunctioning. Although some new versions of interfaces are designed to be compatible with previous versions (such as USB 2.0's compatibility with USB 1.0), this can be a source of some problems.

▲ **Port problems:** Check to make sure the motherboard's cabling to the port or the expansion card holding ports is intact, and that the BIOS recognizes the port. If a port has been added through an expansion card, make sure the BIOS recognizes the expansion card.

▲ **Power problems:** Make sure that devices requiring external power are getting power. If you are using a port that provides power to devices, such as a USB or FireWire port, make sure that the devices attached are not drawing too much power, causing the port to shut down.

▲ **Driver-related problems and configuration problems:** Use Device Manager to make sure that Windows recognizes the device and that the device or the interface controller have not been disabled or have resource conflicts. Make sure you have the latest device drivers, and that the device is configured properly. You can check the

---

FOR EXAMPLE

Downloading Drivers

The CD that comes with the device may or not be the latest driver, and because device drivers are often updated by manufacturers, you should check at the manufacturer's website to make sure you have the latest driver for your device and operating system. A newly downloaded driver will typically come in the form of a setup/application file that you can just double-click to install. If the download contains just the raw driver files (such as DRV and INF), you will need to manually install the driver. You manually update a driver by clicking the Update Driver button on the device's Properties box (which you can open through the Device Manager).

---

configuration through a device's Properties dialog box, which you can also access through Device Manager. Depending on the device, special software may be needed for it to fully operate, so you should check the device documentation to understand how to properly configure the device. In some cases, Plug and Play may have problems assigning resources and configuring devices, and simply reinstalling device drivers or forcing Plug and Play to reconfigure all devices may resolve these problems. In a methodical approach, you can reinstall devices one at a time to help pinpoint a problem.

In addition to examining the Device Manager, POST beep codes may provide a clue to the problem in some cases. You can also use Windows hardware troubleshooting wizards which will guide you through a series of troubleshooting questions. To access the troubleshooting wizard, open the device's Properties dialog box and click Troubleshoot on the General tab.

SELF-CHECK

1. What common connector type is used for both serial and parallel communications?

2. List four I/O interfaces commonly used today.

3. What is a device driver?

4. What types of problems may affect the functioning of an I/O device?

9.2 Examining Popular I/O Interfaces

Adding new peripherals and upgrading I/O devices are popular PC upgrades, and you should be familiar with the various I/O interfaces used to connect devices to the PC.

9.2.1 Legacy Serial Interface

The legacy serial interface (also referred to as RS-232C) is slow: the maximum specified speed for a standard RS-232 serial connection is 115 Kbps and actual speeds are dependent on the peripheral and other transmission qualities). However, the serial interface is good for synchronizing devices, and was most popularly used for connecting external modems. Today, high-speed serial interfaces, such as USB and FireWire, are phasing out the use of the traditional serial interface.

Distinguishing features of serial communications include:

▲ **Serial ports:** PC serial ports are either a DB-9 or DB-25 male connector. PCs use only nine pins in a serial connection, which is why many PCs use the DB-9 connector in place of the DB-25 with its unused pins. You will occasionally find the DB-25 plug on many older PCs, multipurpose adapter cards, and some modems. Serial ports have a maximum data transmission speed of 57Kbps and support a maximum cable length of 50 feet.

▲ **Logical resource assignment:** Serial ports are assigned a logical device name (COM1, COM2, COM3 or COM4) that is associated with default resource assignments. Logical device names are assigned during the POST process by the system BIOS. The BIOS searches the I/O addresses for devices in a preset order and assigns them a logical name in numerical order each time the system boots. Table 9-2 lists the system resource assignments for the common serial ports found on most PCs. (On systems with four serial ports, you may need to switch I/O port and IRQ assignments to accommodate them, especially if you plan to use them simultaneously).

▲ **UART chip:** Serial devices are controlled by a **Universal Asynchronous Receiver/Transmitter (UART) chip.** This specialized integrated circuit

Table 9-2: Serial Port System Resource Assignments

Logical Device	IRQ	I/O Address
COM1	IRQ 4	3F8h
COM2	IRQ 3	2F8h
COM3	IRQ 4	3E8h
COM4	IRQ 3	2E8h

is found either on the device adapter card or on the motherboard (if a serial port is mounted on it). The UART chip controls all actions and functions of the serial port.

▲ **Flow control:** Flow control, or handshaking, describes the protocol used to control the dialog of two serial devices. In general, flow control manages the data flow by sending a character or signal to stop it. Usually the flow control method used also has a means for restarting the data flow. After a serial device such as a modem is connected to the PC, each is designated as either the *Data Terminal Equipment (DTE)* or the *Data Communications Equipment (DCE)*. When you connect a modem to a PC, the modem becomes the DCE and the PC is the DTE. These designations determine which device initiates and controls the conversation between the two devices at various points in their interaction

▲ **Serial cables:** A serial cable can be up to 50 feet long (compared to the standard 15-feet limit of a parallel cable). Beyond that distance, the data signal begins to lose its strength and data errors can occur. Serial cables come in two common wiring configurations:

- **Standard serial cable:** A **standard serial cable** is used to hook various peripherals like modems and printers to a computer. Also called a modem cable, or a straight-through cable, in this cable, all the pins are connected one to one without any twists or other arrangements

- **Null modem serial cable:** A **null modem** (or **modem eliminator**) **cable** is used to hook two computers together without a modem, in a DTE-to-DTE arrangement. The transmit wires on one end are wired to the receive pins on the other side, as if a modem connection existed between the two computers.

If you're having a serial port problem, the cause is usually a system resource conflict. System resource conflicts include problems such as a serial device that fails intermittently or doesn't work at all, another device that stops working when the serial device is installed, or the PC locking up during the boot sequence. You should also make sure that the serial device is using the proper straight-through or null-modem cable.

9.2.2 Parallel Interfaces

The legacy parallel interface on a PC uses a DB-25 female connector on the PC to transfer data to peripherals. Parallel ports were originally designed specifically for printers. However, other devices were adapted to them, including other types of output devices, input devices, and storage devices, all taking advantage of the bidirectional capabilities of IEEE 1284 parallel devices.

Distinguishing features of parallel communications include:

▲ **Parallel ports:** The **IEEE 1284** standard incorporated the two existing parallel port standards into a new protocol, creating an all-encompassing port model, which specifies maximum transfer rates of 4MBps, although actual maximum data transfer rates are around 2MBps. The three parallel port types specified in IEEE 1284 are:

- **Standard Parallel Port (SPP):** Allows data to travel one way only— from the computer to the peripheral (typically a printer).
- **Enhanced Parallel Port (EPP):** Allows data to flow in both directions, but only in one way at a time. This lets the printer communicate information such as that the printer is out of paper or its cover is open to the processor or adapter. An EPP port increases bidirectional throughput from 150KBps to anywhere from 600KBps to 2MBps.
- **Enhanced Capabilities Port (ECP):** Allows bidirectional simultaneous communications over a special IEEE 1284–compliant cable. Many bidirectional cables are EPP cables, which do not support ECP communications. An ECP port is designed to transfer data at high speeds to printers. It uses a DMA channel and a buffer to increase printing performance.

Most parallel PC ports use a DB-25 female connector, and most parallel cables and printer cables use a DB-25 male connector on one end and either a DB-25 male connector or Centronics-36 connector on the other. Maximum cable lengths range from six to ten meters, depending upon the type of data transfer (unidirectional, bidirectional, EPP, ECP, and so on).

▲ **Logical resource assignment:** Parallel ports are assigned logical device names: LPT1 and LPT2 which use default resource assignments (Table 9-3).

Trouble with a parallel port usually originates from the device attached to it. Because a parallel port is virtually featureless, it either works or it doesn't. However, problems may be caused by using the wrong type of cable for the port (SPP, EPP, or ECP) or, less likely, a system resource conflict, if more than two parallel ports are on the PC. Printers don't use IRQs or DMA channels, but other parallel port devices do.

Table 9-3: Parallel Port System Resource Assignments

Port	IRQ	I/O Address	DMA Channel
LPT1	IRQ 7	378h	DMA 3 (ECP capabilities)
LPT2	IRQ 5	278h	n/a

9.2.3 Universal Serial Bus (USB)

The USB interface was designed to replace the older, slower serial and parallel ports on a PC, including the PS/2 mouse and keyboard ports. Multiple USB devices can connect to a single USB port by using USB hubs, which can support 7 USB devices. The USB interface incorporates a USB mass storage device class, a set of standards for reading and writing to storage devices such as hard drives, optical drives, and USB flash drives.

Distinguishing features of the USB interface include:

▲ **Multiple device support:** The USB interface supports up to 127 devices on a system, with maximum cable lengths of five meters. These devices connect both to the PC directly or into at least one USB hub (Figure 9-12). A USB port uses a single IRQ, which is shared by all the devices attached to that port.

▲ **High-speed data transfer:** USB version 1.1 supported data transfer speeds of up to 12MBps for faster devices and a 1.5MBps (188KBps) sub-channel speed for lower-speed devices. The newest version, USB 2.0, which is also known as the Enhanced Host Controller Interface (EHCI), supports three data transfer speeds:
- Low speed: 1.5Mbps
- Full speed: 12Mbps
- High speed: 480Mbps

▲ **Variable bandwidth:** The USB interface has a 1.5MBps subchannel that slower devices (mice, keyboards, and so on) can use, which frees up the rest of the bandwidth for faster devices.

▲ **Four types of data transfer:** USB supports four kinds of data transfer: bulk, interrupt, isochronous, and control. Bulk transmission is used for

Figure 9-12

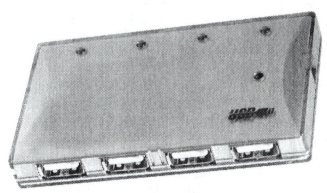

USB hub.

devices that send a large amount of data to the PC, such as printers, scanners, and digital cameras. Interrupt transmission is used for essential data that must be transmitted immediately, such as data from a mouse or keyboard. Isochronous transmission is used for streaming data that must be relayed in a specific order, such as that from a video camera. Control transfers are used for configuring and managing device setup.

▲ **Plug and Play:** USB was designed to be Plug and Play—just plug in the peripheral, and it should work (providing the software is installed to support it). When you install a USB device, generally, you install the driver and software for the USB device first, and then plug in the device while the computer is on. Doing so allows the computer to recognize the new component and configure it properly.

▲ **Hot-swapping:** USB devices can be attached and detached from the PC without powering the PC down, known as **hot-swapping** or **hot-plugging**.

▲ **Device powering:** The USB port provides 5V on a single wire to power low-powered devices, such as keyboards. Devices don't need to use this power. Devices that require more power have external power cables.

▲ **USB host controller:** The USB 2.0 architecture requires a USB host controller (installed as an expansion card or built into the motherboard) that controls communication between the PC and the USB device. The host (the PC) and the device (such as a digital camera) use different types of connectors (Type A for the host, and Type B, or mini-B, for the device.) However, a new extension to USB 2, called USB On-The-Go (OTG), will allow devices to communicate directly with each other. USB OTG specifies two additional connectors, the mini-A, and a universal mini-AB port to fit both mini-A and mini-B connectors.

USB 2 is backward compatible with earlier USB versions (USB 1.0 and USB 1.1), so you can use a USB 2 device with an older USB port on your PC, although it will be limited to the transfer speeds the port supports. A recent extension to USB is a high-speed wireless interface called Certified Wireless USB, which uses a wide range of radio frequencies for communication. It is designed for use by PC peripherals as well as consumer electronics applications and specifies transfer speeds of 480MBps at a range of three meters and 110MBps at a range of ten meters.

A USB port will shut down if too much power is drawn from it, so if you have many devices attached to a single port, check the power consumption used through the Properties dialog box for the USB hub. If you have problems with a USB device and have multiple USB devices connected, you can reinstall all the drivers for all attached USB devices (you may need a PS/2 mouse and keyboard to work with the PC during this procedure), and then re-boot to allow Plug and Play to reinstall and configure the devices. Note that although USB 2 devices should be compatible with a USB 1.x port, some devices may have problems.

You can use a USB 2 to USB 1.x adapter on a USB 1.1 port to remove any possible compatibility issues.

9.2.4 IEEE 1394/FireWire

The **IEEE 1394** standard is a high-speed serial bus protocol also known as the i.Link (Sony), Lynx (Texas Instruments), and the FireWire (Apple), which are proprietary, licensed versions of the IEEE 1394 standard. The generic name is High Performance Serial Bus (HPSB), but it is commonly referred to as FireWire. Although initially popular for digital video equipment because of its high data transfer rate, FireWire is being used more and more as a universal, high-speed data interface for devices such as hard drives, CD-ROM drives, and digital video editing equipment.

Distinguishing characteristics of the FireWire interface include:

▲ **Multiple device support:** Up to 63 FireWire devices can be linked via hubs to a FireWire port (maximum cable length is four and a half meters).

▲ **High-speed data transfer:** FireWire supports four speeds:
  - S100: 100MBps
  - S200: 200MBps
  - S400: 400MBps
  - S800: 800MBps (specified by the latest version, IEEE 1394b which uses a 9-pin connector and compliant cable).

▲ **Two types of data transfer:** FireWire supports two modes of data transfer: asynchronous, used for standard data transfer and storage, and isochronous (real-time) data transfers—data is transferred within certain time constraints (such as multimedia data where the audio and video must arrive together).

▲ **Variable bandwidth:** Similar to USB, FireWire is designed to cope with devices that require high and variable amounts of bandwidth.

▲ **Plug and Play/hot-swapping:** FireWire devices are Plug-and-Play and hot-swappable.

▲ **Device powering:** FireWire uses two wires for providing up to 12V for external device powering. Some devices that are externally powered use a 4-pin connector that only connects to the data lines.

▲ **Peer-to-peer architecture:** FireWire is designed for peripheral to peripheral data transfer.

9.2.5 Wireless Interfaces

Infrared (IR) and radio frequency (RF) are the two main wireless interfaces used with PCs today; primarily for supporting mobile, handheld devices such as PDAs.

Although most desktop computers don't have wireless ports, you can easily add them with an expansion card. Common I/O peripherals that are available with wireless interfaces include printers, keyboards, and mice. Installing a wireless device involves installing any receivers that are needed and configuring the device's software. For example, if you want to configure your computer to talk to your PDA, all you need to do is tell the Palm Desktop software on the PC to communicate with your Palm via an infrared connection. Some devices, such as keyboards and mice, may have a synching button that you press, or reset, to synchronize the device with the PC. Wireless devices require batteries for operation. RF devices are designed to work within a specific frequency band, typically in the 900 MHz or 27 MHz ranges. One popular RF interface is Bluetooth.

IrDA (short for **Infrared Device Association**) is the trade organization for the Infrared device industry that has established a number of standards defining and prescribing the use of the IR connection. IR uses an invisible band of light at the low end of the electromagnetic spectrum, just short of the beginning of the visible light part of the spectrum. Infrared ports, or receivers, send and receive data at a very slow rate (maximum speeds range up to 16MBps). Other characteristics of IR transmission include:

▲ Infrared communications take place within a short distance. The operating range of most IR systems is between 1 and 50 feet, but you can usually adjust the operating power to fit the distance at which you plan to use the device.

▲ IR devices are line-of-sight devices; they must have a clear, unobstructed path between their transmitters and receivers. If anything blocks the path, you must move the obstruction or the controller to reopen the line of sight.

▲ The IR signal transmission pattern is a cone about 30 degrees wide, and devices must be oriented to each other inside the transmission cone. However, some IR devices now use broadbeam IR technology that frees you from having to be directly in front of the system case and its

FOR EXAMPLE

Bluetooth

Bluetooth is another wireless technology, especially popular with cell phones, that uses radio frequencies to communicate. Its absolute maximum range is 100 meters, and most devices are specified to work within 10 meters. Bluetooth 1.0 has a maximum data transfer rate of 1MBps and Bluetooth 2.0 has a data transfer rate of 3MBps. Bluetooth-enabled devices are becoming more and more popular, and you can find mice, keyboards, headsets, barcode scanners and printers with the Bluetooth interface.

receiver port. Broadbeam IR allows you to use the keyboard with a wide range of operating angles.

▲ Competing IR devices in the vicinity, such as a TV remote control, can interfere with the connection.

SELF-CHECK

1. What features make installing a USB device easier than installing a serial or parallel device?
2. List six features that USB and FireWire share.
3. What devices typically used serial and parallel interfaces?
4. What are the benefits and drawbacks of using IrDA?

9.3 Examining Input/Output Devices

A variety of I/O devices can be used with a PC. Some are essential to the PC's operation, such as keyboards, pointing devices, and monitors; others may be essential business or multimedia tools. To be able to select an appropriate device, it is important to understand the basic technologies used with these devices.

9.3.1 Keyboards

The **keyboard** enables a user to communicate with the computer via keystrokes. Popular keyboard styles include:

▲ **Enhanced (also known as AT Enhanced):** 101 keys, including 12 function keys, separate cursor and screen control keys, and a numeric keypad. This style keyboard may even include buttons for controlling a CD-ROM drive, the sound, and other built-in features of the PC. Enhanced is still the most common keyboard type in use.

▲ **Windows:** 104 keys, including keys to pop-up the Windows Start menu and a key to show the pop-up shortcut menu (Figure 9-13).

▲ **Natural/ergonomic:** Enhanced keyboard with a built-in wrist-rest and an arched or bowed keyboard shape; this keyboard may also separate into segments (Figure 9-14).

Early keyboards connected to the PC through a DIN-5 connector. PS/2 ports have been until recently the standard connection for keyboards and mouse devices, but today keyboards may have a USB, FireWire or use a wireless connection.

Figure 9-13

Windows 104-key keyboard.

Wireless keyboards (and mice) work with a receiver that typically plugs into a USB port. IR keyboards need to be placed within a specified range and angle of the receiver, while RF keyboards don't; depending on the design, they can be used some distance away from receiver, as far as 100 feet.

Keyboards are simple devices and usually either work or don't. Most problems are environmental, caused by dirt, dust and spills; you should not eat or

Figure 9-14

Natural/Ergonomic keyboard.

drink near the computer. If you spill a liquid on your keyboard, you could short-circuit it.

To clean a keyboard, use a commercial keyboard cleaner as these don't leave residue behind and/or compressed air. If you do have to clean a keyboard that's had a soft drink spilled on it, remove the key caps before you apply a cleaner. It makes it easier to reach inside. You can clean a keyboard by soaking it in distilled, demineralized water and drying it off.

If your keyboard has failed, the POST display will usually show a short message, such as "Keyboard failure." If your keyboard is not working, but there is no POST message, check the Device Manager to see if your keyboard has been recognized. For PS/2 keyboards, check for system resource conflicts in Device Manager. The keyboard is usually assigned IRQ 1 and I/O address 060h.

A failed keyboard can be repaired, but a keyboard is far less valuable than the time it would take to troubleshoot and repair it. You can use a multimeter to determine whether you have an electrical failure in the keyboard or on the system board, by checking the voltages of the keyboard connector pins on the motherboard. If any of the voltages are out of range (near +2 volts to +5.5 volts, depending on the pin), the problem is likely in the keyboard circuits of the motherboard. See the keyboard's documentation for the specific voltage and pinouts; otherwise, the problem is probably in the keyboard.

Keyboard-related problems may occur during the POST (Power-On Self Test) process. The boot process has two means of indicating the source of the problem: Audible beeps are emitted before the video system is available and POST error messages after the video system is enabled. In most cases, if a keyboard failure occurs, an error code in the range of 300 to 399 displays, indicating the keyboard error. The most common reason for a keyboard POST or boot error is a keystroke detected during the POST processing. This could be a stuck key, an accidentally-pressed key.

FOR EXAMPLE

Legacy USB Settings

Most PC USB keyboards are configured to be used while the operating system is running. However, sometimes you need to work with the keyboard to configure CMOS settings or use a command line utility (before the OS is loaded). If you try to do this and find your USB keyboard isn't working, you may need to configure CMOS settings to allow the system to recognize USB devices outside of the Windows environment. To do this, you will need to reboot the PC using a PS/2 keyboard and enter the BIOS setup utility. In the CMOS settings, look for an option called "Legacy USB support" and enable it.

9.3.2 Mice

Older PCs used a serial port to connect with a serial mouse, or a special expansion card to connect with a bus mouse. A mouse today is typically connected through a PS/2, USB, or wireless (IR or RF) interface. FireWire mouse devices are also available.

There are several different types of mouse devices:

▲ **Mechanical mouse:** The **mechanical mouse** uses a rubber ball that moves as the user rotates the mouse. As the ball moves, it rotates a set of rollers, which in turn drive sensors that translate the ball's movement to move the screen pointer around the display. As the user moves his hand, the distance traveled and the speed of the ball is detected by the rollers and sensors, and the screen pointer moves a relative distance and speed accordingly.

▲ **Trackball:** An upside-down version of the traditional, mechanical mouse, called a **trackball,** puts the ball on the top of the mouse. The user manipulates the ball with his or her fingers or thumb.

▲ **Optical mouse:** Also known as the opto-mechanical mouse, an optical mouse uses either optical sensors and LEDs or a digital capture "eye" to sense the distance and speed of the mouse's movement. This type of mouse "sees" its movement over a surface and translates it into movement of the on-screen pointer. Early optical mouse units required a special hard plastic or metal mouse pad that had a grid of intersecting lines printed on it. As the mouse moved, an LED reflecting off the shiny surface and grid lines were used to detect direction, speed, and distance. Today the optical mouse works with a digital capture apparatus that literally takes around 2,000 pictures per second of the surface under the mouse to determine its movement. This means that any surface can act as the mouse pad, and a mouse pad is no longer needed. Inside the optical mouse is a *digital signal processor (DSP)* that compares the captured images to detect even the slightest movement. Unlike its mechanical predecessors, the optical mouse has no moving parts to pick up dirt that can impair its performance. This also means that you don't have to clean it.

If you have a mechanical mouse, you should periodically clean its moving parts—the ball and rollers inside the ball housing. Cleaning should be part of routine maintenance because a dirty mouse can cause the screen pointer to move erratically or not at all. To clean a mechanical mouse, remove the ball and clean it and the ball rollers with a cotton swab and mild soap. You can use tweezers to remove lint caught in the rollers, and compressed air to blow debris out of the mouse cavity.

9.3.3 Touch Screens and Other Pointing Devices

A **touch screen** is a computer screen that has a film over it that is sensitive to touch. With touch screens that are used with PCs, touching a box drawn on the touch screen does the same thing as double-clicking that box with a mouse. These screens are commonly found on the *tablet PC* (a laptop designed to be held like a pad of paper).

There are three primary systems used to detect a touch on the screen:

▲ **Capacitive:** This system places a capacitive layer over the glass face panel of the monitor that holds an electrical charge. When an object touches the screen (such as a human finger), the charge of the spot that was touched transfers to the other object; therefore, there's less charge at that location. Circuits in the corners of the monitor screen calculate the location of the touch exactly using the relative differences in the charge amount at each corner. A capacitive monitor transmits almost 90 percent of the light from the monitor compared to only about 75 percent of the light from a resistive system.

▲ **Resistive:** This touch screen system uses a normal glass panel covered with conductive and resistive metallic layers, which are kept apart with spaces. A scratch-resistant layer covers all of these layers. When a user touches the screen, the conductive and the resistive layers are forced together and the coordinates of the contact result in an exact X (horizontal) and Y (vertical) location. Unfortunately, the metallic layers restrict the amount of light emitting from the monitor.

▲ **Surface acoustic wave (SAW):** This type of touch screen system is indicated by the tiny holes along the top and side of the monitor's front bezel. Behind the holes are two sets of transducers, one to send and one to receive signals from each other. If the receiving transducer sees that the signal has been interrupted by some object touching the screen, it can locate it precisely. Because the SAW system places no metallic or conductive layers on the screen, it is able to emit 100 percent of the monitor's light. The stimuli that make contact with the screen can be almost anything on a resistive or SAW system. However, on a capacitive system, the object must be able to absorb an electrical charge, which means it must be conductive.

In addition to the touch screen and mouse, other pointing devices for the PC include:

▲ **Joystick:** Popular with flight and navigation games, and as a backup mouse.
▲ **Touchpad:** A reliable alternative to the mouse that is typically integrated into the keyboard of a laptop.

▲ **Digitizing tablets:** Used with drawing or CAD (computer-aided design) software to create line or vector graphics; these are also popular alternative devices used to replace mice. These have a flat sensing screen that you touch and tap with a pen-like device.

9.3.4 Scanners

Another technique for inputting data to a PC is through a **charge-coupled device (CCD)**. A CCD converts light (and shades of light) into electrical pulses. The largest classes of input/output devices that use CCDs are scanners and digital cameras. Optical scanners (their full name) use CCDs and a light source to convert analog images, such as the printed side of a sheet of paper or a photograph, into a digitized version of that image.

In scanning, the source image, such as a photograph, is interpreted as a grid of tiny dots, called pixels, each with a different shade or color (black and white scanners will only see shades of black and white). The scanner shines a light onto the source image, and for each pixel, the scanner senses and records a numeric value that represents its color. These values are processed by the PC and scanner software to reproduce the scanned image in digital form. Scanners typically record one line of pixels at a time, with sensor mechanisms moving, or scanning, down the source image.

The most popular home scanners are flatbed scanners; these have a flat glass plate, beneath a protective cover, that you place a sheet of paper on to be scanned. Flatbed scanners (Figure 9-15) are the most popular because they are

Figure 9-15

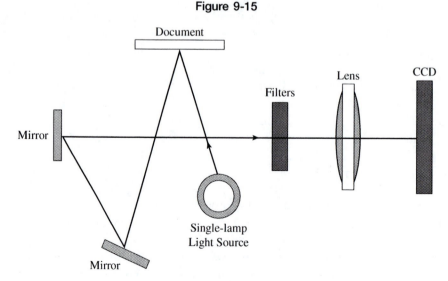

A typical scanner and its components.

inexpensive and for their price produce the best results for scanning single photographs or documents.

The basic components of a flatbed scanner are:

▲ **Glass plate and cover:** The glass plate is the transparent plate that the
original is placed on so that the scanner can scan it. Although originally
made of glass, there are scanners with cheaper, clear acrylic plates. The
cover comes down over the original (in the case of flatbed scanners) and
keeps out stray light that can affect the accuracy of the scan. Most often,
the side of the cover that sits on top of the original is white so that any
part of the glass plate that the original doesn't cover is shown as white
in the document as it is scanned. (Flatbed scanners are the only types of
scanner that use a glass plate and cover.)

▲ **Scanning head:** The scanning head is the component that does the
actual scanning. It moves down the page underneath the glass plate,
controlled by the computer and moved by the stepper motor. It contains
several components, including:

- **Charge Coupled Device (CCD) Array or Contact Image Sensor
  (CIS):** All scanners in use today use one of these two devices to convert the light energy into a data stream. A charge coupled device (CCD)
  array is a device inside a scanner that converts photons (particles of
  light) into electricity. The more light that falls on one of the photosites
  (single cells within the CCD array), the more electricity that site produces and thus the brighter the representation of the image on the
  computer. Any scanner that uses a CCD uses a lens to focus the light
  coming from the mirrors within the scanning head. Some cheaper scanners use a technology known as a contact image sensor (CIS). This
  technology replaces the mirrors and CCD array with a sensor that is as
  long as the glass plate is wide. The light source is a set of LEDs that
  runs the length of the glass plate as well. Either of these two devices
  (depending on the type used) will determine the overall resolution of
  a scanner. The resolution is the definition of how many pixels a scanner can use to make up a square inch of an image. For example, a
  scanner's resolution is given as a number such as 300 × 300 dpi. That
  means that the scanner uses 300 × 300 = 90,000 dots to represent
  one square inch. The higher the number, the higher the quality of the
  scan (but the higher the file size when transferred to the computer).

- **Light source and mirrors:** The light source in a scanner is the
  bright white light that is used to illuminate the original as it is being
  scanned. The light from this light source bounces off the original
  and is reflected off several mirrors and into the CCD or off the original and into the CIS. For a CCD scanner, the light source can be a

fluorescent bulb, a cold cathode fluorescent lamp (CCFL), or a xenon lamp. Their differences are cost, trueness of color reproduction, and bulb life. If you are using a scanner with a CIS, they most often use multicolor LEDs as their light source.

- **Stabilizer bar:** The stabilizer bar is what the scanning head rides on inside a flatbed scanner. It is a long stainless steel rod, usually about one-half inch in diameter that is securely fastened to the case of the scanner. It provides a smooth ride as the scanner scans down the page. If the scanning head were to wobble or stutter as it makes its pass, the image would look funny and the scan would be of no use. Thus, the smooth ride produces a smooth image.

▲ **Stepper motor:** The stepper motor moves the scan head incrementally down the page during the scan cycle. Often, the stepper motor is located either on the scan head itself or attached to a belt to drive the scanner head.

Besides the flatbed scanner, other types of scanners include:

▲ **Sheet-fed scanners:** A sheet-fed scanner (Figure 9-16) is similar to a flatbed scanner, but instead of a moving scan head, the scan head remains stationary and the paper is fed past it. (There are also sheet-feeder attachments for some business-quality flatbed scanners that will turn them into sheet-fed scanners.) The main advantage of a sheet-fed scanner over a flatbed scanner is speed. Sheet-fed scanners are designed to scan large numbers of documents in a short amount of time at the sacrifice of quality. Many sheet-fed scanners can scan 50–150 pages per

Figure 9-16

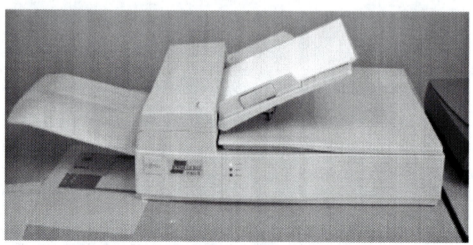

Sheet-fed scanner.

minute. Their image resolution typically isn't as good because the CCD can't read the image that quickly at a high resolution. Thus, fewer pixels are scanned per inch to be able to move the paper that quickly.

▲ **Handheld scanners:** A handheld scanner is a small portable device. With it, you can scan a sheet (held stable on a flat surface) by moving the scanner down the page.

▲ **Combination scanner/printer/copier/fax:** These devices combine the components of a flatbed or sheet-fed scanner with those of a printer and fax machine.

▲ **Film scanners/slide scanners:** These are designed especially to scan from 35 mm film; either negatives or slides.

▲ **Drum scanners:** Drum scanners are very expensive, professional scanners that mount the source image on a cylinder, or drum. Drum scanners can reach the very high resolutions required in the printing and publishing industries.

Other specialized devices that use optical scanning technologies include barcode readers and biometric devices:

▲ **Barcode readers:** A **barcode reader** operates similarly to a scanner. It is used to read barcodes on a flat surface, and operates by emitting a light source aimed at the bar code and reading the light patterns reflected back. A barcode reader may be a handheld device or may have a form factor similar to a flatbed scanner. Different barcode reader technologies may use different types of light sources to aim at the barcode, such as LED or laser. Barcode readers, also called barcode scanners, typically connect to a PC via a USB or PS/2 port.

▲ **Biometric devices:** A **biometric device** captures biometric information about an individual (unique biological traits such as fingerprints or irises) and uses this information to identify or authenticate the individual. Optical scanning is one of the most popular methods used for reading biometric information. A biometric scanning device may be a separate device, although some computing or telecommunications devices have built in sensors—typically fingerprint sensors—used to validate the user of the device. USB flash drives, mobile phones, and laptops are available with fingerprint sensors.

Some of the characteristics and features used to rate and compare scanners include:

▲ **Interface:** Although older scanners often used a parallel port, scanners today are typically connected to a PC through a USB or SCSI interface.

▲ **Sensor type:** CCD or CIS

▲ **Resolution:** Scanners are built to sense a certain number of dots per inch (DPI); typically somewhere between 1200 × 1200 dpi (this is horizontal × vertical) or 4800 × 4800 dpi and higher. The optical resolution (actual resolution) of a scanner is based on the number of sensors per row in the CCD or CIS array. However, many scanners are also advertised with an "enhanced" or "digital" resolution. In enhanced resolution, the scanner software inserts "interpolated" pixels between sensed pixels, giving these interpolated pixels values between the two adjacent pixels. This increases the apparent resolution of an image; because it is artificially derived, enhanced or digital resolution is considered lower quality than the same resolution derived optically.

▲ **Color depth:** The **color depth**, or **bit depth**, represents the number of individual colors that each pixel can display. It is always expressed as the number of bits used to describe each color in the color set. All scanners offer a minimum of 24-bit (true color) scanning, which supports 16.7 million colors. However, the human eye can only discern around 16 million colors (and has trouble distinguishing the color of adjacent pixels at about that level). So although higher bit depth is better—to a point—but past 40 bits, you aren't going to notice much difference.

The general procedure for installing a scanner is as follows; however, be sure to read your device's installation instructions first, as there are exceptions to every rule:

1. **Attach the device using a local or network port and connect power.** Connect the scanner to either the host computer with its power off (if it is a stand-alone device) or to the network (if it is a network device). However, USB scanners usually require that you install the software before connecting the scanner. After you have connected the scanner, connect it to a power source and turn on the device.

2. **Install and update the device driver and calibrate the device.** Boot up the computer and wait for Windows to recognize it. It will pop up a screen similar to the one shown in Figure 9.17. This wizard will allow you to configure the driver for the scanner (depending on the device). You can insert the driver CD-ROM that comes with the device, and the wizard will guide you through the device driver installation. If Windows fails to recognize the device, you can use the Add Hardware Wizard to troubleshoot the installation and to install the device drivers. After the driver is installed, the scanner will function; however, some scanners will require that you calibrate the device. Calibration is the process by which a device is brought within functional specifications, and a scanner may

Figure 9-17

The Windows Add Hardware Wizard.

need to be color calibrated with the monitor so that the final scanned image accurately represents the source image. Many scanners include a test pattern, called an IT8 scanner target, that can be scanned in and the color on the screen corrected for variations in color.

3. **Configure options and default settings.** Scanners may require setting options such as configuring sheet feeders within the driver software. These settings and how to change them can be found in your hardware's manual.

4. **Print/scan a test page.** Run the scanning software that came with the scanner. Place a single page on the scanner. Press the Scan button on the scanner (or in the software) to initiate a test scan. If the scan comes through on the screen, congratulations! Everything was done correctly.

Common problems you may experience with scanners include the following:

▲ **Scanner won't turn on:** Many times when you go to power up the scanner, it won't turn on. The simplest explanation is that the power cord has become unplugged. Check that both ends of the power cord for the scanner are plugged in correctly.

▲ **Strange noises from scanner:** Many people mistake noises coming from the scanner as a problem when in reality it is just the normal operation of the scanner. The scanner will make noise when first turned on as it performs its own internal calibration. The stepper motor will run, and the light source will turn on and off.

▲ **Scanner won't scan:** Sometimes, for whatever reason, a scanner won't scan. You click the Scan button in the software but nothing happens. The first thing to do is to try again. Many people give up when they first notice an error. However, strange things can and do happen with computers, so if at first you don't succeed, try, try again. If that doesn't solve the problem, try shutting down and rebooting the computer. Software isn't always written with the greatest care, and bugs can and do happen. Something that doesn't work after multiple tries may work after a reboot. After you've exhausted those possibilities, examine the simple things. For example, many scanners contain a scanning head lock to keep the scanning head from moving during shipping. There is always a possibility that this lock could have been switched back to the lock position by accident.

9.3.5 Digital Cameras

A **digital camera** uses CCDs (similar to scanners) as well as lenses and natural light sources to take pictures of objects, similar to the way a standard camera works. However, in a digital camera, the CCD replaces the film and records the picture as a pattern of bits.

Digital cameras typically use a USB or FireWire connection and come with software that allows you to pick which pictures you would like to download, so you only download the pictures you want to keep.

Characteristics and features used to rate and compare digital cameras include:

▲ **Resolution:** As with a scanner, the maximum optical resolution in dpi is determined by the number of cells in the CCD, and camera resolutions range up to 3264 × 2448 dpi and higher. For digital cameras, resolution is expressed in millions of pixels, called **megapixels**, calculated by multiplying the horizontal depth by the vertical depth. A 3264 × 2448 camera resolution would have 7,990,272 total pixels (3264 × 2448), or 8 megapixels (MP). Some digital cameras have resolutions higher than 16MP.

▲ **Lenses and zoom:** Higher-end cameras may have detachable lenses that you can exchange specialty lenses similar to a regular camera. Many digital cameras have zoom functions. As with scanners, some zoom functions may not be optical (enabled by lenses); they may be digital zoom. Digital zooms add interpolated pixels to the picture, in much the way scanners with enhanced or digital resolutions add interpolated pixels, to make the image larger.

▲ **Storage media:** Most digital cameras use flash RAM, typically in the form of memory cards, to store pictures.

▲ **Traditional camera features:** High-quality digital cameras share many of the features associated with traditional 35mm cameras, such as aperture, focus, and exposure settings.

9.3.6 Other Common Input/Output Devices

Other devices that can interface with a PC include:

▲ **Digital video cameras:** A **digital video camera** (or **digital camcorder**) operates similarly to a digital camera, but has far greater storage capacity to store the multiple sequences of photos needed for moving video. Common digital video storage options are miniDV (small tape cartridges), flash memory, Digital8, and DVD-R. Digital video cameras typically connect to your PC through a FireWire interface.

▲ **Webcams:** Webcams are small digital video cameras that are designed to be attached to a computer during operation, and popularly used for budget video broadcasting to the web. They can also be used for security systems and video chat and telephony over the Internet.

▲ **PDAs:** A **Personal Digital Assistant (PDA)** such as the Palm handheld and other pocket PCs can be considered a computing device in and of itself and not so much a peripheral. However, they are peripherals for a PC to the extent that they allow PC data to be transferred to them and carried with the owner. As such, PDAs require proper installation and configuration to the PC. The PDA must have a method of connecting to the host PC. Most often, this is done with either serial or USB (although, as previously mentioned, some use a wireless interface). Software or a driver must also be installed on the host PC to facilitate the transfer of information between the PDA and host PC. In the case of the Palm, a piece of software known as the Palm Desktop functions as a repository for the Palm data on the PC. Additionally, pieces of software known as conduits facilitate the communication between software on the PC (such as Microsoft Outlook) and the applications on a PDA. Conduits direct information from the host PC's application to the PDA and vise versa.

▲ **MP3 players:** MP3 players are used to store and play audio files (usually through headsets). Because one of the most popular audio compressions is MP3, these digital audio players are commonly known as MP3 players, although many players can store and play other types of audio files. A main distinguishing factor between types of MP3 players is the type of storage they use, either flash memory or hard drives. MP3 players with magnetic hard drives use miniature one-inch disks, and are more susceptible to damage by physical wear and tear.

▲ **Video projectors:** A **video projector** is used to display visual information, typically from a PC or other media device such as a DVD player, onto a screen. The main components in a projector are the video decoder and the light engine. The video decoder converts analog signals to digital. The light engine may include components such as a lamp, lenses, and optics for projecting the image. Projectors may display images by shining light through an image (transmissive) or by bouncing light off an image (reflective). There are several technologies used for projectors:

- **CRT:** CRT projectors are transmissive, and shine light through phosphor-coated picture tubes. CRT projectors are analog: their images aren't displayed in pixels.

- **LCD:** Liquid crystal display (LCD) projectors are also transmissive, and shine light through transparent LCD panels.

- **DLP:** Digital Light Processing (DLP) projectors are reflective. They use reflective DMD (Digital Micro-mirror Device) chips to bounce light and images off of.

- **LCoS:** Liquid crystal on silicon (LCoS) projectors are reflective; they use a combination of LCD panels and micro mirrors to project images.

LCD, DLP, and LCoS projectors are digital, and their displays can be compared like monitors, in terms of aspect ratios, resolution and display standards. Projectors are also compared in terms of brightness, colors, contrast ratios, types of projection screen, lenses, and their sizes and mounting options and portability. They typically can support several types of video signals, using ports such as DVI, for connecting to HDTV set-top boxes, S-video and composite video (video signals carried on a single cable), and component video (video signals carried on three RCA cables, one each for red, green, and blue, or RGB, signals.)

SELF-CHECK

1. Why are scanners similar to digital cameras?
2. What is the most commonly used keyboard format?
3. How does an optical mouse work?
4. Not including the mouse, identify four other pointing devices.

9.4 Working with Sound

Sound, beyond the little system speaker on the front of the system unit, is added through an adapter card in an expansion slot. Most new computers come with a sound system (a sound card, a CD-ROM or DVD, and a set of speakers). For older systems, sound can be added to a PC with a multimedia upgrade kit (CD-ROM, sound card, microphone, and speakers) or as a single card and speakers.

9.4.1 Sound Basics

For a computer to record and play back a sound that approximates the quality of sounds humans are used to hearing (voices and music, for example), computers must be able to convert between analog sound waves and digital sound waves. Analog sound waves are essentially the types of sounds humans here, digital sound wave are their computerized approximation. Analog sound waves have two primary qualities: amplitude (the height of the wave) and frequency (how many distinct waves occur in a given time frame). Amplitude determines how loud a sound is, and frequency determines pitch. Frequency is measured in cycles per second, or Hertz (Hz).

To convert an analog sound into a digital sound, computers sample the sound, taking small measurements of amplitude at specified time intervals. (Sampling is therefore also measured in terms of cycles per second, in Kilohertz (KHz). The higher the frequency of sampling, and the more data storage (in bits) allotted for each sampling, the closer a digitized sound wave comes to reproducing the original, analog sound.

In general, a 44KHz sampling rate that records 16 bits per sample is considered CD-quality audio; high-end sound cards may record 32 bits at up to 192KHz sampling rates.

9.4.2 Components of a PC Sound System

The following components are common to PC sound systems:

▲ **Sound card or onboard audio chip:** Motherboards typically contain some level of sound support integrated as an audio chip. **Sound expansion cards**, or **sound cards**, combine all ports and signal processors required to convert audio information into and from digital form into a single card (Figure 9-18).

▲ **Amplifier:** After the sound card has converted digital audio into an analog (audible) signal, the signal must be amplified before it can be played back on speakers. Most sound cards include a weak amplifier that is

Figure 9-18

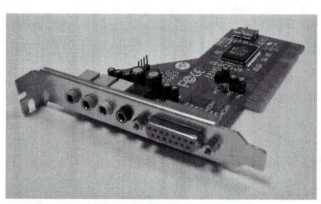

Sound card.

capable of driving a set of headphones or a set of small PC speakers. Some PC speakers include an amplifier in one or both of the speakers, taking the burden off the sound card.

▲ **Speakers:** PC speakers are available as small passive systems that are powered from the sound card's headphone output or as active (amplified) three-way surround-sound systems that rival many home theatres and somewhere in-between. Some computer monitors have speakers that are integrated into their bezels or that snap onto their sides. USB speaker systems do not require a separate sound card—all the sound processing is contained inside the speaker itself.

9.4.3 Examining Sound Cards

In addition to input/output ports, common components of a sound card are:

▲ **Analog to Digital Converter (ADC):** Converts analog audio data, such as a live voice or a musical instrument, into digital data that can be stored on a PC.

▲ **Digital Signal Processor (DSP):** Reduces the load on the PC's CPU for processing audio. This is common on most new sound cards.

▲ **Digital to Analog Converter (DAC):** Converts stored digital audio data into audible (analog) information that can be played on speakers or headphones.

▲ **Synthesizer:** Many of the sounds that a sound card produces are generated on the card using a synthesizer chip.

Sound card features and characteristics include:

▲ **Interface:** Sound cards are installed in expansion card slots on the motherboard. Older systems may have an ISA sound card, but more commonly a PCI or PCIe sound card.

▲ **Number of bits:** The bit depth used for each sample: typically 16-bit, 24-bit, and 32-bit.

▲ **Maximum sampling rate:** The frequency with which the sound card samples waveforms; commonly 92KHz or 192KHz.

▲ **Wavetable synthesis:** In wavetable synthesis sound cards use wavetables to reproduce the complex harmonic sounds of specific instruments. In a wavetable, short audio clips of instruments are stored that the sound card can load into memory and play when that instrument is defined by a digital audio file. Most sound cards today employ wavetable synthesis, although it may be hardware wavetable support, using wavetables stored in ROM memory chips on the card, or software wavetable support, which loads wavetable clips from files installed on the hard drive by the card's configuration software.

▲ **Recording and playback standard:** There are two recording and playback standards commonly used today: SoundBlaster, and the General **MIDI (musical instrument digital interface) standard.** Most sound cards in use today support both the SoundBlaster and General MIDI standards for recording and playback. (An older, 8-bit AdLib standard has all but disappeared.) Most sound cards are CD quality, which means that they capture and reproduce digital audio at the same resolution (CD-A) used for audio CDs. The two standards in use today are SoundBlaster and MIDI.

▲ **Input/output ports:** Sound cards typically sport a variety of ports for connecting to audio equipment; high-end cards may even include additional circuit boards or external hubs with an extended set of ports. Ports you will commonly find on sound cards include:

- **1/8" mini-jacks:** Sound cards have a variety of 1/8" mini jack ports to use with audio equipment; a typical sound card would include mini-jack ports for Line Out (for sending audio to headphones or speakers); Line In (for importing audio from devices such as CD players); Digital Out (for sending audio to digital devices); Microphone, and Speaker. Some sound cards will also have a separate jack for headphones.

- **MIDI port:** MIDI (musical interface digital interface) ports are typically used to connect to digital musical instruments such as synthesizers. The MIDI port is usually a 15-pin D-shaped connector (that may double as a game port/joystick port) or it may comprise two DIN connectors for input and output to MIDI devices.

In addition to these external ports, many sound cards also have general purpose USB or FireWire ports, and internal ports that you use to connect to other devices inside the PC, such as video cards. Some common internal ports are:

▲ **Telephone answering device (TAD):** An MPC-3 connector (Molex) connector used for connecting to an internal modem; this allows you to configure a modem to act as an answering machine or to send and receive voice mail over the modem.

▲ **CD In/Aux In:** MPC-3 connectors to connect to an internal CD drive or other devices.

▲ **Sony/Philips Digital Interface (S/PDIF):** Sony/Philips Digital Interface Format (S/PDIF) connectors are used for digital input and output to devices such as CD or DVD drives. S/PDIF connections use an RCA jack and coaxial cable, or may use optical cable with special Toshiba link (TOSlink) connectors.

▲ **Mic Con:** To connect to an internal microphone.

Sound cards are installed in the same way any expansion cards are. Some sound cards may need to be connected to other internal elements, such as a CD-ROM drive, and you will need to follow the manufacturer's directions. After you have installed the sound card, you connect any other needed audio components, such as speakers and microphones. When you power the PC back on, you should run the setup software that came with the sound card to properly configure the card.

FOR EXAMPLE

MIDI Files and Wavetables

MIDI is the standard language used by most digital keyboard synthesizers. Unlike most sound files (such as AU, AIFF, or WAV files), which are recordings, MIDI files are actually text files that describe instrument factors such as whether a note is playing or not, reverb, vibrato, pressure on a note, and so on. The sound cards interpret the text within a MIDI file and combine this with waveforms from its wavetables. For example, if a MIDI file specifies a piano C note, the sound card loads the waveform for a piano from its wavetables and plays the note using that waveform.

SELF-CHECK

1. What is sampling?
2. What are the three main components of a sound system?
3. List four common components found on a sound board.
4. What connector types are common on sound cards?

9.5 Understanding Display Technologies

Display systems convert computer signals into text and pictures and display them on a computer monitor or other screen. Most monitors are either **cathode ray tube (CRT)** (the same technology found in television sets) or **liquid crystal display (LCD)**. PCs may also connect to a projector display or to other audiovisual devices through specialized video ports provided by video cards.

9.5.1 CRT Monitors

In a CRT monitor, a device called an electron gun shoots a beam of electrons toward the back side of the monitor screen (Figure 9-19). The back of the screen is coated with chemicals called phosphors that glow when electrons strike them. The beam works from top to bottom and left to right, one row at a time. The

Figure 9-19

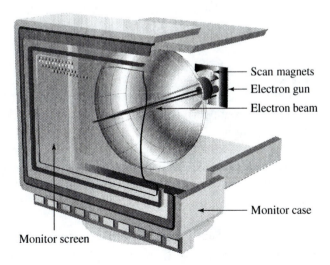

A CRT monitor.

phosphors or dots are illuminated in patterns that create images on the CRT's face. It takes only a fraction of a second to create the image on the CRT. However, the brightness of the illuminated dots fades just as fast, requiring the entire display to be refreshed by repeating the laser and dot illumination process many times per second to keep the image on the CRT's screen.

On a color monitor, each dot carries one of three colors: red, green, or blue. Three dots (one of each color) are arranged together to create a *pixel* (a *picture element*). Three electron beams illuminate a pixel's dots in varying degrees, and this mixture of color intensities produces different color shadings on the screen.

There are two ways to measure a monitor's image quality:

▲ **Dot pitch:** The **dot pitch** is shortest distance between two dots of the same color on the monitor. In CRT monitors, this distance is calculated as the measure of space between holes in the shadow mask or the horizontal distance between wires in the aperture grill (discussed below). Usually given in fractions of a millimeter (mm), the dot pitch tells how "sharp" the picture is. The lower the number, the closer together the pixels are, and, thus, the sharper the image. Common dot pitch sizes on color monitors range from .15 mm to .30 mm.

▲ **Refresh rate:** The **refresh rate** (technically called the *vertical scan frequency*) specifies how many times in one second the scanning beam of electrons redraws the screen, measured in draws per second, or Hertz. CRT monitors generally have refresh rates of 60Hz and higher, but lower refresh rates than 75Hz tend to cause an uncomfortable "flicker" effect.

CRT monitors are analog, and use signals in waveforms. A **digital-to-analog converter (DAC)** on the video card or the motherboard translates digital information from the PC into analog form, for the CRT to display. Inside the monitor is a controller board that communicates with the video adapter card, directs the drawing of the CRT's display, and responds to the adjustment controls on the monitor to adjust the display. The monitor's internal controller also determines the technology used in creating the display. Two technologies that control the illumination of the CRT's phosphor are:

▲ **Shadow mask:** A **shadow mask** is a metal screen with thousands of holes. The mask is placed so that the holes are directly in line with the dots of each pixel. The shadow mask absorbs unwanted electrons and prevents the phosphor material between the pixels from being illuminated, which leaves a black border around each pixel.

▲ **Aperture grill:** An **aperture grill** is composed of very thin vertical wires and lets more electrons through than the shadow mask, creating a deeper color display. Horizontal wires hold the vertical wires in place to keep the verticals from vibrating.

Other monitor features that affect the computer display include:

▲ **Interlacing:** Interlaced monitors use two passes to draw the screen, drawing only the even count lines on the first pass and only the odd count lines on the second pass. An interlaced monitor usually has more screen flicker than a non-interlaced monitor, which draws the entire screen in each pass.

▲ **Resolution:** One important factor that affects image quality of any monitor is resolution. Resolution means the number of pixels that are available to produce an image. The more pixels available for use in creating the display, the higher the resolution, resulting in a much better display. Resolution is stated as the number of pixels available horizontally on the screen by the number of rows of pixels available vertically on the screen. For example, 800 × 600 represents 800 pixels in each horizontal row and 600 vertical pixel rows (of 800 pixels each) on the screen. Resolution determines the size and quality of the image displayed on the monitor and it is a major factor in determining the amount of video RAM, or memory, that should be on the video card to support the display. Each pixel in a monitor's resolution requires a certain amount of data to encode exactly how the pixel should appear. For example, nearly 6MB of video RAM is required to generate a true color image using 1,600 × 1,200 resolution. Higher resolutions require more pixels: A CRT monitor using 640 × 480 resolution uses 307,200 pixels to create its display. The same monitor set to a resolution of 1,280 × 1,024 uses 1,310,720 pixels in the same display space. As the pixel count increases, a CRT monitor adjusts the size of each pixel and the amount of space around it decreases.

▲ **Aspect ratio:** The **aspect ratio** of a monitor describes the relative number of horizontal pixels to vertical pixels in the resolutions it supports. The standard aspect ratio for nearly all monitors and resolutions is 4:3 (read as 4 to 3) although 16:10 aspect ratios are becoming more popular. Resolutions with a 4:3 aspect include 640 × 480; 800 × 600; 1,280 × 768.

▲ **Size and viewable area:** Monitor screen sizes are measured diagonally from a top corner to the bottom opposite corner. However, depending on the design CRT screen, the curved corners and edges of a CRT screen may not really be usable as part of the working screen. Today, manufacturers are required to list the actual viewable area of a CRT monitor, which is also measured diagonally.

▲ **Color depth:** The common color depth settings are 8-bit, 16-bit, 24-bit, and 32-bit color. 8-bit color can express a maximum of 256 colors (2^8), 16-bit color depth can express 65,536 colors, 24-bit color can support 16.7 million colors and 32-bit color supports over 4 billion colors. 24-bit or 32-bit are often described as a "True Color" setting.

9.5.2 LCD Monitors

Liquid Crystal Display (LCD) monitors work by applying electrical charges to liquid crystals sandwiched between two polarizing sheets (Figure 9-20). Electrical currents, and the polarizing sheets, force the molecules to align themselves in patterns related to the electrical field, blocking light and acting as shutters. LCD screens are more compact, thinner and lighter than CRT monitors, and they consume much less power. They were first used for laptops but are rapidly suc-

Figure 9-20

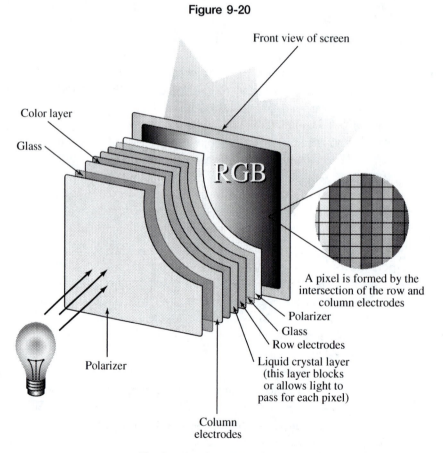

Front view of screen

Color layer

Glass

RGB

A pixel is formed by the intersection of the row and column electrodes

Polarizer

Glass

Row electrodes

Liquid crystal layer (this layer blocks or allows light to pass for each pixel)

Polarizer

Column electrodes

The layers of an LCD display.

ceeding CRTs in popularity. Some manufacturers have stopped making CRTs except for very high-quality professional-use versions or budget versions.

LCDs use digital (bit-based) signals to display screen images and require the video card to be able to support digital output (through the use of a Digital Visual Interface, or DVI, connector). The advantage is that because the video signal never goes from digital to analog, there is no conversion-related quality loss. However, many have an analog interface to work with older video adapter cards that output analog video signals.

There are two main types of PC LCD displays:

▲ **Active matrix:** An **active matrix,** or **thin film transistor (TFT) screen** uses a grid of tiny transistors and capacitors to control and retain information about each pixel. A transistor behind each pixel, when switched on, activates two electrodes that align the crystals and turn the pixel dark. This type of display is very crisp and easy to look at.

▲ **Passive matrix:** A **passive matrix screen** (Figure 9-21) has two groups of transistors: one along the top edge of the display, containing one transistor for each vertical column of pixels, and the other along the left side of the display, containing one transistor for each horizontal row of pixels. Wires form a matrix that interconnects the transistor rows and columns. To darken a particular pixel, power is sent to the transistors on the same row and column as the pixel and down the wires to the intersection point where the pixel sits. This method uses less power than an active matrix screen, but it is slower and produces a lower-quality

Figure 9-21

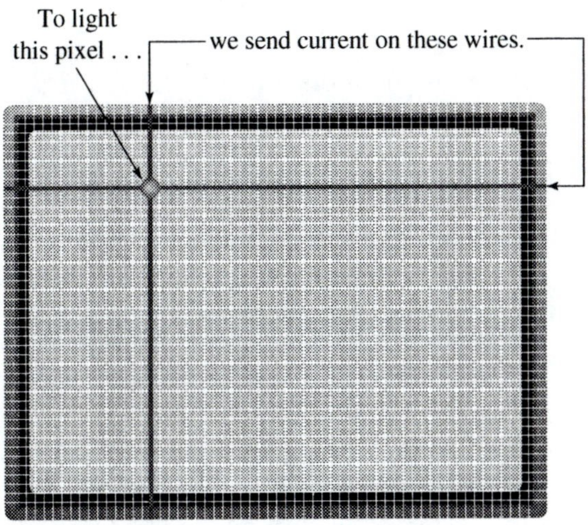

Passive matrix LCD display.

image. Passive matrix displays are usually either the older *Double-Layer Supertwist Nematic (DSTN)* or the newer *High-Performance Addressing (HPA)*. HPA improves the response of the display over DSTN, but both produce an inferior image compared to active matrix (TFT) screens.

Both types of LCDs are flat and about 1/2-inch thick. TFT displays produce the best image and cost the most. The main difference between active matrix and passive matrix is image quality. In passive matrix displays, the response of the screen to rapid changes is poor and subject to an effect known as *submarining:* If you move the mouse pointer rapidly from one location to another, it will disappear from the first location and reappear in the new location without appearing anywhere in between.

LCD displays differ from their CRT displays in several ways:

▲ **Dot pitch:** In LCD, the dot pitch is the measure of space between two LCD cells of the same color on the LCD panel, rather than the width between holes or wires in a shadow mask or aperture grill.

▲ **Resolutions:** LCD screens have a fixed number of pixels and so have a fixed "native resolution." Although they can display other resolutions, the native resolution of an LCD is clearer and sharper than non-native resolutions.

▲ **Size/viewable area:** Because LCD screens don't have the same curvature as CRT monitors, their size and viewable areas are the same.

▲ **Viewing angle:** LCD screens can be viewed only from a certain range of angles. Active matrix screens have a wider viewing angle than passive matrix screens. HPA and DSTN screens are hard to see except by looking straight at the display. In some cases this is an advantage working with secure data.

▲ **Response times:** LCD monitors are evaluated in terms or response times, in milliseconds (ms) for updating pixel information rather than refresh rates. Common response times are 12 ms and less.

▲ **Dead pixels:** Because the pixels in an LCD monitor are created from tiny circuits, a failed circuit can result in a "dead" or nonresponsive pixel, which looks like a dark dot on the screen.

9.5.3 Display Standards

The **video adapter**, also called the **graphics adapter**, is circuitry that converts the graphic images from a software application or operating system into a series of instructions that tell the monitor's internal controller how to draw the image on the screen and the colors to use. In a motherboard with onboard, or integrated, video, the video adapter is integrated into the motherboard's circuitry.

Table 9-4: Video Display Standards

Standard	Resolutions Supported	Colors Supported
Monochrome Display Adapter (MDA)	720 × 350	Mono (text only)
Color Graphics Array (CGA)	320 × 200	4
	640 × 200	2
Enhanced Graphics Array (EGA)	CGA resolutions	
	640 × 350	16
Video Graphics Array (VGA)	CGA and EGA resolutions	
	320 × 200	256
	640 × 480	16
Super VGA	CGA, EGA, VGA 640 × 480 up to 2048 × 1536	256, 32K, 64K, or 16 million+ (ranges from 4-bit to 32-bit color)

Most motherboards, however, include an expansion slot for adding a video adapter card to handle graphics. The video card and monitor must use the same display standard to work properly. Video display standards (Table 9-4) describe standard graphical modes that specify certain resolutions and color depths used with PC monitors and video adapters cards. Common display standards used include:

▲ **Monochrome Display Adapter (MDA):** MDA displays mostly text on a monochrome monitor. This adapter is still used for servers, process control, and monitoring systems where the display contains only text and a color display is not needed. A variation of the MDA that integrates graphics is the Hercules-based Monochrome Graphics Adapter (MGA).

▲ **Color Graphics Adapter (CGA):** This adapter was the first color adapter. It's capable of displaying four colors. CGA monitors support 320 × 200 (four colors) or 640 × 200 (two colors). In this case and those that follow, as the number of colors increases, the resolution usually decreases. This trade-off must take place so that the video RAM is not exceeded.

▲ **Enhanced Graphics Adapter (EGA):** This adapter supports 16 colors at a resolution of 640 × 350. EGA cards (and for the most part CGA) are obsolete.

▲ **Video Graphics Array (VGA):** The VGA standard supports up to 640 × 480 with 16 colors or lower resolutions with 256 colors.

▲ **Super VGA (SVGA):** Most of the video standards that followed VGA and support resolutions and color depths higher than those of the VGA standard are grouped under a general SVGA standard. SVGA video cards support several resolutions and up to 4 billion colors (although 16.7 million colors is commonly used as the standard).

9.5.4 Video Adapter Cards

Monitors require a lot of data stored in memory to be operated on and passed back and forth from the CPU and to be stored in memory. Early PCs and video adapter cards relied on system memory and RAM for processing video. Today, video adapter cards typically have their own onboard processor (a *graphic processing unit,* or GPU) and their own special video memory, and are often referred to as graphic accelerators). Factors that affect the speed of the video display system include: the CPU speed, expansion bus speed, the video memory, and the video card's circuitry. In their time, PCI and AGP buses were the fastest expansion buses used for video adapters, but today the fastest is PCI Express.

Video memory (often referred to generally as **video RAM** or **VRAM**) is used to store image data for processing by the video adapter. The more video memory an adapter has, the higher resolutions the adapter can support, and the better the image quality it can display. VRAM on a card may or may not be expandable and may also use proprietary technology.

The most common RAM technologies that have been used with video cards are:

▲ **Dynamic Random Access Memory (DRAM):** The DRAM used on early PCs. Because DRAM requires constant electrical refreshing to hold its contents, it didn't work well for video memory.

▲ **Extended Data Output DRAM (EDO DRAM):** Provides a higher bandwidth and handles read/write cycles better than standard DRAM.

▲ **Video RAM (VRAM):** VRAM, not to be confused with generic VRAM, is a special type of DRAM that doesn't need to be refreshed as often. VRAM is *dual-ported,* which means it has two access portals, and the processor and RAMDAC (RAM digital to analog converter) can both be accessing it at the same time. As the saying goes, two doors are better than one, and dual-porting doubles the memory's speed.

▲ **Windows RAM (WRAM):** Also called *Windows Accelerator Card RAM,* WRAM is a dual-ported memory that runs a bit faster than VRAM.

▲ **Synchronous DRAM (SDRAM):** SDRAM is EDO DRAM that is synchronized to the video card's processor and chipset. SDRAM is single-ported (one door) memory that is common on video cards.

▲ **Double Data Rate SDRAM (DDR SDRAM):** DDR SDRAM has twice the data transfer speed of standard SDRAM. DDR memories are becoming more commonplace on video cards, especially on 3D graphics accelerators.

▲ **Synchronous Graphics RAM (SGRAM):** An improvement on standard SDRAM adds features that support faster graphics performance:

• *Block write* copies the contents of a color register into memory in a single clock cycle.

• *Write per bit* allows a single bit of a data block to be changed without rewriting the entire data block.

SGRAM, which is a single-ported memory, is found only on video cards with chipsets that support it.

▲ **Double Data Rate SGRAM (DDR SGRAM):** DDR does for SGRAM exactly what it did for SDRAM: It doubles its data transfer rates.

▲ **Direct Rambus DRAM (DRDRAM):** A newer general-purpose memory type that is used for the PC's main memory (and on video cards) that runs about 20 times faster than conventional DRAM. DRDRAM includes bus mastering and dedicated channels between memory devices. *Bus mastering* allows the video card to take control of the PC's system bus and transfer data into and from system RAM. This improves the performance of some video operations that use primary RAM for certain calculations, such as 3D acceleration.

▲ **Unified Memory Architecture (UMA):** Many lower-cost systems intended for home use integrate graphics support and the video system into the motherboard. UMA is so named because it uses system RAM for video memory. This technology almost always produces inferior graphics performance.

▲ **Multibank DRAM (MDRAM):** MDRAM is a lower-budget RAM that is faster than VRAM and WRAM, and can be added in 32KB blocks.

Today, the most popular memory for video cards is DDR SDRAM. In addition to graphics processing chips and memory chips, many video cards have a digital-to-analog converter (DAC) that translates digital information to analog signals used by CRT monitors.

For even more powerful graphics processing and rendering, video card manufacturers have developed technologies enabling PCs to work with two or more PCI Express graphics cards. ATI Technologies version is called CrossFire and requires a CrossFire-compliant chipset. NVIDIA's technology is called Scalable Link Interface (SLI) and requires an SLI certified motherboard.

DVI port.

Video cards typically have a number of ports for connecting to a monitor or other display devices, such as a TV or projector. The most common monitor ports are:

▲ **HD-15:** The **HD-15 connector** (also called a VGA connector) is a standard monitor connector on virtually all newer monitors and video cards, especially VGA and SVGA. The video card has the female connector into which the male plug of the monitor is attached. The HD-15 is a DB-style plug and connector.

▲ **DVI:** The **Digital Visual Interface (DVI) connector** is used for digital connections to LCD monitors and projectors (Figure 9-22). There are several types of DVI port, including DVI-I, which supports both digital and analog signals; DVI-D, which supports digital only signals; and DVI-A, which supports analog only signals. DVI-I is most commonly used.

Video adapter cards often include a FireWire port for connecting to digital video cameras, and may also include ports and port adapters for transferring signals in standards needed for videos, TV and movies:

▲ **RCA plugs:** A single yellow RCA port is used for analog composite video (composite video carries all data in one signal). Three RCA plugs (red, green, and blue) are used for carrying analog component video, which splits data into red, green, and blue signals.

▲ **S-video:** Used for analog video transmissions using two signals.

▲ **VIVO ports:** A 9-pin S-video type port used for both input and output.

▲ **HDMi:** The HDMi (The High Definition Multimedia Interface) connector is used for combined digital audio/video connections between multimedia devices, such as a DVD player or HDTV.

9.5.5 Working with Monitors

You can compare and rate monitors by various factors: their dot pitch, supported resolutions, screen size, aspect ratio (typically 4 × 3 or 5 × 3), and physical size.

If you are purchasing or upgrading a monitor, you will need to choose a monitor that is compatible with the system's video card and the refresh rates supported by the video card. In addition, many monitors today are multifrequency: they can support several frequencies.

If you are purchasing an LCD monitor, make sure that the system's video card supports it: Not all LCD displays are supported by some video cards. Also, many LCD displays use a digital connection, which requires a video card that supports a digital LCD output.

The monitor connects to the system through a connector on the back of the adapter card or through a connector on the motherboard. The most common monitor connectors are HD-15 and DVI. Older monitors (CGA, EGA, and early VGA) may use a 9-pin connector, although some very high-end monitors use a special cable that connects with a standard HD-15 connector on the video card and a 5-pin BNC connector at the monitor.

When you install a monitor, you will typically have to install supporting software from the manufacturer, which will include its device drivers, and this software may need to be installed before connecting the monitor. Although Windows may have a generic driver for your monitor, this driver may not access the full features of your monitor.

After you connect the monitor to the PC, you may also need to configure a video card for the monitor's refresh rate, which in Windows you can usually accomplish through the Advanced tab of the Display control panel.

A monitor will typically have several external controls, or buttons, for adjusting things such as brightness and contrast.

Special considerations in working with monitors include:

▲ **Cleaning the monitor:** Dust collects on the glass of the monitor and is held there by the static electricity, accumulating over time. Never clean the monitor while it's powered on: The static electricity built up on the screen can be conducted straight to you by the liquid cleaner when you wipe it off. Monitors are usually covered with a special coating that can be permanently streaked if the wrong solutions are used to clean them. Ammonia-based cleaning products can dissolve the coating on the monitor, which may damage the display. You can clean a CRT or LCD monitor with a lint-free cloth dampened with water, although special antistatic monitor cleaners are commercially available. The screen of an LCD monitor is relatively delicate, so you should avoid touching it. Because LCDs are covered with a thin sheet of plastic, avoid any abrasive cleaners and cloths. Use a mild detergent or a low-sudsing, general-purpose cleaner and a lint-free soft cloth.

▲ **Environmental concerns:** CRT monitors contain high levels of lead, and LCD monitors also contain hazardous materials. You will need to check with state regulations if you need to dispose of a monitor. To be safe, send the monitor to the manufacturer or a repair company specializing in monitors or a salvage company to dispose of it properly.

▲ **Energy concerns:** CRT monitors use more power than the entire PC system (LCD monitors use about a third of the power of a CRT monitor). The United States EPA program, Energy Star, or Green Star program certifies PCs and monitors that use less than 30 watts in all power modes and reduce their power consumption by 99 percent in sleep or suspend mode. VESA's Display Power Management System (DPMS) protocol shuts down the parts of the monitor or motherboard that have been inactive for a certain period of time. PCs with both a motherboard and a monitor supporting the DPMS protocol significantly reduce the system's power consumption.

▲ **Electromagnetic emissions:** CRTs produce strong electrical and electromagnetic emissions, which can wreak havoc on other electrical or magnetic systems and have raised health questions for users.

▲ **High-voltage hazards:** CRT monitors use very high voltages and hold other hazards that can cause serious injury or even death, even when the power is off and disconnected. Never use a regular multimeter or other test equipment to measure the voltages on a monitor. If you must open the case to work on a monitor, *do not* wear an ESD grounding strap. Also, unplug the AC cord from the power source and use the buddy system (never work alone on a monitor). If you have to open a monitor, you must first discharge the high-voltage charge on it using a *high-voltage probe*. This probe has a very large needle, a gauge that indicates volts, and a wire with an alligator clip. Attach the alligator clip to a ground (usually the round pin on the power cord). Slip the probe needle underneath the high-voltage cup on the monitor. You will see the gauge spike to around 15,000 volts and slowly reduce to zero. When it reaches zero, you may remove the high-voltage probe and service the high-voltage components of the monitor. (A CRT is also vacuum sealed. If you break the glass, it will implode, which can send glass in any direction.)

> ## FOR EXAMPLE
>
> ### Multiple Monitors
>
> You are not confined to using just one monitor for your work: you can add two or more monitors to the PC; and Windows can be configured to show the desktop spread over all monitors. This is a common practice in professional graphic design stations, where one monitor can be used to view a multimedia file, and the other to view other files or areas of the desktop. If you are connecting multiple monitors to your PC, you will need a video card that supports multiple monitors. After the monitors are connected, you can configure what each will display on the Settings tab of the Display Properties dialog box, which you can open through the Control Panel.

9.5.6 Troubleshooting the Video System

The two elements that you must deal with when troubleshooting PC video are the monitor and the video card.

The most common problems with a video card are refresh rates and resolution and color depth settings. Your monitor and video card documentation should have a recommended refresh rate for the monitor. These problems can be fixed through Windows using the Display Properties settings. If a monitor image is unreadable after changing the refresh rate, reboot the PC into Windows Safe mode, use the lower refresh rate, and reboot the PC into Normal mode.

Some problems may be caused by an out-of-date device driver for the video card, so you should make sure that you have the latest driver for your card.

Some common display problems are:

▲ **Distorted display:** If the displayed image is scrambled or distorted or shows multiple layers of the same image, the monitor is unable to handle the output of the video card. Other symptoms of this mismatch are a blank screen or an irritating high-pitched tone coming from the monitor. Until you can replace the monitor with a better-quality monitor, these problems can be handled by lowering the color-depth and resolution settings for the display and video card.

▲ **Faded or distorted colors or image resolution:** The electromagnetic forces in the monitor or other electromagnetic devices nearby can cause the internal components of the monitor to become magnetized. When this happens, the image resolution and color quality produced by the monitor can be distorted or faded, especially in the display's corners. A process called **degaussing** eliminates most of the magnetization inside the CRT. Most color monitors have a built-in degaussing protocol that can usually be accessed from the monitor's front panel. A monitor should be degaussed fairly regularly, but be careful not to overdo it. Degaussing a circuit too much can damage it.

SELF-CHECK

1. Explain what a refresh rate is.
2. List three benefits that LCD monitors have over CRT monitors.
3. What is a display standard?
4. How do you clean a monitor?

SUMMARY

Input/output devices are peripherals used to input data to the PC and translate or display information the PC has operated on. Common I/O interfaces include the legacy serial and parallel interfaces, high-speed serial interfaces such as USB and IEEE 1394/Firewire, SCSI, and wireless RF and IR. Common ports and connectors are D-connectors, RJ-series connectors, USB, IEEE 1394/FireWire, PS/2, IR ports, RCA jacks, HD/VHD, Centronics, and BNC. The general procedure for installing devices is to locate the drivers, power down and connect the device, power up the PC, install the drivers as prompted, and complete any additional configuration through third-party software. Problems with I/O devices include hardware problems, interface compatibility problems, port problems, powering problems, driver-related and configuration problems. The Device Manager, BIOS and POST errors, and Windows hardware troubleshooting wizards are used to troubleshoot devices.

Legacy serial and parallel ports are assigned logical names (COM1, COM2, COM3, COM4, LPT1, LPT2) that have default resource assignments. Serial communications are controlled by a UART chip. Serial ports were typically used for modems, and parallel ports for printers. There are three types of parallel ports: SPP, EPP, and ECP. Features of the USB interface include support for multiple devices, variable bandwidth, four types of data transfer, use of a USB controller, plug and play, hot swapping, and device powering. FireWire features include multiple device support, variable bandwidth, two types of data transfer, plug and play, hot swapping, device powering, and native peer-to-peer architecture. IR and RF wireless interfaces have slower speeds and are used with a PC for I/O devices such as keyboards and mice.

Common input devices include keyboards, mouse devices and other pointing devices such as touch screens, joysticks, touchpads and digitizing tablets, scanners, barcode readers, biometric devices, digital cameras, digital video cameras, PDAs, Webcams, video projectors, personal MP3 players, speakers, and monitors.

A sound system consists of a sound card or integrated audio circuitry on the motherboard, amplifiers, and speakers. A sound card has a variety of ports, such as one-eighth-inch mini jacks, MPC-3 connectors, and S/PDIF connectors to connect to audio devices.

A display system consists of a video card or integrated video circuitry on the motherboard and a display device, such as a CRT or LCD monitor or a projector. A video adapter card usually has co-processors and video RAM to support video processing, and a variety of ports to connect to video devices.

KEY TERMS

Active-matrix screen

Analog-to-Digital Convertor (ADC)

Aperture grille

Aspect ratio

Barcode reader

Biometric device

Bluetooth

BNC (Bayonet Naur) connector

Cathode-ray tube (CRT)

Centronics

Charge-coupled device (CCD)

Color depth

Color Graphic Adapter (CGA)

Connector

Contact Image Sensor (CIS)

D connector

Data bits

Degaussing

Device driver

Digital camera

Digital video camera (digital camcorder)

Digital Visual Interface (DVI) connector

Digital-to-analog converter (DAC)

Digitizing table

DIN-n connector

Dot pitch

Dynamic range

Enhanced Capabilities Port (ECP)

Enhanced Graphics Adapter (EGA)

Enhanced Parallel Port (EPP)

Flatbed scanner

Flow control (handshaking)

High Density (HD)/Very High Density (VHD) connector

Hot-swapping (hot-plugging)

HD-15 connector

IEEE 1284

IEEE 1394 (Firewire)

Infrared

Infrared Device Association (IrDA)

Infrared port

Input peripheral

Input/output (I/O) peripheral

Interface

Interpolation

Joystick

Keyboard

Legacy port

Liquid crystal display (LCD)

Mechanical mouse

Megapixel

Monochrome Display Adapter (MDA)

MP3 player

Musical Instrument Digital Interface (MIDI) standard

Null modem cable

Optical mouse

Output peripheral

Parallel interface

Parity

Passive matrix screen

Peripheral

Peripheral interface

Personal Digital Assistant (PDA)

Plug and Play

PS/2 port (mini-DIN connector)

RCA jack/connector

Refresh rate

Registered jack (RJ) connector

Resolution

RTS/CTS (Request-to-send/clear-to-send)

Scanner

Serial interface (RS-232-C)

Shadow mask

Signed driver

Sound card

Standard Parallel Port (SPP)

Standard serial cable

Stop bit

Super VGA (SVGA)

Touch screen

Touchpad

Trackball

Universal Asynchronous Receiver/ Transmitter (UART) chip

Universal Serial Bus (USB)

Video adapter (graphics adapter)

Video Graphics Array (VGA)

Video memory (video RAM) (VRAM)

Video projector

Wavetable synthesis

Webcam

XON/XOff

ASSESS YOUR UNDERSTANDING

Go to www.wiley.com/college/groth to evaluate your knowledge of input and output devices.

Measure your learning by comparing pre-test and post-test results.

Summary Questions

1. A parallel port transmits data:
   - (a) one data bit at a time
   - (b) four data bits at a time
   - (c) one sector at a time
   - (d) eight data bits at a time

2. You want to plug a keyboard in to the back of a computer. You know that you need to plug the keyboard cable into a PS/2 port. Which style of port is the PS/2?
   - (a) RJ-11
   - (b) DB-9
   - (c) Din 5
   - (d) Mini-DIN 6

3. A driver that has been certified to work with the Windows operating system is called a:
   - (a) certified driver
   - (b) signed driver
   - (c) verified driver
   - (d) Windows driver

4. The two most common connectors used for serial ports are:
   - (a) Centronics 25- and 36-pin
   - (b) DB-9 and DB-15
   - (c) DB-9 and DB-25
   - (d) Berg and Molex

5. A UART chip is used to control:
   - (a) the Plug and Play BIOS
   - (b) a parallel port
   - (c) a serial port
   - (d) the processor

6. Which peripheral port type was designed to transfer data at high speeds to printers only?
   (a) DVD
   (b) USB
   (c) IEEE 1394
   (d) IEEE 1284

7. What is the maximum speed of USB 2.0 in MBps?
   (a) 1.5
   (b) 12
   (c) 60
   (d) 480

8. Which of the following is an IEEE 1394 type port?
   (a) USB-TG
   (b) IrDA
   (c) Parallel
   (d) i.Link

9. A keyboard error code displayed during the boot sequence would be in what number series?
   (a) 1700–1799
   (b) 300–399
   (c) 100–199
   (d) It may be a number from any series

10. The technology used to detect movement on an optical mouse is:
    (a) a low-grade laser beam
    (b) a digital capture "eye"
    (c) a video detection system that detects movement in the mouse ball
    (d) static electricity sensors

11. Which type of touch screen system transmits 90% of the light from the monitor?
    (a) resistive
    (b) capacitive
    (c) SAW
    (d) All of the above

12. What type of device on scanners and digital cameras converts light to digital impulses?
    (a) CCD
    (b) scan head

(c) optical filters

(d) lens system

13. Which of the following parallel port protocols allows bidirectional simultaneous communications?

(a) ECP

(b) SPP

(c) EPP

(d) TCP

14. What component on a sound card converts analog audio into digital data?

(a) synthesizer

(b) DSP

(c) DAC

(d) ADC

15. The distance between pixels on the CRT screen is measured as:

(a) resolution

(b) interlacing

(c) dot pitch

(d) dot triad

16. What monitor feature indicates how fast the monitor redraws the screen?

(a) dot pitch

(b) refresh rate

(c) refresh signal

(d) hertz

17. What peripheral port type is expandable using a hub, operates at 1.5MBps, and is used to connect various devices (from printers to cameras) to PCs?

(a) USB 2.0

(b) USB 1.0

(c) IEEE 1394

(d) IEEE 1284

18. When installing speakers for a PC, you connect the speaker's cable to (one of) the _____ jack(s) on the back of the PC.

(a) RJ-11

(b) RJ-45

(c) 1/8-inch mini jack

(d) RCA

19. Which of the following is *not* a type of video RAM?
    (a) MDRAM
    (b) UMA
    (c) SGRAM
    (d) WVRAM

20. The I/O address of COM1 is:
    (a) 2E8h
    (b) 3E8h
    (c) 2F8h
    (d) 3F8h

Applying This Chapter

1. You're using your USB port for your scanner. What is the preferred method for swapping your scanner with a previously configured digital camera?

2. You are upgrading the mouse on your PC and have chosen an RF wireless mouse. Explain how this mouse connects to your PC.

3. A friend wants to update their PC for better sound. Explain how they can do this.

4. A customer has been having problems with a USB external floppy drive. When you arrive at the customer's site, you discover a stack of floppy disks sitting on top of the monitor. What do you think may be the problem?

5. A friend wants to purchase a scanner. What type of scanner and what features should she look for?

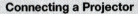

YOU TRY IT

Connecting a Projector

A client wants to use a projector at a conference. Visit a video projector manufacturer website, such as Mitsubishi.com or HP.com, select a projector, and determine what connections it has to interface with a PC.

Comparing Sound Cards

You are selecting a sound card. Select two current sound cards from different manufacturers (such as CreativeLabs.com and TurtleBeach.com) and compare them in terms of at least five key features.

Selecting a Monitor

Your company, an accounting agency, wants to specify a standard PC system for its clerical employees. Select an appropriate monitor, by visiting monitor manufacturer's websites. Describe at least three features of your monitor that make it appropriate for this use.

Troubleshooting a Webcam

You have just installed a USB Webcam, but Windows isn't recognizing the device. What troubleshooting steps will you take?

10
PRINTERS

Starting Point

Go to www.wiley.com/college/groth to assess your knowledge of printers.
Determine where you need to concentrate your effort.

What You'll Learn in This Chapter

▲ Types of printers, their printing processes and components
▲ Printer interfaces and installation steps
▲ Printer maintenance and cleaning
▲ Symptoms and causes of printer problems

After Studying This Chapter, You'll Be Able To

▲ Identify different printers and their key components and supplies
▲ Evaluate and compare printers
▲ Select printers and printer supplies
▲ Install and configure a printer
▲ Clean and maintain a printer
▲ Upgrade a printer
▲ Troubleshoot print image quality problems and failures

INTRODUCTION

A **printer** is an electromechanical output device that is used to put information from the computer onto paper. Other than the display monitor, the printer is the most popular peripheral purchased for a computer. There are several types of printer technologies, each with its own set of maintenance, cleaning, and troubleshooting concerns.

10.1 Examining Printer Technologies

There are three main types of printers used in homes and businesses: impact printers, inkjet printers, and laser printers, each with different advantages and disadvantages. Printers tend to have a longer lifespan than PCs, and many older dot-matrix, inkjet, bubble jet, and even some noisy, old daisy-wheel printers are still in use. Some printers are called **line printers** because they print a line at time, such as impact and inkjet printers. Other printers are called **page printers** because their process prints an entire page at a time.

10.1.1 Impact Printers

An **impact printer** uses some form of impact and an inked ribbon to make an imprint on the paper, similar to a typewriter. An early type of impact printer, the **daisy-wheel printer,** is largely obsolete. Daisy-wheel printers contained a wheel with raised letters and symbols on each "petal." A mechanism called a **printhead** held and rotated the wheel and an electromechanical "hammer," called a solenoid, struck the petal of the appropriate character against the inked ribbon and paper (Figure 10-1). These early printers could only print between two and four characters per second (cps), were very noisy, but were useful for printing multipart forms, documents with many carbon copies. Their print quality is comparable to a typewriter because it uses a very similar technology. This typewriter level of quality is called **letter quality (LQ)**.

The impact printer in most use today is the dot-matrix printer. A **dot-matrix printer** creates characters by grouping the hard-wire pins, or **printwires**, on the printhead into the pattern of a character and then striking the entire group through a ribbon to form the character on paper.

The Dot-Matrix Print Process

The pins in the printhead are wrapped with coils of wire to create a solenoid and are held in the rest position by a combination of a small magnet and a spring. To trigger a particular pin, the printer controller sends a signal to the printhead, which energizes the wires around the appropriate printwire. This turns the printwire into an electromagnet, which repels the print pin, forcing it

Figure 10-1

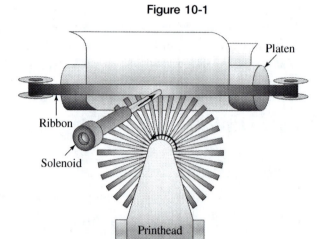

Daisy wheel printer mechanism.

against the ink ribbon and making a dot on the paper. Each pin prints a dot on the page and the pattern of dots creates the printed character (Figure 10-2). The resulting character is less sharp than a character created by a laser printer, but the trade-off of cost and flexibility makes this acceptable for many documents

The typical dot-matrix printer uses continuous feed paper. Dot-matrix printers use a **platen** (a large rubberized roller), under which the paper is fed. The platen provides spring tension to hold the paper in place and move it through the printer. When the platen motor rotates the platen, the paper is pushed up and past the printhead. The paper can also be fed by **form tractors**,

Figure 10-2

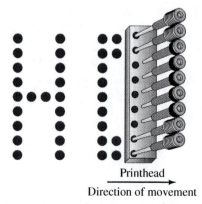

Printhead

Direction of movement

Dot matrix printwires.

or pin-feed tractors, that attach to the platen and are driven by the platen motor. Form tractors provide a more consistent feed mechanism by using the pin-feed holes along the side of the paper to pull the paper and multiple part forms through the printer. Dot-matrix printers use a cloth or polyester ribbon soaked in ink and coiled up inside a plastic case, called a **printer ribbon** (or ribbon cartridge).

Dot Matrix Print Quality and Speed

The quality of a print image is dependent on its resolution. Resolution is the number of dots that are printed in a square inch (dots per inch or **dpi**). The resolution of a dot-matrix printer depends on the number of printwires used to form each character. The most common numbers of printwires in the dot-matrix printer's printhead are 9, 18, and 24. A 24-pin printhead produces **near-letter quality (NLQ)** print. Printers with less than 24 pins are only capable of draft quality print, which produces characters with lots of wide-open spaces between the dots. 24-pin printers can reach resolutions up to 360 × 360 dpi (horizontal × vertical).

The speed of a dot-matrix printer is rated in characters per second (cps). Early dot-matrix printers ranged from 32 to 72 cps, but professional dot-matrix printers can reach speeds of 500 cps and higher. The actual speed realized from the printer depends largely on its mode of operation. Dot matrix printers typically have a number of modes for printing, such as draft or letter quality.

Dot-matrix printers are fairly rugged, able to print multi-part forms, and their continuous paper feed is useful in areas such as computing and data logging. However, their image quality can be quite poor compared to the quality produced with a daisy wheel and they are noisy.

10.1.2 Inkjet Printers

With an **inkjet printer**, tiny drops of ink are sprayed onto a page and form patterns that resemble the items being printed. Two of the main technologies used for ink-jet printing are:

▲ **Thermal inkjet:** A **thermal inkjet printer** produces an image by heating ink into steam and using the force of the bubble that is created to "jet" the droplet of ink onto the paper. These are sometimes called bubble jet printers.

▲ **Piezoelectric inkjet:** A **piezoelectric inkjet printer** uses a piezoelectric crystal, which flexes, or changes its shape, very slightly under applied voltage, to force the droplet of ink onto the paper.

Inkjet printers are considered line printers because they print a line at a time.

Inkjet Printer Components

The main components of a typical inkjet printer are:

▲ **Printhead/ink cartridge:** The printhead contains many small nozzles or jets (usually 100 to 200) that spray the ink in small dots onto the page. The printhead may be disposable, in which case it is part of the ink cartridge, or built-in (fixed-head). Disposable heads are replaced whenever the ink cartridge is replaced. The ink cartridge typically includes several small chambers, typically one for each of the *CMYK* (cyan, magenta, yellow, and black) print inks. Many color inkjet printers have separate cartridges for color and black ink cartridges; and some may have a cartridge for each color. Printers designed for printing photographs may have up to five colors in the ink cartridge.

▲ **Head carriage, belt, and stepper motor:** The **printhead carriage** is the component that moves back and forth during printing and holds the printhead/ink cartridges (Figure 10-3). A **stepper motor**, also called a carriage motor or carriage stepper motor, is motor that can move in very precise, small increments. A **carriage belt**, placed around two wheels or pulleys, is driven by the stepper motor and moves the printhead back and forth across the page while it prints. To keep the printhead carriage aligned and stable while it traverses the page, the carriage rests on a small metal stabilizer bar. When the printhead is not printing, it is held in place at its maintenance station. To keep the ink

Figure 10-3

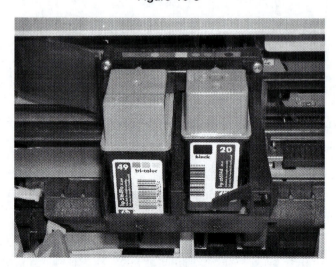

Inkjet printhead carriage.

Figure 10-4

Inkjet pickup rollers.

flowing freely, before each print cycle, the maintenance station pulls ink through the ink nozzles using vacuum suction. This expelled ink is absorbed by the pad.

▲ **Paper-feed mechanism:** The paper-feed mechanism picks up paper from the paper drawer and feeds it into the printer. This assembly consists of rubber pickup rollers that feed the paper into the printer (Figure 10-4); separator pads, small cork or rubber patches that help keep the paper in place (so only one sheet goes into the printer); and a pickup stepper motor that drives the pickup rollers. The paper may be held in a paper tray, a small plastic tray in the front of the printer or in a paper feeder at the back of the printer. Paper-feed sensors (Figure 10-5) tell the printer when it is out of paper, as well as when a paper jam has occurred during the paper-feed process.

▲ **Control, interface, and power circuitry:** Inkjet printers have onboard circuitry for printer control, printer interfaces, and printer power. The printer control circuits, usually on a small circuit board, run the stepper motors and are also responsible for monitoring the printer status. The interface circuitry makes the physical connection to the PC (parallel, serial, SCSI, network, infrared, and so on). The power circuits use a transformer to convert household current into the voltages the printer uses. The printer's circuitry also contains onboard print buffer memory, a small amount of memory (typically 512KB to 16MB) used to store print jobs as they are received from the printing computer.

Figure 10-5

Inkjet paper-feed sensor

The Inkjet Print Process

If the printer has not printed in a while, the printer's control circuits activate a cleaning cycle, a set of steps that purge the printheads of any dried ink. The paper feed mechanism positions the paper properly; then the printhead stepper motor moves the carriage and printhead across the page in small increments. At each step, the printhead sprays dots of ink on the paper as dictated by the control circuitry. At the end of a pass across the page, the paper-feed stepper motor advances the page a small amount, and the process repeats. Some printheads print in one direction only, others print in both directions across the page. After the page is finished, it is ejected into the output tray. If more pages need to print, printing the next page begins. After printing is complete and the final page has been ejected from the printer, the printhead is parked (locked into rest position) and the print process is finished.

Inkjet Print Quality and Print Speed

Inkjets range from 150 × 150 dpi to over 5760 × 1400 dpi on photo-quality printers. Inkjet printer speeds are rated in pages per minute (PPM) rather than characters per second (CPS) because the inkjet doesn't form each character separately. Rather, it prints in horizontal lines across the page. It takes several passes across the page to complete a complete line of text. Inkjet printer speeds range from 2 PPM to 20 PPM and higher, with color printing generally slower than black and white printing.

Inkjet printers are probably the most popular printer type in use for home users. They produce a better-quality print without the noise level of the dot-matrix printer and at a lower price than a laser printer. However, ink cartridges are relatively expensive, especially if they include the printhead, and the total cost per printed page may be quite higher with an inkjet than a laser printer.

10.1.3 Laser Printers

A laser printer uses toner and a complex printing process to produce high-quality documents. **Toner** is a dry powder that consists of iron particles coated with a plastic resin that bond to the paper during the print process. Toner is supplied to the printer in a removable cartridge that contains many of the most important parts used in the printing process, including a **photosensitive drum** (a mechanism that places a charge on the drum) and a roller to develop the final image on the page.

Laser printers are considered page printers because they form and print all the text and graphics for one full sheet or page at a time. Many are capable of duplex printing, printing both sides of a page at one.

The Laser Printing Processes

Three different printing processes are used in laser printers, each directly attributable to one or more manufacturer(s):

▲ **Electrophotographic (EP) process:** This process, which was the first laser printer technology, was developed by Xerox and Canon. It is the technology used by all laser printers in one form or another. A laser beam produces an electrostatic charge and a dry toner to create the "printed" image.

▲ **Hewlett-Packard (HP) process:** The HP process is essentially the same as the EP process, with the exception of some minor operating procedures. It's similar enough to be considered the same process, yet different enough to get its own name.

▲ **Light-emitting diode (LED) process:** An **LED printer** follows the same basic process as EP, except it uses an array of about 2,500 light emitting diodes instead of a laser to produce an electrostatic charge.

Laser Printer Components

The standard components of a laser printer are:

▲ **The toner cartridge:** The **toner cartridge** holds the toner in a medium called the developer (also called the carrier), which carries the toner until it is used by the print process. This cartridge also contains the photosensitive drum (Figure 10-6).

Figure 10-6

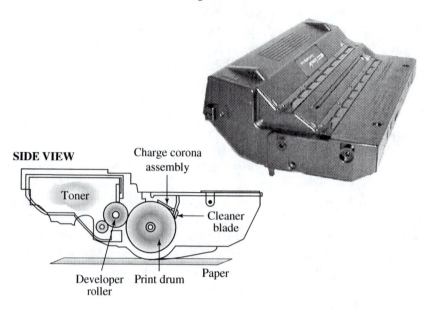

SIDE VIEW

Charge corona
assembly

Toner

Cleaner
blade

Developer   Print drum   Paper
roller

Toner cartridge.

▲ **Photosensitive drum:** The drum inside the toner cartridge is coated with
a photosensitive material that can hold a static charge when not exposed
to light but *cannot* hold a charge when it *is* exposed to light. During
printing, the laser beam is reflected onto the surface of the drum to create a pattern of charged and not-so-charged spots, representing the image
of the page to be printed. The drum also contains a cleaning blade that
continuously scrapes the used toner off the photosensitive drum to keep
it clean. In some laser printers, the toner and photosensitive drum are
replaced separately instead of as a single unit.

▲ **The laser scanning assembly:** The **laser scanning assembly** shines on
particular areas of the photosensitive drum. When it does that, the drum
discharges, but only in that area. As the drum rotates, the laser scanning
assembly scans the laser across the photosensitive drum. Laser light is
damaging to human eyes. Therefore, this assembly is kept in an enclosure and will operate only when the printer's cover is closed.

▲ **High-Voltage Power Supply (HVPS):** The **high-voltage power supply
(HVPS)** converts house AC current into the high voltages used in the
printing process. This high voltage is used to energize both the primary
corona and the transfer corona.

▲ **DC Power Supply (DCPS):** The **DC power supply (DCPS)** converts
house current into three voltages: 5VDC and −5VDC for the logic cir-

Figure 10-7

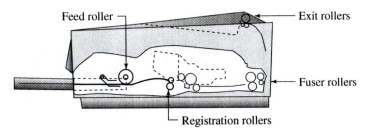

Feed roller — ⌐   ⌐— Exit rollers

Fuser rollers —

Registration rollers

Paper transport rollers.

cuitry and 24VDC for the paper transport motors. This component also runs the fan that cools the internal components of the printer.

▲ **Paper transport assembly:** Inside the laser printer are four types of rollers that move the paper through the printer. Each rubberized roller or set of rollers is driven by its own motor. The four roller types in the paper transport system are the feed roller (or the paper pickup roller), the registration roller, the fuser roller, and the exit roller. Most paper jams in a laser printer occur in the paper transport area (Figure 10-7).

▲ **Primary corona:** The **primary corona** is a charged roller (or in earlier laser printers, a corona wire), also called the *main corona* or the *primary grid,* that forms an electrical field that uniformly charges the photosensitive drum to –600V to reset it prior to receiving the print image and toner.

▲ **Transfer corona:** A **transfer corona** roller (or in earlier printers, a transfer corona wire) moves a page image from the drum to the paper. The transfer corona charges the paper; the charge pulls the toner from the drum onto the paper. As the paper exits the transfer corona, a static charge eliminator strip reduces the charge on the paper so that it won't stick to the drum. (When working on a printer with a transfer roller, be careful not to touch the roller with your bare hand or arm. The oils from your skin can spot the transfer roller and cause improperly charged paper, which appears as defects in the printed image.)

▲ **Fusing rollers:** The toner is melted permanently to the page by the **fusing rollers** that apply pressure and heat (between 165 and 180 degrees Celsius) to it. The fuser—not the laser—makes the printed pages hot.

▲ **Interface controller:** The **interface controller** is the motherboard of the laser printer, and it has architecture and components like a PC motherboard. The controller communicates with the PC and the printer control panel (a button panel for users), controls the printer display, houses the memory in the printer, and forms the image printed on the page.

Figure 10-8

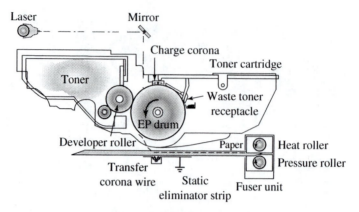

Laser print process.

Memory expansion is possible on virtually all laser printers. Adding memory allows the printer to reproduce larger documents or graphics in higher resolutions or to support additional soft fonts.

Laser Printing Steps

Six major steps are involved in printing a page on a laser printer.

1. **Cleaning:** Before a new page is printed, any remnants from the previous page are cleared away. First, the drum is swept free of any lingering toner with a rubber blade. Any toner removed in this step is not reused but is put into a used-toner compartment on the cartridge. The charges on the photosensitive drum are then cleared. In modern laser printers, this is done by another drum; older models use an erase lamp (the drum, being photosensitive, loses its charge when exposed to light).

2. **Conditioning:** The entire drum is uniformly charged to −600V by the primary corona inside the toner cartridge. This charge conditions the drum for the next step.

3. **Writing:** The laser printer controller uses a laser beam and a series of mirrors to create the image of the page on the drum. The laser beam is turned on and off in accordance with the image to be created on the drum. At the spot where the laser's light contacts the photosensitive drum, the charge is reduced to about −100V. After the image has been transferred to the drum this way, the controller also starts the page sheet through the printer, stopping it at the registration rollers.

4. **Developing:** The developing roller, located inside the toner cartridge, has a magnet inside of it that attracts the iron particles in the toner. As the developing roller rotates near the drum, the toner is attracted to the

areas of the drum that have been exposed by the laser, creating the print image on the drum.

5. **Transferring:** The back of the paper sheet (waiting at the registration rollers) is given a positive charge by the transfer corona that attracts the negatively charged toner from the drum onto the paper as it passes. After this step, the paper has the image of the page on it, but the toner, which is held only by simple magnetism, is not yet bonded to it.

6. **Fusing:** The fusing rollers apply heat and pressure to the toner, which melts and presses it into the paper to create a permanent bond. Fusing rollers are covered with Teflon and treated with a light silicon oil to keep the paper from sticking to them.

After the paper completely exits the fuser, it trips a sensor that tells the printer to finish the printing process with the cleaning step. At this point, the printer can print another page, and the process can begin again. Color laser printers work similarly to black and white laser printers; although some may print one color at a time in several passes.

The LED printer uses the same process as any other laser printer, with one major exception. It uses a row of small light-emitting diodes held very close to the photosensitive drum to expose it. Each LED is about the same size as the diameter of the laser beam used in laser printers. These printers are basically the same as EP process printers, except that in the exposure step, they use LEDs instead of a laser. An LED printer with a 600 dpi resolution has 600 LEDs per inch.

Laser Print Quality and Speed

Typical laser printer resolutions are 300 × 300 dpi, 600 × 600 dpi, and high-quality lasers can be 1200 dpi or higher. Laser print speeds range from 5 to 100 ppm. Color laser printers generally print more slowly. Laser printers are faster than ink jet printers and reach higher resolutions. They are more expensive than inkjet printers, although they have become more affordable for the home user. In high-volume printing, a laser printer usually has a lower cost per page than ink jets.

FOR EXAMPLE

Getting Ready to Print

Before a laser printer can begin printing, the controller must sense that the printer is ready to start printing: toner cartridge installed, fuser warmed to temperature, and all covers in place. Printing cannot take place until the printer is in its ready state, usually indicated by an illuminated Ready LED light or a display that says something like 00 READY (on HP printers).

10.1.4 Other Types of Printers

Besides the dot matrix, inkjet, and laser printer, other printer types are:

▲ **Solid ink:** The inks used by a **solid ink printer** are like large rectangular coloring crayons that are inserted into individual "tanks" on the printer. The process that prints an image on a solid ink printer is similar to that used in the laser printer process. The solid ink blocks are melted by the print head onto the print drum and after the image is formed, paper is passed over the print drum, and the image is transferred to the paper. Because the inks are transferred first to the drum and then to the paper, the printer is able to achieve a high degree of registration.

▲ **Thermal:** A **thermal printer** uses specially treated paper that changes color in reaction to the heat of the print head. There are both monochrome (gray) and color thermal printers:

• **Monochrome thermal printers:** Monochrome thermal paper is chemically treated to darken when heat is applied.

• **Color thermal printers:** Color thermal printers are very high quality and very quiet. Similar to monochrome thermal printing, these printers use a fairly expensive, chemically treated paper that reacts to absorb color from a color ribbon when heated. As the paper passes through the printing mechanism, it is pressed against a multi-colored ribbon that has banks of cyan, magenta, yellow, and black (CMYK). As heat is applied, small dots of the dyes on the ribbon are pressed onto the paper, a variation of the solid ink printing process. However, only one color is applied at a time and the paper makes additional passes through the printer for other colors to be applied.

▲ **Dye sublimation:** A **dye sublimation printer** produces photo-processing-lab quality prints. The dye part of this process is on rolls of transparent film with red (magenta), blue (cyan), yellow, and gray (black) dyes embedded in the film. The printer head is heated and then passed over the film, causing the dyes to vaporize and permeate the glossy face of the special print paper and turn back to solids. Dye sublimation printing is done in smooth forms of color, not pixels. Similar to other printer types, heat is an important part of the printing process. (Technically, both dye sublimation and solid ink printers use a form of thermal (heat) process to create images.)

▲ **Multifunction printers (MFPs):** An **MFP** is a printer with additional functions such as scanning or faxing. Some printers are available with add-on components to add functionality.

SELF-CHECK

1. How does a dot-matrix printer print?
2. Name two types of inkjet printers and describe how they are different.
3. What are the three main types of laser printing processes?
4. What is the laser in a laser printer used for?

10.2 Working with Printers

Printers use an I/O interface to connect to a PC. After connected, they communicate with the PC through driver software that utilizes special printer languages to translate data from the PC into commands the printer uses. Printers are complex devices with many mechanical parts, and need regular cleaning and maintenance to ensure that they perform properly. Other important aspects of working with printers include understanding the supplies they use and how a printer can be upgraded by replacing or adding printer components.

10.2.1 Printer Interfaces

A **printer interface** is the collection of hardware and software that allows the printer to communicate with a computer. The hardware component of an interface is its port and related cables. The **printer interface software** includes the printer's driver and the driver's use of a **page description language** (PDL), which translates the data sent from an application into printer-ready commands.

The interface hardware and software standard must be matched on both the printer and the computer. For example, an HP LaserJet 4L has only a parallel port. Therefore, you must use a parallel cable as well as the correct software for the platform being used (for example, a Windows XP HP LaserJet 4L driver if you connect it to a computer running Windows XP).

Printer Interface Hardware

Each printer has at least one interface, but some printers have several, to make them more flexible in a multiplatform environment. If a printer has several interfaces, it can usually switch between them on the fly so that several computers can print at the same time. Popular hardware interfaces for printers include:

▲ **Parallel:** When a printer uses parallel communication, it is receiving data eight bits at a time over eight separate wires (one for each bit). Parallel communication was the most popular way of communicating from computer to printer for many years, mainly because it's faster than serial. A parallel cable consists of a male DB-25 connector that connects to the computer and a male 36-pin Centronics connector that connects to the printer. Most of the cables are less than 10 feet long. Parallel cables should be IEEE 1284-compliant. Older serial printers may require that you use the parallel port in a slower SPP mode (refer to Chapter 9); most PCs shipping today with a parallel port have the parallel port configured to use the higher, bidirectional ECP mode.

▲ **USB:** Currently, the most popular type of printer interface USB. USB is convenient for printers in that it has a higher transfer rate than parallel and it automatically recognizes new devices.

▲ **Network:** Some printers (primarily laser and LED printers) have a special interface that allows them to be hooked directly to a network. These printers have a network interface card (NIC) and ROM-based software that allow them to communicate with networks, servers, and workstations. The type of network interface used on the printer depends on the type of network to which the printer is being attached. For example, if you're using a Token Ring network, the printer should have a Token Ring interface.

▲ **SCSI:** Only a few types of printers use SCSI interfaces to the PC, and most of them are high-end laser printers, dye-sublimation printers, or typesetters used in professional or industrial applications. When these printers were introduced, they all came with an option for a SCSI interface. At the time, SCSI was a preferred interface because it had relatively large throughput compared to other interfaces of the time. Because of the advent of higher-speed peripheral connection methods, such as IEEE 1394/FireWire and USB 2.0, SCSI interfaces for printers are rapidly becoming obsolete.

▲ **IEEE 1394/FireWire:** The IEEE 1394/Firewire interface has recently become very popular. This high-speed serial interface currently supports devices with a maximum throughput of 800MBps, and professional-grade printers used for tasks such as graphics and typesetting that need to receive hundreds of megabytes of camera-ready art and graphics have IEEE 1394 ports.

▲ **Wireless:** The latest boom in printer interface technology is wireless. Some printers either have built-in 802.11 interfaces or are hooked to 802.11 bridges with their built-in network cards. There are also Bluetooth-enabled printers and IR-enabled printers that allow people with PDAs or laptops with Bluetooth or IR transmission to print to them without a wired connection, as long as they are within range of the printer.

The most common interfaces for printers today are USB and parallel. Although parallel is a legacy interface being replaced by faster interfaces like USB, there are still many parallel printers in use.

Printer Interface Software

Printer interface software translates software commands into commands the printer can understand. Interface software includes the printer language and the driver software. The driver software understands and controls the printer, and uses a printer language to work with the printer. One type of printer language is a page-description language (PDL), which describes the whole page being printed by sending commands that describe the text as well as the margins and other settings. The controller in the printer interprets these commands and turns them into laser pulses (or pin strikes). Common PDLs include:

▲ PostScript, developed by Adobe.
▲ Printer Control Language (PCL), developed by Hewlett-Packard for its LaserJet series of printers.
▲ Windows GDI printers use the Windows operating system's GDI (graphical device interface). In general, the Windows GDI describes the page to be printed essentially as a large bitmap, rather than a series of commands.

Page description languages move some of the processing from the computer to the printer, whereas the Windows GDI processing occurs on the PC's side.

The driver software controls how the printer processes the print job. When you install a printer driver for the printer you are using, it allows the computer to print to that printer correctly. When you need to print, you select the printer driver for your printer from a preconfigured list. The driver you select has been configured for the type, brand, and model of printer as well as the computer port to which it is connected. Each printer driver is also configured to use a particular printer language. If the wrong printer driver is selected, the computer will send commands in the wrong language and the printer will print garbled output: typically printer language commands print literally as text instead of being interpreted as control commands.

10.2.2 Installing a Printer

Windows 9x operating systems handle printing differently from the newer Windows operating systems. Windows 9x printing defines three components: the printer, the print driver, and the print spooler. The print driver and print spooler are both software elements. A print spooler allows print jobs to be stored in a buffer area (typically on a hard drive as a temporary file) as a **print spool** and be printed in sequence, in a queue. Windows 2000 and XP define two main components: the print device (the actual printer), and the printer, which is actually the software (printer driver and spooler) that controls the print device. Regardless of the Windows operating system that you are using, from a user standpoint, you install two elements: the printer hardware and the printer software (the driver and other control software).

The general steps for installing a printer are as follows:

1. **Prepare the printer for use.** Set the printer up according to the printer manual, and install any toner cartridges and appropriate paper for the printer. If you are working with a laser printer, connect the printer to a power source, turn it on, and print a self-test (before connecting to a computer). A self-test is an embedded diagnostic test embedded in the laser printer. The self-test will confirm that the printer is working, independently of any PC interface. Depending on the printer, you initiate the self-test either through a button on the printer or through its display panel.

2. **Connect the printer to the PC.** If the printer is not hot-swappable, you will need to power the printer off before connecting its cable to the PC. Additionally, if you are using a USB you will typically need to install the printer's setup software on the PC first. Make sure to read the manufacturer's manual for any special setup steps.

3. **Finalize printer setup.** Windows should recognize the printer automatically, as most printers today are Plug-and-Play, and guide you through the printer setup process. If Windows does not recognize the printer, use the Add Printer Wizard. In Windows XP, you can access this through Control Panel's Printers and Faxes applet. Depending on the printer, the setup process may include steps for calibrating the printer. A calibration routine will guide you through printing out sample pages that test and confirm the output is properly aligned and so forth.

4. **Configure printer options.** You configure a printer's settings through the printer's Properties dialog box (in Windows XP, you can access this through the Control Panel's Printers and Faxes applet). Printer configuration options include printing defaults for elements such as page layout, printer maintenance, color management and sharing.

5. **Print a test page.** The final step in confirming that a new printer is working properly is to print a test page to test the output of the printer. To do this in Windows, click the Print Test Page button on the General tab of the printer's Properties dialog box (Figure 10-9). This will send a test page to the printer. If the page prints, your printer is working.

Connecting a Printer to a Network

You can connect a printer to a network through one of two ways:

▲ **Share a printer on the LAN.** A printer that is connected to a networked PC can be shared over the network. After printer sharing is enabled on the PC, anyone on the network can print to it (as long as the PC is running).

▲ **Print server device.** A print server device is a network-ready device with several ports (typically USB ports) for connecting non-network-ready

Figure 10-9

Printer's Properties dialog box.

printers. This allows printers connected to the device to be accessed by other PCs on the network.

▲ **Direct network connection.** To connect a printer directly to a network (without connecting it to a PC), you will need a network-ready printer. A network-ready printer has a network interface card (NIC); and the printer is cabled directly to cables running the network. A printer with a wireless NIC will need to be positioned within range of a wireless network access point.

10.2.3 Upgrading Printer Components

Most printers (especially laser printers) can be upgraded with different capabilities to add functions or to increase the printing capacity of a printer. Each manufacturer includes a list of all the accessories, options, and upgrades available for that printer with the printer documentation. Some of these options include:

▲ **Memory:** Most laser printers have built-in RAM memory (usually 8MB or more). Adding RAM or expanding the memory on a laser printer improves its ability to process large image files sent to it and allows the PC's CPU to be freed sooner in the print transfer and go on about its business. Most manufacturers of mid- to high-end laser printers have optional memory upgrades available for their printers. For the most part, printer memory is specific to the make and model of printer being upgraded. You can check with the manufacturer of the printer to see what kind of memory it takes and how best to upgrade it. The procedures are slightly different for each make and model of printer.

▲ **Hard drives:** Many printer manufacturers offer an optional hard disk drive that can be installed inside the printer, or through a PC card slot on the printer. A printer hard drive is used to store fonts (a **font** is software that describes the style of printed characters) and the print queue. This frees the PC's system hard drive and reduces the transfer time between the PC and the printer. A font stored on the printer is called a **printer-resident font.** Fonts that reside on a PC and are sent only to the printer when required are called **soft fonts.**

▲ **NICs:** Some printers can be equipped with a NIC, which must usually be made by the printer's manufacturer. The NIC in a printer has a small processor on it to manage the NIC interface (functions that the software on a PC would do). Some printer NICs have embedded web servers installed that allow clients to check their print jobs' status as well as toner levels from any computer on the network.

▲ **Trays and feeders:** Some printers can accommodate larger paper trays, or multiple paper trays, that can be loaded with different types of paper, stationery, and envelopes. Special feeders are designed to manage more difficult types of print media, such as envelope feeders.

▲ **Finishers:** A printer finisher is used for folding, stapling, hole punching, sorting, or collating the sets of documents being printed. This particular option, although not inexpensive, is becoming more popular on laser printers to turn them into MFPs.

▲ **Firmware:** Printer firmware is the manufacturer's printer software stored in ROM or Flash memory chips. It is often upgradeable, by either replacing the chip or downloading and installing or flashing new firmware.

10.2.4 Printer Supplies

Just as it is important to use the correct printer interface and printer software, you must use the correct printer supplies. The quality of the final print job has a great deal to do with the print supplies. These supplies include:

▲ **Print media:** The **print media** is what you put through the printer to print on. Print media includes:

• **Paper:** Printers are designed to work with specific types of paper. For example, if the wrong paper is used, it can cause the paper to jam frequently and possibly even damage components. If the paper is too

---

FOR EXAMPLE

Ink Cartridge Refill Kits

Ink cartridge refill kits (advertised with a syringe and a needle) have several problems. The kits don't use the same kind of ink that was originally in the ink cartridges. The new ink may be thinner, causing the ink to run out or not print properly. And some inkjet printers are designed for the printhead to be replaced at the same time the ink is. Finally, the hole the syringe leaves cannot be plugged and may allow ink to leak out. A refilled cartridge may also void the printer's warranty. Although the printer manufacturer's cartridges may be more expensive, you will save money in the long run by avoiding ink-cartridge related problems.

---

thick, it may jam in feed mechanisms. A paper that is too thin may not feed at all. Paper characteristics include its composition (what it is made of), weight, and caliper (thickness). The weight of a type of paper is described as the weight in pounds (lb) of 500 sheets of the standard size of that paper. For best results with any printer, buy the paper that has been designated specifically for that printer by the manufacturer.

- **Transparencies:** Transparencies are transparent sheets used for presentations made with overhead projectors. They are difficult for printers to work with, and different brands or models of printers specify the type of transparencies it can work with. For example, if you use the wrong type of transparency with a laser printer, it may melt and wrap around the fuser.

▲ **Print consumables:** A **print consumable** is a printer component that needs to be replaced on a regular basis, primarily ink and toner supplies, such as dot matrix printer ribbons, and inkjet cartridges, and toner cartridges. You should always purchase the brand or type of consumable made specifically for or recommended for the type of printer you have.

10.2.5 Printer Maintenance

Regular preventive maintenance and proper care of a printer extends its life. To keep a printer working and reliable:

▲ **Protect the power source:** Plug the printer into a surge protector or UPS (uninterruptible power supply). Never plug a laser printer into a conventional PC UPS. Laser printers draw a lot of power at startup, and few UPS units have enough power to handle the demand. If you use a UPS for a laser printer, be sure the UPS can handle the peak loading (peak power requirements) of the laser printer.

▲ **Use the right type of paper:** Always use the type and weight of paper recommended for the printer to avoid print feed path jams. Some printers prefer laser paper that is finished on one side. Determine the heaviest paper recommended for the printer and never use anything heavier than that to avoid paper jams and damage to the paper-handling mechanism of the printer.

▲ **Clean the printer regularly and maintain the paper transport:** The printer documentation will specify the best cleaning methods and supplies.

Dot Matrix Printers

To properly maintain a dot matrix printer:

▲ **Clean and vacuum.** Manufacturers typically recommend cleaning the ribbon path every six months to remove ink buildup; and you should occasionally vacuum out paper particles that accumulate inside the printer.

▲ **Maintain the drive belt.** Drive belts can loosen over heavy usage; consult the printer's manual to for instructions on adjusting belt tension.

▲ **Avoid heat buildup:** Excessive heat can damage the printhead, so you should make sure the printer has plenty of airflow around it.

Inkjet Printers

To properly maintain an inkjet printer:

▲ **Clean the printheads.** Inkjet nozzles can become clogged by dried ink if they are not used regularly. To unclog the nozzles, use the printer's head-cleaning utility, which you access through the printer's Properties dialog box (Figure 10-10), or sometimes through buttons on the printer. After the head-cleaning test, run a nozzle test (also typically available on the Properties dialog box). This prints out patterns or blocks of color so that you can see if there are any overly light portions, indicating that ink is not coming through one or more nozzles. You may have to run the head-cleaning several times before all the nozzles are cleared.

▲ **Align the printheads:** When you install a new ink cartridge, most printers automatically realign the printhead; however, you may need to do this manually; which you can usually initiate through the Properties dialog box or buttons on the printer. Printhead alignment is the process by which the printhead is calibrated for use. A special utility that comes with the printer software is used to do this. You run the alignment utility, and the printer prints several vertical and horizontal lines with num-

Figure 10-10

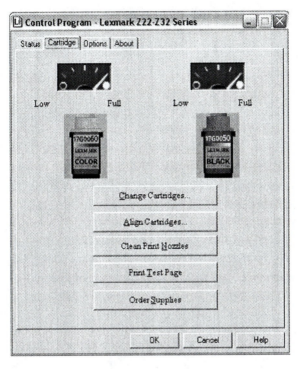

Inkjet printer utilities.

bers next to them. It then shows you a screen and asks you to choose the horizontal and vertical lines that are the most "in line." After you enter the numbers, the software understands whether the printhead(s) are out of alignment, which direction, and by how much. The software then makes slight modifications to the print driver software to tell it how much to offset when printing. Sometimes alignment must be done several times to get the images to align properly.

Laser Printers

Laser printers have their own special needs when it comes to maintenance.

▲ **Run the printer cleaning utility regularly:** When you change the toner in a laser printer, run the printer's self-cleaning routine, if available. This typically involves sending a page (printed with a large black rectangle) back through the printer. This reheats the printed page, making it slightly sticky so that it will pick up any stray particles of toner or paper along the paper transport.

▲ **Clean the corona wire:** Usually packed with the toner cartridges (of printers that use corona wires) is a cleaning brush that you can use to clean the transfer and primary corona wires. You can also use a cotton swab and rubbing alcohol, but make sure before cleaning a corona wire to check the manufacturer's instructions for the correct procedure, if any (some printers are designed without access to the corona wire).

▲ **Replace the ozone filter:** During the print process, laser printers that use corona wires, as opposed to rollers, produce a gas called ozone. Machine components can deteriorate in the presence of ozone. These printers have an ozone filter that also captures toner and paper dust. Replace or clean this filter as per the manufacturer's documentation.

▲ **Clean the mirrors:** Inside the laser printer are at least two mirrors that reflect the laser onto the drum. Using a clean, lint-free cloth, periodically clean the laser mirrors—with the power off, of course. Although most printers will not power up with the cover open, never look directly at the laser and never operate the printer with its cover off.

▲ **Clean the fuser cleaning pad and roller:** The fuser cleaning pad and the fusing roller can also become dirty and leave unwanted toner particles on the paper. Check these printer parts regularly and clean them as necessary.

▲ **Clean spilled toner:** If you ever have a toner spillage accident or see toner spilled inside the laser printer, don't use a regular vacuum to clean it up. Toner is fine particles of iron and plastic. The particles are so fine that they seep through the walls of most vacuum bags and get into the motor, where the plastic particles melt. Very few PC vacuums can be used to clean a laser printer. Special types of vacuums and vacuum cleaner bags are made for working with toner. If you get toner on your skin, never use warm or hot water to clean it off. Warm water may cause the toner to fuse to your skin. First wipe off as much of the toner with a dry paper towel or soft cloth, rinse with cold water, and finish by washing with soap and cold water.

▲ **Ventilation:** Make sure that the laser printer has plenty of airflow around it: Excessive heat can damage heat-sensitive, internal components.

▲ **Upgrade firmware:** This process is somewhat unique to each manufacturer, but in general it involves downloading a compressed or self-extracting file and running the utility with the printer online.

▲ **Toner cartridge care:** Because the photosensitive drum is very sensitive to white light, keep the toner cartridge away from strong light. Also, never ship a printer anywhere with a toner cartridge installed! If the printer is a laser printer, remove the toner cartridge first. If it's an LED page printer, there is a method to remove the photosensitive drum and toner hopper (check your manual for details).

10.3 Troubleshooting Printers

In addition to being the most popular peripheral purchased for PCs today the printer is also the most complex peripheral, as far as troubleshooting is concerned. Some troubleshooting steps will apply to all printers, although different types of printers (dot-matrix, ink jet, or laser) will have problems specific to them.

10.3.1 General Printer Troubleshooting

Printers can experience similar problems to other peripherals, such as a failed or incompatible interface, corrupt or out-of-date driver, and resource conflicts. If your printer is not printing, the first thing to check of course is that it is powered and online. In addition to the problems that may face any I/O device, other issues common to printers include:

▲ **Paper problems:** Make sure that the printer has paper and that the feed tray, roller, or slide is in its proper position for operation. If you find a paper jam, clear it, but also notice the point at which the jam occurred and check the rollers and paper feed mechanism carefully. Most paper jams happen in the paper pickup area, so look there first.

▲ **Printer selection:** Make sure that the correct printer is selected in the Print dialog box.

▲ **Low disk space:** If your hard drive is full, it may not have enough space for Windows to print. Windows uses free hard drive space to temporarily store print jobs.

▲ **Network queue problems:** A networked printer that receives simultaneous requests for printing from different users will queue the jobs, and sometimes a print queue will jam; you can review and clear the queue in the print server software and retry printing the document.

▲ **Software problems and conflicts:** Printers can stall because of a problem with software: If the printer status shows no problems and you can't find any other problem, try restarting the system.

Beyond a printer not printing, the most common failure is a bad print image. Regularly cleaning the printer and its printing mechanism or printhead as directed by the printer's manuals helps to avoid this problem.

10.3.2 Dot-Matrix Printer Problems

Some of the most common dot matrix problems are:

▲ **Low print quality:** Problems with print quality are easy to identify. When the printed page comes out of the printer, the characters are too light or have dots missing from them. Table 10-1 details some of the most common print quality problems, their causes, and their solutions.

Table 10-1: Common Dot-Matrix Print Quality Problems

Characteristics	Cause	Solution
Consistently faded or light characters	Worn-out printer ribbon	Replace the ribbon with a new, vendor-recommended ribbon.
Print lines that go from dark to light as the printhead moves across the page	Printer ribbon-advance gear slipping	Replace the ribbon-advance gear or mechanism.
A small, blank line running through a line of print (consistently)	Printhead pin stuck inside the printhead.	Replace the printhead.
A small, blank line running through a line of print (intermittently)	A broken, loose, or shorting printhead cable	Secure or replace the printhead cable.
A small, dark line running through a line of print	Printhead pin stuck in the out position	Replace the printhead. (Pushing the pin in may damage the printhead.)
Printer makes a printing noise, but no print appears on the page	Worn, missing, or improperly installed ribbon cartridge	Replace the ribbon cartridge correctly.
Printer prints garbage	Cable partially unhooked, wrong driver selected, or bad printer control board (PCB)	Hook up the cable correctly, select the correct driver, or replace the PCB (respectively).
Print appears "wavy" or out of alignment	Printhead not aligned	Use alignment procedure from owners manual to calibrate printing.

▲ **Paper jams:** Paper jams occur for two major reasons: an obstructed paper path, and stripped drive gears. Obstructed paper paths are often difficult to find. Usually it means disassembling the printer to find the bit of crumpled-up paper or other foreign substance that's blocking the paper path. A common obstruction is a piece of the *perf*—the perforated sides of tractor-feed paper—that has torn off and gotten crumpled up and then lodged in the paper path. It may be necessary to remove the platen roller and feed mechanism to get at the obstruction.

▲ **Stepper motor problems:** Stepper motors move the printhead back and forth as well as advance the paper (these are the carriage motor and main motor, respectively). These motors get damaged when they are forced in any direction while the power is on, and are also very sensitive to stray voltages. Damage to a stepper motor will cause it to lose precision and move farther with each step. Lines of print will be unevenly spaced if the main motor is damaged, and characters will be squeezed together if the carriage motor goes bad. If the motor is bad enough, it won't move at all in any direction; it may even make high-pitched squealing noises. If any of these symptoms show themselves, you will need to replace a motor. Stepper motors are usually expensive to replace—about half the cost of a new printer.

10.3.3 Inkjet Printer Problems

The majority of inkjet printer problems are quality problems, most of which can be traced to a faulty ink cartridge and solved by replacing the cartridge. Common inkjet problems include:

▲ **Streaked or patchy printing:** This can occur because of low ink levels for one or more colors. You can usually check an inkjet printer's ink levels in the Properties dialog box; or for some printers, in an LED display on the printer.

▲ **Thin stripes or blank areas on the page:** This typically indicates a clogged nozzle.

▲ **Garbage output:** A document printing garbage, garbled output, prints strings of meaningless characters. This may happen when a printer driver is corrupted, but more commonly when print job is interrupted, for example, by a power loss or software crash. This interruption can prevent the print job information header being sent to the printer. When the printer resumes, it prints out the command codes for the print job instead of using the command codes to manage the print job.

▲ **Smeared images:** If an ink cartridge becomes damaged or develops a hole, it can put too much ink on the page and the letters will smear. The solution is to replace the ink cartridge. (A very small amount of smearing is normal if the pages are laid on top of each other immediately after printing.)

▲ **Print goes from dark to light and then prints nothing:** One print quality problem that does not directly involve the ink cartridge occurs when the print goes from dark to light quickly and then prints nothing. Manufacturers include a small suction pump inside the printer that primes the ink cartridge before each print cycle. If this priming pump is broken or malfunctioning, this problem will manifest itself and the pump will need to be replaced.

▲ **Paper jams:** Although inkjet printers have a simpler paper path than laser printers, and suffer fewer paper jams, they can still occur. Paper jams in bubble-jet printers are usually due to one of two things: a worn pickup roller, or the wrong type of paper.

10.3.4 Laser Printer Problems

Laser printer problems are the most complex of the three main printer types because the printer is the most complex. However, most problems are easily identifiable and have specific fixes. Common laser and page printer problems and their solutions include:

▲ **Paper jams:** Paper can get jammed in a printer for several reasons.

- **Worn paper transport rollers:** Check to see where the jam is occurring to determine which rollers are worn. Most paper jams occur in the paper pickup area. Replace the worn rollers. If an exit roller is the problem, you must replace all exit rollers because even one worn exit roller can cause the paper to jam. Additionally, the drive gear of a pickup roller may be broken or have teeth missing. (Print a test page without paper and look into the paper-feed opening with a flashlight to see if the paper pickup roller(s) are turning evenly and don't skip.) Never put anything inside a laser printer while it's running, and always wait until the fusing area has cooled down before working in this area of a laser printer. (It generates a lot of heat to melt the toner to the paper and stays hot for some time afterward.)

- **High humidity:** If your printer consistently tries to feed multiple pages into the printer, the paper isn't dry enough. The best all-around solution, however, is humidity control and to keep the paper wrapped until it's needed.

- **Static eliminator strip:** A metal, grounded strip called the static eliminator strip inside the printer drains the corona charge away from the paper after it has been used to transfer toner from the cartridge. If that strip is missing, broken, or damaged, the charge will remain on the paper and may cause it to stick to or curl around the photosensitive drum, thus causing a jam.

▲ **Blank pages:** Blank pages are printed when the toner isn't being put on the paper. There are three major causes:

- **Toner cartridge:** There may be no toner in the cartridge, or a refilled or reconditioned toner cartridge may be filled with the wrong kind of toner (for example, one with an incorrect charge). This can cause toner to be repelled from the drum instead of attracted to it. Also, toner is prevented from escaping during shipping by a sealing tape: make sure that this was removed.

- **Corona assembly:** A missing or damaged transfer corona wire or roller prevents the developed image transferring from the drum to the paper and should be replaced.

- **High-Voltage Power Supply (HVPS):** A failed HVPS will prevent both the primary and transfer corona from working.

▲ **All-black pages:** When the primary corona in the toner cartridge malfunctions, it fails to place a charge on the drum and all the toner will stick to it. The solution is to replace the toner cartridge. If that doesn't solve the problem, the HVPS is at fault, meaning that it's not providing the high voltage that the charging corona needs to function.

▲ **Repetitive small marks or defects:** Repetitive marks may be caused by toner spilled inside the printer, or a crack or chip in the drum that accumulates toner. The extra toner gets stuck onto a roller and leaves toner smudges spaced a roller circumference apart. To help you figure out which roller is causing the problem, the service manuals for a printer contain a roller circumference chart (Figure 10-11). You align your smudged paper to this to determine which roller is the problem. Different models of printers will have different-sized rollers and different charts.

▲ **Vertical black lines on the page:** This can be caused by a groove or scratch in the drum (solved by replacing the toner cartridge), or by a dirty primary corona. You will need to replace the toner cartridge.

▲ **Vertical white streaks on the page:** Vertical white streaks running down all or part of the page are caused by foreign matter (likely toner) caught on the transfer corona. The dirty spots keep the toner from being transmitted to the paper.

▲ **Image smudging:** If the ink on a printed page smears when you touch it, you have a fuser problem. The fuser isn't heating the toner and fusing it into the paper. The whole fuser may not need to be replaced. Fuser components, such as a lamp, can be ordered from parts suppliers.

▲ **Repetitive smudging:** Dents or cold spots in the fuser heat roller cause small, repetitive smudged areas down the page. The only solution is to replace either the fuser assembly or the heat roller.

Figure 10-11

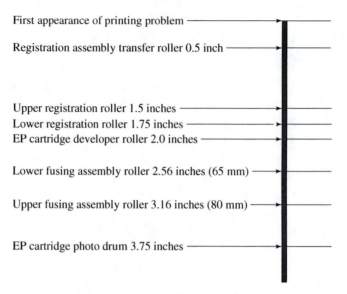

Laser printer roller circumference chart.

▲ **Ghosting:** Ghosting is the appearance of light images of previously printed pages on the current page. This is caused by one of two things: bad eraser lamps (or the charged drum used for erasing) or a broken cleaning blade. Replacing the toner cartridge solves the second problem. Solving the first problem involves replacing the eraser lamps or charged drum.

▲ **Garbage output:** This problem comes from one of two different sources: the printer's driver, as with inkjets, or the formatter board. The **formatter board** is a circuit board in the printer that turns data from the PC into commands for the various components in the printer, and typically includes the printer interface. Usually, problems with the formatter board produce wavy lines of print or random patterns of dots on the page. You can replace a failed formatter board.

▲ **Memory overflow error:** A printer that experiences frequent memory overflow errors has a bad memory board, a memory board that was installed incorrectly, or a memory board that needs additional memory.

Other tools to help in troubleshooting laser printers include:

▲ **Printer resets:** Laser printers can be reset to clear system information such as downloaded fonts; and resetting a printer can help solve software

FOR EXAMPLE

HP LaserJet Self-Tests

Two self-tests common to HP LaserJets are the engine self-test and the engine half self-test. The engine self-test tests the print engine of the LaserJet, bypassing the formatter board. This test causes the printer to print a single page with vertical lines running its length. A print engine half self-test is performed the same way as the self-test, but you interrupt it halfway through the print cycle by opening the cover. This test is useful in determining which part of the print process is causing the printer to malfunction.

problems. There may be different levels of resets for a particular printer, so check the printer documentation to find out how to initiate these, and what they do.

▲ **Error messages:** Manufacturers use different error codes that signify various causes; these should be documented in the user manual or at the manufacturer's website.

▲ **Self-tests:** Most laser printers have at least one self-test routine programmed that perform internal diagnostics. These programs can be initiated through buttons or the printer display without being attached to a PC. They can help determine if the laser print engine is functioning correctly and help determine at which point the printing process is having problems. You will have to check the printer documentation to determine what self-tests it runs and how to perform them.

▲ **Manufacturer's troubleshooting guides:** Many manufacturers have troubleshooting steps to perform for your particular model, either in the printer documentation or at their website. The manufacturer may also provide a diagnostic utility for your printer that you can download.

SELF-CHECK

1. List at least seven types of problems that can occur with a printer.
2. How will a stepper motor problem affect a dot-matrix printer?
3. What are the most common inkjet problems, and how are they resolved?
4. What causes a laser printer to print blank pages?

SUMMARY

Printers may be impact or non-impact, line- or page-printers. There are three main types of printers used in the home and businesses: dot-matrix, inkjet, and laser printers. Printers are compared by their print quality, usually measured in DPI, and print speeds, measured in CPS or PPM. Key components of a dot-matrix printer include the printhead, printwires, printer ribbon, and a paper-feed mechanism such as form tractors. Inkjet printer components include the print-head/ink carriage with spray nozzles, stepper motors, carriage belt, a paper feed mechanism, and control, interface, and power circuitry. Laser printer components include the toner cartridge, photosensitive drum, laser scanning assembly, HVPS, paper transport assembly, primary corona, transfer corona, fusing rollers, and interface controller. Laser printers typically include a formatter board and onboard memory and firmware. Other types of printers include the solid ink printer, thermal printers, and dye-sublimation printers.

Printers connect typically through a USB or legacy parallel port, and can be connected to a network through a NIC on the printer or through a network printer interface device. The PC communicates to the printer through its printer driver and printer language, such as a page description language. Printers are installed much the same as other I/O devices and different manufacturers have special procedures for installing printer software. Printers can be upgraded by adding or upgrading various printer components, such as memory, hard drives, NICS, trays and feeders, finishers, and firmware. Printer supplies consist of print media (paper and transparencies) and consumables, such as printer ribbons, ink cartridges, and toner cartridges.

Printers need regular maintenance and cleaning for optimal functioning and to maintain print quality. Aspects of maintenance include protecting the power source, ventilation, proper paper type and weight, cleaning, maintaining the paper transport system, and upgrading firmware. Best practices differ for each type of printer.

Dot-matrix, ink-jet, and laser printers suffer from different types of problems. General types of printing problems include print quality problems, interface and hardware problems, driver and configuration problems, network and software problems, and device-specific problems. To help in troubleshooting, laser printers often have diagnostic routines, such as the self-test and other tools to help diagnose a problem.

KEY TERMS

Carriage belt	DC power supply (DCPS)
CMYK	Dot-matrix printer
Daisy-wheel printer	Dots per inch (dpi)

Dye sublimation printer

Finisher

Font

Form tractors

Formatter board

Fusing rollers

High-voltage power supply (HVPS)

Impact printer

Interface controller

Laser printer

Laser scanning assembly

LED printer

Letter quality (LQ)

Line printer

MFP (multifunction printer)

Near letter quality (NLQ)

Page description language (PDL)

Page printer

Photosensitive drum

Piezoelectric inkjet printer

Platen

Primary corona

Print consumable

Print media

Print spool

Printer

Printer emulation

Printer interface

Printer interface software

Printer resident font

Printer ribbon

Printhead

Printhead carriage

Printwire

Self-test

Soft font

Solid ink printer

Stepper motor

Test page

Thermal inkjet printer

Thermal printer

Toner

Toner cartridge

Transfer corona

ASSESS YOUR UNDERSTANDING

Go to www.wiley.com/college/groth to evaluate your knowledge of printers. *Measure your learning by comparing pre-test and post-test results.*

Summary Questions

1. Which type of printers can be used with multipart forms?
   (a) bubble-jet printer
   (b) EP process laser printer
   (c) HP process laser printer
   (d) daisy-wheel printer

2. What is the highest quality print a dot-matrix printer with a 24-pin printhead is capable of?
   (a) draft quality
   (b) near-letter quality
   (c) letter-quality
   (d) perfect quality

3. Dot-matrix print speeds are measured in:
   (a) CPS
   (b) CPM
   (c) PPS
   (d) PPM

4. The inkjet printer's circuitry contains onboard print buffer memory. True or false?

5. Which component allows an inkjet printhead to move in small, incremental steps during printing?
   (a) carriage belt
   (b) stabilizer bar
   (c) precision motor
   (d) stepper motor

6. What are the main color inks used in color printing?
   (a) cyan, magenta, yellow
   (b) cyan, magenta, yellow, and black
   (c) red, green, blue
   (d) red, green, blue, and black

7. Inkjet speeds range from:
   (a) 2 PPM to 20 PPM and higher
   (b) 100 CPS to 500 CPS and higher

(c) 20 PPM and higher

(d) 500 CPS and higher

8. What happens in the conditioning phase of a laser printer?

(a) The image is created on the drum.

(b) The erasure lamps neutralize the drum.

(c) The primary corona applies a uniform charge to the drum.

(d) The paper is charged by the transfer corona.

9. Reducing the negative charge on the areas of the drum that represent the image to be printed is done in which step of the laser printing process?

(a) transferring

(b) conditioning

(c) fusing

(d) writing

10. The toner is deposited onto the drum surface in which step of the printing process?

(a) writing

(b) conditioning

(c) developing

(d) transferring

11. Toner is bonded with the paper during which phase of the laser printing process?

(a) writing

(b) transferring

(c) conditioning

(d) fusing

12. Which of the following forms the electrical field that charges the drum?

(a) transfer corona wire

(b) primary corona wire

(c) fusing roller

(d) cleaning blade

13. Which of the following is a page printer?

(a) daisy wheel

(b) dot matrix

(c) inkjet

(d) laser

14. What does PDL stand for?

(a) Printer Description Language

(b) Page Description Language

(c) Printer Definition Language

(d) Page Definition Language

15. If the static-eliminator strip is absent (or broken) in a laser printer, what will happen?

    (a) A dark line will print down the page.

    (b) Blank pages will print.

    (c) The paper will have repetitive smudges.

    (d) The paper will curl around the photosensitive drum.

16. In addition to a printer driver problem, what can cause a laser printer to output garbage?

    (a) faulty formatter board

    (b) multiple paper jams

    (c) missing or broken primary corona

    (d) missing or broken transfer corona

17. If a dot-matrix printer is printing text with wavy margins, what is the likely cause?

    (a) stuck printwire

    (b) wrong parallel port mode

    (c) printhead not aligned

    (d) printer ribbon dislodged

18. You should use a PC vacuum to clean toner from a laser printer. True or false?

19. Which of the following is a print consumable?

    (a) paper

    (b) transparencies

    (c) printer ribbon

    (d) all of the above

20. What is the embedded diagnostic procedure on a laser that can be performed without connecting the printer to a PC?

    (a) page test

    (b) self-test

    (c) reset procedure

    (d) cleaning utility

Applying This Chapter

1. In a small office, the printing process has been working well. Recently, however, users get an error message when they try to print. No changes

have been made to the system. After checking whether the printer is powered on, what do you check next?

2. The paper continuously jams in a laser printer. Where would you look first?

3. A friend is having problems printing with her laser printer. What tools do you suggest she use in troubleshooting?

4. A dot matrix printer in your office is printing pages with characters spaced too closely together. What is the likely cause of this?

5. A new office manager has asked for your advice and input on the paper used for the office printers. What is your advice to him?

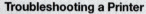

YOU TRY IT

Troubleshooting a Printer

You have just installed a dot-matrix printer to the parallel port on an office computer. It is printing, but exceptionally slowly. Outline your first troubleshooting steps.

Selecting a Printer

You are selecting a printer for your own home or home office use. Review and select a printer from a printer manufacturer, such as HP.com or Epson.com. Describe the model you are choosing in terms of its key features. What are your reasons for choosing this printer?

Working with Special Printing Needs

You are working for a small beverage distributor. The company's graphics department needs a wide-format printer capable of printing posters and other large-format materials for salespeople. Review the printers available from two manufacturers, such as HP.com and Epson.com. What factors do you think will play a role in determining what the appropriate printer is?

Planning Office Printers

You work in the IT department of a business consulting firm and have been asked to help plan the IT needs for a new branch. Your immediate job is to determine the types and numbers of printers that will be needed. How will you go about this? What type or types of printers do you think will be needed?

11
PORTABLE SYSTEMS

Starting Point

Go to www.wiley.com/college/groth to assess your knowledge of portable systems.
Determine where you need to concentrate your effort.

What You'll Learn in This Chapter

▲ Laptop components
▲ PC card and ExpressCard form factors
▲ Common laptop upgrades,
▲ Laptop maintenance and troubleshooting guidelines

After Studying This Chapter, You'll Be Able To

▲ Identify and describe laptop components
▲ Evaluate and compare different types of portable systems
▲ Select and install a PC card
▲ Maintain and manage a laptop
▲ Upgrade a laptop's hard drive or memory
▲ Manage the laptop's power options
▲ Troubleshoot laptop problems

INTRODUCTION

A **portable computer** is any computer that contains all the functionality of a desktop computer system but is portable. Early portable computers, referred to as "luggables," had a small case with a built-in screen and a handle. Today's laptops contain a built-in keyboard, pointing device, and LCD screen in a clamshell design. In a clamshell design, the laptop has two halves, hinged together at the back.

In addition to portability, the primary differences between portable systems and desktops are:

▲ **Cost:** Laptops cost more in general than desktop computers with similar features. The primary reason is that portability requires smaller components and unique (proprietary) designs for those components. Miniature versions of components cost more money than standard size (desktop) versions.

▲ **Performance:** In general, portable systems have lower performance ratings, primarily because their small form factor makes heat a major consideration. CPUs and RAM used in portable devices are designed to minimize heat and tend to have lower speeds. However, advances in CPU architecture have brought laptop performance much closer to desktop performance.

▲ **Internal component upgrades:** Laptops and other portable computing devices have fewer replaceable components than desktops because their small form factor requires precision architecture. In general, the only components that can be upgraded are the hard drives and memory. You can get different brands of memory and hard drives for laptops, but you can't buy a motherboard from one company and the video circuitry from another. Even a floppy drive may be designed to work only with a specific model.

▲ **Quality of construction:** To withstand the bumps and jostles that accompany portability, the materials construction of the laptop case and other components are designed to be extremely durable. Not that this is not important in a desktop—but it is more important in a laptop.

Advances in computer architecture have led to ever smaller portable systems, from desktop replacement laptops to small handheld computing accessories, such as the Personal Digital Assistant (PDA). Four general categories distinguish laptops primarily by size and weight.

Desktop replacement laptops are the largest and heaviest laptops, range from seven to ten pounds, and are designed to handle more powerful, desktop and mobile CPUs and to compete with tower PCs in performance. They tend to be somewhat bulkier and less portable than other laptops. Standard or main-stream laptops are smaller, generally between six and eight pounds. Although laptops are commonly referred to as notebooks, this term is often applied to the next, smaller category of laptops, which range from four to six pounds and are also referred to as **thin-and-light notebooks**. **Ultraportable notebooks** weigh four pounds and less.

Tablet PCs are about the size of an ultraportable, but use a large touchscreen for input and display. The touchscreens are designed to work with handwritten input from a stylus, as opposed to keystrokes, similar to the way you use a paper notebook. A **slate tablet PC** is similar to a large touchscreen whose computing hardware is located behind the display. The **convertible tablet PC** incorporates a keyboard, typically through a hinged clamshell design. It is similar to a note-book with a flip-around screen that allows a user to hold it like a large notebook and write notes directly on the screen with a stylus. Tablet PCs use special oper-ating systems, such as Windows XP for Tablet PC.

In general, the smaller the laptop, the fewer the number of I/O ports it will feature, and the smaller its keyboard and display. Some ultraportables will not contain a DVD or CD-ROM drive. Other mobile computing devices include **handheld PCs (HPCs)** that are similar to very small laptops, with a clamshell design and a mini keyboard and LCD screen. PDAs are flat, palm-sized devices that use a touch screen as a primary inputting device and display.

Because these devices have much smaller processors, memory, and storage capabilities, they run on leaner operating systems, which may be proprietary. Many PDAs and handhelds run a Windows Mobile OS for Pocket PCs (Windows Mobile) or the Palm OS designed for Palm devices. Older PDAs may run an older version of Windows for handheld devices called Windows CE.

11.1 Examining Laptop Components

Laptops are similar to desktop computers in architecture in that they contain many parts that perform similar functions. However, the parts that make up a laptop are completely different from those in desktop computers. They are phys-ically much smaller and lighter, and they must fit into the compact space of a laptop's case (Figure 11-1).

A typical laptop case is made up of three main parts: the display (usually an LCD display), the case frame (the metal reinforcing structure inside the lap-top that provides rigidity and strength and that most components mount to), and the actual case (the plastic cover that surrounds the components and pro-vides protection from the elements). The cases are typically made of some type of plastic (usually ABS plastic or ABS composite) to provide for light weight as well as strength. A few notebooks have cases made of a strong, lightweight metal, such as aluminum or titanium.

Figure 11-1

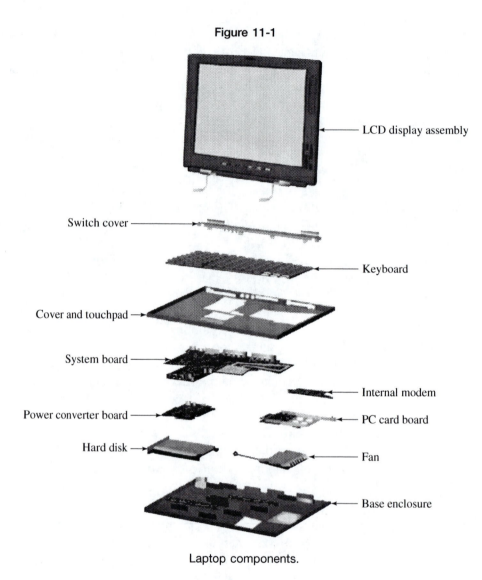

Laptop components.

Laptop cases are made in what is known as a clamshell design. Usually, the display is the top half and keyboard and system hardware in the bottom half.

Laptop parts are designed to consume less power and to shut themselves off when not being used (although many desktops have some components that go into a low-power state when not active, such as video circuitry). Finally, most laptop components are proprietary—the motherboard from one laptop will not necessarily fit on another.

11.1.1 Power Sources

Adaptable, lightweight, and long-life power sources play a large part in the usability of a portable PC system. Essentially, three general types of power sources are available for portable PCs—each designed to provide it with power either in the office or on the road:

▲ **AC adapter:** An **AC adapter** works much like the power supply in a desktop computer to convert the wall socket AC power into DC power. AC adapters are also used to recharge the portable PC's battery. The adapter either is integrated into the laptop (as on some Compaq laptops) or is a separate "brick" with a cord that plugs into the back of the laptop. Some adapters are fixed input, and connect only to and use 110VAC (for use in the U.S.) or 220VAC for use overseas. An **auto-switching adapter** can sense and convert both 110VAC and 220VAC power. You can also purchase adjustable voltage laptop adapters that can output a range of voltages. You select the voltage level on these to match the input voltage needed by your laptop, but you will need to make the adapter support the specific voltages required by your laptop. An accessory called a DC adapter allows a user to plug the laptop adapter into the power source (usually a cigarette lighter) inside a car or on an airplane. These adapters enable travelers to use their laptops while on the road (literally).

▲ **Battery:** The battery is an integral part of any portable PC because without it, the PC would not be as portable. Although very small devices, such as PDAs, may use standard AA alkaline batteries, laptops and tablets use the following types of batteries:

• **Nickel Cadmium (NiCad):** A **NiCad battery** is the most durable type of rechargeable battery. This battery is also the heaviest, yet least expensive, of the portable PC battery types. NiCad batteries can only be recharged a finite number of times (about 700 charge and discharge cycles). After a time, they develop a memory and must be recharged on a special deep-charging machine. NiCad batteries contain especially toxic metals, and have to be recycled by special disposal or recycling companies or facilities.

• **Nickel-Metal Hydride (NiMH):** Unlike NiCad batteries, **NiMH batteries** are environmentally friendly because they don't contain heavy metals that can be toxic. They also store up to 30 percent more power than NiCad batteries of the same weight. Some of the disadvantages of NiMH batteries are that they have a shorter life (around 400 charge-and-discharge cycles, less than a comparable NiCad battery) and cost about 30 percent more than NiCad batteries.

FOR EXAMPLE

Fuel Cells

Fuel cells have been talked about for some time as a potential laptop power source. A fuel cell battery produces electricity like an ordinary battery—using electrochemical reactions. The difference between the two is in the fuel cell's ability to produce electricity as long as it has a fuel source (such as methanol, aluminum, hydrogen, and other substances); an ordinary carbon battery must be recharged periodically. Fuel cell batteries don't store electricity and can't run down like an ordinary battery. Fuel cells convert fuel into electricity; ordinary carbon batteries store electricity that's provided from an external source. The primary advantages offered by fuel cells are that they have a longer life, which means they can run the portable system longer, and they don't need recharging, which could be a real cost savings in the long run. Several manufacturers have developed fuel cell prototypes for laptops, including Ultracell, NEC, and Toshiba.

- **Lithium Ion (Li-Ion or LiON):** Most laptop batteries today are lithium ion. Very lightweight with a long battery life, this type of battery is made with one of the lightest available metals (lithium). **LiON batteries** hold about twice the power of a NiCad battery in about half the weight. Compared to a NiMH battery of equal weight, a LiON delivers twice the run time from each charge and about the same life cycle as NiMH batteries.

Some batteries, called smart batteries, include circuitry that allow it to inform the laptop if it needs recharging or conditioning.

- ▲ **Docking station:** A **docking station** is a laptop peripheral that acts as an extension of the motherboard of a laptop. A docking station may contain components such as a full-size drive bay and expansion bus slots. In addition to providing a connected laptop with full-sized expansion cards and additional ports, a docking station can also provide power to a laptop.

11.1.2 Displays

Laptops normally use liquid crystal displays (LCDs), either active or passive matrix screens that are integrated into the case. These LCD displays are designed to consume less power and be more portable than other display types. A laptop's display takes the most power to run and is the device that drains the battery the fastest when the laptop is running on batteries only.

The graphics display resolution standards supported on laptops are the same as those available on desktop monitors and PCs. The primary standards supported on active displays are:

▲ **Super Video Graphics Array (SVGA):** This is an extension of the Video Graphics Array (VGA) standard that supports 1024 × 768 and higher resolutions.

▲ **Extended Graphics Array (XGA):** The standard in use today is actually XGA-2, based on the original IBM XGA standard introduced in 1990. This standard supports non-interlaced resolution of 1024 × 768 and higher.

▲ **Super Extended Graphics Array (SXGA):** This is an extension of the XGA standard that can support 1280 × 1024 with 1.3 million pixels in the display.

▲ **Ultra Extended Graphics Array (UXGA):** This is a further extension of XGA that supports a 1600 × 1200 resolution.

▲ **Widescreen UXGA:** This is a version of UXGA for widescreen displays, supporting 1920 × 1200 pixels; and a 16:10 aspect ratio.

LCD displays do not produce light, so to generate brightness, many LCD displays have a backlight—a small fluorescent lamp behind, above, or to the side of an LCD display. The light from the lamp is diffused across the screen, producing brightness. The typical laptop display uses a cold cathode fluorescent lamp (CCFL) as its backlight. These are generally about eight inches long and slimmer than a pencil, and are designed to generate little heat. However, they do require fairly high-voltage, high-frequency energy that is provided by an inverter, which is a small circuit board installed behind the LCD panel that converts (and inverts) AC power for the backlight.

Because the number of pixels in an LCD is fixed, LCD screens operate optimally at their **native resolution,** and must use interpolation to display other resolutions, which typically results in some loss of image quality. Higher quality LCD screens offer greater contrast ratios (the contrast between the darkest and lightest pixels it can display). In addition to resolution and contrast ratio, characteristics used to compare and rate LCD screens include their aspect ratio, viewing angle, luminance (how much light a display produces), and response rate.

11.1.3 Keyboards and Pointing Devices

A laptop's keyboard and pointing device are designed to fit within the design constraints of the laptop (low power and small form factor) while remaining usable. That usually means laptop keys are smaller and packed together more tightly. Laptop keyboards are built into the lower portion of the clamshell. They can sometimes be removed easily to access peripherals below them (like memory and hard drives).

FOR EXAMPLE

Dead Pixels

Active matrix displays can suffer from the phenomenon of dead pixels. These are small defects that cause a few transistors in the display to not function, and their corresponding screen pixels are completely black. Manufacturers usually consider a display to be fully operational if 99.999 percent of its pixels are operating: On a 1028×768 display, this is eight pixels. Some manufacturers indicate in their warranties that 99.99 percent is good enough: 79 pixels on a 1027×768 display. Because dead pixels are part of the manufacturing process, if you buy a laptop, you will most likely have a couple, but be aware of your laptop manufacturer's warranty policy.

Because of the much smaller space available for keys, some laptop keys (such as the number pad, Home, Insert, PgUp, and PgDn keys) are consolidated into special multifunction keys. These keys are accessed through the standard keys by using a special function key (usually labeled Fn). To use a multifunction key, or **Fn key,** you press the function key and the key that contains the function you want (for example, press <Function >? for the slash [/] normally found on a numeric keypad on a regular keyboard).

Although some early laptops used trackballs, the most common pointing devices used on laptops today are:

▲ **Touchpad:** A **touchpad** is a device that has a pad of touch-sensitive material. The user draws with their finger on the touchpad, and the on-screen pointer follows the finger motions. Included with the touchpad are two buttons for left- or right-clicking.

▲ **Track point:** The **track point,** also called a touch point or pointing stick, is a pointing device embedded in the keyboard that uses a small rubber-tipped stick (Figure 11-2). The user tilts the tip to move the screen cursor.

Some laptops incorporate several pointing devices, and most laptops today include a mouse/keyboard port and/or a USB port that can be used to add an input device such as a mouse or a standard-sized keyboard.

11.1.4 Internal Components

The internal components of a laptop include its motherboard, I/O ports, expansion buses, memory, CPUs and storage:

▲ **Motherboard:** The primary differences between a laptop motherboard (Figure 11-3) and a desktop motherboard are the lack of standards and

Figure 11-2

Track point pointing device.

the much smaller form factor. Motherboards are usually proprietary to the manufacturer. Almost all interface components are integrated onto the motherboard, including onboard circuitry for the serial, parallel, USB, IEEE 1394, video, expansion, and network ports of the laptop. Many laptops are now embedding wireless LAN chips into their motherboard, and a connector for attaching an antenna to enable the laptop to connect to wireless networks.

▲ **I/O ports:** Laptops have the same I/O interface ports found on desktop computers (serial, parallel, USB, IEEE 1394/FireWire, infrared, RF/Bluetooth, networking, and video/audio ports). The range of I/O ports on laptops depends in general on the size of the laptop, with larger desktop replacement laptops typically integrating a wider variety of ports than

Figure 11-3

Laptop motherboard.

Figure 11-4

Proprietary docking port.

ultraportables or tablet PCs, which are too thin to incorporate legacy serial or parallel ports, and typically use USB, FireWire, and PC card slots. In addition to these standard interfaces, a laptop's I/O ports may include:

- **Combination mouse/keyboard port:** Many laptops come with a combination keyboard/mouse port to connect either an external keyboard or an external mouse to the laptop. On laptops that don't have USB ports, this port is most often used for a standard PS/2 mouse. On those laptops that do have USB ports, this port is typically used for an external keypad or keyboard.

- **Docking port:** Some laptops have a proprietary docking port. A **docking port** (Figure 11-4) is used to connect the laptop to a docking station. A docking station is placed on a desktop, and you plug the laptop into it in order to use the docking station's components and ports. Docking stations may contain hard drive bays, expansion card slots, and a variety of I/O ports. You typically connect full-sized monitors and keyboards to them so that you can use your laptop as a desktop PC. Some docking stations are proprietary, made by the laptop manufacturer specifically for a laptop model, and connect through a special port on your laptop. Universal docking stations may use a USB port. Similar to a docking station, a **port replicator** is a device that allows a laptop a wider range of I/O ports for connecting peripherals that do not travel with the laptop, such as monitors and external keyboards (Figure 11-5).

▲ **Expansion Buses:** Many laptops have integrated video, audio/speakers, and networking circuitry that is not upgradeable. Some laptops use a GPU (Graphics processing unit) manufactured by a popular video adapter, such as ATI or nVidia, to supply the laptop's graph-

Figure 11-5

Port replicator.

ics processing capabilities. Other laptops produced today incorporate small-form factor versions of the PCI expansion bus. The following two primary PCI adaptations are used on systems with smaller physical sizes:

- **Compact PCI (CPCI):** This PCI adaptation is used primarily for industrial computer applications that need a smaller and more robust form factor than is used with desktop PCs. CPCI, an open standard developed and supported by the PCI Industrial Computer Manufacturer's Group (PICMG), is well suited to small, high-speed industrial applications with several high-speed card interfaces.

- **Mini-PCI:** This is a smaller version of the standard desktop PC PCI form. The mini-PCI has all the same features and functions of a standard PCI card while being only about one-fourth the size of the larger standard card. Adapters are available that allow full-sized cards to fit into the mini-PCI slot and vice versa. The mini-PCI is commonly used for internal wireless network adapters on portable PCs and hand-held devices.

Although you can theoretically replace a laptop's mini- or compact PCI card with another, this is not a typical upgrade, as the laptop PCI expansion slots may be difficult to access and doing so may void a laptop warranty. Laptops are more commonly expanded by using one or more types of PC cards: thin, credit card-sized expansion cards that fit into a compatible slot on the laptop.

Figure 11-6

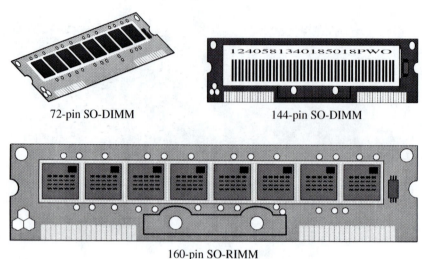

72-pin SO-DIMM   144-pin SO-DIMM

160-pin SO-RIMM

Laptop SoDIMM and SoRIMM memory modules.

▲ **Memory:** Although some laptops may use proprietary memory modules, more typically they will use DDR SDRAM or DDR2 memory in one of the three small-form factor modules:

• **SODIMM:** Small Outline DIMMS (SODIMMS) are available in both 32-bit (72-pin) and 64-bit (144-pin) configurations (Figure 11-6).

• **MicroDIMM:** Designed for ultraportable notebooks, the Micro-DIMM (Figure 11-7) is over 50 percent smaller than a SoDIMM, has 144 pins, and is similar to a DIMM in that it uses 64-bit memory modules.

• **SORIMM:** A smaller version of the RIMM, is similar to the SODIMM, except that it uses Rambus technology.

▲ **CPUs:** Laptops use CPUs designed for mobile computing. When producing a mobile version of a processor, manufacturers are primarily concerned with reducing size, power usage, and heat generation. The packaging of a mobile CPU provides much of the cooling for the processor (nonportable systems normally handle heat with fans and heat sinks) and most CPUs designed for mobile computing incorporate throttling features, which may be enabled or configured in the BIOS. Some laptop CPUs have power management features that reduce the CPU speed and voltage to conserve power. Most CPUs are directly soldered to the motherboard, although some may use the micro-FCBGA

Figure 11-7

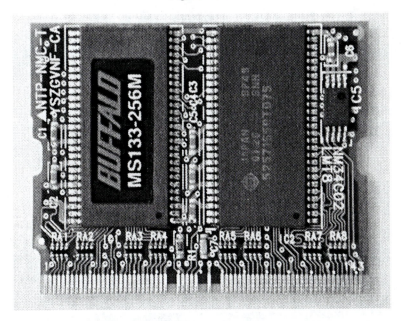

MicroDIMM memory module.

socket. Intel's Pentium family of processors includes the most popular CPUs used in laptop computers. Among these are mobile versions of its Celeron, Pentium III, and Pentium 4 processors, plus the latest Centrino mobile technology bundle, which includes the Pentium M processor. AMD is gaining in popularity among portable system manufacturers with its Athlon XP-M and XP-M Berton, Mobile Athlon 4, and Mobile Duron processors.

▲ **Storage:** Laptops typically incorporate one, and sometimes two, small 2.5 inch form factor hard drives that are less than .5 inches thick. These drives share the same interface technologies (parallel ATA/UDMA and SATA) as desktop computers (Figure 11-8). Because of space limitations, not all laptops have both a floppy drive and a CD/DVD drive. Often there is a drive bay that a user can swap in either a floppy drive or CD/DVD drive. Depending on the manufacturer, these may be hot-swappable drives, or you may need to power off the PC or disable the bus the drive bay uses before replacing the drive. In some cases, the floppy drive is an external device that you connect to either a USB port, or in some cases with a special cable through a proprietary connector developed by the laptop manufacturer. Laptop optical drives are usually are very small in

Figure 11-8

Desktop and laptop hard drives.

form factor, less than .5 inches high (Figure 11-9), but have all the functionality of a desktop unit. The drive mechanism and circuits have all been miniaturized to save space.

SELF-CHECK

1. Identify the different categories of laptops.

2. Describe three ways a laptop can be powered.

3. Describe the pointing devices that portable systems use.

4. A desktop PC uses the expansion bus and cards to expand its functionality. What do laptops use to expand functionality?

Figure 11-9

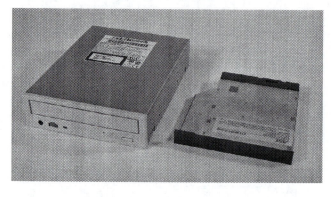

Desktop and laptop CD drives.

11.2 Understanding PC Cards

The industry group **Personal Computer Memory Card International Association (PCMCIA)** developed the PC card bus as a universal expansion bus for adding more memory and peripherals to portable computers using credit card–sized expansion cards called **PC cards** (Figure 11-10).

PC cards are used for flash memory drives, small form-factor hard drives, modems, NICs, and interface adapters for connecting peripherals. Unlike the internal expansion buses on a PC that are used for adding expansion cards, the PC card buses allow you to connect expansion devices through a slot opening in the portable's case. The first PC cards connected to the 16-bit ISA and 32-bit PCI internal expansion buses. The latest generation, ExpressCard, connects to an internal PCI express bus.

11.2.1 PC Card Form Factors and Interfaces

All PC cards are 85.6mm long and 54mm wide, or approximately 3.4 inches by 2.1 inches, and use a 68-pin connector. PC cards are matched to designated slots on the portable PC, and each is defined to one of the three types and sizes of cards (Figure 11-11).

Figure 11-10

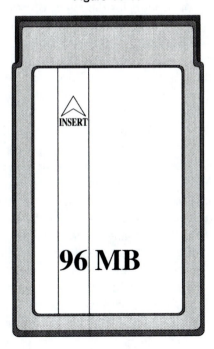

Flash memory PC card.

Figure 11-11

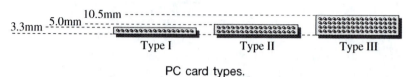

PC card types.

The three PC card form factors are:

▲ **Type I:** At 3.5mm thick, these slots have one row of sockets and are used primarily to add flash memory, or SRAM (static RAM).

▲ **Type II:** At 5.5mm thick, these slots have two rows of sockets and are used to add modems and NICs to a laptop computer. These cards usually have a pop-out connector for an RJ-11 or RJ-45 connector.

▲ **Type III:** At up to 10.5 mm thick, these slots have three rows of sockets and are used to install hard drives or support adapters for external peripherals and hard drives.

Various releases of the PC card standard (from Release 1.0 through 8.0) have defined increased levels of support for the needs of different types of peripherals and I/O interfaces. There are two defined interface standards:

▲ **PC card:** An older 16-bit interface that connects to internal 16-bit ISA parallel buses, and supports up to 20MBps for memory transfers and 7.84MBps for I/O transfers. PC cards use a 5V charge. You will only find PC card slots on older laptops.

▲ **CardBus:** A 32-bit interface that uses PCI-based signaling and connects to internal PCI buses, and offers support for low voltage 3.3 volt operation and bus mastering. CardBus supports transfer speeds up to 133MBps at 33MHz. CardBus cards are not compatible with 16-bit PC card slots, although CardBus sockets can accept 16-bit cards. To support compatibility, CardBus sockets and cards use a low voltage key in their connectors. A low-voltage socket will accept both 5V and 3.3V cards and uses dedicated signal lines to detect which type of card is present and adjust the operating voltage. CardBus cards have a gold grounding strip across the width of the card, near its connector edge, that distinguish them from a 16-bit PC card. CardBus also includes advanced power-management features that can idle or turn off PC cards to increase battery life.

Both interfaces support plug and play and hot-swapping and use the following layers of software to detect and support a PC card when you insert it into the computer:

▲ **Socket Services: Socket Services** software is a BIOS-level interface to the PCMCIA bus slot. When loaded, it hides the details of the PC card hardware from the computer. This software can detect when a card has been inserted and what type of card it is.

▲ **Card Services: Card Services** software is the interface between the application and Socket Services. It tells the applications which interrupts and I/O ports the card is using. Applications that need to access the PC card don't access the hardware directly; instead, they tell Card Services that they need access to a particular feature, and Card Services gets the appropriate feature from the PC card.

11.2.2 Working with PC Cards

PC cards are one of the most common expansion methods for laptops because of their ease of use and flexibility. Many different types of PC cards are available for laptops, including:

▲ Network interface cards (NICs)
▲ Modems
▲ SCSI adapters
▲ IEEE 1394/FireWire cards
▲ USB cards
▲ Sound cards

Most laptops have either one or two Type II slots or one Type III slot, or they may use a stacked slot into which two Type II cards or a single Type III card can fit. A PC card can fit into a socket of its size or higher; for example, a Type I card can fit into a Type II or III socket, and a Type II card can fit into a Type III socket.

PC cards are Plug and Play, so the process for installing one is straightforward. Insert the card into an available slot, making sure the card type matches the slot type. Also, make sure the card is pushed in all the way to ensure that the connection to the bus is good. After the card is installed, Windows should recognize and be able to use the card.

However, with a new card, you should install the manufacturer's setup software to install any needed configuration software or drivers to use the full functions of the card. Sometimes you must run an installation program before installing the card.

FOR EXAMPLE

Hot-Swapping Cards

Hot-swapping lets you change PC cards without shutting down the system. You can remove an existing card from its slot and install a new card while the PC is on and the operating system is running. However, before removing a PC card, you must stop, or turn off, its services to the PC before ejecting it. You do this in Windows XP and Vista through the Safely Remove Hardware wizard, which you can access from an icon on the system tray. In Windows 2000, you can use the Add/Remove Hardware applet in the Control Panel. To physically remove the card, you press an Eject button located next to the PC card slot.

Considerations when installing and configuring PC cards include:

▲ You must have the Card and Socket Services software installed before you try to physically install the card, so the computer can manage the card's resources. Card and Socket Services software is included in all Windows operating systems since Windows 98 SE.

▲ You may have a PC card bus that supports two Type II cards or one Type III. If you have one of these buses, you can have only one or the other situation. If you have a Type II card installed, you can't install a Type III card without removing the existing Type II.

▲ PC cards are too small to have jumpers or DIP switches, so you must configure the hardware through a software configuration program. This program can be a separate program, or it can be built into the BIOS.

11.2.3 Express Cards

ExpressCards are the most current generation of PC cards. They are designed to connect to a laptop's internal PCI Express and USB 2.0 buses. Because they can connect to either of these high-speed serial interfaces, ExpressCards reach the higher transfer rates of these interfaces: 2.5GBps for PCIe transfers and 480MBps for USB 2.0 transfers. ExpressCards also use lower voltages (3.3V and 1.5V) than PC Express cards.

ExpressCards are 5mm thick and their standard length (without extenders to accommodate ports) is 75mm. They use a single row of 26-pin contacts. There are two ExpressCard form factors:

▲ **Express/34:** 34mm wide, these are for narrower applications, such as CompactFlash readers and 1.8-inch hard drives.

▲ **Express/54:** 54mm wide cards that can accommodate wider applications that cannot fit into Express/34 dimensions. Express/54 slots are compatible with Express/34 cards.

Similar to PC cards, ExpressCards are Plug-and-Play, hot-swappable, and designed to accommodate a full range of expansion devices: network cards, storage devices, and interface adapters. You install and remove an ExpressCard in the same manner as a PC card.

SELF-CHECK

1. Describe and compare the different PC card form factors.
2. What are the differences among PC card, CardBus, and ExpressCard?
3. In what circumstances are the PC card and CardBus not compatible?
4. Describe how you would install a new ExpressCard.

11.3 Working with Laptops and Portable Systems

Although laptops and portable systems have similar components and operate in the same ways as desktop PCs, there are two key qualities of laptops that differentiate them from PCS. The first quality is their portability or size. Manufacturers typically employ proprietary engineering to fit all the same components you would find in a desktop PC into a much smaller space. For this reason, most laptop manufacturers require that most repair work be done at an authorized service center, except for some common upgrades, such as replacing a hard drive or memory. The second key quality is the laptop's ability to run on battery power. In contrast to PC maintenance, for laptops there is an important focus on conserving power and managing batteries.

Although the work that a PC technician will perform on a laptop is limited, it is essential to understand laptop power management and common tasks, issues, and constraints involved in working with laptops.

11.3.1 Power Management

Power management and conservation of battery power is a major concern for all portable computing device owners. Virtually all portable PCs now have some kind software battery monitor. In Windows 2000, XP and Vista systems, this can be accessed through the Control Panel's Power Options applet. A battery monitor tracks the reserve power of the battery and reports the battery's strength as a percentage. A report of 70 percent means that you've used only 30 percent of the battery's capacity. Many power-management systems also check whether the PC is in use; if it's not, the power-management system suspends the PC to conserve the battery's power. Conserving a battery and extending its life is a much better—and less expensive—choice than replacing the battery.

Nearly all notebook PCs are configured with the Advanced Configuration and Power Interface (ACPI); older laptops may use the earlier Advanced Power Management (APM) system. ACPI is the newest of these technologies and APM is a legacy technology.

ACPI is configured in the BIOS and APM is implemented through an application programming interface (API). ACPI is a collection of BIOS code routines, where **APM** is an operating system directed configuration and power management technology for portable PCs, as well as desktop and server computers. The benefit of ACPI is that it lets the operating system control the power supply to peripheral devices, such as the CD-ROM, printer, and other external devices. In addition the peripherals also have the ability to use ACPI to power on the PC. For example, if you insert a CD-ROM into a CD-ROM drive, the PC automatically boots up from a power off state.

ACPI defines seven power levels, or states, for a PC:

▲ **G0—Working:** Normal state. In GO, devices that aren't being used can be cycled into and out of lower power states to conserve energy.

▲ **G1—Sleeping:** There are four Sleeping states:
  • S1. The CPU stop processing instructions, but the CPU and memory are still powered.
  • S2. The CPU receives no power.
  • S3: Also called Suspend to Ram (STR). Only RAM is powered. This means that all of the data currently being processed, such as applications running and documents open, are still in memory.
  • S4: The contents of RAM are transferred to hard drive and RAM is powered off. When the system is woken to a working state from S4, RAM is refreshed with its previous contents. This means that any applications and documents are restored to their previous states, and you can continue working on them.

▲ **G2—Soft Off:** Also called S5. Most of the power is off, although some components are still powered, and to restart the PC the boot sequence must be run.

▲ **G3—Mechanical Off:** The PC is fully powered off.

ACPI also specifies different levels of power states for devices and CPUs. Many keyboards have power management keys on their keyboards: A power key used to power on (G0) and soft-power off (G2) the PC; a sleep key used to put the PC into a G1 state; and a wake key used to put a PC that is in a sleep state into a working state.

ACPI power management allows:

▲ The operating system to manage the power states of the PC and motherboard devices, including the CPU.

▲ Helps Plug and Play configure hardware resources.

▲ Monitors system power levels, changes in heat levels or powering, and recognizes when a device is inserted or removed.

▲ Monitors battery levels (with ACPI compliant batteries) and enables the operating system to define battery-level warning points.

▲ Allows interrupt, or "Wake Up" events to be defined that wake the system

The PC or laptop's BIOS must be ACPI compliant, and have ACPI enabled, in order for the operating system to use ACPI power management. A laptop's BIOS will have a configuration screen for changing some ACPI settings. In these settings, you configure ACPI to be enabled or disabled (the default is enabled), and there may be advanced settings to further configure ACPI. For example, you may be able to define the sleep/standby state as S1 or S3. However, you typically manage ACPI settings through the operating system. A BIOS may support both ACPI and APM settings, however, if ACPI is enabled, APM is automatically disabled.

In Windows 2000, XP, and Vista, you configure power management settings through the Power Options Properties dialog box (Figure 11-12), which you access from the Control Panel's Power Options. Power Options lets you configure when and whether your PC can be put into Standby (S3) or Hibernate (S4), and includes settings for turning off power to the monitor or hard drives after defined times of inactivity.

On older systems that use APM, you manage power settings through the BIOS or Windows. APM power levels include:

▲ **Full on:** The normal, working state of the computer, using full power.

▲ **APM Enabled:** APM power management is enabled, and only the CPU and RAM may receive full power.

▲ **APM Standby:** RAM is still powered, but power to the CPU and motherboard devices is stopped.

▲ **APM Suspend:** The power is reduced to its lowest level. This may include hibernating features, writing data in RAM to a hard drive.

Figure 11-12

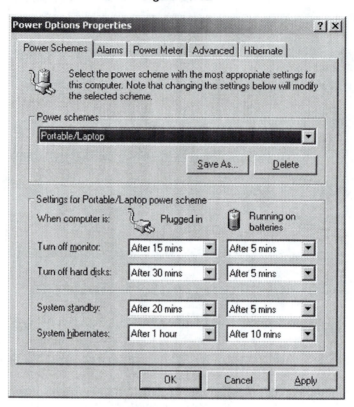

Portable/laptop power options.

11.3.2 Upgrading Laptop Components

The two main disadvantages of portable PCs are that they are difficult to work on and upgrades are expensive. Upgrade parts are expensive because they are usually proprietary and not generally interchangeable between manufacturers— or even between models from the same manufacturer, in many cases.

Due to the complexity of laptop design, most manufacturers insist that all upgrades be performed at an authorized service center. Equipment such as LCD display screens, DC controllers, video boards, and processors is often unreachable in a laptop. Most field service will involve replacing hard drives or other storage, adding memory, configuring PCMCIA cards, or adding a battery to extend useable time.

Before you attempt any work on a laptop, read the laptop manufacturer's warranties and service agreements. For some laptops, even opening the laptop can void a warranty.

If you are going to work inside a laptop, be aware that because of the tight design of parts, you may need to remove the keyboard, screen, or other components in order to have access to the component you are working on. Additionally, unlike some PC components, there is little room for error: be careful of any cables or connections inside the laptop. If you inadvertently remove a connection, you may not be able to determine how to replace it. Make sure that you have the laptop manual, and any other troubleshooting guides from the manufacturer, close at hand to refer to while you are working on the laptop.

11.3.3 Storage Upgrades

The hard drives of some portable computers are under the keyboard for easy interchange or replacement. In these models, replacing the hard drive is easy: Snap out the old and snap in the new. On other models, however, the hard drive is internally blended into the laptop's system. If you really want to increase the hard drive space, you may want to use a less arduous way of increasing the PC's storage capacity. The following is a list of options that you should try before attempting to replace an internal hard drive on a laptop PC:

▲ You can easily add removable storage through an existing port. For example, you can add an external drive via a serial, parallel, or USB port.
▲ You can add a hard drive card in a PC card slot.
▲ You can add a flash memory card in a PC card slot or other card reader.
▲ Depending on the laptop's design, you may be able to remove a floppy drive or optical drive and replace it with a hard drive. Some laptops allow for easy swaps using modular drive bays (Figure 11-13).
▲ You can use disk compression utilities to minimize the space taken up by existing files.

Portable computers don't have standard internal layouts and designs like those provided by the form factors of desktop and tower PCs. Because of this, you typically need an upgrade kit to change the hard drive in a portable PC. The upgrade kit usually includes the new hard drive, a PC card, and data transfer cables. The PC card and cables are used with data transfer software that is also included in the kit to temporarily hold and transfer the data from the old hard drive to the new one.

If you decide to replace or install a new hard drive in a laptop, and you are not using an upgrade kit from the laptop manufacturer, you will need to make sure of the following:

▲ The new hard drive is the correct size: Most laptops have a $2^{1}/_{2}$" side hard drive that is 9.5 or 11mm high. Older, pre 1996 laptop hard drives were typically 18mm high and will definitely not fit in a laptop designed

Figure 11-13

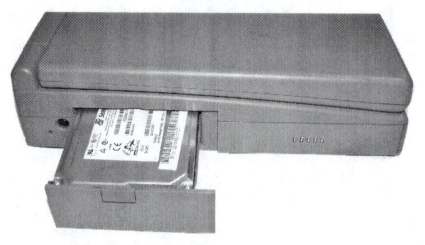

Removing a drive from a modular bay.

for a slimmer drive. Additionally, check the laptop documentation to see if it expects the drive to have built-in supporting brackets; if it does, you may need to purchase a mounting kit to prepare the drive for the laptop.

▲ The laptop has the proper interface connectors (typically parallel or serial ATA) for the new drive.

There are several common ways manufacturers provide for accessing the hard drive: There may be a drive caddy that allows you to easily slide the drive out. If there is no drive caddy, you may need to either lift or remove a keyboard or unscrew a section of the case to gain access to the drive.

The basic procedure for installing a hard drive on a laptop is the same as for a PC. You will need to remove any mounting brackets, disconnect the hard drive's interface connector, and then slide or lift the drive out from its mounting brackets. Installing a laptop drive involves the same basic considerations as installing PC hard drive. When replacing a laptop drive, you typically remove the drive with its mounting brackets; detach the drive interface from the interface connector and the power connector; and finally remove the drive from the mounting brackets. To install the new drive, follow the reverse of this procedure: Slide the hard drive into its mounting brackets, attach the drive interface and power connectors; and insert the drive in the drive bay. Note that a laptop hard drive typically has a ribbon cable made of thin plastic; you will need to be careful to not bend or break it. It will also have a power supply connector that is smaller than a PC power connector.

Many laptops have second, open, modular bays, which, depending on the laptop design and model can be used to install a battery, floppy drive, optical drive, hard drive, or memory card reader. You should read the documentation to determine the exact installation process for your brand of portable computer, but the basic installation process for devices that go into a modular, or accessory storage bay, is the same. You will first need to remove any bay-cover blank or device to open the bay. Slide the new device into place, using any guides that may be present; ensure that the connections are lined up properly and will make good contact and then secure the device in place with either a screw or a latch lever.

11.3.4 Memory Upgrades

One of the most common and easiest upgrades to a laptop is replacing or adding new memory. A portable system will usually have specific instructions on how to do this, as well as the type of memory you can use, along with specifications for the total memory that the laptop can support and the increments that you can use to add it.

It's not uncommon for a laptop to have a specific amount of memory built in, which you can't remove, along with one expansion slot for a new module. However, some ultraportable laptops or tablets may have a fixed amount of system memory that is not upgradeable.

Most laptops use Small Outline-DIMM memory, which you can typically order from either a memory module manufacturer or the laptop manufacturer.

Most RAM upgrades (at least on most high-end and name brand portable PCs) are accomplished through a porthole or trap door on either the bottom or the side of the portable PC (Figure 11-14). The SODIMM is mounted flush to the main board and lies flat to save space.

After installing new RAM in a laptop PC, if the RAM doesn't appear in the BIOS POST display, the RAM probably isn't properly seated. Shut down the notebook and reseat the RAM. Older laptop PCs may use Single In-Line Memory Modules (SIMMs), which are installed in much the same manner as the SODIMM.

Palmtop computers and other handheld computing devices don't have the overall physical size or internal case space to accommodate full-sized memory modules. For these systems, smaller memory modules have been developed, such as the micro DIMM.

11.3.5 Other Upgrades

Other common, upgrades to a laptop include replacing a battery and enabling networking or wireless networking. Less commonly, you may need to replace a faulty LED display.

▲ **Batteries:** Depending on the laptop model, you may be able to upgrade its battery by replacing it with a compatible battery that is longer lasting.

Figure 11-14

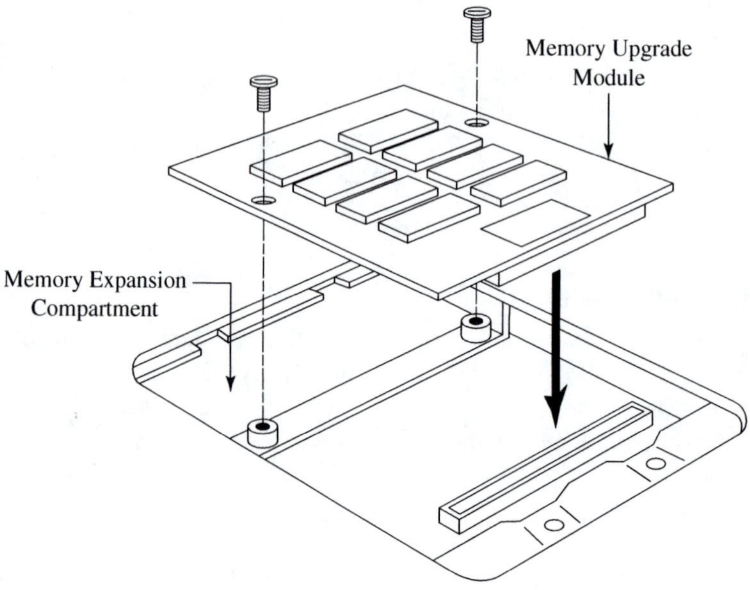

Memory Upgrade
Module

Memory Expansion
Compartment

Installing memory in a case opening.

Batteries are installed in different ways. They can be installed in an accessory device bay (if your laptop has one and supports installing a battery in this manner). Most laptops have the battery installed from the bottom of the computer. The battery is secured by either a single screw or (more often) a simple slide latch that lets you remove the battery without using tools. The laptop's manual will dictate exactly how to remove a battery on that specific model.

▲ **Networking:** Some laptops have network adapters (and RJ-45 ports) built in. If not, you can add a local area network (LAN) adapter though a USB or parallel port, or more commonly through a PC card slot.

▲ **Wireless networking:** Many laptops include wireless LAN adapters (and some may have connectors for attaching an antenna used for amplifying signals), but if the laptop does not, you can use a wireless LAN Wireless LAN PC card. There are different standards for wireless networking, but the two most common are IEEE standards 802.11b and 802.11g. The 802.11b standard operates at either 1MBps or 11MBps over the 2.4GHz radio frequency band. The 802.11g standard operates on the same frequency band, but operates at 1MBps, 11MBps, and 54MBps (and is interoperable with the 802.11b equipment). The

> ## FOR EXAMPLE
>
> ### Wireless Networking with Bluetooth
>
> As you learned in Chapter 10, another popular standard for wireless communication is Bluetooth. The IEEE specification 802.15 describes Wireless Personal Area Networks (WPANs) and is based on Bluetooth. Bluetooth doesn't have the range of cellular communications, nor does it have the bandwidth of current wireless networking standards (WiFi). Bluetooth signals are good only for about 30 feet, and it really helps to have line of sight to make them work. However, Bluetooth is not designed specifically for wireless networking; it's designed for wireless communication and is fast and reliable transferring small amounts of data short distances. It also uses little power compared to cellular or WiFi options, making it ideal for laptops as well as handheld computers. Bluetooth is more popular in cell phones and handheld computers, but it still gets a lot of attention in laptop computers. Common devices are keyboards and mice, printers, cameras, and headsets and microphones.

latest IEEE wireless networking standard, 802.11n promises to reach speeds well over 200MBps. If the reception range on your PC card isn't good, you can increase it by adding an external antenna. These are available from the PC card's manufacturer (although not all PC cards can use external antennae—check with the manufacturer to be sure).

11.3.6 Laptop Maintenance and Troubleshooting

Many problems people have with their computers can be prevented. By taking good care of your equipment, you can dramatically extend the life of your hardware, and laptops are no exception. Two ways to look at preventative maintenance include being careful of what the computer is exposed to (the environment) and taking steps to proactively protect your computer (tools and techniques). Environmental issues refer to all of the external conditions and events that can damage a laptop. Steps you can take to maintain your laptop include:

▲ **Use a proper carrying case.** Laptops get moved around all the time, and if you're going to carry one around, always put it in a carrying case designed for such a purpose. Too many people just stuff them into a backpack or briefcase and then wonder why things like broken screens happen.

▲ **Gentle handling:** Be gentle when opening and closing the laptop cover; because its hinges get so much use from opening and closing, they can weaken and break. Also, when the laptop is closed, the screen is basically face to face with the keyboard. Any pressure or squeezing together of the sides causes the keys to press into the screen. Over time, the keys will mar the coating of the LCD screen, and you'll be left with permanent marks in your display. One way to prevent this problem is to place a screen-sized piece of foam (they usually come between the keyboard and screen when the laptop is shipped) or heavy cloth between the keyboard and screen when you close your laptop. It will keep the display better for longer.

▲ **Heat management:** All laptops have fans to keep the processor and memory cool, and laptop components are designed to run cooler than their desktop counterparts, but overheating can still be a problem. Don't operate your laptop for long periods of time in the sun or in very hot conditions. You can also purchase external cooling devices for your laptop, which help to keep it cooler and extend the life of your system. The most common version is a cooling pad. It sits on your desk (most are about 1 inch high), and the laptop sits on the cooling pad. Inside the pad are fans that circulate hot air away from the bottom of your laptop, the part that usually gets the hottest. There are dozens of varieties of cooling pads, starting off around $15 and going up to several hundred dollars for exotic cooling fan/docking station combos.

▲ **Dust prevention:** Dust and dirt can get into fans, rendering them useless for cooling your computer. Additionally, even small amounts of contaminants can damage laptop components. Make sure the area you're working in is clean and not overly dusty, and keep closed any doors or flaps covering any PC card slots and drives.

▲ **LCD cleaners:** You can't clean an LCD screen the same way you do a TV, with glass cleaner and a paper towel and clean away. Paper towels can be abrasive and scratch the coating on the LCD coating. Also, commercial glass cleaners often contain chemicals that will damage the LCD screen. To clean an LCD screen, you can use a soft cloth slightly dampened with water or a cleaner designed for LCD screens. You can find them at most any office supply store. There are even premoistened towelette versions that are handy to carry with you in your laptop case.

Occasionally, part of a laptop's case will crack and need to be replaced. However, you can't usually just replace the cracked section. Most often, you must remove every component from inside the laptop's case and swap the components over to the new case. This is a labor-intensive process because the screws in laptops are often very small and hard to reach. Often, repairing a cracked case may cost several hundred dollars in labor alone.

Because the technology behind LCD displays is complex, there are almost no service procedures for the display in a laptop. The cost of replacing the display on a laptop is prohibitive to the point that it would be almost as much as buying a new laptop (or an excellent used model). However, when a display is broken, it can be removed by a service technician and exchanged with the manufacturer for a new one. This procedure may be under warranty (depending on the length of the manufacturer's warranty). Replacing an LCD screen is not that difficult, in terms of the service procedure. Although every laptop is different, the procedure for replacing the LCD display follows this generalization fairly closely. You must completely disassemble the laptop, exposing the mounting screws for the display as well as the data connection to the motherboard (usually a ribbon cable); then you must remove the display from its mounting mechanism and install the new display. Some displays are actually orderable only as a complete top-half, including hinge, case, and support frame.

Unique considerations in troubleshooting laptops include:

▲ **Laptop power problems:** If the laptop isn't receiving power, this may be due to a battery or AC adapter. An AC adapter commonly has an LED to indicate it is receiving power from an outlet, and laptops have one or more status lights to indicate whether it is receiving power from the battery or AC adapter. If an AC adapter isn't receiving power from an outlet, make sure the outlet is good. If the AC adapter is receiving power, but the laptop can't be powered by the AC adapter, check the adapter's connection to the laptop. Swap the adapter with a known good one to confirm the problem lies with the adapter and not the laptop. Some laptops may run solely from the battery, which is powered by the adapter. If you are running the laptop just on its battery and it won't start up, the battery may have run out of power, or it may need reconditioning. It can also take a while to start up a laptop if it is in Sleep mode, and you may need to press and hold the power button down for a few seconds to get it to wake up. Check the battery documentation and LEDs to determine if it is charged or if it needs conditioning. Some batteries may need to be periodically reconditioned, which usually involves a routine for fully discharging and recharging the battery, and you must follow the manufacturer's procedure for doing this.

▲ **Laptop LCD display problems:** The most common problem with LCD screens is a dim screen. This is generally caused by one of two things: a failing inverter or a failing backlight. Unfortunately, the only real way to test it for sure is to replace a part, unless you have an inverter power tester available. Many repair shops will be able to test your inverter and see if it is the cause of the problem. There are four things that can cause backlight problems. They are (in order of likelihood): the inverter, the backlight lamp, the video card, and the backlight circuitry on the motherboard. If your screen is flickering, or does not display but your monitor is getting power, the likely culprit is the inverter. (When you replace an inverter, make sure it's designed to work with the LCD backlight in your system. Having a mismatched inverter could cause video display problems, such as a dim or flickering screen). A very faint image on the screen can also be due to a LED cutoff switch that has become stuck. When a laptop is closed and snapped shut, the LED cutoff switch turns off the backlight to the screen. This switch is usually located close to the screen hinges. Check this to make sure it is not stuck. If an LCD display isn't functioning at all, the display may not be powered, or there may be a problem with the video circuitry. If the laptop fan powers on, the problem is likely to be a failure of the video circuitry. A dark screen, white screen, or garbled screen may be due to problems with the connector to the LED screen. Connect an external monitor to the laptop to determine if the video adapter is working. If this monitor does not function, there may be a problem with the video adapter and it may need to be replaced. If the external monitor works, the problem is likely to lie with the LCD assembly, typically a loose connection between the LED screen and the motherboard, which you can fix by reseating the cable.

▲ **Laptop function key issues:** Depending on the manufacturer, your laptop's function key combinations. (Fn + another key) may enable or disable certain functions, such as fan control, display brightness, enabling or disabling a device such as the wireless antenna, touch pad, or external monitor or projector. If a component is suddenly no longer accessible or disabled, this may be due to inadvertently pressing a key combination that disabled the component. To use a function key combination, press the Fn key and then another key, such as a numeric key. The secondary key on the keyboard typically has some color-coded symbol on it that indicates it can be used with the Fn key. However, each manufacturer will program these keys differently, so check the laptop documentation. Instead of having a separate number pad, a laptop keyboard may enable a section of the keyboard to act as a number pad through using the Fn key. (If your laptop keyboard is only producing numbers instead of typing alphabetical characters, a function key combination may be the cause.)

▲ **Touchscreen problems:** Touchscreens (and graphical digitizers) can suffer the same types of problems as regular LCD displays, such as adapter problems and driver problems. Touch screens use special drivers that manage communication with the stylus used to draw on them, and these drivers must be configured properly. To configure a touch screen, run the manufacturer's calibration routine, which should be accessible from the touch screen's Properties dialog box or through the device's Setup or configuration software. This routine will ask you to tap various areas of the touch screen and then uses this information to configure the touch screen. If you are having a problem with the touchscreen responding to a stylus, you may need to recalibrate the touchscreen.

SELF-CHECK

1. Why is power management important for laptops?
2. How is power managed on a laptop?
3. Describe the ways in which a laptop's storage can be upgraded.
4. What maintenance considerations are there for laptops?

SUMMARY

Portable laptop computers are a popular alternative to desktop PCs. Laptops are generally categorized by their size and weight, and categories include desktop replacement laptops, standard or mainstream laptops, thin-and-light notebooks, and ultraportable notebooks. Tablet PCs are similar in size to ultraportables, but use a large touch-screen as its display and primary inputting device. Smaller portable computing devices include handheld PCs (HPCs) and PDAs.

Laptops are powered by AC adapters, batteries, or a docking port. Laptop battery types include NiCad, NiMH, and LiON batteries. Laptop components are specifically designed for lower power usage, lightness and portability, and many components are not designed for easy upgrades or replacements. Memory and hard drives are the most common laptop components replaced. A laptop display is embedded in the laptop case, as is its keyboard. Laptops typically incorporate a touch pad and/or track pad as its pointing device, although a mouse can be added through a USB or combination keypad/mouse port.

Most laptops have integrated audio, video, or networking circuitry that is not easily upgraded, although some laptops use smaller adaptations of the PCI expansion cards, such as Compact PCI and mini PCI to add circuitry. Laptops use small form factor memory modules, such as SoDIMM and MicroDIMM, CPUs designed for mobile systems, and small form factor hard drives.

PC cards are the most popular way to expand a laptop's capabilities, using a 16-bit PC Card bus, or the 32-bit CardBus. There are three PC card form factors: Type I, II, and III. A next generation of the PC card expansion technology is ExpressCard, which uses the high-speed serial technology of PCI Express, and defines two form factors, Express/34 and Express/54.

Almost all laptops use some form of power management to help conserve battery power. ACPI is the current PC power management standard, and defines different levels of power usage for a system, including a Sleep state and a Hibernate state, that can be managed by an operating system. An earlier power management system was APM.

Laptops are not designed for the same upgradeability as desktop PCs, and laptop warranties may be voided if the laptop is opened by a non-certified technician. The most common internal upgrades are hard drives and memory. Although laptops are designed for portability, special care must be taken in handling them to protect them from moisture and accidental bumps. In addition to problems that affect any PC, a laptop may experience problems with its AC adapter or batteries, LCD display or touchscreen. A unique consideration in troubleshooting laptops is its multifunction key combinations. Depending on the manufacturer, certain laptop components, such as the laptop fan or wireless port or antenna, may be enabled or disabled through a multifunction key combination (Fn + another key).

KEY TERMS

Advanced Configuration and Power Interface (ACPI)

Advanced Power Management (APM)

AC adapter

Auto-switching AC adapter

CardBus

Card Services

Compact PCI (CPCI)

Convertible tablet PC

Desktop replacement laptop

Docking port

Docking station

ExpressCard

Extended Video Graphics Array (XGA)

Fn key

Handheld PC (HPC)

Lithium-Ion (Li-ION) battery

Mini-PCI

Native resolution

Nickel-Cadium (NiCad) battery

Nickel-Metal Hydride (NiMH) battery

PC Card

PC card

Personal Computer Memory Card International Association (PCMCIA)

Portable computer

Port replicator

Slate tablet PC

Socket Services

Super Extended Graphics Array (SXGA)

Super Video Graphics Array (SVGA)

Tablet PC

Thin-and-light notebook

Touchpad

Track point

Ultra Extended Graphics Array (UXGA)

Ultraportable notebook

Widescreen UXGA

ASSESS YOUR UNDERSTANDING

Go to www.wiley.com/college/groth to evaluate your knowledge of printers. *Measure your learning by comparing pre-test and post-test results.*

Summary Questions

1. Which of the following is not a benefit of laptop design?
   (a) portability
   (b) increased performance
   (c) desktop replacement
   (d) higher-quality construction

2. Which laptop accessory allows you to power your laptop from a car or airplane?
   (a) AC adapter
   (b) DC adapter
   (c) battery converter
   (d) Automotive Wizard

3. LCD screens display their highest quality at their native resolution. True or false?

4. Which laptop input device is a flat surface that you can draw on with your finger to control the cursor?
   (a) touch pad
   (b) track point
   (c) touch point
   (d) track pad

5. The smallest laptops today still typically carry at least one parallel and one serial port for backward compatibility. True or false?

6. Which of the following is a CPU designed for portable systems?
   (a) Pentium M
   (b) Athlon 64FX
   (c) Itanium
   (d) Xeon

7. What type of battery is able to communicate its status and need for recharging or conditioning to the laptop?
   (a) LiON batteries
   (b) all laptop batteries
   (c) smart batteries
   (d) any battery, if the system uses a power management system

8. Which display standard supports a 16:10 aspect ratio?
    (a) any display standard
    (b) all SVGA standards
    (c) UXGA
    (d) WUXGA
9. There are no common form factors for laptops motherboards. True or false?
10. Which kind of laptop was designed to look and function like a paper notebook?
    (a) HPC
    (b) Tablet PC
    (c) Thin-and-light notebooks
    (d) Notebook PC
11. A modem generally fits in what PC card slot type?
    (a) Type I
    (b) Type II
    (c) Type III
    (d) Type IV
12. A Type I PC card is typically used for what type of laptop expansion?
    (a) add memory to the system
    (b) add network capabilities to the system
    (c) add a hard drive to the system
    (d) connect an external device, such as a CD-ROM drive, to the system
13. Which type of PC card is used most often to add interface connectors for attaching external drives?
    (a) Type I
    (b) Type II
    (c) Type III
    (d) Type IV
14. Which of the following defines hot-swapping?
    (a) installing new devices without the need for a driver
    (b) removing and adding internal devices without rebooting
    (c) removing and inserting PC cards while the system is running
    (d) all of the above
15. Which power management standard is most commonly used today in portable systems?
    (a) APM
    (b) ACPM
    (c) ACPI
    (d) Both a and b

16. Many HPCs produced today run which operating system?
    (a) Windows Mobile
    (b) Windows CE
    (c) Windows XP for Tablet PCs
    (d) Windows XP for HPCs

17. A common laptop upgrade is upgrading internal expansion cards, such as the compact-PCI video adapter card. True or false?

18. What is the most common disk size for an internally mounted laptop hard drive?
    (a) 5.5 inch
    (b) 4.5 inch
    (c) 3.5 inch
    (d) 2.5 inch

19. Which memory form factor was designed for ultraportable laptops?
    (a) MicroDIMM
    (b) SoDIMM
    (c) MiniDIMM
    (d) SORIMM

20. Which wireless IEEE standard operates on the 2.4GHz radio frequency and transmits data at a maximum of 11MBps?
    (a) 802.11b
    (b) 802.11c
    (c) 802.11e
    (d) 802.11g

Applying This Chapter

1. A coworker's laptop is displaying only a very faint image. What could be the problem?

2. Your laptop's hard drive has failed. Describe the basic steps you will follow for replacing the drive.

3. You want to add memory to a laptop that has 128MB RAM. Describe the steps you will follow to upgrade the laptop's memory.

4. After inserting a PC card into a notebook computer, the system does not recognize the card. What could be the problem?

5. A coworker is considering purchasing a new laptop because their current laptop is older and has limited storage. What will you advise him?

YOU TRY IT

Choosing a Laptop

You are going to purchase a laptop for your own personal or work needs. Review current models of laptops available from one or more laptop manufacturers (such as Toshiba.com or Lenovo.com). Select a laptop and describe at least five key features it has that makes this laptop a suitable selection for your needs.

Working with Laptop Batteries

You are working in the IT department of a small manufacturer. A salesperson has asked for a new battery, as her current battery only lasts an hour. What course of action do you take to resolve this situation?

Troubleshooting a Laptop

After you turn on your laptop, your laptop's screen is dark. What troubleshooting steps will you take?

Selecting a Portable System

You are consulting for an engineering company that wants to supply its engineers with mobile computing for fieldwork at construction sites. What options do they have, and what will you advise them?

12
NETWORK FUNDAMENTALS

Starting Point

Go to www.wiley.com/college/groth to assess your knowledge of network fundamentals.
Determine where you need to concentrate your effort.

What You'll Learn in This Chapter

▲ Types of networks, network components, and protocols
▲ Types and features of network transmission media and hardware
▲ Steps for connecting to a network or the Internet

After Studying This Chapter, You'll Be Able To

▲ Evaluate and compare types of network protocols, topologies, and architectures
▲ Identify different types of transmission media
▲ Connect a PC to a network or the internet
▲ Configure a PC for a connection to a network or the internet
▲ Evaluate network connectivity devices
▲ Evaluate internet connectivity choices
▲ Troubleshoot network connection problems

INTRODUCTION

By themselves, computers are powerful tools. When they are connected in a network, they become even more powerful because the functions and tools that each computer provides can be shared with other computers. Networks exist for one major reason: to share information and resources. Networks can be very simple, such as a small group of computers that share information, or they can be very complex, spanning large geographical areas. Regardless of the type of network, a certain amount of maintenance is always required. Because each network is different and probably utilizes many diverse technologies, it is important to understand the fundamentals of networking and how networking components interact. This chapter introduces the fundamental concepts of networking, the components and hardware used in networks, and explains how to connect a PC to a network or the internet.

12.1 Understanding Networks

A network is nothing more than two or more computers connected to each other so that they can exchange information, such as email messages or documents, or share resources, such as disk storage or printers. In most cases, this connection is made via electrical cables that carry the information in the form of electrical signals. But in some cases, other types of connections are used. For example, fiber-optic cables let computers communicate at extremely high speeds by using impulses of light. Wireless networks let computers communicate by using radio signals, so the computers aren't restricted by physical cables.

In addition to the hardware that comprises the network, a network also requires special software to enable communications. In the early days of networking, you had to add this software to each computer on the network. Nowadays, network support is built into all major operating systems, including all current versions of Windows, Macintosh operating systems, and Linux.

12.1.1 Primary Network Components

Networks consist of three primary components—servers, workstations, and network resources.

▲ **Servers:** A **server** is a network computer from which workstations (or clients) access and share files, printers, communications, and other services. Although the term server is usually used to refer to a specific computer, the term also describes the software that performs, controls, or coordinates a service or resource. Additionally, a single computer can act as a multipurpose server and physically house many different software servers. To network clients, each server can appear to be a completely

Table 12-1: Common Server Types

Type	Description
File server	Stores network users' data files
Print server	Manages the printers that are connected to the network and the printing of user documents on the network printers
Communications server	Handles many common communications functions for the network, such as email, fax, or internet services
Application server	Shares network-enabled versions of common application software and eliminates the need for software to be installed on each workstation
Database server	Manages a common database for the network, handling all data storage, database management, and requests for data

separate device when that is not usually the case. Several types of servers can exist on a network, each one performing a different task for the network and its workstations (Table 12-1).

Servers offer networks the capability of centralizing the control of resources and can thus reduce administrative difficulties. They can be used to distribute processes for balancing the load on computers and can thus increase speed and performance. Servers may also be categorized as dedicated or nondedicated servers: **A dedicated server** is assigned to provide specific applications or services for the network, and nothing else. Dedicated servers are often used to provide efficiency and improve network performance. A web server is an example of a dedicated server: It is dedicated to the task of serving up web pages. A nondedicated server is assigned to provide one or more network services as well as local access, for example, serving as a front end for the administrator to work with other applications or services.

▲ **Workstations and clients:** In the network environment, the term **workstation** normally refers to any computer that is connected to the network and used by an individual to do work. In network terms, workstations are also known as client computers. However, a client is any network entity that can request resources from the network; a workstation is a computer that can request resources. Workstations can be clients, but not all clients are workstations. For example, a printer can request resources from the network, but it is a client, not a workstation. Workstations use a NIC to connect to the network, and network client software allows the computer to communicate over the network.

▲ **Network resources:** A **network resource** is any item that can be used on a network. Resources can include a broad range of items, such as printers and other peripherals, files, applications and disk storage.

In addition to servers, workstations, and resources, every network requires two more items to tie these three components together:

▲ **Network Operating System (NOS):** Most networks use a **network operating system (NOS)** to control the communication with resources and the flow of data across the network. The NOS runs on the server. Some of the more popular NOSs at this time include Unix; Novell's NetWare; and Microsoft's Windows NT Server, Windows 2000 Server, and Windows Server 2003. NOSs enable servers to monitor memory, CPU time, disk space, and peripherals.

▲ **Network media:** The **network media** are the transmission media used for the actual network data transmissions and signaling, such as special cabling or wireless radio wave connections. The media is used to connect each network **node:** any addressable network point, including workstations, peripherals, or other network devices. However, the term node is often used interchangeably with workstation. In TCP/IP networks, nodes are often referred to as **hosts**.

12.1.2 Types of Networks

There are many types of networks. The principal ways in which they differ include:

▲ **Resource access model:** How the workstations access the network resources. There are generally two resource access models, peer-to-peer and client/server.

  • **Peer-to-peer:** This type of network includes two or more PCs that are connected to share data files, a printer, or other resources, without the use of a dedicated server managing the network (Figure 12-1). Peer-to-peer networks are appropriate for small (up to ten users), simple, inexpensive networks. This model can be set up almost immediately in Windows, with little extra hardware required. Generally speaking, there is no centralized administration or control in the peer-to-peer resource model. Every station has unique control over the resources the computer owns, and each station must be administrated separately. However, this very lack of centralized control can

Figure 12-1

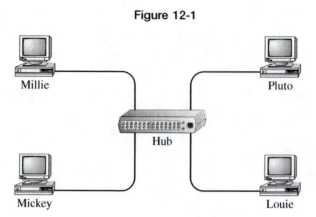

A peer-to-peer network.

make it difficult to administer the network; for the same reason, the network isn't very secure. Moreover, because each computer is acting as both a workstation and server, it may not be easy to locate resources. The person who is in charge of a file may have moved it without anyone's knowledge. Also, the users who work under this arrangement need more training because they are not only users but also administrators.

- **Client/server:** The client/server (also known as server-based) model uses a dedicated, centralized server to manage administrative functions and resource sharing (Figure 12-2). A client/server network is more appropriate than the peer-to-peer model for large networks (25 users or more) that need a more secure environment and centralized control. Using a server makes it easier to share resources, perform backups, and support an almost unlimited number of users. This model also offers better security. Client/server networks require specialized software (the NOS) to manage the server's role in the environment. With the addition of a server and the NOS server-based networks can easily cost more than peer-to-peer resource models.

▲ **Geographical size:** How big the network is in terms of geography. Although a peer-to-peer network typically connects only a few computers, types of larger, client/server networks used by businesses are:

- **Local-area networks (LANs):** A **LAN** interconnects from two to hundreds of PCs, using permanently installed cabling or perhaps a wireless technology.

- **Wide-area networks (WANs):** Several networks may be joined to form a **WAN**. Whereas LANs are limited by cabling to single locales, such as a building or a single floor within a building, WANs can span

Figure 12-2

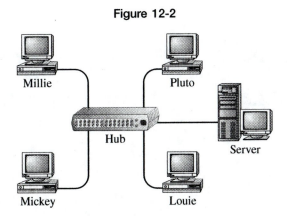

A client/server network.

buildings, states, countries, and even continental boundaries. A corporation may maintain a WAN using dial-up, leased, or other dedicated communication means.

- **Metropolitan area networks (MANs):** A MAN is a network that's smaller than a typical WAN but larger than a LAN. Typically, a MAN connects two or more LANs within a same city but are far enough apart that the networks can't be connected using a simple cable or wireless connection.

▲ **Topology:** The term **topology** refers to how a network is organized in terms of its cabling and signaling. The most common topologies are the bus, star, and ring topologies. Network topologies are discussed further in Section 12.1.3.

▲ **Protocols:** A **protocol** is a transmission standard used for network signaling. Communications over a network are based on communications protocols or rules for sending, receiving, and interpreting the network signals. Network transmissions involve sending data, messages, and tokens, in small groupings called data packets. The size and format of the data packets are defined by the protocol the network uses and its NOS. Popular protocols for LANs are TCP/IP and IPX/SPX. Network protocols are discussed further in Section 12.1.5.

12.1.3 Network Topologies

A topology is a way of laying out the network. Topologies can be either physical or logical. **Physical topologies** describe how the cables are run. **Logical topologies** describe how the network messages travel. Each type differs by its cost, ease of installation, fault tolerance (how the topology handles problems like cable

Figure 12-3

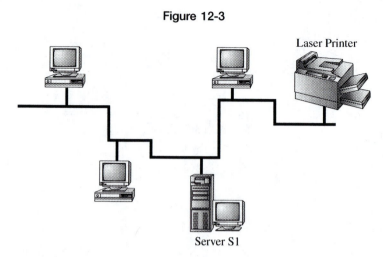

An example of a physical bus topology.

breaks), and ease of reconfiguration (such as adding a new workstation to the existing network). There are five primary topologies (some of which can be both logical and physical), bus, star, ring, mesh and hybrid:

▲ **Bus topology:** A **bus topology** is the simplest physical topology. It consists of a single cable that runs to every workstation (Figure 12-3). In a bus topology, each computer shares the same data and address path. With a logical bus topology, messages pass through the trunk, and each workstation checks to see if the message is addressed to itself. If it is, the network adapter copies the message to the card's onboard memory. Cable systems that use the bus topology are easy to install and use the least amount of cabling. Because of the simplicity of installation, and because of the low cost of the cable, bus topology cabling systems (such as Ethernet) are the cheapest to install. However, if any one of the cables breaks, the entire network is disrupted.

▲ **Star topology:** In a physical **star topology** (Figure 12-4), a cable is run from each workstation to a central device (a hub or switch), which is usually placed in a central location in the office (such as a utility closet). Star topologies are more expensive to install than bus networks because several more cables need to be installed as well as the hubs. However, star networks are easy to configure and have a higher fault tolerance (one cable failing does not bring down the entire network). Some types of Ethernet, ARCNet, and Token Ring use a physical star topology.

▲ **Ring topology:** In a physical **ring topology**, stations are connected in a circle and use a unidirectional transmission path where messages move

Figure 12-4

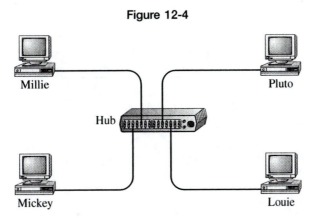

A typical star topology with a hub.

from workstation to workstation. Each station in the ring reads a message and then regenerates it and hands it to its neighbor on a different network cable (Figure 12-5). Unlike a star topology network, the ring topology network will go down if one entity is removed from the ring. Physical ring topology systems are not used commonly today because hardware involved is fairly expensive and the fault tolerance low. (One type of logical ring still exists: IBM's Token Ring architecture; however, Token Ring actually uses a physical star topology.)

▲ **Mesh topology:** The **mesh topology** is the simplest logical topology in terms of data flow, but it is the most complex in terms of physical design. In this physical topology, each device is connected to every other device (Figure 12-6). This topology is rarely found in LANs, mainly because of the complexity of the cabling. Although a mesh topology

Figure 12-5

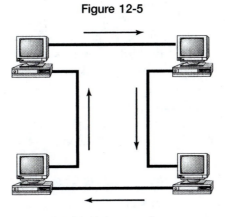

A typical ring topology.

Figure 12-6

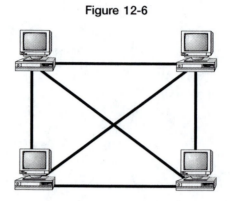

A typical mesh topology.

has high fault tolerance, it is very expensive to install and maintain. In a logical mesh topology, there are multiple ways to get the data from source to destination. The data may not be able to take the direct route, but it can take an alternate, indirect route. For this reason, the mesh topology is found in WANs to connect multiple sites across WAN links. It uses devices called routers to search multiple routes through the mesh and determine the best path.

▲ **Hybrid topology:** The **hybrid topology** is simply a mix of the other topologies. Most networks today are not only hybrid, but heterogeneous (they include a mix of components of different types and brands). The hybrid network may be more expensive than some types of network topologies, but it can take the best features of all the other topologies and exploits them. The most common is a star-bus topology, which operates as a physical star, but as a logical bus.

Each topology has advantages and disadvantages (Table 12-2).

In complex networks, we commonly break networks into backbones and segments (Figure 12-7). A backbone is the part of the network to which all segments and servers connect. A backbone provides the structure for a network and is considered the main part of any network. It usually uses a high-speed communications technology of some kind, such as Fiber Distributed Data Interface (FDDI) or 1 or 10 Gigabit Ethernet. A segment is a general term for any short section of the network that is not part of the backbone. Just as servers connect to the backbone, workstations connect to segments.

12.1.4 Network Models and Standards

There are many different types of communication needed for networking: Applications and operating systems need to communicate with network soft-

Table 12-2: Network Topologies

Topology	Physical/Logical	Advantages	Disadvantages
Bus	Both	Cheap. Easy to install.	Difficult to reconfigure. Break in the bus disables the entire network.
Star	Physical only	Cheap. Easy to install. Easy to reconfigure. Fault tolerant.	More expensive than bus.
Ring	Both	Efficient. Easy to install.	Reconfiguration is difficult. Very expensive.
Mesh	Both	Simplest for data flow. Most fault tolerant.	Reconfiguration is extremely difficult. Extremely expensive. Very complex.
Hybrid	Usually physical	Gives a combination of the best features of each topology used.	Complex (less so than mesh, however).

ware, and network software must be able to work with network hardware and cabling. All of the communications must be managed to work as a whole, and to do so, network communications use protocols, or sets of rules that govern communications. Protocols detail what "language" the computers are speaking when they talk over a network, and if two computers are going to communicate,

Figure 12-7

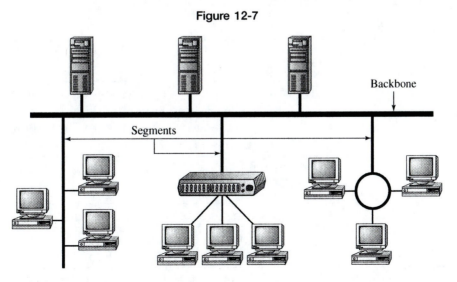

Backbone and segments on a sample network.

they both must be using the same protocol. Network data is transmitted in small chunks called packets, whose size and format and management depends upon the protocol being used.

Because of the complexity of the different types of network communications, the International Standards Organization (ISO) introduced the Open Systems Interconnection (OSI) model to provide a common way of describing network protocols and stages of communication in network transmissions.

The OSI model describes network transmission taking place on seven different layers (Table 12-3), with information exchanged between the layers by appending "header" information to the data packets.

The OSI model describes the general flow of data packets as follows. The data begins its journey when an end-user application sends data to another network computer. The data enters the network through an Application layer interface. The Application layer is composed of special programming interfaces and protocols used by desktop applications. The data then works its way down through layers called the protocol stack. Along the way, the protocol at each layer manipulates the data by adding header information, converting the data into different formats, combining packets to form larger packets, and so on. When the data reaches the Physical layer protocol, it is actually placed on the network media (in other words, the cable) and sent to the receiving computer. When the receiving computer receives the data, the data works its way up through the protocol stack. The protocol at each layer reverses the processing that was done

Table 12-3: The Seven Layers of the OSI Model

Layer	Name	Description
1	Physical	Governs the layout of cables and devices such as repeaters and hubs.
2	Data Link	Provides MAC addresses to uniquely identify network nodes and a means for data to be sent over the Physical layer in the form of packets. Bridges and switches are layer 2 devices.
3	Network	Handles routing of data across network segments.
4	Transport	Provides for reliable delivery of packets.
5	Session	Establishes sessions between network applications.
6	Presentation	Converts data so that systems that use different data formats can exchange information.
7	Application	Allows applications to request network services.

by the corresponding layer on the sending computer. Headers are removed, data is converted back to its original format, packets that were split into smaller packets are recombined into larger messages, and so on. When the packet reaches the Application layer protocol, it is delivered to an application that can process the data.

A network protocol or suite of protocols may define communication at one or more levels defined by the OSI model, and some protocols may define fewer or additional levels for their network transmissions. A network may employ multiple protocols that handle the different levels of communication needed.

To provide for the standardization of protocols, the Institute of Electrical and Electronics Engineers (IEEE) created a series of 802 standards for networks (Table 12-4). These standards specify certain types of networks, although not every network protocol is covered by the IEEE 802 committee specifications.

Table 12-4: IEEE 802 Networking Standards

Standard	Topic
802.1	LAN/MAN Management (and Media Access Control Bridges)
802.2	Logical Link Control
802.3	CSMA/CD
802.4	Token Bus
802.5	Token Ring
802.6	Distributed Queue Dual Bus (DQDB) Metropolitan Area Network (MAN)
802.7	Broadband Local Area Networks
802.8	Fiber-Optic LANs and MANs
802.9	Isochronous LANs
802.10	LAN/MAN Security
802.11	Wireless LAN
802.12	Demand Priority Access Method
802.15	Wireless Personal Area Network
802.16	Wireless Metropolitan Area Network
802.17	Resilient Packet Ring
802.18	LAN/MAN Standards Committee

The IEEE 802 standards were designed primarily for enhancements to the bottom three layers of the OSI model. The IEEE 802 model breaks the ISO Data Link layer into two sublayers: the Logical Link Control (LLC) sublayer and the Media Access Control (MAC) sublayer. In the Logical Link Control sublayer, data link communications are managed. The Media Access Control sublayer watches out for data collisions, as well as assigning physical addresses.

Media access refers to the rules that define how computers put data on and retrieve it from a network cable. Common media access methods include:

▲ **Carrier Sense Multiple Access with Collision Detection (CSMA/CD):** CSMA/CD specifies that every computer can transmit at any time. When two stations transmit at the same time, a collision takes place, and no data can be transmitted for either node. The stations then back off for a random period of time and try to transmit again. This process repeats until transmission takes place successfully. The CSMA/CD technology is also called contention.

▲ **Carrier Sense Multiple Access with Collision Avoidance (CSMA/CA):** Instead of monitoring traffic and moving in when there is a break, CSMA/CA allows the computer to send a signal that it is ready to transmit data. If the ready signal transmits without a problem, the computer then transmits its data. If the ready signal is not transmitted successfully, the computer waits and tries again. This method is slower and less popular than CSMA/CD.

▲ **Token passing:** In token passing, a special chunk of data called a token circulates from computer to computer. A transmitting computer waits for a free token, and modifies it with the data it needs to transmit. The modified token travels around the ring until it gets to the destination computer, which takes the token and data off the wire, modifies the token (indicating it has received the data), and places the token back on the wire. When the original sender receives this token and sees that the destination computer has received the data, the sender modifies the token to set it free and sends the token back on the ring. The main advantage of the token-passing access method over CSMA/CD is that it eliminates collisions. Only workstations that have the token can transmit.

Historically, there are two predominant IEEE 802 models on which existing network architectures have been based: 802.3 CSMA/CD and 802.5 Token Ring

▲ **IEEE 802.3 CSMA/CD:** The 802.3 CSMA/CD model defined a bus topology network that used a 50-ohm coaxial baseband cable and carried transmissions at 10MBps. This standard grouped data bits into frames and used CSMA/CD to put data on the cable. Ethernet is an example of a protocol based on the IEEE 802.3 CSMA/CD standard.

▲ **IEEE 802.5 Token Ring:** The IEEE 802.5 standard specified a physical star, logical ring topology that used a token-passing technology to put the data on the cable. IBM developed this technology for its mainframe and minicomputer networks.

12.1.5 Network Protocols

Four major network protocols are in use today:

▲ **TCP/IP:** The **Transmission Control Protocol/Internet Protocol (TCP/IP)** suite is a collection of protocols. The two most important protocols are TCP and IP. The TCP/IP suite is based on a four-layer model of networking that is similar to the seven-layer OSI model. Figure 12-8 shows how the TCP/IP model matches up with the OSI model and where some of the key TCP/IP protocols fit into the model.

TCP/IP is the only protocol suite used on the internet. TCP/IP was designed to get information delivered to its destination, even in the event of a failure of part of the network. It uses various routing protocols to discover the network it is traveling on and keep apprised of network changes. The TCP/IP suite includes many protocols. A few of the more important include:

• **Internet Protocol (IP):** Handles the movement of data between computers as well as network node addressing

• **Transmission Control Protocol (TCP):** Handles the reliable delivery of data

Figure 12-8

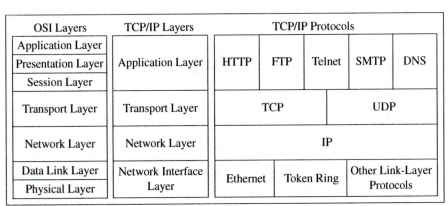

OSI Layers	TCP/IP Layers	TCP/IP Protocols				
Application Layer	Application Layer	HTTP	FTP	Telnet	SMTP	DNS
Presentation Layer						
Session Layer						
Transport Layer	Transport Layer	TCP			UDP	
Network Layer	Network Layer	IP				
Data Link Layer	Network Interface Layer	Ethernet		Token Ring	Other Link-Layer Protocols	
Physical Layer						

TCP/IP and the OSI model.

- **Internet Control Message Protocol (ICMP):** Transmits error messages and network statistics
- **User Datagram Protocol (UDP):** Performs a similar function to TCP, with less overhead and more speed, but with lower reliability

Application layer protocols are built on top of and into the TCP/IP protocol suite and are available on most implementations. These protocols include:

- **File Transfer Protocol (FTP):** Used to send and receive files in client/server mode to or from a remote host
- **Hypertext Transfer Protocol (HTTP):** Used to send World Wide Web (WWW) documents, which are usually encoded in HTML, across a network
- **Network File Services (NFS):** Allows the network node to access network drives as if they were local drives, files, and data; also performs the file access and data-retrieval tasks that are requested of the network
- **Simple Mail Transfer Protocol (SMTP):** Used to send electronic mail (email) across a network
- **Telnet:** Used to connect and log in and manage a remote host

▲ **IPX/SPX:** Although TCP/IP has quickly become the protocol of choice for most networks, plenty of networks still use an alternative protocol suite called IPX/SPX. **The Internetwork Packet Exchange/Sequenced Packet Exchange (IPX/SPX)** is the default communications protocol for versions of the Novell NetWare operating system before NetWare 5. It is often used with Windows networks as well, but in Windows networks, the implementation of the IPX/SPX protocol is known as NWLINK. IPX/SPX is a communications protocol similar to TCP/IP, but is used primarily in LANs. It has features for use in WAN environments as well; before the mid 1990s, most corporate networks ran IPX/SPX because it was easy to configure and could be routed across WANs. The two main protocols in IPX/SPX, IPX and SPX, provide the same functions that TCP and UDP do in TCP/IP.

▲ **NetBIOS:** Short for **Network Basic Input Output System,** this is the basic application-programming interface for network services on Windows computers. (It is installed automatically when you install TCP/IP, but doesn't show up as a separate protocol when you view the network connection properties.) NetBIOS is a Session layer protocol that can work with Transport layer protocols such as TCP, SPX, or NetBEUI. Many Windows computers use NetBIOS over TCP/IP. NetBEUI (Network BIOS Extended User Interface) is a Transport layer protocol that was designed for early IBM and Microsoft networks. NetBEUI is now considered obsolete.

▲ **AppleTalk:** AppleTalk is both a protocol and a proprietary network architecture for Macintosh computers. It uses a bus topology and typically either shielded or unshielded cable. AppleTalk uses CSMA/CA technology to put data on the cable. The AppleTalk suite includes a Physical and Data Link layer protocol called LocalTalk, but can also work with standard lower level protocols, including Ethernet and Token Ring.

Networks use special connection protocols and services to establish, maintain, and release connections over the transmission media. For instance, TCP/IP internet traffic runs over two different analog connection protocols: Serial Line Internet Protocol (SLIP) and Point-to-Point Protocol (PPP). Both work to get you on the internet, but PPP is more commonly used because it is more easily configured; it's also more stable because it includes enhanced error-checking capabilities. Other common connection protocols include X.25, Frame Relay, and ATM (the name is used for both the network and the connection protocol controlling traffic across it).

12.1.6 Network Architectures

Network architectures define the structure of the network, including hardware, software, network protocols used, and layout. We differentiate architectures by the hardware and software required to maintain optimum performance levels. A network architecture's performance is usually discussed in terms of **bandwidth**, or how much data a particular network technology can handle in a period of time. The major architectures in use today are Ethernet, Token Ring, and wireless LAN.

▲ **Ethernet:** Ethernet is network LAN architecture based on the IEEE 802.3 standard and specifies network communications at the physical layer and the media access control (MAC) layer. Various flavors of Ethernet operate at different speeds and use different types of media. However, all the versions of Ethernet are compatible with each other, so you can mix and match them on the same network by using devices such as bridges, hubs, and switches to link network segments that use different types of media. Ethernet comes in four different speed versions: 10MBps (Standard Ethernet); 100MBps (Fast Ethernet); 1000MBps, or 1GBps (Gigabit Ethernet), and 10GBps (10 Gigabit Ethernet). Each of these three versions are broken down into further classes based on the type of cable used (Table 12-5). An Ethernet LAN can support about 500 nodes. Ethernet devices connect to either a hub or a switch that is in turn connected to the network backbone. Ethernet is the cheapest and simplest network architecture, and Ethernet LANs are the most commonly installed type of network.

Table 12-5: Ethernet Versions

Ethernet Version	Classification	Cabling
Standard Ethernet (10MBps)	10Base5	Older, thicker, obsolete cable
	10Base2	Thinner coaxial cable in bus topology
	10BaseT	UTP cable: Uses a physical star topology with hubs at the center of each star; and a logical bus topology
	10BaseFL	Fiber-optic cable
Fast Ethernet (100MBps)	100BaseT4	UTP cable (same as 10BaseT)
	100BaseTX	Category 5 UTP cable; Most commonly used standard today for office networks
	100BaseFX	Fiber-optic cable; commonly used as a backbone connecting workgroup hubs to routers and servers
Gigabit Ethernet (1GBps)	1000Base-TX	Category 5, 5e, or 6 UTP cables
	1000Base-SX	MMF fiber optic, short wavelength laser
	1000Base-LX	SMF and MMF fiber optic, long wavelength laser
	1000Base-CX	150 ohm copper cabling with special 9-pin High Speed Serial Data Connector (HSSDC)
10 Gigabit Ethernet (10GBps)	10Gbase-SR	MMF fiber optic with short wavelength lasers
	10Gbase-LR	SMF fiber optic with long wavelength laser
	10Gbase-ER	SMF fiber optic with extra long wavelength lasers

▲ **Token Ring:** Token Ring networks are exactly like the IEEE 802.5 specification because the specification is based on IBM's Token Ring technology. Token Ring uses a physical star, logical ring topology. All workstations are cabled to a central device called a multistation access unit (MAU). The ring is created within the MAU by connecting every port together with special circuitry in the MAU. Token Ring can use shielded or unshielded cable or fiber-optic cabling and can transmit data at either 4MBps or 16MBps. Token Ring supports about 260 nodes.

▲ **Wireless LAN standards:** There are many standards that have been developed for wireless networking. The majority of the technology in use today for wireless LANs is based on the IEEE 802.11 series of standards for RF transmissions. The three most commonly used 802.11 standards today are:

* IEEE 802.11a
* IEEE 802.11b
* IEEE 802.11g

Although the term WiFi specifically refers to 802.11b, the term is used in general for any 802.11 RF transmissions. The 802.11 standards are essential wireless Ethernet standards and use many of the same networking techniques that the cabled Ethernet standards (in other words, 802.3) use. Most notably, 802.11 networks use the same CSMA/CD technique as cabled Ethernet to recover from network collisions. Similar to Ethernet, the 802.11 standards address the bottom two layers of the IEEE seven-layer model: The Physical layer and the Media Access Control (MAC) layer. Currently, most wireless networks are based on the 802.11b standard. Although 802.11a is faster than 802.11b, it is considerably more expensive and has less range. In addition, 802.11a and 802.11b aren't compatible with each other because 802.11a transmits at 5GHz and 802.11b transmits at 2.4GHz. As a result, 802.11a and 802.11b devices can't receive each other's signals. Other standards for wireless networking include:

* **Bluetooth:** Bluetooth is a RF-based wireless standard that has a total maximum throughput of 2MBps. It isn't fast as far as throughput is concerned, but it is still more than enough for peripheral communications like mice, keyboards, and headphones, and it is possible for two Bluetooth devices to network to each other in a peer-to-peer fashion, but it is impractical to build an entire multistation wireless LAN using the Bluetooth technology. Table 12-6 summarizes the IEEE 802.11 wireless LAN standards in comparison to Bluetooth.

* **Infrared networking:** Infrared is used primarily for short distance, point-to-point communications, like those between a peripheral and a PC. The largest use of infrared wireless is for peripherals using

Table 12-6: Bluetooth and Wireless LAN Standards

Standard	Max Throughput	Frequency Band(s)	Typical Max Range (Indoors)	Typical Max Range (outdoors)
Bluetooth	1MBps	2.4GHz	328ft/100m	N/A
802.11	1-2MBps	2.4GHz	328ft/100m	1500ft/457m
802.11a	54MBps	5GHz	250ft/76m	1000ft/305m
802.11b	11MBps	2.4GHz	328ft/100m	1500ft/457m
802.11g	54MBps	2.4GHz	328ft/100m	1500ft/457m

the IrDA standard. The standard specifies a data transmission rate of 16Mbps (increasing to over 100MBps with updates to the standard) and a maximum range of about 1 meter (1m). As you can see, although it possesses significant throughput, the range is lacking for a wireless LAN standard for large LANs.

Wireless transmissions are essentially broadcast in a wide range of direction available to any nearby, appropriate receiver, and therefore do not require any topology as with wired networks. There are two modes for wireless transmission, however: infrastructure and ad-hoc. In ad-hoc mode, wireless devices transmit directly to each other. In infrastructure mode, wireless devices transmit to a device called a wireless access point (WAP). WAPs allow wired networks to be extended to wireless devices.

In addition to Ethernet, Token Ring, and wireless LANs, other network architectures include:

▲ **ARCNet (Attached Resource Computing Network):** ARCNet was developed in 1977, but was not based on any existing IEEE 802 model. However, ARCNet is an older architecture popular with IBM mainframe networks. Its popularity came from its flexibility and price. It was flexible because it's cabling used large trunks and physical star configurations, so if a cable came loose or is disconnected, the network did not fail. Additionally, because it used cheap, coaxial cable, networks could be installed fairly cheaply. Even though ARCNet enjoyed an initial success, it died out as other network architectures became more popular. The main reason was its slow transfer rate of only 2.5MBps. Although a version of ARCNet that runs at 100MBps was developed, most people have abandoned ARCNet for other architectures. ARCNet is also not based on any standard, which makes it difficult to find compatible hardware from multiple vendors.

▲ **FDDI (Fiber Distributed Data Interface):** FDDI is a standard of ANSI and the International Standards Organization (ISO) for data networks that use ring topology with dual and redundant rings and data speeds of 100MBps. An FDDI NIC contains a laser or diode transceiver that converts its digital data into light to be transmitted on a fiber-optic network or back to a digital signal from incoming light impulses for use by the PC.

12.1.7 Network Addressing

Three types of **addressing** are used in networking to identify the source and destination of data transmissions:

▲ **MAC (Media Access Control) address:** Every NIC or network adapter is assigned a unique ID (called the MAC address) by its manufacturer when it is made. This address is burned into the NIC's firmware and cannot be changed. The MAC address is the basis for all network addressing, and all other address types are cross-referenced to it. A MAC address is a 48-bit address that is expressed as 12 hexadecimal digits (a hex digit is comprised of 4 bits), as in: *44-45-53-54-00-00.* (To display the MAC address (adapter address) of the NIC or NICs installed in a PC, you can use either the WINIPCFG command on Windows 9x and Me systems or the IPCONFIG command on Windows NT, 2000, XP and Vista systems.)

▲ **Network address:** Every network address in either TCP/IP or IPX is assigned both a network portion and a node portion. The network portion is the number that is assigned to the network segment to which the station is connected. The node portion is the unique number that identifies that station on the segment. Together, the network portion and the node portion of an address ensure that a network address is unique across the entire network.

  • **IPX addressing:** IPX addresses use a 32-bit, eight-digit hexadecimal number for the network portion. This number, called the IPX network address, can be assigned randomly by the installation program or manually by the network administrator. The node portion is the 12-digit hexadecimal MAC address assigned by the manufacturer. A colon separates the two portions. Here is a sample IPX address:

Network Address: Node Address

00004567:006A7C11FB56

- **TCP/IP addressing:** TCP/IP uses IP addresses with a dotted decimal notation in the format xxx.xxx.xxx.xxx, as shown here:

    199.217.67.34 IP Address

    The IP address is a 32-bit value represented as four groups of eight-digit binary numbers (or up to three decimal digits) called octets, separated by periods. Each decimal number in an IP address is typically a number in the range 1 through 254, although in some cases 0 and 255 are also acceptable.

▲ **Network/NetBIOS names:** A network name is the name assigned to a workstation or other networked device and used to identify that node by other network users. For example, it is much easier to find a printer with a network name of MAIN_LASER than trying to remember the printer's MAC or IP address. Commonly, network names are NetBIOS (Network Basis Input/Output System) names. NetBIOS uses unique 15-character names that are periodically broadcast over the network so the names can be cataloged by the Network Neighborhood function. NetBIOS names are the names that show up in Windows Network Neighborhood.

Various protocols and services can be used on a network to aid in the correlation and translation of one address form to another.

▲ **DHCP (Dynamic Host Configuration Protocol):** This protocol is used to automatically configure a network workstation with its IP address data. Each time that the workstation is logged on to the network, the DHCP server software, running on a network server or router, assigns or renews the IP configuration of the workstation. Typically, the address that is assigned is from blocks of IP addresses that have been set aside for use by internal networks. An IP address can be assigned as a static IP address (a fixed PC location) or as a dynamically assigned IP address (changeable). A static IP address is permanently assigned to a node when it is added to the network. Static IP addresses work as long as the network doesn't move, the NIC is not interchanged with other PCs, and the network is never reconfigured. Because most networks change (and they change fairly frequently), many networks are configured to assign IP addresses dynamically. Each PC that is attached to the network and is configured to obtain an IP address automatically requests and is assigned an IP address to use for a specific length of time by a Dynamic Host Configuration Protocol (DHCP) server. Beginning with Windows 95, all versions of Windows include a DHCP client. On occasion, a network PC boots up and finds that the DHCP server is not available.

When this happens, the PC continues to poll for a DHCP server using different wait periods. The Automatic Private IP Addressing (APIPA) service allows the DHCP client to automatically configure itself until the DHCP server is available and the client can be configured to the network. APIPA allows the DHCP client to assign itself an IP address in the range of 169.254.0.1 to 169.254.254.254 and a Class B subnet mask of 255.255.0.0. The address range that is used by APIPA is a Class B address that Microsoft has set aside for this purpose.

▲ **DNS (Domain Name System):** DNS is used to resolve (translate) internet names to their IP address equivalents. An internet domain is an element of the Domain Name Server (DNS) naming hierarchy used for creating easy to use names for internet servers. For example, when you request the domain name www.wiley.com from your browser's location line, a nearby DNS server (typically at your ISP) converts it to an IP address, such as 12.168.1.100, which is then used to request the data across the internet.

▲ **WINS (Windows Internet Naming Service):** WINS is Microsoft's network name resolution software that converts NetBIOS names to IP addresses. Windows computers are assigned NetBIOS names, which are converted into IP addresses for use on a network using TCP/IP, the foundation protocol suite of the internet. The use of a WINS server allows nodes on one LAN segment to find nodes on other LAN segments by name.

In general, when a new workstation is added to an Ethernet network, the workstation identifies itself using its MAC address and computer name to the rest of the network. Those devices that need to hold this addressing information, such as a switch or bridge, store the information in their MAC address tables. When requests come in for a particular IP address, the MAC address of the node is looked up and the message is sent to that workstation.

With Token Ring networks, when you add a new node, the node must first establish that its address is unique. The workstation sends out test frames with its ID address, and the system responds with its own test frames that are sent to that address. If no other node responds, the new ID address is accepted and established for the new ring node. If duplication exists, the NIC must be configured with a new address.

12.1.8 Understanding TCP/IP Addressing

With TCP/IP addresses such as 209.110.12.123, you can easily see that it's difficult for most users to memorize these numbers, so host names are used in their place. Host names are alphanumeric values assigned to a host; any host may have more than one host name.

For example, the host 209.110.12.123 may be known to all users as Gemini, or it may be known to the sales department as Gemini and to the marketing department as Apollo9. All that is needed is a means by which the alphanumeric name can be translated into its IP address. There are four methods of so doing:

▲ On a small network, you can use HOSTS files. These are ASCII text files located in the /etc directory of every machine that performs the translation. When a new host is added to the network, every host must have its HOSTS file updated to include the new entry. HOSTS files work with every platform and every operating system, but they require constant manual updating and editing to keep them current—impractical on large networks.

▲ On a large network, you can add a server to be referenced by all hosts for the name resolution. The server runs Domain Name Services (DNS) and resolves Fully Qualified Domain Names (FQDNs) (Figure 12-9) such as www.wiley.com into their IP address. Multiple DNS servers can serve an area and provide fault tolerance for one another. In all cases, the DNS servers divide their area into zones; every zone has a primary server and any number of secondary servers. DNS, similar to HOSTS, works with any operating system and any version.

▲ If the network within which you work is all Microsoft (Windows 2000, Windows XP, and so on), you're accustomed to using NetBIOS names as computer names. On a small network, you can use LMHOSTS files to translate computer names to IP addresses—much like HOSTS does. The big difference is that NetBIOS (computer) names exist only on the Microsoft platform, and LMHOSTS files can't be used with Unix or other operating systems.

▲ If you have a large Microsoft-only network, you can stop editing the LMHOSTS files manually and use a server running Windows Internet Naming Service (WINS). The WINS server dynamically maps NetBIOS names to IP addresses and keeps your network mappings current. Again, this is a replacement for LMHOSTS and works only in the Microsoft world.

Figure 12-9

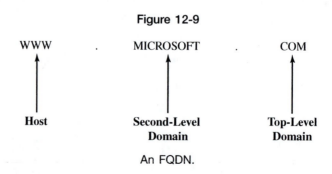

An FQDN.

Whether the files/services are case-sensitive or not depends on the operating system. If you're using HOSTS files in Unix and have a host named GEMINI, you must have the following entry in the file:

209.110.12.123 GEMINI

In Windows, however, neither the operating system nor the HOSTS file is case sensitive, and

209.110.12.123 Gemini

delivers the same result when trying to resolve GEMINI, as do references to gemini, gemInI, and so on. HOSTS files are limited to 256 characters per line, and the pound sign (#) is used as the comment character. Wherever the pound sign is found, the rest of the line is ignored. For example:

#This is the first line

209.110.123.4 MARS #This is the second line

Line one is completely ignored, and line two is processed up to the space following the S. LMHOSTS files also use the pound sign as the comment character.

The FQDNs mentioned earlier identify the host and information about it. The first part, www, identifies the type of service to use. The second part, wiley, identifies the entity, and com identifies the type of entity. Known as a domain, the entity type can be any of the values shown in Table 12-7.

Table 12-7: Common Domains

Domain	Meaning
.biz	Business
.com	Commercial
.edu	Educational
.info	Information
.mil	Military
.gov	Government
.net	Network—ISP
.org	Original—organization
.xx	Two-character country identifier, such as ca for Canada

Dynamic Host Configuration Protocol (DHCP) falls into a different category. Whereas the other services described concentrate on resolving names to IP addresses, DHCP issues IP configuration data.

Rather than an administrator having to configure a unique IP address for every host added on a network (and default gateway and subnet mask), they can use a DHCP server to issue these values. That server is given a number of addresses in a range that it can supply to clients.

For example, the server may be given the IP range (or scope) 209.110.12.1 to 209.11.12.200. When a client boots, it sends out a request for the server to issue it an address (and any other configuration data) from that scope. The server takes one of the numbers it has available and leases it to the client for a length of time. If the client is still using the configuration data when 50 percent of the lease has expired, it requests a renewal of the lease from the server. Under normal operating conditions, the request is granted. When the client is no longer using the address, the address goes back in the scope and can be issued to another client.

DHCP is built on the older Bootstrap Protocol (BOOTP) that was used to allow diskless workstations to boot and connect to a server that provided them an operating system and applications. The client uses broadcasts to request the data and thus—normally—can't communicate with DHCP servers beyond their own subnet (broadcasts don't route). A DHCP Relay Agent, however, can be employed to allow DHCP broadcasts to go from one network to another.

IP addresses are 32-bit binary numbers. Because numbers of such magnitude are difficult to work with, they're divided into four octets (eight bits) and converted to digital. Thus, 01010101 becomes 85. This is important because the limits on the size of the digital number are due to the reality that they're representations of binary numbers. The range must be from 0 (00000000) to 255 (11111111) per octet, making the lowest possible IP address 0.0.0.0 and the highest 255.255.255.255. Many IP addresses aren't available because they're reserved for diagnostic purposes, private addressing, or some other function.

Three classes of IP addresses are available; they're identified by the first octet. Table 12-8 shows the class and the range the first octet must fall into to be within that class.

The class of the address also determines the number of bits in the address that are used to identify the network and the number of bits used to identify the host

Table 12-8: IP Address Classes

Class	Range	Network Address Bits
A	1–126	First octet: e.g. 125
B	128–191	First two octets: e.g. 152.119
C	192–223	First three octets: e.g. 205.19.15

address. Class A addresses use the first octet to identify the network; Class B addresses use the first two octets and Class C the first three octets. For example, if you have a Class A address, you are assigned a network address such as 125 for the first octet. With a few exceptions, this means you can use any number between 0 and 255 as the second octet, any number between 0 and 255 as the third octet, and any number between 0 and 255 in the fourth octet. This gives you a total number of hosts that you can have on your network in excess of 16 million.

If you have a Class B address, you are assigned a network address using two octets, such as 152.119. With a few exceptions, this means you can use any number between 0 and 255 in the third octet and any number between 0 and 255 in the fourth octet. This gives you a total number of hosts that you can have on your network in excess of 65,000.

If you have a Class C address, you are assigned a network address using three octets, such as 205.19.15. You can use any number between 1 and 254 in the fourth octet, for a total of 254 possible hosts (0 and 255 are reserved).

The class, therefore, makes a tremendous difference in the number of hosts your network can have. In most cases, the odds of having all hosts at one location are small. Assuming you have a Class B address, will there be 65,000 hosts in one room, or will they be in several locations? Most often, it's the latter.

Subnetting your network is the process of taking the total number of hosts available to you and dividing it into smaller networks. When you configure TCP/IP on a host, you must only give three values: a unique IP address, a default gateway (router) address, and a subnet mask. The default subnet mask for each class of network is shown in Table 12-9.

When you use the default subnet mask, you're allowing for all hosts to be at one site and not subdividing your network. Any deviation from the default signifies that you're dividing the network into multiple subnetworks.

TCP/User Datagram Protocol (UDP) uses port numbers to listen for and respond to requests for communications. RFC 1060 defines common port numbers for a number of services, generally below 1024. You can, however, reconfigure your service to use another port number (preferably much higher) if you're concerned about security and you don't want your site to be available to anonymous traffic.

Common port assignments are listed in Table 12-10.

Table 12-9: Default Subnet Mask Values

Class	Default Subnet Mask
A	255.0.0.0
B	255.255.0.0
C	255.255.255.0

Table 12-10: Common Port Assignments

Service	Port
FTP	21
Telnet	23
SMTP	25
HTTP	80
NNTP	119
SSL	443

FOR EXAMPLE

IPv4 and IPv6

Most of the current internet is based on version 4 of the Internet Protocol, also known as IPv4. IPv4 has served the internet well for more than 20 years. However, the growth of the internet has put a lot of pressure on IPv4's limited 32-bit address space. Eventually all the addresses will be assigned and the IPv4 address space will be filled to capacity. When that happens, the internet will have to migrate to the next version of IP, known as IPv6. IPv6 offers several advantages over IPv4, but the most important is that it uses 128 bits for internet addresses rather than 32 bits, which means the number of unique internet addresses provided by IPv6 is 340,282,366,920,938,463, 463,374,607,431,768,211,456. The transition from IPv4 to IPv6 has been a slow one. IPv6 is available on all new computers and has been supported on Windows XP since Service Pack 1 was released in 2002. However, most internet service providers still base their service on IPv4. Thus, the internet will continue to be driven by IPv4 for at least a few more years.

SELF-CHECK

1. What types of networks are there?
2. What is the difference between a physical and logical topology?
3. Explain the difference between network models, standards, and protocols
4. What is Ethernet?

12.2 Examining Network Media and Hardware

The network medium is the material on which data is transferred from one point to another. There are two parts to the medium: the network interface card and the cabling. The type of network card you use must support the right connections to the network cabling. Because transmission media have limits to how far they can carry a message before their signal is degraded, various types of hardware devices are used to extend the reach of and manage network signaling.

12.2.1 Network Transmission Media

When the data is passing through the OSI model and reaches the Physical layer, it must find its way onto the medium that is used to physically transfer data from computer to computer, either a cable or a wireless transmission method. The type of network cable used in a network depends on the network's architecture and topology. There are five main types of transmission media: coaxial cable, twisted-pair cable, fiber-optic cable, RS-232 Serial, and wireless. (Coaxial cable and RS-232 cables are older media that are used less often today.) In addition to these standard network cabling methods listed as follows, USB and IEEE 1394/FireWire cables can be used in a limited fashion, typically in home networking, to network devices together.

▲ **Coaxial:** A type of cable that was once popular for Ethernet bus networks is **coaxial cable**, sometimes called thinnet or BNC cable because of the type of connectors used on each end of the cable. Coaxial cable (or coax) contains a center conductor made of copper, surrounded by a plastic jacket, with a braided shield over the jacket (Figure 12-10). Either Teflon-type material or a plastic such as PVC covers this metal shield. Thinnet cable operates only at 10MBps and is rarely used for new networks. However, you'll find plenty of existing thinnet networks still being used. You attach thinnet to the network interface card by using a twist-on connector called a BNC connector. A T-connector on each NIC can connect two cables.

Figure 12-10

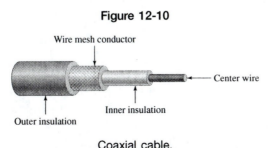

Coaxial cable.

Figure 12-11

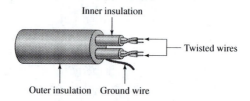

Twisted-pair cable.

▲ **Twisted-pair cables: Twisted-pair cable** is one of the most popular methods of cabling because of its flexibility and low cost. It consists of several pairs of wire twisted around each other within an insulated jacket (Figure 12-11).

Twisted-pair is most often found in 10BaseT Ethernet networks, although other systems can use it. Twisted-pair cabling is usually classified in two types: unshielded twisted-pair (UTP) and shielded twisted-pair (STP). UTP is simply twisted-pair cabling that is unshielded. STP is the same as UTP, but it has a braided foil shield around the twisted wires (to decrease electrical interference). UTP comes in seven grades to offer different levels of protection against electrical interference:

- **Category 1:** For voice-only transmissions, and common in older phone system. It contains two twisted pairs.
- **Category 2:** Able to transmit data at speeds up to 4MBps. It contains four twisted pairs of wires.
- **Category 3:** Able to transmit data at speeds up to 10MBps. It contains four twisted pairs of wires with three twists per foot.
- **Category 4:** Able to transmit data at speeds up to 16MBps. It contains four twisted pairs of wires.
- **Category 5:** Able to transmit data at speeds up to 100MBps. It contains four twisted pairs of copper wire to give the most protection.
- **Category 5e:** Able to transmit data at speeds up to 1GBps. It also contains four twisted pairs of copper wire, but they are physically separated and contain more twists per foot than Category 5 to provide maximum interference protection.
- **Category 6:** Able to transmit data at speeds up to 1GBps and beyond. It also contains four twisted pairs of copper wire, and they are oriented differently than in Category 5 or 5e.

Each of these levels has a maximum transmission distance of 100 meters. UTP and STP cables use an RJ (registered jack) connector. Most telephones

Figure 12-12

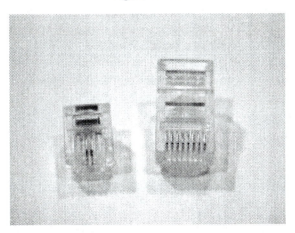

RJ-11 and RJ-45 connectors.

connect with an RJ-11 connector; most Category 2 and higher cables use RJ-45 (Figure 12-12).

▲ **Fiber-optic:** Fiber-optic cabling consists of a thin, flexible glass or plastic fiber surrounded by a rubberized outer coating (Figure 12-13).

Fiber-optic cabling provides transmission speeds from 100MBps to 1GBps and a maximum distance of several miles. Because it uses pulses of light instead of electric voltages to transmit data, it is immune from electric interference and from wiretapping. Fiber-optic cable has not become a standard in networks, however, because of its high cost of installation. Networks that need extremely fast transmission rates, transmissions over long distances, or have had problems with electrical interference in the past often use fiber-optic cabling. Fiber-optic cable may be either single-mode fiber (SMF) or multimode fiber (MMF). The term mode refers to the bundles of light that enter the fiber-optic cable.

Figure 12-13

Inner insulation (cladding)

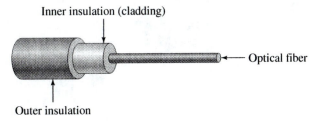

Optical fiber

Outer insulation

Fiber-optic cable.

- **Single-mode fiber (SMF) cable:** SMF cable uses only a single mode of light to propagate through the fiber cable. SMF cable is commonly used as backbone cabling; it is also usually the cable type used in phone systems. Because only a single mode of light travels through the cable, single-mode fiber-optic cable supports higher bandwidth and longer distances than multimode fiber-optic cable. Devices that use single-mode fiber-optic cable typically use lasers to generate the light that travels through the cable.

- **Multimode fiber (MMF) cable:** MMF allows multiple modes of light to propagate. In MMF cable, the light bounces off the cable walls as it travels through the cable, which causes the signal to weaken more quickly. Because of this, it has lower cable distances and a lower available bandwidth. Devices that use MMF cable typically use light-emitting diodes (LEDs) to generate the light that travels through the cable; however, higher bandwidth network devices such as Gigabit Ethernet are now using lasers with MMF cable. MMF cable is most often used as horizontal cable.

The maximum backbone distance using single-mode fiber-optic cable is 3,000 meters (9,840 feet), and the maximum backbone distance using multimode fiber is 2,000 meters (6,560 feet). Fiber-optic cables can use myriad different connectors, but the two most common are:

- **SC (square connector):** SC connectors (Figure 12-14) use a latch to hold the connection and work with either SMF or MMF cables and last for around 1,000 matings.

- **ST (straight tip):** The ST connector (Figure 12-15) uses a BNC attachment mechanism similar to the thinnet Ethernet connection mechanism and has a maximum mating cycle of around 1,000 matings.

Figure 12-14

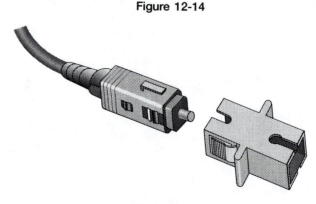

SC connector.

Figure 12-15

Examples of ST connectors.

Other popular styles of fiber-optic connector are the small form factor styles of connectors (Figure 12-16). These allow more fiber-optic terminations in the same amount of space than their standard-sized counterparts. The two most popular are the mechanical transfer registered jack (MT-RJ or MTRJ) and the Local Connector (LC).

▲ **RS-232 (serial cables):** Occasionally, networks use RS-232 cables (also known as serial cables) to carry data. The classic example is in older mainframe and minicomputer terminal connections. Connections from the individual terminals go to a device known as a multiplexer that combines the serial connections into one connection and connects all the terminals to the host computer. This cabling system is seen less and less

Figure 12-16

MT-RJ connector   LC connector

Small form factor fiber-optic connectors.

> ## FOR EXAMPLE
>
> ### Plenum-Rated Coatings
>
> A **plenum-rated coating** on a cable simply means that the coating does not produce toxic gas when burned (as PVC does) and is rated for use in air plenums. A plenum is the space in a building used for circulating air, such as between a suspended ceiling and the actual ceiling. This type of cable is more expensive but may be mandated by electrical code whenever cable is hidden in walls or ceilings. Plenum rating applies to all types of cabling.

as a viable LAN cabling method, however, because LAN connections like twisted-pair Ethernet are faster, more reliable, and easier to maintain.

▲ **Wireless media:** Wireless transmissions are made through the air by infrared light, laser light, narrow-band radio, microwave, or spread-spectrum radio and are used most often in environments where standard cabling methods are too costly or not possible or wanted. However, they are still not as fast or efficient as standard cabling methods. Wireless transmissions are also more susceptible to eavesdropping and interference than standard cabling methods. The three basic types of wireless communications are:

- Radio waves (transmission frequencies of 10KHz to 1GHz)
- Microwaves (transmission frequencies of 1GHz to 500GHz)
- Infrared (transmission frequencies of 500GHz to 1THz)

Each type of transmission medium has its own benefits and drawbacks (Table 12-11).

12.2.2 Network Interface Cards (NICs)

A **network interface card (NIC)** is a card you install in your computer to connect, or interface, your computer to the network. This device provides the physical, electrical, and electronic connections to the network media. A NIC is either an expansion card or built in to the motherboard of the computer. In some notebook computers, NIC adapters can also be connected to the printer port or through a PC card slot.

NIC cards generally all have one or two LEDs that help in diagnosing problems with their functionality. A Link LED illuminates when proper connectivity to an active network is detected. An Activity LED flickers, indicating the intermittent transmission or receipt of data to or from the network.

The primary purposes of the NIC are to serve as a transceiver—a device that transmits and receives data to and from other NICs (installed in the other networked nodes and devices)—and to connect to the network cabling. The NIC also acts

Table 12-11: Cable Types

Characteristics	Twisted-Pair	Coaxial	Fiber-Optic	Wireless
Cost	Least expensive	More than twisted-pair	Expensive	Most expensive
Maximum length	100 meters (328 feet)	185 meters (607 feet) to 500 meters (1640 feet)	10 Miles	Up to 2 miles
Transmission rate	10MBps to 100MBps	10MBps	100MBps or more	2MBps to 54MBps
Flexibility	Most flexible	Fair	Fair	Limited
Ease of installation	Very easy	Easy	Difficult	Depends on the implementation
Interference	Susceptible	Better than UTP; more susceptible than STP	Not susceptible	Susceptible
Special features	Often pre-installed; similar to the wiring used in telephone systems	Easiest installation	Supports voice, data, and video at the highest transmission speeds	Very flexible
Preferred uses	Networks	Medium-size networks with high security needs	Networks of any size requiring high speed and data security	WANs and radio/TV communications
Connector	RJ-45	BNC-T and AUI	Special (SC and ST, and others)	Dish, transceiver, or access point
Physical topology	Star	Bus	Star (typically)	Bus or star
Other information	Five categories of quality	RG-58 and RG-59 family; also called thinnet and thicknet, respectively	Requires special training to configure	Most must comply with FCC regulations

as a translator between the network and the PC. Networks transmit data in a serial data format (1 bit at a time), and the data bus of the PC moves data in a parallel format (8 bits at a time). The NIC converts the signal from serial to parallel format or from parallel to serial format, depending on its direction. The NIC also formats the data as required by the network architecture. NIC characteristics and features include:

▲ **MAC (Media Access Control) address:** Each NIC is physically encoded with a unique identifying address that is used to locate it on the network. This address is 48 bits (6 bytes) long.

▲ **System resources:** A NIC is configured to the computer with an IRQ, an I/O address, and a DMA channel. A NIC commonly uses IRQ3, IRQ5, or IRQ10, and an I/O address of 300h.

▲ **Data bus compatibility:** NICs are designed with compatibility to a particular data bus architecture. ISA (Industry Standard Architecture) and PCI (Peripheral Component Interconnect) cards are the most common.

▲ **Data speed:** The NIC must be compatible with the data speed of the network. The data transfer speeds of a network are determined by several factors, including the cable media, the network topology, and the network connectivity devices that are in use. Many NICs have the capability to sense the data speed in use. A NIC designated as a 10/100 NIC has the capability to autosense between a 10MBps and a 100MBps network. Newer systems now support data speeds of 1,000MBps (or 1GBps), and newer NICs now support an autosensing 10/100/1000 port. Additionally, network cards can send data using either full-duplex or half-duplex mode. Half-duplex mode means that transmission can occur in only one direction at a time (Figure 12-17); the main advantage of full-duplex over half-duplex communication is performance. Network cards (specifically Fast Ethernet network cards) can operate twice as fast (200MBps) in full-duplex mode as they do normally in half-duplex mode (100MBps).

▲ **Connectors:** Several different connectors are used to join NICs to network cabling. The type of connector that is used depends mostly on the type of cable in use. Coax cabling primarily uses a BNC connector. Fiber-optic cabling is rarely used for cabling to workstations because of its cost. The most commonly used connector for networking is the RJ-45 connector.

In most respects, a **wireless NIC** (Figure 12-18) is the same as a traditional NIC, but instead of having a socket to plug a cable into, the wireless NIC will have a radio antenna. On laptops with built-in wireless networking, this antenna may be internal. Wireless antennas act as both transmitters and receivers. There are two broad classes of antennas on the market, omni directional and directional. As a general rule, directional antennas have greater range than omni antennas of

Figure 12-17

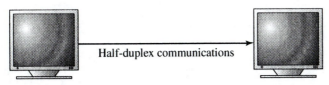

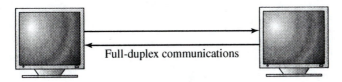

Duplex transmission modes.

because they focus all their power in a single direction. There are wireless adapters that are not NICs. For example, Linksys makes an external USB wireless adapter for notebooks. It is not a NIC because it isn't an expansion card (the C in NIC), so they are generally referred to as "adapters." Additionally, NICs also come in the form of PC cards, generally for laptops, not just conventional expansion cards.

Figure 12-18

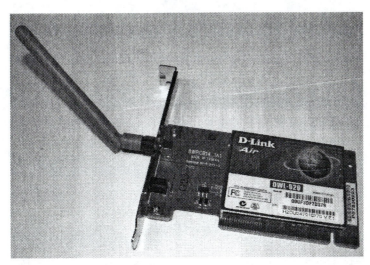

A wireless NIC.

FOR EXAMPLE

Half-duplex or Full-duplex

All network communications (including LAN and WAN communications) can be categorized as half-duplex or full-duplex. With **half-duplex**, communications happen in both directions, but in only one direction at a time. When two computers communicate using half-duplex, one computer sends a signal and the other receives; then, at some point, they switch sending and receiving roles. Chances are that you are familiar with half-duplex communications. If you have ever used a push-to-talk technology, such as a walkie-talkie, you were communicating via half-duplex: One person talks, and then the other person talks. **Full-duplex**, on the other hand, allows communications in both directions simultaneously. Both stations can send and receive signals at the same time. Full-duplex communications are similar to a telephone call, in which both people can talk simultaneously.

12.2.3 Network Connectivity Devices

Network connectivity devices connect network entities and allow networks to extend beyond standard cable limits. In addition to the NIC, the most important and frequently used network connectivity devices are:

▲ **Repeaters:** A repeater is a simple, inexpensive amplifying device that allows a cabling system to extend beyond its maximum allowed length by amplifying the network voltages so they travel farther. Repeaters operate at the Physical layer of the OSI model. Because of this, repeaters can only be used to regenerate signals between similar network segments. For example, you can extend an Ethernet 10Base2 network to 400 meters with a repeater. But you can't connect an Ethernet network and a Token Ring network together with one. The main disadvantage of repeaters is that they just amplify signals. These signals include not only the network signals but any noise (random fluctuations or disturbances in electrical signals) on the wire as well. Eventually, if you use enough repeaters, you could possibly drown out the signal with the amplified noise. For this reason, repeaters are used only as a temporary fix.

▲ **Hubs:** A **hub** is a device used to link several computers together. They are most often used in 10BaseT Ethernet networks. They are essentially multiport repeaters: They repeat any signal that comes in on one port and then copy it to the other ports (a process that is also called broadcasting). There are two types of hubs: active and passive. Passive hubs connect all ports together electrically and are usually not powered. Active hubs use electronics to amplify and clean up the signal before it is broadcast to the other ports. Intelligent hubs are active hubs that can be remotely managed on the network.

▲ **Switches:** A **switch** operates similarly to a hub because it connects several computers (usually twisted-pair Ethernet networks). However, switches don't repeat everything they receive on one port to every other port as hubs do. Rather, switches examine the header of the incoming packet and forward it properly to the right port and only that port. This greatly reduces overhead and thus performance as there is essentially a virtual connection between sender and receiver. A switch functions like a multiport bridge (and in some cases, a multiport router).

▲ **Bridges:** A **bridge** joins similar topologies and is used to divide network segment, by keeping traffic on one side from crossing to the other. For this reason, they are often used to increase performance on a high-traffic segment. For example, with 200 people on one Ethernet segment, performance will be mediocre because of the design of Ethernet and the number of workstations that are fighting to transmit. If you divide the segment into two segments of 100 workstations each, the traffic will be much lower on either side and performance will increase. Bridges are not able to distinguish one protocol from another because higher levels of the OSI model are not available to them. If a bridge is aware of the destination address, it can forward packets; otherwise it forwards the packets to all segments. Bridges are more intelligent than repeaters but are unable to move data across multiple networks simultaneously. Unlike repeaters, bridges can filter out signal noise. The main disadvantage of bridges is that they can't connect dissimilar network types or perform intelligent path selection. For that function, you need a router.

▲ **Routers:** A **router** is a device that connects multiple network types and determine the best path for sending data. They can route packets across multiple networks and use routing tables to store network addresses to determine the best destination. Routers are normally used to connect one LAN to another to create a WAN. The advantage of using a router over a bridge is that routers can determine the best path for data to take to get to its destination. Similar to bridges, they can segment large networks and can filter out noise. However, they are slower than bridges because they are more intelligent devices; as such, they analyze every packet, causing packet-forwarding delays. Because of this intelligence, they are also more expensive.

▲ **Gateway:** A **gateway** is any hardware and software combination that connects dissimilar network environments. Gateways are the most complex of network devices because they perform translations at multiple layers of the OSI model. An example of a gateway is the NT Gateway Service for NetWare, which, when running on a Windows NT Server, can connect a Microsoft Windows NT network with a Novell NetWare network. Another popular example is the email gateway. Most LAN-based email software, such as Microsoft's Exchange, can't communicate directly with internet mail servers without the use of a gateway. This gateway translates LAN-based mail messages into the SMTP format that internet mail uses. A gateway is usually a dedicated server on a network because it typically requires large amounts of system resources.

12.2.4 Other Networking Devices and Hardware

In addition to these network connectivity devices, there are several devices that are involved in the process of moving network data, including modems, DSL endpoints, ISDN terminal adapters, wireless access points (WAPs), transceivers, and firewalls.

▲ **Modems:** A **modem** (MOdulator/DEModulator) is a device that modulates digital data onto an analog carrier for transmission over an analog medium and then demodulates from the analog carrier to a digital signal again at the receiving end. Modems can be used to connect to the internet or to a LAN or WAN.

  • **Traditional (POTS) modems:** Most modems you find in computers today fall into the category of traditional modems. These modems convert the signals from your computer into signals that travel over the plain old telephone service (POTS) lines. The majority of modems that exist today are POTS modems, mainly because PC manufacturers include one with a computer.

  • **Cable modems:** Cable modems connect an individual PC or network to the internet using your cable television cable. The cable modem itself is a fairly simple device. It has a standard coax connector on the back as well as an Ethernet port. You can connect one PC to a cable modem (the PC will need to have an Ethernet NIC installed), or you can connect the modem to multiple PCs on a network (using a hub or switch). A router may also be used to enhance the Ethernet network's capabilities.

▲ **DSL endpoints:** A **DSL endpoint** (also called a modem, although it does not translate signals from analog to digital) is the device that allows the network signals to pass over phone lines at higher, digital frequencies. This modem is usually an external modem (although internal DSL modems are available), and it usually has both a phone line and an Ethernet connection. You must connect the phone line to a wall jack and the Ethernet connection to your computer (you must have an Ethernet NIC in your computer in order to connect to the DSL modem). Alternatively, a router, hub, or switch may be connected to the Ethernet port of the DSL modem, increasing the options available for the Ethernet network.

▲ **ISDN terminal adapters:** Integrated Services Digital Network (ISDN) is another form of high-speed internet access. Your computer accesses ISDN services through an ISDN terminal adapter. The box itself is about the size of a modem and also uses a phone jack and an Ethernet jack. You connect a phone cord from the phone jack to the wall jack where your ISDN services are being delivered. Then you connect an Ethernet cable from your PC to the ISDN TA's Ethernet jack.

▲ **Wireless access point:** A **wireless access point (WAP)** (also called an access point or AP) is essentially a wireless bridge (or switch, as multiple end devices can connect simultaneously). It operates by connecting wireless clients together. In addition, it can connect those wireless clients to a wired network. As with a bridge or switch, the WAP indiscriminately propagates all broadcasts to all wireless and wired devices while allowing filtering based on MAC addresses. The WAP contains at least one radio antenna that it uses to communicate with its clients via radio frequency (RF) signals. The WAP can (depending on software settings) act as either an access point, which allows a wireless user transparent access to a wired network, or a wireless bridge, which will connect a wireless network to a wired network yet only pass traffic it knows belongs on the other side. Wireless access points (Figure 12-19) often include other built-in features. For example, some access points double as Ethernet hubs or switches. In that case, the access point will have more than one RJ-45 port. In addition, some access points include broadband cable or DSL firewall routers that enable you to connect to the internet. A multifunction access point that's designed to serve as an internet gateway for home networks sometimes is called a residential gateway.

▲ **Transceivers (media converters):** Another small device that is commonly seen on a network is the external **transceiver** (also known as a media converter). These are relatively simple devices that allow a NIC or other networking device to connect to a different type of media than it was designed for. Many NICs have special connectors that will allow this, as do hubs and switches. For example, if you have a 100Base-TX switch and would like to connect it to another switch using fiber-optic cabling, you would connect a fiber transceiver to each switch's transceiver

Figure 12-19

A wireless access point (WAP).

port and then connect the two transceivers together with the appropriate fiber-optic cabling.

▲ **Firewalls:** A **firewall** is probably the most important device on a network if that network is connected to the internet. Its job is to protect LAN resources from attackers on the internet. Similarly, it can prevent computers on the network from accessing various services on the internet. It can be used to filter packets based on rules that the network administrator sets. These rules state what kinds of information can flow into and out of a network's connection to the internet. Firewalls can be either stand-alone "black boxes," or can be set up in software on a server or router. Either way, the firewall will have at least two network connections: one to the internet (known as the "public" side), and one to the network (known as the "private" side). Sometimes, there is a third network port on a firewall.

SELF-CHECK

1. Identify six types of network transmission media.
2. What are the two main functions of a NIC?
3. Define "network connectivity device," and cite six examples.
4. What is a DSL endpoint?

12.3 Connecting to Networks

In a business environment, it would be extremely unlikely to find a network that has been planned, set up, and works without any further intervention from network technicians. Networks may suffer security breaches, lag in performance due to unexpected traffic volumes or configuration problems, and users and resources will need to be added and removed from the network on a continuous basis. Network management is therefore a crucial task in maintaining network performance. Common network tasks include connecting, sharing, and managing printers and other resources, backing up important data from network devices such as servers as well as data from workstations. The most fundamental tasks are creating and troubleshooting basic network connectivity.

12.3.1 Creating and Configuring a Network Connection

The network interface card (NIC) is the PC component that communicates with a network. The PC itself only communicates with the NIC through the operating system and the NIC's device drivers and protocols. Installing a NIC in a PC involves physically installing the NIC in an expansion slot on the motherboard and configuring the NIC to interact with the PC and the network and to facilitate the interface of these two. This includes ensuring you have the latest driver for the NIC and performing a software installation of the NIC through its Plug and Play installation or by using the Control Panel's Add Hardware Wizard. When Windows 2000, XP or Vista detects a NIC, it automatically creates a network connection and configures it to support basic networking protocols. You can also create a new network connection through the New Connection Wizard, which you can access through the Control Panel's Network Connections applet. The New Connection Wizard guides you through the process of creating a network connection.

You configure the NIC (system resources, power management, and so on) through the NIC's Properties dialog box. A NIC's configuration settings include some advanced settings. These let you set a variety of device-specific parameters that affect the operation of the NIC. For example, some cards have a parameter that lets you set the card's speed (typically 10MBps or 100MBps) or the number of buffers the card should use. You should consult the manual that came with the card before you adjust these settings.

To configure a client to connect to a network, you may need to manually change the configuration of the network connection in the Local Area Connection's Properties dialog box (Figure 12-20).

The Local Area Connection Properties dialog box lists the protocols, network services, and clients that are enabled for the network:

▲ **Protocol:** To communicate with a network, the PC must be using the same protocols as the network. In most cases, the protocol stack used

Figure 12-20

The Local Area Connection Properties dialog box.

is TCP/IP, but verify this with your network administrator before proceeding.

▲ **Client:** Network clients allow a PC to communicate with specific network operating systems, such as Windows NT, Windows 2000 Server, Windows 2003, or Novell NetWare.

▲ **Service:** Network services include specialized drivers that facilitate specialized capabilities, such as File and Print Sharing for Microsoft Networks and support for file systems on non-Windows servers.

To connect to a network, you must have a NIC or network adapter, and the proper protocol and client for the network must be installed and enabled. Common items listed in the Local Area Connection's Properties dialog box are:

▲ **Client for Microsoft Networks:** This item is required to access a Microsoft Windows network. It should always be present.

▲ **File and Printer Sharing for Microsoft Networks:** This item allows your computer to share its files or printers with other computers on the network. This option is usually used with peer-to-peer networks, but you can use it even if your network has dedicated servers.

▲ **QoS Packet Scheduler:** This item manages the flow of data through your broadband connection.

▲ **Internet Protocol (TCP/IP):** This item enables the client computer to communicate via the TCP/IP protocol. If all the servers on the network support TCP/IP, this protocol should be the only one installed on the client.

Not all networks need all these items, but to connect to a network, the network items that your client requires must be listed here. For example, if Apple Computer or NetWare servers are on the network, the PC must have the applicable clients and linkware to be able to interact with them. Common network protocol suites used for non-Windows networks are:

▲ **AppleTalk:** This is Apple Computer's proprietary network protocol suite.
▲ **IPX/SPX:** This is a Novell NetWare proprietary protocol suite that is used as the native network operating system prior to Version 5 of NetWare, which uses TCP/IP as its native protocol.
▲ **NWLink:** A protocol that allows a pc running a Windows OS to communicate and interact with a Novell NetWare server
▲ **NetBEUI/NetBIOS:** The NetBIOS Extended User Interface (NetBEUI— pronounced "net booey") is an enhanced version of the NetBIOS network operating system. NetBEUI is still used by many manufacturers as a network operating system on local networks that don't connect to the internet.

If a protocol that you need isn't listed, click the Install button to add the protocol that you need. You can also remove network items that aren't needed.

You may also need to configure TCP/IP settings to accord with the network setup: To do this, click Internet Protocol (TCP/IP) and click Properties to display the TCP/IP Properties dialog box. TCP/IP settings include:

▲ **Obtain an IP Address Automatically:** Used if your network has a DHCP server that assigns IP addresses automatically.
▲ **Use the Following IP Address:** If your computer must have a specific IP address, choose this option and then type in the computer's IP address, subnet mask, and default gateway address.
▲ **Obtain DNS Server Address Automatically:** The DHCP server can also provide the address of the Domain Name System (DNS) server that the computer should use. Choose this option if your network has a DHCP server.
▲ **Use the Following DNS Server Addresses:** Choose this option if a DHCP server is not available; then type the IP address of the primary and secondary DNS servers.

In addition to configuring the network connection, you must also usually configure the client computer identification. Every client computer must identify itself to participate in the network. The computer identification consists of the computer's name, an optional description, and the name of either the workgroup or the domain to which the computer belongs. The computer name must follow the rules for NetBIOS names; it may be from 1 to 15 characters long and may contain letters, numbers, or hyphens but no spaces or periods. For small networks, it's common to make the computer name the same as the user name. Larger networks typically use a naming scheme to identify a computer.

In addition, some networks, such as Windows NT/2000/2003 use domains: logical groups of computers with centralized security and administration. Servers and workstations are classified into domains by the role that they play on the network. In the context of a Windows NT Server, Windows 2000 Server, or a Windows Server 2003 network, a domain is a collection of hardware and software resources and the user accounts that have access to them. The resources may include multiple servers, printers, CD-ROM drives, RAIDs, and other devices that are attached to the network.

Every user who wants to access a domain-based network must log on to the domain by using a valid user account. The user account is created on the domain controller—not on the client computer. If the computer will join a domain, you need to have access to an Administrator account on the domain unless the administrator has already created a computer account on the domain. Note that only Windows 2000, XP, and Vista, and Windows Server (NT, 2000, and 2003) com-

FOR EXAMPLE

Workgroups versus Domains

In a Windows network, a domain is a group of server computers that share a common user account database. A user at a client computer can log in to a domain to access shared resources for any server in the domain. Each domain must have one server designated as the domain controller. This server is ultimately in charge of the domain. A peer-to-peer network can't have a domain because it doesn't have a dedicated server computer to act as the PDC. Instead, computers in a peer-to-peer computer are grouped together in workgroups, which are simply groups of computers that can share resources with each other. Each computer in a workgroup keeps track of its own user accounts and security settings, so no single computer is in charge of the workgroup.

To create a domain, you have to designate a server computer as the primary domain controller and configure user accounts. Workgroups are much easier to administer. In fact, you don't have to do anything to create a workgroup except decide on the name you want to use. Although you can have as many workgroups as you want on a peer-to-peer network, most networks have just one workgroup. That way, any computers on the network can share resources with any other computer on the network.

puters can join a domain. (Windows 98 or 95 users can still access domain resources by logging on to the domain as users, but domain computer accounts for Windows 9x clients aren't required.) When you install Windows on the client system, the Setup program asks for the computer name and workstation or domain information. You can change this information later, if you want. The exact procedure varies, depending on which version of Windows the client uses.

12.3.2 Understanding Wireless Network Connections

There are two main access modes used for wireless networking, ad hoc mode and infrastructure mode:

▲ **Ad-hoc mode:** The simplest installation type for wireless 802.11 devices is **ad-hoc mode**. In this mode, the wireless NICs (or other devices) can communicate directly without the need for a WAP. A good example of this is two laptops with wireless NICs installed. If both cards were set up for ad-hoc mode, they could connect and transfer files (assuming the other network settings, such as protocols, were set up correctly). To set up a basic ad-hoc wireless network, all you need are two wireless NICs and two computers. Install the cards into the computers according to the manufacturer's directions. During the installation of the software, you will be asked at some point if you want to set up the NIC in ad-hoc mode or infrastructure mode. For an ad-hoc network, choose the ad-hoc mode setting; then bring the computers within range (90–100m) of each other. The computers will "see" each other and you will be able to connect to each other. (To transfer files, both computers will need to have security settings that will allow it.)

▲ **Infrastructure mode:** The most common use for wireless networking equipment is to provide the wireless equivalent of a wired network. To do this, all 802.11 wireless equipment has the ability to operate in what is known as **infrastructure mode**. In this mode, NICs will only communicate with an access point (instead of each other as in ad-hoc mode). The access point will facilitate communication between the wireless nodes as well as communication with a wired network (if present). In this mode, wireless clients appear to the rest of the network as standard, wired nodes.

Two main concerns in wireless networking are security issues and signal degradation.

▲ **Security concerns and SSIDs:** The SSID (short for Security Set Identifier) is the unique 32-character identifier that represents a particular wireless network. All devices participating in a particular wireless network must be configured with the same SSID. If a wireless network is to have more than one access point that provides access to the same wireless network, the access points must all have the exact same SSID. (Multiple access points with the same SSID spread over a large area allow a user to move around that area while maintaining a connection to the wireless network. This process is called roaming.) Because most access points are configured by default to broadcast their SSID so wireless clients can browse and find them, and because wireless signals can travel long distances (even outside of a building), security is extremely important on wireless LANs. To that end, most access points have one or more of the following security measures in place:

- **WEP/WPA:** Short for Wired Equivalent Privacy, this protocol, when enabled, requires that both access point and workstation are configured with the same 64-bit, 128-bit, 152-bit, or 256-bit encryption key to communicate. This key is manually configured by the network administrator and usually comprises a string of alphanumeric or hexadecimal characters. WEP is vulnerable due to weaknesses in the encryption algorithms. These weaknesses allow the algorithm to potentially be cracked in less than five hours using available PC software. This makes WEP one of the more vulnerable protocols available for security. WiFi Protected Access (WPA) is an improvement on WEP that implements some of the 802.11i standards. An improvement over WPA is WPA2, which implements the full 802.11i standard.

- **MAC list:** Some WAPs are capable of restricting which clients can connect to the AP by keeping track of authorized MAC addresses. The administrator configures the AP with the list of all the MAC addresses of wireless NICs that are authorized to connect to that AP. If a NIC with a MAC address not on the AP's MAC list tries to connect, it will be rejected.

- **Disabling SSID broadcast:** By default, WAPs broadcast their SSID to make it easier for clients to find them. For example, Windows XP and Windows Vista have a built-in utility that allows users to browse for WAPs. However, you can turn this feature off. You then must configure each client with the SSID of the WAP to which client will connect.

▲ **Signal degradation:** Because the 802.11 wireless protocols use radio frequencies, the signal strength varies according to many factors. The weaker the signal, the less reliable the network connection will be, and thus the less usable as well. These factors include:

- **Distance:** The farther away from the WAP you get, the weaker the signal. Most WAPs have a very limited maximum range (less than 100m for most systems). To some degree, this can be extended using amplifiers or repeaters or using different antennas.

- **Walls:** The more walls a wireless signal has to pass through, the more attenuated (reduced) the signal becomes. Also, the thicker the wall, the more it interrupts the signal. In an indoor office area with lots of walls, the range of wireless could be a low as 25m.
- **Protocols used:** The various wireless 802.11 protocols have different maximum ranges.
- **Interference:** Because 802.11 wireless protocols operate in the 900 MHz, 2.4GHz, 5GHz range, interference can come from several sources, including other wireless devices, such as Bluetooth, cordless telephones, microwave ovens, cell phones, other wireless LANs, and any other device that transmits radio frequency (RF) near the frequency bands that the 802.11 protocols use.

12.3.3 Configuring a Wireless Network Connection

There are really two main types of components in 802.11 networks: WAPs and NICs. Wireless NIC installation is just like installing any other network card. But, after it's installed, you must configure it for a connection to a WAP. In general, most wireless equipment is designed to work alone almost without configuration. The only things you need to configure are customization settings (name, network address, and so on) and security settings.

Windows XP and Windows Vista include software to automatically configure a wireless connection and install this software automatically when you install a wireless NIC. The first time you reboot after the installation of the NIC, you will see the Wireless Network Connection Properties dialog box (Figure 12-21).

From this dialog box, you can see any available wireless networks and configure how a computer connects to them. You can also configure several of the properties for how this wireless NIC connects to a particular wireless network:

▲ **Use Windows to Configure My Wireless Settings:** When this is unchecked, Windows will need an external program to configure how it connects to a wireless network, as is the case with some wireless NICs that have their own software program for this purpose. It is usually best to let Windows manage your wireless settings.

▲ **Available Networks:** This list shows all the wireless networks within range. The networks are listed by their SSID. From this list, you can choose which network you want to connect to, and you can configure how your workstation connects by clicking the Configure button. If you don't see the wireless network you are looking for, and you are in range, click the Refresh button.

▲ **Preferred Networks:** This list details any wireless networks you have connected to before and want to connect to again automatically. If there

Figure 12-21

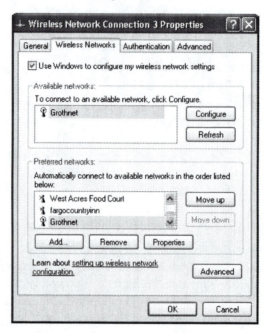

The Wireless Connection Properties dialog box.

is more than one wireless network in range, this list determines the order in which the workstation will try to connect to them.

In addition, you may have to configure the encryption for the connection if the wireless connection you are using requires it. To set up how your workstation uses encryption for a particular connection, click the SSID of the wireless network you want to configure in the Wireless Connection Properties dialog box and then click Configure to open the Wireless Network Properties dialog box (Figure 12-22).

From this dialog box, you can configure several parameters for the specific connection:

▲ **Network Name:** If, for some reason, the SSID of the WAP changes, you can change the name of the WAP you are connecting to in this field. Just delete the old one and type in the new name.

▲ **Wireless Network Key (WEP):** This section contains all the parameters for configuring encryption for this connection. If the network you are connecting to uses WEP encryption, this is the section where you will click the check boxes and configure how the wireless connection uses

Figure 12-22

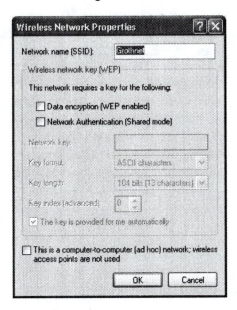

The Wireless Network Properties dialog box.

WEP, the key it uses, and what type of key it is. The following parameters are in this section:

- **Data Encryption (WEP Enabled):** If the network uses a key to encrypt data sent over the network, you should make sure this box is checked (it is checked by default). You will then need to specify the key in the box labeled Network Key. You will also need to specify what type of key it is (ASCII or hex) by selecting the appropriate item from the drop-down list.

- **Network Authentication (Shared Mode):** If your WAP uses shared mode authentication, you must check this box to ensure that your workstation will authenticate to the WAP using the shared key. Often, the key is provided automatically by the WAP during the response to the initial request. If this is the case, you must check the checkbox labeled The Key Is Provided for Me Automatically (the default). Otherwise, uncheck it and enter the key and related information in the appropriate boxes.

- **This Computer Is a Computer-to-Computer (Ad Hoc) Network:** Check this check box if you are connecting to another computer instead of an access point. After you have changed any settings you need to, click OK to save the changes and finish the configuration.

12.3.4 Dial-Up Networking Using a Modem

Any Windows PC that uses a modem to connect to a network—whether it is a LAN, WAN, or the internet—uses a Windows component called Dial-Up Networking (DUN) to make the connection.

In connecting to a network, DUN creates a Point-to-Point Protocol (PPP) connection between two computers over a telephone line. PPP essentially causes the modem to act like a network interface card. It encapsulates the network protocol for transport of the data packets over telephone lines, which allows the connected and communicating PCs to carry out their network interaction. PPP picks up a packet that has been created by one of the other network protocols and acts as an intermediary that carries the data packet over the telephone line. If the packet begins the journey as a TCP/IP packet, it arrives at its destination as a TCP/IP packet.

Regardless of the process used to connect to the internet, either by using a dial-up or LAN connection, after the connection is made, the communication process and the protocols applied are the same. (DUN automatically installs the Dial-Up Adapter and the Client for Microsoft Networks.) The only real difference between establishing a dial-up connection and a network connection is that the network connection remains in place and doesn't require a reconnection each time that access is desired. Also, the user doesn't need to be authenticated except for secure services.

Modems on both the sending and receiving end of network transmissions use controls called the AT command set. On a modem, AT refers to attention, which is used to precede each command that's given to the modem from the AT command set. The AT commands are sent to the modem by the communications program to initialize it. These commands tell the modem information such as how many rings to wait before answering, how long to wait after the last detected keystroke before disconnecting, and at what speed to communicate (Table 12-12). (You can also manually send AT commands to a modem through the Windows communication utility HyperTerminal.)

Other commands can be used to control the modem during the dialing process. For example, if you are in an office or hotel where it is necessary to dial 9

Table 12-12: AT Modem Commands

Command	﹑ Action
ATDT xxx-xxxx	Dial the telephone number (indicated by the letters x) using touch-tone dialing
ATH	On hook (hang up)
ATL	Speaker loudness (volume)
ATZ	Reset the modem to default settings

to get an outside line, that digit can be entered into the string, along with appropriate pauses to wait for a second dial tone. For example, to dial out of an office, you could use the following command string: ATDT 9,,15095551212. This string issues the following command sequence to the modem:

1. Prepare to dial a phone number.
2. Dial 9 to get an outside line, and pause two seconds (as indicated by the two commas) to wait for the outside dial tone.
3. Dial the number 1-509-555-1212.

Many PCs are shipped with an installed internal modem, but a modem can be physically installed inside the PC (in an expansion slot) or externally installed through a serial or USB (Universal Serial Bus) connection. After installed, the modem should be configured as appropriate for the system with its drivers and any additional setup software. Modern modems do not require physical configuration, but some modems have DIP switches or jumpers that need to be set. However, most of a modem's configuration is performed automatically by the operating system.

Modems are used to connect to networks as well as the internet. Windows NT, Windows 2000 Server, and Windows Server 2003 versions support Remote Access Services (RAS), which is the service that is used to manage and control incoming dial-up connections. A remote user may need to dial up the RAS of a corporate server and log on to the corporate LAN and gain access to its WAN.

To connect to a network or the internet using a dial-up connection, you must have a telephone number for the modem to call and any security or configuration information to access the network. You configure a dial-up connection through the Internet Connection Wizard in Windows 2000, or, in Windows XP or Windows Vista, through the New Connection Wizard. After the new connection is named and configured, you can initiate a dial-up connection by double-clicking the connection icon. The configured connection will dial the phone number and manage the modem's operation.

Common connectivity problems when using modems include:

▲ **Phone connection:** Nearly all modems use sound to enable the user to track the connection (handshake) as it is being made. The first of these sounds is the dial tone from the phone line. If the modem is not connecting and you do not hear a dial tone, a problem exists with the wall jack connection or with the phone line itself. You will probably get an error message indicating that you have no dial tone.

▲ **Modem problems:** If the modem cannot complete the handshake with the other end of the connection, the modem may be configured incorrectly in terms of its character length, start and stop bits, and speed.

▲ **Protocols:** Another common problem, especially for new modems, is that TCP/IP or other protocols have not been properly configured. Dial-up connections typically require PPP. Verify that the protocols are enabled and that the proper bindings are set for the protocols.

▲ **Remote response:** The NAS that you are attempting to connect to may be down or having problems. Call your ISP to check this.

▲ **Telephone company problems:** If sufficient static or crosstalk exists on the telephone line, this noise can cause the modem to disconnect soon after completing the connection or can cause enough data retransmissions that the line appears to be exceptionally slow.

▲ **Resource conflicts/device drivers:** If the internal modem will not begin the dial-up process, the problem is probably either a resource conflict or a device driver problem. Modems do not have a default IRQ assignment and must use an unassigned IRQ or share one with another device, such as a USB controller. An updated, newer version of a device driver can often solve a modem/operating system conflict. An external modem uses the resources that are assigned to the COM port that it uses. Conflicts can arise when both an external modem and an internal device have both been assigned the same IRQ. To remedy this situation, move the external modem's connector to a different COM port or reassign the internal device.

▲ **Installation problems:** If the system has not detected the modem on startup after installing an internal modem, use the Add New Hardware icon in the Control Panel to start the Add New Hardware Wizard. Should that fail, open the system case, reseat the modem, or move the modem to another open slot and reboot the PC.

12.3.5 Internet Connection Methods

One of the procedures performed most often by today's technicians is setting up a computer to connect to the internet. The internet is essentially an ad-hoc group of private networks that are connected as a global WAN using public telephone lines and high-speed backbones and use the TCP/IP protocol suite for network communications. The private ISP networks are the access points to the internet and are run by companies called internet service providers (ISPs). They sell you a connection to the internet for a monthly service charge. There are a variety of ways to connect to an ISP, which vary in the hardware and cabling used, and in access speeds:

▲ **Dial-Up/POTS:** In a dial-up internet connection, the computer connecting to the internet uses a modem to connect to the ISP over a standard telephone line, or POTS (Plain Old Telephone Service). Dial-up internet connections are relatively slow, and are technically limited to 56KBps, and practically limited to 53KBps by FCC rules. In reality, the 53KBps speed is for downloads only (from the internet to your computer) and only under ideal conditions. With a POTS internet connection, you are most likely to get speeds around 40KBps with maximum upload speeds (from your computer to the internet) around 33.6KBps. To make a connection with POTS, you must have a modem installed in your computer that is connected to your home phone line. The modem uses software on your PC called a dialer, a special program that initiates the connection with the ISP, takes the phone off hook, dials the ISP's access number, and establishes the connection. Most versions of Windows have a built-in dialer known as dial-up networking (DUN). Other ISPs may have their own dialer program that they give you on disk or CD-ROM when you sign up for their service. Dial-up networking is the most basic type of internet access. Most people use the internet so much that they are moving on to higher-speed methods of internet access. These higher-speed methods are generally lumped together and called broadband internet access.

▲ **xDSL (Digital Subscriber Line):** DSL uses the existing phone line from your home to the phone company to carry digital signals at higher speeds. There are several DSL varieties: Digital subscriber line (DSL), high data-rate digital subscriber line (HDSL), single-line digital subscriber line (SDSL), very high data-rate digital subscriber line (VDSL) and asymmetric digital subscriber line (ADSL), which is currently the most popular. ADSL has become the most popular xDSL because it provides reasonably fast upstream transmission speeds (up to 640Kbps) and very fast downstream transmission speeds (up to 9Mbps). Additionally ADSL allows you to use the phone line for both internet access and voice calls. However, a drawback is that you must be within a certain distance of the phone company's central office (usually less than one mile, but this varies on the type of DSL being used). Also, phone lines in older homes and neighborhoods may not be able to carry DSL signals. To connect using DSL, you use an internal or external DSL endpoint, or modem. External endpoints can be hooked to a hub, switch, or router, which can share the internet connection with multiple computers.

▲ **Cable:** Cable internet provides broadband internet access via the television cable that runs to your home via a specification known as Data Over Cable Service Interface Specification (DOCSIS). It is relatively cheap (usually less than $50 per month) and provides fast internet download speeds (typically between 3MBps and 15MBps). It is theoretically available to anyone with a cable TV connection and a cable provider that provides the service.

▲ **Integrated Services Digital Network (ISDN):** Integrated Services Digital Network (ISDN) is a digital, point-to-point network capable of maximum transmission speeds of about 2MBps, although speeds of 128KBps are more common. ISDN uses the same UTP wiring as POTS, but uses the copper wiring differently. Instead of carrying an analog (voice) signal, it carries digital signals. A computer connects to an ISDN line via an ISDN terminal adapter. An ISDN line has two types of channels. The data is carried on special Bearer, or B, channels, each of which can carry 64KBps of data. A typical basic rate interface (BRI) ISDN line has two B channels. One channel can be used for a voice call while the other is being used for data transmissions, and this occurs on one pair of copper wires. The second type of channel is used for call setup and link management and is known as the signal, or *D channel* (also referred to as the Delta channel). This channel has only 16KBps of bandwidth. BRI ISDN is also known as 2B+D because of the number and type of channels used. In many cases, to maximize throughput, the two Bearer channels are combined into one data connection for a total bandwidth of 128KBps. You can also obtain a Primary Rate Interface (PRI) known as 23B+D, which means it has 23 B channels and one D channel. The total bandwidth of a 23B+D ISDN line is 1536KBps (23 B channels×64KBps per channel+64KBps for the D channel). The main advantages of ISDN are its fast connection, higher bandwidth than POTS, and no conversion needed from digital to analog. However, it is more expensive than POTS, requires specialized equipment at the phone company and at the remote computer. In addition, not all ISDN equipment can connect to every other type of equipment. ISDN is a type of dial-up connection and therefore the connection must be initiated.

▲ **Satellite:** A satellite internet connection uses a satellite dish to receive data from a satellite and relay station that is connected to the internet. There are two types of satellite connection:

- **Unidirectional:** In unidirectional satellite internet, the satellite connection is used for only one part of the connection: the download of information from the internet. The request for information is made via some other transmission method (usually a phone line). The request goes to a relay station, where it is made on behalf of the user. The response is then transmitted back to the user via the satellite. The benefit is that because you use your internet connection for much more downloading than uploading, downloads happen at a much higher speed (usually 500KBps or better). The downside is you still need to use a phone line for part of the connection.

- **Bidirectional:** In bidirectional satellite internet, the satellite is used for both uploads and downloads. However, uploads are still slower than downloads. This type relieves you of needing a phone line for part of the internet connection. But, you still need a satellite dish.

The need for a satellite dish and the reliance upon its technology is one of the major drawbacks to satellite internet. You must keep the satellite dish aimed precisely at the satellite, or your signal strength (and thus your connection reliability and speed) will suffer. Cloudy or stormy days can cause interference with the signal, especially if there are high winds that could blow the satellite dish out of alignment. Another drawback to satellite technology is the delay (also called propagation delay). The delay or latency (typically between 250 and 350 milliseconds) occurs because of the length of time required to transmit the data and receive a response via the satellite. With standard web and email traffic, the delay is acceptable; however, with technologies like Voice over IP (VOIP) and live internet gaming, this delay is intolerable. Satellite internet is best used in remote rural areas where other types of internet may not be practical or available and speeds higher than dial-up are required. In most other cases, land-based internet is preferable.

▲ **Wireless:** There are two main methods for wireless internet access:

- **Wireless LAN:** In a wireless LAN, you connect to the internet through an 802.11b or a g wireless access point, which itself is connected to the internet via a cabled connection (Figure 12-23). WAPs provided by an ISP are often called hotspots. Local wireless is usually available within a particular room or building only. After you leave that area, it is no longer available. Local wireless has an operating range of around 100 meters outdoors and about 30 meters indoors. It usually conforms to either the 802.11b or 802.11g standard and has speeds of 1MBps, 11MBps, and 54MBps maximum.

- **Wireless WAN:** In a wireless WAN, you connect to the internet using a service provider's cellular network system. Many cell phone service providers offer wireless access plans. Service providers use a variety of wireless broadband technologies in their cellular networks, which are typically grouped or categorized in terms of successive generations, such as 1G, 2G, 2.5G, and 3G, with higher access speeds and efficiency. Older technologies may have quite low 64KBps access speeds, while 3G cellular networks support access speeds from 144KBps to over 2MBps. Wireless WANs are designed for mobile computing and internet access, and allow you to maintain a connection within a wide area, such as an entire metropolitan area. You connect to a wireless WAN through an internet-enabled cell phone (often called a smart phone). A portable system can connect via an adapter that a cell phone attaches to, or through a PC card modem. Because cellular networks are proprietary, you must usually use a PC card that is manufactured by your mobile phone provider.

Figure 12-23

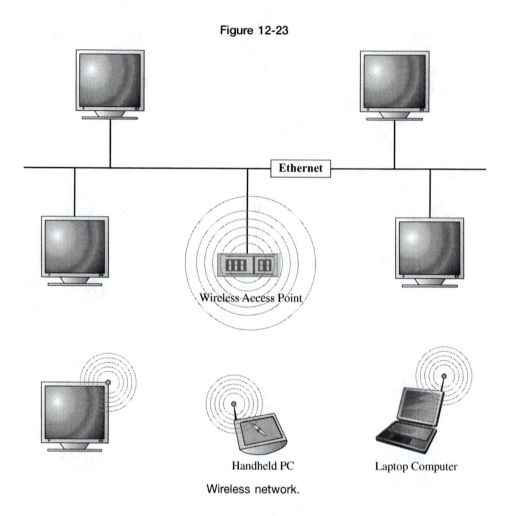

Wireless network.

Table 12-13 summarizes the different connection types and download speeds.

12.3.6 Connecting to the Internet

The following components are needed to connect to the internet:

▲ **Internet service:** You typically connect to the internet through an internet service provider (ISP), who will often provide some or all of the networking hardware and software needed. Many telecommunications and cable and satellite providers offer internet access service, and will typically include some or all of the hardware and software you need.

▲ **Networking hardware:** The networking hardware components appropriate for the type of internet connection, such as modems or NICs, and cabling.

Table 12-13: Common Connection Types and Download Speeds

Designation	Download Speed Range	Description
POTS	2400Bps to 56 KBps	Plain Old Telephone System. Your regular analog phone line.
ISDN	64 KBps to 1.5 MBps	Integrated Services Digital Network. Popular for home office internet connections.
ADSL	256 KBps to 9 MBps	Digital Subscriber Line. Shares existing phone wires with voice service.
Cable	128 KBps to 20 MBps	Inexpensive broadband internet access method with wide availability.
Satellite	128KBps to 16 MBps	Suitable for rural areas without cabled broadband methods.
Wireless LAN (WiFi)	1MBps to 54MBps	Allows a user to roam around a small area like an office or building while remaining connected to the access point and the internet.
Wireless WAN (cellular)	64 KBps to 3 MBps	Allows a user to roam around a metropolitan area while remaining connected to a broadband-level internet service.

FOR EXAMPLE

VoIP

VoIP, which stands for **Voice Over IP (Internet Protocol)** works much the same as a regular telephone. However, instead of connecting to the public telephone network, your phones connect directly to the internet. Because the internet uses the IP protocol, the digital data that represents your voice must be converted into packets that can be sent reliably over IP. Hence the name, Voice Over IP, or VoIP. There are two basic approaches to setting up VoIP: Software—only VoIP systems run on your computer and enable you to talk free with anyone else anywhere in the world provided they are using the same software you are. The best-known software-only VoIP system is Skype. The second approach is to use VoIP services such as Vonage and AT&T CallVantage. These services don't require the use of a computer or special software. Instead, they use a special adapter called an Analog Telephone Adapter (ATA) that connects a normal telephone to the internet. The adapter lets you use VoIP pretty much as if it were a regular telephone.

▲ **Internet access software:** Internet access software is composed of various user applications that access files and other resources located on internet servers such as web pages on web servers. The most popular internet access software includes web browsers, such as Internet Explorer or Mozilla Firefox and email software, such as Outlook Express or Eudora. You can also use software designed for specific types of file transferring or sharing, such as an FTP client or peer-to-peer file-sharing software.

After you install the networking hardware and establish internet service with a provider, you configure and set up an internet connection in Windows, either through the Internet Connection Wizard or the New Connection Wizard, depending on the version of Windows you are using. Alternately, the ISP you are using may provide you with setup software that will automatically configure an internet connection for you. In either case, the internet connection is configured specifically to connect to the ISP's network. The ISP's network typically assigns an IP address to your PC though its network access services (NASs), or modem banks, and RADIUS (Remote Authentication Dial-In User Service) services after a username and password are verified and your user account is authenticated.

In addition to a computer connecting directly to an ISP for internet access, two or more Windows PCs on LAN may share an internet connection, through Windows' Internet Connection Sharing (ICS) feature. However, this feature is designed to be used only on very small networks that don't have a separate router to enable the connection to be shared. Windows XP (Service Pack 2) and Vista also include a feature called the Windows Firewall that provides basic firewall support for home networks.

A PC that connects to the internet through a LAN uses as its primary (or default) gateway the router on the LAN that is used to connect to the WAN (internet).

12.3.7 Troubleshooting Network Connections

In Windows XP and Windows Vista, you can use the Wireless or Local Network Connection dialog box to check the status of the network connection. After you've configured a network connection, a network status indicator icon appears in the notification area of the taskbar. You can quickly see the network status by hovering the mouse cursor over this icon; a balloon appears to indicate the state of the connection. For more detailed information, you can click the status icon to display a status dialog box. This dialog box provides the following items of information:

▲ **Status:** Indicates whether you are connected.
▲ **Duration:** Indicates how long you've been connected.

▲ **Speed:** Indicates the current network speed. Ideally, this should say 11MBps for an 802.11b network, or 54MBps for an 802.11a or 802.11g network. However, if the network connection is not of the highest quality, the speed may drop to a lower value.

▲ **Signal Strength** (for wireless connections): Displays a graphic representation of the quality of the signal.

▲ **Packets Sent & Received:** Indicates how many packets of data you've sent and received over the network. You can click the Properties button to bring up the Connection Properties dialog box for the wireless connection.

If a PC is unable to connect to a network, the status will indicate it is not connected. To troubleshoot this, the first things to check for are:

▲ **The correct login procedure and rights:** To gain access to the network, users must follow the correct login procedure exactly. If they don't, they will be denied access. First, a user must enter the username and password correctly. Additionally, in NetWare and Windows, the network administrator can restrict the times and conditions under which users can log in. If a user doesn't log in at the right time or from the right workstation, the network operating system will reject the login request even though it might be a valid request in terms of the username and password being spelled correctly. A network administrator might also restrict how many times a user can log in to the network simultaneously. If that user tries to establish more connections than are allowed, access will be denied.

▲ **The link and collision lights:** The link light is a small light-emitting diode (LED) found on both the NIC and the hub (Figure 12-24). It is typically green and is labeled "link" (or some abbreviation). A link light indicates that the NIC and hub (in the case of 10Base-T) are making a logical (Data Link layer) connection. You can usually assume that the workstation and hub are communicating if the link lights are lit on both the workstation's NIC and the hub port to which the workstation is connected. (The link lights on some NICs aren't activated until the driver is loaded. So, if the link light isn't on when the system is first turned on, you may have to wait until the operating system loads the NIC driver.) The collision light is also a small LED, typically amber in color. It can usually be found on both Ethernet NICs and hubs. When lit, it indicates that an Ethernet collision has occurred. It is important to know that this light will blink occasionally because collisions are somewhat common on busy Ethernet networks. However, if this light stays on continuously, there are too many collisions happening for

Figure 12-24

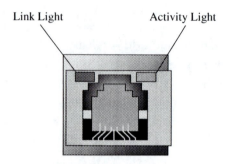

Link Light   Activity Light

Ehternet link light.

legitimate network traffic to get through. This can be caused by a mal-functioning network card or another malfunctioning network device. Be careful not to confuse the collision light with the network activity or network traffic light (usually green). The network activity light indicates that a device is transmitting. This particular light should be blinking on and off continually as the device transmits and receives data on the network.

▲ **The power switch:** To function properly, all computer and network components must be turned on and powered up. Most systems include a power indicator such as a Power or PWR light, and the power switch typically has a 1 or an On indicator. However, the unit could be powerless even if the power switch is in the On position. Thus, you need to check that all power cables are plugged in, including the power strip.

▲ **Operator error:** The problem may be that the user simply doesn't know how to perform the operation correctly; in other words, the prob-lem may be due to operator error (OE). Before you attribute any prob-lem to operator error, however, ask the user to reproduce the problem in your presence, and pay close attention. You may find out that the user is having a problem because they are using an incorrect proce-dure—for example, flipping the power switch without following proper shutdown procedures.

In addition, common connectivity problems specific to using wireless NICs include:

▲ **Interference from other devices:** One of the most common problems of wireless network trouble is interference from other wireless devices. The culprit might be a cordless phone, or it could be a neighbor who also has a wireless network. The simplest solution to this type of interference is to change channels. 802.11b access points let you select one of 11 different channels to broadcast on.

▲ **Wireless antenna problems:** The angle of the antennas can sometimes make a difference in transmission, so try adjusting the antenna angles. In some cases, you may actually need to add a high-gain antenna to the access point to increase its range. These high-gain antennas simply snap or screw on to the access point to provide a bigger antenna.

Additional steps to take in troubleshooting a network connection include:

▲ **Is hardware or software causing the problem?** A hardware problem typically manifests itself as a device in your computer that fails to operate correctly. The solution to hardware problems usually involves either changing hardware settings, updating device drivers, or replacing hardware. Software problems are a little more evasive. Some problems might result in General Protection Fault messages, which indicate a Windows or Windows program error of some type. Also, a program might suddenly stop responding (hang), or the entire machine might lock up randomly. The solution to these problems is generally a software upgrade or reinstallation. Often, network problems can be traced to software configuration, such as in the DNS configuration or a network HOSTs file.

▲ **Is it a workstation or server problem?** If you are able to connect to a network from another workstation, the problem is related to the user's workstation. Look for a cabling fault, a bad NIC, or some other problem. On the other hand, if several people in a group (such as a whole department) can't access a server, the problem may be related to that server. There may be a problem on the server related to user rights and permissions or the server may no longer be running.

▲ **Which segments of the network are affected?** If multiple segments are affected, the problem could be a network address conflict. If all users of the network are experiencing the problem, it could be related to a different device, such as a server that everyone accesses. Or, a main router or hub could be down, making network transmissions impossible.

▲ **Are there any cabling issues?** After you determine whether the problem is related to the whole network, to a single segment, or to a single workstation, you must determine whether the problem is related to network cabling. Check to see if the cables are properly connected to the correct port. Additionally, patch cables from workstation to wall jack can and do go bad, especially if they get moved or tripped over often. This problem is often characterized by connection problems. If you test the NIC and there is no link light, the problem could be related to a bad patch cable. It is also possible to have a cabling problem in the walls where the cabling wasn't installed correctly.

Windows includes and supports a variety of command-line TCP/IP tools and utilities that can be used to monitor or diagnose network problems that affect a single PC, including:

▲ **Ipconfig (IP Configuration):** This command-line utility displays the current configuration for a PC that is connected to a TCP/IP network for Windows NT/2000/XP/Vista systems (Figure 12-25). This utility can also be used to manage the IP configuration of a networked PC.

▲ **Nslookup (Network Lookup Service):** The Nslookup command is a powerful tool for diagnosing DNS problems, and is used to find an IP address or hostname of a particular PC. You know you're experiencing a DNS problem when you can access a resource by specifying its IP address but not its DNS name.

▲ **Ping (Packet Internet Groper):** This internet utility is used to determine whether an IP address is online or reachable. Either an IP address or a domain name can be pinged over a network.

▲ **Telnet:** This is a terminal emulation protocol that is used on TCP/IP-based networks to remotely log on to a device to run a program or manipulate data.

Figure 12-25

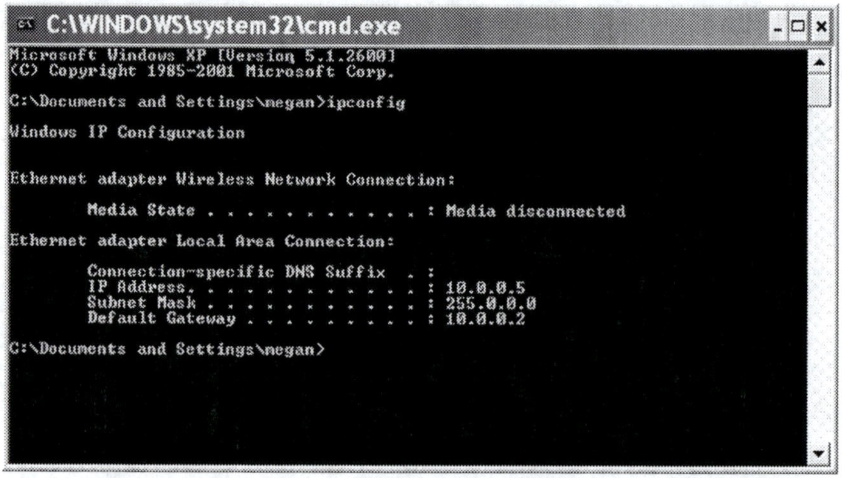

Using the Ipconfig command.

▲ **Tracert (Trace Route):** This TCP/IP utility is used to display the path between one network point and another, and the routers and timing on those routers along that route.

▲ **Nbtstat:** A Windows-only command that can help solve problems with NetBIOS name resolution.

▲ **Netstat:** This command displays a variety of statistics about a computer's active TCP/IP connections. It's a useful tool to use when you're having trouble with TCP/IP applications, such as FTP, HTTP, and so on.

You must be able to determine that a PC is networked before working on it. This requires special considerations and actions on your part. Not recognizing that the PC is on a network can result in damage to the PC and possibly to the network, including the following:

▲ Reduced bandwidth (the data transmission capacity and capability of the network) on the network caused by a faulty NIC signal or improperly set NIC

▲ A loss of data caused by an interruption in the network structure

▲ A slowdown in the general operation of the network

Some of the ways that you can determine whether a PC is networked are as follows:

▲ Look at the back of the PC for a network port with a cable attached to it. If you find one, you have a winner—a networked PC.

▲ If a network cable is not attached to the back of the PC, this doesn't mean that the PC is not a networked PC; the customer may have already disconnected the PC from the network. Question the customer to determine whether you are working on a networked PC.

▲ If no network cable exists, check to see whether a NIC is installed. No NIC—no network. However, if a NIC is in the PC, you can make other checks to determine whether the PC is networked.

▲ If you have access to the hard drive, search it for the telltale signs that the PC has been networked: folders or directories with names like NWCLIENT. Or look in the AUTOEXEC.BAT or CONFIG.SYS files for entries that start networking clients. (This is especially true for Novell software, which places entries in these files.)

▲ Use Windows Explorer to look for network drives. They usually have drive designators of E:, F:, or higher.

Before working on a networked PC, you will need to log off the network and disconnect the PC physically from the network. Additionally, if you will be working with the hard drive, you will need to make sure you have an up-to-date backup of the hard drive.

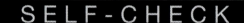

SELF-CHECK

1. What elements are required for a workstation to connect to a network?

2. How do you create a network connection?

3. What are the two modes for wireless network connections?

4. What is the function of the Windows DUN component?

SUMMARY

A network is composed of two or more computers connected to share files and resources. The primary components of networks are servers, workstations or clients, and resources. Peer-to-peer networks do not use a server or NOS; client/server networks do. Categorized by their size, networks may be LAN, WAN, or MAN networks. Networks are also distinguished by their physical and logical topologies. Common topologies are the bus, star, ring, mesh, and hybrid topologies.

Network communications are governed by the protocols used for network transmissions. Models of network communications describe the various layers that communications must occur in, such as the Physical, Data Link, and Network layers. Protocols are specifications for implementing communications, and networks typically use multiple protocols for communicating at different layers. The most common protocols used for networks are TCP/IP, IPX/SPX, NetBIOS, and AppleTalk.

A network's architecture defines the protocols it uses as well as its layout and hardware. The most common network architectures are Ethernet, Token Ring, and wireless LANs. An important aspect of networking is the addressing schemas used to identify nodes on a network. Addressing types include the MAC address, network addressing, and NetBIOS names. Various protocols or services may be used to translate from one address form to another, such as DHCP, DNS, and WINS.

Networking hardware comprises the network transmission media, network adapters or NICs, and network connectivity devices. The five main network cabling types are coaxial cable, twisted pair cable, fiber-optic cable, RS-232 Serial cable, and wireless, although USB and IEEE 1394/FireWire cables can be used in limited fashion to network devices together. NICs are network adapters that are installed in a computer's expansion slots and have two main functions: To act as a transceiver between the network communications and the PC and to connect to the network cabling. Network connectivity devices include repeaters, hubs, switches, bridges, and gateways. Other devices used on networks include devices for internet connectivity, such as modems, wireless access points, transceivers, and firewalls.

To configure a PC to work with a network, the PC must have a network adapter and be configured with the proper client software, and to use the correct protocols. Additional services the network uses should also be enabled on the client workstation to allow it to access network functions. To connect to a TCP/IP network, the workstation must either be configured to obtain its IP address and DNS server address automatically from a DHCP server, or the IP address, subnet mask, gateway address, and DNS address must be configured manually. In addition, the workstation may need to have valid user accounts and rights established by the network administrator. A wireless network connection may need to be additionally configured for encryption and WAP authentication. A network connection is typically configured automatically after installation of the NIC, but can also be created using Windows New Connection or New Wireless Connection Wizard.

Internet connection methods include POTS, using a dial-up modem and DUN, ISDN, xDSL, cable, satellite, wireless LAN, and wireless WAN. To connect to the internet, you need internet service from a provider, the correct networking hardware (DSL endpoints, ISDN terminal adapters, cable modems, and so on) and internet access software, such as browsers and email software.

If a PC is unable to connect to a network, the first troubleshooting steps are to ensure that the login procedure and user rights are correct, check the link and collision LEDS on the NIC, ensure all devices are powered, and to review the user's steps in connecting to see if there is a user error. Connectivity problems can be due to hardware or software problems, workstation, server, or cabling problems. Wireless connections can also experience problems due to signal degradation and interference from other devices.

KEY TERMS

802.11	Bridge
Addressing	Bus topology
Ad-hoc mode	Client/server network
AppleTalk	Coaxial cable
Bandwidth	Dedicated server
Bluetooth	Digital Subscriber Line (DSL)

DSL endpoint

Domain Name System (DNS)

Dynamic Host Configuration
Protocol (DHCP)

Ethernet

Fiber optic

Firewall

Full-duplex communications

Gateway

Half-duplex communications

Host

Hub

Hybrid topology

Infrared networking

Infrastructure mode

Internetwork Packet
Exchange/Sequenced Packet
Exchange (IPX/SPX)

Integrated Services Digital Network
(ISDN)

Local area network (LAN)

Logical topology

Mesh topology

Metropolitan area network (MAN)

Modem

Network Basic Input Output
System (NetBIOS)

Network connectivity device

Network interface card (NIC)

Network media

Network operating system (NOS)

Network resource

Node

NWLINK

Peer-to-peer network

Physical topology

Plenum rated coating

Protocol

Repeater

Ring topology

Router

Server

Star topology

Subnet mask

Switch

Token Ring

Topology

Transceiver

Transmission Control
Protocol/Internet Protocol (TCP/IP)

Twisted pair cable

Voice over IP (VOIP)

Wide area network (WAN)

Windows Internet Naming Service
(WINS)

Wireless access point (WAP)

Workstation

ASSESS YOUR UNDERSTANDING

Go to www.wiley.com/college/groth to evaluate your knowledge of network fundamentals.

Measure your learning by comparing pre-test and post-test results.

Summary Questions

1. Printers, files, email, and groupware can all be categorized as resources. True or false?

2. What is the name of a set of rules that governs the communication between two entities?

    (a) protocol

    (b) service

    (c) server

    (d) client

3. Which access method asks the other workstations for permission to transmit before transmitting?

    (a) CSMA/CD

    (b) CSMA/CA

    (c) Token passing

    (d) Demand priority

4. Which of the following TCP/IP protocols is used to send mail on the internet?

    (a) HTTP

    (b) SMTP

    (c) POP3

    (d) FTP

5. Which topology uses the least amount of cabling, but also covers the shortest distance?

    (a) bus

    (b) star

    (c) mesh

    (d) hybrid

6. Which of the following is a characteristic of a mesh network?

    (a) It controls cable costs.

    (b) It offers improved reliability.

(c) It is required by fire code.

(d) It needs a token to operate.

7. The software facility that is used to resolve the domain name to its associated IP address is DNS. True or false?

8. The address 44-45-53-54-00-00 is an example of which of the following?

   (a) NetBIOS name

   (b) IP address

   (c) IPX address

   (d) MAC address

9. Which device is most efficient at moving packets between similar network topologies?

   (a) gateway

   (b) router

   (c) bridge

   (d) switch

10. What type of cabling is immune to electromagnetic or radio-frequency interference.

    (a) broadband coaxial cabling

    (b) CSMA/CD

    (c) fiber-optic cabling

    (d) twisted-pair cabling

11. Which cabling standard can send data at up to 10,000MBps?

    (a) 10Base-T

    (b) 100Base-TX

    (c) 1000Base-TX

    (d) 10GBase-SR

12. Which of the following devices is responsible for converting the signal between the PC and the network media?

    (a) router

    (b) bridge

    (c) NIC

    (d) hub

13. Plenum-rated cable has which of the following characteristics?

    (a) It has a lower cost than PVC.

    (b) It meets fire codes for installation in suspended ceilings.

    (c) It transmits data faster.

    (d) All the above.

14. What devices transfer packets across multiple networks and use tables to store network addresses to determine the best destination?

    (a) active hubs

    (b) routers

    (c) gateways

    (d) bridges

15. In SMF cable, the light bounces off the cable walls as it travels through the cable, which causes the signal to weaken more quickly. True or false?

16. The command that is used to reset a modem to its default settings is

    (a) ATDT

    (b) ATH

    (c) ATL

    (d) ATZ

17. To connect to the internet using xDSL, you must have a:

    (a) DSL terminal adapter

    (b) DSL endpoint

    (c) DSL-ready NIC

    (d) DSL AP

18. The Windows service that creates a Point-to-Point Protocol (PPP) connection between two computers over a telephone line is DUN. True or false?

19. The default subnet value for a host with a Class B address is 255.255.255.0. True or false?

20. Which of the following is **not** a networking component that can be configured through Local Area Connection Properties dialog box in Windows XP?

    (a) protocol

    (b) service

    (c) server

    (d) client

Applying This Chapter

1. TCP/IP is installed on each PC within a network. You can communicate within the network but are unable to access the internet. What TCP/IP settings must be properly configured for internet access?

2. You have an older NIC that is designed to work with Ethernet, but the network of your office is using fiber-topic cabling. Is this NIC unusable? If not, what must you do to allow it to connect to the network?

3. A friend is interested in setting up his internet access through an ISDN service provider. Explain what his PC will require to make that connection.

4. You have been called to a client location to work on a troublesome PC. What is the first thing you should do before working on it?

5. A user calls you complaining that he can't access the corporate intranet web server. You try the same address, and you receive a Host Not Found error. Several minutes later, another user reports the same problem. You can still send email and transfer files to another server. What is the most likely cause of the problem?

YOU TRY IT

Setting Up a Network

You have been hired by a small business that has ten full-time employees in a small office. They are interested in setting up a network. What are the main choices they will need to make in deciding on a network?

Purchasing a NIC

You have just been hired to work in the systems administration department of a small company, and your first task is to configure a PC to connect to its network. What information do you need to accomplish this?

Troubleshooting a Connection

A PC at your office is unable to connect to the network. What are the first steps you will take in troubleshooting?

Wireless Internet Access

Your company wants to enable its sales force's laptops to have mobile internet connections. What choices do they have for this? What would you recommend?

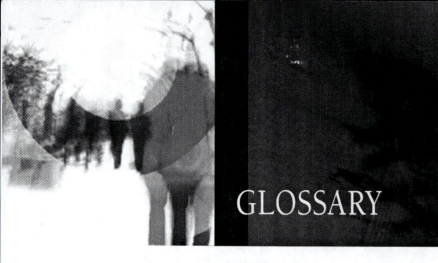

GLOSSARY

802.11 The IEEE standard for wireless networking. Three popular variants are 802.11a, 802.11b, and 802.11g.

AC adapter A small external power supply that converts main electrical power to the low-voltage DC required for a laptop or notebook computer or other device needing its own power supply.

Accelerated Graphics Port (AGP) bus A 32-bit expansion bus on a motherboard, designed for video card use only.

Access time The period of time that elapses between a request for information from a drive or memory and when the information arrives at the requesting device.

Active backplane A backplane that incorporates circuitry to help speed the system.

Active partition The primary disk partition that is checked for boot instructions at startup.

Active termination A method for terminating a daisy chain of SCSI devices.

Active-matrix screen A liquid crystal display (LCD) monitor that has a separate transistor for each pixel. Also called thin-film transistor. Contrast to passive matrix display, which has only one transistor for each row and each column of the display.

Actuator arm A hard drive mechanism that moves the read/write heads as a group.

Address bus The internal processor bus used for accessing memory. The width of this bus determines how much physical memory a processor can access.

Address line Used to carry addresses as opposed to data.

Addressing   Designations that allow PCs to be known by a name or number to other PCs. Addressing allows a PC to transmit data directly to another PC by using its address (IP or MAC).

Ad-hoc mode   In this mode, the wireless NICs (or other devices) can communicate directly without the need for a WAP.

Advanced Configuration and Power Interface (ACPI)   An interface specification for assigning system resources (such as IRQs and memory addresses) and for managing device power conservation settings. The system's BIOS must support ACPI; early motherboards support Advanced Power Management (APM) instead.

Advanced Power Management (APM)   An API specification for managing device power conservation settings to save electricity and/or to extend notebook battery life.

Advanced Technology Attachment (ATA) The set of standards governing Integrated Drive Electronics (IDE) device interfaces.

Alternating current (AC)   Current that reverses direction at regular intervals.

Amps   A unit of voltage.

Analog-to-Digital Converter (ADC)   Converts analog audio data, such as a live voice or a musical instrument, into digital data that can be stored on a PC.

Antistatic bag   A bag designed to keep static charges from building up on the outside of a computer component during shipping.

Antistatic wrist strap   A specially constructed strap worn as a preventive measure to guard against the damages of ESD. Also called an ESD strap.

Aperture grille   A system of vertical wires between electron guns and phosphors for keeping the electron beams aligned on some CRTs. Compare to shadow mask.

AppleTalk   Both a protocol and a proprietary network architecture for Macintosh computers.

Application   Software that performs a useful task such as creating a document or playing a game.

Arithmetic Logic Unit (ALU)   A component of the CPU that performs generic logic and mathematical computations.

Aspect ratio   Describes the relative number of horizontal pixels to vertical pixels in the resolutions it supports.

AT motherboard   A type of motherboard form factor wherein the motherboard is the same size as the original IBM AT computer's motherboard.

ATX motherboard   A motherboard type that has the processor and memory slots at right angles to the expansion cards, allowing the installation of full-length expansion cards. This arrangement also puts the processor and memory in line with the fan output of the power supply, allowing the processor to run cooler.

Audio Modem Riser (AMR)   An type of expansion slot and card designed for modem and sound expansion cards.

Auto-ranging multimeter   A multimeter that automatically sets its upper and lower ranges depending on the input signal.

Auto-switching AC adapter   An AC adapter that can sense and convert both 110VAC and 220VAC power.

Baby AT motherboard   A type of motherboard form factor wherein the motherboard is smaller than the original AT form factor.

Backplane   A system design in which all of the circuitry components, even the CPU and memory, are installed as separate daughterboards.

Backside bus   A set of signal pathways between the CPU and Level 2 cache memory (if present).

Bandwidth   In network communications, the amount of data that can be sent across a wire in a given time. Each communication that passes along the wire decreases the amount of available bandwidth.

Bank   A single module or group of modules whose bit width adds up to the bit width the CPU works with.

Barcode reader   Used to read barcodes on a flat surface, and operates by emitting a light source aimed at the bar code and reading the light patterns reflected back. A barcode reader may be a handheld device or may have a form factor similar to a flatbed scanner.

Basic input/output system (BIOS)   The ROM-based software on a motherboard that acts as a kind of interpreter between an operating system and a computer's hardware.

Berg connector   See floppy drive power connector.

BGA package   A CPU package similar to the PGA package but uses solder balls instead of pins.

Binary number system   A base 2 numbering system.

Biometric device Captures biometric information about an individual (unique biological traits such as fingerprints or irises) and uses this information to identify or authenticate the individual.

Bit The basic unit of information in the binary numbering system, representing either 0 (off) or 1 (on).

Blackout A power drop from 110 volts to zero volts in a very short period of time. It is a complete loss of power for anywhere from a few seconds to several minutes or longer.

Bluetooth An RF-based wireless standard that has a total maximum throughput of 1Mbps.

Blu-ray A next-generation DVD standard that uses a different laser technology for storing up to 50GB in dual layer disks.

BNC (Bayonet Naur) connector A small connector with a half-turn locking shell for coaxial cable; used with thin Ethernet and RG-62 cabling.

Boot block A tiny area in BIOS that is not reprogrammable and contains a program for booting from a floppy disk.

Boot failure The failure of a system to complete the boot sequence.

Boot partition The partition that contains the operating system's executable and support files.

Boot sequence The process that loads an operating system into memory, usually from a hard disk, although occasionally from a floppy disk. This is an automatic procedure begun when you first turn on or reset your computer. A set of instructions contained in ROM begin executing, first running a series of power on self-tests (POSTs) to check that devices such as hard disks are in working order, then locating and loading the operating system, and finally passing control of the computer over to that operating system.

Bridge Joins similar topologies and is used to divide network segment, by keeping traffic on one side from crossing to the other. For this reason, it is often used to increase performance on a high-traffic segment.

Brownout A short period (1 second or more) of low voltage often caused by an unusually heavy demand for power.

BTX motherboard A new form factor motherboard designed for improved airflow and technology standards such as PCI Express and SATA.

Buffer An area of memory set aside for temporary storage of data. Often, the data remains in the buffer until some external event finishes. A buffer can compensate for the differences in transmission or processing speed between two devices or between a computer and a peripheral device, such as a printer or modem.

Bus   A set of pathways that allows information and signals to travel between components inside or outside of a computer.

Bus mastering   A technique that allows certain advanced bus architectures to delegate control of data transfers between the Central Processing Unit (CPU) and associated peripheral devices to an add-in board.

Bus topology   the simplest physical topology. It consists of a single cable that runs to every workstation.

Byte   A group of 8 bits—usually. In some computer systems, a byte may have only 7 bits, or it may have as many as 11. However, 8 bits is the modern standard definition of a byte.

Cache   Memory associated with a disk drive that buffers the data input and output to it. See cache memory.

Cache memory   Fast SRAM memory used to store, or cache, frequently used instructions and data.

Capacitor   An electronic device that stores an electrical charge.

Card Services   Part of the software support needed for PCMCIA (PC Card) hardware devices in a portable computer, controlling the use of system interrupts, memory, or power management. When an application wants to access a PC Card, it always goes through the card services software and never communicates directly with the underlying hardware.

Cardbus   An update to the PC Card standard for expansion cards for notebook PCs, providing speed, bus, and voltage improvements.

Carriage belt   The printer belt placed around two small wheels or pulleys and attached to the printhead carriage. The carriage belt is driven by the carriage motor and moves the printhead back and forth across the page during printing.

Cathode-ray tube (CRT)   A type of monitor in which electron beams strike phosphors and make them briefly glow.

CCGA package   A CPU package similar to the PGA package but uses round posts instead of pins.

CD-Recordable (CD-R)   An optical writable disk that can be written to only once. Although the disk may be written in multiple sessions, once a spot on the disk has been written, it cannot be changed.

CD-Rewritable (CD-RW)   An optical writeable disk format that can be written to and erased up to 1000 times.

Centronics   A type of connector consisting of a solid bar with pins on either side that fits into a trough-style connector.

Charge-coupled device (CCD)   A device in which the semiconductor elements are connected so that the electrical output from one provides the input to the next. CCDs are used in the light-detection circuitry in digital and video cameras and scanners.

Chip creep   The slow self-loosening of chips from their sockets on the system board as a result of the frequent heating and cooling of the board (which causes parts of the board—significantly, the chip connector slots—to alternately expand and shrink).

Chipset   A collection of chips or circuits that perform interface and peripheral functions for the processor.

Circuit   A specific path or loop that electricity is made to flow along.

Client/server network   A network managed by a server running an NOS.

Clock doubling   Technology that allows a chip to run at the bus's rated speed externally, but still be able to run the processor's internal clock at twice the speed of the bus. This technology improves computer performance.

Clock multiplier   The number used to change the working speed of the processor relative to the speed of the external clock.

Clock rate   See clock speed.

Clock signal   Provides the card with the signal of the bus clock so that if can synchronize its communications with the buses of the motherboard.

Clock speed   Also known as the clock rate. The internal speed of a computer or processor, normally expressed in MHz. The faster the clock speed, the faster the computer can perform a specific operation, assuming the other components in the system, such as disk drives, can keep up with the increased speed.

Clock tick   A built-in metronome-like signal that indicates how fast the components can operate.

CMOS battery   A battery used to power CMOS memory so that the computer won't lose its settings when powered down.

CMOS settings   The hardware configuration settings stored on a CMOS chip.

CMOS setup program   A program that modifies BIOS settings in the CMOS memory. You access this program at system startup time by pressing a key combination such as Alt + F1 or Ctrl + F2.

CMYK   A color inking system that mixes cyan, magenta, yellow, and black inks to make the desired colors.

CNR   Slots on a motherboard that allow a motherboard designer to design a chipset with certain integrated features, which allow the addition of a CNR riser card to enhance onboard capabilities.

Coaxial cable   Often referred to as coax. A type of cable used in network wiring. Typical coaxial cable types include RG-58 and RG-62. 10Base-2 Ethernet networks use coaxial cable. Coaxial cable is usually shielded.

Cold boot   A boot started when the system is powered off.

Color depth   The number of bits used to describe the color of each pixel in the display. For example, 24-bit color uses 24 binary digits and has 2 to the 24th power possible values for a pixel—8 bits for red, 8 bits for green, and 8 bits for blue.

Color Graphics Adapter (CGA)   The first color adapter. It's capable of displaying four colors. CGA monitors support 320 x 200 (four colors) or 640 x 200 (two colors).

Column Address Strobe (CAS) latency   A rating for DRAM memory that measures the time in clock cycles for the first bit of a memory request to be sent to the module's pins.

Combination drive   As used with optical drives, drives that support multiple optical disk formats.

Command line utility   A utility program executed through the command line interface (CLI), which is a DOS-like text base interface.

Compact Disk Read Only Memory (CD-ROM)   An optical disk that stores up to 700 MB of data. The ROM portion of the name indicates it is read-only, differentiating it from CD-R and CD-RW.

Compact PCI (CPCI)   Used primarily for industrial computer applications that need a smaller and more robust form factor than is used with desktop PCs.

Complimentary Metal-Oxide Semiconductor (CMOS) chip   An area of nonvolatile memory containing settings that determine how a computer is configured.

Computer   An electronic device that can process data automatically.

Conductor   Any item that permits the flow of electricity between two entities.

Connector   Hardware that allows a port to connect to a cable.

Constant angular velocity (CAV) A constant speed of rotation.

Constant linear velocity (CLV)   A constant speed of reading or writing data, which involves a changing speed of rotation of the storage disk.

Contact Image Sensor (CIS)   An inexpensive alternative to a charge-coupled device (CCD) for digitizing pictures in a scanner or digital camera.

Continuity   The presence of a complete, working circuit.

Control signal line   Used to manage overall communications.

Control Unit   The CPU component that coordinates the CPUs actions.

Controller   A device that allows a peripheral component or hardware device to communicate with the rest of the computer.

Conventional memory   The amount of memory accessible by DOS in PCs using an Intel processor operating in real mode (normally the first 640KB).

Convertible tablet PC   Incorporates a keyboard, typically through a hinged clamshell design. It is like a notebook with a flip-around screen that allows a user to hold it like a large notebook and write notes directly on the screen with a stylus.

Coprocessor   An add-on chip that works with the CPU to expand its instruction set.

Core   See die.

Core voltage   The voltage that a processor uses internally while running at a separate voltage externally.

CPU clock   A type of clock signal that dictates how fast the CPU can run.

CPU clock speed   The setting, in MHz, of how fast the CPU's clock "ticks."

Current   The flow of electricity.

Cutover threshold   A condition in which the line voltage drops below a pre-set threshold, causing sensors to detect the situation and switch the power from the wall to the internal battery. When the power comes back above the threshold, the sensors detect the restoration of power and switch the power source back to the line voltage.

Cylinder   The collective name for all the tracks at the same concentric position on a disk.

Cylinder, Head, Sector (CHS) addressing   A method of accessing each block of data by its cylinder, head, and sector address.

D connector   Any of several types of cable connectors used for parallel or serial cables. The number following the letters DB (for data bus) indicates the number of pins that the connector usually has; a DB25 connector can have up to 25 pins, and a DB9 connector can have up to 9.

Daisy-chaining   A pattern of cabling wherein the cables run from the first device to the second, second to the third, and so on.

Daisy-wheel printer   An impact printer that uses a plastic or metal print mechanism with a different character on the end of each spoke of the wheel. As the print mechanism rotates to the correct letter, a small hammer strikes the character against the ribbon, transferring the image onto the paper.

Data bits   Indicates the number of bits used in the character coding scheme, or data word.

Data bus   The electronic channel on a motherboard that transfers data.

Data line   Transfers one bit at a time.

Data path   A CPU characteristic that measures in bits how much data can be sent to the CPU in a single operation.

Data transfer mode   The protocol used for actually transferring the bytes of data to and from the hard drive.

Data transfer rate   A measure of the amount of data that a system can access over a period of time, typically one second.

Daughterboard   A printed circuit board that attaches to another board to provide additional functions.

DC power supply (DCPS)   Converts house current into three voltages: 5VDC and –5VDC for the logic circuitry and 24VDC for the paper transport motors. This component also runs the fan that cools the internal components of the printer.

DDR2   A type of DRAM that succeeded DDR RAM and supports faster bus speeds.

Dedicated server   A server that is assigned to perform a specific application or service.

Degaussing   To discharge magnetic buildup in a CRT that causes its image to be distorted or discolored.

Desktop replacement laptop   The largest and heaviest laptops, range from 7 to 10 lbs, and are designed to handle more powerful, desktop and mobile CPUs and to compete with tower PCs in performance.

Device driver A small program that allows a computer to communicate with and control a device. Each operating system contains a standard set of device drivers for the keyboard, the monitor, and so on. When you add specialized peripheral devices, such as a network interface card, you must install the appropriate device driver so that the operating system knows how to manage the device.

Diagnostic utility Software designed to help troubleshoot a computer problem.

Die The small chip in the center of the big CPU chip package.

Differential signaling A method of signaling that uses two wires, each carrying the electrical opposite of the other.

Digital camera Uses CCDs, lenses, and natural light sources to take pictures of objects, much as a standard camera works. However, in a digital camera, the CCD replaces the film and records the picture as a pattern of bits.

Digital Subscriber Line (DSL) A digital WAN technology that brings high-speed digital networking to homes and businesses over POTS. There are many types, including HDSL (high-speed DSL) and VDSL (very high data-rate DSL).

Digital video camera (digital camcorder) Somewhat like a still digital camera, except it takes many "shots" per second and strings them all together in a single data file.

Digital Video Disk/Digital Versatile Disk (DVD) Digital video disk when it holds video, or digital versatile disk when it holds computer data. A compact disk format. A standard single-layer single-sided disk can currently store 4.7GB of information; a two-layer standard increases this to 8.5GB, and eventually doublesided disks are expected to store 17GB per disk. DVD drives can also read conventional compact disks.

Digital Visual Interface (DVI) connector A digital video standard that converts analog signals to digital signals and supports both analog and digital monitors. DVI connectors are distinctly different from standard VGA connectors.

Digital-to-analog converter (DAC) Converts stored digital audio data into audible (analog) information that can be played on speakers or headphones.

Digitizing table Used with drawing or CAD (computer-aided design) software to create line or vector graphics.

DIN-n connector A circular type of connector used with computers. (The n represents the number of connectors.)

DIP switch A small switch used to select the operating mode of a device, mounted as a Dual Inline Package (DIP). DIP switches can be either sliding or rocker switches and are often grouped together for convenience. They are used on printed-circuit boards, dot-matrix printers, modems, and other peripherals.

Direct current (DC)   Current that flows without reversing direction.

Direct Memory Access (DMA)   A method of transferring information directly from a mass storage device such as a hard disk or from an adapter card into memory (or vice versa), without the information passing through the processor.

Direct-solder method   A method of attaching chips to the motherboard. The chips are soldered directly to the motherboard.

Disk cache   An area of computer memory in which data is temporarily stored on its way to or from a drive.

Disk caching (disk buffering)   Temporarily stores recently accessed or frequently accessed data to the hard disk to take advantage of its higher access rates.

Disk controller   The electronic circuitry that controls and manages the operation of floppy or hard drives.

Disk image   A single file that contains an exact copy of a hard drive or optical disk, including the drive's structure and files. A disk image can be treated by the operating system as an actual hard drive.

DMA (Direct Memory Access)   A data transfer mode that transfers data directly from a storage device into memory (or vice versa), without the information passing through the CPU.

DMA channel   Dedicated circuit pathway on the motherboard that makes DMA possible.

Docking station   A hardware system into which a portable computer fits so that it can be used as a full-fledged desktop computer. Docking stations vary from simple port replicators that allow you access to parallel and serial ports and a mouse to complete systems that give you access to network connections, CD-ROMs, and even a tape backup system.

Domain Name System (DNS)   Used to resolve (translate) Internet names to their IP address equivalents.

Dongle   A special cable that provides a connector to a circuit board that doesn't have one. For example, a motherboard may use a dongle to provide a serial port when there is a ribbon cable connector for the dongle on the motherboard, but there is no serial port.

Dot pitch The distance between two phosphors of the same color on a CRT monitor.

Dot-matrix printer An impact printer that uses columns of small pins and an inked ribbon to create the tiny pattern of dots that form the characters. Dot-matrix printers are available in 9-, 18-, or 24-pin configurations.

Dots per inch (dpi) A measure of resolution expressed by the number of dots that a device can print or display in one inch.

Double Data Rate SDRAM (DDR DRAM) A type of DRAM that transmits data twice during the clock cycle.

Double-pumped Clock-doubled; memory chip can perform reads and writes twice during a clock cycle, thereby doubling the effective memory executions per second.

Drive fault tolerance The ability of a drive to recover from an error condition.

Drive geometry The organization of a drive into a specific number of cylinders, read/write heads, and sectors.

Driver A small program that allows a computer to communicate with and control a device.

DSL endpoint The device that allows the network signals to pass over phone lines at higher, digital frequencies. This modem is usually an external modem (although internal DSL modems are available), and it usually has both a phone line and an Ethernet connection.

Dual BIOS motherboards Motherboards that have a second, backup BIOS.

Dual Inline Memory Module (DIMM) A memory module that is similar to a SIMM (Single Inline Memory Module), except that a DIMM is double-sided. There are memory chips on both sides of the memory module. DIMMs have since been introduced with chips on one side of the memory stick.

Dual Inline Package (DIP) chip A standard housing constructed of hard plastic, commonly used to hold an integrated circuit. The circuit's leads are connected to two parallel rows of pins designed to fit snugly into a socket; these pins may also be soldered directly to a printed-circuit board.

Dual-channel memory Memory that is accessed from a memory controller that has two channels.

Duplexing A fault-tolerant technique that writes the same information simultaneously onto two different hard disks, each connected through a separate host adapter.

DVD±R Digital video disk-recordable. An extension to the digital video disk format to allow one-time recording. There are two competing formats: DVD+R and DVD-R. Many drives can write in either format; blank disks, however, are one format or the other.

DVD±RW Digital video disk-rewritable. An extension to the digital video disk format to allow multiple rerecordings. There are two competing standards: +RW and -RW. Some drives support both and are designated +/-RW.

DVD-RAM A format for writing to DVD blanks. Waning in popularity and nearly obsolete; requires a disk caddy.

DVD-ROM A type of DVD that is read-only.

Dye sublimation printer Produces photo-processing-lab quality prints. The dye part of the process is on rolls of transparent film with red (magenta), blue (cyan), yellow, and gray (black) dyes embedded in the film. The printer head is heated and then passed over the film, causing the dyes to vaporize and permeate the glossy face of the special print paper and turn back to solids. Dye sublimation printing is done in smooth forms of color, not pixels.

Dynamic disks A Windows 2000/XP alternative to partitioning and formatting that allows volumes to be created from multiple hard drives.

Dynamic Host Configuration Protocol Protocol that is used to automatically configure a network workstation with its IP address data.

Dynamic RAM (DRAM) A common type of computer memory that uses capacitors and transistors storing electrical charges to represent memory states. These capacitors lose their electrical charge, and so they need to be refreshed, during which time they cannot be read by the processor.

Dynamic range The ability of a scanner to distinguish between light and dark.

Electromagnetic interference (EMI) Any electromagnetic radiation released by an electronic device that disrupts the operation or performance of any other device.

Electronically Erasable Programmable Read Only Memory (EEPROM) A memory chip that maintains its contents without electrical power, and whose contents can be erased and reprogrammed either within the computer or from an external source. EEPROMs are used where the application requires stable storage without power but may have to be reprogrammed.

Electrostatic discharge (ESD) The exchange of electrons that occurs when two objects of dissimilar charge come in contact with one another, to standardize the electrostatic charge between the objects.

Embedded computer Tiny computing device embedded in consumer appliances, such as cell phones and microwave ovens.

Encoding The process of translating data from binary to flux transition patterns recordable and readable from magnetic media.

Enhanced Capabilities Port (ECP) A parallel port specification that allows for high-speed, two-way communication between the computer and the peripheral attached to the port, usually a printer or scanner.

Enhanced Graphics Adapter (EGA) Supports 16 colors at a resolution of 640 × 350. EGA cards for the most part are obsolete.

Enhanced Parallel Port (EPP) Allows data to flow in both directions, but only in one way at a time.

Erasable Programmable Read Only Memory (EPROM) A memory chip that maintains its contents without electrical power, and whose contents can be erased and reprogrammed by removing a protective cover and exposing the chip to ultraviolet light.

Error Correction Code (ECC) An error detection and error correction mechanism used to check and correct minor data loss.

ESD mat A grounding mat used for preventing electrostatic discharge.

ESD strap See antistatic wrist strap.

Ethernet A shared-media network architecture. It operates at the Physical and Data Link layers of the OSI model. As the media access method, it uses baseband signaling over either a bus or a star topology with CSMA/CD. The cabling used in Ethernet networks can be coax, twisted-pair, or fiber-optic. *See also* Carrier Sense Multiple Access/Collision Detection, Open Systems Interconnect.

Even parity A technique that counts the number of 1s in a binary number and, if the total number of 1s is not even, adds a digit to make it even. See also parity.

Expansion bus An extension of the main computer bus that includes expansion slots for use by compatible adapters, such as memory boards, video adapters, hard disk controllers, and SCSI interface cards. Also called an I/O bus.

Expansion card A device that can be installed into a computer's expansion bus. Holds circuits and controllers for controlling specific types of peripherals and ports and adapters to attach the peripheral.

Expansion slot One of the connectors on the expansion bus that gives an adapter access to the system bus. The slot is made up of several small copper channels that grab the matching "fingers" of the expansion circuit boards. The fingers connect to copper pathways on the motherboard.

ExpressCard   A next generation expansion card for laptops that uses a serial ATA bus.

Extended CHS (ECHS)   A method of addressing and translating a drive's geometry to values acceptable to the system BIOS.

Extended Data Out (EDO) DRAM   A type of DRAM technology that increases performance over FPM DRAM by eliminating memory wait states.

Extended ISA (EISA)   A PC bus standard that extends the traditional AT-bus to 32 bits and allows more than one processor to share the bus.

Extended memory   A logical division of system memory comprised of all memory above 1MB.

Extended partition   A nonbootable partition on a hard drive that can be assigned multiple logical drives.

Extended Video Graphics Array (XGA)   Supports non-interlaced resolution of 1024 × 768 and higher.

External bus   See expansion bus.

External cache   A separate expansion board that installs in a special processor-direct bus containing cache memory.

Fast Page Mode (FPM) DRAM   A type of early DRAM technology, typically used at time of 486/Pentium transition, and compatible with memory buses with speeds under 66MHz.

FAT16   A 16-bit version of the FAT file system.

FAT32   A 32-bit version of the FAT file system.

FC-PGA package   The Flip Chip-PGA. A processor form-factor type in which the internal processor die in the package is put in with the die toward the top so that the heatsink and thermal grease that are normally applied to the insulation of a package can be used directly on the part that is putting out the heat. It makes for much more efficient cooling of the processor.

FDISK   A system utility used for creating and managing FAT partitions for DOS and Windows 9x.

Fiber optic   A type of network cable that uses a central glass or plastic core surrounded by a plastic coating.

Field Replaceable Module (FRM)   See Field Replaceable Unit (FRU).

Field Replaceable Unit (FRU)   The individual parts or whole assemblies that can be replaced to repair a computer. Also called a Field Replaceable Module (FRM).

File allocation table (FAT)   A table maintained by FAT file systems that lists all the clusters available on a disk.

Finisher   A printer device that finishes sets of documents being printed, by folding, stapling, hole-punching, sorting, or collating them into their final form.

Firewall   A device whose job is to protect LAN resources from attackers on the Internet. Similarly, it can prevent computers on the network from accessing various services on the Internet. It can be used to filter packets based on rules that the network administrator sets.

Firmware   Any software stored in a form of read-only memory—ROM, EPROM, or EEPROM—that maintains its contents when power is removed.

Flash BIOS   BIOS stored on a Flash memory chip.

Flash memory   A type of non-volatile RAM that can be written to with electrical pulses and then holds its data indefinitely. Sometimes used for storing system BIOS settings; more commonly used today for flash RAM portable storage devices and digital camera memory chips.

Flashing   Updating or imprinting the memory on a Flash memory chip.

Flatbed scanner   An optical device that can be used to digitize a whole page or a large image.

Floppy disk   A flat, round, magnetically coated plastic disk enclosed in a protective jacket and used for removable data storage.

Floppy disk controller   The electronic circuitry that controls and manages the operation of floppy disks.

Floppy disk drive   A device used to read and write data to and from a floppy disk.

Floppy drive cable   A 34-wire ribbon cable that connects the floppy drive(s) to the floppy drive controller.

Floppy drive interface adapter   An adapter that is supported through the chipset, which integrates the floppy drive controller functionality.

Floppy drive power connector   A small, flat connector, also known as a Berg connector, commonly used to power floppy disk drives and other small form factor devices.

Flow control (handshaking)   In communications, control of the rate at which information is exchanged between two computers over a transmission channel. Control codes or particular characters are exchanged to maintain and coordinate data flow between two devices so that data is only transmitted when the receiving device is ready to accept the data. Flow control can be implemented either in hardware or in software. Also referred to as handshaking.

Flux transition   The presence or absence of a magnetic field in a particle of the coating on the disk.

Fn key   A laptop function key used in conjunction with other keys in order to extend the smaller laptop keyboard's functionality.

Font   Software that describes the style of printed characters.

Forced perfect termination   A technique used to terminate a SCSI bus.

Form factor   The size and shape of a component such as a case or motherboard.

Form tractors   A mechanism used to feed paper by pulling it through a series of gears and sprockets.

Formatter board   A type of circuit board that takes the information a printer receives from the computer and turns it into commands for the various components in the printer.

Frequently Asked Questions (FAQ)   A document that lists some of the more commonly asked questions about a product or component. When you're researching a problem, the FAQ is usually the best place to start.

Frontside bus   A set of signal pathways between the CPU and main memory.

Full-duplex communications   Communications where both entities can send and receive simultaneously.

Fusing rollers   In a laser printer, applies pressure and heat (between 165 and 180 degrees Celsius) to the page.

Gateway   Any hardware and software combination that connects dissimilar network environments.

Half-duplex communications   Communications that occur when only one entity can transmit or receive at any one instant.

Handheld computer   Smaller computing devices designed primarily for portable personal information management.

Handheld PC (HPC) A handheld device that is basically a shrunken laptop. HPCs run on an operating system called Windows CE.

Hard drive A storage device that uses a set of rotating, magnetically coated disks called platters to store data or programs.

Hardware A computer system's physical equipment.

HD-DVD A next-generation DVD format that stores up to 45 GB in a triple-layer disk.

HD-15 connector Also called a VGA connector. Is a standard monitor connector on virtually all newer monitors and video cards, especially VGA and SVGA. The video card has the female connector into which the male plug of the monitor is attached. The HD-15 is a DB-style plug and connector.

Heat spreaders Two aluminum sheaths that cover the chips on a DIMM/RIMM to help prevent overheating.

Heatsink A device attached to an electronic component that removes heat from the component by induction. It is often a plate of aluminum or metal with several vertical fingers.

Hexadecimal number system The base-16 numbering system that uses the digits 0 to 9, followed by the letters A to F, which are equivalent to the decimal numbers 10 through 15. Abbreviated as hex.

High Density/Very High Density (HD/VHD) connector Has a shell similar to D-connectors and is used for SCSI devices. It may have 50 or 68 pins and latches or screws to hold the connection in place.

High memory area (HMA) In an IBM-compatible computer, the first 64KB of extended memory above the 1MB limit of 8086 and 8088 addresses. Programs that conform to the extended memory specification can use this memory as an extension of conventional memory, although only one program can use or control HMA at a time. Also called expanded or reserved memory.

High-level formatting Preparing a drive for use by a particular operating system by creating a file system on it.

High-voltage differential (HVD) signaling An early implementation of SCSI differential signaling.

High-voltage power supply (HVPS) A component that provides the high voltages used during the EP print process. It converts house AC currents into higher voltages that the two corona assemblies can use.

Host   In TCP/IP networks, nodes are often referred to as hosts.

Host adaptor   An expansion board, or circuitry on a motherboard, that controls and coordinates a hard drive.

Hot-swapping   Connecting or disconnecting a device while the PC is running. Also called hot-plugging.

Hub   A device used to link several computers together. Hubs are most often used in 10BaseT Ethernet networks. Hubs are essentially multiport repeaters: They repeat any signal that comes in on one port and copy it to the other ports (a process that is also called broadcasting).

Hybrid topology   The hybrid topology is simply a mix of the other topologies.

HyperTransport   A combination serial/parallel bus using a point-to-point architecture and packet transmissions, similar to PCIe.

I/O voltage   The external voltage of the processor.

IEEE 1284   The IEEE specification governing parallel printer ports and defining the available modes: SPP, Bidirectional, EPP, and ECP.

IEEE 1394 (FireWire)   An IEEE standard for a digital Plug and Play bus, used for a variety of external devices, including digital video cameras and external hard disks. Also known as FireWire.

Impact printer   Any printer that forms an image on paper by forcing a character image against an inked ribbon. Dot-matrix, daisy-wheel, and line printers are all impact printers, whereas laser printers are not.

Industry Standard Architecture (ISA)   A 16-bit bus design first used in IBM's PC/AT computer in 1984.

Infrared   A method of wireless transmission that uses part of the infrared spectrum to transmit and receive signals. Infrared transmissions take advantage of a frequency range just below that of visible light, and they usually require a line-of-sight connection between transmitter and receiver.

Infrared Data Association (IrDA)   A trade association of more than 150 computer and telecommunications hardware and software suppliers, including Hewlett-Packard, Apple Computer, AST, Compaq, Dell, IBM, Intel, Motorola, Novell, and others.

Infrared networking   Used primarily for short distance, point-to-point communications, like those between a peripheral and a PC.

Infrared port A small, usually dark red, plastic window located usually on the front or side of the case. External IR ports can be attached to the PC through adapters to other ports.

Infrastructure mode In this mode, NICs will only communicate with an access point (instead of each other as in ad-hoc mode). The access point will facilitate communication between the wireless nodes as well as communication with a wired network (if present). In this mode, wireless clients appear to the rest of the network as standard, wired nodes.

Inkjet printer A nonimpact printer that sprays a mist of liquid ink through tiny jets in the print head to form characters or graphics on the page.

Input peripheral Used to input data to the computer. Includes keyboards, mice, scanners, bar-code readers, Webcams, digital cameras.

Input/output (I/O)peripheral Has combined inputting/outputting functions, such as a Personal Digital Assistant (PDA) and touch screen.

Input/Output (I/O) address A memory address reserved for transferring data to and from a device.

Instruction set 1. The set of machine-language instructions that a processor recognizes and can execute. 2. An instruction set for reduced instruction set computing (RISC) may only contain a few instructions; a computer that uses complex instruction set computing (CISC) may be able to recognize several hundred instructions.

Insulator A device or material that offers resistance to the flow of electricity.

Integrated motherboard A system board that has most of the computer's circuitry attached, as opposed to the circuitry having been installed as expansion cards.

Integrated Services Digital Network (ISDN) A telecommunications standard that is used to digitally send voice, data, and video signals over the same lines.

Interface bridge Circuitry that translates signals between two different interfaces.

Interface controller The motherboard of the laser printer.

Interface The point at which a connection is made between two hardware devices.

Internal bus The motherboard buses that connect motherboard components.

Internal cache   Cache memory located in the CPU.

Internetwork Packet eXchange/Sequenced Packet eXchange (IPX/SPX)   The main protocol suite used on Novell NetWare networks before Netware 5.

Interpolation   A method of creating extra bits of data between two real bits by averaging them. Interpolation is useful for increasing the resolution of pictures, for example.

Interrupt Request (IRQ)   Signals that an event has taken place that requires the processor's attention, and may come from the keyboard, the input/output ports, or the system's disk drives. In the PC, the main processor does not accept interrupts from hardware devices directly; instead interrupts are routed to an Intel 8259A Programmable Interrupt Controller. This chip responds to each hardware interrupt, assigns a priority, and forwards it to the main processor.

Interrupt   A request from a device (other than the CPU) to the CPU for a service, action, or special action.

ISO 9660   A file system for optical drives, used primarily by CDs.

ISO image   A disk image of an optical drive.

Jaz disk   A form of Iomega Zip disk that holds 1 or 2GB of data; no longer manufactured.

Joystick   Input device that is popular with flight and navigation games, and as a backup mouse.

Jump address   The address on the BIOS chip that references the first instructions for the CPU to use in the booting sequence.

Jumper   A small plastic and metal connector that completes a circuit, usually to select one option from a set of several user-definable options. Jumpers are often used to select one particular hardware configuration rather than another.

Keyboard   Enables a user to communicate with the computer via keystrokes.

Land Grid Array (LGA) package   A CPU package similar to the PGA package but uses contacts called lands instead of pins.

Lapping   A process by which the heatsink or water block surface is sanded flat using a very flat surface (like a sheet of glass) and progressively finer grits of sandpaper until the surface is as flat as it can get. This helps minimize the very small air gaps that occur between the processor and heatsink due to the uneven metal surface of the heatsink, thus creating the largest possible surface area for the greatest heat transfer efficiency.

Laser printer   A printer that's based on the same technology as that used by photocopiers. A laser and a rotating mirror create an image of the page on a rotating photosensitive drum. This image is converted into an electrostatic charge that attracts and holds the toner. Electrostatically charged paper is rolled against the drum, and the toner is transferred to the paper and fused to the paper using heat. The last step is to remove the electrostatic charge from the drum and collect any excess toner.

Laser scanning assembly   The assembly in an EP process printer that contains the laser. This component is responsible for writing the image to the EP drum.

LED printer   A printer that essentially uses the same general print process as a laser printer, except it uses LEDs to expose the photosensitive drum.

Legacy port   Includes serial ports, parallel ports, and PS/2 keyboard and mouse ports.

Letter quality (LQ)   A category of dot-matrix printer that can print characters that look very close to the quality a laser printer might produce.

Level 1 cache   Any cache memory that is integrated into the CPU.

Level 2 cache   Any cache memory that is external to the CPU.

Line conditioner   A device that produces "perfect" power of 110V/60Hz, removing most of the stray EMI and RFI signals from incoming power and reducing any power overages down to 110V.

Line power   Electrical power that comes out of the standard wall socket.

Line printer   A printer that prints single lines at a time.

Lines   In reference to parallel motherboard buses, lines refers to the signaling wires.

Liquid cooling   Technology whereby a water block is used to conduct heat away from the processor (as well as chipsets). Water is circulated through this block to a radiator, where it is cooled.

Liquid crystal display (LCD)   Work by applying electrical charges to liquid crystals sandwiched between two polarizing sheets. Electrical currents, and the polarizing sheets, force the molecules to align themselves in patterns related to the electrical field, blocking light and acting as shutters. LCD screens are more compact, thinner and lighter than CRT monitors, and they consume much less power.

Lithium-Ion (Li-ION) battery   Very lightweight with a long battery life. LiON batteries hold about twice the power of a NiCad battery in about half the weight.

Local area network (LAN)   A network that is restricted to a single building, a group of buildings, or even a single room.

Logic board   A sheet or board containing computer circuitry.

Logical Block Addressing (LBA)   A type of addressing that assigns a unique ID number to a sector, as opposed to using a CHS address.

Logical drive   A separate storage area within a partition accessed through the use of a drive letter. Also referred to as a volume.

Logical geometry   The numbers of cylinders, heads, and sectors that the drive controller reports to the system.

Logical topology   Describes the way the information flows. Logical topologies are the same as the physical topologies except that the flow of information, rather than the physical arrangement, specifies the type of topology.

Low-level formatting   Factory processing of a hard drive that creates its logical organization units such as the tracks and sectors.

Low-voltage differential (LVD) signaling   A low-voltage implementation of SCSI differential signaling.

LS-120   A high-capacity floppy disk and drive that stores up to 120MB. Uses an IDE interface rather than a standard floppy interface.

Magnetic disk   Stores data in transitions between positive and negative magnetic charges on a disk surface.

Mainframe   Also called enterprise servers, mainframe computers are powerful, shared computers that many users can work on through different terminals.

Master Boot Record (MBR)   A system file that records data about a hard drive's partitions.

Mechanical mouse   Uses a rubber ball, which moves as the user rotates the mouse. As the ball moves, it rotates a set of rollers, which in turn drive sensors that translate the ball's movement to move the screen pointer around the display. As the user moves his hand, the distance traveled and the speed of the ball is detected by the rollers and sensors, and the screen pointer moves a relative distance and speed accordingly.

Megapixel   One million pixels, typically used to refer to the maximum resolution of a digital camera.

Memory   The primary random access memory (RAM) installed in the computer. The operating system copies application programs from disk into memory, where all program execution and data processing takes place; results are written back out to disk again. The amount of memory installed in the computer can determine the size and number of programs it can run, as well as the size of the largest data file.

Memory address Areas of system memory (DRAM) set aside for a device to use.

Memory card A credit-card (or smaller) sized Flash memory storage device that fits into a card slot on a digital media device or PC, and commonly used with digital cameras.

Memory slot A connector on the motherboard used for attaching RAM memory.

Mesh topology The mesh topology is the simplest logical topology in terms of data flow, but it is the most complex in terms of physical design. In this physical topology, each device is connected to every other device.

Metropolitan area network (MAN) Connects two or more LANs within a same city but are far enough apart that the networks can't be connected using a simple cable or wireless connection.

MFP (multifunction printer) An MFP is a printer that combines printing capabilities with other functions, such as copying, scanning, or faxing.

Micro-Channel Architecture (MCA) An early 32-bit expansion bus.

Microcode Microprograms embedded in a CPU that operate on the CPu's instruction set.

MicroDIMM An extremely small DRAM form factor, only 45.5 millimeters (about 1.75 inches) long and 30 millimeters (about 1.2 inches, a bit bigger than a quarter) wide. It was designed for the ultralight, portable subnotebook style of computer. The module has 144 pins and is similar to a DIMM in that it uses 64-bit memory modules.

Microdrive A tiny IBM hard drive that stores up to 8GB and connects via a CompactFlash memory card slot or PC Card Type II slot.

Micro-PGA package A micro-PGA package is similar to the PGA package but packs more pins into a smaller area.

Mini-PCI Smaller version of the standard desktop PC PCI form. The mini-PCI has all the same features and functions of a standard PCI card while being only about one-fourth the size of the larger standard card.

Mirroring A fault-tolerant technique that writes the same information simultaneously onto two different hard drives that use the same host adaptor.

Modem   A device that modulates digital data onto an analog carrier for transmission over an analog medium and then demodulates from the analog carrier to a digital signal again at the receiving end. Modems can be used to connect to the Internet or to a LAN or WAN.

Molex connector   See standard peripheral power connector.

Monochrome Display Adapter (MDA)   Displays mostly text on a monochrome monitor. This adapter is still used for servers, process control, and monitoring systems where the display contains only text and a color display is not needed.

MP3 player   A USB device. Two types of portable MP3 players, based on the storage they use: flash memory or hard drive.

Multicore   CPUs with more than one processing core.

Multimeter   An electronic device used to measure and test ohms, amperes, volts, and farads.

Multiplexing   The use of two or more types of signals through a communications line. A multiplexed bus may use one line for carrying both data and address information.

Multitasking   A feature of an operating system that allows more than one program to run simultaneously.

Multithreading   The ability of a program to send multiple tasks to the processor at the same time. This allows an application to execute more quickly, but it requires the support of a multithreaded operating system.

Multiword DMA   A category of DMA transfer mode that transfers transfer several words (2 bytes) at a time.

Musical Instrument Digital Interface (MIDI) standard   A serial interface standard and communications protocol that defines the connections between a computer and a synthesizer. MIDI devices can be used to create, record, and play back music.

Native resolution   The primary resolution supported by an LCD display, which has a fixed, or native, number of pixels.

Near letter quality (NLQ)   A category of dot-matrix printer that can come close to the quality of a laser printer, but still is lacking somewhat in print quality.

Network adapter   See Network Interface Card (NIC).

Network basic input/output system (NetBIOS)   A Session layer protocol that opens communication sessions for applications that want to communicate on a network.

Network connectivity device Any device that facilitates connections between network devices. Some examples include hubs, routers, switches, and gateways.

Network Interface Card (NIC) A PC expansion board that plugs into a personal computer or server and works with the network operating system to control the flow of information over the network. The network interface card is connected to the network cabling (twisted-pair, coaxial, or fiber optic cable), which in turn connects all the network interface cards in the network.

Network media Transmission media used for the actual network data transmissions and signaling, such as special cabling or wireless radio wave connections.

Network operating system (NOS) The software that runs on a network server and offers file, print, application, and other services to clients.

Network resource Any item that can be used on a network.

Nickel-Cadium (NiCad) battery Most durable type of rechargeable battery. This battery is also the heaviest, yet least expensive, of the portable PC battery types. NiCad batteries can only be recharged a finite number of times (about 700 charge and discharge cycles).

Nickel-Metal Hydride (NiMH) Environmentally friendly because they don't contain heavy metals that can be toxic. They also store up to 30 percent more power than NiCad batteries of the same weight, but they have a shorter life (around 400 charge-and-discharge cycles) and cost about 30 percent more than NiCad batteries.

NLX motherboard A motherboard form factor that uses a riser card to hold expansion cards.

Node Any addressable network point, including workstations, peripherals, or other network devices.

Nonintegrated motherboard A type of motherboard wherein the various subsystems (video, disk access, and so on) are not integrated into the motherboard, but rather placed on expansion cards that can be removed and upgraded.

Nonvolatile memory Memory storage that retains its information when the power is turned off. Examples of nonvolatile storage include disk drives and flash RAM devices. Compare to *volatile storage*.

Nonvolatile storage Data storage that retains its information when the power is turned off.

Northbridge   A subset of a motherboard's chipset or circuitry that manages high-speed peripheral communications. The Northbridge subset is responsible primarily for AGP communications and processor-to-memory communications.

NTFS   A file system for Windows NT 4, 2000, and XP.

Null modem cable   A short serial cable that connects two personal computers so that they can communicate without the use of modems or network cards.

NWLINK   The Microsoft version of the IPX/SPX protocol.

Odd parity   A technique that counts the number of 1s in a binary number and, if the total number of 1s is not odd, adds a digit to make it odd.

Ohms   A unit of electrical resistance.

Operating system   The software responsible for allocating system resources, including memory, processor time, disk space, and peripheral devices such as printers, modems, and monitors. All applications use the operating system to gain access to these resources as necessary. The operating system is loaded into the computer as it boots, and it remains in memory until the computer is turned off.

Optical disk   A disk that stores and reads data in patterns of reflectivity rather than magnetism, such as a CD or DVD.

Optical drive   A type of storage drive that uses a laser to read from and write to the storage medium.

Optical mouse   A mouse that must be used on a mouse pad containing a special grid. The mouse shines a small beam of light on the grid that conveys mouse movements back to the computer.

Output peripheral   Used to display or otherwise translate data the PC has operated on. Includes monitors, printer, speakers, and projectors.

Overclocking   Changing the internal speed or front-side bus speed of a system so that it runs faster than intended. Overclocking pushes the CPU past its stated limit, often causing overheating and instability.

Page description language (PDL)   Translates the data sent from an application into printer-ready commands.

Page file   See swap file.

Page printer   A printer that holds the entire page in memory until it is ready to output the entire image to the paper in one operation.

Parallel bus   Made of group of wires that transmit one or more bytes at a time.

Parallel interface   Transfers data 8 bits at a time as opposed over multiple wires. The most common peripheral connected via a parallel connection is a printer.

Parity   A simple form of error-checking used in computers and telecommunications. Parity works by adding an additional bit to a binary number and using it to indicate any changes in that number during transmission.

Partitioning   Sectioning the hard drive memory space into separate areas, which can then be assigned to hold logical drives.

Passive backplane   A backplane design that functions as a holder only, with no additional circuitry on the backplane itself.

Passive matrix screen   An LCD screen that uses only one transistor per row and column, resulting in a display that is less bright than an active matrix display.

Passive termination   A simple method used to terminate a SCSI bus that works using resistors.

PC Card   A term that describes plug-in cards that conform to the Personal Computer Memory Card International Association (PCMCIA) standard. A PC Card is about the size of a credit card and comes in three types: Type 1 (thinnest), Type 2 (medium thickness) and Type 3 (thickest). The modern standard is called *CardBus*.

PC card   Credit card-sized expansion cards that fit into a compatible slot on the laptop.

PC Memory Card International Association (PCMCIA)   A nonprofit association that developed a standard for credit card–sized plug-in adapters designed for portable computers.

PCI-Express (PCIe)   A new full-duplex serial standard based on the older PCI local bus. PCI Express doubles the data transfer rates of the PCI bus and allows multiple 1X lanes to be combined for use by a single device, such as a 16X PCIe video card.

PCI-Extended (PCI-X)   An upgraded version of PCI designed primarily for high-end workstations and servers which offers faster bus speeds and data throughput.

Peer-to-peer network   Computers that are hooked together and have no centralized authority. Each computer is equal and can act as both a server and a workstation.

Peripheral   Device that is not part of a PC, but is connected to the outside of the PC and increases its functionality.

Peripheral Component Interconnect (PCI) bus   A specification introduced by Intel that defines a local bus that allows up to 10 PCI-compliant expansion cards to be plugged into the computer. One of these 10 cards must be the PCI controller card, but the others can include a video card, network interface card, SCSI interface, or any other basic input/output function. The PCI controller exchanges information with the computer's processor at either 32- or 64-bits at a time and allows intelligent PCI adapters to perform certain tasks concurrently with the main processor by using bus-mastering techniques.

Peripheral interface   Method of connecting a peripheral or accessory to a computer, including the specification of cabling, connector type, speed, and method of communication used.

Personal computer (PC)   Also called microcomputers, these computers are used by individuals in home or business settings.

Personal Digital Assistant (PDA)   A tiny, pen-based, battery-powered computer that combines personal organization software with fax and e-mail facilities into a unit that fits into your pocket. PDAs are available from several manufacturers.

PGA (Pin Grid Array) package   A type of IC package that consists of a grid of pins connected to a square, flat package.

Phase-change cooling   A cooling system wherein the cooling effect resulting from the change of a liquid to a gas is used to cool the inside of a PC.

Photosensitive drum   The large cylinder in a laser printer to which the page image is written before being transferred to paper.

Physical topology   The physical layout of a network, such as bus, star, ring, or mesh.

Piezoelectric inkjet   An inkjet printer that uses piezoelectric crystals to force ink onto a page.

PIO (Programmed Input/Output) mode   An early ATA data transfer mode.

Pipeline   The sequence of steps a CPU takes to perform an operation.

Pipelining   In processor architecture, a method of fetching and decoding instructions that ensures that the processor never needs to wait; as soon as one instruction is executed, the next one is ready.

Plastic Pin Grid Array (PPGA)   A form factor package type that has pins arranged so the processor can be inserted only one way into its socket. It also has a nickel-plated copper heatsink on top. This package type is used primarily by early Intel Celeron processors with 370 pins that fit into a Socket 370.

Platen   The hard rubber roller behind the paper that absorbs the impact of the print head striking the ribbon and paper on a dot matrix printer.

Platters   The disks within a hard drive that are coated with magnetic media and comprise the physical storage medium.

Plenum rated coating   Coaxial cable coating that does not produce toxic gas when burned.

Plug and Play   Sometimes abbreviated as PnP. A standard that defines techniques designed to make PC configuration simple and automatic. A user can plug in a new device, and the operating system will recognize it and configure it automatically when the system is next started.

Pocket hard drive   Small, portable hard drives that typically connect via a USB port to the PC.

Port replicator   A device containing standard computer ports to which a notebook PC can attach, used to avoid constantly connecting and disconnecting the individual peripherals from a portable computer.

Portable computer   Any computer that contains all the functionality of a desktop computer system but is portable.

POST card   An expansion card whose function is to record and report POST errors.

Power   The amount of work an electrical current is capable of producing.

Power line   Used to carry small amounts of voltage for powering devices.

Power On Self Test (POST)   A set of diagnostic programs, loaded automatically from ROM BIOS during startup, designed to ensure that the major system components are present and operating. If a problem is found, the POST software writes an error message on the screen, sometimes with a diagnostic code number indicating the type of fault located. These POST tests execute before any attempt is made to load the operating system.

Primary corona   In a laser printer, the charging wire or roller that applies an electrostatic charge to the paper.

Primary partition   A basic drive partition that can contain only one logical drive.

Print consumables   Products a printer uses in the print process that must be replaced occasionally. Examples include toner, ink, ribbons, and paper.

Print media   What you put through the printer to print on. Includes paper, transparencies, envelopes, etc.

Print spool   A holding tank for print jobs waiting to be sent to the printer. Using a print spool frees up the application quicker from which you are printing.

Printer   An electromechanical output device that is used to put information from the computer onto paper.

Printer emulation   The ability of a printer to change modes so that it behaves like a printer from another manufacturer. For example, many dot-matrix printers offer an Epson printer emulation in addition to their own native mode. Most laser printers offer a Hewlett-Packard LaserJet emulation.

Printer interface   The collection of hardware and software that allows the printer to communicate with a computer.

Printer interface software   Includes the printer's driver and the driver's use of a page description language (PDL).

Printer resident fonts   Fonts that are housed in a printer's onboard memory.

Printer ribbon   A fabric strip that is impregnated with ink and wrapped around two spools encased in a cartridge. This cartridge is used in dot-matrix printers to provide the ink for the print process.

Printhead   The part of a printer that creates the printed image. In a dot-matrix printer, the printhead contains the small pins that strike the ribbon to create the image, and in an ink-jet printer, the printhead contains the jets used to create the ink droplets as well as the ink reservoirs. A laser printer creates images using an electrophotographic method similar to that found in photocopiers and does not have a printhead.

Printhead carriage   The component of a bubble-jet printer that moves back and forth during printing. It contains the physical as well as electronic connections for the printhead and (in some cases) the ink reservoir.

Printwire   Hard-wire pins in a dot matrix printer that are used to form characters by striking an ink ribbon against paper.

Process   In CPU manufacturing, used to describe the size, in nanometers or microns, of transistors used.

Programmable Read Only Memory (PROM)   A blank ROM chip that can be programmed with data or instructions.

Proprietary design   A design style for computer components that is unique to a particular manufacturer and is not licensed to other manufacturers.

Protocol   A predefined set of rules that dictates how computers or devices communicate and exchange data on the network.

PS/2 port (mini-DIN connector)   A small round connector with six pins used for connecting a legacy mouse or keyboard to a system. Also called a mini-DIN connector.

Radio frequency interference (RFI)   Electromagnetic radiation produced by many electronic devices, including computers and peripherals, which can interfere with other signals in the radiofrequency range.

Rambus DRAM (RDRAM)   A proprietary type of DRAM developed by Rambus, Inc.

Random Access Memory (RAM)   Memory that is accessed nonsequentially.

RCA jack/connector   Used to transmit both audio and video information.

Read Only Memory (ROM)   A type of computer memory that retains its data permanently, even when power is removed. Once data is written to this type of memory, it cannot be changed.

Read/write head   Component of a floppy- or hard-drive that reads and writes data to and from a magnetic disk.

Redundant Array of Independent Disks (RAID)   A method of using several hard drives in an array to provide fault tolerance in the event that one or more than one drive fails.

Refresh rate   Technically called the *vertical scan frequency*. Specifies how many times in one second the scanning beam of electrons redraws the screen, measured in draws per second, or Hertz.

Registered jack (RJ) connector   Most often used in telecommunications. RJ connectors are typically square with multiple gold contacts on the top (flat) side. A small locking tab on the bottom prevents the connector and cable from falling or being pulled out of the jack accidentally. Common types include the RJ-11, a commonly used four-wire (two-pair) connector most often used for voice communications, and the RJ-45, an eight-wire (four-pair) connector used for data transmission over unshielded twisted-pair (UTP) cable and leased telephone line connections..

Registers   Components of the CPU used for storing data temporarily.

Repeater   A simple, inexpensive amplifying device that allows a cabling system to extend beyond its maximum allowed length by amplifying the network voltages so they travel farther.

Resistance   The quality of impeding the flow of electricity. Some materials are more resistant to the flow of electricity.

Resistor   An electronic device used to resist the flow of current in an electrical circuit.

Resolution   The number of pixels that are available to produce an image.

RIMM   A type of memory module that uses Rambus memory.

Ring topology   In a physical ring topology, stations are connected in a circle and use a unidirectional transmission path where messages move from workstation to workstation. Each station in the ring reads a message, and then regenerates it and hands it to its neighbor on a different network cable.

Riser card   An expansion card that adds further capabilities to an existing expansion card or bus. The riser card may also allow an expansion bus to change direction (e.g., from horizontal to vertical).

Rotational latency   The time it takes for the area of a hard disk containing the required information to rotate to a position under the read/write head.

Router   A device that connects multiple network types and determine the best path for sending data. They can route packets across multiple networks and use routing tables to store network addresses to determine the best destination. Routers are normally used to connect one LAN to another to create a WAN.

RTS/CTS (request-to-send/clear-to-send)   Sends signals to specific pins to stop and start the data flow. The RTS signal indicates when a device is ready to send data, and the CTS signal indicates that a device is ready to accept data.

Sag   A momentary drop in voltage lasting a few milliseconds.

Scanner   Divides the picture into a grid, and then a sensor determines a numeric value based on the amount of red, green, and blue that is bounced back when a light hits that area. These values are processed by the PC and scanner software to reproduce the scanned image in digital form.

SCSI terminator   A device on the SCSI interface used to prevent signals echoing on the bus.

SECC package   A processor packaging type similar to a SEPP, except the entire expansion card is placed inside a plastic case to protect it.

SECC2 package   Similar to the SECC package type, but the SECC2 plugs into the Slot 1 connector and does not use the thermal plate.

Secondary storage   Non-volatile data storage devices, such as hard drives and CD-ROMs.

Sector   A portion of one of the concentric tracks on a hard drive, usually capable of storing 512 bytes of information.

Sector translation   A method of translating physical geometry to logical geometry using a translation table.

Seek time   The time it takes an actuator arm to move from rest to active position for the read/write head to access information.

Self-test   An internal diagnostic routine of a printer which can be initiated without connecting the printer to a PC.

Semiconductor   Any material that, depending on some condition, is either a conductor or nonconductor.

Serial Advanced Technology Attachment (Serial ATA)   A serial (one bit at a time) hard drive communication standard.

Serial bus   Transmits bytes one bit at a time over a single wire or line.

Serial interface (RS-232-C)   Once a standard for I/O communications, the serial interface involves sending bits in a serial fashion, one bit a time.

Server   A network computer from which workstations (or clients) access and share files, printers, communications, and other services.

Shadow mask   A metal screen with thousands of holes. The mask is placed so that the holes are directly in line with the dots of each pixel. The shadow mask absorbs unwanted electrons and prevents the phosphor material between the pixels from being illuminated, which leaves a black border around each pixel.

Shadowing   Placing a copy of the BIOS in memory.

Signed driver   A driver that has been digitally "signed" by Microsoft with a special value that only Windows can read. This signature tells the Windows installer that the driver being installed has been tested for security and stability on the chosen Windows platform and that the driver is from a reputable source.

Single Data Rate (SDR) DRAM   See Synchronous DRAM.

Single Edge Processor Package (SEPP)   A processor packing type where the processor is placed on a special expansion card, which then fits into a Slot 1 connector.

Single Inline Memory Module (SIMM)   Individual RAM chips soldered or surface-mounted onto small narrow circuit boards called carrier modules, which can be plugged into sockets on the motherboard. These carrier modules are simple to install and occupy less space than conventional memory modules.

Single word DMA   A data transfer mode in which data is transferred one word (2 bytes) at a time.

Single-ended (SE) signaling   A SCSI data transfer method that sends voltages over a single wire for each bit in the signal path.

Slate tablet PC   Like a large touchscreen whose computing hardware is located behind the display.

Slocket   A circuit board that plugs into a slot 1, but has a socket (typically a Socket 370) on it. It allows Socket 370-based chips to be plugged into slot 1 motherboards.

Slot   A CPU mounting mechanism that connects a CPU package on a circuit board that connects to a motherboard slot.

Small Computer System Interface (SCSI)   A high-speed, system-level parallel interface for connecting devices (including the host adapter) on a single, shared cable called the SCSI bus.

Small Outline DIMM (SoDIMM)   A small DRAM form factor.

Smart card   Device that looks like a standard credit card but that actually contains an embedded microprocessor and/or flash memory chip. The card can be programmed to contain various types of data.

Socket   A CPU mounting mechanism that connects a CPU package directly to the motherboard and establishes a connection through pins, soldered balls or lands.

Socket services   Part of the software support needed for PCMCIA hardware devices in a portable computer, controlling the interface to the hardware. Socket services is the lowest layer in the software that manages PCMCIA cards. It provides a BIOS-level software interface to the hardware, effectively hiding the specific details from higher levels of software. Socket services also detect when you insert or remove a PCMCIA card and identify the type of card it is.

Soft font   A font that is contained in a computer file and sent to the printer whenever a document requiring that font must be printed.

Software Programmed instructions that control the hardware in a computer system.

Solid ink printer Uses solid ink blocks that are melted by the print head onto the print drum. After the image is formed, paper is passed over the print drum, and the image is transferred to the paper. Because the inks are transferred first to the drum and then to the paper, the printer is able to achieve a high degree of registration.

Sound card Device that converts computer signals into sound.

Southbridge The subset of the chipset that is responsible for providing support to the myriad of onboard peripherals (PS/2, parallel, IDE, and so on), managing their communications with the rest of the computer and the resources given to them.

Spanning Combining two or more drives into a single logical volume.

Spike An electrical power overage condition that exists for an extremely short period of time, a few milliseconds.

Spin speed The speed at which a disk spins, measured in revolutions per minute (RPM).

Spindle The rod onto which platters are mounted in a hard drive.

Standard Parallel Port (SPP) Allows data to travel one way only—from the computer to the peripheral (typically a printer).

Standard peripheral power connector A type of connector used to power various internal drives. Also called a Molex connector.

Standard serial cable Used to hook various peripherals like modems and printers to a computer. Also called a modem cable, or a straight-through cable, in this cable, all the pins are connected one to one without any twists or other arrangements.

Standby power supply (SPS) A backup power supply that provides power from its batteries only when the power drops below a preset threshold.

Standoffs Small metal or plastic spacers that hold the motherboard away from the motherboard mounting plate in the case and prevent the components of the motherboard from touching the mounting plate and shorting out. The subset of the chipset that is responsible for providing support to the myriad of onboard peripherals (PS/2, parallel, IDE, and so on), managing their communications with the rest of the computer and the resources given to them.

Star topology   In a physical star topology, a cable is run from each workstation to a central device (a hub or switch), which is usually placed in a central location in the office (such as a utility closet).

Static RAM (SRAM)   A type of computer memory that retains its contents as long as power is supplied. It does not need constant refreshment like dynamic RAM chips.

Stepper motor   A very precise motor that can move in very small increments. Often used in printers.

Stop bit   Used in certain serial communications to indicate the beginning and end of data words.

Striping   Splitting file data into separate portions that are stored on separate physical drives.

Subnet mask   A group of selected bits that identify a subnetwork within a TCP/IP network.

Super Extended Graphics Array (SXGA)   An extension of the XGA standard that can support 1280 × 1024 with 1.3 million pixels in the display.

Super VGA (SVGA)   Support several resolutions and up to 4 billion colors (although 16.7 million colors is commonly used as the standard).

Super Video Graphics Array (SVGA)   This is an extension of the Video Graphics Array (VGA) standard, that supports 1024 × 768 and higher resolutions.

Supercomputer   Expensive and fast computers used for intensive processing.

Superscalar   1. A microprocessor architecture that contains more than one execution unit, or pipeline, allowing the processor to execute more than one instruction per clock cycle. 2. For example, the Pentium processor is superscalar, with two side-by-side pipelines for integer instructions. The processor determines whether an instruction can be executed in parallel with the next instruction in line. If it doesn't detect any dependencies, the two instructions are executed.

Surge   An electrical power overage condition that exists for up to several seconds.

Surge protector   A regulating device placed between the computer and the AC line connection that protects the computer system from power surges.

Swap file   On a hard disk, a file used to store parts of running programs that have been swapped out of memory temporarily to make room for other running programs. A swap file may be permanent, always occupying the same amount of hard disk space even though the application that created it may not be running; or it may be temporary, created only as and when needed.

Switch Operates very similarly to a hub because it connects several computers (usually twisted-pair Ethernet networks). However, switches don't repeat everything they receive on one port to every other port as hubs do. Rather, switches examine the header of the incoming packet and forward it properly to the right port and only that port. This greatly reduces overhead and thus performance as there is essentially a virtual connection between sender and receiver.

Synchronous bus (local bus) Designed to operate synchronously with the system clock.

Synchronous DRAM (SDRAM) Also called Single Data Rate (SDR) DRAM; the first generation of DRAM synchronized to speed of systems in which it will be used.

System BIOS The BIOS used by the system, as opposed to BIOS specific to and incorporated in separate hardware peripherals.

System bus (Frontside bus) The main PC motherboard bus that carries addresses and data between the chipset's Northbridge and the CPU.

System partition The partition that contains the specific hardware files needed to select an operating system.

System resources Communication channels or addresses that are used by the CPU to manage system devices such as expansion cards.

Tablet PC A laptop designed to be held like a pad of paper. A slate tablet is a flat tablet PC, and a convertible tablet PC incorporates a keyboard in a clamshell design.

Tape cartridge A self-contained tape storage module, containing tape much like that in a video cassette. Tape cartridges are primarily used to back up hard disk systems.

Tape drive A removable media drive that uses a tape cartridge containing a long polyester ribbon coated with magnetic oxide and wrapped around two spools with a read/write head in between.

Test page A testing page a printer produces to verify print quality and functioning.

Thermal contact patch A tape-like substance attached to the heatsink or water block to facilitate the best contact with the processor.

Thermal grease A compound used to allow the heatsink or water block to make the best contact with the processor.

Thermal inkjet An inkjet printer that uses heat to create vapor bubbles that force ink onto a page.

Thermal interface material (TIM)   Material used to allow the heatsink or water block to make the best contact with the processor. Includes thermal grease and thermal contact patches.

Thermal printer   Uses specially treated paper that changes color in reaction to the heat of the print head. There are both monochrome (gray) and color thermal printers.

Thin-and-light notebook   A category of laptop that typically weighs between 4 and 6 lbs.

Throttling   A thermal management feature that slows the CPU or turns the PC off when the CPU reaches a certain temperature.

Token Ring   Token Ring networks are exactly like the IEEE 802.5 specification because the specification is based on IBM's Token Ring technology. Token Ring uses a physical star, logical ring topology. All workstations are cabled to a central device called a multistation access unit (MAU). The ring is created within the MAU by connecting every port together with special circuitry in the MAU.

Toner   A powdered blend of metal and plastic resin particles, used in laser printers to create an image on a page.

Toner cartridge   The replaceable cartridge in a laser printer or photocopier that contains the electrically charged ink to be fused to the paper during printing.

Topology   Refers to how a network is organized in terms of its cabling and signaling.

Touch screen   A computer screen that has a film over it that is sensitive to touch.

Touchpad   A touch-sensitive rectangular pad that functions as a mouse alternative for moving an on-screen pointer.

Track point   A pointing device that uses a small rubber-tipped stick. When you push the track point in a particular direction, the onscreen pointer goes in that same direction. It allows fingertip control of the onscreen pointer, without the reliability problems associated with trackballs.

Trackball   Contains a movable ball that you rotate with your fingers to move the cursor on the screen. Because it doesn't need the area of flat space that a mouse needs, trackballs are popular with users of portable computers.

Tracks   Concentric rings of data areas recorded onto a hard or floppy drive during a low-level format.

Transceiver Also known as a media converter. Transceivers are relatively simple devices that allow a NIC or other networking device to connect to a different type of media than it was designed for.

Transfer corona The wire or roller in a laser printer that applies a positive charge to the paper so that the negatively charged toner will be attracted to it.

Transistor Abbreviation for transfer resistor. A semiconductor component that acts like a switch, controlling the flow of an electric current. A small voltage applied at one pole controls a larger voltage on the other poles. Transistors are incorporated into modern microprocessors by the million.

Transmission Control Protocol/Internet Protocol (TCP/IP) The protocol suite developed by the DoD in conjunction with the Internet. It was designed as an internetworking protocol suite that could route information around network failures. Today it is the de facto standard for communications on the Internet.

Twisted pair cable A type of network transmission medium that contains pairs of color-coded, insulated copper wires that are twisted around each other. A twisted-pair cable consists of one or more twisted pairs in a common jacket.

UDF A file system for optical drives, used primarily by DVDs.

Ultra Extended Graphics Array (UXGA) A further extension of XGA that supports a 1600 × 1200 resolution.

Ultraportable notebook A category of laptop that is typically 4 lbs or less and features fewer I/O ports.

Uninterruptible power supply (UPS) A backup power supply that supplies power through a continually recharged battery.

Universal Asynchronous Receiver/Transmitter (UART) chip Pronounced "you-art." An electronic module that combines the transmitting and receiving circuitry needed for asynchronous communications over a serial line.

Universal Serial Bus (USB) A standard from Intel and Microsoft for a high-speed serial peripheral bus designed to remove the need for almost all the connectors on the back of a personal computer. USB supports up to 127 devices on a single interface, and devices can be connected/disconnected without shutting down the PC.

Upper memory area Free area of memory that can be used for loading drivers and programs into the upper memory area.

USB flash drive   A small, typically pen-shaped Flash memory storage device that connects to the PC through a USB port.

VESA Local Bus (VLB or VL-bus)   An early bus designed for supporting video cards.

Video (graphics) card   Used to enhance a computer's graphic capabilities and work with the PC's monitor.

Video adapter (graphics adapter)   An adapter that provides the text and graphics output to the monitor. Some video adapters are included in the circuitry on the motherboard rather than as separate plug-in boards.

Video Graphics Array (VGA)   Supports up to 640 × 480 with 16 colors or lower resolutions with 256 colors.

Video memory (video RAM) (VRAM)   Pronounced "vee-ram." Special purpose RAM with two data paths for access (conventional RAM has just one). These two paths let a VRAM board manage two functions at once: refreshing the display and communicating with the processor. VRAM doesn't require the system to complete one function before starting the other, so it allows faster operation for the whole video system.

Video projector   Used to display visual information, typically from a PC or other media device such as a DVD player, onto a screen.

Video RAM (VRAM)   Specialized DRAM used on video cards. Has two data paths for access, rather than just one as in conventional RAM. These two paths let a VRAM board manage two functions at once—refreshing the display and communicating with the processor. VRAM doesn't require the system to complete one function before starting the other, so it allows faster operation for the whole video system.

Virtual memory   A memory-management technique that allows information in physical memory to be swapped out to a hard disk if necessary to free up RAM to hold other data instead.

Virus   A program intended to damage your computer system without your knowledge or permission.

Voice Over IP (VoIP)   A technique for routing telephone calls over the Internet instead of over traditional phone carriers.

Volatile memory   Data storage that loses its information when the power is turned off. Dynamic random access memory (DRAM) is the most common example.

Volts A unit of electrical potential, or pressure.

Volume A named portion of drive space.

VRM Voltage regulator module that supplies and regulates voltage supplied to the CPU.

Warm boot A boot started when the system is powered.

Water block An aluminum device mounted to the processor with two small connectors for a water inlet and outlet, which are in turn connected to a small pump and radiator for processor cooling.

Water cooling Using water to cool a computer processor. See *water block*.

Watts A unit of power.

Wavetable synthesis A method used by a sound board to simulate musical instruments. Wavetable synthesis uses digitized samples of real orchestral instruments, which are edited and mixed to produce music. FM synthesis is cheaper than wavetable synthesis but is also of much lower quality.

Webcam A low-cost video camera used to capture live images for display on a website. Webcams are used to display traffic information, activity inside a person's apartment, fish tanks, scenic views, and street scenes.

Wide area network (WAN) A network that crosses local, regional, and international boundaries.

Widescreen UXGA A version of UXGA for widescreen displays, supporting 1920 × 1200 pixels; and a 16:10 aspect ratio.

Windows Internet Naming Service (WINS) Microsoft's network name resolution software that converts NetBIOS names to IP addresses.

Wireless access point (WAP) Also called an access point or AP. A WAP is essentially a wireless bridge (or switch, as multiple end devices can connect simultaneously). It operates by connecting wireless clients together. In addition, it can connect those wireless clients to a wired network.

Word In binary communications, multiple bytes associated together.

Word size A CPU characteristic that describes the size of word that a register can store.

Workstation High-end microcomputers typically used for tasks that involve intensive processing. May also refer to any computer that is connected to the network and used by an individual to do work. In network terms, workstations are also known as client computers.

XON/XOFF   One of the two most common forms of flow control, it sends control characters to stop the flow of data (XOFF) and restart it again (XON). This is the software method of flow control.

Zip disk   A popular removable storage device from Iomega Corporation, capable of 100MB to 750MB of storage on relatively cheap, portable, 3[1/2]-inch disks.

Zone bit recording (ZBR)   Disk organization method in which there are fewer sectors per track on the inner parts of a disk and more on the outer parts.

Zoned CLV (ZCLV)   With zoned CLV, a disk is divided into sections with different CLV speeds.

INDEX